EUROPEAN U... ...ALISM

The International Political Economy of New Regionalisms Series

The International Political Economy of New Regionalisms Series presents innovative analyses of a range of novel regional relations and institutions. Going beyond established, formal, interstate economic organizations, this essential series provides informed interdisciplinary and international research and debate about myriad heterogeneous intermediate level interactions.

Reflective of its cosmopolitan and creative orientation, this series is developed by an international editorial team of established and emerging scholars in both the South and North. It reinforces ongoing networks of analysts in both academia and think-tanks as well as international agencies concerned with micro-, meso- and macro-level regionalisms.

European Union and New Regionalism

Regional Actors and Global Governance
in a Post-Hegemonic Era
Second Edition

Edited by

MARIO TELÒ
Institute for European Studies, Universite Libre de Bruxelles, Belgium

ASHGATE

Published by
Ashgate Publishing Limited
Wey Court East
Union Road
Farnham
Surrey GU9 7PT
England

Ashgate Publishing Company
Suite 420
101 Cherry Street
Burlington, VT 05401-4405
USA

Ashgate website: http://www.ashgate.com

British Library Cataloguing in Publication Data
European Union and new regionalism : regional actors and
    global governance in a post-hegemonic era. - 2nd ed. - (The
    international political economy of new regionalisms)
    1. European Union 2. Regionalism - Europe 3. Globalization
    4. Europe - Politics and government - 1989-
    I. Telo, Mario
    320.4'4049

Library of Congress Cataloging-in-Publication Data
European Union and new regionalism : regional actors and global governance in a post-
hegemonic era / edited by Mario Telo. -- 2nd ed.
        p. cm. -- (The international political economy of new regionalisms
series)
    Includes index.
    ISBN 978-0-7546-4991-5
    1. European Union--Congresses. 2. Regionalism--Congresses. 3. Globablization--
Congresses. I. Telo, Mario.

HC240.E8557 2007
337.1'42--dc22

Reprinted 2009
ISBN: 978-0-7546-4991-5

2007003828

Mixed Sources
Product group from well-managed
forests and other controlled sources
www.fsc.org Cert no. SA-COC-1565
© 1996 Forest Stewardship Council
FSC

Printed and bound in Great Britain by
MPG Books Ltd, Bodmin, Cornwall.

Contents

List of Figures and Tables

*This book is dedicated to our colleagues and friends in
Asia, Africa and Latin America*

Notes on Contributors

Catherine Børve Arnesen is associate professor at the Department of Public Governance at the Norwegian School of Management BI (NSM- BI) in Oslo and is the director of the Centre for Media Economics (www.bi.no/sfm). She holds a Doctorate in Economics from NSM- BI. She has published academic articles and book chapters related to her research interests, which include regulation, European telecommunications policy, strategy and comparative studies.

Kjell A. Eliassen is a professor of Public Management at the Department of Public Governance at the Norwegian School of Management and director of the Centre for European and Asian Studies. He has published eighteen books and several articles related to his research interests: EU institutions and decision making, European affairs, telecommunications and public management. His most recent books include: *European Telecom Liberalisation (1999), a new edition of Making Policy in the European Union* (2001) and *European Telecommunications Privatisations* (2007).

Andrew Gamble is Professor of Politics at the University of Cambridge. He is a Fellow of the British Academy and a co-editor of *New Political Economy*. His books include *Regionalism and World Order* (1996) (co-edited with Tony Payne), *Politics and Fate* (2000), and *Between Europe and America: The Future of British Politics* (2003). His current research, supported by the Leverhulme Trust, is on Anglo-America and the problem of world order.

Björn Hettne is Professor at the Department of Peace and Development, Göteborg University. He is author of a number of books on development theory, international political economy, European integration and ethnic relations. He is currently the president of the Academic Council of the GARNET PhD School, EU 6th Framework Program. He was Program Director of the United Nations University WIDER project on new regionalism and co-edited the five volume series *Globalism and the New Regionalism*, 1999–2001, Macmillan.

Richard Higgott is Professor of Politics and International Studies and Director of the ESRC, Centre for the Study of Globalisation and Regionalisation at the University of Warwick, Coordinator of the Network of Excellence GARNET on 'Global Governance, Regionalism and Regulation. The Role of the EU' (EU 6th Framework Program, 2004–2010) and editor of the *Pacific Review*. With Morgan Ougaard he published *Towards a Global Polity* (Routledge 2002) and is currently completing a book called *From Colonialism to Global Governance. A Geneology of Political Development*.

George Howard Joffé served as Deputy-Director and Director of Studies at the RIIA in London. He is affiliated to the Centre of International Studies at the LSE and to the Centre of International Studies at Cambridge University. He also teaches at the School of Oriental and African Studies at London University. His publications include 'The Middle East and the West' in Robertson, B. A. ed. *The Middle East and Europe: The power deficit* (1998, Routledge) and 'The European Union and the Maghreb in the 1990s' in Zoubir, Y. ed., North Africa in Transition: state, society and economic transformation in the 1990s (University Press of Florida, 1999).

Pablo Medina Lockhart is researcher at the IGEAT-Université Libre de Bruxelles, Institute of Geography and co-author (with Christian Vandermotten) of 'Electoral Geography of Europe' in *Le Vote des Quinze. Les élections européennes de juin 1999*, Presses de Sciences Politiques, Paris.

Thomas Meyer is Professor at the University of Dortmund, Director of the Friedrich-Ebert Stiftung, Bonn-Berlin and Director of Neue Gesellschaft. His main research areas include: social democratic theory and practice, comparative research on fundamentalism, theory of politics. Among his recent books is *Fundamentalismus in der modernen Welt*, Suhrkamp, Frankfurt, *Identity Mania. Fundamentalism and the Politicization of Cultural Differences*, London: Zed, and with co-author, Hinchman, Lew, *Theory of Social Democracy*. Cambridge: Polity, 2007.

Pier Carlo Padoan is Professor of Economics at the University of Rome, La Sapienza, and visiting professor at the College of Europe, Bruges. He is currently Deputy secretary general of the OCDE, Paris. His main research areas include: international economics, international political economy and European integration. He has published more than 100 articles and books. He was executive director for Italy at the IMF and director of the Fondazione Italianieuropei, Rome.

Sebastian Santander has a PhD in political science, is Assistant Professor at the Department of Political Science and researcher at the Institut d'études européennes of the Université libre de Bruxelles. His articles have appeared in journals such as *Journal of European Integration, European Foreign Affairs Review, Études internationales* (Québec*), Annuaire Français des Relations Internationales* (Paris), *Relazioni, Studia Diplomatica* (Belgium), *Revista de Derecho International y del Mercosur* (Buenos Aires). He published *Globalisation, gouvernance et logiques régionales dans les Amériques*, Paris/Brussels, Cahiers du GELA-IS/L'Harmattan, 2004.

Alberta M. Sbragia is the Director of the Center for West European Studies as well as the UCIS Research Professor of Political Science at the University of Pittsburgh. She was Visiting Associate Professor at the Harvard Business School, served as the Chair of the European Community Studies Association (1993–1995) and as the co-chair of the American Political Science Association (APSA) in 1999. She has published extensively on the institutional evolution of the EU, edited

Euro-Politics: Politics and Policymaking in the 'New' European Community (The Brookings Institution) and served on the editorial board of numerous journals in the United States, Canada, and Europe. Her current work examines the role of the European Union in global environmental politics.

Reimund Seidelmann is Professor for International Relations/Foreign Policy at Giessen University/FRG, honorary professor at Renmin University in Beijing/ PRC and has an international chair at the Institut d'Etudes Européennes at the Université Libre de Bruxelles. His main areas of research are European security and integration, peace and conflict theory, EU-China relations and, more particularly, Eastern Europe. He has directed a number of research projects (among them, GARNET and NESCA, including European and East-Asian universities, 6th FP, EU Commission) and published several books and scientific articles.

Fredrik Söderbaum is associate professor at the Department of Peace and Development Research (Padrigu) and Director of Centre for African Studies (CAS) at the School of Global Studies, Göteborg University, as well as research fellow at the UNU-CRIS, Bruges. He is published, mainly on the topic of regionalism, in journals such as *Global Governance, New Political Economy, Journal of Modern African Studies, Journal of European Integration, European Foreign Affairs Review, European Journal of Development Research. Recent books include The EU as a Global Player. The Politics of Interregionalism* (co-edited with Luk van Langenhove, Routledge, 2006), *The Political Economy of Regionalism. The Case of Southern Africa* (Palgrave, 2004), *The New Regionalism in Africa* (co-edited with Andrew Grant, Ashgate, 2003), and *Theories of New Regionalism* (with Tim Shaw, Palgrave, 2003).

Mario Telò is President of the Institute for European Studies, Professor of Political Science at the Université libre de Bruxelles and member of the Belgian Royal Academy. He is honorary Chair Jean Monnet, coordinator of the GARNET PhD school, and served as expert for the Presidency of the EU Council and the EU Commission. Among his recent books, *Europe: a Civilian Power? EU,Global Governance and World Order*, Palgrave, 2005, and L'Etat et L'Europe, Labor, Brussels, 2005.

Göran Therborn is Professor of Sociology at the University of Göteborg and Director of the SCASS (Swedish Academy of Advanced Social Studies), Uppsala. As political sociologist, he particularly focuses his comparative research on the Welfare State and unemployment in western Europe. Among his recent books is *European Modernity and Beyond. The Trajectory of European Societies, 1945– 2000*, Sage, 1995.

Álvaro Vasconcelos is Director of the Institute for Security Studies, Paris and Honorary President of IEEI, Lisbon and the main driver of the 'Euro-Latino-American Forum'. He also works on new regionalism in the international system after the Cold War. He leads the Euro-Latino-American Forum which celebrated its 15th anniversary in 2005. He recently co-edited (1998) *La politique étrangère et de sécurité commune. Ouvrir l'Europe au monde*, Presses de Sciences Politiques, Paris, and is coordinator of the network Euromesco, on Mediterranean EU policy.

Foreword

Regionalism – A New Paradigm?

George Howard Joffé

There is little doubt that the end of the Cold War has forced analysts of the state as the vehicle through which international relations is expressed to reconsider their assumptions of the basic paradigms involved. Although globalization has been highlighted as the obvious alternative, particularly from the point of view of the global economy and, latterly, in terms of the new knowledge economy, the reality of the contemporary world seems to be better expressed in terms of regionalism. In other words, the political, social and economic characteristics originally attributed to states seem increasingly to be expressed through regional constructs in which the traditional Westphalian state is now embedded.

Of course, this classic concept of the state – autonomous, sovereign and freed of all constraint – never reflected the reality of the international scene, despite the role it has played in realist and neo-realist theory for many decades. Indeed, some of the contributors to this volume highlight the ways in which, over the past forty years or so, new paradigms have emerged to account for the increasing restraints on the freedom of action of states. In addition, since the Second World War, there has been a growing momentum towards the creation of supra-state institutions that have a normative role in contributing towards such developments. The balance of power between the superpowers, however, prevented the emergence of genuinely new political constructs designed to respond to the conditions created by the evolution of international law and commerce.

Only in Europe – for quite specific reasons connected with a long and bloody history of conflict between Germany and France – did such a structure emerge. Yet, even here, the European Community emerged within the context of the Cold War, in part as a pragmatic response to the superpower confrontation. It was only in the 1990s that the profound theoretical implications of what European statesmen had achieved over the previous thirty to forty years began to become apparent. Furthermore, it has only been since 1990 that the implications of hegemonic stability and the role of the United States could have become a central concern of students of international relations, as a consequence of the end of the Cold War, balanced by a new interest in the alternative concept of regionalism.

It is therefore, perhaps, no accident that the second major initiative in modern regionalism took place in March 1991 when Mercosul-Mercosur was founded as an experiment in common political and economic development involving Brazil, Argentina, Uruguay and Paraguay. Drawing on the experience of the European Union, it sought to encourage parallel initiatives in political evolution and economic development and integration without engaging in a close federal structure to achieve its objectives. Yet other experiences in regionalist approaches since then have emphasized the variety of different models that exist, alongside the European experience. This study examines five of them – the European Union itself, Mercosul-Mercosur, the North American Free Trade Area (NAFTA), the Association of South East Asian Nations (ASEAN) and African regionalism – some of which predate the end of the Cold War, although all of them were only able to develop their full potential after its end.

The novelty in the current concept of 'New Regionalism', unlike earlier concepts during the Cold War period, resides in its potential as an alternative to hegemonic stability, within a globalized context, in which the region becomes the nexus of activity both at the state and the supra-state level. Without denying the state and the cultural specificities associated with it, regionalism binds states – that are usually contiguous – together through their voluntary derogation of sovereign rights into a collective economic endeavour. Such an endeavour may also, should the partners wish it, become a political project as well so that the collectivity retains a significant autonomy of political and economic action within the structures created by economic globalism.

The success of the regional model is attested to by the vitality of the initiatives that have been undertaken to date. The models discussed here are only the most prominent of a far wider range of initiatives that have either been started or revived during the past decade. Their continued vitality demonstrates that regionalism is becoming a permanent and prominent feature of the contemporary international system, providing a degree of theoretical order to a world that appeared to be increasingly confused and confusing in the aftermath of the Cold War. Regionalism, in short, may become the preferred response in a post-modern world through which the threats and benefits of globalization are mediated.

In this context, the role of the European Union is primordial. Not only is it the vehicle in which many of the ideas that inform modern economic regionalism were first tested, it is also becoming an experiment in new forms of political cooperation. Its formal structure as a network of sovereign states is being gradually transmuted into a new political construction as states gradually cede sovereign power over economic policy, monetary control and external foreign policy in a series of bold constitutional initiatives. Quite where this experiment will lead is unclear. Will the Union become a global competitor with the United States, as some fear? Or will it become the 'civil society of civil societies' that many anticipate – a political and social model for others to follow?

Whatever the outcome, there can be little doubt of the future role of regionalism inside the future international system as a theoretical and practical construct. Nor can there be any doubt that Europe will retain its particularity as the innovator in finding solutions to the future relationship between state, nation and the individual in a world in which the certainties of the past find no echo.

This distinctive collection of original contributions by leading specialists stems from an international and international multidisciplinary network coordinated by Mario Telò with the aim to combine European studies and international relations. On the one hand, it situates the EC/EU and its external relations in the framework of the development of different forms of regional arrangements. This combination offers an original development of European integration studies and a vigorous response to the conventional wisdom on European international identity, by considering various scenarios for the evolving international identity of the EU: a continental trading state, a new mercantilist fortress or a new civilian power. On the other hand, it supplements the current literature in international relations by dealing with regionalism as a possible new paradigm for international relations in the contemporary world.

This innovative textbook provides a clear insight for graduate and undergraduate students and researchers, ideal for courses that include issues of regionalism, world governance, EUs evolving continental and global role.

Preface to the Second Edition and Acknowledgements

The essays included in this second edition trace an intellectual journey over the course of ten years towards a mature and distinctive understanding of the contribution provided by the European Union and other regional associations to global governance and multilateralism. This is a new book which builds on the first edition. All the chapters have been updated and revised, some entirely rewritten, many extensively by the authors. Furthermore, the book entails three new chapters, by Björn Hettne, Fredrik Söderbaum and Richard Higgott. The volume actually results from two-stages of international and multidisciplinary research networking. The edition of 2001 was the first issue of a research project on 'Europe, New Regionalism and Global Governance (EUNRAGG)' launched in 1997 by the Université Libre de Bruxelles, Institute of Sociology (which sponsored the first steps) and Institute for European Studies (IEE), in cooperation with several international institutions including the Royal Institute of International Affairs, the Oslo Centre of European and Asian Studies (Business Institute), and the Institute for International and Strategic Studies, Lisbon. The second stage started in 2001 at the ECPR Conference in Canterbury and led to the current 'GARNET Network of Excellence', coordinated by Richard Higgott, University of Warwick (in the context of the 6th framework programme of the European Commission, DG research, 2005–10), focusing on 'Global governance, regionalization and regulation. The role of the European Union'.

The authors wish to extend their gratitude to all the scholars and students who contributed as discussants to the research project, from the very beginning. First of all, F. Cerutti (University of Florence), J. Nagels, P. Pierson-Mathy, F. Nahavandi, E. Remacle, P. Winand, (ULB), G. Ross (Harvard CES), F. Attinà (Un. Catania), G. Edwards (Oxford University), A. Viñas (European Commission). The Canterbury Conference of the European Consortium for Political Research. The project was possible thanks to the positive dialogue with further scholars and scientific institutions, namely P. Leslie (Queens University, Canada), P. Guerrieri (Rome, Sapienza), the PADRIGU (Gotheborg University), led by Björn Hettne, and continued in cooperation with the UN-CRIS (Bruges) directed by L. Van Langehove. In 2003/4, EUNRAGG merged within the 'GARNET'.

Furthermore, the editor would like to thank the institutions which gave him the opportunity to present drafts of his work in progress, and particularly: the IEE, Centre of Excellence J. Monnet of Brussels; F. Laursen and the IPSA/ Mexican Political Science Association (Manzanillo Conference, 1998); the ECPR Conferences of Canterbury (2001) and The Hague (2004), the UN-CRIS led by L. Van Langenhove, the European–Japanese networks and namely the professors of the Universities of Kyoto (I. Otake), Tokyo (Mori and Soji), Chuo (T. Furuki) and the International Christian University (T. Ueta); the Institute of Social Science of New Delhi (A. Giri and A. Mathew), the Euro-Latino American Forum set by the IEEI of Lisbon (A. Vasconcelos); the Institute Sorensen of São Paulo and the INTAL, Buenos Aires (F. Peña); the Institute of European Studies of Macau (Sales Marques and Ceu Esteves); the UNESCO, Caracas (F. L. Segrera); the SDIC, University of Bologna (G. Antonelli and P. G. Ardeni); the Forum on the Problems of Peace and War, Florence; the University of Florence, Political Science (U. Gori) and the Institute Sant'Anna of Pisa (B. Henry, A. Loretoni); the Centre d'Etudes Européennes, Institut d'Etudes Politiques, Paris (J. L. Quermonne); J. H. H. Weiler; the Center for European Studies, Harvard and particularly the 'Boston Group'; the Center for European Studies, University of Berkeley (V. Aggarwal and its network); the Geneva University/ECPR summer school (G. Nivat, N. Levrat, R. Schwok, J. Caporaso, A. Moravcsik, R. Ginzberg and the students); the Garnet PhD School, the European Commission (Action J. Monnet); the IPSA/RCEU network led by P. Leslie and H. Wallace; and, finally, the Portuguese Presidency of the European Union of 2000 (and particularly M. J. Rodrigues, special adviser to the Prime Minister and responsible for the 'progressive governance experts network' as well).

Of course the editor and the individual authors are entirely responsible for what is asserted in the chapters of the book.

We are particularly indebted to those who had a special role in the compiling and amending of this book including G. Joffé, former Director of the Royal Institute of International Affairs, M. May and her staff, J. Fitzmaurice, and last but not least, Jeannine Lowy and Tiziana Telò, whose precious help in the editing of the manuscript resulted in the first and second edition of this volume, respectively.

Mario Telò,
Bruxelles,
January 2007

List of Abbreviations

ACC	Arab Cooperation Council
ACM	Arab Common Market
ACP	African, Caribbean and Pacific countries
AEC	ASEAN Economic Community
AFTA/FTAA	American Free Trade Area (or Free Trade Area of the Americas)
ALALC	Latin American Association of Free Trade
ALADI	Latin American Association for Development and Integration
AMU/UMA	Arab Maghreb Union
APEC	Asia-Pacific Economic Cooperation
APT	ASEAN + Three (China, Japan, South Korea)
ARF	ASEAN Regional Forum
ASEAN	Association of South-East Asian Nations
ASEM	Asia–Europe Meeting
BENELUX	Belgium, Netherlands, Luxemburg
CACM	Central American Common Market
CAEC	Council for Asian Europe Cooperation
CAEU	Council for Arab Economic Unity
CAO	Eastern African Community
CAP	Common Agricultural Policy
CARIFA	Caribbean International Free Trade Association
CARICOM	Caribbean Community
CCASG	Council of Cooperation between Arab States of the Gulf
CEPAL	Economic Commission for Latin America
CEEAC	Economic Community of Central African States
CEPGL	Economic Community of the Great Lakes Countries
CER	Closer Economic Relationship
CFSP	Common Foreign and Security Policy
CIS	Commonwealth of Independent States
COMESA	Common Market for Eastern and Southern Africa
CSCE	Conference on Security and Cooperation in Europe
CUSA	Customs Union of Southern Africa
CUSFTA	Canada–USA Free Trade Agreement
DG(s)	Directorate(s) General
EAEC	East Asian Economic Caucus
EBRD	European Bank for Reconstruction and Development
EC	European Community (subsequently EU)

ECB	European Central Bank
ECFA	Economic Commission for Africa
ECHO	European Community Humanitarian Aid Office
ECLA	Economic Commission for Latin America
ECOWAS	Economic Community of West African States
ECSC	European Coal and Steel Community
EDF	European Development Fund
EEA	European Economic Area
EEC	European Economic Community
EFTA	European Free Trade Association
EIB	European Investment Bank
EMU	Economic and Monetary Union
EMP	Euro-Mediterranean Partnership
EP	European Parliament
EPC	European Political Cooperation
ESCAP	Economic and Social Commission for Asia and the Pacific
ESCWA	Economic and Social Commission for West Asia
EU	European Union
FDI	Foreign Direct Investment
FTA	Free Trade Area
FTAA	Free Trade Area of the Americas
FTCE	Free Trade Agreement of Central Europe
G7	Group of Seven most wealthy countries (United States, United Kingdom, France, Germany, Italy, Japan and Canada)
G8	G7 and Russia
GATT	General Agreement on Tariffs and Trade
GCC	Gulf Cooperation Council
GSP	Generalized System of Preferences
ICT	Information and Communication Technologies
IGC	Intergovernmental Conference
IMF	International Monetary Fund
LAS	League of Arab States
MAI	Multilateral Agreement on Investment
MERCOSUR	Mercado Comùn del Sur (MERCOSUL in Portuguese; Common Market of the South)
MFN	Most Favoured Nation
NAFTA	North American Free Trade Agreement
NATO	North Atlantic Treaty Organization
NGO	Non-Governmental Organization
NTBs	Non-Tariff Barriers

OAS	Organization of American States
ODA	Overseas Development Assistance
OAU	Organization of African Unity
OECD	Organization for Economic Cooperation and Development
OPEC	Organization of Petroleum Exporting Countries
OSCE	Organization for Security and Cooperation in Europe

| PRC | People's Republic of China |
| PTAs | Preferential Trading Arrangements |

SAARC	South Asian Association for Regional Cooperation
SADCC	Southern African Development Coordination Conference (subsequently SADC)
SEATO	South-East Asia Treaty Organization
SELA	Latin American Economic System
SPC	South Pacific Commission

| TEC | Treaty of European Community |
| TEU | Treaty of European Union |

| UDEAC | Customs and Economic Union of Central Africa |
| UN | United Nations |

WAEMU	West African Economic and Monetary Union
WEU	Western European Union
WTO	World Trade Organization

Introduction: Globalization, New Regionalism and the Role of the European Union

Mario Telò

This volume stems from the work of an international and multidisciplinary research group. The group includes political scientists, internationalists and social scientists who do not neglect to recognize the international economic structures shaping the new power hierarchies among states and regions. It also includes political economists who take into account the weight of the political factors in the changing globalized economy.

We begin by observing that globalization and new regionalism are not only economic but also multidimensional and political processes. Of course, the book neither deals with the pros and cons of free trade nor with the theory of international trade; its subject matter is also not international politics itself. Its particular focus is the *comparative analysis of regional organizations and their interrelations with the globalized economy and world politics of the post-Cold War era*. To focus on the political and strategic dimension of regionalism involves going beyond controversies among economists on the regionalism versus globalization relationship. It involves instead explaining the flourishing of regional organizations through endogenous and exogenous factors, and studying their current and potential impact on global governance. Regionalism and globalization are two components of the same historical process of strengthening interdependence and weakening the state's barriers to free trade, even if there can also be conflicting tendencies. This is shown by trade blocs, strategic traders and by current asymmetries and uncertainties of global multilateralism.

The group of scholars included here combines two peculiar approaches. Some of them are outstanding specialists in international relations. Many of them are prominent specialists in European integration studies, and they approach regionalism and globalization from a EU point of view. All focus on the comparison of regional arrangements with the EC-EU and the evolution of the EU as both a workshop of institutional innovation and an international entity after the end of the Cold War. Consequently, the book offers, on the one hand, a theoretical framework for new regionalism and a comparative analysis of other regional organizations, bearing in mind the European experience. On the other hand, it shows the characteristics of the European Union as a global player and also its proactive relationship with other regional organizations. The open question is to what extent this can be considered a significant part of its current and potential role as a new kind of 'civilian power', in the uncertain world politics of the early twenty-first century.

1   Three types of regionalism in the history of the twentieth century

The resurgence of regionalism must be placed in a broader historical perspective, including *three waves of regionalism during the twentieth century*. The world experienced the tragedy of both an aggressive nationalism and an imperial regionalism during the inter-war period. The international economy was characterized by the crucial fact that the British-centered hegemonic multilateral stability came to an end, which was already perceptible *in nuce* with the consequences of the Great Depression of 1873 and the Age of Empires. The crisis publicly crashed with the First World War and the international system came to its demise in August 1931, with the end of the Gold Standard's basis for the pound being one of the direct consequences of the Great Depression of 1929. After the failure of the International Economic Conference in 1933, it was finally realized that the UK could no longer play the role of hegemonic power and that the US could not, as yet, take over the role. The end of the long era of the self-regulated market and of free trade was an international event.[1] The American economic crash of 1929 had a huge global impact. It undermined the apparent economic boom of the 1920s, which J. M. Keynes had warned of ten years earlier, in *The Economic Consequences of Peace*. International economics shifted from open trade order and the first seeds of international liberalization (including the Most Favoured Nation Clause, MFN) to state protectionism, discriminatory and regionalist imperialisms.[2]

The parallel crisis in the fragile League of Nations peace system, the breakdown of the first steps towards a farseeing European unity design, namely the Briand-Stresemann dialogue, and the parallel Japanese expansion in East Asia, heralded the end of the first attempt to construct a modern multilateral collective security system able to cope with the challenges of the twentieth century. During the 1930s and the early 1940s, the world experienced the difficult times of both economic and political 'malevolent regionalism', as a result of German and Japanese attempts to become regional hegemonic powers. The military and fascist regimes of Japan and Germany replaced the former 'pax Britannica', holder of a cooperative king of balance of power, with new conflicts for regional domination, in Asia/Pacific and Europe respectively, provoking the outbreak of the Second World War.

Until then, in spite of its financial and economic strength, the US was not able to take the place of the declining UK as the hegemonic power in the international system. Post-war American hegemony took the form of an accelerated move towards a more institutionalized multilateralism, whose domestic roots are to be found in the New Deal pattern of regulated capitalism. Despite the evolving global system having its centre in European colonialism for four centuries, the main globalization tendencies no longer come from Europe since the Second World War. The 1944/47 multilateral political and economic institutions – the new monetary system based on the convertibility of the US dollar, the International Monetary Fund and the World Bank, the GATT, the United Nations and so on – provided an effective framework to overcome the catastrophic instability of the inter-war period. Between 1944 and 1947, these institutions attempted to include both former and potential enemies.

The beginning of the Cold War (1947) was a fundamental historical change, breaking universalistic perspectives.. However, this new type of US-centered multilateralism has for three decades, been the basic architectural principle for international cooperation and growing interdependence. The golden age of international economic growth only became possible due to harmony between the American design and practice of a 'trading state' and national Keynesianism (Clarck, 1997). The double aim of containing the Soviet threat and of creating a transatlantic community made it possible to harmonize the interests and ideals of the US New Deal, associating realism and idealism, namely peace, prosperity and democracy. This was typical of the new stable hegemonic international system (Ruggie, 1993).

A second type of regionalism, an economic regionalism, was set up during the 1950s and 1960s, which was compatible with such American-centered hegemonic stability and its vision of multilateralism. Particularly important was the regional integration of the European Community, which was inconceivable without taking into account the huge impact of American hegemony. Even if less successful elsewhere in the 'free world' and in the third world, regionalist experiments took place, for example in Asia, Africa and Latin America. During these decades the US, in spite of free trade ideology, tolerated many forms of national and regional protectionism abroad, which is clearly proven by the EC (for instance, Customs Union, Common Agricultural Policy, Lomé Convention, and so on), and the Latin American (supported by CEPAL and its ideology, and so on.) examples. With the exception of the EC, the results have been very poor.[3] Too many inward-looking economic policies, too weak institutional settlements, the legacy of colonialism and the weight of underdevelopment do explain the failure or the marginal impact of such a second type of regionalism.

As far as the EC is concerned, the harmony between transatlantic stability, which was centred on the trading state, the open market and national growth, started to decline with the end of the Bretton Wood Gold Standard system (1971) and the two oil crises of the 1970s.. There is no doubt that the end of the dollar as an international factor of stability undermined the American hegemony and also the idea of a 'Trilateral' Directorate of the capitalist world. This Directorate, the famous 'triad', including Japan, Europe and the USA, was supposed to rescue the former stability path but only announced the coming epoch of transition.[4] The first plans for a European regional monetary union (the 'Werner Plan') began in the early 1970s, even though the single European currency was not established before 1999. Step by step, a new regionalism is emerging and not only in Western Europe.

However, the question of the relationship between American leadership and new regionalism seems to be crucial in the new era of transition in the current international system. On the one hand, the scientific and public debate of the 1980s on the declining role of the US, though overemphasized, allowed one to speak of a 'post-hegemonic' international system from then on.[5] On the other hand, the collapse of the USSR in 1991 and the consequences of 9/11 confirmed the strength of the tendency towards a sole superpower. The successful New Economy of the 1990s and the 'wars against terrorism' confirm the leadership of the US as far as military, politics, economy and technology are concerned. Nevertheless, limits of unipolarism are evident and no new international order has yet been established. The parallel and opposing tendencies towards the decentralization and globalism of the world economic and political system are continuing within this uncertain framework. Regionalism shows as resilient to global changes and is about to evolve in many areas of the world, according to new patterns, trends and agendas. In continuity and discontinuity with the past, it is a matter of *a third, post-hegemonic, regionalism* as a component in a new turbulent and heterogeneous world system.

This volume focuses on this complex phenomenon and its theoretical implications. The current globalization process entails a broader and deeper (even if highly differentiated) new type of regionalism. During the last twenty years the world has witnessed, in parallel with the boom in international trade and foreign investments, the simultaneous development, or revival, of numerous and varied regional arrangements and regional organizations: the most well-known are the EU, NAFTA, ASEAN, Andean Community, MERCOSUR, SADC, SAARC and so on.[6]

Is this new regional dimension of international society a transient feature or is it able to constitute a long-term third trend between the anarchy of nation states and the international markets and globalism as developers of world governance? What is the balance between the economic and political dimensions of new regionalism and what are its systemic and domestic causes? To what extent is current multilevel, regional and global, multilateralism conflicting with unipolarism and, at the same time, is it unable to hinder moves towards fragmentation? Can it lead to an upward trend towards a new kind of multilateralism, including not only continental states and emerging economies (such as India and China) but also five or six regional trading blocs and regional entities and thus contribute to a new post-hegemonic stability? Which particular role does and could the European Union play in the foreseeable future, as an international entity supporting regionalism world wide? To what extent do its external relations and responsibilities have an impact on regional arrangements towards enhanced coherence and institutional consistency? And finally, what is the difference between the EU approach to regionalism and inter-regionalism and that of the US?

2 Domestic and systemic causes of new regionalism

This book offers, first of all, *a general overview of the common causes and features of new regionalism*. Important schools of thought are in conflict over two salient scientific issues. Firstly, what is the balance between domestic and systemic factors of regional integration? Secondly, how does regionalism interact with globalization? Let's start by examining the first divergence of opinion. On the one hand, domestic factors play an important role in developing new regionalism: the will of nation states, and mainly of regional leaders, to rescue their sovereignty and recover their international bargaining power, or the wish of minor states to balance the regional leader within a common framework. The second cause is the private interest of export industries and economic branches, of social groups, lobbying and networking on a national and regional basis. Thirdly, there is the internal functional spillover as a consequence of successful – even if limited to relatively marginal sectors – cooperation agreements. Political parties, groupings, associations, NGOs, may underpin regional construction according to their respective interests and ideologies. Finally, there is the desire of less developed countries to gradually cope with global competition by cooperating and converging with regional leaders.[7]

The so-called 'domino theory' stresses the importance of mutual emulations and reactions as far as the development of regional organizations is concerned, particularly emphasizing the 'multiplier effect' induced by the recent evolution of the EU and NAFTA, in Latin America and world wide.[8]

On the other hand, many scholars focus on the impact of systemic, exogenous, economic and political causes, which make it easier to underline what is common among regional organizations and to analyze variations provoked by the influence of national or subnational causes. As R. O. Keohane points out, without an overview of common problems, constraints and challenges set by the international system, we would miss the analytical basis to better understand the weight of domestic factors and distinguish them from external causes.[9] The particular approach of this volume combines both these classical schools of thought. It focuses, however, not only on the controversial economic effects of regionalism on globalization, but mainly on the political dimension of regional agreements and their impact on world governance.

The main systemic even if ambiguous explaining factor is globalization. The influence of the global system on national societies and on the regions of the world increased during the twentieth century and was accelerated after 1945, and even more particularly in the two last decades.[10] International forces, political actors and multinational companies are working on and shaping the relations and hierarchies between states, economic interests and regions of the world. From an economic point of view, regional arrangements provide clear advantages in terms of location (trade and investment, saving in transport and economy of scale). Furthermore, regional adjustments ease the recovery of the developing regions of the world, namely after hard financial crises, and also help them to cope gradually with the constraints of international competitiveness. Finally, larger regional markets make it possible for large companies to expand and to train for world competition. Whatever their institutional features are, preferential trade arrangements, regional arrangements and regional organizations have proliferated. Regionalism stands more and more in the centre of the globalized economics and world politics.

There are two dominant contradictory explanations for this boom. The first explanation is based on the GATT-WTO vision of regionalization as part and antecedent of systemic globalization. In other words, regional trade liberalization and cooperation arrangements are seen as necessary intermediate steps, enabling nations and companies to cope with the risks and opportunities of the global market and to accept new multilateral rules. Of course, this assessment is partially correct. In many cases, regional cooperation is certainly a good preparation for an open international economy, as proven, for example by the conclusion of the Uruguay Round (where integration into the EU induced some member states to accept the GATT deal)[11] or by the high impact of NAFTA on investments liberalization, or by the dynamics of ASEAN. As authoritative illustration of such a harmonic school of thought, Larry Summers argues that regional liberalization is the best way towards liberalization and globalization and that regionalism did not only damage the multilateral world trading system, but will increasingly be the decisive drive towards liberalization (and also the reverse).[12] By contrast to such an optimistic vision, a second classical and varied school of thought emphasizes *regional and subregional discriminatory agreements as reactions to globalization*. For instance, according to Bhagwati[13] regionalism slows down world-wide global liberalization and threatens the multilateral trade system. Furthermore, Bergsten[14] is of the opinion that it sets unilateral priorities in conflict with global ones, as illustrated by the example of the European Monetary Union. According to other comments[15] regional trading blocs will cause geo-economic conflicts, with potential for political consequences.

The chapters in this book highlight many facts which cast some doubts on this controversy. Our goal is firstly to explain the resurgence of regionalism at the end of the twentieth century and its common features and variations, independent of any qualitative appreciation of its potential to damage trade liberalization. The aim is secondly to go beyond this controversy, namely concerning the systemic causes of regionalism and its political dimension and consequences.

For example, many contributors stress the impact of the *fragile evolution of multilateral global trade bargaining on the strengthening political dimension of new regionalism*. On the one hand, the aforementioned GATT agreement in Marrakesh (1994) welcomed regional free trade agreements (article XXIV) as a step in the right direction. On the other hand however, the problems raised by the hard bargaining of the Uruguay Round, the failure of the WTO to commence a 'Millennium Round' in Seattle (1999) and to bring to a final compromise the 'Doha Round' in 2006, provoked uncertainty for many actors and a changing balance between regionalism and multilateralism. Fear of over-asymmetric globalization strengthens discriminatory agreements and competition on a regional basis. Region building is seen by many actors as a willingness to react to uncertainties and to compete better with other regions and economic powers. The question remains open whether new regionalism and inter-regionalism can better provide the rare public goods of governance and stability or instead damage global economic liberalization.

In this framework the meaning of the changing attitude of the USA towards regionalism needs also to be correctly interpreted. Firstly, the decision to create NAFTA and the project FTAA are new chapters in the economic foreign policy of the only remaining superpower. These can be seen as new leverages within a general multiple strategy, including regionalism, multilateralism and bilateralism. Even if not particularly successful, the participation of the US in many interregional groupings and projects (APEC, Free Trade Area of the Americas and so on) was expected making the asymmetries of the globalized or regionalized world's economy clearer. The Hettne paper and the book's chapters regarding Asia and Latin America show several conflicts between such US global multidimensional trade policy/foreign policy and new regionalism.[16]

Another systemic issue mentioned in many chapters is the complex impact of financial, technological and market globalization on the traditional territorial state power.[17] New regionalism can be seen as an attempt by states to react by strengthening regional control when traditional centralized national sovereignty no longer functions and to bargain collectively with extra-regional partners. The re-emerging geographical – or territorial – dimension of political regulation and external relations is often regional, instead of national. However, territorial logic interacts critically with functional logic. Domestic social factors, political pressures and democratic participation are strengthening a new bottom-up demand for the rescue of a territorial authority, as granting a better balance between *global* economy and *regional* values. States are attempting to revive political regulation by pooling authority at regional level, both as a voluntary and original decision and as an imitation of neighbour states or of models imported from abroad. According to a part of the literature, regionalism makes a partial rescue of national authority easier. In many areas of the world, new regionalism also limits the fragmenting and disintegrating impact of subnational regionalism, ethnic fundamentalism and the proliferation of movements for national self-determination by creating a new supranational framework. Even if in an oscillating way, in most cases domestic democracies have been reshaped.

To some extent, the success story of the manner in which the European Union copes with both traditional internal conflicts and national diversities, by transforming states' functions and structures, plays an important role as a reference (neither as a model nor as a counter-model) for new regionalism elsewhere.

Many chapters consider a further systemic question: how did world-wide economic and financial crisis, namely the one of 1997/98, affect regional cooperation? The biggest post-Second World War depression could be seen either as pressure towards greater integration or as a factor of the weakening regional cooperation of states, which was tempted to return to inward-looking policies or aggressive regionalism. Even worse: ethnic conflict, social chaos and political fragmentation can provoke not only re-nationalization but true disintegration as far as many parts of the globe are concerned.[18] However, many authors of the present book observe that the financial and economic crisis of 1997/98 did not halt new regionalism and that regional organizations proved to have an edge to go on. Furthermore, the fact that many countries belonging to the same region share the same problems and receive the same policy recommendations from world organizations (that is, liberalization, transparency, new regulatory frameworks, increased infra-regional trade, fiscal and monetary cooperation) is encouraging them to strengthen their cooperation at regional level. This is for the very simple reason that it seems easier to achieve domestic reforms and face external constraints if part of the national power is shared at regional intergovernmental level.

Ultimately, a salient political systemic cause of the growing political dimension of regionalism (summarizing the two former explanations) is the impact of the double transformation of the *hegemonic stability*, which existed after 1944/45. This combined American interests, the economic expansion of the Western world and the political goal of containment. Let us emphasize again that the above mentioned troubles of the American leadership during the 1970s (end of the Bretton Woods system and oil crises) and 1980s, allowed some international relations scholars to raise the huge question of a 'post hegemonic' stability. The second political transformation to be mentioned, because it is particularly useful in understanding the political dimension of regionalism, is the end of the Cold War and of the West–East confrontation. The unification of the world economy, with the end of its political division, the erosion of the previous blocs of alliances and the changing geopolitics of the world's power, the combination of fragmentation and the creation of new economic giants, were all features of this time. Most of the security challenges of the post-Cold War era are regional, and thus the answer must be, at least partially, regional. It is true, that, in some places new regionalism is a matter of the resurgence of old regionalist organizations born in the 1950s and 1960s, but they were for years in lethargy until the mid 1980s–early 1990s. The end of the bipolar world certainly played an important role in giving them a broader scope. Indeed, for many decades, communism figured as a potential alternative model for many developing countries. Its collapse turned out to be a huge unifying factor, not only for the world economy and financial market (linking the former second world to the west and shaping the former third world), but also for political democratization and for world culture, changing world wide, for example, attitudes towards economic liberalization. Many chapters inevitably address two questions. Is a strengthened regionalism a type of substitute, somehow replacing East–West cleavage with multi-regional trading bloc competition? To what extent does it interfere with the transforming political dimension of international order?

In fact, new regionalism matters, namely inwards, by conditioning states' and companies' strategies, and outwards by affording a dynamic contribution to the changing international system. It is not a transient but instead a structural phenomenon of international relations. Its problems and challenges are analyzed in the following chapters. Unipolarism and unilateralism, nationalist and local fragmentation, growing world economic players and new mercantilist policies provoked by fears of marginalization, unstable transnational functional dynamics – all of these can play, directly or indirectly, either a supporting or a conflicting role in the development of regional cooperation and new regionalism.

This volume is divided into three parts: a theoretical part, a second which includes a comparative analysis of new regional organizations and of the EU and a final part, focusing on the EU as a global actor, strengthening new regionalism world wide. The question is whether and how EU external relations provide a conscious and effective contribution towards extending and deepening regional cooperation elsewhere. This open question applies, first of all, in the so-called 'near abroad' (Mediterranean and Eastern Europe). It applies, secondly, in other continents where international relations could evolve from structural anarchy to regional or inter-regional regime building.

3   The political dimension of new regionalism as an alternative to the theory of hyper-globalization and to new medievalism

The new regionalist research paradigm is theoretically challenged by many views sharing the thesis that the political dimension of regional integration is unlikely.[19] Among these are the approaches of the 'globalizers' and the 'new medievalists'.

Let us follow A. Gamble starting with the first one. What is called in France *la pensée unique* and by business utopians 'hyper globalization' entails a new liberal vision of the cosmopolitan global economy, that of fast convergence of national economies, gradually rendering states and politics superfluous.[20] Some new Marxist and former dependence theorists paradoxically agree with new liberals in emphasizing such an interpretation of globalized capitalism,[21] even if that is sometimes complemented by the radical utopia of periphery uprising[22] or by catastrophic forecasts.[23] Whatever the abuse of the concept may be, a huge economic change entailing important political implications comes into focus. Transnational companies, global financial markets, private and public cosmopolitan networks are increasingly taking fundamental decisions and creating new authorities. As a consequence, many national governments only have to choose whether to adjust, or not, to the constraints of the globalized economy.

In this theoretical framework, the crisis in the classic principle of territorial sovereignty (established for five centuries in the main European states and theoretically founded by J. Bodin, N. Machiavelli, T. Hobbes) is accelerating since the nation state is seen as simply obstructing economic development. Consequently, regionalization is considered only as a gateway to a global economy. As a consequence of the feeling of loss for a territorial political authority, competitiveness is taken into consideration only at the level of sectors and companies.

However, such an approach has for many years now been a subject of harsh scientific criticism. The main issue raised by critical literature is that 'hyper-globalizers' do not answer that very simple question: what remains for political power and political bodies? Political bodies does not necessarily mean nation state, but instead actors and institutions embedding capitalism in governance; that is, state and non-state, formal and informal, institutionalized and non-institutionalized authorities.[24] Secondly, as said before, globalization is not only a technocratic bias. On the contrary, it includes both globalism, one or more global political projects, supporting various national and regional interests, and world politics, that is controversial public opinions and political alternatives.[25] Consequently, why should political projects not provoke political reactions? Regional arrangements are driven to a stronger political dimension. A third criticism is also that such discourse about globalization often becomes a kind of 'rhetoric ideology', instrumental to domestic goals of national elites whose menu of policies is certainly changing, but not however their ability to choose it.

The mentioned critics converge in underlining that timing and forms of globalization are the subjects of policies, conflicts and political decisions: that politics matters. Many of the contributors show that global, national and regional politics matter. When national authorities are overcommitted, new regional ones intervene as managers of the globalization process. Everywhere in the world, regional agreements are about to be founded and reinforced by state decisions. The emerging economic and political geography is regional rather than global, even if regional does at all mean against globalization, as Higgott well points out.

We come again with new arguments to the very controversial question addressed by economists: how and in which form consolidated and deeper regionalist projects are compatible with globalization. Pessimistic assessments of new realists (whether new Marxist or liberal) stress that the deepening of regional arrangements will inevitably provoke regional blocs, which will mean a zero sum game within global trade. In the worst scenario, hegemonic state-centered trade blocs will conduct tough economic conflicts, likely to shift towards demands for military security and, according to S. Huntington, 'holy wars'.

Our alternative, third approach, as illustrated by Gamble, Padoan, Hettne and Meyer, forwards various arguments against both harmonic and catastrophic scenarios, namely against subordinated identification and trivial opposition of regionalism and globalization. Gamble is particularly clear about the different ways in which regionalism intersects with globalization and especially globalism. Some years ago R. Keohane (1984) emphasized the fact that, within complex interdependence, and beyond hegemonic stability, new transnational institutions and regimes are mediating conflicts, making a positive sum game possible and economic welfare more likely for a larger number of countries. Many authors are convinced that new institutionalism provides the best theoretical framework for overcoming controversies of the nineties and elaborating new regionalism.

Such an approach must absolutely not be confused with '*Panglossian* optimism'. During these last two decades and particularly after 1989, from behind the embryonic cores which are apparently committed to 'open regionalism', new *strategic traders emerged*, including EU, MERCOSUR, ASEAN.[26] These established themselves within the globalized economy, like USA and Japan. Regional cooperation often becomes a means of enabling regional companies and national economies to be internationally competitive, to weaken competitors and to strengthen the bargaining power of nations and groupings of nations within the WTO and multilateral negotiations. The US and EU are particularly proactive regarding programmes of training, research, investment, public procurement, infrastructure, projects to maintain legal and managerial control over firms, setting international negotiation agendas. They are the two main global players and it is obvious that other regional organizations are about to emulate them.

A part of the answer to the question of the remaining room for strategic traders is whether economic differences and variations tend to adapt or to survive within such a global economy. In fact, a huge convergence process occurred in world capitalism during the past decades. The US economy was able to impose its model everywhere and was able to marginalize different forms of capitalism, even if deeply rooted in very divergent historic national traditions. However, the existing capitalist diversity has not much to do with regionalism before 1945 (Germany, Japan) and this book shares the view that there could be substance behind trade disputes: 'one of the forces driving the current regionalism is an attempt to protect models of economic and cultural organization'.[27] The same economic pattern of global development is still giving birth to various regional mix of sociocultural environments, institutional and legal frameworks and strategic policies, beyond national limits. By way of conclusion, we do not need to share catastrophic scenarios if we question the scientific credibility of the globalizers' vision.

This book pays critical attention to the 'new medievalist' paradigm as well. Current globalization is characterized by transnational networking, overlapping decision levels, declining distinction between the sources of authority and growing uncertainty about where sovereignty is located.[28] In this sense, the EU could be seen as the first post-modern state, because the European 'regulation of deregulation'[29] helps to weaken traditional kinds of political authority and became in fifty years the first factor in the transformation of the nation state. The second factor was the internal process of fragmentation and the empowering of subnational regions and entities – also supported by the EU. Nation state crisis includes political apathy, the growth of subnational regionalist movements, the privatization and mediatization of power and so on. Moreover, in Europe, but particularly in other continents, private domestic and international violence and criminal networks mean the decline of state monopoly of force. The weight of transnational links and growing functional loyalties are giving birth to a geocentric technology, mainly a communication technology, unifying the world and opposing national politics. Nation states are no longer able to form a protective shell and ought to be forced to share their authority. The result is a kind of confused multilevel global system of authority where states are involved with other entities (cities, particularly 'global cities', companies, subnational and transnational interregional bodies, private and public networks, international organizations and so on), but no longer as dominant actors. Summing up, according to this approach, supranational regions are nothing but a factor in the decline of states.

This new trans-nationalism would exacerbate the conflict between the principle of territorial sovereignty (political power) and the functional but non-territorial principle of interdependence. The continual tension between the two principles would constitute (in the new medievalist vision) the very nature of the modern world system. After seventy years of a 'kind of political diversion' (1917–89), such a reconfiguration of space-time would unify the contemporary world system.

The criticism of such an approach by this volume (A. Gamble and others) brings the reader back to the importance of political regionalism. Some of the current changes are permanent, some are transient. The state's authority is certainly declining, but is far from over in crucial sectors such as defence, security, and welfare. Its role as main framework of democratic legitimacy is even enhanced. The nation state changes rather than loses its role in several areas of governance. More generally, the unbundling of territoriality is only partial. New systems of law and forms of governance, which globalization itself does not provide, are demanded. Regional governance is often politically strengthened, as a complementary or subsidiary level of national and local governance. External challenges may push regional authorities to a better political coordination orienting the multilevel fragmented governance.

Finally, many authors agree with the declining salience of both mentioned intellectual challenges, represented by hyperglobalization theories and new middle age concepts. Indeed, they emphasize the impact of the current gap between demand and supply of good governance and government. Contrary to unipolar (empire, hegemony) and multipolar tendencies, they suggest a third scenario: a kind of new political economy of the partially globalized world demanding 're-regulation' at regional and global level, by reinforcing regionalized democratic governance as a part of a renewed multilateral and UN system. Many authors in this book find both the analytical and normative sides of such an approach very interesting. Indeed, the evolution of some regional arrangements, and particularly of the European Union, shows that regional 're-regulation' is likely to strengthen the multilevel system of authority', rebalancing it in favour of public centrally coordinated governance.[30] However, this process I find highly controversial as its achievements are concerned in the various regions of the world. Whether new regionalism can support a new post-hegemonic multilateralism (at both political and economic levels) and balance unilateral strategies of world governance demands to be better explored from the points of view of both comparative studies and first of all, of international political economy.

4   The political economy of new regionalism: are strategic regional traders providers of good world governance?

While recognizing many evidences of US leadership, many authors welcome the concept of a 'post-hegemonic world' as a general framework of emerging new regionalism. According to Padoan, the current global redistribution of power causes institutional imbalances, since the single superpower can no longer provide an equilibrium between increasing demand and diminishing supply of international public goods. To what extent could the proliferation of regional arrangements provide the partial supply of a new multilateral equilibrium? Even when taking into account international literature on political economy, many authors come to the controversial question of the *ambiguity of new regionalism*, either conflict-oriented regional blocs or cooperative regional agreements as a precondition for cooperation on a global level. However, while pure economic rationale would support world-wide trade agreements in the current fragile globalization, regional agreements exist and increase. Do their optimal size and internal cohesion have an impact on their contribution to world governance?

The number of countries demanding regional integration is important. It is a matter of fact that if associated with adjustments and reallocations, trade flows increase within regional agreements. Padoan proposes a 'gravity model', emphasizing the advantages of *geographic proximity*: limited transfer costs, common policies, common social and environmental standards, giving comparative advantage to regions within world competition. Other writers in this book, such as Vasconcelos, Eliassen/Børve, Söderbaum, also agree in their chapters, that regional trade liberalization enables members – especially the poorer – to reap some of the benefits of trade, via larger markets and improved efficiency, without exposure to non-regional competition.

The trade-off between increasing size and internal cohesion could become problematic. Simple trade agreements and monetary clubs can both provoke an asymmetrical internal redistribution of benefits and affect the expected improvement in the welfare of members. However, domestic consensus and political support for regional agreements (and also for their changing size) are possible only through the notion of 'cohesion'. Cohesion involves balancing the inequalities and asymmetrical effects of liberalization and implying 'a relatively equal social and territorial distribution of employment opportunities, wealth and income, corresponding to increasing expectations' (Padoan). The optimal size is achieved if the cohesion's costs do not outweigh benefits and if marginal costs (management, decision making, dramatically increasing with the number of member states[31] and demand for majority voting rules) equal marginal benefits, decreasing with the club's size.

The increasing demand for integration in regional clubs ('domino effect') due to globalization implies explicit and implicit admission fees, both in the case of trade and in monetary agreements. However, the marginal benefits, namely the security effects, are particularly relevant in case of an external threat (for example, trade war and monetary instability). The number of members is viewed as crucial to the success and deepening of regional organizations. The 'optimal size' varies in commercial or monetary clubs. According to this model, the international political economy is combined with a new institutionalist approach: importance of institutions as actors of internal cohesion, qualified majority voting rules, issues linkage, trust-building through repeated game and 'diffuse reciprocity' (Keohane, 1984).

Under these conditions regional groups can contribute to global governance. While globalization produces market instability, new regionalism can provide an answer to the demand for public goods and even better conditions for new multilateralism at global level:

a) National actors are better fostered to adapt and to adjust. An agreement between national and regional levels is a good precondition for an international regime, since international organizations interact better with the regional level.

b) Regional agreements imply issue linkages (economy and security, monetary and trade), providing exchange of information and stability. This could be very useful for stabilizing international regimes.

c) The national actors relatively long-term commitment to regional rules makes their propensity to adjust stronger, provided that the advantages of integration are relevant and consistent with domestic political equilibrium.

However, some final caveats. The main challenges are the contradictory implications of *the reduction in the number of actors* of negotiation within the international arena. On the one hand, it can help international cooperation without any hegemonic power, because bargaining between states is more difficult and less efficient than between regional blocs. On the other hand, regionalism might lead to a less cooperative regime: preferential trade agreements and selective market access increase the costs of exclusion and inter-regional conflicts. Furthermore, many member states demand regional clubs to provide them with better protection against global instability, which can consequently weaken the global multilateral system. If it is true that multinational enterprises and several transnational agents increase global interdependence, the convergence of policies and the diffusion of knowledge and innovation, asymmetrical capital mobility can, on the other hand, provoke protectionism in some countries or regional organizations. Furthermore, competition for location sites for multinational activities demands territorial regulation at either national or regional level. Competition among varying regulations can cause deterioration of rules or of rule enforcement, decreasing the costs of investment to the detriment of environmental and social costs.

Summing up, the economic perspective of new regionalism is remaining so ambiguous and open – cooperative and/or conflict oriented – that no clear theoretical conclusion could be drawn through a mere political economy approach. The multidimensional features of new regionalism, including the cultural and political interplay with globalization have to be further explored as key theoretical variables.

5 Economic rationale, identities, strategic actor hood: impact of the cultural and political factors on new regionalism

Even though the influence of cultural differences is increasing in both international and infra-national conflicts after the end of the Cold War, we can neither observe nor foresee a growing consistency between civilizations and regional blocs. T. Meyer's chapter provides an analysis of the current theoretical debate on the relationship between cultural, political and economic factors, which shape the globalized world. Its main conclusion is that regional arrangements present a high degree of internal differentiation in styles of civilization (traditionalism, fundamentalism and modernism), the combination and balance of which change with the evolution of history. Furthermore, cultural global interdependence and trans-regional similarities are more important than tendencies towards regional cultural cohesion. This means that the catastrophic concept of a genetic mutual exclusion of main cultures is not in tune with the facts, and that the concept of culture, underpinned by Huntington's idea of 'civilization's clash', is obsolete.[32] Of course political instrumentalizations of cultural values are also possible at subnational, national and regional levels, particularly in the hard times of economic and social crisis. However, fundamentalism is not in itself a consequence of culture and there is no evidence that regionalism can better channel cultural fundamentalism.

The fact that regional blocs do not correspond to civilization but instead include a variety of infra-state cultural groupings is particularly clear if one observes the three partners of the transatlantic triangle: the European Union, NAFTA and MERCOSUR. All three belong to the same Christian and Western culture, but are differentiated along West–West and North–South cleavages.

The attempts to strengthen cultural factors as a background for a politics of identity at regional level are openly rhetoric: for example the call for 'Asian values' by Mr. Mahatir, Malaysian Prime Minister, or for a 'Christian Europe' by some Catholic democratic leaders. The so-called 'fault lines' are not set between cultures but within cultures. Regionalism can be an opportunity for cross-cultural convergence, for practical examples of 'trans-culturality', to allow internal differentiation, for cross-cultural overlapping and for cluster building of a new kind. This can be seen in the fact that for instance, ASEAN incorporates peoples belonging to six different religions. Also NAFTA still includes a historically very difficult border – a state border but also economic and ethnic borders, between perhaps two of the most distant neighbors in the history of the world, Mexico and the US. After its planned eastern (and southern) enlargement, the widening EU includes very varied subnational cultures, linguistic groupings and also various social and economic standards. New regionalism is likely to hinder the politics of exclusive national identity, impeaching political leaders from using ethnic or religious fundamentalism for their own aims, in times of economic crisis and growing social deprivation and exclusion. Moreover, new regionalism helps to diminish the conflict between states and changing stateless subnational identities. It often allows management of the negative implications of the 'principle of self-determination', offering cultural or ethnic demands a broader and more encompassing alternative to sovereignty.[33]

However, the new century has shown that issues of collective identity increasingly matter and new regionalism is not at all the result of a mere rational choice of convergent rational actors, multinational companies, and domestic interest groups: 'cognitive regionalism'(see Higgott) underlines that it is a social construct. Many liberals and marxists underestimate the importance of identities and of the cultural and political dimension. The previous paragraph has shown that new regionalism goes beyond free trade arrangements. Some regional arrangements, such as SAARC, fail precisely because of political tensions provoked by the instrumentalization of religious differences. Australia is excluded from ASEAN in spite of high trade and economic interdependence. Although it improved in 2005, the status of the relationship between the EU and Turkey is still a special and problematic one. Last but not least, the call for a western identity in the war against Islamic fundamentalism after 9/11, is affecting regional cohesion and particularly inter-regional cooperation in the Mediterranean.

Political regionalism and interregional political dialogue are developing between two extremes poles: on the one hand, regional building processes based on mere free trade areas and, on the other hand, instrumental attempts to create some kind of regional civilization, or 'regional nationalism' (religiously or ethnically homogeneous), as a mutually exclusive background for new regionalist blocs. Many regional organizations already show, behind business networking and intergovernmental *fora*, a variety of tendencies towards regional public entities in the making: economic and social life diversities, cross-border political culture even if keeping national and local peculiarities. In normative terms, new regionalist organizations can set strict criteria for admission and enforce a commitment by member states to democracy, rule of law and human rights. Democratic regionalism and culture are the best reciprocal link and mutual support between international democracy and national democracy. When based on democratic core values, and shared institutions, they support the feeling of common belonging in spite of national and local different identities. Studies on the impact of regionalism on domestic democratization have shown how salient this issue already is. Constructivist approaches in international relations[34] and particularly new institutionalist views provide arguments for that multidimensional new regionalist scenario. Under such conditions, transnational cultural networks and trans-cultural dialogue can strengthen cross-cultural multilateralism and trans-regional coalitions. These help regional blocs to communicate with each other and to build a consensus, contributing to multilateral global governance. Björn Hettne chapter provides evidence of the political relevance of this stake as the competing inter-regional relations respectively set by US and EU are concerned.

In conclusion on this issue, even if cultural and political identity matters, new regionalism, in itself, does not have very much to do with scenarios of civilization clash. Of course, a populist leadership can instrumentalize it in order to support policies of regional fundamentalism and regional nationalism. Rather it has to do with alternative understanding of interregionalism along the transatlantic geopolitical and strategic rift. The role of the cultural and political dimensions is a distinctive feature of EU inter-regionalism. It can also ease both internal deepening and dialogue/cooperation between distinct regional entities. The institutional features and particularly national and supranational democratization seem to be crucial variables in linking regional policies, public spheres and cultural identities and international policies of regional organizations. In many areas, cultural interdependence can be strengthened by new telecommunication technologies and also provide an input into the development of civil societies and pluralism within the southern countries. This would have the consequence of enhancing the possibility of security partnerships.

6 Converging on a new institutionalist research agenda

As a final theoretical conclusion, the political and cultural dimension of regionalism and inter-regionalism are not only salient topics for comparative research. They support our institutionalist and constructivist approach by overcoming both the limits of the views of globalizers/new medievalists and the limits of a mere economic analysis. Several chapters in this volume confirm that, more than the simple descriptive concept of governance, new institutionalism, and namely sociological, historical and discursive approaches,[35] are theoretical frameworks which can make bridging between European integration studies, comparative regionalist studies and international relations easier. Governance is 'an organizing collective action', but it is vague and dated, not because it includes informal and non institutionalized kinds of authority (Rosenau, 1995), which is very appropriated. The problem is that the concept of global governance was conditioned in its origins by the optimistic, post-Westphalian, post-modern, intellectual climate of the early 1990s. This climate is over. War, security and state-politics are back in the global agenda. New institutionalism looks at the best way to face the challenge raised by the revival of Realpolitik and realist thought. Institutions are interesting because they change the behavior of states: they are the rules of the game that permit, prescribe, or prohibit certain actions and by doing so they inevitably raise the challenge of democratic legitimacy. The kind of regional and inter-regional institutionalization can vary of course, as its depth, solidity and formalization. Contrary to the state, international institutionalization can work without organization. Regional and global multilateral institutions, far beyond their instrumental functions, may strengthen and deepen states' cooperation: they limit uncertainty, risks of defection by providing member states with information about the preferences and intentions of partners; they encourage participants to adopt strategies that overcome collective action dilemmas, namely the security dilemma; the existence of a multilateral regime in an issue-area makes issues linkage easier; institutions increase mutual trust and credibility of commitments; once established, institutional dynamics and organizations matter is fostering critical transnational public opinion, and in some cases institutions (including regional entities) become to some extent autonomous as far as their life is concerned, towards political actors in their own right.

The more the majority of regional associations of states converge in deepening their institutional dimension and somehow pooling sovereignties of their member states, the more they can seriously challenge the Westphalian concept of world order and provide a contribution to a new multilevel multilateralism in the making.

Notes

1   K. Polanyi (1944); C. P. Kindleberger (1973); R. Gilpin (1981).
2   J. G. Ruggie (1993).
3   E. Haas (1975).
4   L. Thurow (1992).
5   R. O. Keohane (1984 and Preface to the second edition, 2004), R. Gilpin (1981). In the framework of a discussion focused on the so-called American decline, see also P. Kennedy (1985). R. Keohane, R. Cox, S. Gill and others transferred A. Gramsci's concept of hegemony to the international relations theory. Contrary to imperialism and dependence theories and according to Gramsci (1975), a hegemonic power dominates not only thanks to its economic strength and military, but also to its cultural and political supremacy, creating active consensus of both allies and subordinate states, even if at its own costs. Keohane, following Ch.Kindleberger (1973), adds that an hegemonic power is ready to cover the costs of providing the world with international public goods, as financial stability. See the excellent book edited by K. O' Brien and A. Clesse (eds.), *Two Hegemonies*, Ashgate, 2002
6   For a detailed description of existing regional organizations, see the Appendix by Santander. Recent literature includes: on new regionalism B. Hettne, Andras Inotai and Osvaldo Sunkel (eds.) *The New Regionalism Series. Vol. I–V*, Basingstoke, Macmillan 1999–2001; F. Laursen (ed.) *Comparative Regional Integration. Theoretical Perspectives*, Aldershot Ashgate 2003; Peter Katzenstein, *A World of Regions: Asia and Europe in the New American Imperium*, Ithaca, Cornell, University Press, 2005; F.Söderbaum/Tim Shaw, *Theories of New Regionalism*, Palgrave, 2003, *The EU as a Global Player*. F. Söderbaum/Luk van Langenhove, (eds.) *The Politics of Interregionalism*, Routledge, 2006, L.Van Langenhove, M.Farrell, B. Hettne (eds.), *Global Politics of Regionalism*, Pluto Press, London, 2005; J. Ténier, *Intégrations régionales et mondialisation*, Paris 2003.
7   European Commission and World Bank (1998), *Regionalism and Development. Report*, Brussels, 1997, Studies series, n. 1.
8   R. Baldwin (1993).
9   R. O. Keohane, The World Political Economy and the Crisis of Embedded Liberalism, in J. H. Goldthorpe ed. (1984), *Order and Conflict in Contemporary Capitalism*, Clarendon Press, Oxford.
10   I. Clarck (1997) and L. Fawcett and A. Hurrell, eds. (1995).
11   D. Piazolo (1998), pp. 251–71.
12   Larry Summers, ed. (1991) and particularly his article, *Regionalism and the World Trading System*.
13   J. Bhagwati and P. Arvind, Preferential Trading Areas and Multilateralism: Stranger, Friends or Foes? in Bhagwati and A. Panagariya, eds. (1996).
14   F. Bergsten (1996), pp. 105–20 and F. Bergsten (1997).
15   B. Buzan, *Regions and Powers*, Cambridge University.Press, 2003 and D. Lake and P. Morgan (eds.) Regional Orders ,Pennyilvania University Press, 1997.

16 See S. Haggard, Regionalism in Asia and in the Americas, in E. D. Mansfield and H. V. Milner eds. (1997).
17 See B. Badie (1999).
18 Among others, I. Wallerstein (1991).
19 For an introduction to this scientific discussion, E. D. Mansfield and H. V Milner (1997); Louise Fawcett and Andrew Hurrell (1995); W. Coleman and G. Underhill (1998), D. A. Lake and P. M. Morgan (1997).
20 K. Ohmae (1993) The Rise of the Region State, in *Foreign Affairs*, n. 78, Spring.
21 S. Latouche (1998).
22 S. Amin (1997).
23 J. Gray (1998).
24 P. Hirst and G. Thompson (1996).
25 According to Gamble's chapter, regionalism is also a state project, a system of policies, just like *globalism* is a policy of a certain political authority, whereas 'regionalization and globalization are complex processes of social change'. On the political origins of globalization, see D. A. Lake, Global Governance, in A. Prakash and J. A. Hart (1999) pp: 32–51. *Planispheres* 2 and 3 show different global strategies towards regionalism (see *Appendix*). See the chapter by Padoan.
26 L. C. Thurow (1992).
27 C. Crouch and W. Streeck (1997), *Introduction. The Future of Capitalist Diversity*, pp. 1–18.
28 H. Bull (1977) and S. Strange (1996)
29 G. Majone (1997) From the Positive to Regulatory State, in *Journal of Public Policy*, 17/2, pp. 139–67. For the concept of 'regulatory regionalism', see the chapter by R. Higgott.
30 R. Cox ed. (1997); Prakash and Hart (1999), Ruggie (1998).
31 M. Olson (1965).
32 S. Huntington (1996) pp. 122–49 and the theoretical debate, which follows in *Foreign Affairs*. See also B. R. Barber (1995) and the literature quoted by Th Meyer.
33 L. Fawcett and A. Hurrell, eds. (1995) Conclusion, pp. 309–27.
34 The concept of a 'shared sense of communal identity' has been proposed by C. A. Kupchan, Regionalizing Europe's Security, in E. Mansfield and H. Milner (1997). On 'cognitive regionalism' see the chapter by R. Higgott.
35 For a brilliant analysis of the differences between these approaches and the traditional 'rational choice institutionalism', see Vivien A. Schmidt, 'Comparative Institutional Analysis', in T. Landmann and N. Robinson (eds) *Handbook of Comparative Politics* (Sage, forthcoming).

PART I
Theoretical Perspectives

Chapter 1

Regional Blocs, World Order and the New Medievalism

Andrew Gamble

The end of the Cold War and the reunification of the world economy have fuelled debate on the future shape of world order. Many of the changes that have taken place since then appear contradictory. There has been a marked trend towards globalization and the creation of a more interconnected world economy and world society. This has often been associated with the erosion of the power of nation states to govern their economies, and the rise of new forms and agencies of global governance. At the same time there has been a substantial regionalization of economic activity and the strengthening of regionalist projects launched by core states or groups of states. The hopes that had been briefly expressed after 1991 for a new world order which would transcend the conflicts of the past were dashed after the events of 9/11 brought awareness of new perils and new insecurities, and the application by the United States and its allies of a new security doctrine and the declaration of a new kind of war, a war on terror.

This chapter examines four different futures for world order, based on contrasting perspectives on the forces which are currently shaping it. These are:

- Borderless world – a cosmopolitan global economy, in which states wither away, and a benign global governance is instituted through markets and democracy
- Regional blocs – division of the world into protectionist spheres of influence and rival civilizations controlled by a few great powers
- American Empire – a world dominated by a unilateralist United States
- New medievalism – a world in which there is no single source of legitimacy, but a complex set of levels and networks and jurisdictions shaping governance and identities.

1 Borderless world

The lack of agreement on the present nature of world order is a sign that a fundamental change is taking place in the way in which the world is ordered, but that we lack an adequate language to describe what is going on or to identify the new principles (Gamble, 2000). The old images and concepts remain powerful and seductive, none more so than the conventional international relations view of international politics as relations between states. However imperfectly the basic principle of the modern state system may have been realized in practice since it was enunciated in the Treaty of Westphalia in 1648, it has provided the dominant perspective on international politics for 350 years. This basic principle is the claim of supreme authority over a given territory. All local, particular and personal sources of authority are consolidated into a single public power within a defined territorial space. This public power has two key spatial dimensions: the boundary between the public and the private, and the boundary between the internal and the external (Ruggie, 1993). This principle of territorial sovereignty depended on the repudiation of those existing universal forms of religious and political authority which denied it. The new doctrines claiming exclusive sovereignty for the prince over all matters within a territory, including its religious affiliation (*cuius regio eius religio* and rex in regno suo est imperator regni suo) did not go uncontested, but they were increasingly in the ascendancy from the sixteenth century onwards. They helped justify the dividing up of the world into states which claimed absolute sovereignty over the territory they controlled, recognizing no superior jurisdiction.

1.1   Globalization

This way of conceiving the international state system has had to be rethought because the idea of territorial sovereignty no longer captures the contemporary nature of political rule (Ruggie, 1993). The rethinking has been gathering pace since the 1970s as more and more changes appeared which did not fit easily within the assumptions of the Westphalian perspective. It has produced an extensive literature around the new trends of globalization and regionalization, raising the question of whether the era of the nation state is finally over. The nation state has been declared an anachronism, facing forces which it can no longer control. A global economy is emerging, dominated by new actors, such as transnational companies, banks and NGOs. States are increasingly subordinate and reactive.

Yet globalization, as many have recognized, is not a new theory. Global economic forces and global markets have existed since the emergence of capitalism. In *The Communist Manifesto* 150 years ago, Marx put forward one of the earliest and boldest theories of globalization, and he has been followed by many later writers, most recently world system theorists (Wallerstein, 1974, 1984). World systems theory emphasizes the contradictory character of the world system as a (relatively) unified economy and a (relatively) fragmented polity. For theorists of globalization the world economy is best characterized as a global rather than an international economy. An international economy is made up of separate national economies, controlled to a greater or lesser extent by states. Nation states are at the centre of this world. They derive their legitimacy and their power from their control over discrete national territories, populations and resources. Flows of goods, people and capital have to be sanctioned by political authority.

A global economy, by contrast, is one in which the fundamental units are not nation states and national economies but patterns of production and consumption organized by transnational companies, operating across national borders, and not reliant on any particular national territory or government. Economic decisions are shaped not at the level of national governments but through the workings of the global financial markets and the patterns of international trade and production. Governments have to adjust their societies and economies to the changing requirements of the global economy, or risk impoverishment and isolation.

1.2 Hyper-globalization

The tendencies towards the creation of a global economy have existed since the beginning of capitalism, but they have been stronger in some periods than others. Since the collapse of the Bretton Woods system in 1971 the balance between transnational economic forces and national governments moved in favour of the former. The international state system and the principle of order which it embodied came under severe strain. Supporters and critics of the new global economy have argued that in this changed environment national governments lose their autonomy and become ciphers for global economic forces. A new cosmopolitan society emerges, unified around a single set of political, social, economic and ideological principles, in which there is no room for fundamental alternatives. History has ended (Fukuyama, 1992).

Strong versions of globalization (or hyper-globalization, as it is sometimes called) claim that borders are becoming obsolete. The nation state is no longer an appropriate unit of analysis or agent of governance because economic activity in the global economy no longer coincides with political or cultural boundary lines (Ohmae, 1995). Yet the nation state, although increasingly irrelevant, can still obstruct the development of the global economy. It uses its centralized powers to raise taxes and redistribute resources according to the pressures of special interests. The result is a cumbersome, inefficient bureaucracy which makes national government the enemy of the wider public interest in maximizing the conditions for prosperity and growth. The enthusiasts for hyper-globalization want the powers of the nation state to be dismantled and the growth of region states encouraged. Region states are ports of entry to the global economy, typically urban conglomerates and their hinterlands, with populations of between 5 million and 20 million people; their borders are defined economically, rather than politically. They depend on the existence of resources and skills which are located close together, but not necessarily within a single national jurisdiction. Competitiveness is determined at the level of sectors and firms, not at the level of the national economy. The key policy issue is whether national governments have the will and ability to embrace the global economy and resist pressure for national policies of protection and subsidy. The only role for governments is to become market states (Bobbitt, 2002) and facilitate the globalization of their national economies. By doing so, they bring nearer the nineteenth-century dream of a global cosmopolitan society which is coordinated and managed without the need for politics, and in which national attachments have become insignificant.

1.3 Critics of neo-liberalism

The globalization thesis does point to some important and real changes which have been taking place in the world economy and have led to a weakening of nation states and an erosion of their sovereignty, but critics argue that at least in its hyperglobalist form it is exaggerated. There is little evidence that a global economy is emerging which overrides the modes of governance organized through nation states and exists independently of them (Hirst and Thompson, 1996). Global economic forces and global markets are always embedded in governance, both state and non-state (Peters and Pierre, 2000). Forms of governance have been changing, but the global markets themselves lack the capacity to supply their own internal mechanisms of governance.

In discussing globalization it is important to distinguish between, first, the trends which are extending and deepening connections of many different kinds (Perraton et al., 1997), and second, the normative political project, globalism, better known perhaps as neo-liberalism (Harvey, 2003), which promotes particular policies while ruling out alternatives. Globalization rhetoric has been increasingly adopted by state elites to justify substantial changes in domestic policies, particularly on public spending, welfare and industrial intervention (Hay and Marsh, 2001). But how constrained are national policies? Even if some of the changes which globalization highlights have altered the limits within which national governments may act, some argue that at most it has changed the menu of policies from which governments have to choose, rather than the ability to choose itself (Hirst and Thompson, 1996). From this perspective states still operate in an international rather than a global economy.

2   Regional blocs

The second perspective starts from this claim, that the new global economy has regional and national foundations (Zysman, 1996). Politics and the state remain of vital importance to the way in which the global economy develops and to the institutional and cultural variety within it. Far from globalization sweeping away all political structures, it is creating new ones. The political response to globalization has been the setting up of new structures and new projects. The emerging economic geography is regional rather than global, and a distinctive aspect of the emerging world order is the creation or consolidation of regionalist projects (NAFTA in the Americas, the EU in Europe and ASEAN in Southeast Asia).

The existence of these regionalist projects is clear enough, although they are very different from one another (Gamble and Payne, 1996; Hettne and Soderbaum, 1998; Breslin and Higgott, 2000). A key theoretical and practical question is what they signify. Are they compatible with globalization, even steps towards it, or do they foreshadow a turn away from the cosmopolitan world economy and a return to closed, antagonistic regional blocs? The latter view has its roots in realist perspectives in international relations, both liberal and Marxist. At its heart is a pessimistic assessment of the workings of the international state system. Left to themselves, states will be single-minded and ruthless in the pursuit of their security; the normal state of international relations is conflict.

2.1   The inter-war crisis

This is not a new view. Writing in the 1940s, E. H. Carr analyzed how the world order sustained by British hegemony in the nineteenth century had fallen apart in the twentieth. Carr described this world order as 'the golden age of continuously expanding territories and markets, of a world policed by the self-assured and not too onerous British hegemony, of a coherent 'western civilization' whose conflicts could be harmonized by a progressive extension of the area of common development and exploitation' (Carr, 1946: 224). The First World War had shattered this world beyond repair. During the 1920s there was a tendency towards disintegration and fragmentation of larger political units, particularly in Europe, but this was quickly followed by the reorganization of the world into a system of regional blocs:

> The more autarky is regarded as the goal, the larger the units must become. The United States strengthened their hold over the American continents. Great Britain created a sterling bloc and laid the foundations of a closed economic system. Germany reconstituted Mittel-Europa and pressed forward into the Balkans. Soviet Russia developed its vast territories into a compact unit of industrial and agricultural production. Japan attempted the creation of a new unit of 'Eastern Asia' under Japanese domination. Such was the trend towards the concentration of political and economic power in the hands of six or seven highly organized units, round which lesser satellite units revolved without any appreciable independent motion of their own. (Carr, 1946: 230)

Carr analyzed the trend towards regional blocs in terms of power politics, distinguishing between military, economic and ideological forms of power, and interpreted world politics as a struggle for power between rival states. Classical Marxism reached similar conclusions in its analysis of the formation of regional blocs in the 1930s (Sweezy, 1942; Brewer, 1990).

2.2   Hegemonic breakdown

One of the implications of Carr's analysis was that the breakdown of the world order in the 1930s and the formation of regional blocs followed inevitably from the collapse of British hegemony. This argument became the main theme of the hegemonic stability school which developed in the 1970s. The Great Depression in the 1930s was explained by the lack of a state capable of providing world leadership (Kindleberger, 1973). The institutions of the liberal world order collapsed because of the inability of Britain to continue to play the role of hegemon and supply the public goods necessary to stabilize the global economy, and because of the absence of any other power able or willing to fill that role. The Second World War created the conditions for the emergence of a new hegemon, the United States, which produced the successful reconstruction of the world economy and the long period of prosperity in the 1950s and 1960s. But the gradual erosion of the economic supremacy of the United States meant that its hegemonic power began to decline in the 1970s, and it was no longer able to guarantee the conditions for a stable liberal world order. The results were the recessions and economic instability of the 1970s and 1980s. If no power is able to supply the public goods which a liberal world order requires then states will respond with mercantilist and protectionist policies, as they did in the 1930s. Many observers in the 1930s concluded at that time that the future belonged to national economies and regional blocs.

   One of the characteristics of regional bloc scenarios in the first half of the twentieth century and again today is that the nature of the conflict between the blocs is assumed to be a zero-sum game in which each bloc competes to increase its relative share of territory, resources and wealth within a global total which is fixed. In this neo-realist perspective regionalism simplifies and intensifies this conflict, by combining the most important states into more or less cohesive groups under the leadership of the dominant state in each region. The pressure on a region to become cohesive increases in relation to the success of other regions in unifying themselves. As each regional power seeks to maximize its wealth and extend its territory, the risk of economic wars rises, because in a zero-sum world each regional power calculates that conflict will yield more benefit than cooperation.

2.3   Critics of regional blocs

Gloomy forebodings of economic wars and holy wars (Huntington, 1993) have reappeared in the last ten years; but they are challenged by other scenarios which predict a future of increasing prosperity and peace, the settling of the ideological conflicts which have dominated world politics for 200 years and the universal acceptance of a common set of ideas about economic and social organization associated with the idea of a cosmopolitan global economy. On this view the clash of civilizations predicted by Huntington will not materialize because there is only one civilization – Western civilization – which is adapted for survival. The ethic of ultimate ends contained in Confucianism, Islam and Christianity all belong to the pre-modern stage of social development, and are destined to be left behind.

Liberal institutionalists further argue that as the world economy becomes more interdependent, it becomes rational for states to prefer cooperation to conflict (Keohane, 1984). States increasingly face common problems which can only be handled through agreement on new institutions and rules. As interdependence deepens, so the risk of major economic or military conflict should decline. Democracies do not fight one another, so as democratization spreads, the less likely it becomes that conflicts between states will be settled in the future by resort to arms. New transnational institutions develop to mediate conflicts. These theories reject the assumption that states face a zero-sum game. Instead, they assume that there is a positive-sum game in which states can cooperate either through competition or through intergovernmental negotiation to increase the total output of goods and services available for distribution. Economic welfare can be improved for everyone so long as positional goods such as territory and resources do not become the focus of competition. An earlier Marxist version of this argument can be found in the theories of ultra-imperialism, the peaceful joint exploitation of the world by the united finance capital of the great powers (Brewer, 1990).

2.4   Regionalism and globalization

If the world is not facing a return to regional blocs, what explains the recent growth of regionalism and how far is it compatible with globalization? One of the problems is the different levels of analysis at which these concepts operate. Regionalism is a type of state project which can be distinguished from other types of state project such as globalism. Globalization and regionalization are not state projects but complex processes of social change which involve distinctive new patterns of social interaction between non-state actors (Gamble and Payne, 1996). State projects like regionalism typically seek to accelerate, to modify, or occasionally to reverse the direction of social change which processes like globalization and regionalization represent.

In practice, regionalism as a set of state projects intersects with globalization. The relationship between the two has come into particularly sharp focus with the end of the Cold War. The global economy in the 1990s developed not two but three cores: North America, the European Union and East Asia. The former core around the Soviet Union has disintegrated, allowing the three embryonic cores within the former capitalist world economy to emerge as the constituent elements of the new order, each with its own regionalist project. The relationships between these three cores and between the cores and their peripheries is both complex and diverse. No single pattern has become established. What they all share, however, is a commitment to open regionalism; policy is directed towards the elimination of obstacles to trade within a region, while at the same time minimizing trade barriers to the rest of the world. Policy debate has been conducted not between advocates of free trade and of protection, but between advocates of free trade and of strategic trade. The strategic traders have argued that maintaining and improving international competitiveness needs to be the central goal of economic policy. Instead of insulating the economy from foreign competition, the aim is to expose it to competition while at the same time ensuring that it is able to meet it. Strategic trade arguments deny free trade arguments that an optimum specialization of labour dictated by comparative advantage will arise spontaneously. Rather, states must act strategically to protect key sectors and ensure that they become international leaders in those areas (Reich, 1991; Thurow, 1992).

All the current regionalist projects, even NAFTA, have been driven to some extent by a strategic trade view. One of the benefits of greater regional cooperation has been the possibility of enabling regional companies and sectors to be successful in global markets. The emphasis is placed on training, research, investment, public procurement and infrastructure, and the need to maintain legal and managerial control over firms. Strategic trade assumptions have always been important in some states, but they have become more prominent recently. Free traders regard them as a diversion from the task of building a non-discriminatory open world trading system, and dispute claims that states are equipped to plan strategically in the way that companies attempt to do (Krugman, 1994; Wolf, 2005).

The strategic trade argument has also influenced the models of capitalism literature which argues that there are distinctive models of capitalism that are regionally or nationally specific (Albert, 1991). The dominant Anglo-American model, with its emphasis on free trade, arm's-length banking and a laissez-faire policy regime, contrasts with the Japanese and Rhenish models, which emphasize strategic trade, long-term investment, and corporatist and partnership modes of corporate governance and policy formation. Such models, however, are ideal types. Although there are some significant differences between national institutional patterns which give rise to competing strategies for coping with competitive pressures in the global economy, they are easily exaggerated. Strategic trade considerations, for example, have always been important in some sectors of the United States, particularly defence, while some sectors in Europe and Japan have been governed entirely by the rules of free trade. More recently the idea of national models has been further challenged by the Varieties of Capitalism approach, which seeks the source of variation at the level of companies and sectors (Hall and Soskice, 2001).

The new regionalism is contained within quite narrow ideological parameters, reflecting the continuing ideological and cultural leadership of the United States. The competition between models or varieties of capitalism of the last twenty years is much less fundamental than the earlier conflict between national capitalisms. Charles Maier, for example, has argued: 'Viewed over the whole half century the American international economic effort of the era of stabilization centred on overcoming British, Japanese, and especially German alternatives to a pluralist, market-economy liberalism' (Maier, 1987: 1183). That battle was won, and although important differences remain, they do so within a shared set of neo-liberal assumptions. One of the forces driving current regionalist projects is an attempt to protect what survives of different models of economic and cultural organization. A limited regionalism which does promote some diversity within the capitalist world has been the result.

3 American empire

The third perspective does not accept that the growth of new regionalism in recent years indicates that the US is in decline or that the world is fragmenting into regional blocs. Instead it sees a world in which the US is currently extending its power and transforming itself into an Empire (Rapkin, 2005; Cox, 2004). The huge military preponderance of the US since the demise of the Soviet Union means that no other power is capable of challenging the US militarily, and the determination of the US to maintain its global reach and a network of bases and dependent powers in every continent is undimmed. By providing a security umbrella for its closest allies, the US makes it unnecessary for those allies to acquire large military forces themselves. The US intervenes in every continent to secure its basic geo-political objectives, access to markets and resources, particularly oil. At the same time the US continues to dominate the world economy through its financial power, and the world-wide operations of its transnational companies, and its lead in many of the new technologies of the latest phase of industrial development.

The US has acquired a position of dominance which many observers consider exceptional in the international state system, because for fifteen years it has had no serious rival. Japan has remained dependent upon the US for its security, while the EU, although no longer dependent upon the US as it was during the Cold War, has failed to develop an effective defence and security policy, and in particular has failed to raise its military spending to anything like the US level. Although relations between the US and the EU have therefore grown more distant in the recent past, particularly during the Iraq war, the EU is not seen in Washington as a serious rival to the US, more as an irritant, and even then many EU states have continued to collaborate with the US through NATO on issues of common concern.

New powers such as India and China have the potential eventually to rival the US, but it will not happen quickly, and in the meantime the US continues to dominate the international state system, acting unilaterally and without consent, as in Iraq, whenever it judges one of its vital geo-political interests is threatened. It has begun to act much more as an imperial rather than a hegemonic power, and some observers have found this praiseworthy, and indeed urged the US to go further and openly proclaim its imperial mission (Ferguson, 2004).

3.1 Critics of empire

Popular though the designation of the US as a new empire has become, particularly following the ascendancy of the neo-conservatives in Washington, the elaboration of the Bush doctrine of pre-emptive action, the declaration of an axis of evil, and the invasion of Afghanistan and Iraq. But there have always been powerful sceptics of the idea that the US is a new empire or if it is that it can sustain itself as one. Firstly, the US is an incoherent empire. It lacks many of the capacities it would need to be a truly effective imperial power (Mann, 2003). Secondly, a long-lasting empire requires the ability to impose direct territorial rule and imperial jurisdiction. The Americans have always been good at going in but have rarely stayed. The number of territories permanently administered by the US is not increasing. The US continues to be torn between an imperial and a hegemonic logic, as Britain once was, and the hegemonic logic is still extremely powerful – preserving a rules-based multilateral regime for the ordering of the international state system and the global economy (Ikenberry, 2004). This has often involved the use of military force, but it has not involved permanent US occupation of territory. This makes the US a very different kind of empire from those in the past. Finally the US may be supreme in the military sphere (although even this supremacy has its limits as the difficulties the Americans have encountered in subduing insurgencies in Iraq and Afghanistan demonstrates). But it is far from supreme in other areas, and is unable to impose its will, but must work through coalitions, negotiation and compromise. These areas include the global economy, where the US cannot dictate in areas like trade, but must bargain with the EU, Japan, and new groupings involving India, China and Brazil. US trade and budget deficits also indicate a long-term structural weakness, of the kind which heralded British decline in the past. Other crucial areas include all those issues which arise from the interdependence of the global economy and global civil society – such as climate change, pollution, drugs, crime and terrorism (Nye, 2002). The idea that a unilateralist America can impose its own solutions to these problems looks fanciful. The return at some stage to more consensual, multilateralist approaches seems inevitable.

4 New medievalism

All three perspectives so far seem inadequate in various ways to grasp the implications of globalization and regionalization for the changing shape of world order. An alternative approach is new medievalism, a term first employed by Hedley Bull (1977). New medievalism is best thought of as a metaphor which draws attention to some similarities between contemporary developments and certain features of the medieval political system in Europe. No one suggests that there could be a return to the medieval era. Rather what the concept highlights is whether the principle of exclusive territorial sovereignty so typical of the modern era will turn out to be a unique and aberrant phase in political development (Kobrin, 1996). New medievalism involves contrasting the modern with the medieval state system and arguing that some of the features of the latter are becoming salient again (Tanaka, 1996).

The fundamental aspect of old medievalism in Europe was that there was no ruler with supreme authority over a particular territory or a particular population. Authority was always shared: downwards with vassals, upwards with the Pope – and, in Germany and Italy, with the Holy Roman Emperor. The source of authority was religious, not secular; it was derived from God. The medieval system was theocratic, and this gave it its unity. In 1400 European Christendom still thought of itself as one society (Mattingley, 1964). Authority was multiple and boundaries were overlapping. No centre of universal competence was recognized. There were three separate systems of law – canon law, customary law and civil law – based on three different traditions – Christian, German and Roman – making the administration of justice complex. Political authority was organized through elaborate hierarchies, a chain of dependent tenures and fiefs. Such interlocking relationships promoted stability because sovereignty was distributed not concentrated, with the functions of the state split up and assigned to different levels and locations, such as manors and cities. All this made the centre extremely weak. Monarchs were not supreme authorities ruling their subjects as they subsequently strove to do. They had to rely for financial resources on their own personal domains. Their vassals owed them military service but not taxes, while the existence of the vassals and their local authority meant that monarchs had no way of communicating directly with the whole population. The absence of a mechanism to integrate and consolidate authority at the centre of the feudal system posed a permanent threat to its stability and survival, and made conflict endemic (Anderson, 1974).

Critics of the idea of a new medievalism point to major differences between the medieval and the contemporary world order. Firstly, European medievalism was only one, local, political and cultural order in the world at that time. In place of the separate and largely self-sufficient civilizations of this period there now exists an increasingly interdependent global system, and Europe and East Asia, for example, are interdependent parts of this system rather than separate worlds. Secondly, there is no theocratic basis to the modern state system, except for a few Islamic states, and no universal doctrine in the way that Christianity was a universal doctrine for Europe, although neo-liberalism has pretensions in this direction. Thirdly, the Westphalian system of discrete territorial sovereignties is still strong; indeed, in some respects, with the creation of many new nation states following the breakup of the Soviet Union, it has grown stronger. The modern conception of the public power as the capacity to create new laws and impose obedience to them has been challenged and weakened in some areas, but remains intact in others, and is even being strengthened (Anderson and Goodman, 1995).

But there is still some value in the idea of a new medievalism. It focuses attention on the implications of the evident weakening of states in the last twenty-five years, which have seen boundaries become blurred and the source of authority less distinct. States have been obliged to share authority with other actors, and their ability to command the exclusive loyalty of their citizens in some areas has diminished. Hedley Bull identified five major trends which gave support to the idea of a new medievalism, all of which have grown in importance since he wrote.

- *Regional integration* – the European Community (EC) being the most prominent example at that time. Bull speculated as to whether the EC was developing into a new super state, in which case it would not disturb the traditional international state system, or whether it was a new hybrid, in which sovereignty would be shared between the Community and the member states indefinitely, producing perpetual uncertainty about where sovereignty was located. Bull here anticipated the more recent discussion of the European Union as a new type of political system, the first post-modern state (Ruggie, 1993; Anderson and Goodman, 1995; Telo, 2005).
- *Disintegration of existing states* – principally as a result of new secessionist movements (Nairn, 1981). Again, Bull noted that this trend would be of significance for new medievalism only if the disintegration stopped short of the creation of new states. In that case, the basic principles of the Westphalian system would be upheld, not denied. Of interest to the perspective of new medievalism is the intermediate stage, in which existing sovereignty is questioned but new sovereignty is not fully asserted, creating uncertainty as to where sovereignty is actually located, as well as the increasing number of 'failed states' (Fukuyama, 2005).
- *Revival of private international violence* – Bull was thinking primarily of the growth of international terrorism, but others have also talked about the spread of disorder, corruption, business mafias and private violence more generally. One of the crucial aspects of territorial sovereignty was the claim to monopoly of the means of coercion. Only states were recognized as having legitimacy to wage war or to coerce their citizens. States have not lost this legitimacy, but in some areas their ability to enforce their claims to a monopoly of the means of violence has weakened. The growth of international terror organizations equipped with new techniques and strategies is one example (Hoge and Rose, 2005).
- *Growth of transnational organizations* – Bull detected an explosion in such organizations, ranging from companies, political movements and religious associations to international and intergovernmental agencies. He argued that every organization should be classified as national, multinational or transnational in terms of three dimensions: who controlled it, its personnel and the geographical scope of its operations. The increasing number of organizations defined as transnational in terms of all three criteria suggested a growing divide between a geocentric technology and an ethnocentric politics. The nation state could still be considered strong in certain areas, such as the deployment of military forces and the ability to command the loyalty of citizens, but transnational civil society has been growing in importance (Scholte, 2005).

- *Technological unification of the world* – particularly in communications, transport and cultural networks, captured in ideas such as the global village. As Bull pointed out, a better term is global city, since this way of life – nervous, tense, agitated and fragmented – is more characteristic of urban than of village life. The emergence of new economic and cultural spaces which are global rather than national is another potential challenge to the state system and its authority, because it allows citizens to escape its control (Rosenau, 1990). But even here many spaces remain obstinately national and local.

4.1 Multi-level systems of authority

Although Hedley Bull was sceptical as to how far any of these trends would actually lead to permanent changes in the international state system, the metaphor of new medievalism has proved powerful, and its relevance has if anything increased in recent years. Susan Strange's observation that the world is beginning to look more like the European middle ages with multi-level systems of authority than the Westphalian system of territorial sovereignty, has been developed by Robert Cox (Cox, 1996), who has enumerated a number of ways in which this is true. Cities are once again meaningful centres of global interaction and exchange. Provinces and sub-national regions are achieving autonomy as states lose efficiency. Macro-regions are taking on some of the roles performed by states. The loyalty of companies is now multiple rather than unique, and a new global consumerism is being established which promulgates universal norms of economic and political conduct and assists the convergence of tastes and hierarchies of values.

These trends lead to the emergence of a new world order which is characterized by a multi-level structure and the breakup of the old state system. The new order is a complex structure of political–economic entities: micro-regions, traditional states and macro-regions with institutions of greater or lesser functional scope and formal authority, and world cities. The development of this new order poses a fundamental challenge to the old system because it sets up rival transnational processes of ideological formation as well as institutions for concertation and coordination, and multilateral processes for conflict management, peacekeeping and regulation. States are involved in these processes, but not always as the dominant agents (Scholte, 2005; Cerny, 1990).

This new world order exacerbates the conflict which has always existed in the world system between the principles of interdependence and territorial sovereignty. Interdependence is non-territorial, and is characterized by competition in the world market, global finance unconstrained by territorial boundaries, and global production. The territorial principle is state-based and grounded in military and political power. For Cox, one has not risen at the expense of the other. The two principles define the nature of the modern world order and there is a perpetual tension between them.

4.2   Unbundled territoriality

John Ruggie has taken the idea of new medievalism one stage further by arguing that the term is useful if it helps us to understand that we are living through a major transition as significant as the one between the medieval and the modern eras. The inability of many theorists, journalists and politicians to understand the EU is attributable to its being the first post-modern international political form. It is neither national nor supranational; instead, there are overlapping layers of economic and political space. Ruggie strongly attacks neo-realists who argue that unless the EU becomes a unified state it has no real significance in the international state system, and that since it was primarily a by-product of the superpower conflict, the disappearance of that conflict has removed its rationale. What this ignores is the growth of new institutions, new jurisdictions and new spaces which signal a new form of political rule which cannot be fitted into the old categories.

Ruggie accepts the arguments of Jameson and Harvey that it is not just the international state system which is in crisis but modernity itself. Capitalism is moving into its third great phase of expansion. The first was the national market; the second was the imperial system; and the current phase is the production and manipulation of signs, images and information (Jameson, 1984, 1989). Central to this new phase of capitalism is the reconfiguration of space–time experiences, the first major upheaval since the Renaissance (Harvey, 1989). The experiences, Ruggie argues, have changed; but the perceptual equipment is lacking to make sense of them. Crucial to the concept of space in the modern era was single-point perspective, developed by Filippo Brunelleschi in 1425. Its original application was in painting, but it came to influence the form of all intellectual enquiry. In international relations it helped shape the concept of sovereignty, the viewing of all political relations from a single fixed point.

The specific spatial and temporal coordinates of modernity have been overturned by what Ruggie, following Halford Mackinder, terms the spatial and temporal implosion of the globe. Mackinder, writing at the beginning of the twentieth century, declared that the age of Columbus (the age of European expansion) was over and predicted the emergence of a unified post-Columbian world system (Mackinder, 1904). The Bolshevik revolution delayed that outcome for seventy-five years, but with the collapse of the USSR there is now no major barrier to the integration of all territories and states into a single world system. The ideology of globalization is a reflection of that.

This new stage in the development of the world system will be characterized, Ruggie argues, by a new system of rule of which the EU is the first harbinger. The basis on which the international political system is segmented into units and spaces is changing. The old mode of differentiation – territorial sovereignty – is being 'unbundled' by the globalization of the economy and culture. Instead of one perspective there are now multiple perspectives, and instead of one identity there are multiple identities. It is impossible to grasp the contours of this world with the categories of modernity. In this sense the intellectual perspective which is required is one closer to that of medieval times in Europe than of the modern period.

4.3   The future of the nation state

There remains an uneasiness about using the concept of new medievalism. Contrasts between old and new medievalism often seem much greater than the similarities. At the time of the European middle ages the world system was not unified and interdependent in the way that it is now; the extent of the division of labour and of interdependence was low. It was a period before the monopolization of government functions by sovereign nation states (Hirst and Thompson, 1996). The extent of the integration of modern economies and societies means that no return to that earlier era is possible. Nor is there anything comparable in the contemporary world system to the universal doctrine of Christianity. A new secular universal doctrine embracing human rights and environmentalism has begun to be elaborated, but it is a long way from enjoying the authority that Christianity enjoyed in medieval Europe. Other features of medieval universalism, such as a common elite language, are also less developed. Further criticisms focus on the extent to which nation states have actually been weakened. In some areas state powers have increased (Anderson and Goodman, 1995). The unbundling of territoriality is therefore only partial. Distinctions have to be made between the different roles which states perform. In security, defence and welfare, nation states' loss of sovereignty is much less marked than in economic policy.

New medievalism does focus attention on systems of rule, which globalization does not. But the conditions for rule in the contemporary world system are clearly vastly different from those prevailing in the European middle ages. Different modes of governance – markets, hierarchies, networks and communities – are required to sustain and coordinate such a complex global division of labour and organize the distribution of work and income among sectors, regions, classes and households. A politics-free cosmopolitan society is a fantasy. What is required are new forms of governance to handle the increasingly serious problems of the world system – population pressure, climate change, environmental sustainability, global poverty and ethnic conflict (Held, 1995, 2004; Gamble, 1993, 2000).

The authority and the competence of nation states have undoubtedly been weakened in certain areas in the last twenty-five years. The nation state is on the defensive against a world economy it cannot control, and against institutions such as the EU which it originally constructed to remedy its own weaknesses. It has suffered a loss of will and capacity. It can no longer financially maintain the public services which were so confidently established only a few decades ago; nor can it maintain public law and order (Hobsbawm, 1994). Not all states in all parts of the world suffer the same incapacity and incompetence. But the nation state does appear weak in relation to many of the problems it faces. The paradox is that it is still indispensable within the governance structure of the world system (Pierre and Peters, 2000).

The key test of the thesis of new medievalism is whether this weakness of the nation state is transient or permanent. If the factors which cause it are transient then the nation state may re-emerge with enhanced powers and legitimacy. If they are permanent – as most analysts suspect – then the nation state might just wither away as some neo-liberals hope, or, more probably, it might, as the new medievalism thesis suggests, be gradually changed into one of several overlapping areas of governance (Bache and Flinders, 2004). One of the causes of the weakness of the state is that the era of national protectionism has ended, an era which enhanced the powers of national government and gave meaning to the concept of a national economy as an object of public policy. The 1980s and 1990s have witnessed a reconfiguration of the relationships between states and the global economy, with the emergence of new regions and speculation about regional blocs. As yet, the trend towards the formation of regional blocs remains weak, certainly compared with the 1920s and 1930s, and the new forms of regional political structures that have been established are more in tune with the governance mechanisms of the new medievalism than with those of the old international state system (Hettne and Soderbaum, 1998).

4.4 *Reregulating the economy*

New medievalism is consistent with different scenarios for the future of world order. Robert Cox has speculated that we may be witnessing a new phase in the alternation between deregulation and reregulation (Cox, 1996). Karl Polanyi argued that the conscious deregulation of the nineteenth century meant overreliance upon the market as the mode of governance (Polanyi, 1944). The state was steadily withdrawn from direct involvement in economic activity and was confined to the role of enforcing the rules of the market. Once established, markets were regarded as self-regulating. The consequences of self-regulating markets, however, were so socially destructive that resistance multiplied and the nation state found a new legitimacy as the regulator of the economy and the guarantor of minimum levels of welfare.

Polanyi expected that this would be irreversible, but it has not proved so. The regulated system lost legitimacy in the 1970s because it was unable to cope with the problems of accelerating inflation, decelerating growth and the consequent tendency for public spending to outpace revenues. At the same time, it had to deal with the emergence of an increasingly global economy, manifested particularly in the financial markets. As a result, in the last thirty years there has been a pronounced swing away from regulation and new experiments with deregulation, privatization and the dismantling of public sectors and public programmes have proliferated, particularly in Britain and the United States. Neo-liberal doctrines of globalization have codified many of these policy ideas into dogmas which are routinely expressed in the conditions for financial assistance imposed on national governments by international agencies like the IMF and the World Bank.

Cox asks whether the same pressures that led to the imposition of social control in the nineteenth century will develop again, as a result of the increasingly destructive nature of neo-liberal policies and the self-regulating market throughout the world system. This time, however, control would need to be reimposed not at the national level but at the global level. The practical difficulties in the way of such a development are immense, since the conditions for world government are nowhere fulfilled, and the systems of rule within the world system remain so fragmented. Nevertheless, pressure for some form of reregulation is growing as problems and perils accumulate. But such reregulation, if it occurs, is likely to strengthen rather than replace the multi-level system of authority that now defines the international state system, rebalancing the various modes of governing the global economy, and thus privileging certain national strategies and institutional patterns over others.

5 Conclusion

'New medievalism' is at best a metaphor but, used properly, it can provide insights into the changing forms of governance of the world system. One of the key tests for this perspective is whether the EU is a peculiar and unique phenomenon, as peculiar and unique as the Holy Roman Empire, or whether it is the first embodiment of a new form of political rule which might be a model for other regionalisms (Telò, 2005); or whether it is embryonically a new unified regional bloc, a United States of Europe. Nationalist opponents of European integration still believe, despite much evidence to the contrary, that it is the last of these. They want a return to exclusive national sovereignty, but their critics believe that the rights of self-determination which the nationalists seek can now only be achieved by recognizing the fundamental changes in the way in which political, economic and social space is now structured.

One of the paradoxes of the current debate is that there is a double movement. On the one hand there are pronounced trends towards globalization in finance, production and commerce. On the other, the legitimacy of the nation state as the preferred locus of political rule has never been stronger, and many nations, as in eastern Europe, still seek self-determination and the creation of their own independent state. The fears about regionalist projects and the revival of fears about the formation of blocs is in part the anxiety that the pluralism and overlapping authorities so characteristic of the present time will not last, and that there will be a swing back to unified centralized political authority.

The contrasts made between different periods are often oversimplified. Since the world system began there have always been four types of order present: cosmopolitan, organized around markets; imperial, organized around security; hegemonic, organized around rules; and territorial, organized around legitimacy and frontiers. Their relative weightings have changed in different periods, but they have always coexisted. What we are witnessing today is a rebalancing of these types of order. Realist conceptions of international relations for too long have obscured the fact that there have always been rival and overlapping sources of authority and order. There never was a pure Westphalian world. If new medievalism can help us appreciate that fact, it will have served a useful purpose.

Chapter 2

The Political Economy of New Regionalism and World Governance

Pier Carlo Padoan

After the breakdown of the Bretton Woods arrangement the international system has been moving into a structure often referred to as unipolar, that is, characterized by the presence of a single superpower, the United Stares – holding military and economic power to impose unilateral choices on the rest of the system with no other country or group of countries able to seriously challenge them. Over the past few years, however, the distribution of power, especially economic power, has been changing as new global players such as India, China, Russia, and Brazil have shown economic and political dynamism as well as ambition to play a leading role in world affairs. Long term projections place India's and China's GDP at levels that could match those of the US in twenty years' time. Irrespective of whether such projections are accurate they show that the world is moving away from a unipolar structure and will be increasingly characterized by a multipolar one. A parallel and related phenomenon is the proliferation of limited agreements,[1] be they regional or bilateral, which involve very diverse groups of countries. So, in spite of increasingly integrated markets, a system of global governance is still not available. This, however, does not mean that there is no governance of the global system. The interaction between nation states, regional agreements, and the global dimension, may well lead to the establishment of a system of governance which may provide some form of international order. If and how this can take place remains one of the main challenges in understanding global relations. Starting from this perspective, the chapter seeks to offer suggestions on how to link the three levels of analysis: national, regional, and global in the process of global governance. The discussion will take a dual approach. The 'top-down' approach which considers the influence the higher levels exert on the lower ones: how the globalization of the international system affects the evolution of regional agreements, and how the latter influences the domestic policies of nation states.[2] The 'bottom-up' approach which looks at the opposite direction of influence: how the development of regional agreements shape the characteristics of the new international system.

1 The global system in institutional disequilibrium

As it moves away form a unipolar structure the global system remains in what has been called a post-hegemonic condition (Gilpin, 1987): that is, a situation in which no single country can provide unilaterally the public goods required for the operation of the system itself. This can also be expressed by saying that the international system is in 'institutional disequilibrium' in the sense that there is an excess demand for international public goods which, in turn, is the result of a decrease in supply, because of the redistribution of power away from a hegemonic structure,[3] and an increase in demand because of increased globalization. The current configuration of the global system, however, is, as mentioned, also often described as one of 'regionalism',[4] which should be understood not so much as the result of concentration of trade and investment activities around major integrated regions (Europe, North America, Asia) but rather as a policy option pursued as a response to the failure of the post-hegemonic world in providing international public goods. Regionalism may be 'conflict oriented' or 'cooperative'. In the first case regional agreements provide collective goods for countries included in each region and exclude non-members from their consumption (an example of this would be a discriminatory trade agreement). Cooperative regionalism, on the contrary, could be understood as the formation of regional agreements as a precondition for cooperation at a global level, that is, with a view towards multilateralism. To proceed from this point one needs to consider two factors: firstly, the conditions for cooperation without hegemony, that is, within a multipolar world; and secondly, the interactions among domestic, regional, and international policy.

The theory of international cooperation without hegemony offers a list of conditions that must be met if agreements to supply international public goods are to be reached:[5]

1) the number of actors involved must be small
2) the time horizon of actors must be long
3) actors must be prepared to change their policy preferences
4) international institutions must be available.

Condition 1 allows for the possibility of dealing with free riding. Condition 2 allows for repeated interaction among players, which is both necessary and unavoidable in an increasingly interdependent world. Condition 3 requires nation states to be prepared to adjust to the international environment to reach agreements. Condition 4 relates to the fact that institutions support cooperation as they facilitate exchange and information among different actors.

Conditions 1 to 4 imply, among other things, that cooperation is achieved if nation states adjust both their economic and their political *equilibria*. This leads us to the interaction between international and domestic politics. Robert Putnam (1988) has suggested that international regime formation requires that an agreement be reached at two levels of political activity: both level I, that is, between national governments, and level II, that is, between each national government, the legislator, and domestic interest groups. So, while commitments made at political level II must be consistent with the agreement struck at level I, the opposite relation must hold as well: Level I agreements must be designed so as to be consistent with the specific level II agreements in each of the participating countries.[6]

Regionalism adds a third level of politics, regional politics, to be understood as the definition of a common regional policy which operates between domestic and international politics. The answer to the question whether regionalism will assume benign or malign characteristics, then, requires looking at the role regional (level III) politics can play as a bridge between level I and level II politics. This, in turn, requires a closer look at the conditions that must be met in order for regional agreements to be consolidated, that is, the conditions in which level II politics can be 'melted' into level III (regional) politics also through a transfer of sovereignty from the national to the regional level. Once this is accomplished, international (level I) politics interacts with regional (level III) rather than with domestic (level II) politics.

De Melo, Pangaya and Rodrik (1993) develop this point analytically. Their framework considers regional integration as both an economic and a political process which is the outcome of a relationship between national governments and domestic pressure groups (level II politics in Putnam's terminology). They show that the formation of supranational institutions – regional agreements – has a positive effect on the economic efficiency of national economies when these integrate because of the lower impact of domestic pressure groups on the policy stance of the supranational institution, compared to the corresponding impact on national governments. Without integration, national governments would provide excessive intervention – excessive, that is, with respect to the economically optimal – because of the strong influence of domestic pressure groups (the so-called 'preference dilution effect'). However, if there are large differences among national preferences concerning the degree of government intervention, the incentive to integrate may be insufficient (the 'preference asymmetry effect'). To operate efficiently, supranational institutions must be designed so as to minimize the weight of countries whose domestic pressure groups demand a high degree of government intervention (the 'institutional design effect'). The first effect relates to the increased role of national systems when international regimes are weak. The second effect relates to the role of differences in national systems in favouring or hindering international regime formation. The third effect underlines the point that regional politics requires the formation of some kind of supranational institution, to avoid the risk of being captured by special interest action.

The 'two-level' approach is a useful first step in trying to establish relations between national systemic and regional mechanisms of cooperation. The next step requires looking more closely at level III. More specifically, the following questions arise: firstly, why are regional agreements formed and why do they expand (or contract)? Secondly, how do countries respond to the formation of regional agreements?

2 Economic aspects of regional agreements

The establishment of a regional agreement requires the selection of those who are to join and also those who are to be excluded; regionalism is as much a question of cooperation and integration as it is of exclusion. The extent of membership, therefore, must be determined. When is the optimal number of members reached? Why does it change over time?

Standard trade theory gives a precise answer to the question of number: the optimal size of a trade agreement is the world. Short of full liberalization, however, partial elimination of barriers following integration will generally improve the allocation of resources and welfare. Although the welfare gain might be partially curtailed by trade diversion, which could offset gains from trade creation, reallocation of resources generated by the integration process allows the exploitation of national comparative advantages. Differences in national resource endowments will lead to a deepening of specialization patterns which will benefit all countries involved in the integration process. Factors of production will be allocated in sectors where the country enjoys a comparative advantage, while production in other sectors will stop or be reduced. The process will, of course, involve adjustment costs and temporary unemployment, the severity and duration of which could be alleviated by appropriate financial support. Once reallocation is completed, inter-industry trade, that is, trade in goods belonging to different sectors (for example, textiles and food products), within the region will increase. Note that the benefits of integration, in such a framework, could be equally obtained by the reallocation of factors among countries, that is, by migration and/or capital movements.

Within traditional trade theory the reason why the organization of international trade falls short of global liberalization is usually found in the presence of special interests that, given imperfect political markets, have the resources and the ability to obtain protection from national or regional governments.

'New trade theory' has pointed at another possible source of gains from integration, deriving from the exploitation of (static and dynamic) gains from trade.[7] The larger market generated by integration allows (oligopolistic) firms to exploit increasing returns. This leads to further specialization within the same sectors, as competition rests both on lower costs deriving from expanded production and on product (quality) differentiation. Intra-industry trade, that is, trade of similar goods between countries, will be generated. Welfare gains from integration will ensue from lower costs and broader quality range as well as the exploitation of dynamic returns to scale generated by the learning process following the introduction of new technologies. In this case, too, costs could arise from integration; however, they would be permanent, rather than temporary. In addition to the standard adjustment costs, economies of scale could generate agglomeration effects as both capital and labour would concentrate in specific areas, leading to permanent core–periphery effects within the region. Employment opportunities would concentrate in some areas, exacerbating the asymmetrical distribution of net benefits (Krugman, 1993).

In general, trade integration would increase both inter- and intra-industry trade and, in both cases, increased competition would activate pressures to resist adjustment and/or demand for compensatory measures on the part of countries and regions most severely hit by the asymmetric distribution of net benefits.

The emergence of inequalities generated by the process of integration raises the issue of 'cohesion', which may be defined as '[a principle that] implies … a relatively equal social and territorial distribution of employment opportunities, of wealth and of income, and of improvements in the quality of life that correspond to increasing expectations' (Smith and Tsoukalis, 1996: 1). An important implication is that, without cohesion, political support for a regional agreement is likely to fail.

Consensus to the regional agreement, and ultimately its size, will then depend on the degree of cohesion among its members. Cohesion problems will be greater the larger the asymmetric distribution effects, and therefore the larger the impact of scale effects generated by integration. These effects, in turn, will be greater the larger the diversity among members of the integrating region. Once the costs for cohesion management (that is, the costs that must be borne to offset the asymmetry effects) exceed the benefits from integration, the widening process will come to an end. The number of members will have been determined.

Monetary integration, too, both when it implies fixing exchange rates and when it takes the form of full monetary union, can produce an asymmetric distribution of net benefits. (Economic) benefits from monetary integration stem from three sources (see, for example, de Grauwe, 1992): the elimination of transaction costs, the elimination of currency risk and the acquisition of policy credibility for inflation-prone countries. The first two benefits can be fully obtained only with monetary union. The third benefit has to be weighed against the costs of real currency appreciation, which hits high-inflation countries once they credibly enter an exchange rate agreement (Krugman, 1993). If the latter are also the peripheral countries from a trade point of view, the adverse effects of real and monetary integration will cumulate, leading to further demand for compensation. Low-inflation countries, on the other hand, would be adversely affected by entering a monetary agreement with excessively expansionary partners, so that ultimately they would refuse the latter permission to join (Alesina and Grilli, 1993). In both cases the extension of the monetary agreement will stop short of global integration. Again, the number of members will be determined.

To conclude, economics can provide several contributory elements to the understanding of the extension of regional membership; however, a satisfactory theory of regional integration should explain the optimal number of members through the interaction of economic, institutional, and political variables. One way of approaching the issue is to consider regional agreements as clubs.

3   Regional agreements as clubs

The economic analysis of club formation started to develop in the 1960s with the contributions of James Buchanan (1965) and Mancur Olson (1965), and since then has been applied to several economic and political issues such as community size, production of local public goods, two-part tariffs, congestion problems, political coalitions and international organizations (Casella and Feinstein, 1990). The literature has been surveyed by Sandler and Tschirhart (1980), Frey (1984), Cornes and Sandler (1985) and Bolton et al. (1996).

Club theory deals with problems related to the establishment of voluntary associations for the production of excludable public goods. Optimal membership is determined by marginality conditions, when the spread between an individual member's cost and benefit is maximized. Marginal costs and benefits are functions of the size of the club.[8] Costs are related to management and decision-making activities; hence management costs should not be confused with congestion costs arising, for example, from cumulative effects such as those discussed in the previous section, which will be considered as factors affecting the level of net benefits from club provision. Marginal costs increase with the extension of club membership because management problems rise with the number of members.

As Fratianni and Pattison (1982) stress, decision theory suggests that the addition of new members will raise the costs of reaching agreements in a more than proportional manner. Costs will also rise more than proportionally for organizational reasons and because, for political balance, each new member will have to be given equal opportunity, irrespective of its economic size, to express its viewpoint (Ward, 1991). Institutional arrangements alter the behaviour of costs. For example, a shift from a unanimity rule to a majority rule in decision making within the club lowers marginal costs. On the other hand, individual members' marginal benefits decrease with this change, assuming that the equal-sized share of total benefits from integration increases more slowly as the number of members rises, because congestion lowers the quality of the club good.

Optimal club membership is obtained when marginal benefits (B) equal marginal costs (C). We can consider the following simple rule. The incentive for a change in the extent of a regional agreement emerges whenever there is a discrepancy between marginal benefits and marginal costs of the club. Note that this allows us to consider possible (and not at all unrealistic) contractions in the size of the club (here determined by the number of members Q).

A trade agreement responds to some of the crucial requisites for the definition of a club: it produces freer trade, virtually a public good; it guarantees partial exclusion of non-members from free trade benefits; and, in the case of a customs union, it guarantees the benefits of a common external trade policy. To the extent that standards and regulation contribute to the determination of comparative advantage, groups of countries sharing common standards and regulation are forms of trade clubs.

Marginal benefits of a trade club may be thought of as depending on both exogenous and endogenous components, that is, on the size of the club itself. The first include the 'security' effect of trade agreements. This implies that membership in a trade club is more valuable in the presence of a possible outside threat. This may be a genuine military threat, as Gowa and Mansfield (1993) have argued. The present global environment, however, may present other forms of threat, such as those deriving from the formation of regional and aggressive trade blocs. In such a case the incentive for joining a trade club lies not only in the trade creation and/or scale effects benefits but also in the 'insurance' that club membership provides against the harm that a trade bloc war could produce to small, isolated countries (Perroni and Whalley, 1994; Baldwin, 1993). A larger club membership will benefit existing members as well as new entrants. If the size of the alliance increases it reinforces resistance to the outside threat. This implies that the value of a club rises with the degree of conflict in the global system.

Exogenous factors also include purely political benefits from trade agreements, for example, the fact that members will be admitted to the club in so far as they share the same political beliefs as the existing members, for example, the full acceptance of democratic rules. This element has played a crucial role in the enlargement of the European Community starting from the one to the southern countries, Greece, Portugal and Spain (Winters, 1993). Indeed the issue of 'where Europe ends', which is largely determined by political and cultural values, can be treated along the lines discussed above.

A monetary agreement, whether in the form of a currency union or of an exchange rate agreement, also responds to the requisites of a public good. The public good nature of a single currency is well established in the literature. Globalization and outside threats increase the benefits of a monetary club as capital mobility and deeper financial integration increase the desirability of monetary unions as a protection against destabilizing capital movements (Eichengreen, 1994). Outside threats may come from 'aggressive' behaviour (or behaviour perceived as such) as part of foreign monetary policies. For example, Henning (1996) argues that one of the driving forces behind European monetary integration has been the espousal of an aggressive macroeconomic policy attitude by the United States. Finally, one should include the 'non-economic' benefits of monetary membership, which play a relevant role in the success, or failure, of monetary agreements (Cohen, 1993).

Marginal benefits increase, other things being equal, with the level of economic activity. The pressure of rising inequality due to integration will be lower the more sustained the level of economic activity, as more sustained growth will benefit all club members. Another way of looking at this component is to recall that protectionist pressures increase in times of economic depression.[9] Also, more favourable macroeconomic conditions make it easier to implement the necessary policies for members of a monetary club (for example, higher growth makes fiscal adjustment less costly).

Let us now consider the endogenous determinants of club size, that is, the number of club members. Marginal benefits are related to club membership and decrease with club size because of rising congestion problems in club formation, as discussed in the previous section. Marginal benefits, other things being equal, decrease with the diversity of countries wishing to join the club: increasing diversity implies larger congestion costs in the case of a trade club or increasing divergences in the preference for a stable macroeconomic policy in the case of a monetary club.[10] This explains why members of a monetary club must fulfill appropriate requirements (for example,, the 'Maastricht conditions' for euro membership), and why new members may lower the quality of the public good if their monetary and fiscal policies are not consistent with macroeconomic stability.[11]

Marginal costs also include exogenous and endogenous components (depending on club size). Marginal costs are determined by management problems. In the case of the EU, as Baldwin (1994) describes (see also Widgren, 1994), voting rules are complicated by the increase in the number of members, and hence by the increasing diversity of preferences, as each member country will use its voting power to increase the welfare of its citizens. Exogenous components can be thought of as associated with the amount and quality of international cooperation already existing among club members in other areas; that is, if institutions linking countries involved in negotiating the agreements already exist, this will facilitate the formation and management of the new institutions. While several reasons can be advanced to support such a claim, it is a well-established fact in international relations theory

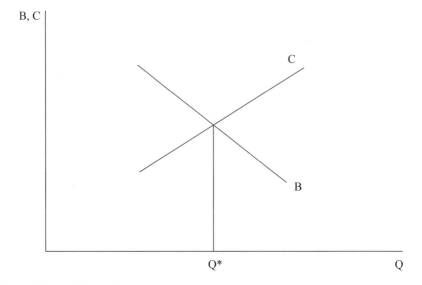

Figure 2.1   Club equilibrium

that institutions provide information about other actors' behaviour, thus facilitating communication and information exchange.[12] In the case of monetary unions, the exogenous component may be thought of as representing the costs associated with the loss of monetary sovereignty as perceived by club members. A simple representation of club equilibrium is offered in Figure 2.1. The equilibrium club size is Q* where the marginal cost and benefits curves intersect.

Starting from Q*, optimal club membership will vary according to a number of factors. There will be an enlargement process if the degree of outside conflicts increases, thus raising the insurance value of membership; if the strength and efficiency of institutional arrangements among members other than trade relations increase; if diversity among countries – both members and candidates – decreases; and/or if the voting system becomes more flexible. The first two factors can be represented by a shift of the B curve to the right; the third factor may be represented by a shift of the C curve to the right.[13]

Finally, as suggested by Mansfield and Branson (1994), the presence of a leader (or k-group in Schelling's terminology) may increase the degree of cohesion of a regional agreement. This could also be represented by a shift of both curves to the right, as a regional leader would increase the value of the club good (for example, by providing monetary discipline or unilateral access to domestic markets) and lower management costs.

In conclusion, equilibrium club size will vary because exogenous conditions and/or endogenous conditions change. This last point needs to be further clarified. Changing endogenous conditions here means that, as a result of changes in the international environment, countries outside the agreement become willing to undertake the alterations in their domestic political economy necessary in order to be 'admitted to the club', that is, to become 'more similar' to the current club members, thus decreasing the degree of diversity. This is the basic insight in Baldwin's (1993) 'domino theory of regionalism', where the demand for integration increases in countries previously not interested in joining a regional agreement. However, the final regional equilibrium will depend on both demand for and supply of membership. Linking the regional to the national level requires examination of this point.

4 Narrowing diversity: the demand for integration

As noted above, we may think of an integration 'equilibrium' as the outcome of the interaction between 'demand for integration', that is, the decision of individual countries to apply for membership of integration agreements and to undergo the necessary adjustments for that request to be fulfilled, and the 'supply of integration', that is, the willingness of regional agreements to accept new members. Let us take a closer look at the determination of the demand for integration.

Economic integration delivers benefits and costs, both economic and political, to the integrating countries. We have already briefly reviewed costs and benefits as discussed in the economics literature; here we consider them from the point of view of individual countries, in other words, as country-specific, as they reflect the economic and political structure of each country. A given level of integration, exogenously determined,[14] will deliver different costs and benefits according to the initial level of market liberalization. From integration theory we know that costs of integration (Ic) are decreasing, and benefits of integration (Ib) are increasing with the degree of integration, that is, with the degree of liberalization of the economy. Costs derive from the adjustment an economy has to undergo in the reallocation process that integration requires. They are initially high as one can assume that the production structure of a closed or isolated economy is quite distant from the one that is optimal in an integration equilibrium. Hence resource allocation may be quite distant from, and distorted in comparison to, an allocation consistent with trade liberalization. Costs can be measured both in terms of markets and sectors that must be restructured and in terms of the political resistance to change; that is,. the Ic curve reflects both economic and political costs. Similarly, integration costs will be greater the higher the degree of protection and the larger the share of the economy that is not exposed to international competition, that is, the non-tradeable sector. Benefits increase with the degree of integration as beneficial effects of international competition spread over a larger part of the economy through a better resource allocation. The Ib curve also reflects political benefits in terms of the support of the interest groups that are likely to be favoured by liberalization.[15] Finally, benefits will be larger if members of the integrating region are also part of an alliance – not necessarily a purely military one (Gowa and Mansfield, 1993).

Figure 2.2 describes these elements. The respective positions of the Ic and Ib curves depend on the share of the non-tradeable sectors (a larger non-tradeable sector shifts the Ic curve to the right), and on the presence of an alliance, an outside threat, elements that would shift Ib to the right. The Ib curve would also shift to the right if a larger number of sectors of the economy would benefit from increased liberalization. As shown, there is a critical level of integration – T* – beyond which

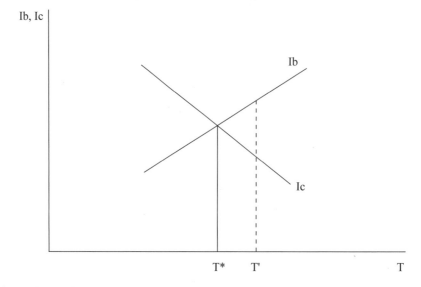

Figure 2.2   Costs and benefits of regional integration

benefits are larger than costs, making it expedient to pursue the integration option. The level of liberalization is exogenously determined by the characteristics of the agreement (for example, the level of the tariff for a trade club or the degree of financial liberalization for a monetary club), say at level T'. Joining the agreement implies accepting this level of liberalization. At T' net integration benefits (Ib – Ic) may be positive or negative. In the first case it would obviously be beneficial for the country to join the agreement (or to ask for membership). In the second case positive net benefits would materialize only following a shift in the position of the two curves (the Ib to the right and/or the Ic to the left), which could be seen as the consequence of a shift in domestic preferences with respect to the integration option.

5   Interaction between supply of and demand for integration

Net integration benefits for a particular country are only a necessary condition for membership. Entering a club requires the payment of an admission fee. The justification for a club admission fee is obvious. New club members must guarantee that they will behave according to club rules and will not lower the quality of the club good. Hence the admission fee requires a policy change in any country wishing to join the agreement. We may think of two examples of policy change as admission fee. In the case of a monetary club the admission fee may be explicit (as in the case of the fulfillment of the Maastricht conditions for joining the euro). In the case of a trade club a policy change is needed to rule out support to the domestic industry through instruments such as subsidies, transfers, deregulation and so on. In short, the admission fee to the club must be paid to obtain the reputation necessary to be accepted into a club.

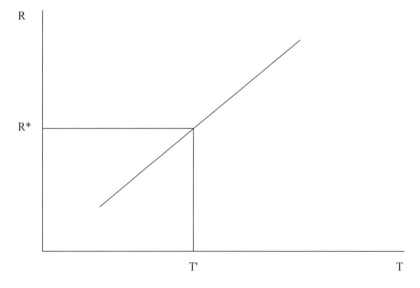

Figure 2.3   Integration and reputation

We can assume that the cost of reputation (R) increases with the degree of liberalization (integration) as deeper integration requires deeper transformation in policy,. In short, membership in a club implies an exogenous degree of liberalization T' and a corresponding amount of reputation R* that must be obtained (the club admission fee). These two elements determine the conditions of the supply of membership. Matching up the two elements, the level of liberalization and the reputation level, produces a new threshold in the choice process, illustrated in Figure 2.3. The value of T' determines a critical value of reputation (R*) which must be reached in order to gain access to a club. Reputation can be obtained by implementing an adjustment programme, which in our framework can be, very simply, represented by an inverse relationship between R and X, the policy variable controlled by the government, hence a proxy of the intensity of state intervention in the economy. This implies that a minimum level of R requires a maximum level of X.

To complete the picture, we must take into account the consequences of the admission fee for domestic political equilibrium. A government faces a domestic problem, which may be represented by assuming that the policy-maker maximizes the probability of staying in power. In order to obtain this goal the government will use X to maximize P, the government's popularity, to which the probability of staying in power is positively related. We can assume that there is a minimum level of popularity (P*) which is required to stay in power for a given institutional and political setting. The way in which X influences (directly) P reflects the social and institutional characteristics of the country. The amount of X necessary to obtain a given amount of P will increase with the degree of social sclerosis in Olson's (1965) sense (which is larger the larger the number and strength of interest groups, and the greater the degree of fragmentation of the society), the size and power of the nation state bureaucracy and the degree to which government is divided (Milner, 1997).

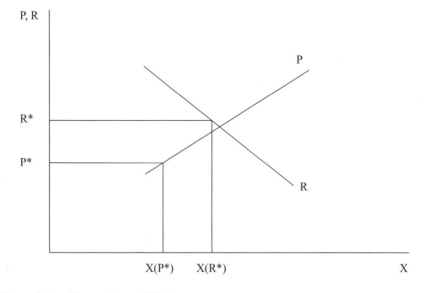

Figure 2.4   Domestic equilibrium

A minimum level of popularity implies a minimum level of X, X*. The position of the P curve is influenced by the nature of the state. A strong state, where the degree of social sclerosis is low, will obtain a higher amount of P out of a given amount of X than a weak state where the degree of social sclerosis is high.[16]

The framework is now set to answer the question: under what circumstances will a country find it desirable to apply for membership of an integration agreement? A positive answer requires that a positive net benefit from integration is obtained. This is larger the more market-oriented is the economy, the stronger the integration process in place (a higher value of T'), the stronger the outside threat and the stronger are the non economic ties with the integration partners. As the net integration benefits must be set against the amount of the admission fee, the pattern described boils down to one choice. The government may set the amount of X, its policy variable, at a value that is consistent with the integration option.

We may now recapitulate the steps in the domestic policy process. The intersection between benefits and costs from integration determines a minimum level of integration, T*. This leads to a minimum level of reputation, R*, to be obtained (the admission fee). Figure 2.4 brings together the reputation function and the popularity function, both determined, although in an opposite relationship, by the level of the domestic policy variable X. To use Putnam's (1988) terminology (see also Guerrieri and Padoan, 1989) the upper and lower bounds to X, established respectively by the reputation – X(R*) – and the popularity – X(P*) – constraints, determine a 'win set', that is,. a set of feasible policies that are consistent with both domestic and international policy goals.

If the reputation constraint is more binding than the popularity constraint – X(R*)<X(P*) – a win set does not exist. The emergence of an integration option, however, may be exploited by the government to force an adjustment on the

domestic economy, by lowering the popularity constraint below the reputation constraint. This is the familiar case where international politics is used as a leverage to impose change in the domestic political and economic arena. This option will be more attractive the larger the benefits promised by integration. This option will also be more easily pursued the more powerful the domestic interest groups that will benefit from integration (whose relative position and size determines the relative position of the Ib and Ic curves). As the country adjusts towards the liberalization level T' and the reputation level R* requested by club membership, the diversity between existing and candidate members decreases and this allows for an expansion of club size (the endogenous component of club size determination increases).

6 From top-down to bottom-up

In the sections above we have followed a 'top-down' approach, suggesting some linkages between the collapse of the post-war international (hegemonic) system – which has produced a state of institutional disequilibrium – and the emergence of regionalism, which can be thought of as a response to the excess demand for international public goods. We have then suggested that the formation of regional clubs has increased both the supply of and the demand for integration. The latter is signalled by the willingness of an increasing number of countries to adjust their domestic political economies in order to pay the entry fee to regional clubs (the 'domino effect').

It is now appropriate to follow a 'bottom-up' approach to examine a question raised earlier: namely, is the spreading of regionalism leading to a more cooperative global system – that is, to the formation of a 'global multilateral regime'?

Let us first clarify that a global multilateral regime should not be understood as an extension at the global level of the regional model of integration, a 'club of clubs'. This should be obvious if one reflects on the fact that regional agreements do form to the extent that there is an exclusion vis-à-vis other countries. If there is no limit to club membership the (excludable) public good nature of a club vanishes by definition. It follows that a global multilateral regime should be understood as a situation of cooperation among clubs, which, however, maintain their specific identity. Is such a scenario feasible?

This issue can be addressed by reconsidering the conditions for cooperation without hegemony, mentioned above. One could start by asking whether the spreading of regionalism makes the fulfillment of such conditions easier. Condition 2 (a long time horizon) is likely to be fulfilled, especially in a context of issue-linking. If club A attaches a high priority to, say, economic integration, it will be willing to strike a long term deal with club B that attaches high priority to, say, energy security. A and B would benefit from an agreement that combines more of both. Condition 3 seems more problematic Why should club A be willing to change its preferences so as to form a larger club with club B when the one reason for the existence of club A is the aggregation of similar national preferences that might be significantly different from those of countries belonging to club B.

However, condition 3 could be fulfilled more easily by the spreading of globally integrated markets. Consider the case of international investment as an example. The most powerful forces of global integration are represented by the activities of multinational enterprises (MNEs). One relevant aspect is that these activities not only increase the degree of economic interdependence, but may also lead to convergence in governments' policies (through reciprocity). The relevance for economic convergence derives from the fact that MNEs are powerful vehicles of innovation diffusion. In a world in which technological progress is the key determinant of growth and competitiveness, the degree of diffusion of knowledge is the crucial factor for the dissemination of the benefits of growth.[17] MNEs, however, may also become a powerful factor in 'political' convergence. As Froot and Yoffie (1991) have shown, MNE activities decrease the incentives for national governments to supply protection to their economies. In a world of highly mobile capital, MNE activities are one typical response to protectionist barriers – whether erected to protect nations or regions. As the amount of foreign investment in protected areas increases, the rents from protection increasingly accrue to foreigners, that is, to the owners of foreign capital in the region, rather than to domestic residents. Hence protectionist governments receive a decreasing share of political support in exchange for their intervention, and their benefit from this form of political exchange decreases. On the other hand, the benefits from both reciprocal market access and international diffusion of knowledge increase. In short, in a world of countries or regions, each pursuing a policy of protection, international mobility of capital tends to weaken the strength of protectionist policies and, indirectly, to decrease the differences in national or regional political economies and preferences.

This is true as long as this process is symmetrical, that is, if capital mobility is a two-way activity. If capital flows only in one direction, the government of a region or country where foreign capital does not penetrate will be able to preserve the political benefits of protection. Only as long as investment flows in both directions do global market forces represent a powerful vehicle of economic integration. Further, if capital integration is not symmetrical, the region where foreign investment does not penetrate will also lose part of the (potential) benefits of innovation diffusion and of growth associated with it. It follows that in a world of high mobility of capital new incentives emerge to attract foreign MNE activities. This reinforces the incentives of industrial sectors to obtain liberal policies on a reciprocal basis.

Support may not come only from business groups. As several scholars show, lobbying activity by trade unions interested in creating new employment opportunities does not necessarily take the form of requests for more protection. Rather, unions will be interested in policies that attract capital, and so may lobby governments for more rather than less openness. This is one of the consequences of the fact that globalization has produced a new form of competition – competition for location sites – which requires (and is also dependent on) regulation: in the first place, because location advantages may be created by the investment of regional development funds, the overall amount of which may be afterwards judged excessive, and secondly, because of 'competition among rules', that is, regulations affecting locational incentives such as environmental and labour market regulations. The attempt to attract foreign investment might create an incentive to relax rules, or rule enforcement, so as to decrease the private costs of investment at the expense of social costs, a problem facing both NAFTA and Europe.

To summarize, increasing capital mobility may indeed represent a powerful element of convergence of preferences in the sense that it creates incentives in domestic politics to pursue more open and less protection-oriented (more 'market'-oriented) policies, which tend to favour cooperative international policies. This last and crucial point stems from the fact that, by definition, MNE operations are global and MNEs themselves can be less and less considered as tied to a specific country or region. This reinforces the need to establish regimes that will facilitate the operation of market forces at a global level: that is, globalization increases the demand for international public goods.

Condition 1 – a small number of actors – is, by definition, fulfilled by the spreading of regionalism. What is less clear is whether such a condition does indeed lead to deeper global integration. Krugman (1993) has argued that the formation of regional blocs leads to conflict rather than cooperation, and he has also shown that, under specific conditions, the number of regional actors less conducive to cooperation is three. It remains unclear whether a small number of actors leads to more or less global cooperation. One approach to address the issue has been suggested by Oye (1992). He posits that, in a post-hegemonic, multipolar world, regional (and national) actors tend to pursue 'unrestricted', that is,. selective, bargaining vis-à-vis each other in order to obtain selective market access and, to this purpose, are ready to reciprocate with their partners to obtain liberalization of their domestic markets. He also notes that a strong incentive to pursue unrestricted (selective) bargaining comes from globalization as selective market access is a form of competition in global markets (which are not uniform markets). In addition, selective market access reinforces the incentives of third parties to barter over market access, as the formation of preferential agreements increases the costs of exclusion. This line of argument (which is very similar to the 'domino approach' to regionalism) may be reinforced by the exploration of issues in the literature on the political economy of protection and liberalization. Grossman and Helpman (1996) suggest that domestic lobbying for domestic liberalization will come from pro-free trade groups that see domestic opening as a condition of obtaining market access abroad as the result of reciprocal bargaining. They also suggest that the predominance of protectionist interest groups arises from the fact that industries seeking protection are usually declining industries where the prospective market size is not big enough to compensate for entry costs, hence the potential for free-riding is much lower and the possibility of organizing collective action larger. On the contrary, industries that benefit from liberalization usually face expanding markets where free-riding firms would be able to enter without contributing to the lobbying effort. However, if 'sunrise' markets expand fast enough, the incentive to pursue reciprocal domestic liberalization may overcome the free-riding costs. In addition, the value of sunk costs investment in lobbying for protection declines over time in 'sunset' industries. This point can be extended to bargaining between regional agreements by noting that, if reciprocal liberalization is carried out on a regional basis, it will benefit firms belonging to the regional agreement which, in principle, have already paid an admission fee. Therefore, participation in a regional agreement that engages in selective bargaining partially offsets the free-riding problem. In other words, reciprocal bargaining between regions may be more efficient than reciprocal bargaining between countries. On the other hand, Winters (1999) has argued that regionalism may make the multilateral system more fragile because, among other things, countries joining a regional agreement are doing so because they want more and not less protection; hence they would oppose regional policies leading to a more open and multilateral system.

We finally come to condition 4, the role of institutions. This condition could be a decisive one in a world of regional aggregations which will continue to remain distinctive entities. The role of global institutions is to provide a forum and a common language, to keep the possibility of compromise permanently open so that members, countries or regional actors, can reach agreement on specific issues. The role of institutions could be strengthened if the benefits of issue linkage are exploited. As most of the international institutions have specific missions to carry out, issue linkages involving different institutions could help reach cooperative solutions. In short, a global multilateral regime would be significantly reinforced if such linkages were strengthened.

7 Summary

The points developed in this chapter may be summarized in the following steps:

Step 1   The international system is in a state of 'institutional disequilibrium' in the sense that there is an excess demand for international public goods. This is the result of a decrease in supply, because of the redistribution of power away from a hegemonic, unipolar, structure, and of an increase in demand, because of increased globalization.

Step 2   The excess demand for international public goods spurs the formation of regional agreements. Regional agreements are a source of supply of (partially excludable) international public goods (club goods). At the same time, globalization provides incentives for the formation of regional agreements based on norms and standards that contribute to the build-up of regional comparative advantage. To the extent that globalization is conducive to instability it is itself a source of spreading regionalism.

Step 3   Regionalism and globalization increase the demand for integration and encourage structural adjustment at country level. The demand for integration increases because access to the global market (globalization) requires new standards for the domestic economy and regional standards are a source of comparative advantage, but also because clubs offer protection against global instability. Domestic adjustment and demand for integration will respond positively to the supply of integration (as provided by existing regional agreements) to the extent that they are not inconsistent with domestic political equilibrium.

Step 4   A global multilateral regime should not be understood as an extension at the global level of the regional model of integration, a 'club of clubs'. Regional agreements as clubs do form to the extent that there is an exclusion of other countries from joining the club. If there is no limit to club membership the public good nature of a club vanishes by definition. So a global multilateral regime should be understood as a situation of cooperation among clubs, which, however, maintain their specific identity.

Step 5   Cooperation among clubs is possible if conditions of cooperation under anarchy are fulfilled. Condition 3 (adjustment of preferences) and, to some extent, condition 2 (a long time horizon) are unlikely to be fulfilled.

Step 6   The fulfillment of condition 1– a small number of actors – does not necessarily imply that regionalism leads to the construction of a new global system. However, this might be obtained under unrestricted bargaining. The incentive to pursue unrestricted (selective) bargaining comes (also) from globalization as selective market access is a form of competition in global markets. Issue linkage may also reinforce the incentive to cooperative solutions.

Step 7   Condition 4, the role of institutions, could be a decisive one in a world of regional aggregations which continue to remain distinctive entities. The role of institutions could be strengthened if issue linkages are exploited. As most of the international institutions have specific missions to carry out, issue linkages involving different institutions could help reach cooperative solutions.

8 Conclusions

Two main features are likely to characterize the evolution of the international system in the foreseeable future, the emergence of new world leaders, such as China and India, which strengthens the trend towards a multipolar system, the formation of regional agreements as a strategy to fill the gap between demand and supply of governance. We have argued that while there are strong incentives for the formation of regional agreements, incentives for cooperation among a limited number of players are weak to say the least. It is hardly imaginable that global governance can develop out of an aggregation of regional agreements, a 'club of clubs', so we should expect regional blocs and large national players to coexist and pursue independent and, possibly conflicting, policies for some time to come. In such a framework the role of international global institutions remains crucial. The role of institutions is to provide a forum and a common language, to keep the possibility of compromise permanently open so that members, countries or regional actors, can reach agreement on specific issues. As most of the international institutions have specific missions to carry out, issue linkages involving different institutions could strengthen the emergence of a global multilateral regime.

Notes

1   On regionalism see, among others, de Melo and Panagariya, 1993; Winters, 1999; Baldwin, 1998.
2   In this chapter globalization is defined as the increasing elimination of barriers that separate local and national markets of factors and products from one another, accompanied by an increasing mobility of capital.
3   On hegemonic stability theory the standard reference is Kehoane, 1984.
4   For an analysis of the characteristics of regionalism see Winters, 1996.
5   See the articles in Oye, 1986, in particular the paper by Axelrod and Keohane; also Guerrieri and Padoan, 1989.
6   See, for example, Guerrieri and Padoan, 1988; Mayer, 1992; Milner, 1997; Grossman and Helpman, 1994.
7   For a survey see Baldwin and Venables, 1994.
8   A more extended analysis is presented in Padoan, 1997.
9   It can be argued that the operation of an international trade regime is influenced by the operation of an international macroeconomic regime. See Guerrieri and Padoan, 1988.
10 Collignon (1997) shows that the benefits of a currency union, a clear example of a monetary club, decrease with the increasing divergence in preferences among the union members for active stabilization policies.
11 This is also consistent with the view (see Bayoumi, 1994) that the incentives for non members to join a monetary union are larger than the incentives for union members to accept new countries.
12 See Powell, 1994, for a survey of the role of institutions in international cooperation.
13 A more formal treatment is contained in Padoan, 1997.
14 For instance membership in a trade agreement implies that all member countries adopt the same level of tariff.
15 The role of interest groups in determining international agreements is analyzed in Grossman and Helpman, 1996; Milner, 1997.
16 See Alesina and Perotti, 1995, for an empirical survey of the role of government institutions in determining fiscal policy behaviour.
17 On this point see Padoan, 1997. A formal assessment is provided by Grossman and Helpman, 1991.

Chapter 3

Cultural Difference, Regionalization and Globalization

Thomas Meyer

1 Theories on the increasing global role of the cultural factor

There is a widespread consensus in Political Science today that the cultural factor is going to play an increasingly crucial role in the national and trans-national political arenas after the end of the ideological cold war. According to this view the politics of identity will be topmost on the political agenda in the new era of globalization in all parts of the world and in the relations between them. Some even argue that the cultural factor is about to outrank economic and political strategic interests in the arena of global political conflicts. A whole variety of causes for the unprecedented prominence of the cultural factor has been advanced in the last one and a half decades. Samuel Huntington has initiated this debate with his famous prognosis that cultural differences will form the main axis of political conflict at a global scope as they are essentially irreconcilable in an era when the different cultures of the world are doomed to come in ever closer touch with each other.[1] This argument was – despite the host of sharp and profound criticism offered ever since its first introduction into the academic and political debate – able to develop a paradigm-building power that exercises its open or hidden influence even among the ranks of some of its critics.

Benjamin Barber has argued that economic globalization is perceived by most relevant social and political groups within Third World countries as a direct threat to their traditional cultural identities. In response to this perceived thread a radical resort to religiously founded political fundamentalism is one of the most frequent answers in the world of today.[2] Consequently, the increasing impact of fundamentalism is as direct outflow of the basic processes of market globalization themselves. Barber and Huntington share the basic hypothesis that the cultural factor in the form of political fundamentalism is able to play an increasingly independent role in the world politics of the future.

A counter- approach to this has recently been developed by *Robert W. Cox*. He offers a direct economic interpretation of the expected new role of the cultural factor as a much more convincing interpretation of the underlying historical factors and forces.[3] Cox states that the libertarian character of the globalizing economy of today with necessity causes the social and economic depravation and exclusion of considerable social sectors in all parts of the world. They experience their common class fate of social and economic exclusion under the form of a challenge of their cultural identity due to the lack of more adequate ideological forms of expressing it in the post Cold War period.

Whatever the particular approach of these authors may be and whatever factors they identify as last causes they share the view that the foreseeable future of the globalized world will be marked by an triangular interaction between economic, political and cultural factors in which cultural differences and their political expression and instrumentalization are to play a peculiar role of conflict generation and aggravation.

What are the real causes underlying this new constellation? The discussion about this goes on. The key question that remains is, however, whether the cultural factor is a power in its own right or in some or another way a derivate from economic or genuine political conflict constellations so that it could be coped with as soon as mutually acceptable solutions will be found for the principal political and economic conflicts of the global era. The answer to this question will contribute in no small measure to our understanding of the process, the risks and the positive prospects of globalization and the chances of alternative political strategies. If, as Huntington and some others see it, the cultural conflicts are of such a nature that there will never be a political way to reconcile them, the world order under globalization will take a very different route compared to a scenario in which they are understood as variables that depend largely upon the state of economic and political relations, such as a fairer globalization and a more multilateral global governance.

2 Huntington: The (still) leading paradigm

How can the competing hypotheses be evaluated in the light of empirical research data and what need a theory about the political role of the cultural factor look like to be in tune with them? It is often misunderstood that the crucial point in Huntington's theory is not that there are cultural conflicts, whatever their real nature may turn out to be in the light of an intricate empirical analysis. The generative idea of his theory is the assumption that all of the great cultures/civilizations of the world are based on *mutually exclusive 'genetic' value programmes* in particular with respect to those norms that underlie the construction and legitimacy of social and political order. According to Huntington it is particularly in the fields of social and political basic values such as equality/inequality, individualism/collectivism, gender-relation, religion-politics- relation, freedom and tradition, pluralism and regulation where the 'fault lines of civilization' separate distinct cultures sharply from each other. As these values are exactly the crucial pillars both for social relations in each society and for the structure of its polity and the legitimate political processes there can be no sustainable coexistence between the cultures either within a society or between states in a peaceful global order.

In the final analysis there can be only three modes of interrelation between mutually exclusive value sets as conceived ass meta-structures of cultures by Huntington:

a. Separation/apartheid.
b. Hierarchies of dominance.
c. Conflict/war.

Huntington himself, in his prognosis of the future development of the relation between different cultures in the global arena, favours a mixture between modes 2 and 3: the 'west' should try to contain and dominate the Islamic and Confucian part of the world or otherwise prepare for a global cultural war in which the decision on the lasting hierarchies of dominance and subordination will have to be taken by way of force.

The discourse about 'Asian values' including 'guided democracy', 'culturally interpreted' human rights, 'Confucian Dynamism' as the new Protestant ethic for the global economy of the 21st century are heavily influenced by this theory which they quote as a western corroboration of their claims.[4] The picture of Islam as an 'essential fundamentalism' (Benjamin Barber) unable to cooperate and understand the rest of the world which must, in the last instance, be contained forcefully, is another result of this line of thinking. A cultural type of cold war thus looms large with a triangular conflict constellation as its core pattern: Confucianism vs. westernism vs. Islam. This cultural conflict pattern in this view intervenes heavily with both the economic and the political process of globalization. It impedes an undisturbed global economy and an equitable political multilateralism.

The surface of a variety of conflicts in the post-communist world appears to deliver some evidence for the Huntington paradigm, in particular in former Yugoslavia, the central Asian states, the Middle East and the New Wars between informal terrorist groups and some of the 'western' states like the US, the UK and others. But how about the empirical basis of the fault line theory of cultures?

3 Cross-cultural empirical data

Huntington's model is, fortunately for the prospects of cooperative global governance, regionalism and inter-regionalism, not in tune with the relevant facts that have been produced by more recent comparative research.[5] In addition it is built on a gross methodological misconception, which believes that even clear cases of political instrumentalization of real and ascribed cultural differences for the purposes of power building are the inevitable political consequences of cultural determinants. This misconception is quoted by the respective actors for reasons of justification. And, finally, the very concept of culture/ civilization which is underlies these theories is completely obsolete in empirical respect und unfit even for a rough description of present day cultural reality.

The available results of empirical and historical research on present day intra and inter-cultural differentiation with respect to the socio-political core values that determine the political space for their peaceful co-existence can be summed up in a nutshell as follows.[6]

All present day cultural units, be they defined as religious-cultural or ethno-cultural, are marked by a very large degree of internal differentiation, the macro- level of which might be called mutually contradicting styles of civilization, that is, patterns of giving actual meaning to what the respective cultural tradition has to say to the challenges of the presence. It is one of the most convincing results of world-wide research in fundamentalism that every single culture of the world of today presents itself as a *dialectical social discourse system* in which three principal styles of civilization , try to give actual relevance to the traditional topics and are struggling for hegemony:[7]

- Traditionalism which aims at an utmost defensive adaptation of only the absolutely unavoidable measure of elements to modern culture and societal development.
- Modernism/liberalism which interprets the tradition more or less consequently in the light of the predominance of the values of individualism, pluralism, activism and rationalism and allows for major differences in the interpretation of the reference culture.
- Fundamentalism which is a self-contradictory modern form of fight against modernity as it makes use of some of the most effective outcomes of modernity, such as: weaponry, organization and mass communication, simply in order to fight against the basic values of modernism; particularly against difference, openness, relativity; pluralism, democracy, gender equality and individual rights.

Fundamentalism is the most conspicuous among the styles of civilization in some of the present day cultures, in particular Islam. By way of a retrieval of past stages in the development of its respective mother-culture it dogmatizes one particular historical pattern of its interpretation as the absolutely certain fundament of cultural identity and political legitimacy. Nobody, who wants to be recognized as a true member of the respective cultural community, is allowed to doubt this dogmatized version.. Varying models of closed society and closed polity are constructed upon the basis of such pretended absolute certainties of cultural identity. They all tend to varying degrees of comprehensiveness and consequence towards some form of theocracy. Internal cultural differences are considered to be altogether destructive, alien to the true nature of the given cultural heritage and poisonous seeds of modernism within it.

However, it is a clear result of current research that no religion or culture, including Islam, is inescapably fundamentalist by its very nature. Nowhere can fundamentalism rightfully claim to be the unchallenged expression of the cultural identity of a community. Every culture – including, for example, Buddhism, Hinduism, Judaism, Islam, Christianity, Confucianism – today presents itself in this dialectical shape – including, above all, the 'west' itself. The relative political and social size and influence of each of the three competing *styles of civilization* within each culture is constantly changing faster, or slower. The pattern of such changes depends highly upon the historical situation, the socio-economic constellation, the acceptance and performance of the political class that succeeds in establishing itself as the key interpreter of the tradition[8] and the ways and the speed of change in a given society as induced by globalized communication and economy.

The relative dominance of fundamentalism in many parts of the world of Islam is itself but a product of the specific historical development of the respective societies in the last couple of decades. Since the middle of the nineteenth century tendencies to modernize the Islamic tradition have been prominent in Egypt, British India and other Islamic countries. From the 1920s until the 1960s Islamic secularism, often under the form of socialism, has been one of the most dynamic forces in Islamic culture.[9] It is only since the 1970s that fundamentalist Islam has become the most visible force in large parts of the Islamic world. As *Bassam Tibi* has demonstrated, in present day Islam the three principal styles of civilization are all vivid in the course of a dialectical interplay according to the experiences that the individual societies and their relevant sub-milieus are undergoing. Paradigmatically they are represented by the mainstream style of civilization in three relevant countries: traditionalism in Saudi Arabia, modernism in Turkey and fundamentalism in Iran.[10]

In this respect empirical study corroborates three generalizations:

a. It is not the cultural identity itself which determines the social and political role of the different cultures but the social and political forces that control its mainstream interpretation in a given historical, social and economic context.
b. All cultures in the modern world provide a vast scope for internal differentiation and modernization.
c. The contradicting styles of civilization obviously do have more in common with their counterparts in other cultures than with their rivals within their own culture of origin. Culture-based coalitions for political actions, thus, can reach out to trans-national and trans-cultural levels. A fact which is particularly illustrated by the multilateral networks of civil society institutions.

Cross-cultural comparison of the relevant socio-political values in sixty-five societies which belong to all the great cultural traditions have come to quite informative results with respect to their capacity for trans-cultural political co-operation. As aggregated national-level data they are particularly useful in the negative sense as refutations of Huntington-type generalizations about the dividing effects of different cultural identities. On a more positive note, they are, however, still of a limited value for understanding the political role of culture in the world of today: the crucial units of cultural identity-building turn out to be sub-national socio-cultural milieus within every individual society.[11]

Hofstede's and Inglehart's cross-cultural data on the distribution of socio-political basic values in sixty-five, respectively forty countries have yielded informative results. They can be summed up as follows:

a. In the value dimensions of power distance (that is, acceptance of *equality/ inequality*), *individualism/* collectivism, femininism/ masculinism (that is, soft or hard *modes of social coordination*) and uncertainty avoidance (that is, *openness*, tolerance) the maximal score differences between countries sharing the same culture and the average difference between countries of different cultures as a whole are roughly the same. Some of the countries with the largest overall score difference belong to the same cultures, for example: Portugal-Denmark, Greece-Sweden, Portugal-Great Britain, whereas some of the countries with the closest similarities in their basic value profiles belong to different cultures, for example, East-Africa-Thailand, Arab Countries-Mexico, Brazil-Turkey, Portugal-South Korea.

b. These data demonstrate that there is no such thing as 'fault lines' between cultures in the social reality of the distribution of socio-political values in the world of today. It needs to be stressed here that it is exactly this set of socio-political values which underlies the basic pattern of social relations in a society and its polity. It becomes obvious that these sets of socio-political values cannot be invariantly determined by religion-based cultural traditions. There are some characteristic differences in values like individualism and equality, but not in big measures. According to the data their differences appear to be more dependent on the socio-economic level of modernization of different societies than on their affiliation with variant cultural tradition. More striking are the cross-cultural similarities in all the other value dimensions and a considerable degree of overlapping between most societies from all cultural strands in all the researched value dimensions.

c. *Inglehart* has shown that the key value set of *post-materialism* – which expresses such crucial values as *participation in politics and job, a more personal and humane society, civil liberties, and individualism* – cross-culturally varies exclusively with the level of the GNP of a society. This value set is of a particular relevance for the cultural identity of any society as it has a major impact simultaneously on political culture, the political process, the preferred structure of the polity and the acceptance of economic, ecological and civil rights and security policies. This research indicates an increasing tendency of cross-cultural convergence in one of the most crucial value dimensions as post-materialism is most prominent amongst the younger generations but once acquired most probably sustained throughout their lifetime.

Following *Pierre Bourdieu's* studies in the formation of *habitus* and socio-cultural milieus beneath the macro-level of the socio-cultural unit of the society as a whole, cross-national and cross-cultural studies have been carried out in order to analyze the structure and the dynamics of socio-cultural milieu building in European, North American and Asian societies.[12] As a result of these studies it can be summarized that in all societies there is a strong *internal* cultural differentiation into ten to twelve relatively homogeneous sub-groups, *socio cultural milieus*, the individual members of which share a universe of values concerning work, consumption, partnership, meaning of life, politics, family, leisure, life style, religion and everyday-life aesthetics. The members of such milieus consciously and unconsciously distinguish themselves strictly from those of the other milieus, the more so the greater their distance to them is on a dynamic axis of value modernization. Social stratification along the lines of income, profession and formal education in all compared societies of today only works as a loose frame within which a variety of socio-cultural options is open for the individual to join one amongst three or four milieus at a given status level. The main difference between the milieu-cultures is created by the degree to which their generative value set is traditional hedonistic, semi-modernized, modernized or post-modern. Thus, what matters in the process of cultural identity building in the world of today is not so much the macro-level of the great cultural traditions, but the meso- level of the dynamics of socio-cultural milieu formation.

The members of all these different milieus still may share some very basic values at the macro-level which makes it meaningful for them to coexist in the same polity. But, then again, what defines value patterns at the macro-level is more the history and stage of development of a society than the meta-identity of *religio*-cultural or *ethno*-cultural belonging. The more advanced the milieus are on the value change axis the more values and attitudes they tend to share with members of corresponding socio-cultural milieus cross-nationally and also cross-culturally. Their cultural distance with respect to social and political values may be greater to some of the milieu groups of their own community than to their counter-parts in societies with different cultural traditions. Though they may still share some of the religious cults and sotereologies (M. Weber) with them they will not be sharing the socio-cultural orientations that are relevant for their economic, social and political actions in real life.

Thus, it is mainly the sub-national milieus at the meso-level that are relevant for that dimension of cultural identity-building that has the main impact on political orientations and action. In this field it is cross-cultural value formation that matters most. All this gives proof of the fact that fundamentalism as the most effective and most widespread form of a non-cooperative *politics of identity* anywhere in the world can rightfully claim to be the pure and constant expression of the cultural identity of the respective community. Though, in the event of certain constellations of social, economic and political crises, in a given society, fundamentalism may gain dominance over the competing traditionalist and modern currents, in the world of today it is nowhere the genuine expression of the cultural identity of entire cultures or societies. It is this, however, exactly this unfounded claim on which Huntington's entire theory is built.

4 Cultural difference and shared citizenship: national, regional and global

We know from history and from research that civic identity is nothing that exists prior to common political deliberation and decision making procedures. There is, as Habermas has put it, a situation of mutual causation. It starts as a process of political deliberation with a certain feeling that we belong together already, and then in the course of that process of deliberation and decision making this consciousness and feeling of belonging together, of a common identity of our civic aspirations and fates is structured and reinforced. This is a process of circular causation – we know this from the European Union also – that needs to be set in motion. And once it is set in motion, it can work not without obstacles, not without setbacks, but gradually with success. The amount of overlapping of cultural values necessary to set this process in motion, will gradually increase.

Citizenship in a democratic polity requires, at the level of political culture, only that all citizens are ready and able to transcend the horizon of their cultural-religious identity in their role as citizens of that polity.[13] They need to develop a certain sense of *political identity* as members of one and the same polity that is strong enough to pave the way for a sufficient degree of solidarity and cooperation among all citizens, whatever their cultural affiliation. All comparative studies in the political culture of stabile and fragile democracies since the 1950s have demonstrated, that in order to make a democracy work and have a sustainable citizenship, it needs to be embedded in a shared *political* culture.[14] Such a democratic political culture in order to sustain democracy needs, according to *Galston*, to encompass such core elements as: independence and openness, loyalty, respect of the rights of others, recognition of cultural difference and political judgement.[15] From the point of view of empirical research in democratic political culture some additional features are required, like trust in fellow citizens, cognitive knowledge of the political systems citizens belong to and a sufficient degree of affective identification with its political project and their own role as citizens, active tolerance, the competence to balance limited political conflict with basic democratic consensus, capability to realize a clear cut difference between political conflict with fellow citizens and their recognition as human beings.[16] Though the simultaneous achievement of all these goals is rarely the status quo in a given culturally diverse society, the described criteria can serve at least as a hallmark for the direction in which the political culture of culturally diverse societies needs to move. Otherwise political cooperation and stability will become difficult.

Obviously outright fundamentalists are prone to obstruct this process. Required as a prerequisite for the co-existence of different ethno-cultural or cultural religious identities is, thus, the 'de-fundamentalization' of those who are still inclining towards a fundamentalist concept of identity. The very meaning of democratic cooperation under the rule of law, national or trans-national, is to make just that minimum set of rules binding for all that are necessary to guarantee the maximum of liberties for all individuals and groups to secure their autonomous decision about their own ways of believing and living. Hence, all collectives of citizens are obliged to all other citizens to define and practice their own cultural identities within this framework of rights, norms and rules as far as they wish these identities in turn to be recognized by all the others. This is what the *Universal Cultural Basic Rights*, as laid down in the UN Covenant of 1966, all are about.

This requirement is, as we have seen earlier, in no way in a contradiction to the great variety of cultural identities as it exists today. Due to the process of internal differentiation each of the current cultural traditions manifests its contents and claims at three clearly distinct levels:

1. the *metaphysical* level of *believing*, on which the 'last' questions about the meaning of life and death are answered (religions);
2. the level of individual or group *ways of life*, where the ethics, aesthetics and pragmatics of everyday life find there, sometimes temporary expression (*everyday life culture*); and
3. the level of social and political basic values that establish *ways of living together* (political culture), likewise nationally, regionally and trans-nationally.

The concept of political citizenship and the shared orientations of political culture are entirely situated on level III. There is, as the empirical evidence has shown, nothing in the core of any of the world's religions or cultures that would in principle stand in the way to convergence on level III. Overlapping values have the space for as much divergence as any of the cultural traditions need in order to define and live up to their cultural identity.[17]

The potentiality for such convergence at level III is, as the empirical data prove, sufficiently given in all the different cultures, and in most societies it is manifested and working well. In order to allow the overlapping consensus at level III to gain strength it is not only helpful, but under normal conditions, a necessity, that different cultural communities do not encapsulate themselves in parallel societies without civic and everyday life interaction with each other. As political cultural, bridging social capital[18] and trust are built through civil society activities for culturally diverse societies culturally-overlapping cooperation at the level of civil society and the life world are imperative. Recently the paradigmatic study by *Ashutosh Varshney* has corroborated this experience through convincing empirical data.[19]

5 The ambivalent role of the cultural factor

In the light of this analysis it becomes obvious that the *cultural factor* can play three substantially divergent roles in multilateral contexts of political action:

a. *Identity politics*. There is always a strong temptation for political and religious leaders in power or aspiring for power to use the cultural factor as a resource for a variety of purposes such as the justification of authoritarianism and the denial of human rights in the name of the true identity of the culture they aim to represent. In this sense it can be a resource of mobilization and the resort to violent action against the ruling elite by leaders of opposition movements in the name of a restoration of a more genuine cultural identity of a country against foreign influence or against cultural minorities or deviant groups within the country.
b. *Trans-cultural and trans-national cooperation*. At the same time the trans-cultural patterns of cultural differentiation can facilitate 'cross-cultural' multilateralism at the civil society level along the lines of shared styles of

civilization. this trend will play an increasingly relevant role Thus, increasing interaction between trans- governmental organizations and international institutions on the one hand and trans-societal networks at the level of the civil society on the other will be one of the factors shaping global politics in the era of globalization. A representative example for this case was the Parliament of World Religions in Chicago 1994 and it's declaration 'Towards a Global Ethics'.

   c. *Framing the fight against exclusion.* Obviously, unfair social and economic consequences of economic globalization with large scale intra-national and trans-national exclusion will, due the want of attractive alternatives in a post-ideological era, foster a tendency of religious and cultural language to frame the expression of protest against exclusion by the least powerful economic and political actors.

All these three tendencies most probably will play their unpredictable role with their relative weight depending, among a a variety of other factors, on the perceived fairness of the economic and political quality of globalization. The overlapping consensus that is required to make the tendency of trans-cultural cooperation increasingly strong can be forcefully supported through new ways of regional cooperation as the history of the European Union has proven so impressively. The political success of regional cooperation does not depend on common religious belief or identical lifestyle cultures but on shared political convictions, fairness and a pragmatic sense of cooperation. Necessary for the beginning of it are only some shared political core values and the credible promise that the envisaged cooperation will benefit all participants in an equitable way. The interaction of these twin ideas can create a sufficient basis of political identity, inter-regionally, intra-regionally and even at the global level. This is highly likely, whereas in the case of the South Asian region a long history of close interaction between culturally diverse milieus has been passed already.

   Regarding the cultural preconditions for regional political cooperation it is a misconception that the common values that are required do not include the metaphysical doctrines of salvation or of shared religious practices in everyday life but just agreement on political values such as liberty, equality, tolerance and so on. Even in the European case it was not a historically given cultural identity that made political co-operation possible but a political construction based on the experience that overstressing the role of religious and cultural divergence would seriously harm the interests of all the involved actors.[20] The comprehensive religious identity which European societies once shared never prevented war and conflict and served finally in the age of confessionalism as a powerful source for European civil wars. In addition, the same religious and cultural resources lent themselves at differing stages of European history to substantially contradictory sets of socio-political values, ranging from outright authoritarianism to liberalism, socialism and anarchism.

   Only when all relevant European societies started to share democratic political values and human rights systematic regional co-operation at the political level was made possible and finally with the process of European unification became a success story. Newly emerging systems of regional co-operation like SAARC and ASEAN include almost all the divergent religions of the world, some of them large majority communities in some countries and minorities in others. Most of them have an age old record of cultural diversity and how to manage it in the framework of the nation state. In this respect they are well accustomed to the concept of political identity on the basis of a wide range of cultural diversity and well equipped for the coping with cultural difference in an era of globalization.

6 Concepts of global citizenship as resource of global governance

The cultural divergence of today is by no means an obstacle to world-wide efforts to bring the unleashed economic forces of the liberal world market back under the control of shared socio-cultural values such as have been put into force in the UN Covenant of 1966 on Universal Civil, Political, Social and Economic Rights. These rights by themselves can be said to constitute a kind of *passive global citizenship* as they manifest a mutual recognition of all citizens of the world to respect and protect the basic human rights of each citizen. This is one of the basic features of citizenship. To come to full mutual guarantee of these rights, however, would require a step forward to active global citizenship, that is, the creation of a global structure of shared political responsibility and decision making that allows for appropriate measures of global governance in favour of active measures to protect universal citizen's rights.[21] Like national political identity cosmopolitan citizenship needs to be based on shared political values and not on common cultural identities. Civic identity is build around a common sense of belonging and responsibilities related to political problems and solutions that concern all those individuals who are subjects of a shared polity. Citizenship is a pattern of cooperation between individuals in establishing binding frames and rules for running their lives. This specific pattern of cooperation of citizenship consists in the mutual assurance of equal rights, obligations and opportunities for active political participation in decision making. The question for further progress in global governance, thus, is not, whether or not, but in which final ways citizenship rights can best be implemented at the regional and global levels of the emerging system of a global polity.

In the pre-global era of democratic culture, citizenship was organized in the nation state as the appropriate arena in which political problem causation and the power of political problem resolution were co-extensive, so that addressees and the authors of political jurisdiction were generally coterminous. This idea of the existence of coterminous political arenas was the core idea of legitimacy of a democratic nation state, as long as the scope of political problem causation and that of political competence were roughly the same. This was the main condition of political legitimacy in the era of the democratic nation state. Under this condition, national citizenship and democratic legitimacy were in accordance with each other. In the era of globalization it is exactly this basic condition that has changed fundamentally in a variety of aspects.

The present-day political community of fate in many respects is regional and global, whereas the principal patterns of political deliberation and governance are still mainly national. However, in some regions, like Europe, and in a few issue respects like trade, they are increasingly trans-national. The modern idea of legitimacy requires that problems that are political in nature need to be tackled through procedures based on democracy and universal basic rights. Hence, political legitimacy in a globalized era requires new trans-boundary forms of governance and citizenship. They are emerging already, and in some respects they are in place, yet at the global level they are only at an embryonic stage of development. What are the prospects for further progress in global governance in a realistic evaluation and what is their relation to the cultural factor?

The first, of course, is Huntington's negative approach with its proposition that there can be no common regional let alone global community of political values. Due to the absolutely relativist basic assumption of his approach there never can be such a thing as a trans-cultural civic identity. Citizenship at the global level would need to be underpinned by certain political values, which are shared by all people of the world to a sufficient degree. But sharing core political values is impossible due to the 'fault lines' of civilization. No common ground is in sight for a global civic identity, or a global concept or reality of citizenship. There can be only competing cultural and political identities. A new 'ultra- realism' of continued nation state politics in the era of globalization ensues.

The second concept is that of Yasemin Soysal.[22] Her approach is widely discussed in political science. She says that the concept of citizenship by its very nature is linked to the concept and the existence of the nation state. Therefore it needs to be replaced in a globalized world by a human rights approach. But universal human rights are entitlements of individuals, independent of their specific affiliations and therefore they entail rights of protection and participation wherever a person may live. This concept regards the European Union in the first place but refers finally to the global arena as well. We should, Soysal argues, discuss the whole matter of political belonging and entitlements rather in terms of universal human rights than citizenship. You can allow people to enjoy their human rights wherever they live, whoever they are, independent of their citizenship titles. This concept may be meaningful in a situation where trans-national and global structures of governance are in place already, global participation in national institutions of decision making cannot, however, be a substitute for them.

The third approach, the concept of *post-modern citizenship*, is favoured in civil society initiatives which are part of the anti- or alter- globalization movement. Post-modern citizenship is a form of citizenship that is only related to political issues and political responsibilities in individual issue areas and is completely detached from statehood-structures. Citizens are entitled to participate in deliberation and decision making wherever issues of concern for them may emerge. There is no need to institutionalize structures of trans-national political participation. For the same reasons we discussed concerning Soysal's approach this concept is not entirely convincing.

The fourth is the concept of *cosmopolitan citizenship*.[23] It refers to some form of multiple citizenship related to overlapping political authorities in a multi-level global polity. Cosmopolitan citizenship thus is a form of multiple institutionalized citizenship. Everybody remains citizens in a nation state and, additionally, becomes citizens in the existing or emerging regional systems of political cooperation and increasingly in a global polity. It is the basis of a historically unprecedented global civic identity. It requires overlapping consensual political norms, and also some common cultural norms such as liberty, equality, solidarity and mutual recognition.

The models of global governance presently under discussion, that would give global citizenship its institutional underpinning and its resources to act are in their own ways related to these concepts of citizenship with the exception of Huntington's, which does not lend itself in any way to democratic global governance.[24]

The *first* is the model of a *democratic subsidiary world republic* with a large measure of statehood, as the final aim of global governance. This is discussed, for instance, by the German political philosopher Otfried Höffe. It has an impact on the discussion in the political arena in some of the Social Democratic parties. Global statehood would render a great amount of power to centralized global bodies and make democratic participation at the global level almost impossible. Therefore it might rather increase the problem of lacking democratic control instead of solving it. It would require a substantial sense of global citizenship and a strong form of institutionalization.

The *second* is the model of a world-wide '*demarchy*' (mix of democracy and anarchy), as offered by several Anglo-Saxon authors.[25] It is under discussion, particularly within the world-wide civil society and anti- or alter- globalization movement. This model of democracy is identified with the present insufficient forms of representative government which lead to the new concept of 'demarchy', which draws on the concept of civil society governance. Civil society here will stepwise replace the failing structures of representative democracy instead of extending them to the regional and global arenas. There is no place for organized supra-national power in the concept. It is hardly conceivable that there can be democratic control, particularly of economic power, without organized political power. Additionally, civil society, even if organized in world-wide networks, is never fully legitimized to act on behalf of the entire society. This idea rests on a post-modern concept of citizenship and the spontaneous ability of citizens in all parts of the world to exercise it jointly in different issue fields of their common concern amid all kinds of cultural differences.

The third concept is that of cosmopolitan democracy as framed among others by David Held and the Commission on Global Governance led by Ingvar Carlsson.[26] The model of global governance proposes a four-pronged approach to global democratization:

1. To extend, to democratize and make more inclusive the principal trans-national institutions, such as the United Nations, by way of creating a new Economic Security Council, a People's Assembly, and an assembly for Civil Society Associations, plus more equality and more inclusiveness in all of these institutions.
2. The functional area of issue-related regimes needs to be democratized, being made more inclusive and more equal in the respective procedures of decision making – such as the WTO, the ILO or the World Bank.
3. The systems of regional political cooperation need to proliferate and develop dense networks of inter-regional political cooperation.

4. A crucial role for global civil governance in all policy areas. In this four-column approach of global governance political regionalization is attributed an outstanding role for one of its democratic backbones. In this concept global citizenship seems to be conceived as a composition of modern and post-modern elements.

Obviously all three of these strategic designs of democratic global governance draw on concepts of global citizenship that require, institutionalize and reinforce new forms of multi-level political identity, i.e. new forms of citizenship at the national, the regional and the global level that are built amid continuous patterns of cultural diversity among the citizens addressed. The EU itself is a prominent case in point.

7 Citizenship, multiculturalism and integration in the EU

For most of the European societies the problems connected with social and political integration of multicultural communities have gained top relevance in recent years following a series of serious signs of disintegration even in countries like the Netherlands that have for a long time been considered as outstanding examples of admirable success stories in intercultural social integration. This development appears in the wake of three interrelated experiences that have started to puzzle European political elites:

1. Right wing populism is reaping the fruits of failing integration and at the same time actively contributes in its turn to it. It is in almost all European countries about to become a growing threat to democracy and integration particularly hitting the democratic parties of the centre left.
2. Apparently all the standard models of handling the challenge of balancing immigration and integration practiced in various European countries have failed.
3. In response to failing integration fundamentalist tendencies among cultural minorities, particularly the Muslim community as the largest group almost everywhere in Europe are on the increase.[27]

Whereas centre left parties up until recently have displayed a conspicuous inclination to ignore emerging problems of failing integration and stigmatize the related discourse as typical right wing propaganda, they started after a series of electoral failures in countries like Austria, the Netherlands or Denmark to realize that they need to address these issues in a more serious and open minded way. The two most typical standard models to balance immigration and integration in Europe have been the French model of *assimilation* and the Dutch model of unrestrained *multiculturalism*. As empirical studies have demonstrated, both models for different reasons have failed. The French model of civic assimilation leaves little space for legitimate cultural differences and at the same time does not succeed in assimilating the migrants sufficiently in social and economic terms. Consequently, it ends up with massive protest activities, social anomy and severe signs of disintegration. The Dutch model of unrestrained multiculturalism with the government supporting all the different cultural communities in their efforts to build closed parallel societies produces social and economic disintegration and increasing alienation between the majority society and its cultural minorities. Other societies like Germany have just begun to acknowledge that they are de facto immigration societies and need to develop sustainable integration policies. However, the same experience also reveals that the integration of the vast majority of diverse cultural minorities can be sufficiently successful under the condition that they are given opportunities to social and economic participation and leeway to live their own cultural identities in a democratic framework.

Two questions arise in this situation: *first*, what are the conditions for successful social and political integration of culturally diverse societies in the framework of a democracy under the rule of law; and second; is there enough potentiality in modern democracies to accommodate all of the diverse cultural religious traditions by way of a successful strategy of integration.

European experiences with failed integration suggest that all of the pursued one-dimensional strategies are under-complex. What is needed is a more complex *integrationist approach* that comprises three dimensions:

a. the *recognition* of different ethno-cultural and cultural-religious identities
b. the insistence on the need to accept and develop an overlapping political culture of democratic cooperation among all communities and
c. the *fair participation* of all of them in the available social, cultural and economic opportunities.

As empirical comparison spanning all cultures has shown under certain conditions that every culture is able to generate currents of fundamentalism alongside the omnipresent modernizing and the traditionalist ones. As soon as a community perceives their own members as excluded from the benefits of the society, particularly when combined with the humiliation of its cultural identity claim its inclination to take refuge behind fundamentalist identity politics may grow quickly.[28] This seems to hold as true at the level of national societies as at the regional and global levels of social relations.

It holds likewise true for all the different religio- cultural and ethno-cultural communities. In each of them fundamentalism declares war on the two rival currents of modernism and traditionalism and outside enemies of other cultural persuasions, unswervingly defending the goal of redeeming the real identity of the traditional culture from its sullied state and resurrecting it by taking over the reins of political power and achieving absolute supremacy, so that society is once and for all rid of the tortuous contradictions of modernization.

Most recent European experience reveals the strong relation between social exclusion and denied recognition of cultural communities on the one hand hand and the inclination of affected sub-groups within them to resort to fundamentalist forms of socio-cultural identity building or even aggressive identity politics.[29]

8 Identity politics as a power strategy

All brands of Fundamentalism – be they Christian, Jewish, Muslim, Hindu or Buddhist – tend to establish a closed system of thinking that artificially excludes differences, doubts, alternatives and openness. Thus they aim at providing security, assurance of orientation, firm identity and absolute truth for their own members at the expense of outsiders. Thereby they arrive at some self-manufactured certainty of their belief system immunized against doubt. Modern day fundamentalism serves in its militant forms as legitimization for intellectual, religious and political claims to power and supremacy over those who differ and guarantees strong forms of unconditional recognition of those who submit to its claims. The closed systems of faith and schemes of order of a fundamentalist mould represent a return of the absolute in politics to the extent that they assume a role in the public sphere and shut out criticism, all alternatives, doubts, and open dialogues on their cognitive claims between equals. What generally follows is the total – or sometimes in developed democratic civilizations only selective – disregard for human rights, pluralism, tolerance, law and the democratic majority principle in the name of an absolute truth to which the fundamentalists in each case believe themselves to be uncompromisingly committed. In the culture of the west we have been witnesses to a variety such fundamentalist movements recently: Protestant Fundamentalism in the US, Ethno-Fundamentalism in the Balkans or Germany, and, without overt religious features, Marxism-Leninism in its many forms.

By the end of the twentieth century modern day fundamentalism has turned out to be an unparalleled formula for success in the politicization of cultural differences in all civilizations, even if it reveals facets that are just as diverse as the very modernization against which it revolts in the various centres where it emerges as the dominant force. With the end of the East-West conflict and the related grand ideologies, the different cultural patterns have actually become more conspicuous than ever. Hardly had this rather unspectacular fact succeeded in somewhat imprinting itself in the public consciousness in the few years following the end of the ideological age than it itself became the object of political exploitation. Fabricated partly for political ends, over accentuated in part to ensure recognition, taken in by disoriented publics with a shudder of relief at their safe distance from the terrible misfortune, cultural self-awareness and with it the awareness of cultural differences seem as of now to take over the legacy of the great ideological confrontation which had dominated the twentieth century.

The politicization of cultural differences constitutes a threat in foreign policy and a temptation in the domestic. In many cases challenges on both fronts automatically extend into each other, as exemplified with classic clarity in South Asia where the same cultural differences between the two nuclear powers, India and Pakistan, dominate both external relations and domestic politics within the two societies, proving equally explosive in both cases once politicized with the intention of creating antagonisms. Nevertheless it is never cultural differences per se, but almost always their political exploitation which often enough follows in the wake of economic conflicts, despair and degradation or denied social and political recognition.

In the course of the last three decades of the twentieth century the politicization of cultural differences has proved to be a universal instant recipe that is forever useful in stirring up public opinion inside the respective communities that can then be converted into political support. Problems which can and must be resolved through political means such as fair co-operation, mutual security, economic progress, meaningful division of labour and social inclusion that are in fact underlying the dissatisfaction of the frustrated communal groups are obscured and re-interpreted as mere cultural conflicts. Social and economic conditions which have outraged many are projected as the outcome of the degeneration of cultural identity, the deliberate intermingling of cultures or the subjugation of one's own cultural by that of the powerful others. Viewed from this perspective, the politics of cultural identity, by ousting others from the domain of their rights, appears to be the indispensable basis for the welfare of 'one's own kin'.

The politicization of culture takes place both from within as well as from without. The former represents the strategy of fundamentalism which seeks to convince us that the afflictions of the world can be wholly cured only when claims to certainty, held out by charismatic fundamentalist leaders in each case, rule the world without fear of contradiction. The latter represents the strategy of those like Huntington who, without being fundamentalists themselves, pave the way for fundamentalist action by declaring that the divergent civilizations of the world are by their very nature nothing but fundamentalist action programmes which compel even non-fundamentalists to pay back in the same coin if they do not want to jeopardize their own powers of assertion in the supposed global clash of civilizations.

As long as socio-economic exclusion and denied recognition are the basic features of many societies and, moreover, the world society as a whole, there are, therefore, great risks that the politicization of cultures is becoming a self-sustaining process and the cultural factors tend to exceed political control. Hence, a purely culturalist counter-strategy trusting in dialogues and symbolic recognition alone will hardly prove successful, as the above explanation for the growing strength of fundamentalism underlines. What needs to be fought are the tangible causes of fundamentalism with credible policies, lest people be driven into its embrace.

9 The politics of recognition: Basis for fair globalization and multilateralism

Obviously it is social experiences and life-situations that prove decisive in defining the cultural ways of life of the groups, in terms of their affiliation to a great religious-cultural tradition. Included in these formative experiences are crises, ruptures and deprivations, as the case of fundamentalism reveals. However, social values regarding ways of living together that are shared by all the existent cultures create space for the coexistence of different cultural identities as ways of believing and living in all the relevant political arenas: national, regional and global. Today, however, against the actually given opportunities for mutual understanding, the risk is imminent that the politicization of cultures is becoming a self-sustaining process. Those who are pursuing it from within and those who are working on it from outside are playing into each others' hands, their explanations and prognoses corroborating each other deceptively, their energy being mutually reinforcing. Contrarily, all cultures of today's world prove to be social discourse spaces which are intrinsically highly diverse and dynamic. In all of them, to a varying degree, fundamentalism occurs, in none of them is fundamentalism the unchallenged expression of the culture's identity as a whole. But in all of them too, Islam not excluded, liberal traditions emerge and build a solid basis for intercultural cooperation.

Like any national society, regional systems of political cooperation and the emerging global order require some common values and norms of living together. Such basic commonalities exist in the heart of all the cultures, though expressed in different languages, symbols and images. More often than not they are hardly obvious but need to be discovered and brought to the full light of day. It requires purposeful efforts to recognize, develop and bring those elements in the various cultures close to each other that facilitate understanding and common action, particularly since they almost always manifest themselves in diverse forms.

As noted, common citizenship demands that all five categories of universal basic rights (civil, political, social, economic and cultural) be equally respected. Only a policy of *integration through recognition* can manage to satisfy the conditions for a satisfactory implementation of these rights. Such a strategy is complex but necessary in order to develop the liberal and democratic potentialities in each culture and tame the omnipresent fundamentalist temptations they also comprise. The political strategy that is required for the achievement of these objectives is a four- pronged politics of recognition:

1. The recognition of diverse cultural identities.
2. The recognition of democracy under the rule of law and universal basic rights as a binding legal framework by all cultural communities; that is, the emergence of a common political culture.
3. The fair participation of all in the social and economic resources and opportunities both of their own society and of the global society.
4. A fair multilateralism in the making of those political decisions that affect all of them.

As stated at the beginning of this chapter the cultural factor in the world of globalization is and certainly will remain both powerful and ambivalent. We do not have the power to wish its often irritating and unpredictable role away from the political agenda. It is, after all, more probable then not that libertarian market politics that produce exclusion nationally, regionally and globally in combination with hegemonic political power strategies and, even more so, hidden or open claims to cultural superiority will play directly into the hands of actors and communities that promote fundamentalist identity everywhere in the world. It is one of the unavoidable consequences of globalization that their networks are worldwide effective so that all attempts to guard the centres of wealth from the severe threats to peace and security they pose will be in vain.

To sum up: there will be an increasingly powerful trade off, either the politics of globalization builds on the emergent trends of overlapping social and political values of all the world civilization and pursues a credible politics of recognition including the dimension of fair participation in world resources and decision making or the countervailing tendency of identity politics will proliferate at all levels: within most of the nation states, the regions and in the global area. In that sense the future of fair political globalism and regionalism indeed depends on the way in which the cultural factor is taken into account.

Notes

1   Huntington, 1996.
2   Barber, 1995.
3   Cox/ Sinclair, 1996.
4   Lee, 2005.
5   For details see Meyer, 2001.
6   Marty/Appleby, 1991; Hofstede, 1994; Inglehart/Abramson, 1995; Sigma-Institut, no year.
7   Marty/Appleby, 1996.
8   Weber, 1974.
9   Tibi, 2002.
10 Tibi, ibid.
11 Flaig/Meyer/Uelthöffer, 1993.
12 Sigma.Institute, noyear.
13 Kymlicka, 2000: 35.
14 Almond/Verba, 1963.
15 Galston, 1991: 221ff.
16 Almond/Verba, 1993.
17 For the idea and theory of overlapping consensus see Rawls, 1993.
18 Putnam, 2000.
19 Varshney, 2002.
20 Delanty, 1995.
21 The Commission on Global Governance, 1995.
22 Soysal, 1994.
23 Held, 1996.
24 Compare Meyer/Hinchman, 2007.
25 Dryzek, 1995; Hirst, 1995.
26 Held, 1996.
27 Heitmeyer, 1997.
28 Tibi, 2002.
29 Heitmeyer, 1997.

Chapter 4

Alternative Models of Regional Cooperation? The Limits of Regional Institutionalization in East Asia

Richard Higgott

Introduction

There is a large range of literature on regionalism (the creation of formalized regions with agreed membership) and regionalization (the process by which regional economies and societies become more integrated).[1] There is also a large body of literature on regionalism and regionalization in East Asia and the Pacific; notably on ASEAN and APEC, and of late on 'East Asia' as a voice of the region. Indeed, if the volume of literature written on a region was an indicator of the strength of regional institutional development then the Asia Pacific would be a highly institutionalized region. There is also a growing body of literature comparing regionalism and regionalization in Europe with East Asia in particular.[2] Finally, there are also large bodies of scholarly literature in economic and political science on the theory and practice of institutionalism and international organization.[3] This last body of literature is evolving and it is not settled on many issues.

Notwithstanding the recent major work of Peter Katzenstein (2005) we are no closer to a genuine comparative study of the theory and practice of regionalism. There are lessons to be drawn from different regions but this does not amount to what we might call settled comparative theory of regionalism. Specifically, there is as yet little or no substantial analysis of the importance of the theory and practice of institutionalism as a significant predictor of enhanced regionalism in an East Asian context. There is a range of reasons for this. From the perspective of the scholar of institutionalism and international organization, East Asia until recently has simply not been a region where they could ply their craft in a meaningful way. The laboratories were to be found either in the multilateral organizations, or in the study of the European project – for many, the one exercise in regionalization worthy of theoretical study. For the analyst-cum-practitioner involved in the various regional discourses taking place in the Asia Pacific, and East Asia in particular, since the closing decades of the twentieth century, the very idea of 'institutionalizing' this dialogue in a meaningful way, or certainly on the basis of some European model was largely unthinkable. Indeed, senior members of the Asian regional policy community were often heard to rail against what they saw as the dangerous excesses of European legal formalism and the prospect of a 'Brussels in Asia'.

Since the turn of the century there has been a change of mood in East Asia. Driven by a number of factors in the wake of the financial crises observers have focused on the enhanced dialogue on regional monetary cooperation, especially following the Chiang Mai agreement, and the development of the ASEAN + 3 (APT) as a sign of a new interest in enhanced cooperation in the region. This chapter is not just another review of the state of East Asian regionalism.[4] Rather it takes the theory and practice of institutions and institutionalization seriously and asks exactly what are the prospects of such institutionalism in East Asia in the early twenty-first century. This is done in a comparative context with the theoretical literature on institutionalism embedded in the empirical context in which it has found strongest expression to-date – the European project. At this time in the history of the EU, the comparison with East Asia warrants further interrogation especially since the normative advocacy of institutionalism in East Asia would appear to be strengthening at the very time when limits of this process in Europe, in the wake of the defeat of the constitution, are being questioned more strongly than at any time in the last twenty-five years.

Does the history of the European project tell us anything about the utility and limits of regional institutionalism in East Asia? If so, does it do so in a way that takes us beyond the early 1990s' dichotomous analytical impasse that gave us the 'No Brussels in Asia' school of thought on the one hand and the 'No serious regional cooperation in Asia until it adopts the European model' on the other (for discussions see Segal, Maull and Wanadi, 1995 and Breslin, 2005). Does a comparative reading of the European and East Asian institutional projects instead now allow us to offer a more dynamic explanation or regionalization in East Asia that sees a process of adaptation, or what Acharya (2004) calls 'norm localization', rather than one of either mere rejection or mimicry? Yes. The often Eurocentrically smug, analyses of the 1990s – that saw European regionalism overcoming the negative constraints of state sovereignty on the one hand while Asia hovered on the edge of perilous security and regional disorder on the other (Friedberg, 2003/4; Buzan and Segal, 2004 – were crudely overdrawn.

The chapter is in four parts. Firstly it discusses the current state of the theory and practice of regionalism in comparative perspective. Secondly, it locates the theory and practice of institutionalism in a regional setting. Finally in parts three and four, it asks how relevant contemporary European institutional cooperation might be for understanding the way forward in East Asia. In so doing, it recognizes not only the significance of the European project to date, but also the limits of that project as a vehicle for transcending sovereignty and advancing supranationalism on the one hand and the potential for regional transformation in East Asia on the other. Europe, certainly for the time being, would appear to have gone about as far as it can down the institutional path. East Asia is only at the first step on that path. The interesting policy question is not whether East Asia will become more institutionalized rather than what form that institutionalization might take. The interesting scholarly question is what are the key drivers that might assist or impede that process of regional institutionalization? Just as Europe is questioning the status of the institutions and practices that characterized the European project in the closing decades of the twentieth century, so too is Asia, especially since the financial crises of 1996–97. The 'Asia Pacific way' characterized by weak informal norms of consensus-based decision making and non-interference are giving way to calls to establish substantive institutional practices of decision making, especially in the domains of trade and monetary relations at both regional and bilateral levels even though the practical direction and application of initiatives such as ASEAN Plus 3 and a putative East Asian Community remain to be determined. In this context, the issue of regional 'leadership' and institution building is identified as the key issue for early twenty-first century East Asian regionalism. At its core, the degree and the nature of regional leadership in the emerging Asian integration process that can be provided by China and/or Japan will prove crucial to the success of the current endeavours to secure enhanced regional economic (and political) institutional cooperation in the region. The presence of, or absence of, the emergence of some kind of collective leadership, or at least consensual cooperation, is the major instrument for, or obstacle to, any advancement of regionalism in Asia. Without a 'historic compromise' between China and Japan economic integration will remain a distant prospect.

1 Theorizing regionalism: Europe and Asia compared

Regionalism is invariably conceptualized with comparative reference to Europe even though it is clear that policy learning and the politics of emulation (or in many cases the politics of avoidance) are major features of current deliberations about regionalism in other parts of the world, and especially East Asia. This is especially the case as regionalism is increasingly seen as a response to the growing internationalization of the division of labour and production, or what we now call globalization. The time lag between European developments and the construction of regional orders elsewhere has meant that region-building elites have had the opportunity to learn from the European experience. As often as not this has led to a desire for avoidance of, rather than the emulation of, the 'Brussels model'. The less institutionalized approach that emerged in Asia in the early 1990s represented a deliberate choice to avoid the legal formalism of the EU (see Higgott, 1998a).

So, whether viewed negatively or positively, the European experience looms large. This search for 'European correspondence' is an obstacle to the development of analytical and theoretical studies of regional integration elsewhere (Breslin, 2005). The oft-repeated characterization of Asian regionalism as 'loose' or 'informal' reflects a teleological prejudice informed by the assumption that 'progress' in regional organization is defined in terms of EU-style institutionalization. An assumption remains that the EU is *the* paradigmatic case of regionalism against which all other regional projects are judged. For some, the Union's longevity, institutional complexity and policy reach means that it is more than just an international organization. Indeed, Hix (1994 and 1999) argues that the EU is a political system rather than an integration project. This is an extreme position (see Rosamond, 2000), but it raises the issue of whether the EU is in fact an instance of integration, and thus of regionalism, at all and thus of any comparative use for trying to explain the direction of regionalism in Asia in the twenty-first century.

This dominance of the EU on our mental maps imposes an understanding of regionalism as bound up with 'formal institutionalization'. But to equate mature regionalism with the creation of supranational politico-institutional bodies equivalent to the European Commission, the European Parliament and the European Court of Justice prejudices any conclusions we might want to make about the emergence of a world order based on alternative forms of regional organization and cooperation. This approach also assumes that key political economy questions pertaining to economic cooperation can only be addressed in this context. This emphasis on institutional regionalism proceeding through a mixture of intergovernmental dialogue and continual progressive treaty revision is at the heart of the now classic model of economic integration developed over forty years ago by Bela Balassa (1962). Balassa used the term 'economic integration' to refer to the creation of formal cooperation between states and the forward movement from a free trade area to a customs union, a common market, a monetary union and finally total economic integration.

Belassa's four stages of regional economic integration

- Free trade area (with the removal of trade restrictions).
- Customs Union (with a common external trade policy towards non-members.)
- Common Market (with free movement of factors of production between member states).
- Economic Union (harmonization of economic policies under supranational control)

This view of regionalism, with its teleological reasoning, also informed the early neo-functionalist versions of integration theory emanating from American political science (Webb, 1983). In these explanations of regional cooperation neo-functionalists saw 'spill-over' leading to economic and (ultimately) political integration. They theorized the transcendence of the state system rather than its survival. Economic and political integration was driven by *rational actors*. For a while neo-functionalists used Europe to generalize about the prospects for regional integration elsewhere (Haas, 1956 and 1964; Lindberg, 1966; Schmitter, 1971; Nye, 1968 and 1971). But this was short-lived. The publication of Haas's auto-critique, *The Obsolescence of Regional Integration Theory* (1975), suggested the very idea of producing replicable models of *regionalism* was misconceived. Two problems with integration theory had emerged:

- The European experience from the creation of the European Coal and Steel Community through to the achievement of the Common Market was not replicated. Analogous projects such as the Latin American Free Trade Area and the East African Common Market failed.
- Integration theory in Europe had underestimated the pervasiveness of nationalist sentiment and the inter-governmental direction community policy making had taken (Wallace, 1996 and Moravcsik, 1994 and 1998).

Explanations of European integration remained complicated by the domestic politics of the member states.

But, the dissolution of 'integration theory' was not just a consequence of the discrepancies between theoretical predictions and empirical 'reality'. It was also marginalized by a growing distaste for grand predictive social theory and a growing interest in explanations that privileged international 'interdependence' as the forerunner to globalization (see Katzenstein, Keohane and Krasner, 1998). It was only with the emergence of the single market programme in the mid-1980s that we saw a partial revival of neo-functionalist integration theorizing. An activist Commission, under Jacques Delors, offered an empirical reinstatement of the neo-functionalist idea of supra-nationalism and the single market was suggestive of a number of spill-over into social policy, economic and monetary union and political integration more generally (Tranholm-Mikkelsen, 1991). More traditional state-centric accounts of integration, clinging to outdated realist state theory, failed to capture the 'everyday' regulatory complexity of the European policy process (see Rosamond, 2000).

Interestingly, this reawakening of European integration occurred more or less simultaneously with the appearance of regional free trade areas elsewhere. The appearance of schemes in North and South America, the Asia Pacific and Southern Africa were suggestive of a new regionalized world order, which would be triadic, with Europe, the US and East Asia as the nodal points. The drivers of this process were twofold:

- The revised, essentially looser, geopolitical security structure that followed the end of the Cold War enhanced trans-border activity and inter-state exchange.
- The growth of globalization: especially, but not only, the liberalization of global trade and the deregulation of global financial markets questioned economic relations founded on the premise of national territory (Held *et al*, 1999; Scholte, 2005).

Both drivers stressed the fuzziness of the distinction between the 'domestic' and the 'international'. Regional cooperation was thought to enhance global competitiveness. This general assumption is crucial to comparative analysis of the European and emerging Asian Experience. Nowhere did regionalism appear to be getting stronger throughout the first half of the 1990s than in East Asia and the Pacific. For many, the growth of ASEAN and the so-called 'Asian way' to regional cooperation was a new form of regionalism explained by the need to respond to globalization (see Acharya, 1997 and 2001). The development of APEC in the early 1990s strengthened this view (see Higgott, Leaver and Ravenhill, 1993) while the financial crises of the late 1990s challenged it.

2 Beyond Europe: Regionalism in Asia after the financial crises

The financial crises of the late 1990s proved to be a watershed for both the analysis and practice of regionalism in East Asia. It provided clarity of observation and represented a political reality check on a number of issues of regional and global economic management that had been obscured during the heady 'Asian miracle' era of the early 1990s. Despite the hype that accompanied its development throughout the 1990s, the much-vaunted APEC initiative seemed incapable of even delivering short-term palliative responses to the regional financial crises, posing serious questions about APEC as an emergent mode of regional organization in the Asia-Pacific (see Ravenhill, 2001). This reading was further justified by the abortive Japanese initiative to establish an Asian Monetary Fund (AMF) in the wake of the crises. The collapse of this plan in the face of US opposition highlighted the fragility of a Pacific-wide regional project that seemed dependent on US blessing.

It can, of course, be argued that APEC was only ever a trade-led initiative, neither intended nor equipped to deal with financial crises (Harris, 2002). On the other hand, an argument can be made that the crises opened the way for less idealistic, more pragmatic thinking about regionalism in Asia (see Higgott, 1998). In the longer term the crises pushed states to think again about how best to build a regional order capable of preventing financial crises (or at least competent to deal with those crises when they arise). The creation of a network of currency swaps and other financial arrangements arising from, and subsequent to, the Asian Development Bank meetings in May 2000 reflect this approach to regional cooperation.

The discussions that have taken place since that time suggest a growing regional self-definition of 'East Asia' as a valid economic space with a discernible political voice. Analytically, this suggests that such policy initiatives do not simply arise just as rational spill-overs from financial integration. Rather they depend also upon an emergent sense of collective identity that frames the way in which policy elites respond to exogenous shocks. This highlights the centrality of two important variables in the study of regionalism often over-looked in the economic literature on regional integration.

- The importance of identities in region building;
- The catalytic impact on regionalization of exogenous political as well as economic challenges emanating from the rapid growth of globalization.

Events in Asia since 1996 allow us to identify roles that nascent regional organizations play as mediating layers of governance between the nation state and global institutions. In the Asian case this has involved the increasingly less passive acceptance of dominant western ideologies, preferences and economic models bound up with the philosophies and actions of the international financial institutions. This is not dissimilar to the situation in Europe, where the purpose of such a mediating layer, certainly in the late twentieth century, involved the protection of the 'European social model' against the assimilating tendencies of deregulated Anglo-American capitalism (Hay and Rosamond, 2000).

We thus need to treat institutions (such as regular forums for regional dialogue) as socio-political venues or sites rather than just capsules in which rational economic action takes place. Observers of regional cooperation in Asia need to recognize the salience of the relationship between institutionalized interaction on the one hand and the emergence of regional identities and interests on the other. Rationalists need not just follow well-worn state-centric paths. Strategic action by state actors may still be, indeed certainly is, important, but such action must continue to be placed within a wider complex of actors (both state and non-state) and institutional venues that conspire to influence the development of regionalism (Hurrell, 1995a). It is in this context that the role of institutions, and indeed the theory that underpins institutional growth and activity, is more important than has traditionally been thought to be the case in the dialogue on regionalism that prevailed in Asia prior to the Asian financial crises.

3   Why institutions matter and why Europe is different

> Institutions are the rules of the game in a society or, more formally, the humanly devised constraints that shape human interaction. … Institutions reduce uncertainty by providing structure to everyday life … institutions define and limit the set of choices of individuals' (North, 1990: 3-4). Institutions are '… persistent and connected sets of ruled (formal and informal) that prescribe behavioural roles, constrain activity and shape expectations' (Princeton political scientist, Robert Keohane, 1989: 3).

As processes of economic globalization deepen they need to be institutionalized if they are to avoid increased hostile and negative responses. The continued liberalization of trade, the deregulation of finance and a limited role for the state in the process of market globalization requires trusted and legitimated structures (institutions) if globalization is to continue. The level at which these institutions will flourish is yet to be fully determined. What is clear is that this cannot be either/or global or regional. It has to be both. It is a multi-level enterprise in which the failure of institutionalism at the global level is likely to enhance institutional thinking at the regional level. As problem solving at the global level becomes more difficult, enhanced collective action problem solving at the regional level becomes more attractive.

But much that we have learned about institutions is in danger of being unlearned. We are correct to point to deficiencies in the UN. We are correct to want to reform it and the international economic institutions such as the IMF, World Bank and WTO. What is alarming, however, is a growing willingness to question the very utility of institutions – as ways of organizing international behaviour – that is growing in key quarters of the global policy community. Social science has demonstrated the theoretical and practical importance of institutions as the reducers of uncertainty and transactions costs and the importance of their role in making promises credible. We may be cynical about institutions and distrust them but most of us recognize that if they did not exist we would be re-inventing them in one way or another. Institutions facilitate deal-making between actors that may be in adversarial situations. But, institutionalism as a trust-enhancing commitment to principled behaviour lacks support at the global level. It is difficult for societal actors to give loyalty to transaction cost reducers!

Institutional principles developed in the twentieth century

- Institutions lower transactions costs by the provision and sharing of information
- Institutions reduce uncertainty
- Institutions help make promises and commitments credible
- Institutions facilitate deal-making
- Institutions enhance compliance
- Institutions are vehicles for learning and socialization
- Institutions help shape collective identities.[5]

These principles do not give us a clear-cut definition of what constitutes an institution. It is not, for example, always easy to distinguish, in practice, between an institution and a norm of behaviour. Moreover, for some analysts the concepts of 'organization' and 'institution' are interchangeable while for others not all institutions are organizations. For economists for example, 'property rights' are an institution, and an important one in explaining stability and predictability of market behaviour under conditions of globalization. For political scientists a key institution for global problem solving is multilateralism.

It is, therefore, worth recalling the standard definition of multilalteralism as the management of trans-national problems with three or more parties making policy on the basis of a series of acceptable ' … generalized principles of conduct' (Ruggie, 1993: 11). The key principles identified by Ruggie are indivisibility, non-discrimination and diffuse reciprocity. It was expected that over time, decision-making underwritten by these principles would lead to collective trust amongst players within an institution. A key element in the development of trust would come from the willingness of the institutional hegemon – that is the strongest member of the institution – to agree to be bound by these principles. That is, to accept the principle of 'self-binding' (Martin, 2003).

But it is not sufficient simply to identify the principles inherent in multilateralism. We must also understand the degree to which these processes do, or do not, deliver outcomes; the prominence of an international organization (pace APEC) does not always correlate with a high rate of success in problem solving in a given area of international relations. Ambitious organizations might try to structure rules and behaviour in some of the key policy areas of contemporary global politics but often to little avail. Thus, the decreasing salience of the principal international institutions has been a growing factor in the search for regional solutions to collective action problem solving.

Recently, insight has moved beyond the 'institutionalist' literature on institutions to take more account of history, culture and identity. Powerful insights into the inter-subjective socio-legal context for inter-state behaviour have also emerged (see

Kratochwil and Ruggie, 1986). These approaches, finding fullest expression in the constructivist theorizing of the late twentieth century (see Wendt, 1992 and 2000) which focused less on the role of international institutions as actors and more on their role as norm brokers (see Finnemore, 1996). States not only use international institutions to reduce uncertainty and transaction costs. They also use them '... to create information, ideas, norms and expectations ... [and] ... to legitimate or delegitimate particular ideas and practices' (my emphasis) (Abbott and Snidal, 2001:15). Institutions are thus more than arbiters, and trustees, they are also norm producers, brokers and 'enforcers'. This is an important theoretical insight that has only partially found its way into the analysis of East Asian regionalism to date (see Acharya, 2004).

This discussion of institutionalism has clear implications for the prospects of enhanced institutionalization taking place in East Asia in the contemporary era in other ways too. In the language of institutional theory, to what extent are the processes that are in train in East Asia maximizing information sharing, generating transparency in decision making and advancing the institutional ability to generate credible collective action problem solving in a given issue area, eventually (in some if not all instances) leading to the development of enforcement/compliance mechanisms and dispute resolution procedures? This is not only a question for East Asia. There is a general issue at stake. Are we in danger of unlearning these principles in the early twentiy-first century? Specifically, is the USA unlearning the message about the role of institutions at the very time when other parts of the world (including Europe, and notwithstanding the current problems with the constitutional settlement) are learning of their importance?

But the need for institutions is particularly important in those regions of the world in which the market economy is less embedded and where these questions will continue to cast massive policy shadows. East Asia needs to learn the principles of institutionalism that flourished in the twentieth century. This is not to suggest that their implementation will follow the same paths in the twenty-first century. Indeed, what makes East Asia so interesting is precisely the fact that it is a vehicle for adaptation of some of the key principles of governance behaviour that developed countries took on board during the twentieth century. The approach adopted by the EU to institutionalization is unlikely to be replicated in Asia.

If we look at the EU, then, a major purpose of it as an institution has been to create 'credible commitments' amongst its member states in areas where the need for collective action problem solving has been accepted (Moravcsik, 1998). It has done so via a pooling and delegation of sovereignty in key areas. This is the main difference between the EU and other regional integration schemes in the modern era. Pooling and delegating sovereign decision making is what has given the EU institutional capacity. Relevant key elements of the development of the EU that makes it different from other systems to date can be noted:

1. Europe does have a substantial element of integrated governance system, linking institutional structures, policies, legal instruments that bring together the national and supranational level of decision making and policy implementation necessary for the success of any governance system.

2. In individual policy areas (for example, trade and competition policy) Europe has a sophisticated regulatory framework unequalled at the global level. Only Europe has developed a competition framework based upon the adoption by each state of common standards, procedures and laws. This is a framework that will not pass easily to the global trade community embodied in the WTO.

3. The EU governance model relies heavily on the rule of law (see Stone Sweet, 2004). The role of the European Court of Justice (ECJ) is crucial in ensuring a system that is both effective and fair. The ECJ has a key role to play in ensuring the legal provisions of the Treaty of Rome (and subsequent amending treaties) are upheld by the member state governments, the supranational institutions, and by organizations and individuals.

4. Access to the ECJ for private individuals as well as member states and the supranational institutions makes it distinctive from other international governance models. Contrast it with the WTO, where only states can make a complaint to the Dispute Settlement Body. If these legal principles of direct effect and supremacy were to be fully incorporated into other international agreements, and particularly in systems of global governance, there would be a radical change in the effectiveness, the capacity and the fairness of international and global governance.

5. The EU, for all its shortcomings has managed to instil a spirit of cooperation amongst a diverse group of member states, succeeded in proving that cooperation need not be zero-sum and can be learned. In essence, cooperation within the context of an international governance system produces results where the participants can perceive cooperative action as a public good. This is not to suggest, of course, that cooperation among sovereign states or between states and non-state actors is either automatic or easy. Successful cooperation to date has depended on a public-sector push and an emerging supranational structure.

6. The EU has evolved towards a model of governance with a degree of democratic legitimacy. Despite real criticisms and a literature on the democratic deficit (for a discussion see Bellamy, 2005 and Moravcsik, 2004) the EU strives to address the imbalance between the supranational and the national democratic structures.

7. Europe exhibits some common and distinctive features in its national social models. Its models of the welfare state face common internal and external challenges arising from globalization. Within the academic and the policy communities, the debate about European socio-economic convergence versus national diversities has aspired to building a competitive 'European knowledge society' consistent with social cohesion. Such a modernization process does impact (if only in a limited way) on the co-ordination of national social, economic, employment, research, technology, public health and enterprise policies.

8. While the European Union has emerged as a major actor in the world economy, with a reasonably developed and coherent set of trade policies, it is not as successful as a global political actor. For the EU to be taken seriously in the

international arena, and to exert influence in the international institutions that currently form the global governance system, it needs a regional political identity as an effective and legitimate actor able to represent the interests of all member states. But finding legitimacy among its citizens and in public discourse within the EU on the one hand, and among the actors and institutions of global governance on the other has proved difficult and events can and do derail these processes (see Reuber and Wolkersdorf, 2002).

9. The European Union has built a dense web of cooperative relations with countries and regions in other parts of the world. These form a set of bilateral and multilateral relations linked to trade, aid, investment and other forms of development cooperation. Determined by historical, political and geographical factors, these links demonstrate distinctive priorities, value systems and normative considerations in the negotiation processes and decision making frameworks, all of which shape the European approach to reform of the global governance system. Inter-regional cooperation has increased in both the scope and density of the agreements. Although often misunderstood, the Asia-Europe (ASEM) process, EU-Mexico, EU-Mercosur, and the Cotonou Agreements constitute examples of the increased aspirations of a regional group to build a density of relations and foster trust and understanding fundamental to a global governance framework.

These developments, and the networking and bargaining surrounding them, provide many lessons for regional and global governance in general and for the prospects of institutionalization at the regional level in particular. European experience (and European scholarship, see Higgott, 2005b) can make a serious theoretical and practical contribution to our changing theoretical understanding of sovereignty. European approaches to governance have developed flexible and multidimensional concepts of sovereignty in the international system which contrast with the often bounded, state-based/intergovernmental characterizations of sovereignty and international relations as understood by most US practice and scholarship and reflected in many other parts of the world where state consolidation rather than sovereignty pooling remains a principle pre-occupation of a governing regime. Institutions, especially regional ones, are the essential conduits between the state and the global economic and political orders. Enhanced global economic integration requires innovation in thinking about governance at the regional as well as the global level.

It remains important to make an intellectual leap to overcome these more bounded notions of sovereignty that beset decision makers in all East Asian states. The repressive potential of the state remains considerable, especially given the changing dynamics of international security in the post 9/11 era. We need to escape from a bounded notion of sovereignty and narrow definitions of security and state-interest if the global and regional integration process is to deliver better governance at both regional and global levels. Central to overcoming these limitations must be the recognition that sovereignty can be disaggregated and redistributed across institutional levels from the local to the global with the regional level, if the EU experience is anything to go by, capable of playing an important intermediary role. Thus the importance of institutionalism is no mere theoretical indulgence. How seriously we take it, and in what domains, will determine the nature of regional cooperation in the early years of the twenty-first century. Institutions will be important interlocutors in the relationship between globalization and regionalization, especially as the recourse to regionalism becomes an increasingly common response to globalization.

Some early depictions of globalization missed the complex interplay in the relationship between the 'global' and the 'regional' in the foreign economic policies of states. These analyses made judgements on technical and economic change and then extrapolated from them into the socio-political sphere in a manner for which the evidence was, at best, flimsy. Nowhere was this better illustrated than in what is often called the 'hyperglobalist' literature (pace Oman 1999) which saw the declining salience of state actors and state borders in the rise of what Kenichi Ohmae (1995), with a breathless McKinseysque cartography, labelled 'region states'. In so doing he prematurely reduced the state to the role of a passive actor in cross-border processes. The 'hyperglobalization' thesis misconstrued how economic space is politically and socially (re)constructed over time. At the very least, economic regionalization requires governments to sanction the relaxation of barriers to trade and investment, or, more proactively, to facilitate the provision of incentives to investment and trade sponsorship.

States are reasserting themselves, but not in the same way in all parts of the world (Weiss, 2001). In some parts of the world regionalization, seen here as a meso-level process of state-led governance and regulation, continues to grow in influence in the early stages of the twenty-first century. But this regionalism will not necessarily follow the European model leading to some 'sovereignty pooling'. Europe's regional present is not Asia's regional future. Rather, we are seeing the rise of 'regulatory regionalism' (Jayasuriya, 2004) as state actors develop selective, issue-specific, strategies to manage regional stability and enhance regional competitiveness in the face of recognized limitations in the institutional structures of global economic and political management of the second half of the twentieth century.

5 The new regionalism: Some important lessons from and for East Asia[6]

It may help if we embed our discussion in the wider context of what has come to be known as the 'new regionalism' that, as Breslin (2005: 6) rightly notes, is 'a framework, not a theory'.[7] At its core, new regionalism is a response to globalization and especially a recognition of the inseparability of what Wallace (1990) called 'informal' and 'formal' integration and Higgott (1997) identified as *de facto* and *de jure* integration. The former refers to integration via the emergence of transnational space among private market actors. The latter sees integration led by the authority of governmental actors through agreement or treaty. New regionalism captures the importance of the ideology of regionalism; that is region building as a political project rather than one driven simply by gravity models of economic integration. The new regionalism also has structural consequences beyond the region in which it has taken place; witness the growth of institutions and organizations, or at least discourses, attempting to mediate between regions (such as the ASEM process). If this occurs in a formalized way we speak of inter-regionalism.

It is increasingly accepted that *regionalization* refers to those processes of integration that arise from markets, private trade and investment flows, and from the policies and decisions of companies rather the predetermined plans of national or local governments. *Regionalism* refers to those state-led projects of cooperation that emerge as a result of intergovernmental dialogues and treaties. But, as in the relationship between regionalization and globalization, these are not mutually exclusive processes. Failure to recognize the dialectic between globalization and regionalization can mean that we impose a regional level of analysis on something that is actually global or vice versa. We must also consider the salience of extra-regional relations when considering regionalization.

The growth in intra-regional trade in East Asia is the consequence of the fragmentation of production across national boundaries. With components produced across a region, the traded component in the production of a commodity increases dramatically. But the final goods produced as a result of intra-regional trade still have to be sold somewhere, be it inside or outside the region. Is this regionalization or globalization? The dichotomy does not help. The answer is both: the processes of developing regional production networks are themselves driven by global processes and are contingent on global markets.

How we map economic and political space is also a concern. Strict national or sovereign parameters should be avoided when identifying regionalization. In addition to looking for a correlation between the national state and regional membership, we should also examine the wider groups and classes of actors that are involved in processes of integration. The growth of trans-national networks and alliances that integrate elites, but not usually the wider populations, of a given country is the key here. Nowhere is this better illustrated than in the context of the development of APEC, where throughout the 1990s and early twenty-first century there has been a clear disjuncture between the enthusiasm for the process amongst intellectual, corporate and bureaucratic elites (if not all political ones) and the lack of knowledge and disinterest, if not hostility, towards the project in the wider communities of the member states.

New regionalisms are invariably defined by the rejection of the old, 'old' in terms of both theory and practice. At the level of practice, the first key feature of the 'new' is the sheer number of formal regional arrangements. There are few countries that are not members of at least one regional organization and most are members of more than one. This upsurge in regional activity can be explained in several ways:

- The promotion of export growth strategies has advanced the reality of increased economic regionalization. In this regard, the increased adoption of varieties of domestic neo-liberal policies is an explanatory variable for regional initiatives.
- An understanding that state actors are but one set of agents among many is at the heart of newer approaches. Moving away from this old 'statist' approach is a defining characteristic of 'new regionalisms'. Newer

perspectives recognize the complex cocktail of state actors, interstate and global institutions and non-state actors (especially multinational corporations, emerging civil society organizations and NGOs) that all have an effect upon regional outcomes.
* The need to respond to globalization or *participate* in the global economy is a driving factor for governments, both weak and strong.

Hence it is the meso level, between globalization and the nation state, especially in a European context, that most effort has been applied to the management of trans-territorial, or multi-territorial collective action problem solving. While moves toward regionally integrated problem solving have been more active in Europe than in other parts of the world, this is not only a European phenomenon. Elsewhere, the growing linkages between different regional integration schemes, such as the FTA between the EU and Mercosur, or the development of the ASEAN Free Trade Area, for example, are evident (Sampson and Woolcock, 2003.)

There is also a growing tendency to devolve competencies from state level to local levels in countries participating in integration processes. As a result, political authority becomes increasingly dispersed while economic activities become more globalized. In addition, non-state actors become increasingly involved in governance. This is not simply an academic observation. It is also replete with policy implications. We should stop thinking in terms of hierarchical layers of competence separated by the subsidiarity principle. We cannot ignore the strong tendency towards networking arrangements at all levels of governance shaping, proposing, implementing and monitoring policy together. In this context, we can identify at least four different ways of trying to explain contemporary regionalism:

Four contrasting approaches to regionalism

1. De facto Regionalism: Informal, market-led and leading to enhanced economic integration. This is principally *rationalist-economic* in analytical orientation.

2. De Jure Regionalism: Formal, rule-governed, state-led enhanced institutionalized cooperation. This approach is principally *legal-political* in analytical orientation.

3. Instrumental Regionalism: Initially informal and interest-led. Built on the identification of the interest to be gained by the development of a common policy towards third parties in a given issue area. This is principally a power politics *realist* analytical orientation.

4. Cognitive Regionalism: Initially informal. Built on shared cultural, historical and emotional affiliations which distinguish 'insiders' from 'outsiders'. This is principally *socio-cultural* in analytical orientation.

The salience of these approaches varies over time. Trying to find a 'one size fits all' explanation is pointless and rather than building (or joining) regional arrangements to enhance independence from the global economy (as they once did), many developing states now see regionalism as a measure to ensure continued participation in the global economy. Thus, and by extension, the distinction between *de facto* and *de jure* regional activity becomes less salient in the contemporary era. While markets remain the key drivers of economic *regionalization*, state-led initiatives to enhance integration into the global economy lead to the pursuit of more strongly politico-strategic regional policies (*regionalism*).

But, for a range of reasons that we are only just coming to understand, East Asia, notwithstanding a growing keenness for enhanced regional cooperation, is unlikely to repeat the four-stage sequential process of integration outlined by Balassa in a European context. Globalization has had the effect of enhancing trans-border activities and inter-state exchange. Moreover, the security driven disciplines of the Cold War era that ensured tight bi-polarity have disappeared and the growth of a neo-liberal ideology (and practice) of freer trade and financial deregulation amongst global economic actors have combined to challenge traditional economic relations once founded on the premises of 'national economies'. In their place we had a growing recognition in the last quarter of the twentieth century of regional projects as a response (both defensive and offensive) to the power of global markets and the need to ensure the flow of FDI into a region in the search for competitiveness.

The difference of the Asian regional experiment in the twenty-first century is that it is less trade-led than the European project of the twentieth century. Of course, *de facto* market led integration is strong. Intra regional trade at 26.5 per cent of regional GDP in 2002 is larger than that for any developing region (Evian, 2005: 5). But such has been the success in liberalizing trade in goods under the GATT that the need to free up trade in goods on a regional basis has become less pressing. This is not to suggest that trade is not the motor of growth in East Asia. It remains so. Rather, it is to suggest that it is not the only motor of the regional economic discourse.

Much of the hyperbole surrounding the evolution of APEC in the first half of the 1990s saw only the benefits of free trade. But the export-oriented countries of East Asia needed little convincing of these benefits and discussions in APEC in the first half of the 1990s missed the major changes taking place in the global economy and the potentially adverse effects they could have. What was not understood until the financial crises of 1997–98 was the manner in which dramatic increases in deregulated, unrestricted capital mobility could lead to the kind of catastrophic volatility seen in these crises. Since that time we have seen two seemingly opposing, but nevertheless compatible, trends. These trends are the gradual movement towards enhanced monetary cooperation in East Asia on the one hand, and the growing interest in bilateral trading arrangements on the other. What makes them compatible is that both are wrapped up in the wider recognition of the importance of 'East Asia', as opposed to the 'Asia Pacific', as the 'voice' of region.

Of course, the US remains the dominant presence in the region, defined as the Asia Pacific (in both economic and military terms), but it is also an unwitting exogenous catalyst in the 'East Asianization' of the Western Pacific seaboard. APEC, rather than being a potential instrument for trade liberalization at the Asia Pacific level, has come to be seen in large sectors of the policy communities of East Asia as but an additional site at which the US might advance its own agendas, such as for further capital market liberalization and, since 9/11 as a vehicle for advancing the US security agenda (see Higgott, 2004). The US suggestion for an Asia Pacific Free Trade area was resisted by East Asian leaders at the November 2006 APEC Summit in Vietnam.

As is well known, since the late 1990s, regular ASEAN summits have been expanded by the participation of Japan, China and South Korea in ASEAN Plus Three (or APT) meetings. The first East Asian summit took place in Kuala Lumpur in December 2005. Asian policy elites appear no longer to want their policies controlled from Washington when economic crises occur; hence the search for 'purpose-designed', East Asian responses to economic policy uncertainty. In this regards, 'instrumentalism regionalism' is driving the growing regional interest in monetary cooperation. There is recognition of the need to cooperate in the face of the shared common problem of financial volatility. This is a stronger urge than a desire to liberalize trade on a regional level. Initiatives emanating from this mode of thinking, especially those in the monetary domain discussed in include not only the 2001 Chiang Mai Initiative to create a regional liquidity (swap) fund but also the Asian Bond Fund Initiative (ABF), proposed in June 2003, and the suggestion of a regional stock exchange, both of which have the aim of reducing the distances between the individual national markets and exchanges. One clear benefit of this process is the raising of standards and regulatory norms and practices in the region. The CMI and the ABF collectively enhance, although they do not guarantee, the regional capability of resisting financial volatility.

In terms of 'cognitive' influences in East Asia, the changing leadership role of the United States is important. It represents a growing 'other' in the Asian regional foreign policy context as regional players move to secure greater autonomy *vis-à-vis* the erstwhile regional hegemon. The nascent nature of regional cooperation, when accompanied by the fear of being on the receiving end of asymmetrical agreements in times of low trust in the multilateral trading system, has also seen governments in Asia developing bilateral strategies. This can be seen in the proliferation of preferential trading agreements in the region (see Dent, 2006).

What the Asian crisis told us was that there was no consensus on how to manage the international economic order in the closing stages the twentieth and the early stages of the twenty-first centuries. The major financial institutions were caught between competing nationalist and liberal views of how the world should work. The international financial institutions (IFIs) were found wanting in both theory and practice by the events in East Asia and the crisis provided a learning experience at the multilateral level – globalization requires institutional capability for prudential regulation and it does so at a range of different levels. While most regional analysts recognize that regulation is best pursued at the global level, regional level initiatives of the type outlined in the Manila framework and discussion of an Asian Monetary Fund will continue to evolve.

Where early regionalism might have been identified as a defensive mechanism to reduce dependence on the international economy, the 'new regionalism' sees it as more pro-active. It is a means of greater access to global markets, not securing regional autarchy. Regionalism is also now more multifaceted and multidimensional than in the past. States engage in any number of overlapping endeavours without sensing contradictions in such a process. Where the defensive legacies of the earlier phase remain – among political elites sceptical of the unregulated nature of contemporary global capitalism – this does not imply a regional resistance to all elements of the globalization process. Indeed, the extent to which regional organizations act as a spur to global economic liberalization is an important question. APEC was designed to facilitate wider global processes and could be read as a (seemingly failing) attempt on the part of its Caucasian members to prevent the emergence of a specific 'East Asian' regionalism.

We should also consider the impact of joining (or forming) regional organizations for many developing states. On one level, the formal criteria established for membership by organizations – *pace* EU requirements in 2004 – force policy change on aspirant members. In the process of liberalizing to meet EU standards, these economies have become more open to the global economy. Thus regionalism can be seen as a pathway to globalization. This is a key distinction between current and old explanations for regional projects. Rather than building (or joining) regional arrangements to enhance independence from the global economy, many developing states now see regionalism as a measure to ensure continued participation in it but with emerging regionalism as a meso-level comfort zone.

Thus regionalism can be simultaneously a response to, and a dynamic behind, globalization. We are dealing, in short with mutually reinforcing and co-constitutive rather than contending processes. Regional regimes are not barriers to globalization. Rather, the regional project is both part of and a facilitator of globalization and a regional counter-governance layer in the world political economy. This relationship between regions and neo-liberal paradigms and economic policies stands at the heart of the new assessments of regionalism and regionalization at the beginning of the twenty-first century.

Trends in East Asian regionalism

Since the turn of the century several broad trends have emerged:

- The growing malaise of APEC, notwithstanding the trappings of multilateral diplomacy, as the foremost regional construct has continued.
- The growth of bilateral Free Trade or Preferential Trade Areas (PTA or FTA) in the region continues to strengthen.
- The development of an East Asian understanding of regionalism (embodied in the development of the ASEAN + 3) and the first East Asian Summit
- Closely linked to the above point, the development of an East Asian interest in mitigating the prospects of further financial volatility at a regional level via the gradual development of policies promoting monetary regionalism.

The defining issue in the development of these regional trends is not 9/11. Rather, it is the Asian financial crises of 1997/8. For most Asian states these crises, their aftermath, and Asian responses to US policy in the period since then provide the most salient component of an explanation of current trends and policies.

Bilateral trade policy and regional theory

While the rhetorical support for markets remains strong, the impact of politics on markets is never far away. And the growing interest in bilateral trade arrangements is determined by a number of factors. In the economic domain, the WTO had not fared well since its inception and the unbalanced diet that is the Doha MTN Round has proved particularly indigestible in many parts of the world giving rise to the growth of interest in bilateral preferential trading relationships (PTAs). This interest was (is) not simply a US phenomenon. But, if the Europeans started it, and other, smaller and weaker states also began to explore it, it has been the role of the US, as the strongest partner in any bilateral relationship, which has been disproportionately influential. In the politico-security domain, the offer of preferential bilateral trading relationships in return for support in Iraq in particular and the war on terror in general has been a major instrument of US foreign policy.

The Asian interest in bilateral agreements reflects a general appreciation of the success of GATT in reducing tariffs and, albeit to a lesser extent, non-tariff barriers in the second half of the twentieth century on the one hand, but a concern about the direction of the WTO in the twenty-first century on the other. But the benefits of regional-multilateral free trade agreements are much less significant in economic terms than they were thought to be. Industry leaders in the region (*de facto* agents of market-led economic integration) are acutely aware of the degree to which manufacturing is now more global than regional. Building large, multi-member, regional trade blocs in an era of globalization is deemed less relevant. Rather bilateral trade arrangement – in many ways a defining feature of the regional political economy in the early twenty-first century – are felt to give regional policy elites greater control over national trade policies. This reflects Asian fears that their influence over deliberations at the WTO is not always as great as they would wish. As such, bilateral free trade agreements are statements of sovereignty. East Asian leaders also see them as a useful policy tool with both extra-regional and inter-regional payoffs for the states concerned. The effects of this trend can be, at one and the same time, to enhance regional convergence in one area of activity yet exacerbate regional divergence in another.

If bilateral economic cooperation in the trade domain is a fact of life in East Asia in the early years of the twenty-first century, the key issue for this chapter is the degree to which it might enhance the regional project overall or detract from greater regional economic policy coordination and integration.. This is clearly not an either/or situation. Elements of both enhanced cooperation and increased competition are present in the contemporary regional policy process. In a 'structural argument', bilateralism can bolster the economic foundations of the region with the prospect of enhanced cooperation at the regional level. It can provide a regional 'lattice' of technical and institutional arrangements to reinforce the regional project (Dent, 2004).

By contrast, a 'process-led argument' in favour of bilateralism suggests that it has the effect of enhancing the broader discourse on regional economic cooperation and integration. No state, it is argued, pursues just a bilateral or multilateral trade policy. Bilateral activity should be seen as a compliment to other initiatives such as the development of an ASEAN Economic Community and the APT, both of which have different, but complementary agendas and functions. This is a position advanced by Singapore and Thailand as part of their trade strategies (see Desker, 2004).

In sum, support for enhanced economic cooperation and integration at the regional level is a possible outcome of the trend towards bilateralism in East Asia, but it is not inevitable and strong counter-veiling tendencies and outcomes are equally possible. We have little or nothing in the historical or scholarly armoury to make a strong prediction one way or the other at this stage. The risks may outweigh the opportunities. The degree to which the positive outcome might prevail will in part be determined by the success or failure of activities in other areas of the policy domain and with other putative economic initiatives, such as monetary cooperation, where the collective regional urge in East Asia in the early twenty-first century is stronger. But the jury is out on the strength of these arguments for the foreseeable future.

Opponents argue that the increasing recourse to bilateral initiatives has the effect of undermining the wider regional project in East Asia.. Intellectual and technical capability and political will (key components of institution building) are finite resources that cannot be indefinitely sub-divided without diminishing their utility and effectiveness.. At the ASEAN level, bilateral activities must inevitably be in competition for attention with attempts to upgrade the ASEAN (AFTA) to the ASEAN Economic Community (AEC) by 2020 (Hew and Soesastro, 2003). A longer-term outcome of this competition in the trade domain could be the consolidation of existing asymmetries, enhanced inter-state rivalry amongst regional neighbours and a diminution of the region's ability to present a united front to other global actors in other policy domains.

Monetary regionalism and cooperation

Narratives of the development of cooperation in this area abound (Deiter and Higgott, 2003; Hamilton-Hart, 2005; Pempel, 2005a) but several points about regional monetary policy as an example of cooperation can be drawn out. Nascent regional cooperation, when accompanied by the fear of asymmetrical agreements in times of low trust in the multilateral trading system, has seen governments developing bilateral strategies. But the search for a new voice of Asian regionalism, remains problematic. Dialogue at the Asia Pacific level has faltered. APEC's identity crisis persists.. However, the regional dialogue has moved on dramatically since the time of the financial crises of 1997/8. It is the crises of late 1990s that have contributed to the evolution of a new type of regionalism in Asia. Before the crises trade-led regionalism in the Asia-Pacific had been driven by the Caucasian members of APEC. But even prior to 9/11, Asian observers had increasingly evaluated APEC as a tool of American foreign policy. The resistance of Asian policy makers to a strengthened APEC was caused by their fear of American dominance (Kahler, 2000: 568). They became increasingly critical of the lack of tangible benefits that

APEC provided (Ravenhill, 2001). The manner in which the US has treated APEC in the wake of 9/11 has confirmed these initial Asian perceptions.

The debate about cooperation at the level of East Asia, writ small to mean ASEAN, continues with discussions about the creation of an AEC to integrate the activities of AFTA, the ASEAN Framework Agreement on Services, and the ASEAN Investment Agreement. But it is at the level of East Asia – writ large to include ASEAN, China, Japan and South Korea – that a dialogue on how best to mitigate the kind of volatility experienced during the financial crises of 1997/8 has developed most rapidly. Notwithstanding the failed attempt to establish an AMF in 1998, the principle behind the proposal did not die. By the end of 1999, the worst of the Asian crisis was over and East Asian policy circles once again addressed the topic of regional cooperation. The regular ASEAN summits were expanded by the participation of Japan, China and South Korea, the new body being called ASEAN+3 (or APT) with the first East Asian Summit taking place in Kuala Lumpur in December 2005. Since then, steps in the search for a new monetary regionalism have been frequent and numerous. They represent a contribution to a regional institutional economic architecture that departs from previous cooperation models in Asia.

Efforts to secure monetary cooperation are very much part of the wider exercise of soul searching that has been taking place both within ASEAN, and between ASEAN and its other East Asian partners, since the turn of the century. The crucial point of these exploratory exercises is not their immediate significance. Nor is the point to underestimate the difficulties of such policy coordination in the region. Rather I suggest we would be naive to think that Asians will not continue to develop greater regional institutional mechanisms for the common management of financial questions. To see ASEAN + 3 as but an exercise in extended conference diplomacy, reflecting weakness rather than strength, would be misleading. True, in the opening years of the twenty-first century, it is too early to see what kinds of institutional structures will eventually be embedded in the region, but the range of interactions developing is unprecedented. ASEAN + 3 have moved on from initial leadership meetings. Considerable deepening has taken place with regular ministerial meetings across most policy domains (economics and finance, agriculture, forestry, tourism and so on) (see Stubbs, 2002; Suzuki, 2004 and Thomas, 2004).   In T. J. Pempel's perceptive view,

> ... a strikingly contradictory view of the East Asian region emerges. ... [D]espite the overwhelming structural impediments to integration, East Asia has in recent years become considerably more interdependent, connected and cohesive. [It is] ... a region that has developed an increasingly dense network of cross border cooperation, collaboration, interdependence and even formalized institutional integration (Pempel, 2005: 2).

In keeping with earlier analysis of the importance of a concept of 'East Asia' (Higgott and Stubbs, 1995) what we are seeing is a trend later picked up by others (Bergsten, 2000; Webber, 2001; Rapkin, 2001); namely, the emergence of a voice of region beyond that of the sub-regions – Southeast and Northeast Asia – but more restricted than that of the Pacific as a mega region. The voice of region that is emerging in the global political economy is an 'East Asian' one. When looked at collectively, the processes in train represent a more systematic package of activities than would at first sight appear to be the case. The whole will be greater than the sum of its parts if momentum is maintained. The degree to which this is likely to be the case will be conditioned by the structures of regional leadership that emerge in the early twenty-first century.

5 Institutionalizing East Asia: The leadership issue

Leadership is one of the most difficult analytical concepts in the lexicon of the modern day policy sciences. It is a little understood popular and populist concepts. The key distinction drawn in this section is between what we might call structural/ institutional leadership and agency oriented/political leadership. The two are of course not distinct but do provide a useful way of identifying the problems and prospects for leadership in the enhancement of Asian regional cooperation over the short to medium term. Specifically, a twofold classification allows us to distinguish between leadership and hegemony.

Leadership is not the same as economic and military preponderance. Leadership can be intellectual and inspirational as well. If we look at the development of the EU, for example, then we can see both kinds of leadership over the life of the organization, pace the intellectual leadership of figures such as Schuman and Monnet in the crucial agenda setting period of the 1950s and a quasi cooperative hegemony of France and Germany as the economic core of Europe in the following era. From such a judgement it is easy to suggest that part of the problem that Europe faces at the moment is the absence of either kind of leadership. From this position we can also ask a series of similar questions about leadership in Asia in the early twenty-first century. Several specific questions come to the fore in this context:

- From where will the leadership come to take the cooperative dialogue in East Asia forward at this time? Where are the necessary actors to be found? Where are the Schumans and Monnets?
- What are the structural constraints on actor based leadership emerging and can they be overcome? To-date, the leadership and political resolve required to advance regional institutional cooperation, of the kind seen in Europe in the second half of the twentieth century has yet to emerge in East Asia.
- What are the roles for the principal actors in the region over the short (five years) to medium (twenty years) period? Will the USA play a supportive role in building East Asian cooperation in the twenty-first century as it did in the building of the European Union in the second half of the twentieth century? Can China and/or Japan play the kind of role that Germany and France played in the EU?

The USA and the question of hegemony

To talk of regionalism in East Asia without addressing the specific question of the role of the USA is not possible. To do so is to miss the context of the US in East

Asia since the Second World War, especially when compared with its role in the reconstruction of western Europe. This is especially, but not solely, the case since the advent of the Bush administration and the policy changes emanating from the events 9/11. US policy towards the region is shaped by its own agenda which, since 9/11 has, become increasingly a security driven agenda at the expense of what we might call the neo-liberal economic agenda that underwrote its policies towards the region prior to then.

In historical terms the US role, as an exogenous actor, in the development of a European community was pivotal (see Latham, 1997). Within a Cold War context US foreign policy pro-actively supported the European project. Regional cooperation in Europe may have taken place without US support in any circumstances, but we will now never know what form it would have taken. But we do know that the US, via a range of initiatives, gave considerable impetus and assistance to the early collaborative efforts of the European project. This is not the contemporary case in East Asia. Indeed, Mark Beeson (2005: 978–81) would argue that one of the key reasons for the slowness of enhanced economic cooperation in East Asia has been precisely because of the constraining role played by the USA in the Cold War context. Moreover, American hegemony and the geo-political setting in the contemporary era remain, as Beeson notes:

> ... still crucial influences on regional processes, they are having an inadvertent rather than intentional impact. Whereas the EU sprang from a highly successful attempt to reconstruct Western Europe on a new integrated basis, in East Asia American foreign policy is having a more ambivalent impact on the region that is gradually moving to assume greater autonomy despite, rather than because of, American policy.' (See Beeson, 2005: 970. But see also Beeson and Higgott, 2005).

If the Cold War in Europe was centripetal, in East Asia it was centrifugal. For fifty years, US policy split the region along ideological lines and built a structure of bilateral 'hub and spoke' relationships between it and its major East Asian partners on the one hand and propagated Cold War divisions on the other that rendered impossible any leadership pretensions of the regions two major powers. Japan for the second half of the twentieth century subordinated any leadership ambitions to its asymmetrical bilateral relationship with the USA. Indeed, Japan's rise to become the world's second largest economic power in the 1980s and 1990s was achieved at the expense of its own regional leadership ambitions. Similarly, the absence of China (for Cold War reasons) was not in a position to contribute to East Asian wide regional cooperation. For most of the second half of the twentieth century, both states, China for ideological reasons, Japan for its own particular debilitating historical reasons, were effectively denied regional leadership ambitions.

The historical balance sheet on US economic leadership in the post-Second World War era is mixed, or perhaps more precisely divided into two eras. In the first era it provided massive reconstruction funding, especially for Korea and Taiwan (see Stubbs, 2005). It also provided relatively open market access for the rapidly growing Japanese economy and other NICS in the first three decades after the Second World War without receiving a reciprocal openness from these trading partners. This is traditionally explained as part of a wider grand strategy in the

Cold War context. From the early 1970s, however, this benign (Kindleberger-esque) reading of US hegemony needs to be revised. From that time have seen a well documented recourse to an increasingly aggressive US economic policy aimed to manage access to the US economy for East Asian exports and open East Asian markets to US exporters. This has taken place through a range of strategies variously described as 'aggressive unilateralism' (Bhagwati and Patrick, 1990), strategic trade policy (Krugman, 1986) and the recourse to sectoral protectionist activities with euphemistic names such as Voluntary Export Restraints, Orderly Marketing Arrangements, Structural Impediments Initiatives and the like and, since the 1980s a more or less permanent pressure on the major countries of the region to progressively de-regulate their financial markets.

In contemporary terms, it is perhaps inevitable in the wake of 9/11 that we should see the robust reassertion by the US of the geo-security agenda over the geo-economic agenda that prevailed in the 1990s. US attitudes towards regional projects are now, ambiguous, to say the least. This is not only the case with regards to Europe in the wake of the war in Iraq but also in its attitudes towards enhanced regional cooperation in an East Asian context. While keeping a sense of perspective, we should note that the principal contemporary trends are not substantially different to those that were developing prior to 9/11. The US, since the time of the Asian financial crises and the attempts to establish an AMF, has opposed (or at best feigned indifference to) regional initiatives that run counter to its perceived regional interests.

But economic relationship between the USA and East Asia are becoming less economically asymmetrical and, as a consequence, the ability of the US to set the regional agenda is becoming less convincing than at anytime in the last two decades. As such, the likelihood that it will actively support greater institutional cooperation in the region should not be taken for granted. Indeed, there are obvious signs of concern in the US foreign economic policy community that events in East Asia, especially closer regional economic cooperation, have the capacity to '… develop in a way that excludes the US' (Marcus Noland *The Financial Times*, 14 September, 2005: 6; but see also Munakata, 2003: 10).

Resulting from a secular trend over the last thirty years, US GDP is now only 80 per cent of that of East Asia. East Asia's share of total world trade is, at approximately 25 per cent almost double that of the US at 13 per cent. As of 2003, East Asian exports are double those of the US; inter-regional trade in East Asia is strengthening rapidly and the US share of East Asian export trade has declined to 25 per cent. Holdings of foreign currency reserves in East Asia are now more than 20 times those of the United States. US technological superiority notwithstanding, when judged by the increase in its share of patent registrations, East Asia is making some inroads into US preponderance (see Ravenhill, 2005: 12–13).

Of course, quantitative indicators alone are not definitive, especially when dealing with a concept as illusive as hegemony. East Asian aggregate performance does not axiomatically find its way into enhanced political leverage over the US given that the region does not formulate policy towards the US on the basis of an 'East Asian' interest or via regional institutional policy-making machinery capable of reflecting any such aggregate interest. Decision-making resides firmly at the level of the constituent states not at the level of the wider regional collective. In this context the agenda setting abilities of the US far outweigh those of any single East Asian state individually or, even given the probability of some enhanced cooperative decision making emerging in the region from a successful EAS, collectively for years to come. For East Asia to minimize the asymmetry in decision making with the USA to accompany the declining gap in material capability, it needs to enhance its _collective_ decision making capabilities. For this to occur, leadership endogenous to the region needs to strengthen. How this might be achieved is, of course, the single most important regional policy issue for the future.

Geo-politics, leadership and East Asian cooperation

East Asian responses to US economic policy are not insignificant. Major strides have been made by East Asian states in using existing institutional opportunities to defend sectoral interests, for example, via the WTO Dispute Settlement Mechanism (see Pekkanen, 2004) although the region remains basically under-represented in the Bretton Woods institutions that still reflect the configuration of global power at the end of the Second World War. However, Japanese and Chinese leadership aspirations continue to grow and the discursive practices of regionalization continue to evolve in a non-trivial manner. Whether the Asians will be successful or not in their endeavours, there can be little doubt that the continued exploration of cooperation as a way to combat vulnerability is an established item on the regional policy agenda in the early twenty-first century and it demonstrates a marked contrast with the late twentieth century. Take three examples.

Firstly, if we consider APEC as the dominant regional initiative of the closing decade of the last century, then during this period we saw the US strongly pro-active; Japan as a passive/reactive actor in the organization; and China giving its support to the EAEC initiative of the Malaysians rather than APEC. But the Asian financial crises exposed the limitations of the progressively excessive expectations that were heaped on APEC from the time of the first summit in 1993 until the crises of 1996–97. Secondly, the AMF initiative of the late 1990s, initiated by the Japanese met with resistance (albeit low key) from the Chinese and outright hostility from the USA.

From that time on, rose-tinted lenses and soft rhetoric have been replaced by harder realist lenses as APEC lost its appeal for Asian policy makers in particular. No significant economic initiatives have emerged from APEC since that time. Other factors diminished its attraction as an 'institution' for Asian leaders; especially the 'securitisation' of APEC following 9/11 (Higgott, 2004). APEC's potential to be anything more than a vehicle for general dialogue, notwithstanding detailed technical work in its sub-groups and committees by some of its members has always been over-hyped. East Asian regional support for APEC has always been constrained by national interest concerns that eschew any serious commitment to APEC's core analytical and policy concepts of 'open regionalism' and 'concerted unilateral liberalisation'.

Thirdly, and most significantly, in the early twenty-first century the major regional agenda item to date has been the attempt to develop enhanced monetary cooperation, especially since the Chiang Mai initiative, as the major exercise in regional cooperation in the twenty-first century. In this initiative we see, for the first time, a position where both the Japanese and the Chinese are strongly supportive of this regional project. While the USA is opposed, it is not minded to develop strong countermeasures. China and Japan are not, it should be stressed, engaged in a concerted coordination of their foreign policies. Rather, we have seen it is a coincidence where both powers recognize that the regional agenda for enhanced monetary policy coordination can be supported and advanced comfortable in the knowledge that it is a positive sum, not a zero sum, game. This cooperation reflects the primacy of *instrumental* regionalism. At the risk of labouring the point, in contexts where Japanese and Chinese instrumental interests cohere, this will be a powerful force for regional cooperation in East Asia. In contexts where they are at odds, it will be very counter-productive.

China and regional cooperation

How the relationship between China and the rest of the region plays out in the long run is the key to security, cooperation and institution building in East Asia in the twenty-first century. This issue is best approached by posing a question rather than offering unsustainable assertions regarding future behaviour. 'Does increased wealth and power lead to greater cooperation or greater competition?' This is the perennial question for international relations. It is central to the relationship between China and Japan. The evolution of their respective economies, over the last two decades at least, has been complementary, rather than competitive in terms of what they produce for the global market and what they take bilaterally from each other. China is Japan's second largest trade partner after the USA. Japan is both the largest trade partner and the largest source of ODA to China and, since 2001, Japanese FDI third only to that of Hong Kong and the USA (Taniguchi, 2003).

Longer term, however, it is likely that the relationship will become increasingly competitive as they compete (both bilaterally and with the USA) in their search for inputs into their respective economies – especially in their search for sources of energy and other resources. The year 2004 saw China overtake Japan as the world's second largest oil importer. It is also now, depending on statistical interpretation, the world's second largest economic power in PPP terms and the world's third largest trading power. It has also been argued that US policy fuels rather than cools the competition between the two Asian superpowers as it grapples to adjust to changes in the global power structure brought about by China's rising role (see Johnson, 2005.)

Of course there are also still strong, residual nationalistic antagonisms between the two countries that cannot be assigned to the historical past. Aaron Friedberg's (1993/4) suggestion that the region is 'ripe for rivalry' could be countered by T. J. Pempel's (2005) recent assertion that the region could just as easily be 'ripe for cooperation'. But how it turns out will depend on how the regional conversation is managed in the coming decades. In essence there are thus two scenarios for consideration.

In the worst case scenario, contemporary strains in the relationships between the regional great powers are seen as fundamentally irresolvable. There are several factors that we might anticipate in this scenario:

1. The unwillingness of Japanese policy makers to distance themselves and their country sufficiently from the atrocities of the Second World War continues, and remains unacceptable to the rest of the region. The historical roots are deep and continue to cast ominous policy shadows over its relationships with the key players in East Asia in a way that has long ceased to be the case in Germany's relationships with the rest of Europe for example.

2. Japan sides with US in attempting to block China's greater participation in the regional economic order and political orders and this is seen as a fundamental act of hostility by the Chinese government. Note here certain signalling activities by Japan such as its support for the US approach towards Taiwan and other factors such as Japan blocking Chinese participation in the Inter-American Development Bank.

3. A conflictual rather than peaceful outcome to the increasing contest for energy supplies amongst the US, China (and Japan) must remain a possibility if not necessarily a probability. Demand in both countries and the region in general (not to mention India) will grow rapidly. But, provided the increased pressure is 'lateral', and brings on gradual structural reform of the system rather than provokes direct confrontation between these rising great powers, then there is hope for a non-conflictual outcome.

The worse case scenario also assumes certain, resistant, courses of action by the USA towards greater regional economic cooperation in East Asia. In grand strategic terms, Asian economic cooperation is not nearly as useful to the USA in the twenty-first century as European integration was in the second half of the twentieth century. There is no longer any need to demonstrate the superiority of the market economy. The alternative has vanished. But successful economic integration in Asia today from China (more so than Japan notwithstanding parallels with the 1980s) is a challenge to US competitiveness (and for some analysts its security). Indeed, Asian regionalism is seen by much of the current US policy community as but a vehicle for China's ambitions. If Asia were to emancipate itself from American 'guidance', Washington's hold on the region would deteriorate sharply. Most importantly, US-China competition for scarce energy supplies could impact adversely on the US's wider geo-political objectives in say the Middle East or Latin America. As Shambaugh persuasively argues (2005:90–1) the Sino-US relationship, notwithstanding China's strengthening position in the region, does not have to be zero-sum. How the US takes it forward is yet to be determined, and the omens in the early twenty-first century have not been promising.

Thinking more positively, there is an alternative, more favourable scenario that can be developed around the rise of 'regulatory regionalism'; the key elements of which are enhanced regional economic dialogue and interaction both *amongst* the states of Northeast Asia (China, Japan and South Korea) and *between* these states and the states of Southeast Asia through the development of the ASEAN + Three process leading to an East Asian Community.

Regulatory regionalism

This is not the kind of regional cooperation that has its antecedents in a European intellectual context. Rather it links national and global understandings of regulation via the region as a 'meso' level. Effectively, regionalism is a transmission belt for global disciplines to the national level via the de-politicizing and softening process of the region in which regional policy coordination – evolving regional governance – becomes a link between the national and the global. It is emerging as a genuinely multi-level exercise. It reflects several trends where:

1. Regional policy coordination to mitigate risk is delegated to the state. It is sovereignty enhancing. Indeed, there is a strong relationship between state form, the global economic and political orders and the nature of regional governance emerging. This compromise is inevitable if the continuing tension between nationalism and regionalism in East Asia is not to jeopardize the cooperative endeavour. Again, it is instrumental regionalism.
2. The meshing of multilevel process of regulation reinforce the connections between the international institutions (especially the IMF and World Bank) and regional institutions such as the ADB and the emerging instruments of regulation developing in the context of monetary regionalism at the level of ASEAN + Three, such as the ASEAN regional surveillance process (ASP) and the regularized meetings of regional central bankers (EMEAP).
3. The transmission of internationally agreed codes, emanating from the perceived best practice of international institutions such as the IMF, help enforce market standards, and do so much more than sceptics concede (see Manupipatpong, 2002).

It is in the area of monetary regionalism, not regional trade liberalization, where cooperation is advancing most rapidly. It is not *de facto* trade led regionalism driving the agenda – this is taken care of now much more at the global multilateral and bilateral levels. The key to monetary regionalism is closer integration through the development of *common* national 'regulation' rather than regional institution building. Nor is it simply de jure state-led cooperation driving the agenda. The discourse of regulatory regionalism carries fewer negative connotations for sovereignty and regime autonomy than 'regional institution building'. Institution building throughout the pre-crisis days in East Asia carried with it the implications of sovereignty pooling of the European Cartesian legal formalist variety that alarmed Asian regional elites. Regulatory regionalism in the twenty-first century does not have the same echoes. It is instrumental regionalism built on trans-regional networks of regulators. While it reflects a different understanding of regionalism to that which prevails in Europe, it nevertheless demonstrates perhaps a greater interest in the development regional institutions and inter-regional relationships to enhance collective action problem solving under conditions of globalization than is to be found in contemporary US foreign economic policy as the brief comparison set out below suggests.

Americans and Europeans project sharp differences in their approaches towards world politics in general and global and regional institutional cooperation in particular. The US and the EU, for example, differ on questions of 'partnership', 'burden sharing', and 'exceptionalism' as approaches to global management. For the Bush Administration, what secures contemporary world order is 'primacy', '*Real-politik*' and freedom to manoeuvre. For Europeans it is 'globalization' and 'interdependence'. The EU disposition for multi-level-governance and 'sovereignty pooling' is incomprehensible to US policy makers. The '*acquis communautaire*' (the body of common standards and regulations that have developed over the life of the European project) notwithstanding perpetual complaints about excessive bureaucracy and the rejection of the constitution, are generally accepted in Europe. Europe, in theory if not always in practice, exhibits a stronger normative attitude towards multilateral governance structures and constitutional and regulatory frameworks that transcend the nation state.

Those states of greater Europe that are not members of the EU, for all its shortcomings, are still keen to join it. With the benefit of the longer term historical perspective, what looks like weakness through traditional state-centric, realist, power politics lenses actually looks like strength through the newer lenses of the increasingly diffused and networked nature of power in the contemporary global era (see Hall and Biersteker, 2002 and Slaughter, 2004).

Similar differences towards regionalism and multilateralism in East Asia may also be found with the US in the early twenty-first century. East Asia also places a greater stress on multilateral and regional cooperation than the US, although there may be a marked disconnection between theory and rhetoric on the one hand and application and practice on the other. But we live in an era of the 'new regionalism' in East Asia that has progressed apace since the financial crises of the latter part of the 1990s. The key elements of this new regionalism are enhanced regional economic dialogue and interaction both *amongst* the states of Northeast Asia (China, Japan and South Korea) and *between* these states and the states of Southeast Asia. This tendency is not, of course, unproblematic and the behaviour of China in East Asia over the medium to longer term is crucial. But the continual war of words between China and Japan over the past has not stopped China replacing the USA as Japan's major trading partner.

In this positive scenario, while the USA remains the dominant presence in the region, defined as the Asia Pacific (in both economic and military terms), it does so as a more passive actor, but also, ironically, as an exogenous catalyst in the 'East Asianization' of the Western Pacific. The USA becomes the 'other' enhancing the growth of a cognitive understanding of East Asian regionalism. Similarly, while the growth of bilateral initiatives may be sub-optimal in terms of pure economic theory, they should not cause alarm if they lead to competitive liberalization, domestic reform and enhanced regional knowledge and transparency. This is the positive gloss that might be put on what one scholar calls the 'Sino-Japanese FTA Race' (Munakata, 2003: 6)

When looked at collectively the processes in East Asia may actually represent a more systematic package of regional governance activities than would at first sight appear to be the case. The APT process is being institutionalized through the evolution of an over lapping multi-dimensional process of regional conference diplomacy strengthening, and indeed creating, links between the states of Northeast Asia and Southeast Asia (Suzuki, 2004). Whether Asians will be successful or not in their endeavours, there can be little doubt that the continued exploration of cooperation as a way to combat vulnerability is an established item on the regional policy agenda in the early twenty-first century, as even the normally sceptical *Economist* in a recent editorial was prepared to acknowledge (March 26–27, 2005).

Of course, the future of successful regional discourse seems dependent not only on Japanese economic reform, but also on a willingness of the PRC to continue its new found regional cooperative economic role that has developed since 1997 (see Shambaugh, 2005). If this continues in a positive way and trust can be built in the region between the major actors, then regionalism will grow as an important activity as a meso-level instrumental expression of the desire to optimize sovereign decision making by states confronting the rigours of global competition. If Japanese and Chinese *instrumental regional interests* can be privileged over *cognitive regional differences* this could be a powerful force for regional cooperation in East Asia. Without their input and indeed eventual leadership, ASEAN-driven attempts to secure East Asian regionalism will amount to little. The extent to which either player is committed remains problematic and for both, but especially Japan, it is in many ways a function of their relationship with the United States. Japan remains a reluctant regional institutionalist and the US does nothing to dissuade it from that position.

These alternative scenarios are not merely determined regionally. They need to be located in the overall discussion about globalization and regionalization in the early twenty-first century. There is a general principle that we can draw about power and regionalism from a comparative discussion of Europe and Asia. Again, it is better put as a question than offered as an assertion. 'Is it likely that we are entering an era where large sections of the global community look less to the major multilateral institutions – so much the playthings of the major powers – as vehicles for collective action problem solving and more towards the development of regional activities and communities?' If so, then the growing salience of the regional dialogue is a positive trend in international relations in general and in East Asia in particular.

Regionalism is an effort to transcend a uni-polar world in which the hegemonic power shows an increasing reluctance, in contrast to times past, to engage as an 'altruistic', as opposed to what Jagdish Bhagwati (2003) calls a 'selfish' hegemon. To this extent, although this is not the intended outcome, contemporary US foreign policy can act as a catalyst to regional consolidation in Asia. Growing discontent with US policy in, and towards, the East Asian region (especially since the Asian financial crises) has been a significant factor in the enhanced regional dialogue of the twenty-first century. Taken to extremes, it is not impossible to envisage a situation in which the world does become more multi-polar. Not necessarily multi-polar in the traditional realist sense of other regions combining to 'balance' against the US, but multi-polar in the sense that the US becomes less salient as an actor in the development and activities of other regions. That we even raise these questions is testament to the magnitude of change that has taken place in thinking about the strength of the glue holding contemporary global order together in the early twenty-first century.

The US having won the Cold War through a combination of hard power and soft power now seems to hope that raw material power will be sufficient to intimidate other great powers. This assumes that China, Japan (and East Asia) as well as Europe, Russia, India, Brazil and Latin America are not capable of developing policies and strategies to mitigate the influence of US economic and military power. US hegemony, or primacy in the military sphere, is not preventing the development of multi-polar initiatives in geo-political and economic domains, as the nature of regional institution building without US participation attests.

None of this should allow us to underestimate the continuing power and influence of the USA in the East Asia. A growing Asian rhetorical resistance to US policy in the region (agency driven sources of power and leadership) should not cause us to neglect the residual and continuingly strong structural influences from the US, what Nye (2002) would call 'soft power', especially strong support for the broad neo-liberal economic agenda. Moreover, for most states of the region, notwithstanding the increasing role of China, the US remains the major bilateral relationship; although not an easy one. The Bush administration has been the most self-regarding US administration any Asian post-colonial leaders have known.

Conclusion

Both the practice and theory of regionalism are undergoing a period of significant change. The key element is a shift from a Cold War to post-Cold War/globalization era. During the Cold War, regional theory was statist, European-influenced and stressed inter-governmental bargains. In the era of globalization it is more complex, multidimensional and, notwithstanding the increased salience of security issues post-9/11, still primarily economically focused. In the first era, the 'economic' and the 'political' were largely treated as separate issue areas for investigation and action. In the second era, politics and the economics are more clearly linked and the state is joined by a series of other significant, non-state actors in the practice of regionalism as the relationship between state authority and market power becomes fuzzier.

In addition, the early Balassian model, based on a reading of the evolution of the EU, no longer stands scrutiny in the context of globalization, where guarding against the volatility and erratic mobility of capital is in many ways now a factor of as great, if not greater, regional concern than guaranteeing the openness of the trade regime. Balassian style theory pays insufficient attention to the possibility of different routes to, or different agendas for, regional cooperation. It is also silent on the significance of socio-cultural factors – especially the role of identity in region building – to be relevant in an era of globalization. In this sense, the contemporary discussion in East Asia illustrates the differences between the two eras and two approaches to theorizing regional integration and offers us an alternative reading of regionalism in a wider global context.

East Asia is a region of economic experimentation. The glue of regionalism at the level of the Asia Pacific – embodied in APEC – has come unstuck since the time of the Asian financial crisis. Events post-9/11 have exacerbated this trend. Moreover, Asian policy communities have learned that globalization and regionalization are not mutually exclusive activities but rather exist in a dialectical relationship. Regionalism is not an alternative to globalization. Following this logic allows us to explain the emergence of a multiplicity of policy responses to recent economic issues in the Asia-Pacific. These responses reflect, in part at least, Asian resistance to western driven models. Specifically, the financial crises of the late 1990s forced regional scholars and policy makers alike to examine not only their national economic policies, but also their very understanding of regionalism.

The regionalism we see emerging in East Asia in the twenty-first century is not the kind of regional cooperation with a European intellectual pedigree. It is clearly unrealistic to imagine the development of institutions involving the transfer of elements of state sovereignty to regional institutions. Rather it is a 'regulatory regionalism' that links national and global understandings of regulation via the intermediary regional level. This regulatory urge is not simply restricted to trade. Indeed, it is in the area of monetary regionalism that it is advancing most rapidly. The key to monetary regionalism is closer integration through common national 'regulation' rather than regional institution building. In discursive terms, 'regional regulation' carries fewer negative connotations for sovereignty and regime autonomy than 'regional institution building'. Institution building throughout the pre-crisis days in East Asia carried with it the unwanted implication of European style 'sovereignty-pooling'.

In the absence of global structures of economic governance we must expect policy makers to explore more manageable alternatives. State-centric, power politics approaches to the management of the world order under conditions of globalization are becoming less salient. More diffuse networked understandings of power, with loosely institutionalized regulatory actions providing a *modus operandi* for cooperation are becoming increasingly attractive. The role of institutional capacity – especially institutions as transaction cost reducers and vehicles for the enhancement of norm compliance – cast increasingly long policy shadows over current regional activities in East Asia. It is here that the current discourse on regionalism (and multi-level governance for all its faults and all its detractors) offers the bones of an alternative model. The European experience, or that of the multilateral international organizations, is not simply an 'off the shelf' export model. Some key elements, especially those of a sovereignty pooling nature will be resisted. But other elements will be adjusted and/or localised in a specifically East Asian fashion. The degree to which East Asia can develop institutional capacity in the absence of some sovereignty pooling is the key research and policy question for the future. Meso-level, regulatory regionalism can enhance cooperation only so far. East Asia will not mirror what we understand by the term institutionalism in Europe in the second half of the twentieth century, but neither will it be trivial. For both the scholar and the practitioner of regionalism and institutionalism, these are indeed interesting times in East Asia.

Notes

1   See *inter alia*, Coleman and Underhill, 1998; Fawcett and Hurrell, 1995; Gamble and Payne, 1996; Grugel and Hout, 1998; Mansfield and Milner, 1997; Mattli, 1999.
2   For reviews of this literature see Beeson, 2005, Higgott, 1998a and 2005 and Acharya, 2005.
3   Katzenstein, *et al*, 1998; Simmons and Martin, 2002; Kratochwil and Mansfield, 2005; Higgott, 2006.
4   The literature on the state of the contemporary regional project in East Asia is large. For a flavour see Beeson, 2004 and 2006; Higgott, 2005; Pempel, 2005; Ravenhill, 2005; Stubbs, 2002; Knight, 2004.
5   See for discussions of institutions and institutional theory see Keohane, 1984, 1989, 2002, Simmons and Martin, 2002, Higgott, 2006.
6   There is a plethora of activity in East Asia in the current era. It is difficult to keep up with the panoply of bilateral initiatives to secure FTAs in the region. For reviews see Dent, 2004; Soesastro, 2005 and Defraigne *et al*, 2005.
7   A term first used, according to Breslin (2005) by Andrew Hurrell (1995). The growing body of litereature that we can gather under the rubric of the 'new regionalism cannot be reviewed here. But see *inter alia*, Gamble and Payne, 1996; Hettne *et al*, 1999, 2000 and 2001; Breslin *et al*, 2000; Soderbaum and Shaw, 2003 and Breslin, 2005.

Chapter 5

Interregionalism and World Order: The Diverging EU and US Models

Björn Hettne

The US and the EU are dominant actors in the international system. Hence the transatlantic alliance still to a large extent defines world order. However, their relation has been breaking up since the end of the Cold War and the two have even come to represent different world order models: unilateralism (now often called imperialism) and interregionalism (an emerging international phenomenon). There is actually a role for regionalism in both models, but of very different kinds: neo-Westphalian in the US case, post-Westphalian in the EU case. The US strategy emphasises bilateralism in regional contexts, creating weak regions held together mainly by trade relations, whereas the EU strategy, as it has been developing so far, encourages multidimensional intra-regional links as well as institutionalized inter-regional relations – interregionalism.

What is interregionalism? Interregionalism is a recent phenomenon in international relations. There is no consensus as far as definitions are concerned. Some use the concept broadly to describe the EU relations with other regions: group-to-group dialogue (Edwards and Regelsberg, 1990). More recently it is used as a systemic international phenomenon, namely linkages built among regions in general: the new interregionalism (Hänggi, 2006).

In the analysis of US-EU relations in different regional contexts and in order to clarify the contrast between the two approaches, I find it important to distinguish between interregionalism as a formalized relation between regional organizations, and relations among regions in a more general sense: transregionalism. The latter could include relations between all kinds of regional actors as well as a formal regional organization, on the one hand, and other diverse actors, state and non-state, on the other. A growing and increasingly dense global network of transregional and interregional links ultimately implies a regionalized world order, which can be termed regional multilateralism or, for short, multiregionalism.[1]

In this chapter a comparison is made between the EU and the US approaches to regionalism, defined as the ideology and project of building regions, and interregionalism, defined as a formal relationship between organised regions. With such a narrow definition of interregionalism only the EU has an authentic interregionalist policy, whereas the US at the most uses regionalism in its own national interest by getting access to or remaining in control of different regions or prevent other powers, like the EU, from gaining international influence. For the EU regionalism is a preferred form of political organization, for the US regionalism has simply an instrumental value. This difference is one important dimension of the emerging transatlantic rift, which could prevented by a less unilateral/bilateral approach on the part of the US, and by a more consistent and responsible attitude on the part of the EU. For the US this means less unilateralism in terms of decision making – and less bilateralism in terms of diplomatic relations. What the 'lame duck' period after the November 2006 election implies will be discussed later. The EU in contrast is committed to multilateralism in terms of decision making and plurilateralism/regionalism in terms of diplomatic relations: the group-to-group approach.[2]

The chapter is structured as follows. Firstly, the historical relationship between Europe and the US is briefly reviewed with the focus on more recent EU-US relations. These relations are sometimes referred to in regional terms as European – North American, but the actual counterpart to the EU is the US not North America (NAFTA). This is a significant fact which deserves to be carefully analysed. Secondly the qualitative difference between the two actors – a nation state with superpower status and a regional institutionalized polity – is analyzed in terms of actorship. The complex relationship between the two actors is explained by differences in actorship. In order for a region to be an actor, to achieve actorship, particular preconditions are needed. Thirdly the concept of world order is elaborated in some detail in order to analyze the principal differences between the two models: Pax Americana and Pax Europaea. Fourthly, the preferred world order model from the EU perspective is outlined, followed by, fifthly, the US preferences as far as global governance is concerned. Sixthly we look into the encounters between the policies and practices inherent in the two models as they take shape in different regional contexts. Finally, we conclude by some thoughts on the future world order.

1 The uncertain Atlantic Alliance

Where to start an account of European – US relations? Perhaps from the very start, since the relationship between Europe and America has gone through a number of fundamental transformations all of them having created an important legacy. The US was born in an anti colonial revolt against European imperialism, it grew economically by means of protectionism and industrial policy, it grew bigger as provider of goods during the European civil war, it established itself as a superpower in divided Europe, it became the champion of multilateralism and free trade after the war, and encouraged European integration as a geopolitical strategy against the rival superpower. In spite of so much shared history as well as shared enemies and threats, the differences in terms of values are substantial. The alliance has therefore always been 'uncertain' (Smith, 1984) but the current uncertainties are inherent in the new context created by the end of the Cold War. Between the US and Europe the close relationship, historically manifested in NATO has grown increasingly strenuous. Joint operations are difficult to agree on and when they are implemented they leave bitterness behind. NATO itself has therefore been marginalized, as shown in particular after 9/11, when the NATO declaration of support was completely disregarded by the US.

After the Cold War the relations thus became more complicated and tense as Europe in the form of the EU asserted itself as a world power. There was divergence and a conspicuous lack of interregionalism as here defined (Aggarwal and Fogarty, 2006). Attempts were nevertheless made to institutionalize relations. The rather symbolic Transatlantic Declaration (1990) was replaced by the New Transatlantic Agenda – TNA (1995) and later complemented by the Transatlantic Economic Partnership – TEP (1998).

The two powers meet in various regional arenas, but whereas the EU tries to form or consolidate regional groups, the US tries to break them up through bilateral agreements (Mexico, Chile, Paraguay), and the 'disaggregation policy' (dealing directly with the nation states) in Europe. This aspect of the decline of Atlanticism will be discussed in section 6.

Transatlantic links between Europe and North America include EU-US, EU-Mexico, and EU-Canada links which here are termed transregional (or hybrid interregionalism being between a regional organization and a state), whereas EU – MERCOSUR and EU - ASEAN relations exemplify authentic interregional relations.

In the EU – Canada relationship it is Canada rather than the EU that has tried to focus on the interregional possibilities (EU – NAFTA). The obvious reason is that Canada wants to reduce its dependence on the US. Apart from this there seems to be a stronger cultural affinity between Europe and Canada than between Europe and the US. The Framework Agreement of 1976 is the oldest formal relationship of the EU with any industrialized country. It is noteworthy that both parties in the 2004 (Ottawa) Partnership Agenda spell out their commitment to 'an effective multilateral system' and 'international rule of law'.

The EU 'global agreement' (1999) with Mexico was based on a wish from the EU to maintain a role in this large Latin American market and for Mexico (as for Canada) to reduce its extreme dependence on its Northern neighbour.

Does the EU–NAFTA relationship have any future? There are many problems among which are the extremely asymmetrical structure of NAFTA which places 'the fate of NAFTA essentially in the relationship between the US administration and the Congress' (Aggarwal and Fogarty, 2006). Aggarwal and Fogarty provides a detailed analysis in explaining why the EU has neglected this link by employing different theories: functionalism, interest group preferences (pluralism), great power politics (realism), and EU identity-building processes (constructivism). They find that no theory predicts a strong transatlantic interregionalism. There are thus reasons to believe that the Atlantic Alliance will fall apart, and that Nato will become marginalized (Hodge, 2005). It is remarkable that both the EU and NATO are building up rapid response forces (Economist, Nov 24, 2006:26). Thus both the EU and the US are distancing themselves from NATO. The Atlantic Alliance seems doomed. For reasons to be discussed further on this does not preclude bilateral cooperation in crisis situations where the interests of both are threatened and when they can agree upon the adequate response. The latter condition seems most problematic.

2 Regionalism and agency

When comparing the external actions of the EU and the US one problem to address is that while the US operates as a large nation state, the EU is a different kind of political animal: a regional institutionalized polity. The question is how such a polity can be an actor in world politics. Regions are not simply geographical or administrative objects, but should be conceived of as subjects in the making (or un-making); their internal cohesion as well as their boundaries are shifting, and so is their capacity as actors (actorhood). When different processes of regionalization in various fields of action and at various levels intensify and converge within the same geographical area, the cohesiveness and thereby the distinctiveness of the region in the making increases. This will make its presence felt in the outer world and it will also have an impact on this world. Thus agency in the context of regionalism (or regional actorship) can be understood as an outcome of regional cohesiveness/identity (regionness), presence and actorness (Bretherton and Vogler, 2006). Building on Bretherton and Vogler my analytical framework for the study of regional agency is built around what is seen as three interacting dimensions of actorhood: *regionness*, international *presence* and purposive *actorness*. By actorhood (or actorship) I refer to the general phenomenon of being able to act towards the outside world more or less effectively. This capacity to act can increase or decrease over time, depending on changes in the underlying variables which may go in different directions. An actor can thus also lose its actor capacity due to changes in any of the underlying variables.

Internal integration, cohesion and identity is summarized in the concept of regionness. Presence is an expression of the impact of the region on the external world due to size, demography, economic strength, that is, factors which do not depend on a purposive policy to influence, whereas actorness is a variable based on conscious organized efforts to shape the external world in accordance with the values, interests and identity of the actor.

The process of regionalization shaping cohesiveness and regional identity can in general terms be described in terms of levels of 'regionnes'– that is, successive orders of regional social space, system, society, community and institutionalized polity. Increasing regionness implies that a geographical area is transformed from a passive object to an active subject – an actor – increasingly capable of articulating the transnational interests of the emerging region (Hettne, 1993, 2003; Hettne and Söderbaum, 2000).

The concept of regionness defines the position of a particular region in terms of its cohesion; this can be seen as a long-term endogenous historical process, changing over time from coercion, the building of empires and nations in history, to voluntary cooperation: the current logic of regionalization. The political ambition of establishing regional cohesion and identity has been of primary importance in the ideology of the regionalist project. The approach of seeing region as process implies an evolution of deepening regionalism, not necessarily following the idealized stage model presented here, that mainly serves a heuristic purpose. Since regionalism is a political project, created by human actors, it may fail. In this perspective decline would mean decreasing regionness. From this perspective Europe now seems to have reached an impasse, facing decline in terms of regionness with an impact on actorhood.

Actorness, usually referring to external behaviour, implies a larger scope of action and room for *manoeuvre*, in some cases even a legal personality. The concept of actorness (with respect to the EU's external policies) has been developed by Bretherton and Vogler (2006).[3] Capacity to act is of course relevant internally as well, for instance in relation to what I have referred to as security regionalism, development regionalism and environmental regionalism, three areas where increased regional cooperation may make a difference (Hettne, 2001). Actorness is closely related to regioness, the latter implying an endogenous process of increasing cohesiveness, the former a growing capacity to act that follows from the strengthened presence of the regional unit in different contexts, as well as the actions that follow from the interaction between the actor and its external environment. Actorness is thus not only a function of regionness but an outcome of a dialectic process between endogenous and exogenous forces.

Europe as external actor is more than the EU foreign policy, and more than even EU's policies in different areas taken together. Simply by existing, the union due to its relative weight – demographically, economically and so on – has an impact on the rest of the world, its footprints are seen everywhere. Bretherton and Vogler use the concept 'presence' to signify this phenomenon. Furthermore, they usefully relate presence to 'actorness', or capacity to act. A stronger presence implies more capacity to act, unless we are dealing with a sleeping giant (which anyhow must wake up sooner or later). Actorness implies consciousness. In the near abroad presence is particularly strong, and can develop into outright absorption of new territory (enlargement). Bretherton and Vogler identify five requirements for actorness: (1) commitment to shared values and principles; (2) ability to formulate coherent policies; (3) capacity to undertake international negociation; (4) access to policy instruments; and (5) legitimacy of decision processes.

This is for a regional actor. A strong, functioning state like the US, of course, possesses these requirements and can use them to rule by either hegemonic power, or by dominance based on the use of force. This makes the third requirement less important ('we do not negotiate about our lifestyle').[4]

The unique feature of regional (as compared to great power) actorness is that this has to be created by voluntary processes and therefore depends more on dialogue and consensus-building than on coercion. This way of operating is the model Europe holds out as the preferred world order, since this is the way the New Europe (as it was organized by the EU) developed.

4 Conceptualizing world order

This chapter tries to clarify the impact of global regionalization on world order. What is then meant by world order? The concept is rarely defined. In recent books on international relations the concept often occurs in the text (sometimes even in the title), but is absent in the index, which means that it is given a common sense meaning in no need of being defined, or used merely as an attractive slogan, but not really meant to be thought of as an analytical concept. Hedley Bull focused on international order, which meant the system of states, and saw world order as both a more general and a more normative concept, but he left it at that (Bull, 1997). According to Robert Cox, who is one of the few who has used the concept in a conscious way for analytical purposes, it is genuinely trans historical (there is always a world order of some sort, but not necessarily an orderly one). However, this order is seen as an outcome of underlying factors – social forces and political units – which then gain more analytical importance for understanding world order (Cox, 1996). The concept is, furthermore, commonly used normatively in a more political sense, which is to say it describes not primarily the actually existing order (or historical orders) but models and/or utopian projects. It has even been used as a political slogan.

In order to be able to compare alternative models, I propose a non-normative and mainly political definition of world order as constituted by three dimensions: structure, mode of governance and form of legitimization. Structure is the way the units of the system are related, that is, different forms of polarity determined by the distribution of power and resources; mode of governance refers to avenues of influence on decision making and policy making; legitimization is the basis on which the system is made acceptable to the constituent units. On the structural dimension, I make a further distinction between the unipolar, the bipolar and the multipolar. Polarity can define relations between regions as well as great powers and these relations are not necessarily hostile (as postulated in realist theory).

In the area of governance, the distinction I draw is between the unilateral, the plurilateral and the multilateral. The difference between plurilateral and multilateral is especially important. A plurilateral grouping of actors is exclusive, whereas multilateral by definition implies inclusion, provided the rules of the game are accepted by all parties. Multilateralism is therefore often seen as preferable, but, for many purposes, regionalism, as a form of plurilateralism defined by geographical proximity, is just as useful. By contrast, unilateralism undermines collective arrangements and may even be a path towards imperialism. By relying on unilateral decision making, which means prioritizing the 'national interest' over collective security, structural anarchy is promoted for as long as no single power is able to impose its will on the whole of international society. In that eventuality the structural result, to the extent that such a policy ultimately succeeds, will be unipolarity (or imperialism). Finally, in terms of legitimization, I discern a declining scale from the universally accepted rule of international law, through hegemony exercised by one great power (which normally means 'acceptable dominance'), to pure dominance, legitimized only by the national interest of the dominant power and relying on coercion, prevention and pre-emption. The dividing line between hegemony and dominance is not a very sharp one, but trends in one direction or the other can easily be established within the general diplomatic/political international debate. For example, the preparedness to accept dominance increases in dramatic crises such as 9/11.

With the help of this framework a comparative analysis can be made between alternative models, as well as of changes in and of world orders over time. The concepts of international order and world order are often used as pseudonyms. Here international order connotes a more state-centric conception, whereas world order connotes a more complex multidimensional and post-sovereign order. An international system can furthermore be less than globally encompassing, for instance Europe as a regional international system in the nineteenth century.

World order of course implies a system including the whole world and all human beings. The degree of order within a region or in the international system can vary; thus different security theories speak of regional security complexes, anarchies, anarchic societies, regional security communities, and so on. The security agenda is broadened, which makes regional approaches to security more relevant.

A well functioning multilateral world order will require a certain degree of institutionalization which counters unilateral action, limited bilateral solutions, or ill-considered political or military reactions which aggravate a sensitive security situation. The degree of order within a particular region or in the international system can vary; different security theories speak of regional security complexes, anarchies, anarchic societies, regional security communities, and so on. Regional approaches to security are fully compatible with, and even necessitating multilateralism. After 9/11 there existed, to an even greater degree than in connection with the first Gulf war, the possibility of an institutionalized multilateralism, an international regime based on the premises of international law and extensive participation by states and other transnational actors. But this multilateralism was false. By 'false multilateralism' is meant political and military actions that take place in the guise of multilateralism but which in reality are an expression of more limited interests: *plurilateralism* if it is a matter of a group of major powers; *regionalism* if it is a geographically united bloc; or *unilateralism* if a superpower or regional major power is in reality acting alone. A certain kind of regionalism (interregionalism) may, however, be supportive to multilateral principles (regional multilateralism, or multiregionalism). But this is a long-term perspective and will depend on the strength of the political project of taking regionalism as the crucial element in reorganizing world order. This is the European approach to world order.

5 Interregionalism as world order: Pax Europaea?

What impact will or could Europe – or rather the EU – have on the future world order? One possible form of world order could be a 'neo-Westphalian order', governed either by a reconstituted UN system, in which the major regions of the world have a strong influence; another alternative would be a more loosely organized global 'concert' of great powers and the consequent marginalization of the UN. The relevant powers in both models will be the regional powers of the world. In the former case, supported by the EU, the UN will make use of the old idea of complementary 'regional arrangements' (Henrikson, 1995; Hettne and Söderbaum, 2006). In the latter case, supported by the US, regionalism will suffer from imposed or hegemonic regionalism, and the regions as such will be far from the ideal of security communities. It will thus be a multipolar and plurilateral world, but the concert model will be lacking in legitimacy.

Regionalism would, however, put its mark on a future post-Westphalian governance pattern, which would be more in line with EU preferences. In such a world order, the locus of power would move irreversibly to the transnational level. The state system would be replaced or complemented by a regionalized world order and a strengthened global civil society, supported by a 'normative architecture' of world order values, such as multiculturalism and multilateralism.

The EU emphasis on interregionalism may in the longer run prove to be important in the reconstruction of a multilateral world order in a regionalized form, here called multiregionalism, meaning a horizontalized, institutionalized structure formed by organized regions, linked to each other through multidimensional partnership agreements. The EU's ambition is to formalize these as relations between regional bodies rather than as bilateral contacts between countries; but, for pragmatic reasons, the forms of agreement show a bewildering variety. The EU's relations with the various geographical areas are furthermore influenced by the 'pillared approach' in its own internal decision making, creating artificial divisions between, for instance, foreign and development policy (Holland, 2002). The development of the pattern has also been influenced over time by shifting bilateral concerns among additional members: for example, the United Kingdom and South Asia, Iberia and Latin America.

Even so, a multipolar system in which the EU constitutes the hub and driving actor does already exist in an embryonic form. The partnership between the EU and ASEAN is a prominent example of a formal interregional relationship. Relations between the EU and Mercosur and between the EU and the grouping of African, Caribbean and Pacific (ACP) countries further extend the global web that has the EU at its centre.

There is thus a clear pattern in the EU's external policy, namely, to shape the world order in accordance with Europe's (more recent) experience of solving conflicts through respect for 'the other', dialogue, multilateralism based on international law, and institutionalized relations. Thus Europe is referred to as a 'civilian power' (Telò, 2006). This can also, more critically, be called 'soft imperialism' since, despite fine diplomacy, it is often felt as an imposition in other parts of the world (Hettne and Söderbaum, 2005). The policy varies along widening circles from integration (making certain neighbours EU members), to stabilization (by entering privileged partnerships with the 'near abroad'), bilateral agreements with important great or middle powers and partnership agreements with other regions. These four foreign policy relations lead to four types of counterparts: prospective members, neighbors, great powers, and more far away regions.

Enlargement policy covers acceding countries (Bulgaria and Romania), candidate countries (Turkey and Croatia) and potential candidate countries in the Western Balkans (Albania, Bosnia-Herzegovina, Kosovo, former Yugoslav Republic of Macedonia, Serbia and Montenegro).[5] The enlargements have either concerned well integrated European countries, whose entry for various reasons were delayed, or 'southern' less developed countries to be integrated into the European mainstream, mainly for security reasons.

The European neighbourhood policy (ENP) offers a privileged relationship with the EU's neighbours (distinct from integration/enlargement).[6] A crucial component of the ENP is the commitment to promote democratization and human rights in combination with the principles of good governance, rule of law, market economy and sustainable development. The 'near abroad' of the EU and Russia coincides to a large degree. The neighbourhood plays a most important role in the EU's more coherent and comprehensive security strategy (Charillon, 2004). The Barcelona process is a strategy of cooperation between the EU and its Mediterranean neighbours (Euro–Med), where peace is the first priority, in accordance with the basic concern for stability. Thus the general method involved in the foreign policy towards Near Abroad is a soft form of imperialism (asymmetric partnership) based on conditional ties; the prize ranging from assistance to full membership. The success story is the transformation and integration of Central and Eastern Europe, which in fact implied a large number of resolved and prevented conflicts. For countries not supposed to become a member the policy is a rather weak way of influencing the external world. Thus, actorness shifts from one context to another.

The EU has also developed a series of *bilateral* relationships with the United States, Russia, Canada, Mexico, China, Japan, India and South Africa. In some cases this completes and in other cases it replaces genuine region-to-region links. Among the bilateral partners the USA is the most powerful, in fact the challenges and problems posed by its military superiority cannot be balanced and its imperial policy influenced according to the old realist recipe: balance of power politics. What remains is what has been called 'soft balancing', which can be seen as a form of civil power, implying different kinds of non-violent resistance. This policy was practiced by both small and big powers in connection with the Iraq war and may increase in importance if the 'imperial' policies of the USA continue. During the last decade *interregional* cooperation has become an increasingly important component of the EU's foreign policy relations, which is realized through a large number of interregional arrangements especially with more far away counterparts in Africa, Asia and Latin America, where the EU interests often clash with those of the US, particularly in Latin America. In spite of massive contacts on the level of civil society, the formal interregional transatlantic links (EU–NAFTA) are institutionally weak or nonexistent, as was discussed in section 1.

In the Middle East, where the US is predominant there has been an opening for the EU in the Gulf area (with The Gulf Cooperation Council – GCC) in the last couple of years. The Strategic Partnership with the Mediterranean and the Middle East was adopted in 2004 bringing all relationships with Middle Eastern states under one umbrella.[7]

The EU relations to ACP (Countries of Africa, Caribbean and the Pacific) are rooted in colonial and neocolonial relations, which now, as for instance in the Cotonou agreement (June 2000), are described in more symmetric terms, as 'partnerships'. The background to this is the gradual abandoning of the 'pyramid of privilege' implied in the Yaoundé-Lomé-framework that since the mid-1960s defined the relationship between the EU and peripheral regions, originally selectively favoured in accordance with former colonial interests. ACP is not a regional organization. The EU is therefore trying to encourage cooperation within the three constituent regions, stressing as an article of faith that regional integration is the best development strategy (see the contribution by Fredrik Söderbaum).

In its cooperation policy with Africa, the EU has always paid special attention to regional integration and cooperation. The main reason for this is its own character as a regional body with a relatively long and successful experience. This implies that it has a unique expertise as regards the technical and practical aspects of regional integration.[8]

6 Unilateralism as world order: Pax Americana?

Before 9/11 one could still discuss several alternative world orders (Hettne and Odén, 2002). After the terrorist action there seemed to be fewer alternatives; there was a clear trend towards one distinct world order model: Pax Americana. This order, now in retreat, was unilateral rather than multilateral or regional, and unipolar rather than multipolar. However, we do not know how stable and durable a new order will be. Unilateralism is particularly provocative and, arguably, therefore inherently unstable.

Regionalism, implying a multipolar world order structure, as preferred by the EU, is unacceptable to the United States, which, furthermore, has made it very clear that multilateralism, although desirable, has its limitations set by the USA's own security interests. This is wholly in line with the traditional realist security doctrine and therefore not new. The US has always applied multilateralist policies and solutions only to the extent that they coincided with 'the national interest' and this interest must first of all, according to the doctrine, be backed up with hard power. According to Chalmers Johnson 'a vast network of military bases on every continent except Antarctica actually constitutes a new form of empire (Johnson, 2004: 1). However, the foreign policy of the Bush administration went beyond classical realism (type Kissinger or Brzezinski) towards reinforcing what the neoconservative think-tank, the *Project for the New American Century*, described as 'a policy of military strength and moral clarity' (inspired by Ronald Reagan). This formulation captures the essence of neo-conservatism: military strength and willingness to use it, and a moral mission to change the world in accordance with American values, first of all liberty. The opportunity, 'the unipolar moment', came after the end of the Cold War and this thinking is thus older than 9/11. The concept was coined by American publicist Charles Krauthammer (1991–92) and stood for the US policy of taking advantage of its military superiority by shaping the world order in accordance with the US national interest. Later the concept became 'the unipolar era', expressing the confidence of the neoconservatives.

The 'war' against terrorism came in a number of cases to mean a strengthening of the state and the military. The violent polarization between regimes that, from a democratic viewpoint, are dubious, and their more or less fundamentalist opponents, created the premises for a further proliferation of terrorism. The multilateralist world order, as distinct from what might be expected of a loose and temporary alliance (ad hoc multilateralism), must grapple with these structural conditions in a more systematic way. It must also be built on political pluralism, a co-existence between civilizations instead of 'the clash of civilizations'. To achieve this will require much time, patience and resources. The alternative is a repressive world order which breeds terrorism with different faces in different regions. This will also impact on the role of regional institutions.

To my mind, it is wrong to call the present world order 'unipolar', since the remaining superpower has to fill the power vacuum created by the collapse of the other. As shown in Iraq, there is no automatism involved. Furthermore, to dub this ideological structure 'neo-conservatism' is hardly an appropriate description of what seems rather to be a militant revolutionary doctrine, rejecting the multilateral world order model and the role of the UN as the protector of this order. Neo-conservatism, or 'militant libertarianism', and isolationism, however different these typically American doctrines may seem, are both sceptical to subsuming national interests to international cooperation and collective security and constitute different expressions of the specificity (the 'exceptionalism') of the USA as the home of a 'chosen people'.

The foreign policy of President Bush has been discussed in terms of 'imperialism' based on domination, whereas the Clinton administration is seen as less overtly imperialist, more hegemonic (Lieven, 2004). The concept of imperialism has been used academically, pejoratively and positively by different people. Some are also warning against reviving the concept (Telò, 2006). A minimum academic definition of imperialism should to my mind contain a unilateralist, exploitative, coercive and systematic (the sustainability problem) relationship with the external world, seen as an object for political and military action by a great power (designed by its political class). Yet most analysts in the new literature on imperialism question the dimension of sustainability and point to the problem of overstretch (Kennedy, 1987; Burbach and Tarbell, 2004; Falk, 2005).

Before 9/11 the unipolar moment was just one ideological current within the USA. From the US point of view, the question of multilateralism revolved around a realistic balancing between legality and effectiveness, and priority was always given to the latter. Unilateralism maintained the upper hand. This has also marked the US approach to regionalism, which has always been subordinated to the national interest. This is clear, for instance in the cases of NAFTA and APEC and the latter's support for regional cooperation in Southeast Asia. All can be explained by specific, perceived national interests: NAFTA was a globalist policy, APEC an instrument for hegemonic control in Asia-Pacific, and support for regional cooperation in Southeast Asia a part of the anti-terrorist struggle. Thus, the US has 'resigned itself to regionalism' (Telò, 2006:129) in spite of its scepticism in order to promote national interests such as an open trading system or geopolitical control.

The interregionalism of the EU is certainly also interest-driven. But in this case there is no unitary national interest, but rather a collective, negotiated interest based on the European integration experience. In what follows we shall look into the competitive relationship in various regional contexts.

7 US and EU regional encounters

As we have seen the EU and the US approaches to regionalism differ a lot, something which also explains the bewildering status of global regionalism. Looking at the existing patchwork of trans-and interregional agreements there is so far, in terms of structural outcome, no clear picture on the horizon. Transregional arrangements are in principal voluntary and cooperative. They are also very diverse and difficult to categorize. Few are interregional in the proper sense of the word, some relations are transregional, some bilateral (hybrid relations between a regional organization and a great power). That the EU constitutes the hub of interregional arrangements is in full accordance with its regionalist ideology, encompassing not only trade and foreign investment but also political dialogue and cultural relations between the regions. The US on the other hand does not value regional relations as such, but cannot but operate in an increasingly regionalized world. In discussing the EU-US encounters in various regions I will follow the categorization of EU foreign policy relations made in section 4.

To what extent has the EU control over itself? With the so called Eastern enlargement the EU got a number of members more interested in the Atlantic community than the European Union. This means that the commitment for deepening is weakened and that regionness actually is on the decline. The members joining with the 'eastern enlargement' were coldly received, to say the least, and as far as Turkey is concerned the attitude in several EU countries is even hostile. In this case the US has actively supported the Turkish candidature.

We have already (in section 4) made a distinction between EU's relations with the 'near abroad' and more far away relations. The frontier between 'Europe', as organized by the EU, and surrounding areas is unclear, some of these areas (or countries in them) being new members or applicants, others defined (through a political discourse) as being 'non-Europe' (but 'near abroad'). The area in question is large and includes much of the post-Soviet area where Russia of course has its interests as a reemerging great power. Since the CIS (Commonwealth of Independent States) did not take off, the EU has also to deal with Ukraine, Belarus and Moldova (the European part of the post-Soviet area) independently. In view of the fear for the former superpower, but now regional power, the expectations in these states are that the US will play a more protective role.

Here Europe does not only meet the US but above all Russia. The relations between EU and Russia are rather similar to the ones between the EU and the USA, in the sense that Russia also prefers bilateralism, although the EU has a Partnership and Cooperation Agreement (PCA) with Russia which covers human rights, the economy, trade, security and justice issues In the rest of the post-Soviet area, that is, the European part (except of course the Baltic subregion now part of the EU) and Caucasus/Central Asia, the EU presence is weak (Dannreuther, 2004). The strategic partnership between EU and Russia implies a substantive geopolitical room for manouvre for the latter.

The Mediterranean 'region' has no formal existence, it is a social construction shaped by the EU's security concerns, particularly in the south. North Africa is linked to France through colonial legacy. Regarding the countries involved in the former peace process (Israel and the eastern Arab countries) the US influence is what counts, and the EU has consequently taken a low profile. This is particularly clear after the Hamas victory in the Palestinian election.

Few observers would consider the EU response to the Balkan crises (Bosnia, Kosovo and Macedonia) an unqualified success. Instead the US involvement, after some hesitation, became massive, providing a dilemma for the new Europe, since the Balkan subregion must be seen as forming part of Europe rather than constituting its permanent 'near abroad'. The dividing line between what is 'Europe' and a 'non-Europe', close enough to constitute the 'near abroad', is ultimately a political issue. To define the Balkans out of Europe might be tempting but politically incorrect and also dangerous. At present Bosnia is under the protection of the EU militarily. In the case of Kosovo, NATO played the military role (to the frustration of the US).

Today, the whole world is becoming more and more integrated through regional formations interlinked by transregional and interregional relations. The most important transregional/interegional complex is the Triad: North America, Europe and East Asia. Furthermore, Southeast Asia and East Asia are increasingly merging into one region as symbolized by the East Asia summit in Kuala Lumpur (December 2005). This growing region is dominated by the two rival great powers, China and Japan, with which both the US and the EU have bilateral relations. With Japan the US has a privileged special relationship whereas China is courting the EU. Transregional links within the Triad are constituted by APEC (Asia-Pacific Economic Cooperation), and ASEM (Asia-Europe Meeting) as well as the various transatlantic agreements between the US and the EU discussed in section 1.

Unsurprisingly, the Triad relations are sometimes rather tense, due to power balance concerns, trade competition that risks degenerating into trade wars, and the somewhat different economic ideologies in the three regions. In the new, larger East Asia there are thus competing transregional institutions expressing the rivalry between the EU and the US: APEC where the USA is the driver, and the ASEM process, involving the EU and ASEAN plus China, Japan and South Korea (but so far excluding Myanmar). Behind the ASEM is the felt need by European and Asian partners to relate to and perhaps try to balance the US dominance. ASEM has been seen as 'the missing link' in the Triad, since Europe had been excluded from APEC by the US. Consequently the US is not welcome as a member in the ASEM process. This process has been seen as instrumental in forming the APT region. ASEAN + Three, or APT, is now emerging as a new regional formation covering both Southeast and East Asia, and actually socially constructed in the process of maintaining an interregional relationship between Asia and Europe (Gilson, 2002), at the same time as being a response to various urgent needs in the regions, such as maintaining or restoring financial stability (Higgott, 2002) and controlling communicable diseases such as SARS (Fidler, 2004). APEC, on the other hand, seems to be losing importance even in the area of trade liberalization (*Financial Times*, Nov 14, 2006).

Central Asia is a 'pre-regional' area in which the US and Russia competes for influence whereas the EU is almost absent.[9] Relations between EU and South Asia have been rather weak, but are now becoming more important as the region stabilizes politically and becomes successful in terms of economic dynamics. This also means a greater US interest in the region.

Europe's relations with Latin America were intensified in the 1990s after a long period of neglect or simply focusing on individual countries. The EU—Mercosur relationship, on the level of the core/intermediate relation, is another clear example of interregionalism, since there exists an agreement between two regional organizations (the EU-Mercosur Interregional Framework Co-operation Agreement – EMIFCA, 1995), which is also built on three pillars, of which the first includes a political dialogue, the second a substantive financial support to Mercosur's institutional development and the third economic and commercial cooperation (Santander, 2006). The closer links between the EU and Latin America are growing as the US seems to lose interest in its own backyard, or perhaps is too preoccupied with other areas.

Over the years the ACP countries have been marginalized in the European-led interregional system, but interestingly they have made efforts to act as a collective unit, while the EU makes efforts to regionalize and differentiate the group, the first principle based on territorial, the other on developmental criteria (LDCs, landlocked countries, island countries, and so on). To this confusing picture comes the fact that the meaning of development has not remained the same from Yaoundé to Cotonou. The trend has been towards neoliberal strategies and political conditional ties in spite of the language of partnership. Of the African, Caribbean and Pacific regions the US has considered Africa as a European concern.

To sum up, interregionalism, as practiced by the EU, has the purpose of building and consolidating regional orders, whereas the US regional activities rather have the purpose of preventing strong regional formations to grow.

Conclusion

The EU is, in terms of regionness, so far the only example of 'an institutionalized regional polity', at present lingering between intergovernmentalism and supranational governance, but with an uncertain future, due to a new wave of Euro-scepticism and the decreased coherence and consistency following the inflow of new members. The frustrated attempt to make a European Constitution even gave rise to speculations about a possible break-up of the Union.[10]

On the other hand, there was an agreement on a common European security policy, marking a significant disassociation from the USA and the NATO framework. The stress is here on prevention rather than preemption, thus holding on to 'civilian power', at the same time as the transatlantic relationship is cautiously referred to as 'irreplacable'. The UN charter is, however, in this document described as 'the fundamental framework' for international relations and international action. Thus the EU muddles through, used as it is to be forced to act in crisis situations. As long as joint management of various problems makes sense this is likely to continue, adding to the ambiguity of the nature of the union.

The way the EU deals with the external world has been different from that of an ordinary great power driven by geopolitical interests. This is because the civilian power employed in the EU's own region-building is also being projected in its external relations as the preferred world order model. This thesis on a correspondence between internal and external is clearly stated by Ian Manners with regard to normative power: 'The concept of normative power is an attempt to suggest that not only is the EU constructed on a normative basis, but importantly that this predisposes it to act in a normative way in world politics'.[11] This concept is different from the idea of Europe as civilian power in the sense that the latter is meant to modify the structural conditions in which all actors operate (Telò, 2006: 228).

In spite of the ideological commitment to systemic interregionalism, weakened over the years, it cannot be said that the EU external policy has developed in a coherent and consistent way. On the contrary, different policies have been applied in different contexts and at different points in time by different constellations of actors. The US, following a more consistent realist line, is dominant in most arenas, particularly in the Middle East, Central Asia, but challenged by the EU in the US backyard – Latin America. The element of competition with the US is particularly obvious in the cases of Asia and Latin America (ALA), where the European presence has increased substantively, leading to stronger actorness.

The European global interests in a more realist sense, are not hidden, though. According to a statement from the Commission (quoted from Bretherton and Vogler, 1999:129): 'the EU can commit itself to supporting only economic and social organization models which contribute to the objectives of its cooperation policy and which comply with the political and social values which it means to promote' (Agenda, 2000). Some would call this a kind of imperialism as well (Hettne–Söderbaum, 2005). It is rather obvious that the EU policies have failed to instill confidence in the partners, whether Arabs, Indians, Latin Americans or Africans. However, the outcome is, in spite of all contradictions, a pattern of governance with its own distinctive characteristics and the potential of becoming a world order. This world order, the outcome of multiple processes of regionalization, could be called 'multiregionalism'. In terms of the definition of world order suggested in section 3 this world order would be multipolar, plurilateral (regionalized) and compatible with established international law, in contrast to the unipolar, unilateral, and national interest-based model proposed by the neoconservative establishment, now less and less established, so it seems.[12]

The question is to what extent the potential of the former model (Pax Europaea) today (in contrast with two decades ago) is realized by European politicians and other decision makers, as well as the increasingly sceptic European public. This is a question of future European regionness and actorness, which by no means are necessarily advancing.

Just like the US, the EU applies its own experiences in conflict resolution and development on neighbourhood relations, as well as on the world as a whole. Two different kinds of power, hard and civil, thus face each other. Coercion may be replaced by influence, and imposition by dialogue. What has worked in Europe may ultimately prove to have wider relevance. Indeed, the European model may have relevance even if Europe no longer seems to believe in it, judging from the debate on the new constitution.

It is important to note that the differences behind the two models do not express varieties of national mentality – Europe versus America – but constitute contrasting world order principles held by political groupings in both areas. It is therefore reasonable to expect coexistence, whether uneasy or not, and the emergence of hybrids formed somewhere between these competing world order models. Even so, changes in the US are of much more importance. Ever since the election of the second George W. Bush administration, there has emerged in the USA a call for a return to multilateralism: the 'USA and its main regional partners must begin to prepare for life after Pax Americana' (Kupchan, 2004). The two years remaining after the November 2006 Congress election will have to be based on domestic (and therefore also international) compromises. Such a shift would bring Europe and the US closer again, but it will not eliminate the difference between the models of interregionalism/multiregionalism and a global concert of regional powers; or between a post-Westphalian and a neo-Westphalian world order. That the US would be the one to make the most concessions and adaptations as compared to its current foreign policy line is due to the fact that this line (Westphalianism) is incompatible with the post-sovereign trend associated with globalization (post-Westphalianism). However, in respects other than security the US, by necessity, is also becoming a multilevel actor. Convergences or at least some compromises cannot therefore be completely excluded.

Interregionalism thus forms part of the EU's foreign policy, the EU being the hub of a global pattern of interregional relations. On the other hand, if regionalism is a global phenomenon, and there are different regionalisms in different parts of the world, it is reasonable to expect that these emerging regions, to the extent that they develop actorhood (with varying degrees of actorness) establish some kinds of links with each other. Thus interregionalism can also be explained from the point of view of the transformation of the global system.

This point is reinforced by the fact that southern regions also (ASEAN, Mercosur, SADC) establish interregional relations, encouraged by the EU. Of course these regions, albeit harbouring potential structural changes in world governance, are still embryonic, and therefore it is possible to read different trends of theoretical significance into them. In other words, the problem lies in the ontological status of what we call interregionalism. The problem is that there is a lack of consensus regarding interregionalism. The existing definitions to date are ad hoc and rather provisional, not based on a systematic overview of the phenomenon to be conceptualized and theorized.[13] To my mind it is important that the concept interregionalism is reserved for formal relations between regions as juridical or at least quasi-juridical entities, since this would be a new political phenomenon, signifying a post-Westphalian era. It does not imply post-sovereignty, however, since the regions get their actorhood from the pooling of national sovereignties. Maybe one should, in the shorter term at least, rather talk about a neo-Westphalian phenomenon.

Interregionalism can be seen as one of the more regulated forms that globalization may be taking. As compared to market-led globalization in a Westphalian world of nation states, it is more rooted in territory; and in contrast to traditional multilateralism, it is a more exclusive relationship, since access to regional formations is limited by the principle of geographical proximity (pluri-lateralism). Interregionalism, not to speak of multiregionalism, is a long-term, non-linear and uncertain trend which certainly will include setbacks, the outcome of which we can not know. It is, however, likely that interregionalism has become a systemic feature of the world order, and that this dynamic may continue even without the support of the EU group-to-group dialogue.

Notes

1   Multilateralism thus comes in many forms, as helpfully clarified by Mario Telò (2006). By regional multilateralism I primarily refer to relations among regions, not intra-regional conditions.

2   This is referred to as Old Interregionalism by Hänggi (2006:32) in contradistinction to the New Interregionalism which is world-wide and systemic. The classic description of the group-to-group approach can be found in Edwards & Regelsberger, 1990. The EU group-to-group approach of course continues, albeit in diluted form, in the new era, so the distinction must not be exaggerated (cf the discussion on old and new regionalism in Hettne, 2005). The relevance of the old interregionalism for world order was for instance pointed out in 1987 by the then West German Foreign Minister, Hans-Dietrich Genscher describing the EU approach as a 'landmark on the road to a new world order' (Edwards & Regelsberger, 1990: 13).

3   It was originally coined by Gunnar Sjöstedt (1977).

4   Interestingly, this difference is diminished, see Hill & Smith, 2005.

5   See http://europa.eu.int/comm/enlargement/index.htm.

6   The ENP covers Algeria, Armenia, Azerbaijan, Belarus, Egypt, Georgia, Israel, Jordan, Lebanon, Libya, Moldova, Morocco, Syria, Tunisia, Ukraine and the Palestinian Authority. With regard to the Mediterranean, the ENP builds on the Barcelona process and the Euro-Mediterranean Partnership from 1995 (http://europa.eu.int/comm/world/enp/index_en.htm).

7   See Helle Malmvig 'An unlikely match or a marriage in the making? EU-GCC relations in a changing security environment' , *DIIS Brief November 2006* (Danish Institute for International Studies).

8   Kennes, 1999: 27).

9   See the special issue of *International Affairs*. Vol. 80, No. 3, May 2004.

10 The expectations regarding the future of the EU are highly contrasting. For a good summary of various positions see McCormick, 2007.

11 Quoted in A. Linklater, 'A European Civilising Process', in C. Hill and M. Smith (eds., *International Relations and the European Union* (Oxford: Oxford University Press, 2005: 375).

12 The nature of a multipolar order is of course impossible to predict. Major powers except the US and Great Britain have expressed sympathy for multipolarity (Walt, 2006: 111), but there is also fear for the Triple Alliance of repressive powers (Mann, 2005: xxi).

13 Important steps have been taken in Söderbaum & Langenhove (2006); and Hänggi (2006).

PART II
Comparative Analysis of Regional Groupings

Chapter 6

Between Trade Regionalization and Various Paths towards Deeper Cooperation

Mario Telò

The second main topic of this book is the comparison between the existing regional organizations, their complexity and ambiguities. Five main case studies are particularly taken into account: two in the Americas (NAFTA and MERCOSUR), one in Asia (ASEAN), and finally the African case; comparative references are made to other regional groupings (Communidad Andina, SAARC, among others), while always keeping the EU experience in mind as an advanced workshop of regional cooperation and integration.

New regionalism is in many respects a multiple and highly differentiated reality, firstly, because of the great variety of institutional and informal features it covers. We are witnessing the revival of old regional organizations and the birth of new ones. Such differences suggest a basic methodological question: is the observer confronted with a variety of institutional forms of regionalism or with different forms of the same pattern? All the chapters embrace the general idea of European exceptionalism; namely that distinctive historical, cultural, and societal features underpin the European path to regional integration and the unique institutions of the EU.[1] However, the authors of this book don't share the idea that all what we have learned by comparative research is that the EC/EU is not an exportable regional model. In other words, the EU is not a kind of counter-model either, while the comparison with the successive and various kinds of European cooperation/ integration process has proven to be very useful to the international literature. Even if against any teleological, evolutionistic, Euro-centric vision, thus far we can distinguish between the following forms of regional groupings (combining the inputs of several authors):

a. By *regionalization* we understand the different, private and public, forms of societal and economic networking, association and cooperation within a region. Their number and influence have increased considerably since the early 1980s, according to the *Yearbook of International Organization*.[2]

b. *Regional fora* are the first step towards dialogue among NGOs, mainly open to civil society representatives (business community, NGOs and so on) and intergovernmental cooperation, formal and informal, by institutionalized bodies or looser structures.

c. *State-promoted regional cooperation* involves *de jure* regime-setting, policy decisions by governments, in general, to remove barriers to trade and investments towards a free trade area and set instrumental intergovernmental cooperation, mainly limited to some sectors and branches[3] which could also include dispute settlement mechanisms.

d. A customs union and a common trade policy: these include common external tariff and foreign economic policy (for example, MERCOSUR, the EU and SACU, including five members of SADC). The definition of 'strategic regionalism', competing for defending regional geo-economic interest and asserting distinctive socio-economic and learning models, could also be fit to cope with such a phenomenon.

e. By economic integration, we understand a common market and an economic union, including not only cooperation but also coordination of national macroeconomic policies, through intergovernmental and, rarely, supranational institutions.

f. By a regional polity we don't understand a regional federal state. Even the five types above don't need to be all included. However, several process of deepening are in progress: a socio-political construction (or 'cognitive regionalism', see Higgott chapter), various steps towards political unity (gradually pooling national sovereignties in sensitive policy fields) and a high institutional capacity to minimize internal asymmetries and maximize external influence and power.[4]

Since new regional associations of states as a concrete phenomenon are often still unclear and overlapping within the current transition of the post-bipolar world system, this book's contributing researchers do not aim to create a general theory of new regionalism. On the contrary, the chapters begin by describing, classifying and raising questions and problems. What we can say is that there is no evidence at all that different regional models correspond to an evolutionary 'Balassian' (B. Balassa, 1961) process where the path and the end are established from the very beginning. Extreme variations, steps backward or stagnation are possible. There is no continuum either between the different degrees of formalization of regional cooperation. Finally, different models cannot be explained through the integration theory that was created and developed relating to western Europe and on the basis of the political background of the European nation state, such a peculiar historical construction. However, comparison is very useful and its main goal is not only to stress similarities but also to underline variations. It would be a methodological mistake to isolate a single regional organization and underestimate the systemic trends and the common features within the partially globalized economy. Europe is a laboratory and a reference – even if the kind of high institutionalization found in European regionalism is not to be found elsewhere in the world.[5] Some of the current forms of regionalization do emulate the European patterns, namely the EFTA, Common Market and Single European Act, while some others react against them or consciously avoid the European way.

The main reasons for comparing are the relevant *international factors of new regionalism*; regional organizations do have the same global environment in common. They not only experienced the common challenges of the globalizing economy, but also of the turning points of the evolving world system: 1931, 1944/47, 1971, 1989/91. However, they have quite a different experience with globalization and global institutions; furthermore they interact with the American leadership and the past Soviet policy and regional leaders in different ways. For example, multilateralism became a common rule in the USA–Western Europe relationship whereas bilateralism characterized the USA–Asia relationship, in the framework of the huge heterogeneity of the Asian continent. They have been differently affected by the evolution in American economic and security leadership, for example, think about the 'transatlantic triangle' or the decline of FTAA and APEC. Regional variations can be classified depending both upon the impact of the international system or upon the degree of internal cohesion and domestic pressures.

As far as *internal factors* are concerned, regional organizations all have experience of networks and intergovernmental regimes, policy making and communities. They all give rise to multi-tier, multi-level, multi-channel, multi-actor regional systems, partly informal and partly formal. Continental and sub-continental variations are explained through several historical, political and economic factors, partly exogenous and partly endogenous, including the difference of the states' preferences, the degree of divergence among them, the distribution of capabilities among members of regional organizations and so on.[6]

Finally, 'club size', the balance between widening and deepening of each regional grouping, is important: very often it is a matter of sub-regional organizations, including only a part of the states, belonging to that region of the world. An important transversal question raised by the literature is whether a regional leader is necessary and sufficient to build up a regional organization[7] and to shape membership and borders. The separate chapters provide both analytical and critical assessments to answer these questions.

1 ASEAN, SAARC and the Asian way to new regionalism

The international literature on the Association of South-East Asian Nations (ASEAN) is characterized by a crucial question: how could ASEAN possibly survive the dramatic changes incurred as the security framework of this particularly turbulent region, the domestic post-colonial regime transition for over thirty years, and the financial crisis of the late 1990s? On the one hand, ASEAN had to be flexible enough to cope with the challenges of internal diversity and the political fragility of regimes within Pacific Asia.[8] On the other hand, it had to be sufficiently innovative to be able to face huge strategic uncertainties and the negative regional legacy of bilateral experiences – including arms control.[9] A comparison with the very poor achievements of the South Asian Association for Regional Cooperation (SAARC) is particularly interesting in this respect.[10] In fact, this regional grouping with the largest population world wide seems to have not only a very low degree of integration among national economies and societies and no incrementalism, but was experiencing the worst periods of conflicts between its two leaders (India and Pakistan) during its fifteen-year history. The four main reasons for the stagnation include the legacy of the colonial past, the problems of underdevelopment, the lack of complementarity between national economies and the political tensions within the region. Bilateral issues, and particularly the conflict between the two nuclear powers India and Pakistan, rigorously left off the SAARC agenda, do brake any further progress in regional cooperation. All in all, the results over fifteen years, often intergovernmental summits, many attempts to improve information exchange, coordination, networking and so on, are so modest that, given the present circumstances, the survival of SAARC as a forum in one of the most dangerous regions of the world illustrates the centrality of the hard politics issues and the question of leadership.

Internal asymmetry is only a partial explanation of failures and stagnation. Certainly with 72 per cent of land and 77 per cent of population, India represents the giant of the region. However, even other regional organizations (including MERCOSUR, ASEAN and SADC) are characterized by huge internal asymmetries that do not stop regional agreements from progressing. Clearly a second internal negative factor (common to many regional groupings, including developing countries) must not be forgotten: the lack of functional dynamics of regional economic integration and of complementarity among national economies as exports and imports are concerned.

According to a more convincing political explanation, the absence of mutual confidence-building measures condemns regional cooperation to the margins. Bilateral political understanding between the two major powers of the region – as in Western Europe (France and Germany) and in Latin America (Argentina and Brazil) – largely explains the success of regional agreements elsewhere. In Asia, the common feeling of an external threat, whether political (Soviet and Chinese expansionism, Vietnam War) has been an important early integrative factor for ASEAN countries. However, the end of the Cold War is significantly reducing the impact of systemic political factors within the Asian continent with the consequence of increasing the influence of both economic (the growing fear of marginalization within the globalizing economy) and endogenous factors.[11] By building no security in the post-Cold War era, the South Asian crisis shows that regionalism does not easily substitute bilateralism or global multilateralism either. In Southern Asia, when bilateralism or globalism are unable to provide solutions for regional conflicts, a regional association does not yet offer more than a forum for a dialogue.

Finally, even the limits of another possible positive external factor are clearly showing the case of the still ambivalent and poor influence of the EU policy supporting regional cooperation in Southern Asia.[12] The EU supporting policies are more successful where internal factors of integration are well balanced with external factors, as in the case of ASEAN. The increasing bilateral cooperation between the EU and India (Strategic Partnership of 2004 and Action Plan since 2005) is consistent with the idea of setting inter-regional relations; however, it had to face political challenges: the new situation created by the military *coup d'état* in Pakistan and the anti-Pakistan evolution of SAARC, on the one hand, the triangular competitive relationship (including economic, nuclear and political cooperation) between the US–EU–India, on the other hand.

In its presentation of Asia's most important regional organization, Eliassen/ Borves's chapter raises a methodological issue by proposing the comparison of ASEAN with the EC of the 1970s rather than with the highly institutionalized EU of today. The question is to what extent we can consider the synchronic dimension of their controversial relation to a globalized world by comparing regional organizations to each other. Furthermore, to what extent must a diachronic approach be chosen in order to have a better understanding of the gradual evolution of regional organizations? Out of any Euro-centric understanding, this book aims to combine both of these approaches, which is particularly useful as far as this case study is concerned.

ASEAN states were able to develop their intergovernmental cooperation, in spite of unusual obstacles and extraordinary difficulties. For four decades, ASEAN has been looking for an Asian way to regional cooperation. At only a very first glance, it is similar to the EU insofar as the scope and range of its activities are concerned. The willingness of some members in the early decades to emulate the western European model and, in the 1990s, to react to the danger of diluting ASEAN within the broader interregional liberalization carried out by APEC,[13] played a certain role. In its Jakarta meeting of 1994, APEC adopted an ambitious programme to set up an inter-regional free trade area by 2020. With the setting up of APEC, we were faced, in Asia as in Europe and elsewhere, with competitive concepts of regionalism. Two opposite barriers were paradoxically braking the Clinton administration preference for a comprehensive and more institutionalized APEC as a model of so-called 'open regionalism',[14] that is, ASEAN's fear of being absorbed into an intercontinental US-centered organization and a preference of many Asian states for a very soft, multiple geometry, Most Favored Nation-based, kind of APEC. However, as R. Higgott argues, the Bush Administration ironically transformed the US presence in the Asia–Pacific regional in an external unintended federalizing factor of East Asian regional cooperation without the US. The US seriously affected East Asian regionalism even during the Cold War era. Nevertheless, such an external potential factor was not as unifying in the Asia–Pacific region as in western Europe, which can be explained largely by underlining that the US's preference in Asia was for bilateralism rather than multilateralism.

Considering the internal factors, one has to take into account the great economic disparities among ASEAN countries in terms of industrial and technological development, labour costs, and export capacity. Furthermore, many observers stress the cultural and political heterogeneity of the region and the particular state traditions (populism, religious parties, role of the army, corruption, and so on) as well as the various difficulties of coping with the challenges of both global liberalization and regional cooperation.

As a consequence, ASEAN followed its own way to regional cooperation and, in spite of the aforesaid weaknesses, it is about to undergo an important change. Despite its very political origins, ASEAN can currently be defined as a mainly network-based regional integration. After the end of the bipolar world, the main driving force became the business community. Business networks are demanding further integration and institution building. The project for an ASEAN Free Trade Area has a main instrument: a Common Effective Preferential Tariff. The most likely issue could be similar to the European Free Trade Association,[15] according to Eliassen/Børve's chapter. However, common market, cooperation on security issues, a ASEAN-Charta are on the current agenda. Moreover, Higgott focuses on the growing relevance of the issues related to monetary cooperation. Indeed, the ASEAN way means that transnational private networks, ethnic business, technological clusters, subregional policy communities, and free trade areas are pushing the governments forward. Personal contacts and business networks created along ethnic and cultural lines certainly build a complex multi-tier system using geographical proximity and both formal and informal meetings as a means to strengthen regional interests in global competition. Of course, as a consequence of such an approach, the institutional structure still is, relatively speaking, rather weak. The Council of Foreign Affairs Ministers (taking decisions on the basis of a consensual procedure and in a collegial way), the permanent and ad hoc committees, and the small General Secretariat in Jakarta are still very limited in scope and authority and lack a credible dispute settlement procedure.

Might ASEAN progress as a political entity as well? As far as the political dimension is concerned, a curious process characterizes ASEAN. It was born as an anticommunist security community, even when the bipolar construct was less constraining and more flexible in Asia than in Europe (because of the impact of the USSR–China conflict). Furthermore, the internal divisions on security issues between neutral Indonesia, pro-UK Malaysia and Singapore, the influence of the US and bilateral conflicts between member states were some of the main factors restraining economic cooperation and regional integration. Ten years after its foundation, the Bali Summit of 1976 did essentially reconfirm the primacy of political cooperation as an attempt to defend a non-communist international identity within that turbulent area. Why has there been a change towards economic priorities since 1992? Why the surprising ASEAN revival after the hard financial crisis of the late 1990s?

Regarding post-1992, this book focuses both on internal factors (business networks) and on a changed perception of common external threats acting as a catalyst on regional cooperation, particularly the new need to react to growing international competition and liberalization. This includes the consequences of the troubled Uruguay Round, the implementation of the Single European Act, the creation of NAFTA, and so on. To increase the competitiveness of ASEAN companies became a new *raison d'être* of the regional organization. As a matter of fact, things changed very quickly in the 1990s, as shown both by consolidation and by the simultaneous ability to expand and to include former enemies, such as Vietnam, which joined in 1995, Laos and Burma in 1997, and finally Cambodia. Regarding the post-Hanoi summit (1998) and the ASEAN revival after the deepest financial crisis, namely the current dynamic evolution, the Higgott chapter provides a comprehensive explanation of both economic and political dimensions.

The consequences of the economic and financial crisis of 1997/98 on the evolution of ASEAN looked highly contradictory, at least , at the beginning: it increased inward-looking policies and, later on, there was a growing expectation of a more institutionalized intergovernmental regional framework for settling disputes and strengthening regional cooperation. As for the ability of ASEAN to survive the financial crisis of the late 1990s, the Hanoi Summit in December 1998 succeeded in launching a common anti-crisis programme and in relaunching financial cooperation with Japan. Step by step, a form of intergovernmental watchdog has appeared on the agenda of ASEAN: the Manila network of mutual surveillance could be substituted by something less vague. According to Eliassen/ Børve and Higgott, a kind of 'cognitive regionalism' could work better than the IMF monitoring and constraining system, which failed and provoked a reaction in the name of an increased sense of South-East Asian identity. A regional approach to internal adjustment has indeed been more effective than a global one. Facing common challenges helps to develop a new ASEAN awareness and a social cohesion; oscillating processes of democratization (in Indonesia, Philippines, East Timor) helps to increase and allow regional cooperation to grow. The worst case scenario is that, on the one hand, fundamentalist terrorism and, on the other hand, economic and social crisis could increase infra-regional conflicts as elsewhere in the past decades. Refugee problems between Indonesia and Malaysia, protectionist conjunctural policies, the external consequences of Indonesian forest destruction, and new domestic political instability in the Philippines and Indonesia (as shown by the Atjeh and Moluchs secession movements) could put into question the delicate balance between external and internal politics in the region. At present, economy and politics have closer links than in the past. The Action Plan 1999–2004 of December 1998 has consolidated the achieved steps of cooperation and started providing common answers to common problems: calling for foreign investments, planning infrastructures, and coordinating currency policies. The twentieth century ended with the Thailand's Foreign Minister's concepts of 'flexible engagement' and of 'strengthened interaction' among member states in a reinforced ASEAN. Could joint political will and common interests cope with the current difficult two level game and further implement the ASEAN way of regional cooperation? The main variable is the complex interaction with the unstable economic and political environment.

What has to be further underlined is that the economic dynamics towards a free trade area are also establishing a new political framework and a new security agenda, firstly, with ASEAN states' decision to discuss regional security issues at the Annual Conference. Secondly, we are witnessing the development of a promising 'concentric circles' system with the creation of 'ASEAN + Three' (APT) including China, Southern Korea and Japan. Furthermore, the meetings in 2005 and 2006 of East Asian countries entail relevant potential implications both at regional and global levels. Thirdly, with regard to security issues, it is important to mention the even wider 'ASEAN Regional Forum' (ARF), including China, Japan, South Korea, the EU, the USA, India and the main Asian-Pacific countries, which is asserting an ASEAN pivotal role, at least as a driving force. The ARF was created in 1993–94 in order to pursue and adapt, in the new international context characterized by a form of security vacuum, the original aim of stability and peace in the area. The major challenge for South-East Asian states is to place ASEAN within the framework of the evolving Asia-Pacific security triangle between the three giants, the USA, Japan and China. This attempt is proceeding quite successfully, even though ARF is still far from becoming a kind of East Asian OSCE. The ASEAN Regional Forum still is a weak structure based on consultation. However, in spite of the principle of non-intervention, something new is currently happening. Dialogue with the growing (and often feared) neighbour, China, seems to be improving. The management of this relationship to the potentially regional hegemon, the People's Republic of China, within a multilateral framework, despite its current economic transition, its nationalistic tendencies and its internal uncertainty, is a crucial issue for the regional security agenda. That is why the achievements of the Bangkok Summit of 1994 and the consequent meeting of heads of states were so important in terms of establishing confidence-building measures, preventive diplomacy, and peaceful conflict settlement. Furthermore, the normalization process with Vietnam and the renouncement by the ASEAN countries and China of the use of force as a means of addressing conflicts over territory and natural resources with regard to territorial problems and the natural resources of the Southern Chinese Sea, were important steps forward. The relationship with China and the ability to settle quarrels – a very sensitive issue in South-East Asia – are crucial for ASEAN as a regional peacekeeping organization. ASEAN member states decided, as a consequence of the harsh financial crisis, to drastically reduce their military budgets and defence programmes. The success of the ARF is particularly commendable because, for the first time in Asian–Pacific history, the economic and political competitive influence of both China and Japan is increasing simultaneously. The influence of the USA in the region is still crucial in order to push free trade, establish military cooperation, and campaign for democratization and the rule of law. However, the role of the USA in the region is likely to decline, if not as an economic power, at least as the 'first range' hegemonic power, at least in a scientific understanding (O'Brien/Clesse, 2002 and Keohane, 1984/2004).

The Hanoi Summit of 1998 was a relevant attempt of change regarding the internal obstacles to deeper integration (heterogeneity, non-intervention principle). With reference to Cambodia (traditionally a difficult issue for ASEAN in spite of its participation to the Paris Agreement of 1991), the enlargement had been postponed to 1999, because of the *coup d'etat* by Hun Sen and the divergent points of view between ASEAN countries. The return of Vietnam to regional cooperation after many years of low-profile foreign policy was a success. Not only was there increasing interference during the two main political crises of 1998/99 in Indonesia and Malaysia, but also Thailand and other MS openly proposed, on several occasions, a 'strengthened interaction' going beyond the principle of non-interference, which was typical of the Suharto era. Deeper integration and stronger institutional cooperation have been conditioned by the very heterogeneity and pre-democratic nature of almost all of the national regimes during the previous decades. This explains oscillations as far as democratization is concerned. ASEAN was, for instance, supporting Corazon Aquino's campaign in 1987, criticizing Hun Sen's *coup d'état* in Cambodia, and is pressing the Myanmar junta. However, in spite of the paradoxical post-crisis democratization wave (Indonesia, Philippines), *new regionalism does not yet entail generalized domestic democratization* (as shown also by the *coup d'etat* of 2006 in Thailand). The weight of a very diverse colonial and neocolonial past, the legacy of the Cold War, the cultural, religious, and linguistic diversity, the unique relation between state and society, are together making regional cooperation more difficult than elsewhere, even regarding common problems such as the fight against air pollution, AIDS, pirates and criminality.

In spite of such problems, economic and political regionalism is increasing in East Asia. Not only is China setting up a free trade area with ASEAN before 2015 and Japan is showing a new interest in regional cooperation after the Tokyo Declaration of 2003; but new issues are on the agenda: monetary cooperation, a ASEAN Charta. The normally sacred principle of non-intervention is starting to be questioned although no consensus yet exists on new regional post-sovereign rules. The current prudent interference in the domestic affairs of other member states is justified in the name of the huge external implications of national crises like those of Indonesia (difficult post-Suharto transition era; East-Timor crisis, and so on) or Malaysia (limited democracy, human rights, and media freedom) or Thailand. The democratization of Myanmar, though openly requested by ASEAN member states along with the EU, UN and US, is still an open issue. The European style troika created by the ASEAN Bangkok Summit of 2000 in order to face regional security problems is confronted by the mainly domestic and internal nature of challenges. Summing up, the process of building an internal problem-solving authority will be very gradual.

A more active role within the international arena was part of the huge dynamism of ASEAN during the 1980s, 1990s and into the twenty-first century. On the one hand, it participated in the APEC process and, on the other hand, in the Asia Europe Meeting (ASEM). The process leading to the ASEM was started in 1994 (Singapore project and the Karlsruhe Summit) under the convergent pressure of strategic interests and private lobbying. The question remains about similarities and dissimilarities in the expectations of both partners. ASEAN has three main goals: to achieve an improved international status, to get better access to the EU market, and to attract European investment. Why is the EU interested in taking a step forward beyond old post-colonial patterns of cooperation with developing countries to reach cooperation on an equal basis? There are two main answers: to accede economically and politically to a strategic area of the planet and to strengthen regional organizations world wide.

Both ASEAN and the EU want to complete a kind of world trade triangle (Europe, Asia, North America), diversify markets, enhance their respective bargaining power with the North Americans and, eventually, push the USA towards a global multilateral approach. The first ASEM Summit, at Head of State level, which took place in Bangkok in 1996, succeeded, as is shown by the chairman's statement and the common final document setting a regular – though informal – interregional agenda. Further summits took place in 1998 (London), 2000 (Seoul), 2002 (Copenhagen), Hanoi (2004), Helsinki (2006), plus an irrelevant ministerial meeting in Vientiane. ASEM still pays a high price for its marginal role during the financial crisis of the late 1990s. Notwithstanding the evident limits of institutionalization of a relationship called 'Meeting', both ASEAN and EU are definitely about to take the opportunity to use ASEM as one of the many instruments strengthening their international role after the end of a bipolar era, through interregional cooperation, including political dialogue. The common goals of economic and political cooperation and socio-cultural dialogue have been partly implemented through ministerial meetings, business forums, managerial and youth leader meetings and the new Europe–Asia Foundation project. Of course the 'strategic partnership' between the EU and Japan already set in the early 1990s, between EU and China (2003) and between EU and India (2004) not only are part of the comprehensive concept on interregional relations, but entail a much more relevant substance (which should push ASEAN to be more proactive).

Of course, there are still several problems to be faced which make ASEM seem a fledging organization: first of all, the EU's protectionism; secondly, the very limited people to people dialogue, the lacking inter-parliamentarian cooperation, the limits of ASEF as a framework of transnational relations at the level of civil society, which could help by changing the Asian authoritarian or post-authoritarian regimes; and thirdly, the bad souvenir of the EU's relative passivity during the financial crisis in the region. One should add that the EU wishes to legally strengthen beyond the current low level and widen the ASEM process to include more Asian countries. India is particularly interested, as due to its size and the paralysis of SAARC, it cannot be encapsulated solely within the South Asian framework. However, to include India as a full member and not only as an observer, is not an easy issue for ASEAN. The main challenge is a political one: is the EU-ASEAN relationship able to evolve towards a building block for global governance?

In conclusion, two parallel and linked trends characterize ASEAN's evolution within the current post-hegemonic world. The member states of ASEAN have been able to overcome their worst financial crisis, to enlarge the regional association to up to ten member states and to take further steps (even if they are somewhat delayed) toward a more comprehensive cooperation agenda. One of the main challenges for ASEAN is how to combine its deepening cooperation with both the concentric circles and the troubled global competitiveness. Politically, ASEAN is now focusing on stabilizing territorial integrity and order against domestic fragmentation (particularly within multi-ethnic member states), even though the East Timor crises of 1999 and 2006 confirm that ASEAN states still are reluctant to get involved in the domestic politics of a member state. Moreover, they are establishing a broader, less rigid, regional security dialogue involving the US, the EU, Australia and the two potential regional leaders, China and Japan.

Secondly, the defensive approach of ASEAN states to economic globalization is evolving toward a more strategic view on the one hand, strengthening the 'ASEAN + Three' and East Asian Summits. China is ready to multilaterally cooperate, including at regional level. Even the new role of the economic giant and technological leader Japan is beyond its previous inattention to regional policy[16] (and not limited to a mere bilateral relationship with the USA) and is likely to become a very dynamic factor. An enlarged regional cooperation process is in progress in East Asia where South-East Asia and North-East Asia are joining, both at economic and security levels (Buzan, 2003). While Japan failed to become the leader in monetary cooperation in 2000–03; however, it is a huge source of public financing and private investments, fund against poverty, and so on, for the whole area. Along with historical links and economic interests, trade tensions with the US and the repeated failures of the WTO new rounds between 2000 and 2006, help to explain the Japanese will to become a strong partner of Asian Pacific countries.

Higgott expertly shows how relevant the challenge raised by the conflicting China and Japan will of leadership is.

Coping with the relationship with China is traditionally the main issue at stake for ASEAN countries. Bringing both Japan and China within multilateral global and regional frameworks is crucial for the security of the region. Improving its relationship with the emerging economic and nuclear power and the technology giant really is salient for ASEAN, particularly because of the legacy of historical problems and the countervailing tendencies as far as the transformation of Pacific Asia in a Japan-centered region is concerned.

In spite of the weight of bilateralism and of the tripolar political structure of the region (China, Japan, US), Asian Pacific new regionalism is evolving in new ways in the wake of the local challenges and the problems that are arising within the globalized economy. Against inward-looking strategies, it is also aiming to complement trade and interregional openness with stronger, more specialized regional agreements. Even more than in the past decades, the institutional settlement of ASEAN will be a crucial factor, as it adapts to internal differentiation but also becomes strong enough to cope with domestic concerns, and, particularly, to help to bring the whole region beyond current uncertainties. Economic dynamics was the way for the old ASEAN to revive. However, to settle a regional polity and a 'regional security architecture'[17] is the challenge not only to avoid competition for resources and exacerbating disputes but particularly to compromise between ambitions of leadership.

2 MERCOSUR and the Transatlantic Triangle

Regional groupings in Latin America and particularly the Organization of American States were for decades weak and stagnant. Nevertheless, there are currently examples of vital subregional integration, namely MERCOSUR and the Andean Community.[18] MERCOSUR shows salient similarities with the EU: the customs union, the political aim and its political function of stabilizing domestic democracies of member states. These are part of a post-sovereign political culture which explains, according to many observers, its outstanding success story in such a short time.[19]

The Italian philosopher of the eighteenth century, Giambattista Vico said that the true nature of things is to be found in their birth. As MERCOSUR is concerned, its origin as a 'security community' in Karl Deutsch's words[20] is crucial in order to understand its future developments. Indeed, the first step of the current integration process between the countries of the southern cone of Latin America was a confidence-building treaty between Argentina and Brazil. The countries agreed to abandon their nuclear programmes and their previous mutually suspicious and aggressive political culture like France and Germany did at the beginning of the European construction. However, it is not an 'amalgamated' kind of security community, because national sovereignty still matters more than in Europe.

MERCOSUR is a political association. The democratic conditionality and intergovernmental political cooperation worked quite efficiently, as far as the internal adjustments of the member states were concerned. This was true for Paraguay, when General Oviedo unsuccessfully tried to return to dictatorship (1996 and during the 1999 political crisis) and in the framework of the negotiations with other Latin American states, such as Chile and Bolivia as well.[21] The next challenge is how to integrate the new member, a socialist Venezuela.

If we compare the MERCOSUR achievements with the paralysis of the SAARC because of the dramatic bilateral tension between the two nuclear powers: India and Pakistan, we can see the highly positive effects of the political variable primacy on the economic ones. These include both deepening economic and trade integration ,(common trade policy) and steps towards a political community. Reciprocally, the political dimension has been strengthened and stabilized by the tremendous success of growth in infra-regional trade, and the functional dynamics of integration, thanks to the better harmonization of the national economies.

The main difference between the EU and MERCOSUR is still the institutional settlement of the latter, which is mainly an intergovernmental body, conditioned by the hesitations of one member state, namely Brazil, regarding institutional progress in terms of supranationality. However, we are witnessing a General Secretariat in Montevideo, a permanent representatives' council and an incipient process towards a MERCOSUR parliament. The current debates on deepening integration, namely on a future single currency, macroeconomic coordination and on the powers of a court regulating juridical and economical disputes, have relevant institutional implications.

Listing the obstacles to this, one should not forget the negative weight of the internal structural imbalances between member states – the reason why many observers still consider MERCOSUR as a great Brazil. Within every member state, between *élites* and civil society, social imbalances are also important, which explains the limited support MERCOSUR currently gets from low-income social strata.[22]

As far as the international dimension of MERCOSUR is concerned the chapter by Vasconcelos focuses on the transatlantic triangle, NAFTA–EU–MERCOSUR.

This emphasizes, firstly, the weakness of one of the three sides, namely the one linking the EU and MERCOSUR and, secondly, the problems existing in the Pan-American dimension after the practical failure of the project called the Free Trade Association of the Americas, for a continental free trade area from the year 2005 onwards. The FTAA (ALCA), a common design of the Bush I and Clinton administrations, took important steps forward at the Santiago Summit of the Americas in April 1998, but the US vision of 'open regionalism' looked incompatible with the existence and further deepening of MERCOSUR. The main Latin American variable is the future strategy of the regional power, Brazil that hesitates between its tradition as a diplomatic dwarf, deeper MERCOSUR regionalism or revival of traditional Latin American discourse. The Brasilia Declaration, signed by twelve Latin American states shows Brazil's natural leadership by launching a South American Free Trade Area including MERCOSUR and the Andean Community, by criticizing the Colombia Plan financed by the US, and by wishing a reform of world financial architecture (Cardoso's opening speech). Will such a new Brazilian ambition weaken MERCOSUR? A process of cooperation is started with the

Andean Community in order to establish a common South American FTA. This project has been combined by President Lula with the idea of a large political Community of South American Nations (Cusco, December 2004). The national political cycle of the large majority of states is in favour of a more autonomous Latin America. However, cleavages between Brazil and neighbouring states are far from disappearing and the final form of the Bolivar idea of a Latino American regional integration is an open issue.

A second obvious problem is to what extent can the Euro–Latin American relationship be strengthened beyond the framework agreement of 1995, both as trade and as political ties are concerned. The relationship of the EU to MERCOSUR is often mentioned as an example of the 'Midas approach' of the EU, namely of the dream of replication of its model world wide.[23] Since the very beginning (1991), one month after the Asunción Treaty, the EU forged deep links with the Common Market of the South and in general supported regional integration in the southern part of the continent.

The bilateral agreement of 1992 has been particularly important in helping MERCOSUR to benefit from the EU's experience, as far as regional integration is concerned, by providing technical assistance to the Secretary of Montevideo (missions of the EU public servants), and by setting norms and standards. The EU Council Declarations of Lisbon (1992), Corfu and Essen (1994) explicitly supported the interregional cooperation between the EU and MERCOSUR. In 1995, the European parliament explicitly mentioned the competition between the policies of the EU and the US towards MERCOSUR. The framework agreement of 1995, a third-generation agreement, includes a democratic clause, a *clause évolutive* and a political dialogue. Its precondition is for MERCOSUR to have a legal personality. Its goal is to underline and strengthen the convergences between regional organizations within multilateral organizations. Even education and training are included as matters of regional cooperation. Foreign direct investments by European companies in MERCOSUR countries and interregional trade have dramatically increased during this decade. The EU is the first trade partner and the first foreign investor. The current situation is characterized by a twofold relationship: on the one hand, the so called comprehensive interregional 'Rio process' started in Rio de Janeiro summit of June 1999 (with the Rio Declaration) continued in Madrid (2002), Guadalajara (2004) and Vienna (2006), includes cooperation, political dialogue and fosters convergence not only on free trade but also on social issues (Vienna Declaration, 2006). It has also offered a relevant opportunity for political convergences between EU and Latin America, supporting multilateralism, even in the worst years of the transatlantic rift between the EU and the US regarding Iraq (Guadalajara Declaration, 2004) and entails several relationships: with Central American countries, with Andean Community, with Mexico, Chili and with MERCOSUR. On the other hand, we have witnessed for more than ten years the endless story of the EU-MERCOSUR negotiations for a free trade area. Both parties have responsibilities for oscillations provoking the repeated failures.[24]

Indeed, important obstacles emerged for both the inter-regional Rio process and the EU-MERCOSUR trade negotiations. These include non-tariff barriers (NTB), European agricultural interests, and the implications of ECSC and the MFA (the

Multi Fibre Agreement) as shown already by the huge bargaining difficulties before the Rio Summit and during the trade liberalization bargaining. There is no doubt that the EU has been placing its priorities elsewhere: the global multilateral trade negotiation and the partnerships with Eastern Europe, Balkan and Mediterranean countries. The Helsinki Council of December 1999 strengthened the decision to proceed to a great Eastern European enlargement of the EU within the next decades, which in general limited global policies for the following decade. On the other hand, many European countries and the European Commission underline the importance of MERCOSUR, not only as an economic partner but as a potential strategic political ally in view of a more symmetric multilateral world. The Rio process is a salient innovation under this respect: a comprehensive framework for articulated interregional relations; regular meetings to supervise the implementation of priorities; proactive cooperation in development policies; emphasis on cultural, social and educational issues; supporting regional deep integration. In this respect, this example is crucial for the EU's interregional relations, including with other continents.

The EU member states are still to some extent divided with regard to the progress of relations with MERCOSUR. On the one hand, France, while strongly supporting political alliance with MERCOSUR as part of a world-wide political 'multipolarism', brakes the implementation of a free trade agreement and provoked several mini crises. Spain, Portugal, Italy and even Germany (number one as for exports to and imports from this region) are on the European Commission's side in supporting an anti-protectionist and encompassing approach to interregional negotiations. The need to adjust to the US initiative of 1994 of creating a FTAA has been seen as a challenge, even if not by every European state. However, the FTAA, because of domestic troubles, and a lack of Latino American enthusiasm, is largely over and US are setting bilateral trade relations.

To conclude, MERCOSUR and other Latin American sub-regional groupings, such as the Andean Community, are at a crossroads. Either they will go on deepening (macroeconomic coordination) and strengthening their political dimension (institutional settlement, democracy and protection of human rights, security, and international political dialogue), or they risk being less relevant than national competition policies. The EU and MERCOSUR strategy linking the advancement of interregional negotiations of sensitive subjects between the EU and MERCOSUR with the progress of the Doha Round is becoming worse than problematic because of the uncertainties of the WTO. All in all, after the strengthening global uncertainties, multilateralism, new regionalism, and interregionalism have been challenged as far as this area is concerned. Both regional organizations, the EU and MERCOSUR, are adjusting their strategies: could bilateral interregionalism substitute for a while global liberalization, without being in conflict with it, as a way to more balanced global governance? Of course, if the future confirms that the US commitment to liberalization meets growing domestic obstacles, most probably, the interregional dialogue between the EU and MERCOSUR will be directly fostered.

According to Vasconcelos, it is possible to foresee an evolution of transatlantic relations at the beginning of the twenty-first century. A third strategic scenario is likely to emerge between that based on the hard political 'multipolarism' concept proposed by French President Chirac, and the other one, the declining US vision of the world combining unilateralism, bilateralism and the steps towards interregional FTAs: a less asymmetric transatlantic triangle as a substantive component of a new multilateral world governance. The strengthening of interregional EU–MERCOSUR cooperation is one of the main pillars of such an alternative, a way to combine deeper regionalism, interregional negotiations, and new multilateralism, thanks to common interests, cultural affinities and the emerging shared vision of new multilateralism.

Strategic choices are urgent. The EU and MERCOSUR have shown their political interest in interregional cooperation, as proven by the process started in the late 1990s and continued in spite of obstacles and oscillations for almost ten years. Even if affected by national inward-looking interests, both regional organizations are reacting to the malaise of globalization and the failures of unilateralism in a constructive way, by deepening regional integration and interregional dialogue.[25] However, the current uncertainty depends on the US, but also on the EU options and on MERCOSUR states options.

3   Developing NAFTA: The US between unilateralism, regionalism and multilateralism

It is a controversial issue amongst international scholars whether the US had a long-term interest or not in regionalism and NAFTA.[26]. Many domestic political streams, lobbying and economic interest coalitions have been in conflict for years over a free trade agreement with Canada and later on with Mexico. The very crucial facts are that this agreement was only finalized in the 1990s, after the Uruguay Round and the revival of European integration and that it, more than a decade after its foundation, looks able to survive the troubles of the declining FTAA. Regarding its origins, the weight of the negative US perception of the Single European Act, the doubts provoked by the image of 'the European Fortress, and the willingness to react through a Northern American regionalist policy must be taken into account.

The US decision to sign and implement a Free Trade Agreement with Canada (1989) and to extend it to Mexico (1994) opens, according to A. Sbragia, 'a new chapter in American foreign economic policy'. It raises the question: why such a new referential trade area should appear along regional lines, in spite of a symbiotic relationship between European and American companies and the Atlantic Alliance?

Firstly, after the end of the Cold War, the US could decouple security and economy. Two economic regionalisms on both sides of the Atlantic would not in themselves undermine the troubled transatlantic community strengthened by the 'New Transatlantic Agenda',[27], the (uncertain) revival of NATO and the EU-US dialogue in order to create a free trade area and weakened by different geo-political interests and perceptions. However, the internal rift that emerged during the Iraqi War confirms that more than a decade after its foundation, NAFTA has no political underpinning, as yet, as the EU, ASEAN or MERCOSUR have.

Is NAFTA nothing more than a step towards FTAA? The Miami Conference of 1994 and the Santiago summit of the Americas of 1998 did set up a detailed schedule for a Free Trade Area of the Americas, namely a greater NAFTA that is a continental liberalization process. During the Bush 2 administration, even before 9/11 (see the Quebec meeting of spring 2001), the US regional option took the meaning of a regional way of combining the dream of a FTAA with a political dimension, including the critical approach to the EU presence in Latin America as a not marginal factor.

Coming back to the internal problems of the ongoing NAFTA, the current free trade agreement with the poor Mexico and the rich Canada already emphasizes the problem of huge asymmetries in regional arrangements as far as the US is included. NAFTA is particularly asymmetric and the institutional capacity is so weak that asymmetries are not counterbalanced enough. Last but not least, the bipartisan US consensus in rejecting the Mexican President V. Fox's proposals for a deeper NAFTA clearly shows the very political limits of US regionalism.

As for the institutional features, the comparison with the EU shows not only a very long list of differences but an alternative model. However, some similarities do exist and they go beyond simple free trade. Sbragia's chapter underlines three of the main distinctive and interesting features: the Commission for Environmental Cooperation; the Commission for Labor Issues and the institutionalization of dispute settlements. International literature does agree that 'the selection of an effective mechanism for resolving commercial disputes is fundamental to generate compliance with these mechanisms by parties to preferential trade agreements'.[28] Functional arguments might explain this increasing institutionalization (compared for instance with ASEAN). However, the establishment of such a dispute settlement mechanism is not deepening the integration process amongst the three countries.

In conclusion, though it can be classified as a modest and soft regional agreement, NAFTA goes further than GATT-WTO, it also includes some important foundational norms, which constitute a *de facto* protection, as in the EU. The regionalist choice of the US is very important at the international level, given the amount of Northern American trade, which represents, just like the EU, some 20 per cent of world trade.

As far as the future is concerned, NAFTA is far from being over. Both strategic options and the uncertainties of the global multilateral trade agenda are pushing the US either to more protectionist and inward looking policies or to a strengthening of its own regional alliances, using them to influence trade globalization world wide. In the first case scenario, Mexico and Canada will no longer be able to resist the temptation of achieving deeper trade deals with the EU and with Latin American countries, independently from the US.

4 African regionalism and the Southern African Development Community (SADC)

Like several Latin American and other regional or subregional arrangements, African regionalism is very poor with regard to its achievements, as proven by the rhetoric of the African Union and by the other subregional organizations' inability to regulate the numerous current (around fifteen) military conflicts within the continent. *Longue durée* explanations are specially adapted to cope with the failures of African regionalism, including economic underdevelopment, weakness of states, various consequences of the colonial and neocolonial legacies, division between different metropolitan references, and problems of border conflicts.

However, the controversial regionalist experience started in the 1980s provides an extremely interesting array of variations, success and failures, as is shown by the F. Söderbaum chapter. According to the Lagos Action Plan approved by the OAU summit of 1980, an African strategy has been implemented with the aim of diminishing dependence on the outside. It also aimed to increase African autonomous development through five projects of enhanced and open, rather than protectionist-oriented regional cooperation. These are: the Economic Community of Central African States (CEEAC, founded in 1983), the Preferential Trade Area (1981), changed in 1994 to the Common Market of Eastern and Southern Africa (COMESA), the Arabian Maghreb Union in Northern Africa (AMU, in 1989) and the pre-existing ECOWAS in Western Africa. The SADCC was created in 1980 by the 'Front Line States' in order to increase the isolation of the apartheid regimes of South Africa and Namibia. In 1981, the Berg Report for the Organization of African Unity criticized the last illusion of African self-sufficiency and pointed out that priority should be given to a break with a state-led economy and the illusion of alternative development strategies. It also inaugurated the new era of gradual economic (and, later on, even political) liberalization, which really matured with the end of Soviet communism and its influence in Africa.[29] Global imperatives and structural adjustment programmes inspired by the IMF and World Bank prevailed during the 1980s and 1990s and regional cooperation became marginal. However, globalization and the disintegration of states and societies are inextricably linked in many African countries, leading to a deterioration of traditional problems, including huge external debt, increasing poverty, and ethnic and border conflicts.

Beyond such negative experience and historical obstacles to successful regionalist cooperation, there appears a basic weakness: the structure of demand and production is too similar to generate substantial trade creation.[30] The huge problem for African regional agreements is to be able to cope with both a very low level of economic development (as for industry, technology, productivity, infrastructures, services, and skilled labour) and with a dramatic and broadly diffused fragmentation of political systems.

Nevertheless, regionalism has increased in Southern (SADC[31]) as well as in Western Africa (ECOWAS[32]), as a result of two main exogenous factors: the growing fear of African marginalization in the new international environment, characterized by the two parallel trends towards globalization and regional blocs, and the growing external pressure by the international community and particularly by the European Union's development policy.

The awareness of the first factor is increasing. The long-term plan approved at the Summit of the Organization for African Union at Abuja (Nigeria) of 1991, can be seen as the background to the current new wave of regional integration, at least at the level of rhetoric from heads of states. These include decreasing tariff barriers, building free exchange areas and customs unions, and strengthening sectorial integration, before 2025, towards an explicit emulation of the EU, the EMU and the political union.

Regional arrangements within the southern part of the continent appear to be an interesting case study, particularly after the end of the apartheid regime. Indeed the Southern African Development Coordination Conference (SADCC) became the current SADC (Southern African Development Community) with the signing of the Windhoek Treaty of 1992. The dynamics of the industrial economy of South Africa allows the neighbouring countries to increase infra-regional trade, beyond the mere political priority of the previous anti-apartheid organization. SADC is currently trying to maintain the difficult balance between national adjustment and global competition, regional cooperation, and decreasing international aid. This is characterized by many surrounding regional organizations, with partly overlapping memberships. Namibia is the only member of them all: the Community of Eastern and Southern Africa (nine members); the Southern African Customs Union (five Member States, started in 1910); the Common Monetary Area (four members); and the Cross-Border Initiative (seven members).

SADC shares huge internal asymmetries with other regional organizations. Since the 1994 enlargement, South Africa represents around 70 per cent of SADC's GDP (and 20 per cent of the population), but is not yet able – because of urgent domestic problems – to play the role of regional aid provider and big economic engine. The Democratic Republic of Congo, one of the poorest member states with the largest population, joined in 1998. The GNP per capita of the richest member state (Mauritius) is eighteen times higher than in the poorest one, Mozambique. The divergences on macroeconomic policy are very important.

From Africa's point of view, the last decades of globalization made asymmetries worse within the world economy. The share of sub-Saharan Africa's total net long-term resource flows decreased dramatically, particularly if compared with the increasing share to East/Asia Pacific and Latin American/Caribbean regions. With 3 per cent of the world's population, SADC represents 1 per cent of the world's GDP and 1 per cent of the world global exports. For some years, either according to the rules of the WTO, or through aid-supported structural adjustment programmes, trade liberalization has been progressing. In spite of huge implementation problems, in 1996 SADC approved a protocol calling for the gradual establishment of a SADC Free Trade Area as a means of achieving a significant increase in infra-regional trade, foreign investment, and rate of economic growth. Observers point out how important complementary policies are (education, health, political stability, institutions, infrastructures and so on) to give a country a chance to increase growth and to reduce the destabilizing effects the more closed economies inevitably face.

By comparing SADC and the EU in terms of convergence measures among member states, one can come to the conclusion that in thirty years (1960–90) SADC countries did not reach any convergence at all (per capita incomes). While within the smaller hard core formed by the SACU (Customs Union, South Africa + Four member states) the dispersion of per capita incomes dropped more than half, exceeding the convergence rate realized by the EU countries in the same period. Free trade, currency union, transfers from South Africa, and similar macroeconomic policies did achieve convergence. Deep regional integration looks likely to be the way forward. The question is whether an extension of such convergence factors to all of the members of SADC could allow dispersion to drop and catch-up convergence, including the less developed countries. Such an extension might occur with mutual benefits for both South Africa and other member states. A regional development fund, the development of sectorial coordinated regional activities and more consistent macroeconomic policies is vital to the FTA's establishment.

However, optimistic visions are tempered by the limited results and by some general caveats. The consequences of the huge internal asymmetry are the dominance of South Africa and its interest in fighting the temptation to create a regional trade bloc (on the contrary, regional integration is seen as an alternative to global liberalization by other member states), searching for larger trade partners beyond the SADC, and setting a free trade agreement with the EU, at least in principle implemented from 2000. Such varied and controversial agendas regarding the correspondence between regionalism, bilateralism and globalization are aggravated by political tensions, as demonstrated during the Zaire–Democratic Republic of Congo crisis in 1998/2000. In fact, as a consequence of the divergent appreciation of the Kabila regime, we are currently witnessing the growing and controversial both economic and political leadership of South Africa. Such political problems do undermine the fragile regionalist integration process in Southern Africa and can stop infra-regional trade liberalization issues.

The multiple uncertainties and internal weaknesses of African regional arrangements do enhance the weight of the external factors, namely the impulse coming from the EU.[33] In spite of traditional Pan-Africanism and of various forms of 'shadow regionalization'(Söderbaum), Africa is a part of the world where the balance between the domestic factors of regionalism and external pressures is in favour of the latter. That is one reason why the success and failures of the EU's policies are also interesting from a comparative point of view. The EU African policy is implemented (at least until the new EU-Africa summit at the end of 2007) in the framework of the Kotonou Convention of 2000,[34] the fifth stage of the Lomé process (convention between the EU and the African, Caribbean and Pacific countries, ACP) which started in the 1960s.[35] In spite of its growing importance as far as its scope and complexity are concerned, the Lomé process is generally not considered a success story. Some causes of the failures in increasing ACP countries' exports are linked to the global economy, price trends, and liberalization, resulting in diminishing the relative advantages of ACP. However, the stage of Lomé 5 provides opportunities for some innovative even if controversial guidelines: the special trade relationship between European countries and the seventy-one ACP partners will get, even if gradually, more in tune with the WTO rules and restrict the preferential regime. On the other hand, the problematic conditionality criteria have been gradually strengthened. They now take into account the shortcomings of the past conventions and stress the peculiarities of the EU external policy. Firstly, in keeping with the IMF and the World Bank, European aid will be linked to progress in macroeconomic performance, in adjustment policies and in improvements to the productive capacities of ACP countries. Secondly, progress in fighting against poverty, good governance, and in respect of human rights has been set as fundamental criteria.[36] Thirdly, it is particularly interesting to see how an existing long-term trend was strengthened to make a model out of interregional cooperation with Africa and ACP countries for the integrationist approach of EU external relations. An essential part of the convention is focused on complementing trade and aid by including explicit support for regional cooperation.[37] Free trade partnership with the EU will only be further developed within the next decade under the precondition that regional groupings are already set up among ACP countries. The open question is whether such a new conditionality is able to improve the implementation of cooperation policies and correct the current decreasing competitiveness, broad corruption, and increasing poverty in Africa or not. In several cases it raises a feeling of an unacceptable and useless external pressure, as the Söderbaum chapter argues. Ultimately, there are some doubts about the consistency between a Euro-centered African regionalism, even if formally allowed by WTO, and, on the other hand, the global economy, namely the economic adjustments requested by international markets and the IMF.

5 Regionalization and deep integration

By comparative analysis of regionalism, this book tries to go beyond the vague and quite ideological concept of open regionalism, opposed to the notion of new mercantilism and protectionism.[38] We classify the first aforesaid three forms of regional agreements (economic association, societal intergovernmental fora, free trade areas and cooperation) as soft regionalism, while the latter three illustrate various forms of deeper regionalism (customs union, common market and policies coordination, full integration and political union). Practical experiences often overlap and borders between soft and deep regionalism are not always clear, never definite or final, for example, as far as the conflict settlement mechanisms are concerned. However, whereas NAFTA is the main example of a 'FTA understanding of regional association' and SAARC shows itself to be a mere forum, we classify the EU and MERCOSUR as 'deep integration', including the cognitive dimension of regional awareness and stress on common identity as well. ASEAN, SADC and Andean Community, not only by their political origin and development, also show many dynamics beyond mere soft regional grouping. The latter two also include other important features, respectively, monetary union as a hard core, and a relatively complex institutional settlement. ASEAN offers an alternative way in the making, namely to the sequencing between monetary deepening and trade integration.

In conclusion, deeper regionalism gradually gives birth to *negotiated and rule-based political space* (not yet necessarily democratic but under the influence of the external and internal democratization waves) going beyond the mere functional model, and including confidence-building measures, common rules, policies and procedures, various paths to institutionalization, and political dialogue or cooperation. It often includes security regimes, regarding member states and applicants as well, for example, Germany and neighbours; Spain and Portugal; Italy and Austria; Hungary and Rumania; Hungary and Slovakia; Greece and Turkey; Brazil and neighbours; South Africa and neighbours; Ecuador and Peru;

and Indonesia and Malaysia. Economic cooperation and political dialogue help by overcoming border conflicts and minority problems only if no major bilateral political tension exists (as in the case of SAARC). Deepening regional cooperation does not necessarily entail a multipolar balance of power and an exclusive civilization identity either. The question is whether it can increase multilateralism instead of bilateralism within and outside the region; create common interests and a new understanding of national interest; enhance economic convergence instead of divergence, and encourage peaceful settlement of existing border conflicts. These questions and answers are salient for the development of the political theory, as a gradual revision of the state-centric Westphalian paradigm.

This book stresses how salient the comparison with the European experience is when studying new regionalism. Even if unique and not exportable elsewhere, the European case study is considered as a relevant reference: many regional arrangements have been created in order to emulate the EC–EU or to react to the success story of the EU. Secondly, the EU as a global actor in the making establishes partnerships at world level and supports new regionalism in Latin America, Africa and Asia, both by institutional policies and private networking. We will deepen the following question in the next sections of the present book: to what extent the future of new regionalism, even if not depending on EU, is in various ways linked to the evolving European regional integration/cooperation.

Notes

1   W. Wallace (1994).
2   Edited by Union of International Associations, published by K. G. Saur, München, New York, London and Paris. See the analysis of empirical data provided by Paul Taylor (1993), pp. 24–46.
3   B. Balassa, 'The Theory of Economic Integration: an Introduction', in B. Balassa (1961).
4   Leon N. Lindberg (1963) 'Political Integration: Definition and Hypotheses', in *The Political Dynamics of European Economic Integration*, Stanford University Press.
5   J. M. Grieco, 'Systemic Sources of Variation in Regional Institutionalization in Western Europe, East Asia and the Americas', in E. D. Mansfield and H. V. Milner (1997), pp. 164–86 and S. Haggard, (1997) J. Grieco explains the European exceptionalism by the absence of stable distribution of capabilities and bargaining power of member states.
6   E. D. Mansfield and H.V. Milner (1997), p.18.
7   Grieco's appreciation is that it is neither necessary nor sufficient. See Mansfield and Milner (1997), pp.10–11.
8   ASEAN was created in 1967 by five countries (Indonesia, Malaysia, Singapore, Thailand, the Philippines, joined by Brunei in 1984) in the international environment characterized by the Vietnam War and the fears of a communist expansion in the region (see the Bangkok Declaration). The political aspect dominated the first decades of the organization, as shown by the Bali Declaration of 1976. It was only in 1992, after the end of the Cold War, that the fourth ASEAN summit (see the Singapore Declaration) approved the Framework Agreement on enhancing ASEAN economic cooperation focusing on the project of an ASEAN Free Trade Area before 2002 for six countries, and 2007 for the others. See R. A. Scalapino, S. Sato, J. Wanadi and S. -J. Han, eds.

(1998), *Asian Security Issues: Regional and Global*, University of California, Berkeley; Rosemarie Foot, 'Pacific Asia: The Development of Regional Dialogue', in Fawcett and Hurrell, ed. (1995). pp.228–49; G. Segal (1990), *Rethinking the Pacific*, Oxford University Press, Oxford; M. Leifer (1989), *ASEAN and the Security of South-East Asia*, Routledge, London; C. McIness and M. G. Rolls eds. (1994), *Post Cold War Security Issues in the Asia-Pacific Region*, Frank Cass, London; Garnaut and Drysdale, eds. (1994), *Asia Pacific Regionalism, Readings in International Economic Relations* Harper, Pymble, Australia; K. Clements, ed. (1993), *Peace and Security in the Asia Pacific Region*, UN, Tokyo.

9 Unfortunately we do not have the space here to go into detail on the hard regional security challenges: from North-East Asia to South-East Asia, without forgetting the turbulent China–Russia relationship and the uncertain normalization between Japan and the People's Republic of China, the issue of Taiwan, and relations between India and China. See D. A. Lake and P. M. Morgan (1997), particularly the Asian chapters by S. L. Shirk and Y. Foong Khong.

10 It was born at the Dakka Summit of 1985 following the Bangladesh proposal of 1980. The Institutions of SAARC: the Council of Ministers, the Standing Committee of Foreign Secretaries, the Standing Committees, the Technical Committees (for example concerning agricultural policy), the Committee on Economic Cooperation, the SAARC secretariat of Katmandu and the Documentation Center in New Delhi. See Kant K. Bhargava (1998), *EU-SAARC: Comparisons and Prospects for Cooperation*, ZEI Discussion papers, Bonn. I express my thanks to Prof. P. Battacharaya (University. of Calcutta) and to Fr. Giri (ISS, New Delhi) for their stimulating observations on this topic.

11 The breakdown of the Soviet Union, on the one hand, drastically limits the external component of the South-Asian crisis and, on the other hand, pushes India to a new dialogue with the USA. One should never forget the impact of the 1962 war with China and its consequences (the partial occupation of Kashmir) as far as India's feelings of insecurity are concerned. In the case of Pakistan, the solidarity of the Muslim international community and of fundamentalism can play a more relevant role. With the exception of some UN conferences (on poverty for example) the common external challenges do not yet bring the SAARC countries together.

12 See the Memorandum of 1996: according to the concept of partnership for development, SAARC can benefit from technical and financial assistance from the EU (on the basis of the 443/92) for the purpose of strengthening regional institutions, infra-regional trade, supporting joint policies among developing countries, networking and communications, research, training, and rural and energy policies. Interregional cooperation between the EU and SAARC already goes beyond previous policies of aid to developing countries: partner countries are helped by adjusting their economies to global competition and expanding trade, but also by building safety networks against social exclusion. The SAARC business networks are increasingly active, including biregional dialogue.

13 The APEC (Asia-Pacific Economic Cooperation Forum) was initiated in 1988 and includes, since 1994, government representatives of eighteen states and entities of the many rims of the Pacific Ocean region: USA, Canada, New Zealand, Australia, the ASEAN countries, Japan, South Korea and China; and also Hong Kong and Taiwan. Mexico, Papua New Guinea joined in 1993. Chile followed and Russia joined three years later. R. Higgott, (1995), S. Haggard, 'Regionalism in Asia and the Americas', in Mansfield and Milner, eds. (1997), pp.43–9 and R. Garnaut and P. Drysdale (1994), J. Rüland, ASEAN and the Asian crisis. Theoretical Implications and Practical Consequences, in '*Pacific review*',vol. 13, no.3, pp.421–52. Stubbs, Richard (2002)

'ASEAN + Three: Emerging East Asian Regionalism' *Asian Survey*, 42 (3) 2002: 440–55. Stubbs, Richard (2005) *Rethinking Asia's Economic Miracle: War, Prosperity and Crisis*. Basingstoke: Palgrave, Beeson, Mark, (2005) 'Rethinking Regionalism: Europe and East Asia in Comparative historical Perspective', *European Journal of Public Policy*, 12 (6): 969–85.

14 Or at least, that portion of deep integration agenda which is in the Americas' interest (S. Haggard, p.46) namely building dispute settlement mechanisms.

15 EFTA was founded in 1960 by the European countries rejecting the pattern of supranational integration characterizing the Rome Treaties of 1957 solely in the name of a free trade area (UK, Scandinavian countries, Austria, Switzerland, Liechtenstein). All but Norway, Switzerland, Liechtenstein and Iceland joined the EC and the EU between 1973 and 1995.

16 Foot p.239. As the Higgott chapter points out, East Asian regionalism is moving forward in somehow unexpected ways , which entails theoretical implications. In spite of the first abortive attempt to create an Asian IMF and the remaining closed domestic market (included labour market), Japan is currently coming back to the Asian Pacific region, which is due to be its largest export market, above the American one. For instance, Japan is pushing ahead with a $30 billion Asia Fund to provide low cost loans. As a consequence, even the theoretical issue of a possible common currency has been discussed at the Forum of the Thirteen Countries in Manila in November 1999 where, among others, China's application for membership in the WTO was supported both by ASEAN and by Japan. The ASEAN + Three (APT) and the East Asian summit of 2005 enhanced this highly relevant stream (see B. Fort and D. Webber, eds., Regional Integration in East Asia and Europe, Routledge, London, 2006).

17 Tony Tan (Defence Minister, Singapore), 'Steps for Asia-Pacific security', speech at the Asian Security Conference, Singapore, 17 January 2000. Regarding the gradual merging of the North-East-Asia security complex with South East Asia security complex, see B. Buzan, *Regions and Powers*, Cambridge, University Press, 2003 and D. Lake & P. Morgan (eds.) *Regional Orders*, Pennyilvania University Press, 1997.

18 The Andean Community (since 1997 – the Cartagena Agreement – subsequent to the Andean Pact created in 1969), including Venezuela, Colombia, Ecuador, Peru, and Bolivia, shows a remarkable overdeveloped institutional settlement (an Andean Tribunal for internal disputes, a monetary fund, a customs union – including only Venezuela, Ecuador and Bolivia – Presidential Council, Council of Foreign Ministers, a General Secretariat located in Lima). Only since 1990 has infra-regional trade significantly increased up to 14 per cent. See H. M. Lira (1999), *30 anos de Integracion Andina*, Comunidad Andina, Lima, and E. M. Jimenez (1999), *La relaciones externas de la Comunidad Andina*, Comunidad Andina, Lima.

19 When signing the Asuncion Treaty of 26 March 1991, Argentina, Brazil, Paraguay and Uruguay decided to set up MERCOSUR. It would not formally come into being until 1 January 1995 as a semi-complete free trade area (95 per cent of intra-regional trade is free of customs duties) and as an incomplete customs union (external common tariff covers about 85 per cent of the bloc's products exported to non-member states). Total free trade area and customs union were originally scheduled for 1999/2000 and 2006. However, the financial crisis of 1998/99 caused significant delay. See Haggard, pp.20–48.

20 K. Deutsch, S. Burrell, R. A. Kann, (1957).

21 L. Whitehead (1996), *The International Dimensions of Democratization. Europe and Americas*, Oxford: Oxford University Press, P. Smith, ed. (1995) *Latin America in Comparative Perspective*, Boulder: Westview Press.

22 Grandi, J, Le MERCOSUR en période de transition: évaluation et perspectives in Bibes, *Problèmes d'Amérique latine*, op. cit., p. 80. E. Martinez, Institutional Dynamics and Political Dimension of Europe-Latin America Partnership facing the FTAA Process, draft paper, RCEU/IPSA, Brussels, XII, 1999. R. Bouzas (ed.), *Domestic Determinants of National Trade Strategies. A comparative analysis of Mercosur countries, Mexico and Chile*, Paris, Sc.Po. Chaire Mercosur, 2006.

23 European Council, *Conclusions*, Lisbon, 26/27 June 1992, p. 24. European Commission, *Appui de la Communauté européenne aux efforts d'intégration économique régionale des pays en développement*, Bruxelles, COM (1995) 219 final. Report of the European Commission and World Bank Seminar, *Regionalism and Development*, Bruxelles, 2 June 1998. Communication de la Commission au Conseil, au Parlement européen et au Comité économique et social, *Un nouveau partenariat Union européenne/Amérique latine à l'aube du XXIème siècle*, COM, 105 final, 9 mars 1999, p. 7.

24 J. Dauster (1998), MERCOSUR and the European Union: prospects for an Interregional Association, in *European Foreign Affairs Review*, 3, pp. 447–49 and the papers presented by G. Fonseca; C. Lafer, J. Gama, D. Opertti, M. Soares, R. Lavagna, F. Pena; L. Lampreia, P. Wrobel, R. Altenfelder, A. Valladao, V. Thorstensen, A. Van Klaveren and A. Vasconcelos at the 6th Euro-Latin-American Forum, held under the initiative of the Instituto estudios Estrategicos Internacionais, Lisbon (Lisbon, 25/26 February 2000).

25 The 1999 new programme Avanza MERCOSUR (ahead with MERCOSUR) includes new cooperation in the fields of transports, energy, communications, and the search for foreign investments. In November 1999, according to the *International Herald Tribune*, President Cardoso stated that the WTO's failure in Seattle 'showed how much we have to win by strengthening our ties within MERCOSUR', including a coordinated monetary policy, controls on the cross-border flows of money and a common currency, infra-continental negotiations with Chile and the Andean Community and interregional negotiations with the EU. Members of the Argentinean and Brazilian governments support the idea of a Latin American Maastricht Treaty, refounding the association beyond the imbalances provoked by the Brazilian Real's devaluation of early 1999.

26 'Short term' interpretations underline pressures on Uruguay Round for concluding in 1994.

27 Within the political general framework of NTA (1995, including cooperation for trade, global challenges and peace) the Transatlantic Marketplace (TMP) and a set of Mutual Recognition Agreements (MRA) have been established since 1996, while the exclusive inter-regional proposal for a Transatlantic Free trade Area (TAFTA) failed because it was seen by the EU as an attempt to relegate it to one of the many US inter-regional free trade partnerships (APEC, FTAA, and so on). However, the limited scope of MRAs is to prevent regulations (social, environmental and safety standards) from acting as non-tariff barriers to trade and investment, especially in high tech sectors. A complementary private initiative was the Transatlantic Business Dialogue (TABD). In 1988, in spite of increasing controversial issues (bilateral trade quarrels, D'Amato and Helm-Burton Laws and so on) a compromise solution has been reached in Birmingham.

28 Mansfield and Milner (1997), p.16 and the article by Yarbrough & Yarbrough, Dispute Settlements in International Trade: Regionalism and Procedural Coordination, ivi, pp. 134–62.

29 See F. J. Cardoso (1997). On this topic, Jaguaribe H. Vasconcelos, A. (eds.), *The European union, MERCOSUL and the New World Order*, Cass, London, 2003.

30 The external trade of African countries is mainly (80–85 per cent) oriented to non-African countries.

31 Started in 1980, by Tanzania, Botswana, Lesotho, Zambia, Mozambique, Angola and, later, Zimbabwe, and currently includes fourteen member states. The institutional settlement is intergovernmental: Summits of Heads of States, Councils of Ministers, sectorial Commissions and Coordinating Units led by specific member states and the Secretariat located in Botswana. Söderbaum, Fredrik (1995) *Handbook of Regional Organizations in Africa*, Uppsala: Nordiska Afrikainstitutet.; Söderbaum, Fredrik, (2004a) *The Political Economy of Regionalism. The Case of Southern Africa*, Basingstoke: Palgrave Macmillan.

32 The Economic Union of Western African States – CEDEAO in French – founded in 1975, includes French-speaking countries (belonging to the economic and monetary union UEMOA, based on the Franc CFA), English-speaking and Portuguese-speaking West African countries as well. The intra-regional trade is still very weak. On the contrary, political and security cooperation is progressing, as shown by the ECOWAS Monitoring Group, a regional military organization which can intervene (with ambivalent effects) in peacekeeping missions within the region (as it did in Liberia and Sierra Leone).

33 The European aid, though remaining the most important from North to South (14.6 billion Euros from 2000 to 2004), decreased to 50% from the amount of 10 years ago. The imports from ACP to EU decreased in 20 years from 6.7% in 1976 to 3.4% in 1997.

34 The European Fund for Development (for 2001–2006) has been fixed at a level comparable with the past budget: 13.5 billion Euro, while the previous 12.9 billion Euro. Moreover, one should add 1.7 billion Euro of loans from the European Investment Bank and also several billion Euro (around 9) remaining from previous funds.

35 The development policy of the EC and EU, already included – under pressure from France – in the Treaty of Rome (part four, art 177–181, ex–130) as complementary to the policies of member states, has the following goals: a) economic and social development; b) aid for developing countries' access to the global economy; c) fight against poverty; d) consolidation of democracy and the rule of law; e) and consistency with the UN's and international organizations' commitments. The Association's policy towards non-European countries and former colonies (art. 182–188, ex 131–136) adds the purpose of establishing 'close economic relations between them and the Community as a whole'. The art. 132.2 stresses that associated countries must apply the same trade conditions they apply to the former European colonial power in their trade with each other (and not only for all the EU member states). That means that increasing infra-regional trade among developing countries is one of the EC–EU's goals since the 1950s. The Treaty plans to abolish all customs duties on imports from associated countries in no reciprocal way, the EC/EU contributes to investments, creates a European Development Fund, channels aids by member states, administered by the European Commission (extra budget). This legal background makes the two Yaoundé conventions (1963 and 1968, see *Dictionnaire du Marché commun*, Paris, July, 1968, vol. 3) and the Lomé convention (1975) particularly stable and oriented towards the long term. The more encompassing perspective of the Lomé convention is due, on the one hand, to the impulses of British enlargement (increasing the numbers of partners to 46) and to the influence of the visions of a new economic international order and the opening of Western markets (generalized system of preferences, GSP), particularly asserted by the UN and also by the new German Chancellor W. Brandt, a champion of North–South dialogue. Even if controversial in their achievements, the Lomé conventions were, and remain, a new kind of cooperation between developed countries and 40% of the entire membership of the UN. Africa covers 90% of the population and the economy of ACP countries. The first Lomé convention (1976–1980) has been followed by Lomé II (1980–1984),

Lomé III (1985–1989) and by Lomé IV (1990–1999). The main features of the previous conventions were maintained: the central role of the supranational Commission by negotiating and managing cooperation (a comprehensive cooperation concept, including social, economic and cultural dimensions), ACP exports' duty-free access to the EC market (the agricultural products covered by Common Agricultural Policy, were a great obstacle) without reciprocal obligation, and emphasis on – at least formally – equitable and institutionalized relationship. The importance of the development policy of EC-EU has been substantially strengthened by improving trade agreements (even beyond the GSP) and, by increasing the scope of financial and technical assistance 'to represent the world's biggest institutionalized link between the developed and developing worlds, worth 46. 5 billion in European Development Fund aid (including EIB loans) from 1958 to 1999' (C. Piening, 1997, p. 176). During the same period the global development cooperation policy of the EC-EU evolved significantly, to include countries like India and Pakistan and others, which do not belong to the ACP conventions. The budget has gradually increased over the years and adjusted with a view to helping, in a more appropriate way, the poorest countries and including social and environmental goals. See also G. Edwards and E. Regelsberger, eds. (1990), particularly the chapter on The Lomé Convention. A Model for Partnership, by O. Schmuck. And M. Lister (1998) *The European Community and the Developing World: the Role of the Lomé Convention*, Aldershot: Avebury.

36 K. Arts (2000), *Integrating Human Rights into Development Cooperation: the Case of Lomé Convention*, Vrije Universitat Amsterdam, 2000, particularly chapter 5 on historical developments, chapter 7 on the positive approach to human rights protection, and 8 on the negative approach (sanctions).

37 Already within the previous (IV) Lomé convention (1990–2000) the European Development Fund linked almost 10% of its funding to regional cooperation (the so-called 'Programmes Indicatifs Régionaux') in order to support infrastructures, communications, transport and telecommunications likely to increase multilateralism on a regional basis. Regarding the impact of Washington consensus, see: Söderbaum, Fredrik (2004b) 'Modes of Regional Governance in Africa: Neoliberalism, Sovereignty-boosting and Shadow Networks', *Global Governance: A Review of Multilateralism and International Organizations*, 10 (4): 419–36.

38 F. Bergsten (1997) and R. Lawrence (1996).

Chapter 7

European Union and NAFTA

Alberta M. Sbragia

1 Introduction

As the European Union (EU) continued to forge ahead in fashioning ever more integrative relationships and institutions in the 1990s, its transatlantic interlocutor began to construct a set of new relationships which represented a break with its past. While the Maastricht Treaty, agreed to in December 1991, could be seen as one more step in the institution-building process which had begun with French foreign minister Robert Schuman's famous press conference on 9 May 1950, the American government's decision to negotiate a free trade agreement with Canada and, more dramatically, with Mexico cannot be viewed in such an evolutionary fashion. Although it would be erroneous to see the creation of NAVI'A as analogous to the creation of the European Coal and Steel Community or the subsequent European Economic Community, there is no doubt that the United States has significantly changed its foreign policy in the area of international cooperation.

The coming into force of the US–Canada Free Trade Agreement (CFTA) in 1989 opened a new chapter in American foreign economic policy. Once the bulwark of multilateralism and a staunch supporter of multilateral rather than regional initiatives, the United States committed itself to a free trade area with its wealthy northern neighbour. Even more significantly, in 1994 it agreed to extend that free trade area to its poor southern neighbour. Thus was born NAFTA, the North American Free Trade Area. NAFTA represented an important break with not only the American but also the Mexican past. In fact, the relationship between Mexico and the United States (to which, in the Mexican–American War of 1846–48, Mexico had lost the huge territory now known as the American Southwest) historically had been so tense that the president of Mexico turned to the United States only after having been rebuffed by both European and Japanese leaders in early 1990 (Grayson, 1995: 51).

While many analysts assume that NAFTA resembles the EU, this chapter takes as its starting assumption that the EU is so much more institutionalized and integrated than is NAFTA that direct comparisons of the two are not analytically very productive. Although comparison can be very helpful in understanding both the EU (Sbragia, 1992) and NAFTA, neither is a good comparative interlocutor for the other.

At the most basic level of institutional functioning, NAFTA differs from the EU in that it is not a customs union and therefore does not have an external dimension; has a secretariat rather than an equivalent of the European Commission; does not have a permanent institution such as the Council of Ministers and COREPER;

has no parliament (whether appointed or elected); has no plans for a common currency or the integration of home and justice affairs; and has no equivalent to the European Court of Justice (ECJ) or the supremacy of European law over national law. Furthermore, NAFTA submits business to national treatment rather than to reciprocity (business is regulated by host country rather than home country rules), does not participate in any international fora such as the OECD and the UN, is not a signatory to International trade or environmental agreements, and so on.

The EU is an evolving system of governance, and that evolution, as seen by the contents of the European Constitutional Treaty, is still in progress. It is, in Helen Wallace's words, 'a part-formed political system' (Wallace, 1989: 205). NAFTA is not in any way a system of governance, and perhaps for that reason the literature about NAFTA has been written primarily by economists rather than by political scientists.1 This chapter, therefore, highlights those elements found in both the EU and NAFTA which may become typical of preferential trade arrangements around the world, and not those which are unique to the EU and likely to remain so. Economic integration in Europe has been undergirded by the decision to address the German question through integration rather than by the traditional balance of power approach – by the search for a system of interstate relations which would avoid the 'rivers of blood' (to use Winston Churchill's phrase) which characterize European history. NAFTA, ASEAN and APEC do not have such political underpinnings, and therefore the degree of institutionalization they will experience is very unlikely to proceed along the lines of the EU. None the less, it may be possible to identify certain similarities in the EU and NAFTA which may be viewed as likely to characterize many preferential trading arrangements organized along regional lines.

This chapter briefly explores why the United States decided to pursue a regional strategy rather than continue to view multilateralism as the only appropriate way to liberalize international trade. It then goes on to describe NAFTA in institutional terms and highlights three elements – asymmetry, the linking of environmental protection and trade, and the unexpected institutionalization of dispute settlement – which have characterized both the EU and NAFTA, although to different degrees. Asymmetry, the environment–trade link and institutionalized dispute settlement may in fact come to be characteristic of international trade agreements in the next century. Certainly, they will characterize the relationship between the EU and the new members from the east and south; whether they will characterize the Asia–Pacific Economic Cooperation forum (APEC) is a more open question.

2 Multilateralism versus regionalism

The existence of regional blocs is often viewed as a threat to the multilateral trading system institutionalized around the GATT/WTO. Above all, the members of a regional bloc are seen as having fewer incentives to engage in multilateral tariff reduction than they would have if acting unilaterally. In LeClair's words,

> The formation of a common market eliminates many of the incentives of engaging in
> meaningful multilateral tariff negotiations. The sheer size of the European Union, for

example, makes unimpeded access to the worlds markets less crucial -. It is indeed fortunate for the world trading system that the majority of tariff reductions currently in place were negotiated in the 1947 and 1963 sessions of the GATT; that is, prior to the entrenchment of the European Union. (LeClair, 1997:9)

Furthermore, in the case of the EC/EU, its own external relations have been, in Raymond Vernon's words, 'explicitly Euro-centric, rather than devoted to the establishment of a trading regime that would eventually have global dimensions'. Those relations have been constructed in an ad hoc fashion and in fact are often 'at odds with the GATT approach' (Vernon, 1991: 546).

Critics worried about regionalism worry that the resources required to maintain a regional system are likely to be diverted from the maintenance of a global system. As Kahler has put it,

> The trade and foreign affairs bureaucracy in the [US] government is not large; budgetary stringency and ideological opposition are unlikely to permit substantial growth. A decline in real resources is more likely Adding responsibility for new regional negotiations that may last for years could soon complicate management of the new dispute settlement mechanism at the WTO and reduce the attention devoted to developing a new WTO agenda. (Kahler, 1995: 22)

From Europe's perspective, the new American regionalism gives the United States a powerful bargaining chip in multilateral negotiations, enabling it to use 'the threat of a regional option in order to force concessions from Europe in bilateral or global negotiations' (Kahler, 1995: 23). It has already used its role in APEC to gain concessions from the EU in the Uruguay Round. The fact that the United States may be involved in several groupings, and plays a very significant role in all of them, gives it leverage within the multilateral system different from that enjoyed by the European Union. The asymmetry within these regional groupings can easily work to the advantage of the United States, a point to which we shall return.

It is not helpful to overstate the importance of regional trading blocs in the world outside of international negotiations and institutions. Business is operating according to a somewhat different logic, as the data on foreign direct investment demonstrate. The emergence of a European–American relationship in which firms are both employers and producers on both sides of the Atlantic cuts across the boundaries of preferential trading areas (Sbragia, 1998). As Raymond Vernon points out, one of the key forces discouraging the emergence of regional trading blocs is the multinationalization of large firms. MNCs operate across regional trading groups and represent a force binding regional groups in a non-governmental framework. The emergence of a private transatlantic relationship' (Sbragia, 1998) is an important antidote to the possible regionalization of the world economy.

3 Why NAFTA?

While European integration has been characterized by the understanding that economic integration, along with NATO, would address the security problems of Western Europe, the American position on regional integration, by contrast, is based on the decoupling of security and economic integration. The American shift from a position of viewing regional trade agreements as a threat to the stability embodied, in the American view; in multilateral global arrangements has its roots in the changed security environment after November 1989. It is also a response to the perceived success of the then European Community and its magnetic effect on the nation states of what were once central and Eastern Europe. While the United States supported European economic integration in its formative years (Winand, 1993), it had to react to an integrative initiative which has been far more successful than most would have imagined in the 1950s. The competition between the European Economic Community and the European Free Trade Association (EFTA) was decisively won by the EEC, and the very success of a model based on regional preferential trading arrangements has led the United States to reconsider its own position in support of multilateral rather than regional arrangements.

3.1   The changed security environment

With the end of the Cold War, many of the security concerns which had underlain the American position in favour of multilateral arrangements were eroded and became less relevant. It is important to note that the original American position in favour of multilateralism, while undoubtedly compatible with American economic interests, was also formed by the strong conviction that the protectionism of the inter-war period had been a leading contributor to the Second World War. From the American perspective, it was imperative that the kinds of protectionism which had marked the 1920s and 1930s be prevented from reappearing, if for no other reason than to prevent the need for American troops once again to engage in combat on European soil.

The link between economics and security was spelled out early in the post-war period, and, although becoming less explicit after that, formed an implicit foundation for the American view of foreign policy (Winand, 1993: 1–5, 112). Multilateralism and security were two sides of a coin, for international trade would promote prosperity which in turn would prevent the emergence of those conditions which lead to devastating war. International trade, of course, was also a necessity for American business; so a position in favour of multilateralism satisfied both those concerned with the potential emergence of military conflict and those concerned with American economic interests. The compatibility of multilateralism (understood as global free trade) and security was stated clearly in Secretary of State Cordell Hull's memoirs:

> To me, unhampered trade dovetailed with peace; high tariffs, trade barriers, and unfair economic competition with war Though realizing that many other factors were involved, I reasoned that f we could get a freer flow of trade – freer in the sense of fewer discriminations and obstructions – so that one country would not he deadly jealous of another and the living standards of all countries might rise, thereby eliminating the economic dissatisfaction that breeds war, we might have a reasonable chance for lasting peace (quoted in Ellwood, 1992: 21–2).

The end of the Cold War and the remoteness of military conflict among the member states of the European Community changed the foreign policy landscape as viewed by American policy-makers. Although the Gulf War represented a major military mobilization for the United States, the lack of a Soviet dimension to that conflict represented a very sharp break with the past. The United States was now operating in a different environment, one in which the link between security and foreign economic policy was much more tenuous than it had been.

3.2 The success of European integration

The American decision to pursue a regional strategy rather than continue to focus exclusively on multilateral options was rooted both in the short-term dissatisfaction with the negotiations going on in the Uruguay Round and the longer term lesson learned from the expansion of the EU (Weintraub, 1997; Boyd, 1997: 151). This latter point is of particular interest. In Sidney Weintraub's words,

> It was becoming increasingly difficult to persuade the US Congress that the United States should not itself embark on regional trade agreements because of their inherent discrimination against non-members in the face of the discrimination exporters from the United States faced in Western Europe. It had become evident that regionalism in Europe would not disappear; if anything, it was expanding to additional countries. Preferential regionalism in Europe, so the argument went, could not be purged by US insistence on multilateralism. This was the ideal context in which to argue that regionalism in Europe is best dealt with by regionalism in North America and that one day – some day – the two regionalisms can come together (Weintraub, 1997: 205).

The EU, by its existence and its seeming magnetism to other European countries, was therefore instrumental in changing the long-held American belief in multilateralism as the dominant strategy. Regionalism was in a sense legitimated by the EU and led American policy-makers to envisage a parallel track in which multilateralism and regionalism could coexist. The symbiotic relationship between the EU and NAFTA is such that the existence of both groupings has led to the debate on what the most appropriate contours for a global trading system would look like, and whether multilateralism and regionalism can coexist over the long term.

In a feedback loop, the very success of the EU as a customs union with an institutionalized capacity led the United States to change its own international economic policy so as to incorporate a preferential trading area into its portfolio; after NAFTA, it became a member of the APEC group. The United States has thus joined one group in the Americas and one in Asia; so it is not surprising that the notion of a transatlantic free trade area seems to be perennially under consideration in some policy circles.

The success of the EU can be assessed in many ways. Judged by the criterion of whether it has had an impact on American policy, it has been very successful indeed. Interestingly, just as the United States was in a position to support early efforts at European integration, so by the 1990s Europe was organized enough for Miles Kahler to conclude that 'the Commission of the European Union supported completion of NAFTA and found that its trade creation effects were likely to offset any negative economic consequences' (Kahler, 1995: 21). The institutional capacity implied in that statement is of such a magnitude that it is clear that the EU is indeed a system of governance, while NAFTA, albeit the 'most comprehensive free trade pact ever negotiated', is characterized by very weak institutional capacity (GAO, 1993: 8).

4 Institutions

In terms of institutional depth NAFTA is, in comparison with the EU, very thin. There is no equivalent of the European Commission. The NAFTA commission does have headquarters in Mexico City, but does not exist as a continuous organization and cannot make proposals on its own. It is meant to help resolve disputes rather than to propose legislation or provide NAFTA with the administrative capacity so critical to the EU. The lack of institutional capacity, in Weintraub's words, 'was deliberate. The framers wanted to minimize the political content of the agreement' (Weintraub, 1997: 212).

Two commissions do exist: the Commission for Environmental Cooperation, headquartered in Montreal, and the Commission for Labor Cooperation, in Dallas. Furthermore, a North American Development Bank, headquartered in San Antonio, funds infrastructure at the American–Mexican border. Finally, numerous working groups are in place to negotiate some kind of harmonization in a variety of areas, including the safety of trucks moving from Mexico into the north.

Disputes are settled through arbitration rather than a judicial process. There is no equivalent to the ECJ. As we shall argue, however, the dispute resolution process, although very different from that found in the EU, none the less does provide some institutional similarity.

5 NAFTA and the EU: a search for similarities

5.1 Asymmetry

Peter Leslie has written that most compound political systems are characterized by asymmetry – that is, some units have more power and/or more privilege than others (Leslie, 2000). A key question has to do with the conditions under which such asymmetry becomes unacceptable to the other units of the system in question.

Clearly, asymmetry does exist within the European Union. EU institutions, however, have deliberately tried to minimize such asymmetry. Although Britain, Denmark and Ireland have been allowed to opt out of the Schengen Agreement, in general the *acquis communautaire* has helped promote symmetry. Further, the institutions have attempted to give small countries a degree of power disproportionate to their size. Neither voting weights in the Council of Ministers nor parliamentary representation are calculated strictly according to population, and funds have been allocated to help the poorer members deal with the disruptions inevitably caused by economic liberalization. Most importantly, however, while Germany is the most powerful economy and the largest country in the Union, it does not dwarf the Union's other members.

In NAFTA, by contrast, the United States is the dominant actor in a way very different from the position of Germany within the EU. Simply in terms of trade patterns, trade with the United States dominates NAFTA, whereas trade with its partners is much less important to the United States:

> Although Canada is the number one trading partner of the United States, and Mexico is number three after Japan, the United States conducts only about one-quarter of its trade with its two North American neighbors. In contrast, more than two-thirds of foreign trade in both Canada and Mexico is with the United States. They have very little direct trade with each other. Put bluntly and somewhat simplistically, foreign trade for Canada and for Mexico means trade with the United States (Kehoe, 1994: 7).

Canada was an obvious candidate for a regional partner. It is the largest trading partner of the United States, and US direct investment in Canada is very large. Intra-firm trade is high, as is the incidence of strategic alliances between Canadian and American firms (Weintraub, 1997: 205). When the United States decided to enter a free trade agreement with Mexico, the Canadians decided to join as well (even though Canadian–Mexican trade was small), in order to prevent a 'huh and spoke arrangement ... [in which] the United States would be the hub and Canada and Mexico the spokes and only the United States would have free trade across North America' (Weintraub, 1997: 209).

In some areas, Canada and the United States both enjoy the effects of the asymmetry accompanying the American position. Peter Leslie has offered a revision of Belassa's concept of stages of integration (Leslie, 2000). Rather than thinking of a free trade area, a customs union, a common market, an economic union and complete economic integration (a la Belassa), Leslie argues we should conceptualize economic union in terms of a trade and investment union (the most basic type), a labour market union, a foreign economic policy union, a monetary union and a structural/development union. Using Leslie's typology, NAFTA is a trade and investment union but is definitely not a labour market union. Neither Canada nor the United States would have approved an agreement which would have allowed the free movement of Mexican workers into the rich economies of the north. Nor is it a foreign economic policy union. NAFTA is not a customs union and therefore has no external dimension. A common external tariff is not in force. Nor is there a common commercial policy. Third parties do not negotiate with NAFTA as they do with the EU; they negotiate with the three member states of NAFTA.

In policy terms, both the United States and Canada had much higher standards of environmental and labour protection than did Mexico. Politically, these two issues came to be associated with the debate over NAFTA in the United States and 'side agreements' in those two areas were negotiated. The North American Agreement on Environmental Cooperation entered into effect on 1 January 1994 along with NAFTA. Under the agreement, both governments and citizens can file complaints if compliance with environmental legislation is weak. Table 7.1 indicates the range of projects which the Commission for Environmental Cooperation has undertaken to improve environmental cooperation. A bilateral US–Mexican agreement established the North American Development Bank and the Border

Table 7.1   Regional cooperation projects undertaken by NAFTA's Commission for Environmental Cooperation

Environment, Economy and Trade	Assessing the Environmental Effects of Trade (2003-2005) Trade in Environmentally-Preferable Goods and Services (2003-2005) Financing in Support of Environmental Protection and Conservation (2003-2005) The North American Green Purchasing Initiative's Self-Assessment Tool (2003) Estimating Avoided Emissions Achieved Through Renewable Electricity (2006)
Conservation of Biodiversity	Strategic and Cooperative Action for the Conservation of Biodiversity in North America (2003-2005) North American Bird Conservation Initiative (2003-2005) Terrestrial and Marine Species of Common Conservation Concern (2003-2005) North American Marine Protected Areas Network (2003-2005) Closing the Pathways of Aquatic Invasive Species across North America (2003-2005) North American Biodiversity Information Network (2003-2005)
Pollutants and Health	Cooperation on North American Air Quality Issues (2003) The Sound Management of Chemicals (2003-2005) North American Pollutant Release and Transfer Register (2003-2005) Capacity Building for Pollution Prevention (2003-2005) Children's Health and the Environment in North America (2006)
Law and Policy	Environmentally Sound Management and Tracking of Hazardous Waste (2003-2005) Enforcement and Compliance Cooperation (2003-2005) Sustainable Use and Conservation of Freshwater in North America (2003-2005)
Citizen Submissions on Enforcement Matters	Los Remedios National Park (2006) Species at Risk (2006) Ex Hacienda El Hospital (Mexico, 2006)

Source: The Commission for Environmental Cooperation website: www.cec.org, 3 November 2006.

Environment Cooperation Commission, to help fund environmental infrastructure and community development projects along the border.

Although there seems to be a general view that the Commission for Environmental Cooperation has raised the awareness of environmental issues in Mexico and has led to somewhat greater enforcement, its work has been dogged by complaints

Table 7.2   Regional cooperation projects undertaken by NAFTA's Commission for Labor Cooperation

Labor markets	Employment in the information age Women's employment and Cross-border labor mobility Labor Markets in North America: Main Changes Since NAFTA (2003)
Employment and Labor Law	Employment discrimination and equal pay law Occupational health and safety and workers' compensation The Rights of Nonstandard Workers: A North American Guide (2003) Protection of Migrant Agricultural Workers (2002) Income Security Programs for Workers in North America (2000)
Employment relations	Trends and practices in employment relations Work Violence in North America (2006) Occupational health and safety Corporate codes of conduct
Multidisciplinarity	Data comparability on enforcement, labor standards, and labor market indicators.

Source: The Commission for Labor Cooperation website: www.naalc.org, 3 November 2006.

from the Mexican government that its wishes are not considered early enough in the process of identifying projects. Understaffing has been severe, with the United States assigning only one staff member to oversee implementation.

In the case of labour, the North American Agreement on Labor Cooperation also came into effect with NAFTA. This agreement is a very visible one, as it is 'the first international agreement to link labor issues to an international trade pact' (GAO, 1997: 27). A Commission for Labor Cooperation was established which for a variety of reasons became operational only in September 1995; in 1996 it was funded at only $1.6 million because of Mexico's financial crisis. One of its major functions is to promote awareness in the NAFTA countries of each other's labour systems. As Table 7.2 indicates, the Commission's work includes the dissemination of information on a variety of labour issues.

5.2   Environment – trade linkage

It is striking that although NAFTA is only, to use Peter Leslie's term, a trade and investment union, it has dealt with environmental protection. Although the inspiration for both the EU and NAFTA was the desire to increase trade and liberalize economies, environmental protection became an important impulse for both groups. In the case of the EU, environmental protection represented the first major policy area added to the Community's reach after a customs union was achieved (Sbragia, 1996), while in the case of NAFTA the agreement could not even be ratified without an environmental side agreement. The addition of environmental protection to the NAFTA negotiations 'took US and Mexican policymakers by surprise early in the negotiating process' (Gilbreath and Tonra, 1994: 53). Trade negotiators were forced to deal with an issue which often seems alien to them. Whereas environmental policy was incorporated into the EC through the institutional mechanisms of the Community, and was only later incorporated into an intergovernmental treaty (the Single European Act of 1986), in NAFTA the environmental dimension of economic liberalization was accorded such importance that the environmental agreement was negotiated alongside the trade agreement.

The trade–environment link represents an important issue for thinking about the relative costs and benefits of multilateral and regional agreements and groupings. Economists generally argue that free trade is benefited by multilateral rather than regional agreements. Environmentalists, by contrast, are likely to argue that regional agreements are more likely to lead to increased environmental cooperation and environmental protection.

The difference between the fate of environmental protection in global institutions concerned with trade liberalization and in regional cooperative arrangements such as the EU and NAFTA has to do with the relative power of the 'green' states within those groupings. The 'green troika' of the Netherlands, Denmark and Germany spearheaded the EU's movement in the field of environmental policy and helped to ensure that southern European countries have a more comprehensive framework for environmental protection than they would have adopted on their own (Sbragia, 1996). Similarly, the pressure on American negotiators from a coalition of environmental groups led the American government to give importance to environmental protection which clearly the Mexican government would not have given if operating unilaterally. As Richard Steinberg argues,

> trade–environment rules in the NAFTA are far more developed and environment friendly than in the GATT/WTO, because integration is deeper and green country power more concentrated in the NA ETA .. Unlike the GATT/WTO, which has only the Committee on Trade and Environment to focus exclusively on trade—environment issues, the NAFTA created a broad set of institutions charged with that exclusive focus and with ensuring adherence to specified standards of environmental protection. These institutions perform legislative, judicial and administrative functions ... Like the GATT/WTO, the NAFTA has a dispute settlement process that grants standing only to party governments. But unlike the (GATT/WTO, the NAFTA allows environmental NGOs to take formal action that may indirectly initiate a dispute (Steinberg. 1997: 245, 247, 248).

The focus on trade–environment issues, and the relatively deep institutionalization of that dimension within an organizational framework characterized by lack of institutional capacity, is a striking example of the 'ratcheting up' effect which takes place when wealthy 'green' countries negotiate with poorer 'brown' countries to liberalize regional trade. Trade and environment are now linked when powerful green countries become involved in regional groupings.

5.3 Dispute settlement

One of the surprising features of the European Union has been the emergence of the ECJ as one of its most important institutions. Although the court was originally viewed as a means of settling rather technical disputes, it eventually emerged as an institution which actually 'constitutionalized' the Treaty of Rome (Alter, 1998; Sweet and Brunell, 1998). The role of European law is now so important that it is difficult to talk about European integration without incorporating a discussion of the European legal system. Scholars argue about how best to explain a phenomenon which is so unexpected that it clearly needs to be explained (see, for example, Alter, 1998; Mattli and Slaughter, 1998; Garrett et al., 1998; Mullen, 1998).

Although nothing comparable to the ECJ exists within NAFTA, it is interesting that the dispute resolution procedure has become institutionalized within the Canadian–American framework to a surprising degree. Under the CFTA, either Canada or the United States can request that a binational panel review decisions made by administrative agencies in the areas of anti-dumping and countervailing duties to see if domestic law has indeed been followed. The panel's decision is binding and replaces domestic judicial review. Rather than keep trade disputes within the national bureaucracy – in the US case, the International Trade Administration (ITA) in the Department of Commerce and the International Trade Commission (ITC) – both countries agreed to have trade disputes resolved at the international rather than domestic level. The institutional apparatus agreed to by Canada and the United States was subsequently incorporated into NAFTA (Goldstein, 1996).

The consequences of this dispute resolution procedure have been significant enough to force the American bureaucracy to change the way it handles trade disputes with Canada and Mexico. The decisions have been pro-Canadian and much less protectionist than they would have been if made by the American bureaucracy. Judith Goldstein argues that

> the FTA and later NAFTA have created a dispute-settlement mechanism that can and has fundamentally altered the behavior of the US bureaucracy. This occurred because binational boards – with more liberal preferences – became the last mover in unfair trade cases, a position previously held by the courts. This enabled importers, frustrated by a decision by the US trade bureaucracy, to choose to petition to a forum in which they had a higher chance of getting their preferred outcome. Binational boards institutionalized their preferences by stipulating acceptable procedures with each remand ... The outcome is what Canada and Mexico had hoped for: greater relief from US unfair trade law (Goldstein, 1996: 555).

In this case, we find that administrative agencies and domestic courts – which tended to be deferential to the administrative agencies – were circumvented by the creation of international panels, the decisions of which were binding. The outcome was less protectionist and more favourable to trade than would have been the outcome if national processes had been left to work in their usual fashion.

6 Conclusion

The creation and institutional features of NAFTA reflect the changed international environment in which the United States operates, its reluctance to institutionalize arrangements which may impinge on its sovereignty, the power of environmental NGOs within the American political system, and the basic fact that its market and international power are such that asymmetry is likely to be an important feature of any regional grouping to which the United States belongs. NAFTA is not the beginning of some kind of integration within the Americas analogous to the integration we have seen in Europe; rather, it is a strategy designed to respond to specific challenges facing the United States in its external environment. It allows the United States to pursue a regional strategy which may, under some conditions, actually increase its leverage within the multilateral framework to which it has long been committed.

One of the domestic factors which will limit the future institutionalization of NAFTA is the power of the US Congress. Far more powerful than any European parliament, and much less constrained by the discipline of political parties, the American Congress stands as a bulwark against the kind of integration which would in any way 'pool sovereignty'. To the extent that institutions are created that could override domestic decisions, they will need to be cloaked in the institutions of dispute resolution. The world of free trade is as likely to be characterized by the judge as by the businessman.

Note

1   I thank Lawrence Graham, University of Texas for pointing this out to me.
    I thank also my research assistant, Dana Adriana Puia, for her excellent work on this chapter.

Chapter 8

European Union and MERCOSUR*

Álvaro Vasconcelos

Various models have arisen to describe the international system of the post-Cold War era, from the liberal optimism vigorously defended by Francis Fukuyama in his 'end of history' thesis to Samuel Huntington's pessimistic vision of the 'clash of civilisations',[1] but none has succeeded in explaining the conflictual nature of the modern world. None of these models produced an adequate explanation of regional integration, a *sui generis* phenomenon capable of transcending the traditional conflictuality between nations and facilitated today by the sheer magnitude of the wave of democratization sweeping, in particular in Latin America.

Regionalization was undoubtedly a major trend in the international system of the 1990s, with widely different forms. Three main types may, for simplicity's sake, be identified: open regionalism, as embodied in, for example, the North American Free Trade Agreement (NAFTA), the Asia-Pacific Economic Cooperation (APEC) forum or the Euro-Mediterranean Partnership (EMP) initiative; deep integration, for example, the European Union (EU) and MERCOSUR; and subregional cooperation, for example the Southern African Development Community (SADC).[2]

1 Three types of regionalization

Open regionalism may be characterized as the policy generally espoused by defined poles in the international system, in order to implement their external economic, political and security relations through free trade agreements. Thus, in the 1990s, the United States, the EU and also MERCOSUR multiplied their commercial agreements, mainly with neighbouring countries but also with more distant regions. Open regionalism was – and still is – a vague concept. From the American viewpoint, it means above all the creation of large free trade areas, as for example in APEC or NAFTA; from the European viewpoint, it goes beyond free trade alone to embrace conditionality and political cooperation, as well as development aid.

The processes of deep integration, for example in the EU and in the MERCOSUR, are of a different nature. Deep integration differs from open regionalism in that it tends to focus on one core group in the international system. Not only does it go beyond free trade arrangements, it also implies a change in the relations among states, the establishment of common positions vis-à-vis those outside the group – at least in the commercial field – and eventually the creation of supranational institutions. The existing models of deep integration could also be classified as 'open integration' models. This concept refers to 'integration projects which are based on pluralist societies, and defend the values of political democracy, cultural and religious diversity, free competition, citizen participation, associationism and shared sovereignty, projecting and promoting these values in their external relations'.[3]

Most of the European, American and African countries, as well as some Asian countries, have made some sort of move, in varying degrees of importance, towards regionalization or subregional cooperation. Projects such as these, however, remain dominated by the participating states as key players, whose voice is as decisive in their operation as it is in their foundation. The EU, the most advanced embodiment of supranational constitutionalism in existence today, was created after the Second World War in recognition of the need for survival and reconstruction in the European states.[4]

Most countries will very probably be participating in open regionalism initiatives of one form or another, particularly those promoted by the United States and the EU. As a general rule, these processes are asymmetrical in both institutional strength and economic development. This trend will reveal ever more strikingly the need for the countries of any given region to engage in deep integration processes if they wish to wield even a minimum of influence within the international system. The regional factor is an indispensable element in the continuing evolution of the international order. The hiatus resulting from the rise to power of neo-conservatives in the United States, and Europe's constitutional problems, should not, in the long term, jeopardize this trend, which the European Union and the United Nations system should actively promote. In essence, the objective is to return to the multilateral projects for the stabilisation of the international order which characterized the 1990s.

2 MERCOSUR and its European inspiration

MERCOSUR was founded in March 1991 with the signature of the Treaty of Asunción by Argentina, Brazil, Paraguay and Uruguay. Its motivation lay in the desire to create a common market modelled on the European Community.[5] However, the underlying conditions in the two regions were very different. European integration made its first appearance in the context of disenchantment with national sovereignty, resulting from two world wars. Indeed, Raymond Aron claimed that 'the Europe of the nationalists has been killed by wars waged to extreme lengths.'[6] The construction of Europe is also a product of the specific conditions of the Cold War – notably the Soviet threat – which facilitated support and encouragement from the United States, both at the political and economic level. The European Economic Community developed under the protection of NATO.

MERCOSUR, by contrast, developed in the 1990s as an embodiment of integration under post-Cold War conditions. In Latin America, nationalism – including a pan-Latin American feeling – has persisted, especially in opposition to US policies which, in the western hemisphere, are still often considered to be 'hegemonic' or even 'imperialist'. Nevertheless, while the region has not experienced the tragedies of the European wars which delegitimated nationalism, it was emerging from a long period of military dictatorships which has had the same effect on the authoritarian model of governance. Moreover, trends towards globalization have deprived the concept of absolute sovereignty of all meaning. MERCOSUR is considered the first integration project generated by globalization, having been born from awareness in Brazil and Argentina that it was, and still is, very difficult for developing nations on their own to benefit from globalization, and to overcome the economic and security challenges it brings.

MERCOSUR was set up in answer to the need of its members to transform their 'development' policy of the 1960s and 1970s, founded on industrialization by means of import substitution, into a policy of commercial openness and integration into the international market. This new phase coincided with the acceptance by the Latin American states of the policies of structural adjustment and economic stability produced by the Washington Consensus with a view to resolving the burden of foreign debt.[7] As Felix Peña has stated, the four MERCOSUR founding members have accepted a common aim of reconverting their economies by creating, at the subregional level, a habitat favourable to national attempts to improve both structural and business competitiveness.[8]

Implementing these principles in the aggressively neo-liberal atmosphere of the 1990s implied, for the Brazilian and Argentinean governments, the creation as a first step of a competitive platform, a customs union applying a common external tariff to facilitate openness towards the global market. It also required that liberalization between neighbouring countries may permit the application of a 'pragmatic liberalism' in relation to the outside world,[9] that is to say a process of gradual and controlled opening and adaptation to the stakes of competition on a world-wide scale.

Awareness that globalization required that states implement policies not restricted to the framework of the individual nation state lent impetus to the creation of MERCOSUR. The customs union brought into being in the Treaty of Asunción stands out as a first step towards a common market, and as a move towards clearly defined political objectives.

The MERCOSUR project reflected the internal priorities of the new Latin American democracies as they emerged from the dictatorships and the 'lost decade' of the 1980s. Inspired by the success of the European model – which Latin Americans had been observing and studying closely for some time – it was born when the expectations of the European single market reached their height with the 'Europe 92' programme, which had an international impact comparable only to that of the euro today.

The European single market was seen in Latin America as reflecting a European Community that was 'stronger and more radiant than ever, and much less dependent on the outside world'.[10] It was the image of a successful integration project; but it also brought new difficulties for exporters in the Southern Cone of the South American continent, who feared the 'European fortress', especially European protectionism against Latin American agricultural products. Back in 1992, the EU was already MERCOSUR's main export market, taking almost 32%, and exceeded as a source of imports only by Latin America (see Tables 8.1 and 8.2).

Table 8.1 MERCOSUR main trading partners

		Value ($USm)		Growth (%)		Share (%) by region		
		1995	2000	2004	95/00	00/04	1995	2000	2004
EXPORT	Asia	9171	7971	17537	-13	120	13	9	13
	European Union	18012	20025	30078	11	50	26	24	22
	Intra MERCOSUR	14451	17741	17114	23	-4	21	21	13
	USA	10773	16930	24678	57	46	15	20	18
	Rest of the World	18087	22196	44453	23	100	26	26	33
	World	**70493**	**84863**	**133861**	**20**	**58**			
IMPORT	Asia	7920	10085	15029	27	49	10	11	16
	European Union	21949	21069	20007	-4	-5	27	24	21
	Intra MERCOSUR	14439	17713	17879	23	1	18	20	19
	USA	17635	18693	15696	6	-16	22	21	17
	Rest of the World	17915	20882	26210	17	26	22	24	28
	World	**79 858**	**88 441**	**94 821**	**11**	**7**			
Total Trade	Asia	17091	18055	32566	6	80	11	10	14
	European Union	39961	41094	50086	3	22	27	24	22
	Intra MERCOSUR	28890	35453	34994	23	-1	19	20	15
	USA	28407	35623	40374	25	13	19	21	18
	Rest of the World	36001	43078	70663	20	64	24	25	31
	World	**150 351**	**173 304**	**228682**	**15**	**32**			

Source: Trade SIA of the Association Agreement under negotiation between the European Community and Mercosur; Update on the Overall Preliminary Trade SIA SIA EU-Mercosur and Sectoral Trade SIA's. Inception Report, September 2006

Table 8.2 Trade flows between EU and MERCOSUR (measured in thousands of euros)

YEAR	EU imports from MERCOSUR	EU exports to MERCOSUR
1999	9 191 944	866 242
2000	10 574 162	980 777
2001	12 040 351	840 914
2002	12 182 517	638 612
2003	12 296 726	590 788
2004	13 537 979	582 381

Source: Trade SIA of the Association Agreement under negotiation between the European Community and Mercosur, Update on the Overall Preliminary Trade SIA EU-Mercosur and Sectoral Trade SIA's. Inception Report, September 2006

Although the trade agreement between the EU and MERCOSUR never happened, and although Brazil developed an internationally active commercial policy, particularly aimed at Asia and Africa, Europe continued to be MERCOSUR's main trade partner, absorbing 22.5% of its exports, and also its main provider (21.1% of MERCOSUR imports). MERCOSUR exports for the EU in 2004 measured in terms of value are more than twenty times greater than imports.

The non-fruition of the free trade agreement with MERCOSUR, as well as the signing of free trade agreements with Chile and Mexico, resulted in a decline in favour of those two partners, from 1995 to 2004, of MERCOSUR's share as a recipient of EU exports from 50% to 36%.

2.1 Integration and democratization

MERCOSUR most resembles the European model in the need felt by the states of South America at the end of the 1980s to consolidate their democratic structures, and in the process to overhaul the security concepts espoused by the military regimes throughout the years of dictatorship. According to Helio Jaguaribe, this amounted to establishing a distinction between internal and external security, and preventing the 'army from being induced into interference in the state's internal affairs, instead becoming converted to protectors of the civil authority'.[11] As in Europe after the Second World War, a post-sovereign political culture emerged in the newly democratic states, particularly in the academic and industrial spheres – a development made possible only by the liberation of external and internal policy alike from the geopolitical concepts adopted by the military. The success of MERCOSUR has contributed greatly to the consolidation of this new democratic orientation.

The reconciliation between Brazil and Argentina, made possible by the political transition in these two countries led by Presidents Sarney and Alfonsin, was perceived as being an underlying condition for democratic consolidation. The Treaty of Integration, Cooperation and Development signed by Brazil and

Argentina in 1988 established a focus on the objectives of democratization and development, though not yet at this stage on international competitiveness. The two countries have changed the strategic culture that had hitherto marked their bilateral dealings, and which had seen both countries pursuing aggressive nuclear armament programmes. Those programmes have been abandoned, and the neighbours have stopped regarding each other as enemies.

For Argentina and Brazil, the change in bilateral relations was fundamental in gaining international legitimacy for their fledgling democracies. The creation of MERCOSUR extended this process to Uruguay and Paraguay, traditionally the buffer states between the 'big two' of the Southern Cone. The establishment through this means of international recognition and credibility was seen as a way of underwriting democracy, and thus represented a convergence of international interests among the four countries[12] MERCOSUR was thus born from the democratization of the countries of the region, and is based on the twin principles that the success of regional integration depends on the democratic nature of the regimes involved, and that the consolidation of democracy depends – at least in part – on the progress of integration. As José Luis Simon has argued, 'If democratic politics and integration are intricately linked in the MERCOSUR, this is all the more true for Paraguay, for which integration is much more than mere trade; indeed, the MERCOSUR created the conditions for the implementation of democracy in Paraguay'.[13]

Democracy is undoubtedly the founding principle of MERCOSUR, and the founder governments are fully aware of this, as was apparent from their concerted response to General Oviedo's attempted coup d'état in Paraguay in April 1996. The members made it clear that it was unacceptable for one state in the group to jeopardize the democratic legitimacy of the whole. Shortly after this episode, the fragility of democracy in Paraguay had prompted the MERCOSUR countries to introduce a democracy clause into the constitutional arrangements of the group. The presidential declaration of Potrero de los Funes (in June 1996) not only stated that 'all change to the democratic order constitutes an unacceptable obstacle for the continuation of the democratic process in progress', but made provision for sanctions, ranging from suspension to expulsion from MERCOSUR, to be applied to any country jeopardizing democracy. Following this declaration, the MERCOSUR states have included the principle of political conditionality in their agreements with other countries. Moreover, on 24 July 1998 the democracy clause was extended with the Protocol of Ushuaia to include Chile and Bolivia, countries with which MERCOSUR has association agreements. It is interesting to note that in the EU context a similar democracy clause was introduced only in June 1997, in the Treaty of Amsterdam, in view of the envisaged expansion of the Union to Central and Eastern Europe.

MERCOSUR, in fact, represents the coming together of two projects: one political, defined by the democratic commitment of the participating countries and lacking any hard structure or well-defined contours; the other economic, aimed at liberalization and commercial openness, both among the member states and towards the outside world. MERCOSUR can thus be described as an 'open pole' model within the international system.[14] By the end of the 1990s, MERCOSUR was a success, a 'trade mark' as the Brazilian President then described it, which has undoubtedly given its member states a new credibility.

MERCOSUR and the EU embody essentially the same model of regionalism, namely that of 'open integration'. Not only do MERCOSUR and the EU both set the condition that a state must be democratic in order to join; both project through their external relations, especially with their neighbours, the fundamental values that legitimate their own integration processes. Clearly the EU cannot base its international action upon an essentially Hobbesian idea; this reductive view is neither accepted nor understood by its citizens, who consider that its legitimacy resides in its democratic nature. This assumption has been a component of the European Community ever since its creation – in contrast to EFTA, one of whose founder members was Portugal under Salazar. It was for this reason that neither Portugal nor Spain could initially join the EC; conversely, as soon as the two countries had jettisoned their authoritarian regimes, both considered accession to the Community a fundamental requirement for the consolidation of democracy at home. Due to the nature of Hugo Chavez's regime, Venezuela's joining MERCOSUR on 4 July 2006 caused a degree of anxiety regarding the strength of MERCOSUR's democratic clause, and its international identity. Nevertheless, Venezuela's integration is a process whereby the new member country must accept all of MERCOSUR's conditions, namely concerning the Customs Union, a process that will not be completed until 2014. This timeframe must be employed to reaffirm the democratic clause. The international legitimacy of the integration process itself will largely depend on MERCOSUR's ability to ensure Venezuela's respect for human rights and for democratic legality, and by the way the country will react if and when the latter are infringed.

Since their transition to democracy, Argentina, Brazil, Paraguay and Uruguay and have all attached great importance in their foreign policies to democracy and human rights issues. This commitment was demonstrated by all four MERCOSUR members in their declaration of support for the constitution of the International Criminal Court in Rome, in July 1998. However, the controversy over the fate of the former Chilean dictator Augusto Pinochet has divided the MERCOSUR countries on the potential conflict between the safeguarding of fundamental rights, on the one hand, and state sovereignty on the other. Their past experience of dictatorship has influenced the four countries in different ways. With problems similar to those faced by Chile – of military political crimes committed during the dictatorship and not yet brought to court – Argentina, Paraguay and Uruguay echoed the Chilean government's protest at what they called Britain's and Spain's interference in the domestic affairs of Chile. Brazil took a less critical approach. The opposition of the MERCOSUR countries, and indeed of Latin America in general, to the element of extraterritoriality in US policy towards them was made clear in the common declaration on the Pinochet affair made by MERCOSUR, Chile and Bolivia, in which they denounced the 'unilateral and extraterritorial application of national laws, violating the juridical equality of nations and the principles of respect and dignity of the sovereignty of states and of non-intervention in domestic affairs, and threatening their relationships'. At the same time, however, the signatories to the document 'recognize and encourage the gradual development of international legislation dealing with the penal responsibility of a person guilty of committing international crimes'. MERCOSUR's member states have maintained this perspective of defending multilateral solutions, and of a huge mistrust towards the concepts of extraterritoriality – an attitude which has been reinforced by the unilateralism of George W. Bush's administration.

2.2 Institutional shortcomings

A fundamental difference between the EU and MERCOSUR relates to the latter's institutional shortcomings. Up to now, MERCOSUR has been a purely intergovernmental body, with decisions taken unanimously in the absence of any form of supranational institution. This situation is a result of the sovereignty concept which still dominates diplomacy in the region, and of Brazil's opposition to any system that might place it in the minority. In the EU, by contrast, there exists a complex system of weights and counterweights – the weighted votes system, the provision for blocking minorities, qualified majority voting, a parliament with real (albeit limited) powers – to help balance power across participating states and protect them from excessively strong leadership by any member or members. MERCOSUR's lack of institutions means a lack of any check on strong leadership, and the consensus rule provides only a limited constraint.[15] In Europe, the France–Germany axis is part of a system of multiple and shifting alliances; in MERCOSUR, the Brazil–Argentine axis is the unchanging core. This asymmetry among the countries involved will continue and the enlargement to Venezuela didn't change this. The asymmetry has become more pronounced in the past few years, with the impact of the Argentine crisis. Brazil's relative weight in the equation will tend to increase with the passing of time. The resolution of MERCOSUR's institutional asymmetry remains a deciding factor for the future of the Southern Cone's integration project, a process which must not continue to depend on the kindness, or 'strategic patience', of Brazil, as Celso Lafer has called it.[16] On this issue President Cardoso remarked in 1998 that 'Brazil must take up this challenge. We are going to have to improve the institutionalization of MERCOSUR'.[17]

In recent years there has been talk of setting up a tribunal to handle commercial disputes, and this would undoubtedly be an important step. Lately, however, and somewhat against the grain, a decision was taken in 2004 to create the Parliament of MERCOSUR. Essentially, this new institution aims to promote an approximation of its citizens to the integration process, and its members are elected by direct and universal suffrage in each of the member states. With apparently limited powers, it should nevertheless be noted that one of the goals of this new institution is the preservation of democratic regimes in the member states, in accordance with MERCOSUR's norms, in particular with the Ushuaia Protocol on Commitment to Democracy in MERCOSUR, the Republic of Bolivia and the Republic of Chile. The MERCOSUR Parliament must compile an annual report about the human rights conditions in all member states.

Table 8.3   Trade relations between Brazil and Argentina *

Year	Exports	Imports
1995	4,023,310	5,748,338
1996	5,164,560	7,131,037
1997	6,761,631	8,287,234
1998	6,743,503	8,420,599
1999	5,358,729	6,110,115
2000	6,226,243	7,197,801
2001	4,995,338	6,533,356
2002	2,337,537	5,019,893
2003	4,557,500	4,949,514
2004	7,370,704	5,904,801
2005	9,911,807	6,591,043
2006	8,621,905	4,494,535

* *thousands of dollars*

Source: ALADI – Estadísticas de comercio exterior

3   Crises of the turn of the century

In 1996, 25 per cent of all Argentinean exports and 14 per cent of Brazil's were destined for MERCOSUR countries; the corresponding figures for 1990, before MERCOSUR was established, were 16.5 per cent and 7 per cent respectively. The change has been less marked for Paraguay and Uruguay, for whom Argentina and Brazil were already the leading trade partners. The credibility of MERCOSUR was demonstrated by the significant annual rise in the volume of international investments, up from US$1,284 million in 1991 to US$8,925 million in 1996.

The financial crisis of the late 1990s that first faced Brazil, and later and more seriously Argentina, represented a great challenge for MERCOSUR, with Argentina coming out of the crisis in a much weaker position than Brazil. The Argentine government implemented some tough measures to try and abate the crisis, and the IMF gave Argentina more than $20 billion in emergency aid. But the international help was not enough, however, and by the end of 2001, Argentina verged on economic collapse. This crisis also had serious implications for Uruguay and Paraguay. The crises were followed by political change in both Brazil and Argentina, and this had a powerful impact on the trade relations between the two countries, which from 2004 onwards, from the traditional pattern in favor Argentina, an asymmetric imbalance favours Brazil.

The crises at the turn of the century were followed by political change both in Brazil and Argentina. This created a set of dynamics in the region, whereby internal issues became the basic priority for leaders like Lula, such as the social agenda and the fight against poverty. MERCOSUR remained an important priority of the Brazilian government, but now in the context of a more diverse regional and international agenda. The idea of building a South American Community of Nations, initiated back in the government of Fernando Henrique Cardoso, became a core objective of the Lula Administration, and the group obtained its name at the Cuzco Summit in Peru, in December 2004. The Community is still a poorly defined project and has not as yet approved a founding treaty. This South American priority is quite clear in the enlargement of MERCOSUR to Venezuela, a move that was considered necessary by Brazilian diplomacy, in order not to isolate Chavez, and as an attempt to water down the tension between Chavez and the American administration.

But with Venezuela joining, the need to define the MERCOSUR's international identity becomes more evident. Some may be tempted to respond affirmatively to Felix Peña's question: is MERCOSUR a political project in which economic and commercial concerns remain subordinate to more generic objectives – such as a South American identity – which for some of its members could signify an affirmation of interests in direct opposition to those of the United States?[18] It is certainly from a perspective of South American nationalism that Chavez sees Venezuela's entry. The Lula administration's position is, however, a good deal more complex. If the South American project has attained a new level of priority, it does not signify the affirmation of an anti-United States project. For Brazil, the South American project is integrated, as is MERCOSUR, in its affirmation as an emerging global power and as an important platform, with a view to achieving international integration under more favourable conditions, and to negotiate under more advantageous ones with the United States. There is an apparent contradiction, however, in Brazil's desire for international affirmation as a global power and MERCOSUR's political consolidation, precisely due to the existing asymmetries and the lack of cooperative mechanisms in the realm of foreign policy. This was made apparent in Brazil's campaign for permanent membership of the United Nations Security Council without managing to develop a common platform with its MERCOSUR partners, particularly Argentina. Even the priority Brazil has awarded the South American project is seen by some as a risk of weakening the commitments already made within MERCOSUR, in the process of establishing of a wider cooperative space – a space whose practical effects are somewhat less potent.[19] According to the Lula administration's perspective, there is no contradiction in the project of a South American Community of Nations and the deepening of MERCOSUR, which should function as its hard core.[20] What MERCOSUR does demonstrate, however, is the difficulty in progressing with a deep integration project without a serious effort towards the harmonization of foreign policies. But even where international trade is concerned, deep rifts are emerging among the members of MERCOSUR during the whole Doha Round process, with Brazil bringing together the Group of Twenty to face the European Union and the United States, but with Uruguay actively opposing this strategy. The rifts between MERCOSUR member states are equally evident in other areas, as demonstrated by the so-called 'paper mill crisis' between Argentina and Uruguay. This situation not only shows the current level of disagreement between member states, but also clearly reveals the inability on behalf of MERCOSUR's institutions to provide a platform for resolving differences between member states. For all the above reasons, MERCOSUR appears weaker now than at the end of the twentieth century.

4 The United States and MERCOSUR

The Clinton government, in line with the orientation of the Bush I administration at the end of the 1980s,[21] has given priority to free trade agreements as a structural element of the dominant US position in world trade – and as a vehicle for the world-wide dissemination of American interests and values. 'The trade agreements of the post-Cold War era will be equivalent to the security pacts of the Cold War – binding nations together in a virtuous circle of mutual prosperity and providing the new front line of defence against instability. A more integrated and more prosperous world will be a more peaceful world – a world more hospitable to American interests and ideals'.[22]

The American strategy in the 1990s was to promote global regionalization with the United States as the hub of the world, by means of large-scale agreements such as the FTAA (Free Trade Area of the Americas), APEC or the proposed Transatlantic Marketplace with the European Union (see the planisphere 3 at the end of this volume). However, in so doing it sometimes ran into opposition from powerful isolationist sectors of American society, and from the labour unions, such as AFL-CIO.[23] Some influential political figures favour a more isolationist stance, believing it (perhaps rightly so) to be closer to the instincts and preferences of most Americans. It is this political sensitivity that caused Congress to deny President Clinton the 'fast track' option that would have enabled him to negotiate free trade agreements directly, particularly with Latin American countries.[24] The George W. Bush administration didn't change the American approach towards regionalization drastically, namely in relation to Latin America and Asia, but it awarded it a priority so low that there has been no United States dependent real progress in this process.

For the United States, MERCOSUR remains a trading detour, an optional step in the regionalization of the Americas. Many US politicians see Brazil as the Latin American country that is most independent of US foreign policy, and the only real opponent of the US position on the free trade area. Some even take the view that MERCOSUR, working towards a strong relationship with the EU, is part of a Brazilian strategy of independence, and that Brazil is setting itself up as a kind of Latin American France. Argentina, by contrast, has been more closely aligned with US international security policy. Unlike Brazil, Argentina has participated in military operations led by the United States, such as the 'Desert Storm' campaign during the Gulf War in 1991; and, by way of thanks for this support, President Clinton has granted Argentina the status of leading ally outside NATO, a rank already bestowed on Israel, Egypt, Japan, South Korea, New Zealand and Jordan.

The Brazilian opposition to the FTAA became the official policy of the Lula government in line with the position defended by the eminent Brazilian sociologist Helio Jaguaribe, going so far as to assert that MERCOSUR must say no to the FTAA because 'constitution of the FTAA implies, in practice, the disappearance of MERCOSUR as it would lead to the elimination of customs frontiers between all the countries of America and, as a result, of the common external tariff, which is one of the fundamental characteristics of MERCOSUR'.[25]

The project of FTAA due to the opposition of Brazil and the low priority given to it by the George W. Bush administration was replaced by a number of bilateral agreements between the US and several Latin American countries, namely those on the Pacific coast such as Chile (2003) and Peru (2006). Some member of MERCOSUR are tempted by the signing of bilateral trade treaties with the United Sates, namely Uruguay and Paraguay, but even Argentina signed with the United States a 'Bilateral Council on Trade and Investment', in 2002. Bilateralism is prevailing over the logic of block negotiations, even though one of MERCOSUR's principal factors was its affirmation as a Customs Union, bargaining as one voice with the United States and Europe.

5 MERCOSUR as a strategic partner of the EU

Despite its limited international influence, MERCOSUR is a strategic partner for the EU in building a new multilateralism based upon a more balanced relationship with the United States. This view is strong in Portugal, Spain and Italy for historical reasons, and in Germany because of its large investments in the countries of the region. For many European countries, MERCOSUR's importance lies only in the part it plays in their foreign trade. If Europe were only a trading region, then MERCOSUR would be reduced to a 'backyard' of the United States, in a version of the Monroe Doctrine by which South America was prevented from engaging in political dialogue with partners other than the United States.[26] But even from a strictly economic viewpoint, it would be a mistake to overlook the importance of MERCOSUR for the EU – which is amply demonstrated by the fact that EU member states are the principal investors in the region, with Brazil being the main destination of the European FDI. In 2003, the FDI stock of the EU in Brazil amounted to US$ 47,997 million and to US$ 23,193 million in Argentina. Traditional investors such as France, the Netherlands, the United Kingdom, Italy and Germany, were joined by Spain (the EU member with the largest stock of FDI in MERCOSUR), and Portugal.

A fresh boost was given to relations with Latin America when Portugal and Spain joined the European Community in 1986. Indeed, a declaration about those relations was annexed to the membership treaty. This impetus was reinforced on the Latin American side by the successful consolidation of democracy in the region and by the appearance of regional groups – the Andean Community and the Central American Community, as well as MERCOSUR itself. The European Commission, under the influence of Portugal and Spain, has attempted to promote relations with these groups and with Mexico, taking advantage of Mexico's role as a member of NAFTA and of the Iberian countries' turns to preside over the Council of Ministers. It was in 1992, during the Portuguese presidency, that the first informal ministerial meeting took place between the twelve members of the European Community and the four members of MERCOSUR; and it was in 1995, during the Spanish presidency of the Union, that the EU-MERCOSUR framework agreement and the project for an interregional free trade area were launched.

Table 8.4   Foreign Direct Investment flows to MERCOSUR

	1991-1995 **		1996-2000**		2001-2005**	
	$USm	(% Total)	$USm	(% Total)	$USm	(% Total)
Argentina	3,781.5	58	11,516.1	31	2,980.6	15
Brazil	2,477.4	38	24,823.6	68	16,480.7	83
Paraguay	103.8	2	185.1	1	53.9	0
Uruguay	82.5	1	187.2	1	367.9	2
MERCOSUR	6,445.2		36,757.1		19,883.1	

In the following decade, the consolidation of the Free Trade agreement did not take place, and only almost ten years later, in 2004, did negotiations make significant progress. However, they did so while coming up against the ever-present agricultural and service sector difficulties, as well as the priority awarded by MERCOSUR member states to the attempt to obtain more significant concessions from the World Trade Organization.

Both MERCOSUR and the EU look upon free trade and globalization differently from the United States, which sees these processes in complete accordance with its own interests. For the EU and MERCOSUR the continental and global free trade projects, accompanied by the deregulation, may jeopardize cohesion among member states and lead to a loss of identity conferred by projects that go beyond the establishment of free trade arrangements, whether in the shape of a customs union (as in MERCOSUR), or in the more ambitious form of an economic and monetary union (in the EU), especially regarding the social model on which these groupings are based. However, the EU and MERCOSUR have not been able to give substance to this relation through a trade agreement .In the 1990s Europe was not able to correspond to MERCOSUR's demand of opening its markets for agricultural trade from the MERCOSUR countries. In the first years of the twenty-first century it was the MERCOSUR countries, Brazil in particular, who resisted such an agreement, emphasizing the Doha Round's potential to free up trade to their advantage. The failure of the Doha Round has perhaps created renewed conditions for the relaunching of the ten-year-old EU-MERCOSUR project for a free trade agreement.

6 A common vision of the international order?

The political convergence between the European Union and MERCOSUR derives
above all from the similarity of their open integration processes and their shared
need for a multilateral system. What both the Europeans and the 'Mercosureans'
want to do is build a system regulated by international rules that are as widely
accepted as possible, not only in relation to international trade but also in the
spheres of security, human rights and the environment – particularly important in
today's world, where the Bush administration has developed a unilateralist vision
of the international order after 9/11. What, then, is the alternative to unipolarity and
American unilateralism? The traditional multipolar perspective assumes that the
EU could become a traditional power, like an enlarged France; but this possibility
is not universally favoured. The model projected by the EU in the international
order is not that of a traditional multipolar system with ephemeral alliances,
possibly formed by the five continental superpowers (EU, United States, China,
Japan, Russia), which would reproduce the nineteenth century European balance
of power system on a world scale, and which India and Brazil (or MERCOSUR)
could join later. What is needed is a different kind of system which, in the words of
Jean-Marie Guéhenno, 'would be based neither on the indefinite supremacy of the
United States, nor on the pursuit of independence and sovereignty as the ultimate
goal of a political entity',[27] but would be a kind of institutionalized interdependence
organization. Jacques Chirac, on his visit to Brazil in 1997, said: 'The unstoppable
progress towards a multipolar world would, however, risk slipping progressively
towards the affirmation of antagonistic poles, if some of today's leading actors
attempted to oppose this evolution rather than participate in organizing it'.[28] We
must go further: the European model assumes that the Union will not be transformed
into a superstate, but will be able to influence the creation of international rules,
based on a fabric of interdependent multilateral economic and political institutions,
such as the WTO or the recently founded International Criminal Court, testimony
to the growing role of international law. In short, a multilateral system based on
multiregionalism must be created.

For this to occur, it is important that the new supranational European pole gains a
greater capacity for political intervention, and that similar new poles are consolidated.
To this end, the EU must resist the diminishing of MERCOSUR into a free trade
area or even its dissolution into the world market, and must defend its consolidation
as an open, supranational pole of multiregionalism and multilateralism. It is
essential, moreover, that this political objective be translated into an interregional
trade agreement. Such an agreement between the EU and MERCOSUR would
represent a significant stage in the process of mutual identification as open poles
of the new international system. It is important for the EU that the MERCOSUR
pole be defined with as much precision as possible, and that other such potential
poles, for example in South East Asia with the democratization and enlargement of
ASEAN, and in southern Africa with the development of the SADC, are fostered.

The European Union's aim is to see the emergence of a world that would not
rely on the leadership of a superpower to govern it; a world where the traditional
loci of power would be diminished and lose legitimacy. The poles it would like

to see emerge are not traditional power poles but open poles, equipped with a capacity for military intervention resulting from cooperation between states and legitimated by multilateral institutions, especially the United Nations. In short, a new multilateralism, capable of protecting not only peace but human rights, and of fighting poverty. This new multilateralism, as stated in the sixth Euro-Latin American Forum, is marked by three main characteristics. Firstly, by the sense that the international community and the United Nations (UN) in particular are responsible for the protection of the rights of individuals, above and beyond sovereign boundaries. Secondly, it is marked by regionalism, which has become a structural feature of the international system as a whole. Thirdly, it is characterized by the emergence of a global public opinion, which expresses the desire of civil society to influence or participate in global decision making. This is a sovereignty-altering multilateralism, which changes the position of the state in the international system.[29]

In summary, the European Union's multilateralist project is not a throwback to the traditional multipolar system, characterized by an unstable equilibrium among the powers and the frequent dissolution and reversal of alliances. Western Europe has put an end to this system of permanent rivalry through integration. The European vision of regionalism implies the consolidation of the poles of integration, such as MERCOSUR, and in this respect it differs from the Clinton vision of 'open regionalism', which pulls in the opposite direction to projects of deep integration in Latin America, and even more of the unilateralist vision of the Bush administration.

The international project of the EU consists in building a new multilateralism based on areas of regional integration, and on experience of supranational regulation of the relations between states: in other words, in turning the international system into a 'community' on the basis of the success of its own model, which is then extrapolated into the wider world. This may be a utopian vision; but it is the only vision of the world that can make sense of the common foreign and security policy of the civil power that is the European Union. This vision alone can answer the specific security concerns of its members and unite their diverse interests in a common project. Three essential elements to this project exist today: integration of all countries of the European continent, from Portugal to Russia, in a single community of destiny in a common project of democracy and social justice; in the long term, the extension by inclusion and prosperity of this security area to North Africa and the Middle East; and the formation, with MERCOSUR, of the first link in the chain of interregional agreements.

7 The strategic relationship in new circumstances

MERCOSUR is a regional grouping roughly inspired by the European model. In spite of its shortcomings, it has exerted a notable measure of attraction vis-à-vis its neighbours through the 'power of example'. As it develops further its inherent 'soft power' dimension, notably in conflict and crisis prevention, MERCOSUR and the

EU will potentially come closer and their ability to act together in the international sphere will simultaneously increase.

During the diplomatic battles in the run-up to the war in Iraq, the high degree of political convergence between Latin America and the EU as a whole regarding the international order once more became apparent. France and Germany's positions symptomatically converged with those of Chile and Mexico, the two LA representatives at the Security Council before the war. Chile arguably championed the collective stance of the MERCOSUR members and associates, who unanimously stressed that the Security Council alone could permit the use of force to ensure compliance with its resolutions. This is not to say that MERCOSUR members stand absolutely united when it comes to relations with the United States. While Brazil voiced total opposition to military intervention on the grounds that, in the words of Foreign Minister Celso Amorim, 'the war is bound to aggravate instability in the Middle East and stir up the existing tensions between The West and the Islamic world', Argentina poised as 'neutral'. The fact that MERCOSUR, along with associate members Chile and Bolivia, felt the need to define a common stance in an international issue of such magnitude is, however, important in itself and indicative of the desire to take a more active role in world affairs.[30] Brazil's president Lula actually sought a negotiated solution at the UN level in order to persuade the United States to moderate their impatience, and later deplored that the US had resorted to military force without the Security Council's explicit backing. Another example of this proactive attitude is the 'Friends of Venezuela' initiative launched by Brazil with the participation of Chile, Mexico, Portugal, Spain and the United States.

The common trait is to be found in a clear preference for diplomacy and the defence of multilateralism. At the same time, the fight against terrorism and the region-wide successes in checking proliferation are stressed. As far as the relationship with the United States is concerned, all agree broadly – though with different nuances – that strategic alliance with the United States remains a shared necessity on economic and security considerations alike. There is a marked resemblance, in other words, with the position of the EU vis-à-vis the United States. The panoply of civilian power instruments at its disposal allows the EU to act in world affairs, if not decisively, at least to some extent, MERCOSUR has yet to create such instruments and mechanisms. Equally, it has yet to devise a common foreign policy, and its sphere of action is limited to the commercial and (to some extent) economic arenas. More so than in Europe, therefore, states are in practice the sole actors in international affairs, and therefore the main EU interlocutors, where region-to-region coordination in international affairs and security is concerned.

The main items on any inter-regional cooperation agenda would seem to be the following: the promotion of a proactive multilateral agenda with the aim to bolster the UN's capacity to face major international security issues; the promotion of a 'critical dialogue' with the United States in an effort to lobby American institutions and decision makers in favour of the multilateralist approach with the aim to 'multilateralize' the United States, which remain as indispensable as ever for the resolution of any major international crisis; the joint exploration of the civilian power approach to crisis prevention and management and post-conflict rehabilitation, namely in what concerns the Andean countries; the promotion of a structured region-to-country security dialogue, between the new EU security mechanisms and MERCOSUR and its members and associates, with a focus on peacekeeping and crisis management.[31]

Two unknown factors are essential for the success of EU/MERCOSUR cooperation. On the one hand, the European constitutional crisis has yet to be resolved, and consequently it is still unclear whether the European Union can be equipped with real efficiency and unity in the realm of foreign politics – that is, if it can contribute decisively to the embodiment of a new, efficient multilateralism. On the other hand, it is also unclear whether Lula's second mandate will equip MERCOSUR with the mechanisms of political cooperation, and with an improved desire for greater international activism, combined with the deepening of MERCOSUR. It is equally unclear whether the European Union and Brazil will yield to the temptation of renouncing inter-regionalism in favour of bilateralism, faced with a deadlock on multilateral and block to block negotiations.

Looking back on the last decade of the twentieth century, the 1990s can be defined by a consolidation of regionalism, with the deepening of the EU, the emergence of MERCOSUR and the beginnings of the hemispheric FTA. Working towards their shared vision of a multilateral world order based on regionalism may well be the most relevant contribution that the EU and MERCOSUR can make to international peace and security into the twenty-first century. The failure of the unilateral agenda so tragically revealed in Iraq once more creates a window of opportunity for the new multilateralism agenda. Will the European Union and MERCOSUR be the driving forces for this agenda? Only the future can tell, but it is absolutely essential that they are.

Notes

* The updated version of this chapter has benefited from the work developed in the framework of the Working Group on Global Governance and Multi-Regionalism of the European Union Latin America Relations Observatory (EULARO/OBREAL).

1 Francis Fukuyama, 'The End of History', *The National Interest*, Summer 1989; Samuel P. Huntington, 'The Clash of Civilisation?' *Foreign Affairs*, vol. 72, no. 3, 1993, pp. 22–49.

2 The EMP, comprising the twenty-seven EU countries and the twelve Mediterranean states, is an open regionalism project that could lead to the creation of a vast free trade area in 2010. The SADC was formed in 1992 from the former SADCC (South African Development and Coordination Conference), founded in 1980. It includes Angola, Botswana, the Democratic Republic of the Congo (1997), Lesotho, Malawi, Mauritius (1995), the Seychelles (1997), South Africa (1994), Mozambique, Namibia, Swaziland, Tanzania, Zambia and Zimbabwe.

3 See Guilherme d'Oliveira Martins and Álvaro Vasconcelos, 'A lógica da *integração aberta*, base de um novo multiregionalismo', in Integração Aberta, Lisbon: Euro-Latin American Forum, Institute for Strategic and International Studies (IEEI), 1995.

4 See Marie-Françoise Durand and Álvaro Vasconcelos, *La Pesc – Ouvrir l'Europe au Monde* (Paris: Presses de Sciences Politiques, 1998).

5   Monica Hirst, 'A dimensão política do Mercosul: especificadades nacionais, aspectos institucionais e actores sociais', in *Integração Aberta* (Lisbon: Euro-Latin American Forum/IEEI, 1995), p. 193.

6   Raymond Aron, 'L'Europe face à la crise des sociétés industrielles', in *L'Europe? L'Europe*, texts collected by Pascal Ory (Paris: Omnibus, 1998).

7   The Washington Consensus emerged from a seminar promoted by the economist John Williamson in 1989, organized to discuss the reforms needed to resolve the Latin American debt crisis. It consisted of a set of economic, financial and social policies and reforms, recommended by multilateral institutions such as the IMF and the World Bank, the application of which set the conditions for the grant of loans, renegotiation of external debt and, ultimately, the reinsertion of Latin America in the international financial system.

8   Felix Peña, 'América Latina, el Mercosul y la Comunidad', in *Convergência Natural* (Lisbon: IEEI, 1993), p. 96.

9   Hélio Jaguaribe, speech delivered at the Fourth Latin American Forum, Institute for Strategic and International Studies (IEEI), Rome, 1996.

10 Geraldo Holanda Cavalcanti, 'As opções da América Latina face às transformações de hoje', speech delivered at the First Euro-Latin American Forum, Federação das Indústrias do Estado de São Paulo (FIESP) and IEEI, São Paulo, 1990.

11 Hélio Jaguaribe, 'Uma nova concepção de segurança para o Brasil', *Estrategia: Revista de Estudos Internacionais* (Lisbon), nos 8–9, 1996.

12 Hirst, 'A dimensão política do Mercosul'.

13 José Luis Simon, 'Lessons from Paraguay', *Open Integration Newsletter* (Lisbon: IEEI, 1998).

14 For a more detailed analysis of MERCOSUR as an open pole in a system of undefined polarities, see: Celso Lafer and Gelson Fonseca, 'A problemática da integração num mundo de polaridades indefinidas', in *Integração Aberta* (Lisbon: Euro-Latin American Forum/IEEI, 1995).

15 Guilherme d'Oliveira Martins, *O enigma Europeu* (Lisbon: Quetzal Editores, 1993).

16 Celso Lafer, Conference IEEIbr/IEEI, 'As Novas Realidades e o Potencial de Cooperação entre a UE e a América Latina', São Paulo, 4-5 de September, 2006.

17 Speech by Fernando Henrique Cardoso, delivered at the closing session of the Fifth Euro-Latin American Forum, IEEI, Lisbon, 1998.

18 Felix Peña, 'Dilemas do Mercosul a Cinco' *O Mundo em Português*, n.63, Outubro-Novembro 2006.

19 Felix Peña, Interrogantes sobre el futuro: las negociaciones comerciales tras las elecciones en Brasil e en los EEUU', Novembro de 2006.

20 Marco Aurélio Garcia , Conference IEEIbr/IEEI, 'As Novas Realidades e o Potencial de Cooperação entre a UE e a América Latina', São Paulo, 4-5 de September, 2006.

21 See Alfredo Valladão, *Le XXIe siècle sera américain* (Paris: La Découverte, 1993).

22 Stuart E. Eizenstat, 'Our Future Trade Agenda', remarks before the House of Representatives, 24 September 1997.

23 See Riordan Roett, *The EU and MERCOSUR: US Perspectives*, text prepared for the Fifth Euro-Latin American Forum, Lisbon, May 1998.

24 Before the 'fast-track' option was put in place in 1974, US law already allowed the President to negotiate, within certain stipulations and time limits, commercial agreements and reciprocal tariff reductions with trading partners. The 1974 bill confirmed the power of Congress to delegate authority to the President to negotiate commercial agreements and tariff reductions subject to a consultative mechanism between the President and

Congress during the negotiation procedure, establishing fixed objectives and including a number of procedures enabling agreements to be established on non-tariff barriers.

25 Helio Jaguaribe, *Mercosul e as alternativas para a ordem mundial* (Rio de Janeiro: Instituto de Estudos Politicos e Sociais, 1998).

26 Stuart E. Eizenstat, 'Our Future Trade Agenda', remarks before the House of Representatives, 24 September 1997.

27 Jean-Marie Guéhenno, 'The Impact of Globalisation on Strategy', paper delivered at the 40th Annual Conference of the International Institute for Strategic Studies, Oxford, 3–6 September 1998.

28 Speech by Jacques Chirac, delivered to the Congress of the Federal Republic of Brazil, Brasilia, 12 March 1997.

29 Sixth Euro-Latin-American Forum Report, 'Forging a New Multilateralism. A view from the European Union and Mercosul', Principia, 2001.

30 Statement issued by the Mercosul+2 foreign ministers meeting in Montevideo, 5 February 2003.

31 See *Álvaro de Vasconcelos*, Back to the future? Strengthening EU/Mercosul Relations and Reviving Multilateralism, Chair Mercosul, 2003.

Chapter 9

African Regionalism and EU-African Interregionalism

Fredrik Söderbaum

1 Introduction

There is a strong tendency in the research field that regionalism on the African continent is seen as primitive, weak or simply a failure (Asante, 1997; Mattli, 1999; Mistry, 2003). A closely related misunderstanding is the notion that regionalism in Africa is of little or no relevance for comparative regionalism (as illustrated by the fact that Africa is seldom mentioned in this literature). These weaknesses reflect the general marginalization of Africa in both research and policy as well as the overwhelming dominance of mainstream and Eurocentric perspectives in the research field. The problem is that the dominant mainstream (and largely rationalist) theories of regionalism – such as realism, liberal institutionalism, (neo)functionalism and regional economic integration theory – are based on specific modes of knowledge production and privilege certain research questions at the expense of others. In particular, they have a rather narrow focus on formal and state-centric regional projects and/or official trade and investment flows, often with Europe and the European Union (EU) as a model, marker or comparator. This chapter will show that such assumptions are less helpful for understanding the logic of regionalism in Africa. As pointed out by one authority on African politics, Christopher Clapham:

> The model of inter-state integration through formal institutional frameworks, which has hitherto dominated the analysis of integration in Africa and elsewhere, has increasingly been challenged by the declining control of states over their own territories, the proliferation of informal networks, and the incorporation of Africa (on a highly subordinate basis) into the emerging global order (Clapham, 1999: 53).

Despite the recent fanfare surrounding the transformation of the Organization of African Unity (OAU) to the African Union (AU), at least the more cautious commentators are pessimistic that the new entity will be able to attain its vaunted goals of a highly developed institutional framework – modelled on the EU – with attendant economic and political integration. The largely dismal track-record of OAU and most other regional African ventures, such as the Arab Mahreb Union (AMU), the Common Market for Eastern and Southern Africa (COMESA), the Economic Community of West African States (ECOWAS), the Intergovernmental Authority on Development (IGAD) and the Southern African Development

Community (SADC), only contributes to the general lack of confidence in formal state-led regionalism in Africa. In contrast, witness the wide range of non-state actors and activities, such as transnational corporations, businesses, socio-ethnic and religious networks, civil societies, think-tanks, private armies, and the informal border politics of small-scale trade, bartering, smuggling and crime.

This is by no means equivalent to saying that states and inter-governmental regional organizations are negligible actors or objects of analysis in the study of regionalism. But whereas mainstream theories are often based on highly normative assumptions about the state and how regionalism/regional integration should proceed, the reality of the post-colonial state in Africa is that it cannot be taken for granted; it needs to be problematized, and it is often a different animal than it pretends to be. The perspective advanced in this chapter – the new regionalism approach (NRA) – obviates the artificial separation of state and non-state actors associated with traditional or conventional regional approaches and also recognizes that formal and informal aspects of regionalization are often closely intertwined.

This chapter is not an exhaustive survey of the varieties of regionalism in Africa, especially not a mapping of intergovernmental regional organizations. It seeks rather to pinpoint some general features of regionalism in African in a more comprehensive sense, with an emphasis on the interplay between state and non-state regional actors as well as formal and informal processes. What is today the EU has played and continues to play a crucial role in the construction of regionalism in Africa, as a model/anti-model, as a comparator and as an actor promoting (and sometimes preventing) regionalism and interregionalism on the African continent. The main thread of this chapter is, in the first instance, to make comparative reflections on regionalism in Africa, but at the same time account for (and problematize) the ways the EU is influencing both analysis and policy-making. Most empirical illustrations are taken from Eastern and Southern Africa, but many of the examples apply to Africa more generally.

The analysis proceeds as follows. The next section situates and outlines the general conceptual and theoretical framework, that is, the NRA. The second and most comprehensive section emphasizes three modes of regionalism in Africa: the 'project' of market integration, regime-boosting regionalism and shadow regionalization. The third section analyzes the EU's role as an external actor for promoting regionalism and EU-Africa interregionalism, and the final section looks at the results in a wider comparative perspective.

2 Theorizing regionalism

Mainstream and rationalist schools of regionalism – such as neorealism, intergovernmentalism, neoliberal institutionalism, (neo)functionalism and regional economic integration and so forth – have had a profound impact on the research field (Mansfield & Milner, 1997; Mattli, 1999; Laursen, 2003). There is an impressive research output connected to these schools, and there is no doubt about the fact that they have contributed to a better understanding of regionalism

Table 9.1   Two types of regionalism

	Old regionalism	New regionalism
Actors	Dominated by states and intergovernmental regional organizations	Involves state, market, civil society and external actors
Areas of cooperation	Cooperation in clearly delimited sectors, especially trade and security	Cooperation on a variety of fronts simultaneously, with strong sectoral linkages
Policy orientation	Introverted and often protectionistic	Extroverted, often directly linked with globalization

and regionalist projects around the world. One of the more fundamental problems with these theories lies, however, in that the same underlying assumptions and conceptualizations that stem from a particular reading of European integration influence both the description and prescription of regionalism in the rest of the world. This is problematic because the underlying ontological and theoretical assumptions – such as the notion of unitary or 'strong' states, the influence of regional institutions, and the emphasis on trade and policy-led economic integration – are more relevant in certain contexts than in others. In essence, the often positivistic logic of investigation seems to result in a concern with the methodological approach of regionalism rather than with a systematic concern for the socio-economic circumstances and historical context within which regionalism occurs. This bias helps to explain both why conventional readings and models of European integration are so dominant in the research field as well as why regionalism in Africa is neglected or considered to be primitive.

During the last two decades a series of reflectivist and constructivist approaches to regionalism have been developed, which reject the particular type of knowledge production inherent in mainstream theorizing (see Hettne et al. 1999–2001; Söderbaum and Shaw, 2003). Several of these alternative approaches also challenge the conventional view that regionalism is primarily driven through formal supranational or intergovernmental regional frameworks as well as the overemphasis on the cases of Europe and more recently on North America and the Asia-Pacific. The point is not to reject European regionalism, but to complement the orthodox readings.

This chapter draws on critical and reflectivist thinking and proposes the relevance of what has been established as the new regionalism approach (NRA).[1] This framework emphasizes that regionalism must be placed within its particular historical context. Whereas the old regionalism in the 1950s and 1960s was dominated by the bipolar Cold War structure with nation states as the uncontested primary actors, current regionalism since the end of the 1980s needs to be related to the current transformation of the world. Contemporary regionalism is taking place in a 'post-hegemonic' era. The close relationship to globalization illustrates the fact that number, scope and diversity of regionalism has grown significantly since the end of the 1980s.

In the broadest sense 'regionalism' refers to the general phenomenon ('regionalism in Africa'), but this general concept needs to be broken down into analytical categories. A key is to distinguish regionalism from regionalization. 'Regionalism' represents the *policy and project*, whereby state and non-state actors cooperate and coordinate strategy within a particular region or as a type of world order. It is usually associated with a formal programme, and often leads to institution-building. 'Regionalization' refers to the *process* of cooperation, integration, cohesion and identity creating a regional space (issue-specific or general). 'At its most basic it means no more than a concentration of activity – of trade, peoples, ideas, even conflict – at the regional level. This interaction may give rise to the formation of regions, and in turn to the emergence of regional actors, networks, and organisations' (Fawcett, 2005: 25). As this chapter will show, one of the major weaknesses with the majority of studies in the field of regionalism in Africa is an obsession with the policies of regionalism and little or no concern for processes of regionalization. This chapter also suggests that regionalism and regionalization often impact on one another: regionalism may thus precede as well as follow from regionalization.

The NRA emphasizes the constructed nature of regions. Mostly when we speak of regions we actually mean regions 'in the making and unmaking'. When such constructivist postulation is accepted it is necessary to transcend pre-defined regions (especially the fixation on regional inter-state policy frameworks) in favour of more flexible definitions of regions. Just like nation states, regions are highly subjective (even imagined) phenomena, created and recreated not only through material incentives but also through identities, ideas, cognitive resources, and not the least through our theories. From this perspective the task is to try to understand and assess how and why actors build, construct and deconstruct regions. Hence, regions should not be taken as natural, organic, essential or simply material objects. Instead, from the point of view of NRA, regions are considered to be dynamic settings for social interaction and the research focus is placed on the processes through which they are 'becoming', including for whom and for what purpose.

An important feature of the NRA is the emphasis on a variety of state, market and society actors (including external actors) in regionalism and regionalization. Due to the often close relationship between state and non-state actors this implies at the same time that different actors often come together in a variety of multi-actor coalitions as well as overlapping and competing modes of regionalism/regionalization. This rather general framework can then be used for analyzing regionalism in a wide range of fields, such as security, culture, environment, and as in this chapter, the political economy of development regionalism.

3 Comparative reflections on regionalism in Africa[2]

This section outlines three modes of regionalism in Africa: the project of market integration, regime-boosting regionalism and shadow regionalization. All of them seem to appear, one way or the other, in different combinations on the African continent. The project of market integration draws attention to the overlapping strategies to further African economic integration on different scales (continental, regional and micro-regional) and the preferences to make these policies and strategies compatible with market-dominated forms of economic globalization and capitalism. Regime-boosting regionalism suggests that ruling political regimes in weak states use regionalism as an instrument to enhance the image, formal sovereignty and legitimacy of their regimes (rather than their nation states in a broader sense). Thirdly, shadow regionalization refers to an informal mode of regional interaction, whereby public office-holders utilize their position and come together with business actors in order to engage in informal and illegal market activities.

The 'project' of market integration

The general ideological foundation of regional cooperation and integration in Africa is seen in the visions and series of treaties developed within the framework of the AU, formerly the OAU, most notably the Lagos Plan of Action, the Abuja Treaty, and more recently the Constitutive Act of the AU and the New Partnership for Africa's Development (Nepad) (Asante, 1997; Muchie, 2003; Muthiri, 2005; Taylor, 2005). The common vision is that pan-African cooperation and integration provides a solution both to the Balkanization of the African economies on a continental level and to the marginalization of Africa in the world economy.

In the past the pan-African visions have stressed collective self-reliance and introverted strategies based on protectionism, state-led and planned distribution of resources and import-substitution industrialization. Even if there are still some scattered demands, particularly among a diminishing number of intellectuals, for a revitalization of such 'old' ideas of regionalism, there has clearly been a dramatic shift in regional visions and institutions in Africa during the two last decades. Most analysts and policy-makers continue to emphasize the problems of weak and small African economies (that is, Balkanization) and often they also favour the ultimate goal of the African Economic Community (AEC), whereby sub-continental regional economic communities (RECs), such as AMU, COMESA, ECOWAS and SADC, are building-blocs for continental unity. However, the introverted strategies are now replaced by a vision and strategy whereby Africa 'must unite' in order to exploit the opportunities provided by economic globalization and liberalized markets. There is thus a much stronger emphasis on outward-oriented regional economic integration, compatible with the global trading agenda under the World Trade Organization (WTO), whereby Africa's marginalization and underdevelopment is to be overcome by closer *integration* into the world economy.

The change in thinking is very evident in the case of Nepad. This venture is quite similar to many previous (and failed) recovery plans in Africa in that it outlines a comprehensive list of development projects and programmes. Nepad is different, however, in that it stresses a closer engagement with the North and an improvement in Africa's political-economic leadership. This reflects hegemonic understandings of neoliberal capitalism and 'good governance', as espoused by the World Bank, the International Monetary Fund (IMF), the G8, the EU and large parts of the donor community. According to Nepad's own logic, ascribing to the familiar ingredients of the Washington Consensus and the exploitation of the opportunities of economic globalization will bring access to markets, aid, investment flows and debt relief, all of which are deemed necessary for the continent's recovery (Taylor, 2005).

This overall paradigm has secured a foothold in most of Africa's main regional cooperation and integration schemes, such as COMESA, ECOWAS, SADC and UEMOA. The paradigmatic shift of SADC is significant, and quite similar to the change of thinking within OAU/AU. SADC's predecessor, the Southern African Development Coordination Conference (SADCC) (1980–92), was deliberately designed in order to avoid trade and market integration, and favoured a strategy of dirigist import substitution industrialization coupled with the equitable distribution of costs and benefits. Although there is still some rhetorical association to 'development integration' within SADC, the new venture (launched in 1992) has officially embraced a conventional market-orientation dominated by a commitment to market liberalization and to some extent also to 'open regionalism'. This is in line with the liberal argument that any regional trading bloc in Africa is too small in itself to generate economic development, resulting in the overall intention being to ensure a closer integration of the region (and continent) into the global economy. As two influential economists emphasize: 'regional integration should not be perceived as an alternative to more general trade liberalization, which is crucial if African economies are to grow, but rather as one step in a process of greater integration into international markets' (Jenkins and Thomas, 2001: 168).

There is a simultaneous and perhaps even stronger emphasis on neoliberal policies on the micro-regional level, at least in Southern Africa. Both South Africa and the Southern African region are currently being reconfigured by the implementation of a large number of spatial development initiatives (SDIs) and development corridors (www.africansdi.com; Söderbaum & Taylor, 2003). These are targeted, short-term interventions with the official purpose to crowd-in private investment in order to unlock economic potential, to enhance regional economic integration, and to become integrated into the global economy. The SDIs are governance mechanisms designed to quickly change legislation, change the role of public governance, broaden the ownership base of the economy, and enhance market competition. SDIs are built on the implementation of private and commercial investment projects of assorted kinds and size. In all cases it is an outspoken neoliberal market paradigm that rules investment decisions: 'In order to be selected for inclusion in the SDI process, a project must offer a commercially viable return on investment, ie it must be a bankable project – a project which a commercial financial institution would be willing to back' (Jourdan, 1998: 20).

According to this line of thinking, there is only a need for minimal public and formal institutions since these are basically seen as bureaucratic obstacles of a functioning market economy. The result is a narrow and exclusivist micro-regional governance mechanism, geared primarily towards enhancing privatization, private investment projects and public-private partnerships (PPPs). In fact, all SDIs and development corridors in Southern Africa are surrounded by a rhetoric of people-centred development. In reality, however, the role of public institutions is limited to implementing trade and investment liberalization or to boosting new bankable and commercially viable investment projects, often of gigantic proportions, such as Saldanha Steel, the Mozambique aluminium smelter (Mozal), the Maputo iron and steel project (MISP), and so forth. Even public roads are becoming commercialized, as shown by the N4 toll road between Johannesburg and Maputo. In this process the main function of the state has been reduced to a gigantic investment promotion agency (Söderbaum & Taylor, 2003). This, in turn, implies a loss of public participation and democratic control in the decision-making and implementation process.

The general argument raised in this section is that market integration should be understood as a distinctive 'project', with a highly political content, fashioned and pursued by identifiable actors, institutions and interests. The project is shared and reinforced by a wide range of state and non-state actors from within the region (politicians and policy-makers, think-tanks and researchers, as well as businesses and private sector alliances) as well as by external actors (especially the EU, G8, IMF, World Bank and Western donors).

The strong link between government institutions and the corporate sector is particularly evident in the case of South Africa's business expansion into Africa, especially Southern Africa. As stated by former Minister of Foreign Affairs, Alfred Nzo, the official position of the South African government is that by 'encouraging the involvement of our private sector elsewhere on the continent, we will also be contributing to the transfer of South African expertise and technology to other African countries, which would in turn contribute to their development' (quoted in Patel, 1999: 18–19). It is evident that South African commercial actors have successfully been able to position themselves as an integral part of key policy strategies, such as the 'African renaissance' (today's Nepad), the sub-regionalist visions and discourses of SADC, the Southern African Customs Union (SACU), the SDIs and development corridors. Making such associations provide them with the necessary legitimacy for conducting business activities that otherwise could have been seen as more exploitative.

The South African business expansion would not be possible without the support and legitimacy of the political elite in the host countries, as well as from key powers in the West, especially the World Bank, the IMF and the EU. One of the problems with the South African-centred economic order constructed by state-business elites is the fact that local business often feel discriminated through what they perceive as unfair competition and even a new form of 'imperialism' (Fernando Goncalves, 'The new Great Trek', Southern African Economist, August–September 1997, p. 4). This issue is discussed in policy circles as well as in academic debates. One of the more critical academic studies suggests that the market forces and South African capital are now creating economically what the old apartheid regime failed to do politically some three decades ago, that is, a Constellation of Southern African Economies (CONSAE) instead of the old proposal of a Constellation of Southern African States (CONSAS) (Ahwireng-Obeng and McGowan, 1998; Söderbaum, 2004a).

Market integration is an ongoing 'project', which can never be complete or finished. Likewise, it is by no means a linear or irreversible drive towards 'free' trade and integration into the global economy; there is always real and potential resistance. Resistance or lack of policy implementation may certainly arise for collective action problems and 'failure' to cooperate. It may also arise when the costs of liberalization and market integration exceed the anticipated gains, which can certainly be desirable from a normative point of view, for instance in order to prevent de-industrialization of weak and vulnerable economies. Governments and politicians may have a key role in preventing market integration, but as the next two sections suggest there seem to be more detrimental reasons than to promote development.

Regime-boosting regionalism

Regime-boosting regionalism seeks to strengthen the status, legitimacy and the general interests of the political regime (rather than the nation state per se), both on the international arena and domestically. Many ruling regimes and political leaders in Africa engage in symbolic and discursive activities, whereby they praise the goals of regionalism and regional organizations, sign cooperation treaties and agreements, and take part in 'summitry regionalism', but without having a commitment to or bearing the costs of policy implementation.

In order to understand how certain African regimes use regionalism for regime-boosting purposes, one needs to consider the nature of statehood on the continent. It is widely agreed that most states in Africa are 'weak'. There is also persuasive evidence that weak states tend to place heavy emphasis on formal and absolute sovereignty in their international relations – that is, the maintenance of existing borders and the principle of non-intervention in domestic affairs – because it enhances the power of the governing political elite and its ability to stay in power (Clapham, 1996). In spite of the fact that most states are 'weak', the states system and the old colonial boundaries have, with a few exceptions, remained intact and seemingly everlasting. The result is a somewhat paradoxical situation with 'weak' states and rather 'strong' or at least 'stable' regimes' (Bøås, 2003).

At first glance, regime-boosting regionalism has similarities with more conventional types of regional cooperation, both in liberal and realist thinking. However, it is different since it neither promotes various types of public goods (liberalism) nor broader national and societal interest (realism). Regionalism is instead used as an image-boosting instrument whereby leaders can show support and loyalty for each other, which enables them to raise the profile, status, formal sovereignty and image of their often authoritarian regimes, but without ensuring implementation of agreed policies. In contrast to much of the conventional readings on this topic, this does not represent a complete 'failure' or absence of collective action. From the point of view of the political regimes that favour such discursive strategies, it is a rather 'successful' type of collective action.

There are a variety of regime-boosting strategies. One is the importance of 'summitry' and high-profile meetings and conferences in regionalism. The summits of heads of states of the main intergovernmental regional organizations, such as AU, ECOWAS and SADC, are gigantic and sometimes even majestetic events where the political leaders can show to the world and their citizenry that they are promoting the cause of regional cooperation and that their political regime is 'important' (or at least 'visible') on the international arena. The summits and conferences are important components in discursive and even imaginary constructions of regional organizations, and this social practice is then repeated and institutionalized at a large number of ministerial and other meetings, which in reality involves no real debate and no wider consultation within or between member states (Simon, 2003: 71). Sidaway and Gibb explain the logic of such discursive strategies and practices within SADC:

> formal participation in SADC is another way whereby the states [i.e. regimes] seek to confirm, fix and secure the appearance and power of 'sovereignty'. Rather like the boundaries and colour schemes of political maps, participation in fora such as SADC is a way in which the state is actively represented as a real, solid, omnipresent authority. In doing so, the fact that it is a contested, socially constructed (not simply natural) object is obscured, and states would have us take them for granted as the natural objects of governance and politics (Sidaway & Gibb, 1998: 179).

The overlapping membership of regional organizations on the African continent has been debated for several decades.[3] And the seemingly ineffective overlap is often taken as an indicator of the 'failure' of African regionalism or at least as a poor political commitment to ensure a more appropriate division of labour. Considering that the overlap is such a distinctive feature of regionalism in Africa, it is relevant to assess the negative impacts of the overlap itself, but also to ask in whose interests it prevails, even has been institutionalized. The maintenance of a large number of competing and overlapping intergovernmental regional organizations may arguably by a deliberate strategy in order to increase the possibilities for verbal regionalism and regime-boosting. To the extent that policy implementation is not the main concern such pluralism may actually be a way to construct 'disorder' and competing regional agendas (cf. Chabal & Daloz, 1999). Furthermore, Bach claims that regional organizations constitute a means for 'resource capture' and international patronage:

> Concomitant membership of several groupings often appears of little practical consequence since policies are episodically implemented and financial contributions irregularly paid. Far from being an inextricable source of conflict, overlapping membership can be negotiated and translates into additional opportunities for the pursuit of conference diplomacy, participation in externally funded ventures or support from regional or extra-regional powers (Bach, 2005: 182–83).

Most of the main regional organizations in Africa (such as AU, ECOWAS, EAC, IGAD, SADC, UEMOA[4]) have undergone comprehensive institutional reform during recent decades, and in many cases the EU has been the major source of inspiration and support. In general there are convincing reasons to promote institutional strengthening of regional organizations, since most of them are weak, undersupplied and lack the capacity to ensure policy implementation. But institution-building is not an end in itself and can also be used for regime-boosting purposes.

The institutional reform of the AU is noteworthy, and often praised as an example of a necessary institutional strengthening. In the past the OAU has been criticized for having been used as an image-boosting arena and a mechanism whereby personal rulers and authoritarian elites have been able to praise one another on the African scene (Clapham, 1996). It is at least partly in response to such critique that the architects behind the AU and the African leaders have made strong efforts to emphasize that the AU is different. Although the AU has inherited many of the OAU's institutions, it has committed itself to a new and stronger institutional structure. Whereas the OAU could be compared to a continental/regional model of the United Nations, the AU is loosely modelled on the EU. In addition to the Assembly of Heads of State and the Council of Ministers, the AU also has the African Commission (headed by a Commissioner), and the Pan-African Parliament (launched in South Africa in 2004). It further plans a Court of Justice (to rule on human rights abuses) as well as various financial institutions (a central bank, a monetary fund and an investment bank). All this boils down to that the AU is supposed to more concerned with 'implementation' (for example, Nepad) and with strictures and institutions supposed to safeguard against unconstitutional changes of government and increased emphasis on good governance and democracy. Especially notable in this regard is the African Peer Review Mechanism (APRM), which aims to make African leaders police themselves. Although it is perhaps too early to evaluate the impact of institutional reform, there is a vivid discussion to what extent AU, APRM and Nepad actually represent anything 'new' or if it is just 'another false start' where old practices continue (Taylor, 2005).

The institutional reforms of SADCC/SADC have a longer history and are particularly relevant for this discussion. The allocation of sectoral responsibilities to each member country was an innovative institutional structure at the start of SADCC in 1980. At the time the decentralized structure was seen as a way to provide a sense of 'ownership' to each of the member states and avoid the cost of a regional bureaucracy (SADC, 1997: 63). However, it is openly discussed and also admitted by SADC policy makers that this institutional structure was then captured by governments seeking to promote their own national and more myopic goals. The national ownership mentality of each sector became so strong that it even resulted in competition between countries, with each sector representing 'national pride' and status. Particularly important from a regime-boosting perspective is the fact that even those sectoral coordinating units that lacked the administrative capacity and the funds to function and implement projects and programmes were still seen as important. According to two self-critical evaluations, SADC's type of cooperation 'encourages political (and rhetorical) rather than economic developments' (SADC, 1997: 63; Isaksen & Tjønneland, 2001).

Furthermore, at least until the mid-1990s, the implementation that actually was achieved within SADCC/SADC was first and foremost tied to its project portfolio. Several factors point in the direction of regime-boosting regionalism. It is, for instance, no secret that the majority of the projects in SADC's project portfolio were more a direction of intent, even a 'wishing list' rather than a development plan with a realistic funding plan. Since the majority of the projects (70–90 per cent) have been/are externally funded by the donor community (especially the Nordic countries and the EU), this enabled the SADC regimes to pay tribute to the goals of regionalism without providing the funds for implementation. In addition, the fact that 'the majority of projects are national and lack a clear regional focus' has enabled the participating regimes to design and implement 'national' projects dressed up as regional (SADC, 1997: 63; Isaksen & Tjønneland, 2001).

Ever since the transformation from SADCC into SADC, the organization has been involved in a slow process of gradual institutional reform and centralization. The interesting thing is that symbolic and regime-boosting politics have actually increased in spite of the institutional reforms. Such diplomacy is taking place in the context of increased international pressure on certain political regimes in the region, such as Zimbabwe, Swaziland, Namibia and Zambia. Similarly to many other regional organizations in Africa (for example, OAU/AU, IGAD and ECOWAS), SADC has often been referred to as 'an old boys' club' where political leaders are able to show loyalty to one another. At least some extent this 'club-mentality' seems to prevail, and in response to the critique and 'shaming and blaming' from major powers and agencies in the West as well as from some civil society actors, the SADC leaders have repeatedly condemned sanctions against Zimbabwe, claiming it is intervention in 'African affairs'. The SADC Summit also considered the elections in Zimbabwe in 2002 as 'free and fair', whereas the elections were heavily criticized by international election monitors, the independent SADC Parliamentary Forum and some civil society actors around the region.

Shadow regionalization

An increasing amount of studies in the research field draw attention to the vibrant informal economic processes of cross-border and regional interaction in large parts of Africa (Bach, 1999; Grant & Söderbaum, 2003). These processes arise for many reasons, one is subsistence, as seen by the multitude of small-scale cross-border traders and vendors buying and selling all types of goods, such as vegetables, fruits, staple products, clothes and small home appliances. Sometimes these small-scale informal traders are also ending up building viable business enterprises. There is a rich variety of actors of assorted kinds involved in these processes, but rather than depicting these practices only as a way for poor people to survive, the concept of shadow regionalization adds important elements to the logic at play. Shadow regionalization – or as Bach (1999, 2005) labels it: 'trans-state regionalization' – draws attention to the fact that public officials and various actors within the state bureaucracy may be entrenched in informal market activities with the purpose to promote either political goals or their private economic interests.[5]

Shadow regionalization grows from below and is built upon rent-seeking or the stimulation of patron-client relationships. As such it undermines the regulatory capacity of the state and formal regionalism. The profits involved in shadow networks are considerable. These networks are also inequitable and extremely uneven since they accumulate power and resources at the top, to the rich and powerful, and those who have jobs, rather than to the unemployed, the urban poor and rural producers. Indeed, small-scale cross-border traders have a disadvantage since the economies of scale are 'only for those who can pay the necessary bribes' (Bach, 1997: 162).

It is important to emphasize that these accumulation strategies do not occur just anywhere. Shadow networks arise, obviously, easier in the context of shadow states or in the presence of large border disparities. This shows that certain rentier-classes actively seek to preserve existing boundary disparities (for example, customs, monetary, fiscal and normative) and as a consequence try to resist implementation or rationalization of formal regional economic integration schemes. But in contrast to conventional policy-centred notions about regionalism/regional integration in Africa, this does not imply an absence of *de facto* regionalization. Commenting on the extremely drawn out process of renegotiating the SACU agreement in the post-apartheid era, Sidaway and Gibb (1998: 178) refer to a representative of the South African negotiation team, who claims that dominant rentier-elite fractions in Botswana-Lesotho-Swaziland-Namibia countries 'are dragging their feet because the old formula is advantageous to them'. Hence, the shadow (or 'trans-state') networks depend on the failure of both the formal economy and of formal/policy-led regionalism. Consequently, when political leaders and policy-makers resist formal regionalism, this may very well be a deliberate strategy to maintain *status quo* in order to not disrupt shadow regionalization. As the authority of this kind of analysis eloquently points out:

> The reluctance of most African governments towards effective transfers of sovereignty and their inability to enforce commonly agreed policies stimulate debilitating patterns of regionalisation. Their stringent adherence to the preservation of national sovereignty and territorial status quo nurtures the formation of trans-boundary spaces in a context also marked by the dilution of inter-state relations into socio-ethnic and religious networks. Trans-state regionalisation mirrors the dynamics of deterritorialisation and deinstitutionalisation that are at work within most states (Bach, 2005: 185).

The attempts to restrict shadow and trans-state informal flows have often been unsuccessful. In the current (neoliberal and post-Cold War) context where the state apparatus itself offers less opportunities for private accumulation and where formal barriers between countries have been reduced, shadow regionalization stems no longer only from the exploitation of existing border disparities. Instead it has expanded to more criminal activities, such as new trades in illicit drugs, including heroin, mandrax and cocaine, arms, light weapons and other merchandise of war. In certain respects shadow networks have entered a new phase, whereby they are better understood as 'networks of plunder', profiting from war and chaos or warlord politics (MacLean, 1999; Taylor and Williams, 2001). The networks of plunder can even be actively involved in the creation and promotion of war, conflict and destruction, as seen in the more turbulent parts of Africa, such as the West African war zone, Great Lakes region, the Horn of Africa, and parts of Southern Africa.

4 EU as an actor in regionalism and interregionalism in Africa

In addition to its role as a model and comparator the European Community/ European Union (EC/EU) has a long tradition of support of regional cooperation/ integration and interregionalism. Historically, the EC/EU-ACP partnership has emphasized humanitarian issues and a particular trade-aid relationship with former colonies, but this is now being redefined in a variety of ways, with an emphasis on a partnership 'among equals', a new and more focused interregional trading agenda (compatible with the WTO), and a stronger focus on human rights, governance, democracy and the rule of law.

Article 28 of the Cotonou Agreement outlines the main objectives of the EU-ACP partnership: 'Cooperation shall provide effective assistance to achieve the objectives and priorities which the ACP States have set themselves in the context of regional and sub-regional cooperation and integration, including inter-regional and intra-ACP cooperation'. Given that the ACP framework comprises countries widely dispersed geographically, the EU has developed more specific interregional 'partnerships' with sub-regions of the ACP, such as West Africa, Eastern Africa, Southern Africa, the Caribbean and the Indian Ocean.

Officially the EU's support of regionalism in Africa and the interregional policy through the Cotonou Agreement and the more recent Strategy for Africa is claimed to promote Africa's development and to 'help Africa help itself'. The underlying idea 'is to help the ACP countries integrate with their regional neighbours as a step towards global integration, and to help them build institutional capacities and apply principles of good governance. At the same time, the EU will continue to open its markets to products from the ACP group, and other developing countries' (European Commission, 2004: 10). A closer integration of the African countries and regions into the global economy is, in the EU's official view, considered to be of mutual gain, both for the EU and for the partner regions. In other words, there is a belief that the EU should try to consolidate regional integration arrangements among developing countries *because* regional integration is seen as 'an important step towards their integration in the world economy' (European Commission, 2004: 10). Besides helping developing countries to integrate into the world economy and among themselves, it is also believed in EU circles that regional integration and cooperation can enhance peace, prevent conflict, promote cross-border problem-solving and a better use and management of natural resources.

The EU's self-image and identity as the 'natural' point of reference for regional initiatives is crucial for understanding the EU's role in the promotion of regionalism and interregional partnerships around the world. Indeed, the EU's 'interest' in supporting regionalism and engaging in interregionalism cannot be understood in isolation from its own identity. The EU is (consciously and unconsciously) projecting its own particular regional integration model to the rest of the world. This is justified in several ways, one of the more important reasons is that the EU considers itself as the 'world champion' of regional integration and therefore seems to believe that it has a special mission as well as competence to promote regional integration and cooperation around the globe. Although in official rhetoric the EU does not claim to 'export' the European integration model, its identity as 'the most advanced regional integration project in the world' transpires from a closer analysis of its policies and partnerships (European Commission, 1995). In official documents the European model of integration is repeatedly proclaimed as the most important reference model for virtually all regional initiatives in the world, especially in Africa:

There are a number of lessons that can be drawn from the experience of regional integration in various parts of the world. Probably the most important lesson can be derived from the European experience, not only on account of its long history but also because, to a large extent, it can be considered as the only successful example of regional integration so far (European Commission, 1995: 8).

In a similar fashion, the Prodi Commission (1999–2004) also praises the virtues of the EU model of governance:

Our European model of integration is the most developed in the world. Imperfect though it still is, it nevertheless works on a continental scale. Given the necessary institutional reforms, it should continue to work well after enlargement, and I believe we can make a convincing case that it would also work globally (Prodi quoted in Rosamond, 2005: 473).

It is crucial to point out that these images of the so-called EU model are based on a positioning of the EU according to the Community Method. Rosamond shows that 'policy actors both within and beyond the EU construct the EU in quite particular and arguably partial terms', which neglects the richness and complexity of what the EU actually is (Rosamond, 2005: 473). The important research task, at least from a constructivist viewpoint, would then be to ask 'why these particular constructions?' (Rosamond, 2005: 473).

Apart from competing constructions of what the EU actually is, the other main contentious issue in the discussion on the EU as a model is related to its normative substance. Many of the official statements and proclamations released by the European Commission underline the liberal internationalist and so-called 'civilian' underpinnings of the EU (see Hettne's chapter in this volume; Telo, 2006). The European Commission proudly states that 'the EU is particularly active in promoting the human aspects of international relations, such as solidarity, human rights and democracy' (European Commission, 2004: 1, 3). It is furthermore often stated that the exercise of these values and principles is in accordance with the principles upon which the EU itself is based, and that the Union needs to spread these norms around the world (European Commission, 2000: 1). But the EU-Africa relationship can certainly be further problematized and several analysts challenge the underlying motivations of the EU for spreading these norms and values. For the more cautious observers it is evident that the EU makes use of (and sometimes imposes) a series of different instruments and means on the 'weaker' counterparts. For instance, Mary Farrell argues that for the EU the interregional relationship with Africa is more a means than an end in itself: through building institutions and establishing agreements, 'the EU has established its channels to convey values, priorities and even special interests' (Farrell, 2006: 22–3). Built on agreements and some institution-building, interregionalism legitimizes and enhances liberalization, deregulation, privatization and access, which reflects the extension of economic liberalization in the self-interest of the EU rather than the normative and 'civilian power' agenda stated in the EU's official discourse. This explains in turn why the EU is one of the crucial actors in the 'project' of market integration (which, somewhat ironically, is very different from the way the EU has developed historically). Farrell is particularly critical of the shift of emphasis in the interregional partnership from aid to trade and the emphasis on political dialogue (for example, conditionality), which reinforce (rather than reduce) the power asymmetries between the ACP group of countries and the EU; that is, 'a triumph of realism over idealism' (Farrell, 2005).

Although norms and issues such as human rights, democracy, the rule of law, and good governance were mentioned in earlier agreements, they are now reinserted much more strongly into the new Cotonou Agreement. Given the limited space available suffices it to mention two points. Firstly, these political issues are so closely linked to the EU's economic agenda that their inclusion supports the objectives of economic liberalization rather than any fundamental support for democratization. Secondly, just like much of the economic agenda, political norms are more or less imposed on the African countries with strong political conditionalities attached, and violations of these norms can even be used for 'hegemonic control' by the EU (Farrell, 2005: 271). A similar conclusion is reached by Hurt, who argues that the new EU–ACP Agreement has shifted the relationship further away from one of cooperation to one of coercion, and this needs to be understood within the context of the hegemonic dominance of neoliberalism within political elites (Hurt, 2003).

To the extent that this critical analysis is accepted, the liberal trading agenda as well as the political norms (and conditionalities) can be seen as strategic means for satisfying the EU's underlying material as well as cognitive 'interests'. Together with Björn Hettne I have conceptualized this in terms of 'soft imperialism' rather than the much talked-about 'civilian power' (Hettne & Söderbaum, 2005). As noted above, the EU has frequently been referred to as a 'civilian power', pursuing a norm-driven (or cosmopolitan) foreign policy, which first and foremost stems from the values promoted internally within the Union, such as social pluralism, the rule of law, democracy, and market economy. These values and norms are seen as 'universal' and deemed to be part of a 'civilian' as opposed to a militaristic and 'hard' foreign policy, in the current discussion often associated with the USA. The concept of 'soft imperialism' acknowledges the familiar distinction between hard and soft power coined by Nye (2002), and that the EU is left with the option of soft power, but adds the fact that 'soft power' may also be employed in 'hard' and coercive manner. The difference between civilian power and soft imperialism lies in the overall importance of values and norms, in what ways and for what purpose these are being used, and also whether negotiations are carried out in a symmetric, dialogical way rather than by imposition and in an 'imperial' fashion. Both soft imperialism and civilian appear to be relevant in characterizing the full spectrum of the EU's foreign policy relations, ranging from enlargement, neighbourhood policy to bilateralism and interregionalism (Hettne & Söderbaum, 2005). With regard to EU–African interregionalism, soft imperialism refers to an asymmetric form of dialogue or even the imposition or strategic use of norms and conditionalities with a narrowly defined self-interest rather than for the creation of a symmetrical interregional dialogue and with a greater concern for the 'weaker' counter-part region. It should be evident from the discussion above that, in my view, soft imperialism seems to dominate over civilian power as far as the EU's interregional relationship with Africa and its sub-regions is concerned.

5 Conclusion

This chapter starts out arguing that regionalism on the African continent is often misunderstood both by specialists on Africa and comparative regionalists. This is illustrated by the fact that regionalism in Africa is often seen as weak, 'failed', or simply ignored. Furthermore, the dominance in the research field of a particular reading of European integration in combination with an exaggerated focus on formal and policy-led regionalism go a long way to explain why so many studies have so little of substance to say about regionalism in Africa.

The NRA was suggested as one analytical framework which could overcome the aforementioned weaknesses and provide a more comprehensive perspective on regionalism in Africa. Instead of departing from one particular pre-defined regional delimitation, the NRA seeks to understand how regions are made and unmade, and by whom and for what purpose. The approach emphasizes the constructed nature of regions, in particular how state and non-state actors come together in the interplay between formal and informal regionalization in the context of globalization.

Three particular modes of regionalism are highlighted in the comparative section. The first is based on that the 'old' and protectionist pan-Africanist ideas have been abandoned in favour of a 'new' pan-African strategy whereby state-business elites promote outward-oriented market integration at different policy levels (continental, macro-regional and micro-regional). These regionalist strategies are closely associated with hegemonic understandings of how neoliberal globalization and capitalism should proceed, and gain their strength by the support from the EU as well as IFIs, G8 and large parts of the donor community. Hence, the EU is one crucial actor in the 'project' of market integration (and depending on the assessment and theoretical perspective on this 'project', the EU's role may be interpreted either as civilian power or soft imperialism). One of the more fundamental problems is that there is more evidence on how these strategies and processes reinforce the strength of the already powerful in a hub-and-spoke fashion rather than a people-centred development path.

The gap between rhetoric and implementation in many regional organizations in Africa is often believed to result from the lack of resources, a weak commitment to regionalist projects or collective action problems. The second mode of regionalism highlighted in the chapter, regime-boosting regionalism, suggests a different picture and draws attention to the discursive strategies of political elites in weak states that serve the primary purpose of strengthening the regimes official status, image and legitimacy. Regime-boosting can be a goal in itself, but it may also be closely related to shadow regionalization, which refers to an informal mode of regional interaction, whereby public office-holders utilize their position in order to engage in informal and illegal market activities. The two may be connected in that regime-boosting regionalism provides a façade behind which shadow activities are allowed to prosper.

One criticism raised in this chapter against mainstream approaches to regionalism and regional integration is that they are often developed for and from the European experience, and then more or less re-applied around the world. Breslin and Higgott (2000: 343) are correct in that: 'Ironically, the EU as an exercise in regional integration is one of the major obstacles to the development of analytical and theoretical comparative studies of regional integration'. The problem is not European integration as such, but the dominance of certain constructions and models of it, and the extent to which these have prevented other relevant studies. One problem with the discussion on regionalism in Africa is that the EC/EU has often been reduced to the community method or a common market, with the consequence that there is no or little understanding of the richness and sophistication of European integration studies (cf. Diez & Wiener, 2003). The problem arises from an absence of communication between European integration studies and African/comparative regionalism. Hence, the road towards a more advanced debate on regionalism in Africa lies not in celebrating the differences compared to European integration, but in drawing upon the impressive research being conducted under the broad banner of European integration studies.

Cross-fertilization works in both directions, and regionalism in Africa can also make contributions to European integration studies. Two renowned scholars of European integration, Alex Warleigh and Ben Rosamond (2005), argue that large parts of recent EU studies scholars have considered the EU as a nascent, if unconventional, polity in its own right ('the famous N=1 problem'). This parochialism has contributed little, Warleigh and Rosamond assert, in deepening our understanding of the EU as a political system, and it has ironically also reinforced the notion that the EU is *sui generis*, thereby down-playing the respects in which the EU remains more like other regionalist projects around the world. Warleigh and Rosamond are correct in their assertion that EU studies need to return to the broader ambitions of the comparative (and classical) regional integration theory.

Although informal regionalism is not totally absent in EU studies, a more nuanced discussion of the link between formal regionalism and informal regionalization appears to be one contribution that regionalism in Africa can make to European integration studies. Likewise, regime-boosting is probably not a uniquely African phenomenon (the particularity seems to be related to the character of the African state-society complex and Africa's insertion in the global order). In fact, the EU's sometimes rhetorical commitment to the humanitarian and egalitarian reasons for supporting regionalism and the EU–Africa partnership may be interpreted as discursive and image-building strategies (with other underlying 'interests'). Furthermore, the role of procedures, symbols, summitry, and other discursive practices of regionalism in Asia, Europe, as well as North and Latin America suggest that it is possible to make intriguing comparisons with Africa.

A final comment on the EU's role as an actor is that the EU's self-image and identity is part of the explanation why the EU is so actively promoting regionalism and interregionalism in Africa. The EU considers itself as the world champion of regional integration, which provides it with the (self-proclaimed) legitimacy to spread the EU model of regional integration to other regions. In the EU's official view, the humanitarian, civilian and liberal internationalist content of the EU's policies are emphasized. There is a rich literature on the civilianness and the EU's normative power, and there is also evidence that this model is relevant for comprehending what is taking place. However, the concept of 'soft imperialism' was introduced as an alternative explanation of the EU's underlying interests.

The 'imperial' flavour of the EU's interregional policies towards Africa should be compared to other counterpart regions, such as Latin America and Asia, because it appears that the EU's strategies are closely linked to relative strength of counterpart, that is, suggesting that the EU is more 'civilian' towards other regions.

Notes

1   For the early versions of the NRA, see the five-volume mini-series on New Regionalism edited by Hettne, Inotai and Sunkel (1999–2001). Söderbaum and Shaw (2003) give a comprehensive overview of the main strands within the 'new regionalism' literature, whereas Söderbaum (2004a) provides the most detailed account of the NRA as such.

2   Parts in this section build on Söderbaum (2004a and 2004b).

3   See *Handbook of Regional Organizations in Africa* (Söderbaum, 1995) for an overview. For a more recent database on regional arrangements world-wide, consult Regional Integration Knowledge System (by GARNET/UNU-CRIS) http://www.garnet-eu.org/215.0.html.

4   Internet resources: AGOA, www.agoa.gov; www.afdb.org;AU(OAU)www.africa-union. org; COMESA, www.comesa.int; ECA, www.uneca.org; ECOWAS,www.ecowas.int; IGAD, www.igad.org; NEPAD, www.nepad.org; SADC,www.sadc.int; UEMOA, www. uemoa.int; SDI, www.africansdi.com.

5   Considering the frequent use of the concept of 'shadow state' in the debate on the political economy in Africa (Reno, 1995), it is rather surprising that it is not used more often in the debate on regionalism in Africa.

Chapter 10

Comparison of European and Southeast Asian Integration[1]

Kjell A. Eliassen and Catherine Børve Arnesen

1 Introduction

The main aim of this chapter is to investigate how and why regional organizational structures and integrating mechanisms differ between various regions of the world. There exist numerous studies of European integration, and in recent years also a growing literature on regional integration in other parts of the world, including Pacific Asia. There are, however, only a limited number of studies comparing in a scientific way the European and the Asian models of regional integration or the linkages between these two regions (for example, Robles Jr., 2004; Abad Jr., 2003; Nathan, 2002; Holland, 1994; Higgott, 1995; Milner, 1995), although this theme is touched upon more generally in the analyses of regional integration (for example, Katzenstein, 1996).

In this chapter we will study differences in the organizational structure and integrating mechanisms of regional groupings by comparing the development of the European Union (EU) to that of the Association of South-East Asian Nations (ASEAN). An important characteristic of the new regionalism, as represented by, for example, ASEAN, is the very wide variation in the level of institutionalization, with many regional groupings consciously avoiding the institutional and bureaucratic structures of traditional international organizations and of the regionalist model represented by the EU (Garnaut & Drysdale, 1994).[2] On the other hand, Gills (1997) and others have argued that the European economic model and the Asian one are not so different from one another, neither historically nor in their current forms. 'Institutional' elements, commonly seen as characteristic of the European model, are present in the Asian model too; and the 'network' element, seen as more typical of the Asian model, is substantially present in the European system – for example in the practice of lobbying. The tendency has often been to overstate the differences between the forms taken by regionalism in these two parts of the world.

In the first of the sections that follow, we discuss the revival of regional integration. The next two parts of the chapter contain studies of the different mechanisms of regional integration and types of institutional arrangements adopted in Europe and Asia respectively, taking the EU and ASEAN as examples of two quite successful regional cooperating organizations. Having compared the French-inspired EU model of legal and institutional integration with the ASEAN pattern of network cooperation, it is a natural next step to ask why they differ. In the course of an attempt to explain the disparities, we will investigate the main reasons behind regional integration and why different regions produce different logics of integration. We consider whether varying historical, political, economic and cultural patterns have an impact on the differences between the two regional organizations. The persisting conditions of crisis in the region create both opportunities for and obstacles to greater regional integration. Our analysis will highlight the trends that seem to dominate the current situation, and these will be explained with reference to, among other factors, aspects of state-making in Asia.

Why then, should we compare these two groupings, ASEAN and the EU, rather than any other organizations? ASEAN is perhaps one of the regional organizations most similar to the EU when it comes to the scope and range of the activities covered. We feel that an analysis of similarities and differences between these two institutions of regional cooperation can make an interesting contribution to understanding the role of intergovernmental institutions in various regional responses to the globalization process. Furthermore, regional integration in Europe, as it emerges, has in fact been sub-regional integration: the construction of institutional structures to combine the interests of a group of countries within a wider region (Wallace, 1995). Seen from this perspective, the EU is more directly comparable, in global terms, with ASEAN than with, for instance, the Asia–Pacific Economic Cooperation forum (APEC).

Our investigation will be based on a review of existing studies of European and Asian regional integration in general, and of the attempts to compare the EU and ASEAN. However, before embarking on the comparative analysis, it is necessary to consider the revival of regional integration more generally and the principal varieties of regionalism.

2 The revival of regional integration

Economic and political development across the world in recent years has been characterized by both increased globalization and a reduction in the number and significance of borders for trade and commerce. Simultaneously we have seen an expansion of regional integration within every continent, as well as closer cooperation between the different regional groupings.

The period since the late 1980s has witnessed a resurgence of regionalism in world politics. Old regionalist organizations have been revived and new ones formed; and regionalism, coupled with the call for strengthened regionalist arrangements, has been central to many of the debates about the nature of the post-Cold War international order. The revival of political and academic interest in regionalism has been associated with a number of developments, including the end of the Cold War and the erosion of the Cold War alliance systems; the recurrent fears over the stability of the GATT and the multilateral trading order during the long drawn out negotiation of the Uruguay Round; the impact of increasing economic integration and globalization; changed attitudes towards economic development in many parts of the developing world; and the impact of democracy and democratization (Fawcett & Hurrell, 1995: 1).

The political salience of regionalism increased significantly as a result of developments within Europe, the successful negotiation and ratification of the North American Free Trade Area (NAFTA), and the increased momentum of cooperative efforts within ASEAN and continuing discussions within the Asia–Pacific region over new economic and security agreements, as reflected in the formation of APEC, the Pacific Economic Cooperation Council (PECC) and the ASEAN Regional Forum (ARF) (Garnaut & Drysdale, 1994). We have even witnessed the development of inter-regional cooperation, as for example in the EU–ASEAN cooperation program the EU–Asia cooperation organization (ASEM) (Cho & Chung, 1997). After the turn of the century, the profound problems of developing the global free trade regime further, most recently in the so far unsuccessful Doha round, have further strengthen the drive for both bilateral and intraregional free trade and other trade cooperation agreements all over the world and not the least in Asia with Singapore as one of the most active participants.

Since the late 1980s we have also observed fundamental changes in the functioning of the world economy and how the multinational companies run their operations, characterized by both increased volumes and increased liberalization of trade, not only within trading blocs but also on a global basis. At the same time, rapid technological development has made the world smaller and altered the conditions for commercial operations. Information, telecommunications and media activity have been crucial in shaping the trading environment, and have contributed to a global restructuring of the companies' production and distribution orders.

In many cases, this evolution has resulted in increasing regional integration. One reason for this may be that globalization and liberalization have led to a diminution of national governments' control over their respective national economies, prompting the industrialized countries at least to attempt to gain compensation through a degree of regional control. The next step will be to exercise control not only within their own region, but also across other regions, in order to retain the political control which the individual countries have lost (Oman, 1994).

The revival of interest in regionalism and regionalist projects needs to be seen within a global perspective (Fawcett & Hurrell, 1995: 3; Higgott, 1997). The fact that regionalist projects have emerged in so many parts of the world suggests that broad international forces may be at work, and that any single-region focus is imperfect. While intraregional dynamics remain important, the resurgence in regionalism needs to be related to changes in the global system, for instance the emergence of an economic system in which state policies are shaped to an ever-increasing extent by the structure and dynamics of an increasingly global world economy, and of a political system in which the boundaries between the 'domestic' and the 'international' arenas have become increasingly blurred.

Gradually since the Second World War, but in particular in the last decade, the total scale and scope of global interrelation have grown enormously in nearly every aspect of human life, politically, economically, culturally, socially and regarding everything from environmental hazards and cooperation to military intervention and global arms trade. World-wide economic integration has linked the fate of nations, communities and households across both regions and on the global level in such a way that crises in one country take a toll on jobs, production and investments in the rest of the world. Every day more than 1.2 trillion USD is handled at the foreign exchange markets, transnational corporations account for between 25 and 33 per cent of world output, 70 per cent of world trade and 80 per cent of international investment while overseas production by these firms exceeds considerably the level of world export (Baylis & Smith 2005: 20–1). This makes these firms key players in global trade, investment and production, partly outside the control of the nation states and even the regional or the international organizations. At the same time the external effects of their decisions on investment, production and trade have to be carried by the nation states through their welfare state and regional development policies.

The second important factor behind this wave of globalization is the digital revolution. Digitalization has created a completely new global communication infrastructure with an enormous capacity and flexibility and brought about convergence between telecommunications, communication and IT into a strong and powerful ICT base for a new global information economy and information society. This development influences all from the running of businesses to the spread of new hits in the music industry. Without this digital revolution, the present wave of globalization could not have been so forceful and radical in its process and consequences. Regionalism is both an attempt to protect neighbouring countries from the effects of this globalization process and to deepen the free trade arrangements to take further advantages of the effects on economic growth.

The return of regionalism to the international agenda has, however, not been universally welcomed; nevertheless, both optimists and pessimists agree that regionalism is on the increase. The end of the Cold War had an important impact on global economic change and the transformation of the international system, and this, together with the passing of the Single European Act in 1986, marked the turning-point in the fortunes of regionalism (Fawcett & Hurrell, 1995: 9). These and other contributory factors have resulted in a proliferation of new regional groupings and a recovery of older regional bodies. What distinguishes this wave of regional activity from others is its truly global nature.

The broad term 'regionalism' has been used to cover a variety of distinct phenomena. Rather than trying to work with a single, very broad, overarching concept, it is helpful to break up the notion of regionalism into five different categories: regionalization; regional awareness and identity; regional interstate cooperation; state-promoted regional integration; and regional cohesion (Hurrell, 1995: 39). We will briefly consider what each of these involves.

Regionalization refers to the growth of societal integration within a region and to the often undirected processes of social and economic interaction. Regional awareness and regional identity are inherently imprecise and diffuse notions; it is, however, impossible to ignore them, since they have become more central to the analysis of contemporary regionalism. The emphasis of regional awareness is on language and rhetoric, means by which definitions of regional identity are constantly defined and redefined. Regional interstate cooperation can be of a formal or informal nature; a high level of institutionalization is no guarantee of either effectiveness or political importance. Regional cooperation can entail the creation of formal institutions, but it can often be based on a much looser structure, involving patterns of regular meetings with some rules attached, together with mechanisms for preparation and follow-up. This issue will be discussed in more depth later in this chapter. Regional integration can refer to the legal and institutional relationships within a region in which economic transactions take place, or it can refer to the market relationship among goods and factors within a region (Cooper, 1994: 11). State-promoted regional integration involves specific policy decisions by governments designed to reduce or remove barriers for the mutual exchange of goods, services, capital and people. These policies have drawn a great deal of attention to the processes of integration, on the paths that it might take, and on the objectives that it might fulfill. Regional cohesion refers to the possibility that a combination of the four categories just mentioned might lead to the emergence of a cohesive and consolidated regional unit. It is this potential for cohesion that makes regionalism of particular interest to the study of international relations. These different categories are important aspects of this chapter, and will be used as a general framework for our analysis.

Several different types of regional cooperation exist around the world today. They may be distinguished from one another in respect to how successful they have become, how they are organized and how they operate. The limited scope of this chapter does not allow us to give a full description of the majority of these institutions, or of the way they operate; and it would be impossible to give a general picture of the differences they present. For these reasons we will focus here on the EU and ASEAN, each in its own field a relatively successful example of a particular kind of regional cooperation organization. The EU is based on French-inspired legal and institutional integration models, while ASEAN can be characterized as far more network-based. We will investigate to what extent and how the two organizations differ, both in organizational structure and in integration mechanisms.

There are obviously similarities between the EU and ASEAN; but the focus in this investigation will be concentrated on how the two groupings differ. For example, both are characterized as regional organizations; but the nature of these organizations appears to be different. Again, we can find networks in Europe as well as in Asia; but we will attempt to show here that the nature of the networks is different in the two contexts. Trying to explain these disparities, we will investigate what the main reasons behind regional integration are, and the two regions generate different types of integration logic. We will also conduct an analysis of the varying historical, political, economic and cultural patterns in Europe and Southeast Asia. Before embarking on such an investigation, however, we need to describe the two organizations. We begin in the next section with a description of the European Union.

3 The EU: Institution-based integration

There exist various descriptions of the EU, its history, construction, functioning, decision-making processes, and so on. Since its birth as the European Economic Community in the 1950s, however, it has mainly been analyzed as an example of the *supranational integration* of, or *intergovernmental cooperation* between, (previously) sovereign nation states (Hix, 1994). Analysis of European integration has historically been dominated by two contrasting theoretical perspectives on the nature of politics and the process of change within the EC/EU: neo-functionalism and intergovernmentalism (Rhodes & Mazey, 1995) and in the last decade also neo-institutionalism.

Many see real movement in the direction of a polity, as individuals, corporations and government actors increasingly identify with, and act according to, European-level institutions and processes (Rhodes & Mazey, 1995) or even using the concept 'Europe's nascent state' (From & Sitter, 2006). Others view the EU as the site of an ongoing struggle of give and take between member states, where no real European polity has emerged. However, most of these descriptions share the common feature of a focus on the legal and institutional aspects of the EU. In recent years, moreover, there has been a marked shift away from the traditional emphasis by analysts on national governments as the key actors in EU policy making towards a broader examination of the relative roles of the various actors involved in the EU policy process. The impact of lobbying by organized interests has come under scrutiny (Andersen & Eliassen, 1993; 2001; Mazey & Richardson, 1993; Greenwood, 1997, 2003), and increasing attention has been paid to the role of policy networks at the European level (Bomberg, 1994; Peterson, 1992, 1995).

In addition, the role played by the European institutions themselves has received growing attention as an 'institutional-matter' perspective on EU policy making has begun to gain ground (Bulmer, 1994a; Peterson, 1992, 1995; Peterson & Shackleton 2006). Neo-institutionalist views emphasize institutions as the main actors in European integration. From this perspective, integration is driven by an internal institutional logic, characterized by elite predominance. The neo-institutional approach illustrates how deeply divided or segmented societies can remain stable as a result of behavior and rules that produce 'elite accommodation' (Lijphart, 1984). In the European case, the important new element in regional integration introduced in the Treaty of Rome was the supranational institutions: the European Commission, the European Parliament and the European Court of Justice. This new element meant that, from the outset in the 1950s, the European Community had a potential for taking the initiative that no other regional organization had previously had.

The European Commission acts independently of the national governments and exclusively in the interest of the Union; it has, with very few exceptions, the responsibility for initiating legislation (Edwards & Spence, 1995; Nugent 2001). The main obligations for the European parliament are budget, legislation and control authority. Direct contacts between the European Commission and the parliament are growing, which has created a basis for more autonomous EU decision making, independent of national interests. The European Court of Justice holds a central position in the overall EU system, its purpose being to safeguard the enforcement of European directives in the member countries. The interpretation of European law, and the final decision on its application, are vested in the Court of Justice.

There are several possible reasons why the priority of supranationalism has been maintained in the EU. A central element is the model of strong nation states in Europe which themselves have experienced state- and nation-building processes. Another reason could be the influence of federal models from the United States. Also, the six founding member states can be characterized as relatively homogeneous countries, both politically and economically. However, the existence of supranational institutions has not prevented problems arising, or a lack of dynamism in the development of the EU. That dynamism appeared in the 1980s with another kind of 'supranationality' through majority voting in the European Council.

These point to the other dominant feature of the development of regionalism in Europe: in addition to strong supranational institutions, a major role has been played by nation states and governments, both in the further development of regional integration and in current policy shaping in the EU. This stands in contrast to other attempts at regional integration. The EEC was established as a result of the Treaty of Rome in 1957, and the legal basis of the Community has continuously been changed as a result of new intergovernmental conferences. At the same time, the European Council functions as the EUs most important executive and legislative authority. Economic and political integration is, thus, first and foremost, a result of nation state politics.

The first major revision of the Treaty of Rome, the Single European Act (SEA), was signed in 1986 and entered into force in 1987. The SEA settled a plan for the completion of the internal market and introduced majority voting. It is widely considered a turning-point in the integration process in western Europe. In addition to having a major impact on economic integration, the SEA also gave a new impetus to European political cooperation (EPC). 'For the first time in history, political cooperation received a legal basis' (Regelsberger, 1988). The SEA provided the EC with a legal basis for the internal market, rules for majority voting, an outspoken commitment to further social and economic cohesion, a framework for further development of concerted action in the area of foreign policy and, not least important, a new role for the European parliament through the co decision procedure. This first major revision of the EC's constitutional basis 'brought together in one 'single' act a treaty on European cooperation in the area of foreign policy and institutional and procedural reforms' (Nelsen & Stubb, 1994).

The Treaty on European Union signed at Maastricht on 7 February 1992, effective from 1 November 1993, created a new European Union based on the European Community, marking 'a new stage' in the process of creating an ever closer union among the peoples of Europe (Duff, 1994). The Maastricht Treaty expanded further the scope to include education, culture, public health, industry and some other policy areas within the remit of the EU. Much of the treaty followed well-tried precedent, building on past EC treaties and on the corpus of law and policy made by the common institutions over forty years. In addition, the Maastricht Treaty made a division of policy areas into three 'pillars'. The first amends the EEC, ECSC and Euratom Treaties and is formally named the European Community (governed on a supranational level). The second pillar concerns foreign and security policy and is built upon the existing intergovernmental procedures of EPC. The third covers justice and home affairs. Other provisions of Maastricht were intended to respond to new external challenges, including enlargement.

After the triumph of agreement on the Maastricht Treaty in December 1991, however, the EU was faced with a series of problems concerning its adoption: the ratification process; getting the member countries to cooperate on the foreign affairs front (in the Gulf War and the Bosnian crisis); creating an economic recovery after the worst depression in Europe since the Second World War; and the near collapse of the European Exchange Rate Mechanism, which was designed to serve as the basis for a European Monetary Union (EMU). All of these things to a greater or lesser extent show the inability of the EU to live up to expectations. Was this evidence of a failure of European cooperation, or was it just a minor setback in the process of European integration?

More than fifteen years after the signing of the Maastricht Treaty, during which time it has been followed by the Treaties of Amsterdam and Nice, we have seen that European cooperation has again progressed in a range of areas. The internal market was, following a few setbacks, put into effect as planned. The Schengen Agreement, which deals with the abolition of border controls, has become an integrated part of European cooperation. And the EMU and the Euro currency represent perhaps the most important contribution to a further deepening of the integration process in the years to come. The biggest challenge facing the EU around the turn of the century was the enlargement to the east, to new member states from the former communist countries. The first ten new members joined on 1 May 2004, another two followed on 1 January 2007. This substantial enlargement represented challenges also for the constitutional structure of the union. The union first attempted to solve the problems associated with having twenty-seven member states in Amsterdam, and then with the Nice treaty, without being able to establish sustainable structures (Moravcsik &. Nicolaidis 1999; Wessels 2001). The bold attempt to create an even more ambiguous 'constitutional' solution to this and other challenges came with the Constitutional Treaty. This was at first regarded as a success, but it collapsed when voters rejected the treaty in referendums in France and the Netherlands in 2005 (Laursen, 2006). At the same time, however, political cooperation in fields of foreign policy and defence has developed more rapidly than most observers could have imagined around the turn of the century.

In any case, despite the failure of the Constitutional Treaty in 2005, the EU may be considered quite successful in both the political and in particular the economic arena. Although progress in achieving the objectives of the internal market has varied in line with fluctuations in the world economic cycle,[3] a common European political and economic arena is taking shape. As defined by the SEA, the EU's internal market is 'an area without internal frontiers in which the free movement of goods, persons, services and capital is ensured in accordance with the provisions of this treaty' (Roney, 1995). It is an attempt to remove the physical, technical and fiscal barriers to trade. The Act increased the importance of the European Parliament, established the EU social dialogue, and introduced the qualified majority rule in several political areas that were earlier ruled by unanimity. Although there are difficult policy areas in the EU, for instance employment, energy policy, and matters covered by the second and third pillars, the competence of the Commission has increased within such areas as education, culture, telecommunications, banking, transport, small and medium-sized companies, and the environment (Andersen and Eliassen, 2001). The SEA, the Maastricht Treaty in particular, and to a certain degree also the Amsterdam and Nice Treaties, has broadened the scope and variety of policy issues which will be influenced by the EU. Today almost all national policy areas will have a European dimension.

How, then, does this European situation compare to the development of a regional grouping in South East Asia?

4 ASEAN: Network-based integration

In the Pacific Ocean and in most of Southeast Asia we can find a somewhat different pattern of regional integration, as economic integration in the Asia–Pacific region develops in its own very distinctive way. Our argument here will be that unlike in Europe, where governments have played a key role in forging regional frameworks that have served to shape regional business activity, in the Asia–Pacific region it has been the activities of the business community which have to a great extent forced governments to consider ways of regularizing regional relations. Economic integration in Southeast Asia is a result of trade and business operations, which have forced through a minimum of regional economic integration arrangements (Gallant & Stubbs, 1996; Abad Jr., 2003). Certainly, as one author has noted, the economic interactions we see in the region, including within ASEAN, be they investment choices, trade patterns or capital flows, are not being significantly affected by a regionally based regime (Aggarwal, 1994). This holds true at least for the first part of the 1990s, but then free trade efforts on both Asian and regional level gain momentum and the regional regimes gained further importance.

As we shall see later, in our analysis of different patterns of regional integration, the theoretical explanations of integration used in the European case do not transfer well to Asia. To some extent, network theory might give the best explanation of the Asian integration process. However, during recent years we have observed an emerging need for institution-building in the ASEAN region in particular.

The foundation of ASEAN, on 8 August 1967 by the signing of the Bangkok Declaration, was the most progressive attempt to date to build a formalized regional integration organization in Southeast Asia. When representatives from Indonesia, Malaysia, the Philippines, Singapore and Thailand established the Association, they held out a bold vision of all countries in Southeast Asia cooperating actively towards peace, stability, progress and prosperity in the region. The ASEAN nations came together with the aim of promoting the economic, social and cultural development of the region through cooperative programs, safeguarding the political and economic stability of the region against big power rivalry, and serving as a forum for the resolution of intraregional differences (CEC, 1996). However, the Vietnam War and the threat of communist diffusion towards other parts of the Pacific Ocean were regarded as the proximate reason for the establishment of the organization. ASEAN is thus a good example of how economic regionalism can be a mechanism by which broader security and political goals can be pursued, rather than the stress falling on specific questions of economic integration as in the European example (Fawcett & Hurrell, 1995: 4). Political questions totally dominated the first fifteen years of ASEAN's operations, with the progress of economic cooperation largely of a symbolic character. The latter included the declaration of increased economic cooperation at the Bali summit in 1976, the ASEAN industry project plan, the ASEAN industry cooperation plan and the ASEAN preference trade agreement in 1997 (PTA). An example of the symbolic character of such economic cooperation is that even though 16,000 products were listed under the PTA agreement they accounted for just 1 per cent of all intra-ASEAN trade (Bernard & Ravenhill, 1995).

After the foreign ministers' meeting in Kuala Lumpur on 24 July 1997, ASEAN consisted of nine member states including Vietnam. Two new members were signed up at that meeting: Laos and Myanmar (Burma); Cambodia was not, owing to the *coup d'état* that took place in the month before the meeting. It could look as if this enlargement, and not least ASEAN's new attitude towards the future treatment of Cambodia, namely to monitor political developments and encourage stabilization, led to a somewhat increased institutionalization in the region. It is hard to run crisis-prevention and stabilization work, as well as building confidence, without institutions. Cambodia became a member of ASEAN in 1999. The Melanesian state of Papua New Guinea has observer status in the ASEAN. East Timor on the other hand formally applied for full membership in 2006. The member countries that make up ASEAN today have a combined GDP of more than 700 billion € with an annual growth rate of more than 4 per cent, but there are large economic disparities between the ASEAN members. With a population of some 503 million people, they make up one of the largest regional markets in the world. Through the Bali Concord in 2003, ASEAN has subscribed to the notion of democratic peace, which means all member countries believe democratic processes will promote regional peace and stability. Also the non-democratic members all agreed that it was something all member states should aspire to.

After the end of the Cold War and the move towards political normalization in Indochina, ASEAN was able and indeed obliged to outline new projects inside the economic area, which could increase the importance of the organization for its members. At the fourth ASEAN summit in Singapore at the end of January 1992, the heads of government signed a 'Framework Agreement on Enhancing ASEAN Economic Cooperation', which committed the six to the establishment of an ASEAN free trade area (AFTA). The purpose of this agreement was to reduce all tariff rates for intra-ASEAN trade in industrial and agricultural products to zero within fifteen years. It aimed to promote the region's competitive advantage as a single production unit. The elimination of tariff and non-tariff barriers among member countries is expected to promote greater economic efficiency, productivity, and competitiveness. As of 1 January 2005, tariffs on almost 99 per cent of the products in the Inclusion List of the ASEAN-6 (Brunei Darussalam, Indonesia, Malaysia, the Philippines, Singapore, and Thailand) had been reduced to no more than 5 per cent. More than 60 per cent of these products have zero tariffs. The average tariff for ASEAN-6 has been brought down from more than 12 per cent when AFTA started to 2 per cent today. For the newer member countries, namely, Cambodia, Laos, Myanmar and Vietnam, tariffs on about 81 per cent of their Inclusion List have been brought down to within the 0–5 per cent range.

One problem with AFTA is, however, the lack of bureaucratic preparations inside AFTA. Free trade within a regional organization requires a well-developed administrative apparatus, and ASEAN has only limited administrative capacity. Another problem is the absence of institutions that can enforce the agreement. However, the agreement has so far been more successfully implemented in the present political and economic climate in Southeast Asia that sceptics had thought

ASEAN also established the ASEAN Regional Forum (ARF). The ASEAN Regional Forum is an informal multilateral dialogue of twenty-five members who seek to address security issues in the Asia-Pacific region. (Acharya, 2001; Fukushima, 2003) The ARF met for the first time in 1994. The current participants in the ARF are as follows: ASEAN, Australia, Canada, People's Republic of China, European Union, India, Japan, North Korea, South Korea, Mongolia, New Zealand, Pakistan, Papua New Guinea, Russia, East Timor, and the United States. Bangladesh was added to ARF as the 26th member in 2006.

Unlike the EU, ASEAN is an organization with no supranational authority. New members are expected to blend themselves into the membership and adopt the so-called 'ASEAN way' of defence: a positive attitude, quiet diplomacy and goodwill in consultations to achieve consensus and strengthen solidarity (Chalermpalanupap, 1997). ASEAN membership does increase the importance of the regional dimension in the policy-making process of the new members. However, political cooperation in ASEAN, unlike economic cooperation in the region and unlike political cooperation in the EU, involves little or no internal adjustment. Each member still develops its own political system and its own governmental structure. The reality is that national interests and preferences remain a major determinant of the possibilities of economic cooperation within ASEAN (Acharya, 1997).

The organizational structure of ASEAN is different from the EU in being less formalized and much more moderate. The highest decision-making organ of ASEAN is the Meeting of the ASEAN Heads of State and Government. The ASEAN Summit is convened every year. The ASEAN Ministerial Meeting (Foreign Ministers) and ministerial meetings for different sectors are held regularly. Intergovernmental committees of senior officials, and technical working groups and task forces are also established.

The Secretary-General of ASEAN is appointed for a five-year term, is mandated to initiate, advise, coordinate, and implement ASEAN activities. The members of the professional staff of the ASEAN Secretariat are appointed on the same principle. ASEAN has also several specialized bodies and arrangements promoting inter-governmental cooperation in various fields of societal activity. In addition, ASEAN promotes dialogue and consultations with professional and business organizations and around sixty Non-Governmental Organizations (NGOs) have formal affiliations with ASEAN.

Thus, the major difference between integration in Europe and integration in Asia can be characterized as that between formal and informal integration. Formal integration is described as that which is formalized by the establishment of institutions and common regulations in order to control the relationship between nation states, as in APEC in Asia and the EU in Europe. Although there are examples of formal integration in Asia, 3 the major form of regional cooperation in this area of the world is informal integration. It is mainly the informal track that distinguishes the Southeast Asian pattern from the patterns prevailing in other regions (Peng, 1997), and for this reason it should be given particular attention. The informal track includes the production networks, sub-regional economic zones (SREZs) and ethnic business networks.

What then, are the reasons for the great differences between the integration patterns of Europe and Southeast Asia?

5 Explaining different patterns of regional integration

After having described how EU and ASEAN differ, with a particular focus on variations in organizational structure and institutional mechanisms, two questions arise: firstly, what are the main reasons behind regional integration, and why have these driving forces produced different types of integration logic in the two regions? And secondly, to what extent and how are these differences linked to variations in historical, political, economic and cultural patterns? A further interesting question is why institutionalized cooperation in the Asian region has proceeded so slowly in contrast to the rapidly expanding regional integration in terms of policy cooperation. Why is informal cooperation particularly strong in Southeast Asia?

These are very complicated questions, and there are several relevant elements that have to be taken into account when attempting to answer them. First of all, however, we have to consider the difference between a political and a chronological time perspective when comparing EU and ASEAN. To what extent is it fair to compare ASEAN today with EU today? The EU has both been in existence for longer, and in previous times developed much more rapidly than ASEAN. Perhaps, then, it is more reasonable to seek comparable political time periods, and compare, for example, the EU in the 1970s with ASEAN today. If we do this, then the differences between the two organizations concerning supra-nationality and organizational development remain significant, but the contrast between a successful versus a slow development of regional cooperation is not so marked.

The motivating forces behind regional integration can be explained in political and economic terms. According to Katzenstein (1996), regional integration is attractive on a number of economic grounds. First of all, relations with neighboring countries stimulate increased trade and investment relations. Secondly, such economic relations with neighbours do not demand the kind of reciprocity that the World Trade Organization (WTO) usually does. Thirdly, efficiency and ability to compete at a regional level are usually strengthened by global liberalization. Finally, the effects of regional economies of scale and savings in transport costs can create dynamic effects which reinforce economic growth.

We find good examples of the role and importance of these arguments for regional integration in the European case. The revitalizing of the EU through the single market was a direct consequence of a wish to make Europe competitive compared to the United States and Asia. Eliminating obstacles to the free movement of goods, persons, services and capital across country borders is an important way of increasing competitiveness (EIU, 1997: 99). The aim of the single market was to bring about market integration, shrinking the obstacles to trade and creating such a large domestic market that global companies with a base in the EU could be developed. This would imply restructuring industries and companies on the basis of comparative advantage and economies of scale. Both reduced prices and larger profits would result, which also would benefit research and development as well as the competitiveness of the businesses.

The reasons behind the success of the SEA and the internal market can be explained in economic terms (Balassa, 1961; Kindleberger, 1973; Cooper, 1994; Summers, 1991; Bhagwati, 1993; Krugman, 1993; Young, 1993; Baldwin & Venables, 1994); but it can also be accounted for in terms of political integration theory. The great success of the internal market was seen to confirm the applicability of neo-functionalist theory. From a neo-functionalistic perspective, the treaties of the 1990s represent an integrationist impulse that is likely to strengthen the supranational institutions and responsibilities of the Union. The neo-functionalists state it as a fact that Maastricht was a spillover from the SEA; it followed the logic of the earlier treaty, which made it possible. However, intergovernmentalism has also frequently been used to explain the success of the internal market. From an intergovernmental perspective the EU remains, despite the 1993 initiative, the creation and instrument of national politics and national interests that will continue to constrain integrationist impulses within it.

Likewise, the adoption of the Euro and the EU's Eastern enlargement can be explained both with reference to the interests of the (biggest) member states and as a development that follows the expansive logic of regional integration. Economic and monetary union was seen by many as the logical consequence of the Single European Market; the final step needed to take full advantage of the common market. At the same time, Germany and France played a big part in defining the rules of the common currency, the smaller members joined in order to recapture some of the influence over monetary policy that they had lost by operating in the shadow of the D-mark, and states like the UK, Denmark and Sweden opted not to join the single currency (McKay, 1999). Eastern enlargement followed the EU's long-term pattern and mechanisms of enlargement, but is timing and practical development was shaped by member state interests (Preston, 1996; Nugent, 2004).

ASEAN was in 1967 created mainly as a political cooperation organization, with the aim of stopping the further expansion of communism in the region. From the very beginning, however, economic cooperation was thought to be an important part of this defence against revolutionary movements. Gradually the focus of the organization has been turned more and more on to economic and social cooperation. Thus the economic theories of regional integration fit well in explaining the development of ASEAN. One important difference between EU and ASEAN identified above is the lack of supranational institutions in Asian organizations. At the same time, ASEAN does not cover the same policy areas as the EU, and has not the same degree of free trade among its members. Thus it is challenging to apply the type of political integration theories used in respect of the EU to explain the development of ASEAN.

The ASEAN Free Trade Area (AFTA) attempts to abolish all customs duties among the member countries, which is one step – the first – towards establishing a common market. The Common Effective Preferential Tariff (CEPT) is the main implementing mechanism of AFTA, and encourages member countries gradually to lower tariffs on each others' imports. The aim is to turn ASEAN into a truly free trade area over a fifteen-year period. AFTA involves several areas of cooperation, including the harmonization of standards, the reciprocal recognition of tests and certification, the removal of barriers to foreign investments, macroeconomic consultations, rules for fair competition, and the promotion of venture capital. Nevertheless, the absence within ASEAN of supranational institutions and an ambiguous legislative programme make AFTA more like European Free Trade Association (EFTA) than like the EU single market.

In attempting to find a suitable theory of political integration to describe this development, the intergovernmental perspective may offer the best focus. The liberal intergovernmentalist approach assumes that the member states of the EU remain the key actors in determining outcomes in European integration issues. The driving force for these actors is interstate bargaining, concerned with national interests and member states' capabilities. Within ASEAN, it is certainly the case that national interests and preferences remain a major determinant of the possibilities of economic cooperation. As Kusuma Snitwongse (1990) notes, progress in economic cooperation will require a model of development that is acceptable to all because it promises equal benefit, and, at the same time, a greater political will to sacrifice at least some national interests for the welfare of the whole. Yet, as she concedes, in the case of ASEAN, national interests have priority over regional ones.

Increased trade and global liberalization are not the only ways in which globalization can lead to regional integration. Geographical location and functional dependency can create good opportunities for regional economic growth. A geographical concentration of production is to an increasing extent driven by technological clusters and an innovation and production network which offers clear advantages through regional cooperation (Lorenz, 1992). Patterns of cooperation both between and within companies change rapidly. Intra-Asian trade is growing much faster than trade between Asia and other regions. At the same time, these intra-regional adjustments in production are important in enabling the Asian countries to compete in the American and European markets. Globalization and regional integration are processes so closely linked that they cannot be analyzed separately.

In the Asian region we witness a kind of regional integration based on trade patterns, business operations and investments, sub-regional cooperation patterns, and informal personal contacts. Business networks – here defined as international business systems formed along ethnic and/or cultural lines, as defined by Katzenstein (1996: 35) – are a particularly important form of non-institutional economic cooperation in Asia. The theory of (business) networks in regional integration is, however, not very well developed, except in a few works such as those by Bressand and Nicolaidis (1990) and Richardson (1995, 1996).

Peng (1997) analyzes this form of integration in more detail. He examines three forms of informal cooperation in Asia, including Southeast Asia: (1) production networks based on a multi-tier economic division of labour, which is cooperation along the lines of industrial production; (2) sub-regional economic zones which embody cooperation based on geographical proximity (as for example in ASEAN);

and (3) ethnic business networks representing cooperation along ethnic and cultural lines. All three, Peng claims, are usually overlooked as important forms of regional cooperation, although in the absence of formal economic institutions they are actually driving trade and investment within the region. Their importance apparently exceeds that of formal cooperation (Peng, 1997: 13).

To Peng's three types of informal types of cooperation in Southeast Asia may be added the development of policy communities within ASEAN. If we look at the development of ASEAN in the last thirty years, we see that there has been a continuous growth of both formal and in particular informal policy networks or communities. The total number of official ASEAN meetings is now approaching 300 (Chalermpalanupap, 1997: 7) and numbers of informal contacts and meetings are obviously much higher. We assume that this development of more and more arenas for cooperation and ever more frequent contacts is an important source of an even higher level of political and economic integration within this region in the future.

The same kind of multi-level, multi-channel, multi-actor mixture of formal and informal types of activity has also been found within the study of European policy-making. Several authors have introduced the concept of 'policy networks' to describe the linkages between different interests and EU policy-makers (Heclo, 1978; Richardson, 1995, 2006). The concepts of policy communities and mulit-level governance have been used to underline both the informal aspects of this process (Richardson and Jordan, 1979; Petersen, 1994; Nugent, 1997) and the existence of some kind of continuum of different degrees of formalization of these networks (Cram, 1997; Schmidt, 1998; Héritier, 1999; Kohler-Koch, 2003).

We believe that in addition to the more economically based network theory, this idea of policy communities may add to our understanding of the nature and functioning of the decision-making process within the Southeast Asian community, and that to this end the emerging policy communities in the region should be more closely examined. Perhaps this line of reasoning may also help us towards an answer to the question of how to compare the two models of regional integration.

In summary, informal or non-institutional cooperation is the dominant form of regional cooperation in the Asia–Pacific region at the present. It has served the demands of Southeast Asian countries for international economic cooperation relatively well, and in the near future the prevailing East Asian pattern is predicted to persist (Peng, 1997) Through ASEAN, Southeast Asia has set a successful example of a new form of regional cooperation. Until the end of the 1980s, ASEAN had been quite successful as a regional political organization, but in the economic arena its progress has been very slow. In the 1990s, as we have described, both economic and political cooperation have increased considerably and this development has continued after the turn of the century, but in an intergovernmental way.

6 A comparison of European and Asian integration

The second element in our attempt to explain how organizational structure and integration mechanisms differ between EU and ASEAN involves an investigation of how these phenomena are linked to historical, political, economic and cultural patterns. In comparison with Europe or North America, the Pacific region as a whole is a much more heterogeneous region. When looking at varying historical patterns between EU and ASEAN, we will examine two determinants of Asian regionalism suggested by Katzenstein (1996) in his attempt to account for the relative weakness of the formal political institutions of Asian regionalism by a comparison with Europe: namely, power and norms in the international system; and the character of domestic state structures.

American power in Asia after 1945 was relatively much greater than in Europe, and US foreign policy in Asia did not establish the principle of multilateralism there as it did in Europe (Katzenstein, 1996). American diplomacy in Pacific Asia has overwhelmingly been bilateral and not multilateral. This has made it much more difficult for Asian states to develop broad, interlocking and institutionalized political arrangements of the kind that have characterized the European integration process. However, it has been argued (Acharya, 1997) that it is in fact the Asia–Pacific region's extreme diversity, rather than America's extreme hegemony, which might have inhibited the emergence of multilateral institutions in the immediate post-war period; for the Asia–Pacific nations are remarkably different in terms of their political systems, cultural heritage and historical experience.

Katzenstein (1996) notes that the comparative weakness in the institutionalization of Asian regionalism is also attributable to the character of Asian state structures. Some state structures are better suited than others to deal with public law and formal institutions as the preferred vehicle for regional integration. Neither Asia as a whole or any of its sub-regions possesses equivalents of the Europe-wide institutions, foremost among which is, of course, the EU itself. In the establishment of formal institutions, Asian regionalism has during recent decades experienced a series of very slow, or even false, starts. Even the most successful institution of Asian regional integration, ASEAN, has arguably avoided the elimination of tariffs; until recently it was committed only to negotiating some preferential tariff margins for member states on selected goods. One argument advanced in regard to the slow development in Asian regionalism is that 'only the more developed countries appear to accept deeper forms of integration' (Wijkman & Sundkvist Lindström, 1989).

Also, Southeast Asia is greatly influenced by British, Dutch, French, Spanish and US colonialism. Social forces inherited from the imperial past penetrate these post-colonial states deeply and thus create multiple political connections in intricate network structures. These states have inherited the colonial tradition of 'the rule by law' rather than The West European tradition of 'the rule of law' (Katzenstein, 1996). Southeast Asian countries are constituted legally, but the relation between state and society is governed by social rather than legal norms.

Our discussion of political heterogeneity between the EU and ASEAN is conducted in respect of the political systems in the region, related to the definition in most dictionaries and as defined by Hanks (1986): 'Politics refers to the study of the ways in which a country is governed and power is acquired.' The Pacific region is politically highly heterogeneous. The political systems in the ASEAN countries can most appropriately be described as all composed of some form of authoritarian capitalist or semi-democratic system, but with great differences between one another. All the EU member countries are democratic polities, and the ASEAN countries definitely differ far more in their political systems than do the EU member states. For example, the political difference between Thailand and Myanmar is far greater than the political difference among any two of the European nation states. The stability of the most democratic nations is also fragile. Thailand gave an example of the instability of one of the most democratic systems in the region with the military take over of power in 2006. These differences obviously constitute a major barrier to institutional economic cooperation. All the free trade agreements previously established have been among countries of similar political systems. This can be explained by the fact that political systems are closely associated with modes of production.

An economy is the system according to which the money, industry and trade of a country or region are organized (Hanks, 1986). We will here examine in particular the *degree of liberalization of the economy* and *differences in per capita income*. The high degree of heterogeneity in the Pacific region makes formal economic cooperation difficult, because it greatly increases the transaction costs of institution-building. By contrast, non-institutional economic cooperation in Asia has functioned well in relation to the progressive liberalization of the Southeast Asian economies, especially in trade and investment, which has been under way since the 1960s, accelerating since the 1980s. The informal, gradual and flexible nature of non-institutional economic cooperation makes this approach highly appropriate as a way to open up economies while minimizing the outside shock accompanying liberalization (Peng, 1997: 14).

Economic disparity is the single most important barrier to formal regional cooperation in the Asia–Pacific region. It reflects the divergence in degree of industrialization, technological level, labour costs, export capacity and several other important factors. Within ASEAN there are enormous differences in per capita income/GNP between the member states. There has been no precedent at any time in the world history of a successful free trade agreement among countries with great economic disparity (Peng, 1997: 15). The closest example is the General Agreement on Trade and Tariffs (GATT); but GATT is an organization setting rules, rather than a real free trade area.

As we have pointed out above, Southeast Asians have their own way of conducting economic cooperation through informal means. For instance, economic cooperation based on the multi-tier economic division of labour is particularly strong in Southeast Asia. Sub-regional economic groupings (like ASEAN) and business networks are also playing very important roles in Southeast Asian regional cooperation. Strong informal economic cooperation is an important factor propelling regional integration in the absence of effective regional cooperative institutions.

Cultural heterogeneity can also raise transaction costs. Culture is a concept difficult to define, but may for present purposes be said to be a particular society or civilization, especially considered in relation to its ideas, its art, its customs or its way of life (Hanks, 1986). In investigating cultural aspects, we consider religion and language in the EU and ASEAN respectively.

In the ASEAN countries there are six major religions – Buddhism, Taoism, Hinduism, Christianity, Islam and Confucianism; so far at least all the EU countries are Christian even if you have Christianity in different versions. The next round of enlargement will, however, probably bring in Muslim countries like Albania – let alone Turkey – and religious mixed countries like Bosnia. One may argue, however, that even if there are many divisions within Christianity, they still fall within one religious creed and thus EU so far in the world has manifested itself as religiously homogenous. Also, language diversity in the Asia–Pacific region is much greater than in Europe. Most EU countries belong to the Indo-European family of languages, with the exceptions of Finland and Hungary. The inclusion of Bulgaria will, however, introduce the Cyrillic alphabet in addition to the Latin and Greek. In contrast, there is a greater diversity among the ASEAN countries, where Thailand and Singapore belong to the Chinese–Tibetan language family, and Malaysia, Indonesia, the Philippines and Brunei to the Malay–Polynesian. Cultural heterogeneity also extends beyond religious and linguistic diversity to much broader categories like consumption behaviour, business practices, and methods of management and so on.

The formation of Asian business networks is linked with the strong East Asian cultural tradition (Katzenstein, 1996). Confucianism, which has a strong influence in all the major Northeast Asian societies, Vietnam and the Overseas Chinese societies, has always placed great emphasis on human relations and personal ties. Extensive use of personal networks is an effective way to get around barriers to business in many Southeast Asian countries, both domestically and internationally.

This comparative analysis, comparing EU and ASEAN, can help us to identify elements of Asian and European distinctiveness. It highlights, specifically, the inclusive character of Asian network-style integration in contrast to the continental European emphasis on formal institutions.

7 Conclusion

In the light of this analysis, do the changes within ASEAN and within ASEAN countries outlined above suggest that the association will over time become more similar to the EU?

We have in recent years witnessed tendencies on several fronts towards more comparable development in the two regions. Firstly, the general tendency, described above, for policy networks or communities to develop in nearly all sectors of society in Southeast Asia, establishing in many cases formal organizations and with increased frequencies of interaction which broaden the scope of policy coordination. Secondly, the increase in the number of summits and formal ministerial conferences make ASEAN more like the intergovernmental aspects of the EU. Still, however, ASEAN is not a supranational body and it does not possess a formal legal identity.

ASEAN involvement in policy issues, like free trade through AFTA, will strengthen the tendency towards more organized cooperation. One possible hypothesis could be that further development of free trade agreements between countries and regions creates needs for rules and controlling institutions in order to be effective. It has been predicted that if AFTA becomes a success, a more institutionalized organization will develop (Westerlund, 1997). ASEAN has already attempted to develop new institutional structures along these lines, for example, by adding a protocol for the settling of trade disputes based on a majority voting procedure.

The expansion of ASEAN, with the problems surrounding the membership of Myanmar and the temporary suspension of Cambodian admission in the end of the 1990s, strengthened also the organizational cooperation. Several new meetings, working groups and procedures were institutionalized in this period. There are also interesting elements in the ASEAN decision-making procedures which resemble those of the EU, such as the use of majority voting and flexible consensus.

The comparative study of the EU and ASEAN highlights the existence of significant differences between the two groupings, on the basis of which a quite unique Asian model is likely to develop. As Paul Evans (1994) has argued, institution-building in the Asia–Pacific region, rather than following the pattern established in Europe and North America, is instead 'emerging from unique historical circumstances and will likely evolve in its own particular way'. Although the picture today remains somewhat complex, the period of transition that these countries now are going through may prove to be a key step towards greater and deeper both economic and political integration in the future.

Notes

1   An earlier version of this chapter was presented at a conference on 'Non-state Actors and Authority in the Global System', University of Warwick, 31 October–1 November 1997. The authors would like to thank Solgunn Hoff and Anne Caroline Tveøy who have participated in preparing part of this manuscript, and in addition Pinar Tank and Alice Chamrernnusit for their help in the final editing of the chapter, all employed at the Centre for European and Asian Studies at the Norwegian School of Management in Oslo. We would also like to thank Nick Sitter for valuable comments on the revised version of the chapter.

2   The term 'new regionalism' has been used by several writers, including Telò, Hetne (2000–04) and other authors of this volume.

3   The formal track of the Southeast Asian pattern of integration includes cooperation through regional institutions like APEC, PECC and EAEC (East Asia Economic Caucus), and sub-regional free trade areas like NAFTA, AFTA and the Australia–New Zealand and recently several more free trade areas.

PART III
European Union as a New Civilian Power in the Making?

Chapter 11

The European Union and the Challenges of the Near Abroad

Mario Telò

A distinctive feature of this book is the consideration of possible tensions between the EU's increasing global actorhood and its relations to the near abroad. The two dimensions, regional and global, are not always easy to reconcile. Global responsibilities demand further integration and cohesion, by representing the EU world wide and also more centralized and efficient decision making. The regional dimension, however, entails both issues, deepening and widening; enhanced ability to act at continental and Mediterranean level, but also a tremendous pressure for wider membership, up to now without any strategically defined borders. Since the size matters and the very nature of a regional organization interacts with the internal balance between deepening and enlarging, we will commence by analyzing the evolving relationship of the EC–EU with the 'near abroad', namely with the eastern/continental dimension and with its southern neighbours.

The evolution of European regionalism is confronted with very complex challenges coming from the so-called arch of the crisis, from the east to south of the EU. R. Seidelmann and G. Joffé both contribute to this volume, respectively considering eastern Europe and the Mediterranean. A common problem concerns the complex interrelationship between the economic and political dimension of partnership, and the changing balance between the security challenges (including energy security, hard security, terrorism, and so on) and the other issues. In both cases, even if during the last two decades we witnessed a shift towards dramatic military and civilian crises, new threats are emerging, that is, ethnic fundamentalism, and refugee flows. Secondly, in both cases, even if for different reasons, the original kind of western European regionalism is being challenged because of the implications of multiple applications and decisions of full membership: the eastward enlargement process (2004 and 2007) and the southern one (2004 and the negotiations with Turkey).

1 European Union and the challenge of a continental Europe

Ten years after the fall of the Berlin Wall we are witnessing a new situation as far as continental Europe is concerned.[1] On the one hand, we see an emerging western-centred east–west cooperation. In spite of domestic instability, Russia's step by step integration into western international organizations, growing interdependence, and a change in Russian priorities are making a military conflict between east and west unthinkable. 'In comparison with the past, the new East–West relations in Europe are basically demilitarized, based on economic and political cooperation and on a western-dominated power formula' (Seidelmann). On the other hand, as confirmed by the Kosovo war, nationalism, ethnocentric movements and economic backwardness, in one word, 'Yugoslavization', make the design of a new European peace order not yet established, by highlighting some political limits of the EU. Moreover, one must not underestimate the collapse of Eastern European subregional cooperation:[2] 'Visegrad', 'Black Sea community' and 'Community of Independent States' have not been supported enough by EU, while bilateral conditionality often played a disintegrating role. Last but not least, the new pan-European institutional architecture, shaped after 1989 (the institutionalization of the Organization for Security and Cooperation in Europe, 1990 'Charta of Paris' and revival of the Council of Europe), is largely disappointing as far as the governance of the continent is concerned. Certainly, the EU and NATO are the major actors at continental level and they dominate political and economic developments in Eastern countries. However, since their strategies and interests present both similarities and differences, the first question is to what extent and how is the EU strengthening its role as a regional engine, and to what extent is its role still partially submitted to the leadership of others. However, it is a matter of fact that such huge regional problems already changed from an inter-bloc issue to a major challenge for the EU, and constitute a global issue, concerning also the main world power.

Let us turn to the second question. The EU is becoming more and more like a kind of a magnet from an economic and civilian point of view. Among the twenty-six applications for membership during the history of European integration, twelve were from central and eastern Europe and some more will come. This proves the significant regional influence of the EU and its impact on both domestic policy and the external relations of eastern applying and neighbouring countries.[3] History, security, economy and social links create a high degree of interdependence between the previous two parts of Europe. Since part of eastern Europe still faces obstacles and difficulties regarding democratization, growth and peace, if the EU proves itself unable to manage, control and solve the critical consequences of interdependence, they will consequently have an impact on the EU's inner legitimacy and political support, as shown by the referenda of 2005 held in France and Netherlands regarding the constitutional treaty.

The EU is being challenged to cope with its pan-European responsibilities. On the one hand, the huge political, financial, institutional, social and cultural implications of the eastern enlargement for the continental stability have no precedent in the history of European construction. On the other hand, if the EU, as an organization, fails in managing the enlargement process and partnership with Russia, it will lose the political support of European public opinion. The current situation shows dramatic weakness, as far as EU regional action is concerned, regarding enforcing and settling peace agreements, defending national minority rights, implementing a so-called 'Marshall Plan' for Eastern Europe, setting a common energy policy in partnership with Russia and Ukraine. Seidelmann's paper underlines three major limits of the EU as far as a regional actor is concerned:

In spite of the 'Stability Pact' and the new 'common strategies', approved in 1999 by the Cologne European Council (regarding Russia), by the Helsinki European Council (regarding Ukraine) , the progress achieved by The Western Balkan policy between 2002 and 2004, and during 2006 regarding steps towards an European energy policy, the EU still lacks a comprehensive, cost-efficient, and cohesive political-economic 'grand' strategy towards eastern Europe, the Balkans and Russia in particular.

The Maastricht CSFP project, in spite of the improvements approved in Amsterdam (new Treaty provisions) and in Helsinki (new military means for 'Petersberg tasks' and defence policy) still lacks a satisfying degree of institutionalization and policy implementation.

The EU shows clear limits regarding its diplomatic power in relation to intergovernmental bodies (the several 'Contact groups' for instance), to nation states' power (for example, as the UN security council is concerned) and to the American role in Europe.

According to Seidelmann, in terms of power, the EU shows its dramatic deficits in the case of the remilitarization of local conflicts (as shown by the former Yugoslavia and former USSR experience), particularly in comparison with the enhanced NATO role in Eastern European security challenges.

Ten years after 1989, instead of a homogeneous trend, we are observing not one, but instead many 'eastern Europes'. The 'strategic partnership' with Russia looks as a still insufficient framework for a balanced and dynamic compromise including energy policy, economic cooperation and political dialogue. There is a 'winners group' (such as Poland, the Czech Republic, Slovenia and Hungary, some of the Baltic states), where clear achievements in economic and democratic transition are making of EU 2004 enlargement a recognized success story[5]. There is a various 'losers group' (Belarus, Moldova, but also some of the Balkan countries). Here, the huge problems of economic and political reform have provoked a vicious circle of dependence on the west. Economic crisis, domestic turbulence, foreign and domestic malevolence and the real threat of regional instability and anti-West movements have aggravated this. Ukraine is representing a distinctive transition, including intensive dialogue with EU and refusal of NATO membership. Finally, after the Kosovo war, a new group was born, including Albania, Macedonia, Serbia, Croatia, Bosnia, Serbia, Montenegro and Kosovo, where *ad hoc* plans and new priorities have been agreed with EU, because of political and humanitarian criteria. In conclusion, the general picture is still very differentiated and ambiguous concerning the feasibility of a new peace and democratic order at pan-European level.

As far as the foreseeable future is concerned, two developments are possible, since the Yugoslavian tragedies of the 1990s shattered the rhetorical idealistic approach of a general benevolence and a final victory for democratic values. Either one can conceive the eastern European problems as marginal for the global governance of the world economy and security, or one can emphasize the threat coming from re-emerging nationalisms, pan-Slavonic fundamentalism, both in the Balkans and in the former Soviet Union. The first vision takes into account the dramatic decline of the former USSR as a superpower, the end of the nuclear threat and the transformation of eastern Europe as part of a growing and encompassing

EU, becoming a civilian regional power, organizing the continent in concentric circles, integrating norms and interests. In the second vision, nationalism, fundamentalism and ethnic conflicts will increase regional wild instability, even if not in the 'civilization's clash' picture. The attempt to build collective security institutions in Europe was formerly conceived as a step between traditional defense institutions and cooperative security institutions.[6] But one of the problems is that, in case of military conflict, the EU needs to be complemented by its competitor: the enlarging NATO's more effective parallel role. The second one is the unresolved transition and foreign energy policy of declining Russia.

The issue of the political role of the EU interacts with the challenge of enlargement. Regarding the future of west European regionalism in the new pan-European environment, 1989–91 was a historical turning point. The small-sized, economic and functional European Community has gone. The consequences of continental change are contradictory and potentially conflicting. On one hand, the external demands of a huge expansion process is forcing the EU to increase internal differentiation and consequently to set a new regional integration model. On the other hand, the European Union, including a political union, needs deepening and strengthening in order to cope with external responsibilities and challenges: the achievement of the long institutional reform process is a crucial pillar, under this respect. The large array of instruments and the fluctuation of EU-Ost-Politik of the past decade, from President J. Delors' project of 'concentric circles', to the Copenhagen European Council setting the criteria for eastern enlargement (1993), to the 'Agenda 2000' (1999), to the Helsinki Council's openness, to the enlargement of 2004–07 to ten new central and eastern European member states, show a lack of strategy. The as yet unclear issue of the final eastern border, raises the question of the institutional settlement in a wider Europe and interacts deeply with the hard process of Treaty revision. The debate on hard core, flexible integration and 'enhanced cooperation' has to be seen as a reaction to the growing uncertainties of regional integration within the new geopolitics of a continental Europe. Later on, we will explore the alternative scenarios. The crucial Balkan challenge has clearly shown that only an efficient, legitimized internal political differentiation, included within the institutional framework of the European Treaties, could overcome opposite (even if not entirely contradictory) trends, either towards a kind of Voltairean 'Candide Europe' or towards an unaccountable directorate of major states (according to the path of the 'Contact group').

2 European Union and near abroad: Mediterranean

The second important chapter of the near abroad is the Mediterranean region. At first glance, there are important similarities with the relationship of the EU to eastern Europe:

- Firstly, European policy is ambitious but ambiguous, including both duality (EU openness to external partners belonging to its periphery) and, as far as some countries are concerned, a real (Malta and Cyprus) or negotiated deeper linkage, namely the Union's enlargement (regarding Turkey);

- Secondly, after the end of the world's bipolar structure, increasing differences emerged between the USA and the EU as far as interest and security perceptions in that area were concerned. The EU is not only the dominant trade and economic partner with northern African and southern Mediterranean countries (see tables in Joffé's chapter). Similarly to Russia, the interdependence between western Europe and northern Africa regarding energy provisions (more particularly since gas pipelines are partly substituting oil) is crucial and symbiotic. The USA has mainly strategic security concerns (plus price stability) in that area.[7] Furthermore, almost every EU state is also seriously concerned with regulating immigration, in preventing crime, illegal traffic and terrorism.[8]

These similarities between the eastern and southern challenges explain the new EU project of 2004 of organizing in the medium term a ring of 500 millions friends surrounding the 500 millions 27-EU. The 'neighbourhood policy' will absorb the highly problematic legacy of the 'Barcelona process', which started in 1995, bringing together the northern and southern rims of the Mediterranean (fifteen EU countries plus twelve southern Mediterranean countries). It excluded the US while the OSCE does not. However, the challenge was and remains that the 'Euro-Mediterranean partnership' is particularly asymmetric as regards the respective main concerns and expectations of the two rims: multiple security issues on the one hand, and economic development on the other. In other words, the so-called 'European methodology' is facing particularly hard problems, by looking at increase economic interdependence as a means towards a pacific settlement of security issues in the long run.

Ten years later, the EU itself recognizes that the impact of the European-Mediterranean process is still witnessing a rather modest result. The EC and the EU can be seen as successful past democratizers of the European rim of the Mediterranean region from the very beginning of the integration process (taking the example of young post-fascist democracies like Italy, Spain, Greece or Portugal). However, in the countries where no promise of full membership is possible, 'democratic conditionality' hardly works, including within the multilateral framework of the 'Barcelona process'. For the current decade, with the sole exception of the open-ended negotiations with Turkey (which is raising hopes of a successful gradual replication), according to the pessimistic Joffé's evaluation of the new system of 'positive rewards' very little is happening regarding the democratization of other southern Mediterranean countries.

One of the explanations of the poor results is linked to the hard security implications of the Israeli-Palestinian conflict, aggravated both by the terrorist threats after 2001 and the Iraqi War. For the very first time the EU is playing a true political role in the Middle East with the dangerous Lebanon mission of 2006. Past common statements and actions, concerning the Middle East and North Africa, have largely been marginal. The 'Venice statement' of 1978, the ECP, the Euro–Arab dialogue, the Lisbon European Council's 1992 conclusion (which declared the Middle East a zone of common interest) and finally the CFSP joint actions in the Middle East since 1993, were not particularly successful. This helps explaining why the 'Barcelona process' challenge was very tough.[9] However, some progress cannot be ignored: the 1995 Barcelona Declaration expressed the common consciousness of EU member states, that geographical proximity and European interests in the region demand a more encompassing and long-term strategy than previously. These should bring together all dimensions of a very complex relationship, and reject the catastrophic scenarios regarding intercultural dialogue. The Barcelona process has been structured in accordance with the 'CSCE-OSCE' model (Helsinki process), underlining, even by such formal parallelism, the request of many member states, to balance the eastern commitment with a southern commitment, facing simultaneously both sides of the 'arch of the crisis' almost surrounding the EU.

The 'Barcelona process' is firstly entailing cooperation in security matters, linking peace and domestic democratization, respect for human rights and the common fight against terrorism. The second basket supports a sustainable and balanced economic and social development, largely based on IMF prescriptions, but corrected by pressures for a move towards a common market among EU partners. The third supports a promotion of better understanding between northern and southern cultures and the development of a civil society within the southern Mediterranean states.

As for the poor achievement and the huge deficits of the first basket they are well illustrated by the lacking energy security policy and particularly by the very poor foreign policy in the – indirectly linked – Gulf area, as shown by the Iraqi War. The EU-institutions approach to the conflict proved correct, but Europe didn't take stock of its alternative understanding to democratization and peace building. Furthermore, the balance includes the lack of cooperation in the fight against terrorism, drug trafficking and crime and also the marginal role played in the Middle East peace process, in spite of huge financial commitment and effort in implementing a new Palestinian democracy. Observers mention several explanatory factors:

- The southern Mediterranean states' opposition to the EU interfering in their domestic affairs. Even if symbolic, national sovereignty is very important for authoritarian or semi-authoritarian regimes.
- The political weakness of the EU, not only when military conflicts within the region might tend to affect high-level politics and as such, demand the intervention of the USA, but also as a mere mediator.
- Despite the political differences and the open competition between the US and the EU as the Mediterranean and Middle-East policies are concerned, ten years of initiatives paradoxically resulted in a shared image of disappointment within the world of Islamic partners, which is making a new start difficult.
- Like as in eastern Europe, the bilateral approach of the EU has the consequence of making south-south horizontal cooperation more difficult and present the picture of a new Eurocentric 'hub and spokes' framework.

The pessimistic forecast provided by the Joffé's chapter is strengthened by his analysis of the 'neighbourhood policy' as renouncing to 'horizontal integration' among southern partners as a cause of complications. However, the perspective of individually joining the European Economic Area has been offered in 2006 to the southern partners. Regarding the continuation of the economic basket of the former Barcelona process, the process will continue, despite the new bilateral framework provided by the 'neighborhood policy', for the simple reason that the southern partners of the very near economic giant, the EU, do not really have a big choice. The problems are not limited to the relatively restricted parallel EU funding and EU agricultural protectionism. They include the huge destabilizing impact of deregulation and liberalization, which threaten non-competitive companies and branches, have relevant direct socio-political consequences and negatively interfere with the other baskets of the process. A failure in constructing better cross-cultural understanding would potentially have disruptive consequences, even as far as the other baskets are concerned.

Regarding 'horizontal integration', the EU's strategy to encourage partners to cooperate regionally seems to be particularly unsuccessful in the Mediterranean. The main question is as follows. Is the desired sub-regional cooperation community a matter of voluntary association or rather of a mere external coercion? Of course, there were many previous regional attempts in the Maghreb and the Arab world, independently from any EU pressure. However, for different reasons, they all failed. The failing attempt to create a northern African common market within the Barcelona process ,despite the EU support is addressing the question of the comparative evaluation of the very various impact of inter-regionalist relations established by the EU during the last decades (see Hettne & Vasconcelos).

3 The near abroad and the future of deep regional integration

The Euro-Mediterranean relationship suggests two interesting theoretical developments concerning analogies and differences between deeper regional integration and softer regionalism. The comparison with the EU-Eastern Europe process is useful, even if similarities cannot be overemphasized. For example, it is true that, as far as central Europe is concerned, the EC-EU policy to support the creation of autonomous 'Visegrad' type multilateral common markets, as alternative to EU enlargement, was fragile and contradictory. This is largely because the new post-communist democratic leaderships never welcomed it. They openly desired full membership, which implies bilateral arrangements. However, obviously the expectations held outside of the continent, namely those of the North -African and Euro-Asian countries, to become active and direct part of the EU decision-making process, cannot have the same legitimacy. Art. 49, of the TEU, states that 'every European state can apply to become a full member of the Union'.

Regarding softer regional cooperation with neighbours. The comparison with the US–Mexican relationship is also very stimulating, even if analogies must not be exaggerated. Although they are very 'distant neighbors', they are united by soft regionalism within NAFTA an association whose evolution towards a FTAA is more than controversial. Even if the North-South relationship established within the 'Barcelona process' is as yet much less linking than NAFTA (this occurs between countries which belong to different continents, a fact which obviously limits possibilities of full integration), the new 'neighbourhood policy', launching the scenario of a possible great European Economic Area (see appendix), gives another meaning to Mediterranean 'soft regionalism', by establishing common policies based on shared values (and supported by the constitutional treaty art.56).

Which are the chances of the new EU neighbourhood policy, a kind of third way with enlargement and neither with foreign policy? Multilateral/bilateral regional, continental and even intercontinental, cooperation has maybe some chances of success, provided that it overcomes the limited basis of the security needs of the stronger side and economic needs of the weaker side. Between the Euro-Asiatic Turkey's success in becoming an official and bargaining candidate, and the traditional model of relationship between the EU on one side, and southern/eastern partners on the other side (the duality model), are new and more encompassing institutional paths eventually and gradually emerging as part of a broad regional architecture? An answer to this crucial question must be divided into two parts:

1. There are limits to a positive trade-off between widening and deepening regional organizations. Too broad an enlargement improves geopolitical legitimacy but dramatically weakens efficiency and effectiveness when acting at regional and global levels. Too wide an eastern enlargement, parallel to a Mediterranean enlargement of the EU, would not only dilute the European integration process. Such an enlargement would also seriously jeopardize the EU's ability to play the role of both regional and global actor, providing governance and stability within the continental and world economic and political systems. Last but not least, the internal legitimacy of EU integration would be undermined.

This is one of the main differences with NAFTA, as an open regional agreement centered on a superpower, a would-be hemispheric free trade area of the Americas. Of course, new structures have to be created around the EU, in order to strengthen the feeling of solidarity and common interests and values between the two rims of the Mediterranean region and between a wider EU and former USSR members, first of all Ukraine and Russia. Furthermore, independent and endogenous federative processes among more democratic southern Mediterranean countries and within the boundaries of the former Soviet Union (and the current Commonwealth of Independent States) would help to create a true partnership with the EU. This is in contrast to the centre–periphery dual path, which would inevitably deepen divisions and provoke long term regional and global instability.

In case of the EU's failure to reach a greater institutional ability to clearly set and implement more consistently its common goals and regional strategy, the main engine for the whole process, the first stability factor of the area, would break down. It would probably be substituted by informal intergovernmental and hierarchical bodies, for example, an intergovernmental directorate, and by the sole global superpower. The second answer fosters a deeper theoretical work:

2. The relationship between the EU and the near abroad will be obliged to evolve dramatically within next few decades on the one side, towards a deeper and a wider European Union, and, on the other side an improved continental and interregional partnership. In conceiving these scenarios,

we need to question the concept of 'new regionalism'. To clarify and stress distinctions with both 'imperial regionalism' (colonial legacies) and 'open regionalism' (US model of the W. Clinton era) at the conceptual level is not only important regarding that part of the world, but also regarding the theoretical discussion on EU, regional governance and world order.

Notes

1   For a contrast, ten years after the fall of communist regimes, see M. Emerson (1998), M. Lavigne (1999); A. Mayhew (1998).

2   M. Lavigne, *L'intégration des pays d'Europe centrale dans l'économie mondiale: régionalisation et mondialisation*, paper, Universite de Pau. 1998.

3   The Helsinki Council of December 1999 modified the schedule introduced by the Commission Paper of 1998 'Agenda 2000'. The division between the first group of six candidates (Poland, Hungary, Czech Republic, Slovenia, Estonia, and Cyprus) and a second group (Bulgaria, Rumania, Slovakia, Latvia, and Lithuania) has been overcome. Malta and Turkey have been added to the list of official candidates. Secondly, developments in the former Yugoslavia foresee Croatia and Serbia as future candidates, as well as special association agreements with Macedonia, Bosnia and Albania. Finally, Ukraine would like to join the list of associated countries and later on be a candidate. When possible, Belarus and Moldova could like to do the same.

4   The Amsterdam Treaty provision of 'common strategies' (to be decided by the European Council by unanimity procedure) allow the Council to adopt Qualified Majority Voting by 'common actions' (Art. 13 and 14, TEU).

5   Alan Mayhew (1998) and European Commission (1997), Agenda 2000, Brussels .

6   See C. Kupchan, Regionalizing Europe's Security, in Mansfield and Milner, eds. (1997), p.16.

7   R. Aliboni, ed. (1990) *Southern European Security in the 1990s*, Pinter, London.

8   R. Bistolfi (1995), *Euro-Méditerranée: Une région à construire*, Paris, G. Joffé (1995), Europe and North Africa, in *Cambridge Review of International Affairs*, Winter /Spring, n. 2, pp. 84–103; B. Khader, ed. (1994), *L'Europe et la Méditerranée. La géopolitique de la proximité*, L'Harmattan, Paris; E. Rhein (1996), Europe and the Mediterranean: A Newly Emerging Geopolitical Area, in *European Foreign Affairs Review*, vol. 1, no. 1 July, pp. 79–86; G. Edwards & E. Philippart (1997), The EU Mediterranean Policy: Virtue Unrewarded, in *Cambridge Review of International Affairs*, Summer/Fall, vol. XI, no. 1, pp. 185–206.

9   *Barcelona Declaration adopted at the Euro-Mediterranean Conference* (27 and 28 November, 1995) Barcelona; European Commission (1997), *Progress Report on the Euro-Mediterranean Partnership*, Communication to the Council and the European Parliament, Brussels, 19 February.

Chapter 12

European Union and Eastern Europe

Reimund Seidelmann

Both in the academic as in the political debate the expression 'Eastern Europe'a has become a synonym for an intellectual as well as a political problem and challenge. For the political scientist, the Eastern European problem is not only a specific area or country issue but has revitalized and refocused transformation studies,[1] has become a major issue for theoretical as well as applied democracy studies,[2] has given new thoughts for peace and conflict studies,[3] and finally has emerged as an important issue for integration studies.[4] For the politically concerned, Eastern Europe means on the one side a long-sought and peaceful change towards democracy and peaceful integration and on the other side specific political challenges such as the Yugoslavian conflicts and the deterioration in Russia to which the European political community has not found adequate and effective prevention, control and solution yet. Further, both the past – and eventually continued – Eastern enlargement has revitalized the question about the political-geographical identity of the EU. Now, after the second major round of Eastern enlargement, the relation between the EU and Eastern Europe has two interrelated dimensions: first, Eastern European EU-members have to be fully integrated and turned into active and responsible member states, and secondly, eastern Europe is not within the EU but at the same time an important near abroad area or neighbourhood. But although the management and solution of the Eastern European problems in their duality constitute an important issue for Europe and specifically for the EU's political agenda, this also has a general and global dimension.. The decline or the implosion of the superpower USSR, the reorganization of the European power constellation, and its effects on EU–US and other relations demand a definition of the notion not only of Eastern Europe as a regional but also as a global issue. Therefore – and in contrast to other views – it is seen as both politically legitimate as well as analytically necessary to regard the Eastern European problem not only as a European problem but as subject and object of the general formula not of globalization but of a dialectic interrelation between globalization, regionalism, and the nation state. In order to do so, both the substantial as well as the theoretical dimension of the problem will be discussed with the aim to broaden both the debate on the Eastern European problem and on globalization.

1 Defining the problem as a historical one

To define the problem of Eastern Europe one can start with a historical comparison between the situation during and after the East–West conflict. This not only follows an understanding of political processes as historical ones but allows the Eastern European problem to be defined as a historical challenge towards the EU as well.

Both regarding the structure of the pan-European state system as well as of Western and Eastern Europe, the end of the East–West conflict has led to fundamental and far-reaching changes. Despite all advances in conflict management through detente policies, the old European state system was dominated by the East-West conflict – that is, military confrontation, political power rivalry, and division into two blocs. The dynamic of bloc-confrontation and bloc-integration dominated east-west relations in Europe and constituted an essential, costly, and high-risk problem for the European system as well as a structural, vital, and dominant destabilization of its security order. The end of the east-west conflict has eliminated this old security problem in the political agenda of the European state system; in today's Europe, old security problems such as in the Balkans have reemerged but compared with the old east-west conflict they have a subregional character, are limited in horizontal and vertical terms of escalation, have only minor military effects, and constitute a politically important but not a vital challenge for the regional order as such. In addition, they can be solved in principle by the European Union without external help. But still after and with the end of the east–west conflict eastern Europe still constitutes a problem for the whole region as well as for its main national, multinational, and supranational actors. Three wars in Yugoslavia, an unstable Ukraine, and still-existing conflict potentials between Russia and the newly independent nations of the former USSR are illustrations. Although the new eastern European problem results more from the past and reflects more the present structural deficits of the emerging new European order, it differs from the old one in terms of quality, dynamic, and political relevance. This is both due to the structural change in the regional system in general and its power constellation in particular. In the period of the east-west conflict, the confrontation with the eastern bloc constituted not only, but most importantly, a regional problem and while the eastern bloc was poor in economic power, it nevertheless commanded a military power of equal relevance[5] to the western one. Disarmament, collapse of the Warsaw Treaty Organization, disintegration of the USSR, and the many problems of transition not only downsized but marginalized the military ability of Russia as the successor of the USSR to threaten western Europe. The new asymmetric or western-dominated east-west cooperation, Russia's stepwise integration into the western institutional and power formula underlined by its association to NATO and the change in Russia's political priorities created a constellation in which political will to militarizing conflict with western Europe became unthinkable or counter-productive.[6] In comparison to the past, the new east-west relations in Europe in general and the Russia–west in particular are basically demilitarized,[7] are based on economic-political cooperation, and on a western-dominated power formula. And new Russia's use of the oil and gas 'weapon' to insure influence and improve power position has a significantly different quality and reach. However – and in particular as a consequence of the first steps towards CFSP, ESDP, and an effective crisis intervention force – this new European power formula includes military policing by or through either EU force or combined EU–NATO capabilities as in the case of the two Yugoslavian wars.[8] Military policing through NATO or new EU peace-keeping as well as political actions of EU against non-democratic forces[9] – even when they are part of the national governments – are based on an understanding of the new European order not as a permissive but as an actively self-defending one.

They not only constitute important elements of Europe's new identity, but are also a clear message to eastern Europe. This role of the EU is particularly necessary *vis-à-vis* the political experience that the eastern European subregion proved unwilling and unable to develop effective subregional structures to solve its problems by itself or to establish necessary subregional unity in negotiations and actions. While the Visegrad and the south-eastern Europe/Black Sea as well as other projects to establish subregional cooperation failed to materialize, the CIS project has been stalled because of the old and new Russian problem – that is, the potential revitalization of Russian power projection towards former Soviet republics or within CIS.[10] Thus, the demilitarization or re-politization and further economization of east–west relations together with the collapse of eastern European subregional cooperation resulted not only in downsizing and downgrading the old east–west problem but also in establishing a revitalizing, enlarging, and deepening EU as the dominant pan-European actor, which, together with an enlarging and re-legitimized NATO and supplemented by the new Stability Pact in the Balkans, directly and indirectly controls political and economic developments in eastern Europe. While recent EU steps towards materializing the new European Security and Defense Identity (ESDI) opened a perspective for a more comprehensive EU civic-military power projection mainly towards eastern Europe in general and the Balkans in particular, the establishment of the European Monetary Union (EMU) has illustrated again the interrelationship between the EU's integration process, power projection towards eastern Europe, and redefinition of the EU's global role.

But the disappearance of the old eastern threat problem and the emergence of a new and EU-dominated pan-European power constellation did not mean the establishment of a new order without structural problems in and with eastern Europe. Socio-economic transformation, redefining national sovereignty and dynamics of nation-building, and the many unsolved ethnic, political, and economic conflict potentials within and between eastern European states have resulted in cumulating and mutually reinforcing problems, of which the most important are socio-economic crises, political instability, ecological disasters, and the 'Yugoslavization' – that is, the militarization of domestic and neighbour-to-neighbour conflicts.[11] With the dissolution of the eastern bloc and the disappearance of a politically unifying, pacifying, and economically supportive Soviet Union as well as viz-à-vis the lack of efficient subregional control, these problems turned from intra-bloc to regional ones and also have 'Europeanized' issues such as the Balkans, which traditionally had been marginalized and neglected by Europe's major actors. And with an enlarging and politicizing European Union, which turned from second range to central actor of European affairs, such regional problems turn into a major problem for the European Union and constitute a global challenge as well, which will be discussed hereafter. The fact that the Balkans have been stabilized through a set of different measures such as economic assistance, peace-keeping, civic-society-building, and finally the opening of the perspective for future membership, does not constitute a solution to the problem but a shift from military towards political and economic dimensions of problem solution strategies.

1.1   The EU view

Following an understanding of politics as a matter of norms, interests, and power in the view of the European Union the new eastern European problem has three aspects. Firstly, in terms of interests, it constitutes an economic, socio-migratory, ecological, and a limited law-and-order-threat, and a major challenge for consolidating peace and democracy within and outside the EU in general and to some of its member nations in particular. However, a serious evaluation of probability and expected damage of the specific threat dimensions as well as its cumulated effects on EU interests can lead to the conclusion that these threats are not vital but limited and are presently under relative political control – even if this control seems inadequate and questionable as cost-effectiveness is concerned. All worst case events of the past like the ecological problem of Chernobyl, continued migratory pressure from the east towards the west, the past and potentially future conflicts in Yugoslavia, and the many financial and political crises in Russia proved to be of limited political weight, to be containable within the existing structures and mechanisms, and of important but nevertheless not vital relevance for the European Union. This does not mean to discount the problem in absolute terms in regard to the eastern European states in which they occur. But with regard to EU interests, it means that in contrast to the old eastern problem the new one is limited in relative terms, is second rate in terms of EU's present political priorities, and competes in the setting of the political agenda with many other problems. This view does not mean to underestimate the effects of new and newest eastern European membership for the EU budget in general and EU's CAP in particular; but in principle the EU is able to solve effectively these problems by itself and within its political culture and political strategies.

Secondly, and in terms of norms, the new eastern European problem is a problem of domestic as well as of subregional political order. It still constitutes a problem for democracy, which concerns EU interests as well as its character as a value or democratic community. Both the EU's definition of democracy as well as its normative mission towards Europe are threatened if the socio-economic crises and the specifics of nation-building or power-formation in eastern Europe lead to limit, block, or even reverse the dynamic of democratization or democratic consolidation. Or – as in the case of Yugoslavia – malevolent actors in eastern Europe turn to military aggression either to the inside as in the case of Kosovo or the outside as in the case of Bosnia-Herzegovina. This is not only a problem of outside image and international credibility, but is of importance, but often overlooked inner political relevance for the EU and the integration process in general. And in addition to the problem of democratization such as in Bulgaria and Romania, parts of eastern Europe still show a problem of peace. Although peace-building or the 'civilization' of interstate relations can be regarded primarily as a result of – as well as a condition for – democratization or the development of the 'civic society' it nevertheless depends on the regional pattern, interaction mode, and institutional framework being able and willing to stimulate, support, and secure this peace-building process.

Like democratization and socioeconomic reforms, peace-building efforts in eastern Europe show different stages of development and reach. Experiences with past EU-enlargement towards eastern Europe prove that true democratization leads to such foreign effects and that the EU's and NATO's strategy of incentives had been effective. Russia, however, shows mixed results. While showing an impressive record of peaceful solutions of conflicts with neighbouring states like the Baltics, Ukraine, and the Caucasus states, Russia's unsuccessful policy for solving the Chechnya-problem with military means shows that the 'pacification' of Russian politics has not been completed. Finally, the past and eventually future low-intensity wars or semi-wars in Yugoslavia illustrate that old mechanisms of nation-building, power formation, and militarizing conflicts are still in effect. This means, in other words, that the newly emerging pan-European security system has on the one side led to a remarkable state of demililtarization and peace- and security-building but has on the other side to cope with some important structural deficits or cases of political regression. If one defines the EU as the only effective responsible pan-European actor, such deficits in democratization and peace-building are not only a problem of the countries directly concerned but of the EU as well. The EU's inner democratic legitimacy and political support, which are essential not only for the present state of integration but also for the future integration process, are put into question, if the EU proves unable and unwilling to manage, control, and finally solve the democracy and peace problem of eastern Europe. And this is not only an abstract problem of the better order but might turn into a structural problem of EU integration as well. If in the present political competition between EU, NATO, and major nation states the EU fails to fulfil such a role,[13] In the long run political elites and the public alike within and outside the EU will limit and even withdraw their support for the EU and European integration in general and might finally put the basic idea of the EU as a community for democracy-, wealth-, and peace-building[14] into question. Thus, both the idea of understanding the EU's role as not only an intra-EU but an all-European peace and security maker as well, as the EU's recent steps towards establishing common will and military ability for the projection of its democratic and civic order to the rest of Europe and its neighbouring regions,[15] have opened important perspectives for eastern Europe.

Thirdly, the experience with Eastern European EU members have again raised the question about the political identity of the EU or the necessary consensus in common policies and politics. Although within the EU one can find differences between 'intergovernmentalists' and 'integrationists', there was a basic consensus about the values and well as intra- and extraregional interests of the European Union. As the political development showed the enlargement process in general and eastern European membership in particular not only complicated joint decision making but weakened the consensus about the doctrine that widening should be necessarily linked to deepening and that the EU should look for a greater global responsibility not as a dependent but a more independent actor. Keeping such consensus and turning new Eastern European members into constructive and engaged 'Europeanists' has become a major challenge for continued integration.

Fourthly, the new Eastern European problem is a problem as well as an opportunity for EU power politics. It constitutes a major challenge or test to the EU's willingness and ability to fulfil its new role as the European actor – both to the inside as well as the outside. While this seems relatively easy with cooperation, benevolence-, and democracy-oriented Eastern European actors, the cases of Yugoslavia, Chechnya, Caucasus have shown the EU's limitations in projecting power to the malevolent in the near neighbourhood, in keeping or re-establishing its type of democratic and peaceful order, and to fulfil its political mission or responsibilities towards the greater European region. Worst cases – for example, that of Russia socio-economically further deteriorating, de-democratizing, and re-militarizing its foreign policy – are still conceivable and would put on EU willingness and ability to a new and more far-reaching test than in the case of Yugoslavia. Present EU policies of limited political management – or mostly containment, symbolic politics, and internationalizing – or Americanizing or UN-izing of eastern Europe or the eastern European problem – should not be mixed up with long-term effective solutions or the establishment of a pan-European democratic growth- and peace-community, which are the objectives behind the EU's post-Maastricht efforts in regard to CSFP, ESDI, and enlargement policies. Again, this is not only a problem of legitimacy and concrete interests, but creates a long-term problem for political willingness to turn to the EU – and EU integration – in continuing to establish a new regional order and to define the democratic and integrative project as an attractive model to solve regional problems. In other words, the challenge constituted by eastern Europe is not only a challenge with or towards old, new, and future eastern European member states within the EU but for a comprehensive and cohesive near-neighbourhood policy towards greater eastern Europe – including Russia.

While on the one side the end of the east-west conflict created a historically unique opportunity for widening, deepening, and projecting EU power towards the east, the EU's will and ability to make use of such opportunity has been limited in the past in three aspects. Firstly, although economics, that is, the EU's traditional source of power, has been used to promote and smooth socio-economic transformation, democratization, and de-militarization, the EU still lacks a comprehensive, cost-efficient, and cohesive economic-political strategy towards its eastern European neighbourhood in general and towards Russia in particular.[16] Secondly, the CSFP-project in general and concerning the issue of a common, coherent, and effective policy towards eastern Europe – including Russia, the Yugoslavian states, and so on, – in particular has shown little progress both in terms of institutionalization as well as in terms of implementation of common policies. EU member states' idea to supplement EU efforts in south-eastern Europe through the establishment of the Stability Pact are still far from being effectively realized. Thus, EU political-diplomatic power is still limited both in absolute terms as well as in relation to nation states' power such as Germany's, France's, and others. Thirdly, military power of the EU as EU-power in terms of hard security guarantees, peace-keeping, and peace- and democracy-re-establishing, is, despite all ESDI-rhetoric, still not only marginal in absolute terms but suffered relative marginalization because of NATO's role in and for eastern Europe in general and Yugoslavia in particular.[17] Despite all progress in joint peace-keeping, the EU lacks both effective and sustained political will and military ability to overcome such deficits; despite all political rhetoric of political-military autonomy it is still accepting an anachronistic US responsibility for European affairs because this seems an easier way to manage eastern European security problems than pursuing the build-up of a comprehensive EU power potential.[18] In the absence of a potent competitor for power in eastern Europe and vis-à-vis the fact that the new eastern European problem is primarily an economic-political and less a military-political one such limited and sometimes incoherent and unconcisive power projection nevertheless propelled the EU into dominant power player in the region – challenged less from the outside but more from its major nation state members from the inside. Whether the EU is willing and able to effectively complement its economic power through a truly common foreign and security policy plus an integrated and effective military capacity is still an open question and the new eastern European members show limited political willingness to support constructive progress. Here, the problem is not only to reach breakthroughs but to secure sustainability.[19]

If one finally looks at Europe in a normative and western European oriented understanding of history based on the idea of enlightenment, the new eastern Europe as well as EU's east European neighbourhood not only poses a problem for EU interests, norms, and regional power, but at the same time a challenge and an opportunity to further develop as a civic order. In principle, the EU – as the main product, mean, and source of the European integration process – might develop both will and ability to establish, maintain, and develop a new pan-European order not despite but because of this new and structural problem. But in contrast to the period of the east-west conflict the new eastern European neighbourhood constitutes more a political challenge for order projection towards the east than a forceful external integrator plus policy-stimulator because it does not pose a vital threat to EU interests and power, as discussed above. This means that the objective necessary for a cohesive policy of enlargements, of developing an efficient grand strategy towards a neighbouring subregion, and to establish or gain common control of the necessary political-diplomatic, economic, and military means does not translate into a political top priority, does not produce the sort of comprehensive political willingness, and does not demand that kind of political ability which characterized the European order during the east-west conflict. This, however, does not discount the concept of historical learning through challenges and the concept of the responsibility of power. But given the new constellation of factors, which stimulate and block further integration as well as political will to solve the Eastern European problem, and given the general weight of Eastern Europe in the European political agenda, this means the search for new actors, mechanisms, and dynamics in order to continue – and implement – Maastricht's redefinition of integration and unionizing, to project its historical successes towards Eastern Europe within and outside the EU, and to benefit in a common way from newly established growth opportunities, social stability, environmental and military security, which result from a solution – and not from a management – of the new Eastern European problem.

1.2 The Eastern European view

Although the far-reaching 'westernization' – or the return of eastern Europe to Europe – of eastern European societies and politics as well as EU and western European agenda-setting for control and solution of the new eastern European problem create the temptation to define the eastern European problem as predominantly, perhaps even as, a western problem only, a normative as well as a functional approach demand to define the new eastern European problem in fact as the eastern European problem. This means in analytical terms looking at the eastern European problem not only from a western but from an eastern European view as well; in political terms this means to state that western European nations, EU, NATO, OSCE and so on, can only complement but not substitute eastern European efforts to solve the problem.

To understand eastern Europe, one has to underline the far-reaching political change in terms of norms, interests, and power, which has taken place after and as a consequence of the end of the east-west conflict and the collapse of the Soviet empire. Prepared and sometimes already introduced during detente, eastern European societies regarded the western model as superior compared with their own former Communist model in terms of values and order, socio-economic performance, and peace and security services. When the end of the east-west conflict allowed a fundamental re-orientation and at the same time had fully discredited even a reformed Communist model, 'westernization' in general and democratization, socio-economic transformation towards market economy, and participation in western institutions like EU, NATO, and the Council of Europe seems to be the only alternative to the present crises, the only model for nation-building, -rebuilding, and -redefining. As often in such situations, the western world was not only idealized but regarded as the prime actor to assist socio-economic, military, and political transformation. And following the temptation of the past as well as of populism, eastern European elites often defined the west – and in particular the EU – as substitute for a lack of political will and ability to solve national and subregional problems in their own responsibility.

Apart from these common experiences and this common re-orientation, eastern Europe did not define itself as a sort of regional entity with common problems and goals to be solved through common politics and common institutions but primarily as individual nations on the way towards western Europe. This means that in respecting the newly emerged and emerging political identities in eastern Europe one has to give up the perception of a more or less homogeneous eastern Europe. And this is not only the result of the new thinking in eastern Europe but results from empirical realities as well. In other words, there were and still are many eastern Europes both within and outside the EU; domestic transformation and foreign re-orientation of eastern European states show some patterns and qualities, which vary more than structures, patterns, and modes of western European policies. Regarding the relation between EU and eastern Europe and referring to EU strategy towards eastern Europe, one can classify at least three different types of eastern European nations: the 'winning', 'losing', and 'in between' eastern European countries.

For the former 'winners' such as Poland, Czech Republic, and Hungary and the group of new EU members of 2004, and the late 'winners'of 2007, such as Bulgaria and Romania, socio-economic transition, democratization, and foreign orientation to the west meant to adapt to the western model of a civic democracy, which promises individual freedom and political participation, social market economy, which promises economic wellbeing and social fairness, and 'civic' foreign policy, which promises both security and peace. Orientation to The West as well as a policy of more or less unconditional integration in western institutions like EU, NATO, and the Council of Europe resulted from a strategy combining new norms, traditional interests, and a policy to seek new net power advantages through integration in EU and NATO. Despite the problems in the first years, the strategy of combining transformation, modernization, and integration, or of 'the return to Europe' through adaptation produced substantial success, political acceptance, and inner and outer legitimacy which the old Communist elites could never achieve. It is not by chance that these 'winners' are not part of the Eastern European problem. On the contrary – they benefit from the problem in portraying themselves both to the inside as well as the outside as the 'no-problem' countries.

One of the most prominent 'losers' of the end of the East-West conflict and the resulting changes is Russia.[20] Socio-economic transformation did not solve but aggravated the economic crises; political change led to the typical 'Oblomov' stalemate, and orientation to the west plus association with NATO revitalized the old dispute, whether Russia is European, Eurasian, or something different.[21] While in countries like Poland the combination of transformation, modernization, and integration reinforced each other and resulted in political success, Russia's transformation into two economies, societies, and political camps together with the inner and outer effects of its general decline in power[22] and dependence on the west resulted in economic and political deterioration and a far-reaching crisis of political identity and culture. This, however, creates not only a new inferiority complex in security policies but constitutes a major concern in Russia's neighbours and beyond, which translates such a lack of domestic stability and predictability into a political-military threat.[23] Thus, domestic instability turns into regional instability, which has been illustrated by Russia's military intervention in Chechnya. In fact, Russia has to regard itself as one of the major losers of the post-east–west conflict period in all aspects and constitutes therefore a source of instability for Eastern Europe and the CIS.[24] While special cooperation with the west in general and the EU in particular has been a way to manage these structural problems, Russia's association with NATO[25] has opened a perspective for containing the effects of the Russian problem towards her Eastern European neighbours. It has to be kept in mind that both management and containment, however, do not constitute solutions for the structural problems of such a 'loser' country; this limits the outer effects but leaves Russia because of its size, its military and in particular nuclear, power potential, and geographic position as the most relevant Eastern European problem. And if the EU and Russia are able to establish a partnership in energy production and consumption, this could further stabilize both the situation and the relation between EU and its eastern neighbourhood.

Between 'winners' and 'losers' one has to mention those countries which on the one side have tried to follow some of the models, concepts, and strategies of the 'western' Eastern European countries but tried, partly intentionally and partly for lack of political will and ability, to preserve some of the old patterns and structures or to pursue a third way. The Slovak Republic of the past[26] – that is, until 1998 – is a perfect example of such a mix of westernization, preserving previous formulas, and searching for a political model of its own after separating from the Czechs. Caught between new and old policies, western and eastern orientation, and nation-building and solution of political and economic problems, the Slovak Republic faced a no-win situation. Domestic acceptance was limited, cooperation with Russia did neither solve the security problems of the newly independent nation nor constituted a viable alternative to integration in western institutions, and NATO as well as the EU dropped Slovakia from the first round of eastern enlargement.[27] The case of Croatia reveals a similar dynamic under different conditions. While subscribing to a regressive, that is, militant-chauvinistic-authoritarian formula to reach independence and to pursue nation-building under the 'old' Croatian regime, political elites as well as the population in general used the elections of 2000 for introducing far-reaching political, economic and foreign policy change. Making 'westernization' the main priority meant to subscribe fully to EU standards and to use preparation for EU- and NATO-membership for the structural modernization of the political system, society, and economy as well as fully adapting to the idea of Europe in general and of the Balkans in particular as a peace-in-security order.

Thus, both the 'in-between' strategy of the old Slovakian governments as well as the regressive character of the old Croatian government proved as counterproductive, unacceptable both for the domestic as well as the foreign players, and anachronistic because ignoring the current dominant structures and dynamics. While thus producing irritation towards the inside as well as the outside, these 'in-between' nations constituted only a limited problem to the region. With no major military power projection and a policy which would sooner or later turn to the EU and NATO for support and eventually integration, even problems like a minority policy unacceptable to neighbours and European standards could be regarded as interim ones with no major effects on the general trends, patterns, and structures set by NATO and the EU.

Introducing the distinction between successful policies of consequent westernizations of the 'winner' countries, which become more western than Eastern European countries, the 'in-between' countries as countries, which have not yet found the way towards westernization, and the 'loser' countries follows the basic assumption, that the western and only the western model offers the best – htat is, cost-effective, accepted, and legitimatized – solution for basic problems of the European region and its nation states. Again, this follows European understandings of history as a process of successful learning, political responsibility, and participation in progressive 'civilization', which includes democratization. In addition, introducing the terms anachronistic, counter-productive, or not rational means to follow conceptual traditions which were cultivated in Western Europe. But the past conflicts in greater Yugoslavia, the political debate in Russia as well as developments outside of Europe and in the international system as such, however, should remind the supporter of such a European understanding that this is one but not the generally accepted and pursued concept. Further – and as the history of the old Europe proves – such concepts of general benevolence, enlightened learning, and communality fall short if confronted with the malevolent. While Western Europe in general and EU-Europe in particular was willing and able to not only manage but solve the problem of malevolence within its boundaries, while the westernization of Eastern European nations widens these boundaries to the east, and the combined economic and military power of EU plus NATO creates optimal conditions to limit, contain, and overcome malevolence beyond these boundaries, malevolence as well as political dynamics, in which structural crises lead to domestic and foreign malevolence, are both an existing as well as a potential option for Eastern Europe. While despite all limitations and restraints the EU has developed a grand strategy for political and socio-economic transformation in Eastern Europe, EU definition and implementation of a pan-European order, which provides both peace and security to the inside as well as the outside, which introduces, stimulates, and honours civic cooperation within and between European nations, and which effectively deters political and military malevolence and – if this fails – re-establishes peace through military policing, is not only at a very initial stage but also meets significant dissent within the old EU, the applicant countries and in the US.[28]

The historical approach leads to ambivalent results concerning the question of how to cope with this challenge. On the one side, western and EU-Europe constitute the proof that the creation of a democratic peace- and growth-community is feasible. On the other side, the new problems of Eastern Europe and in particular the re-emerging of the old Eastern European problems in Yugoslavia and so on, proved that malevolence, however anachronistic in historical terms, irrational in rational choice terms, and unacceptable in terms of democratic legitimacy it is, still exists both as a political option as well as a political reality. Now, one can turn to the structural approach to see, whether it assists in finding a solution to this problem.

1.3 The global view

From a global viewpoint the end of the East-West conflict and the disappearance of the mutual military threat with all its consequences for the international system as such had and has different effects in all three dimensions of politics.

Firstly, and in terms of economic and military interests, the marginalization of the Soviet military threat meant a structural change in the agenda of the international community. While the mutual military threat of the East-West conflict not only threatened the survival of the global community as such but structured international politics including North-South, West-West, South-South, and other relations, the end of the East-West conflict eased the military burden, significantly reduced nuclear risks, and allowed kinds of multipolarity and regionalism. In general, the relative demilitarization of the international system, improvements in peace- and security-building regimes, and peace-keeping introduced a new quality of harmonized international control, while at the same time increased 'economization' of international politics including better management and even governance of economic, financial, and monetary globalization and 'civilized' international relations, that is, made military means less relevant for pursuing long-term political interests. In particular, the Soviet Union and then Russia disappeared as a source of global military destabilization, Soviet/Russian economic transformation did not disrupt supply of raw materials to the global market, despite all economic and financial problems Eastern Europe including Russia and the CIS did not turn into a major threat to the world economy, and Eastern Europe's integration and association to the EU as well as NATO did not cause structural change, instability, or disorder to the existing global economic and military structures. In addition, the new Eastern European problems did not cause disruption or structural change but constituted only a marginal problem for global control and governance of the world economy and global security. While the end of the East-West conflict constituted significant progress in terms of both technocratic control of international affairs and a better, that is, more civic global order, the new Eastern European economic, military, and political problem seems of minor relevance in terms of global interests in manageability and governance.

Secondly, and in terms of power, the end of the East-West conflict caused two structural global changes. Firstly, the disappearance of the USSR as military superpower and the monopolarization of global military power projection in the hands of the US established or renewed on the one side military-political unipolarity and on the other side more predictable, effective, and controllable security governance through US-led regime-building, US and NATO efforts in peace-keeping, and use of US military-political power for maintaining global control. Eastern Europe including Russia in particular turned from a regional bloc led by a superpower into integrated and associated parts of the EU and NATO, which meant not only a far-reaching downgrading of power status but an equally far-reaching limitation of will and ability for Russian military power projection. Secondly, the disappearance of the Soviet threat plus the collapse of the Eastern bloc marginalized Western European dependence from US security guarantees. Together with the projection of EU direct and indirect power towards the East and the economic-political nature of most of the new Eastern European problems, which ask for economic-political strategies only the EU could pursue, the power equation between Europe and the US underwent structural change. Despite all limitations in day-to-day operations of the EU and all US symbolic politics and rhetoric of leadership towards and in Europe, the new developments allow, favour, and stimulate both European regionalism as well as the EU to become the pan-European power. Further, EU realization of Maastricht's EMU project illustrates EU willingness to complement its existing economic power projection capability with a significant and supernational monetary power base, which restructured the global monetary system and ended US hegemony. While these two structural changes had and still have major effects on the intra-European as well as the Atlantic power balance, from a global view of political control and better governance they nevertheless did not only pose no major problems but led to more stability and made global control even easier.

Thirdly, and in normative terms, the end of the East-West conflict, the integration and association of Eastern Europe to Western Europe, EU, and NATO, and the new Eastern European problem constitute the most interesting as well as challenging developments. Firstly, the end of the East-West conflict allowed in principle a feasible search for a new and better global order including a reform of global control and governance. It was not by chance that the US, following its idealistic traditions, asked for a New Global Order after ending the Second Gulf or the Kuwait War and the concept of good or better global governance was revitalized after the end of the East-West conflict. Secondly, and as it has been outlined above, both the transition process as well as the new problems of Eastern Europe posed the interrelated political challenge of national democratization and a more peaceful regional and global order. As a test case for these two political challenges, Eastern Europe – because of its Westernization, Europeanization, or integration and association towards EU-Europe – proved that revolutionary domestic and regional transition can be pursued peacefully, that the integration-based EU model of a democratic growth- and peace-community worked not only under regionally limited conditions but is extendable in principle to neighbouring areas, and the specific European strategic mix of democratic values, socio-economic progress, and common peace and security seemed successful in technocratic terms as well as in terms of enlightened learning. The many deficits of EU's day-to-day operations as well as its structural shortcomings both within the integration process as well as concerning the establishment of the new and better pan-European order are both conceptual and operational problems. This means in other words, that the model as such seems not only feasible in historical terms but adequate to produce structural progress in terms of long-sought better order. Although one has to warn against a simplistic transformation of the European model towards other regions and regionalization processes as well as towards globalization and global control, the model itself and the underlying idea of implementing the better order through integrated structures, introduction of common goals, and linking normative approaches with interests and a new definition of power seems an adequate starting point for continuing and revitalizing ideas of better global governance and a new democratic global community. Thus and despite the many shortcomings, deficits, and failures, the model and political approach which underlies the relations between the EU and Eastern Europe have a major significance for policies of global change.

2 Defining the problem in systematic terms

After having looked at the interrelation between the EU and Eastern Europe in a more empirical-analytical way, one can now ask the question: how such an analysis can contribute to the ongoing general theoretical debate in international relations in general and to the discussion on globalization in particular. To start with, one has to refer to two basic assumptions of the past argumentation. Firstly, that politics is a matter of norms, interests, and power; secondly, that present international politics are object and subject of globalization, regionalism, and the nation state. It has to be recalled, that such an understanding of politics is not in line with a school of thinking which reflects the present debate in the US but explicitly seeks its roots in the European traditions of social and state philosophy.

As a first step this means – and this has been already outlined – redefining the new Eastern European problem in systematic terms as a problem of norms, interests, and power and that this is not a cumulating but an integrating formula. This implies on the one hand that neither an idealistic approach of general benevolence nor a realistic approach of power politics is able to explain and to outline adequate solutions. It means on the other hand that a solution of the problem must be based on a grand strategy, which uses power – including military power – in a qualitatively new way – to establish, maintain, and secure a better order, that is, an order, which is based on the idea of common interests to secure domestic support and regional consensus, and which at the same time establishes both democratic norms and peaceful solution of conflicts. In this view, it is important to underline that although of fundamentally different nature these three elements do not necessarily compete with or contradict each other – or in other words that an idealistic approach does not necessarily contradict a realistic solution. The new Eastern European problem is a typical case, where – at least for countries like Poland, the Czech Republic, and Hungary and now of Bulgaria, Romania, and other Balkan countries – these elements can and have reinforced each other. This evaluation is based on three hypotheses, verified in the Eastern European case. Firstly, democratic structures not only allow better solutions of socio-economic crises but are conditions for the development of the civil society, which seeks demilitarization of its foreign policy and peaceful solutions of conflict. Secondly, a policy of integration, that is, common economic, ecological, military, and other interests, from which everybody benefits, legitimizes and stabilizes the establishment of a new European order or EU expansion as a democratic growth- and peace-community. Thirdly, such a policy, based on norms and common interests, not only defines but legitimizes the EU's 'soft' power politics, secures acceptance, and further establishes this specific historical momentum which has characterized EU integration in the past despite its shortcomings, deficits, and set-backs.

The new Eastern European problem can be regarded as a problem of two basic dimensions of politics – the historical or the dimension of time in political calculation, and the concept of political responsibility. Like the demand to interrelate norms, interests, and power for achieving 'better' politics in terms of norms and rational choice, the idea of historical learning and political responsibility aims to improve political thinking by broadening the horizon in terms of time and social approach. The introduction of historical learning in reference to traditional ideas of 'civilization' or 'progress through democracy' in the theory of democracy or enlightenment as well as the idea of 'responsible' policy in reference to an understanding of politics as a part of the '*vita activa*' concept in Western philosophy and religion defines a basic attitude towards policy which differs from the strategy of pragmatism in two aspects. Firstly, the notion of historical learning and political responsibility is based on cost-benefit calculations which ask not only for the short- but for the long-term benefits and weighs the costs of structural reforms against the costs of pragmatic adaptation, to be cumulated over a time period, which exceeds the traditional election terms of democratic political life. Secondly, the notion of responsibility complements political cost-benefit rationality with the even disadvantageous burdens and risks of structural reforms or policies to overcome the causes and not the phenomena of problems. Both dimensions, that is, the time and the social dimension, become important when interrelated. Negatively speaking, policies of giving priority to short-term opportunity costs and placing burdens on the shoulders of others seem to win easier public support – in particular in and through modern media. Positively speaking, only long-term and responsibility-oriented policies are able to shape, correct, and re-establish order, create willingness for necessary but unpopular structural reform, and lead to qualitatively better levels of democratic development or civilizing.

This reference to the idea of historical learning aims not only at the theoretical debate but has important political connotations. It allows the contrast of present 'pragmatic policies' not only with norms but with a historical interpretation of responsibility, which means to call for political will and the creation of adapted political structures and institutions to solve problems like the new Eastern European problem instead of muddling through and referring to US leadership if things get worse. Concerning EU policies and EU integration in general, this means to revitalize the spirit of Maastricht or to learn from the grand designs of Europe-building of the late 1940s and early 1950s. Historical learning *vis-à-vis* the new Eastern European problem instead of 'realistic' pragmatism is not only an opportunity but – as it was outlined already – a political necessity as well. Although the new Eastern European problem is tolerable in terms of EU interests, EU's power position or its role as the dominant actor in European affairs is at stake. In the last years, NATO as EU's main competitor has proven more effective as well as politically convincing in high-profile aspects of the Eastern European problem – establishing institutionalized association of Russia to Western structures, speedy enlargement to the East, and finally solving the greater Yugoslavian or the Balkan problem. If NATO and EU could be regarded as comparable in terms of basic political formula, goal-means-profile, and way of power projection, such a competition in general and political formulas like division of labour through interlocking institutions in particular could be welcomed. But the competition between NATO and EU is not between equal or complementing actors but between qualitatively different actors. NATO is still based on the Atlantic political formula – including US leadership – which conflicts with the EU's Europeanistic understanding of regionalism. NATO still defines power and security as a primarily military matter, which conflicts with the EU's traditional view and Maastricht's vision of 'demilitarizing' European affairs in general and security in particular. Although integrated in military terms, NATO's political rationale is that of an alliance of nation states led by a global superpower and not a supra- and supernationalizing actor based on the federalist or unionist model. And NATO's formula of solving the new Eastern European problem focuses selectively on the military dimension and not on the interrelation between economic growth, environmental rehabilitation, security, and democratic development, which exactly defines the problem. As the case of Yugoslavia documents, the policy of parallel support of EU and NATO constitutes a pragmatic approach of conflict management and conflict containment but excludes a solution of the new Eastern European problem in general and the Balkan problem in particular and, in addition, ignores the qualitative competition between NATO and EU.

The third aspect of the new Eastern European problem results from the thesis that globalization firstly is no more than only a development in international politics and secondly that it is part of a dialectic equation of globalization, regionalism, and the nation state's willingness and ability to continue, increase, or re-establish control of international politics. On the one hand, this understanding recognizes the relevance of globalization and at the same time disagrees with the idea that globalization is the dominant trend and the only problem of international relations. When in recent years the debate in international politics turned to the problem of structural change of the international system and declared globalization as the most important factor of change, and suggested better global governance might be the only way to control it, it revitalized two important insights. Firstly, it re-emphasized that international relations have to deal with the structural change of the system in general. After decades of focusing on the East–West, North–South, and regional conflicts with its implicit exclusions and partial views of the global system, the new debate follows a more integrative or 'global' approach. This means to understand globalization as a phenomenon which afflicts all actors in the international system and which conditions the behaviour of even those actors who ignore, try to escape, or dissociate themselves from the system. Secondly, this system-oriented view leads to the question of how to control structural change like globalization. Thus, the integrated approach of the analysis, which underlines the global quality of the international system, leads to the question how such processes of structural change can be controlled or politically mastered. Following the analysis such a control actually is not so much a matter of foreign policy of a nation state, supra-, or supernational actor, but of ability and willingness of the global actors to establish good or better political common governance of such a globalization.[29]

In general, this new emphasis on structural global change and its political control rightly responds to objective necessity and subjective political will. In particular, however, there are trends in the current debate about globalization which unnecessarily limit both its reliability and validity and lead both to a distorted view of global change and of necessary politics. Firstly, globalization is often regarded as a new phenomenon although it has characterized international relations since decades. Global or globalizing interdependencies both in structures as well as in behavioural patterns can be found in early and later colonialism from the fifteenth to the nineteenth century, in nuclear arms races of the East-West conflict, and in today's peace-keeping missions as well; they differ only in the ways but not in the basics. And while the ways and means of global actors to control such developments have changed, the political message about the limits of the nation state to control such dynamics has remained the same. Secondly, globalization is not only an economic, financial, and monetary but a political and military affair as well. International relations have often been subject to economistic views and theories and such a reductionism seems understandable in periods where military threats are perceived as of less importance and political stability as guaranteed. But a truly systematic and historical approach to structures, mechanisms, and patterns of international relations shows that on the one side global change has never been mono-dimensional and on the other side that there is no primacy of economics and that there still exist issues, segments, regions, and periods in which political and security needs outplayed all economic rationality.

In order to overcome such self-inflicted analytical restrictions globalization has first to be defined as a phenomenon with an economic, military, and political – and even a socio-cultural – dimension. These dimensions can show different patterns and dynamics of globalization, different underlying power patterns, and different rationalities for political control or its absence. Secondly, globalization has to be seen in historical perspective as well. As a historical and crucial phenomenon of the international system, globalization underlies change; in other words there are periods of globalization, de-, and re-globalization. Thirdly, and returning to the beginning, globalization must be interrelated to regionalism and re- or continued nationalization. Regionalism such as the EU constitutes is both result as well as cause of globalization. The idea to integrate in order to create better conditions for realizing interests, power, and norms vis-à-vis a globalizing world is a well-known strategy in international politics and economics as well as to globalize in order to overcome regional protectionism and so on. Both globalization and regionalism demand from nation states to transfer sovereignty, to accept outer limits of their realization of interests and power, and to downgrade its role as dominant actor in international politics. Thus, both developments depend on the nation state's ability and willingness to accept, promote, and control regionalism and globalization – in other words both globalization and regionalism result from nation state behaviour or non behaviour as well as they shape it.

If one finally introduces the idea of a historical responsibility for the better into this debate one has first to discuss models for better global order and governance. Here, one could discuss the thesis, which was presented earlier, that the European model seems in principle a feasible and progress-producing model not only for Western and pan-Europe but for global community-building as well. But understanding politics as part of a 'vita activa' approach or as a responsibility, as it was done in this argumentation, means to complement the search for the best model with the search for strategies of how to create the necessary sustainable political will in and between the relevant actors to define themselves not only as an object of globalization, regionalism, and re-nationalization but to become subject of this dynamic. What is needed is not only the best model for a new global order as well as new regional orders but the political will to re-introduce and revitalize the idea of common active political governance or to refer to the politicians' responsibility to establish, secure, and improve order.

Notes

1   See, for example, Russell Bova, Political Dynamics of the Post-Communist Transition: A Comparative Perspective, in: *World Politics* 44 (1994), pp. 113–38; Samuel Huntington, The Third Wave: Democratization in the Late Twentieth Century, Norman 1991; Philippe C. Schmitter/Lynn Terry Karl, The Conceptual Travels of Transitologists and Consolidologists: How Far to the East Should They Attempt to Go?, in: *Slavic Review*, Spring 1995, pp. 111–27.

2   See, for example, Jan Zielonka/Alex Pravda (eds.), Democratic Consolidation in Eastern Europe: International and Transnational Factors, in press, Dieter Nohlen, Demokratie, in: Dieter Nohlen/Peter Waldmann/Klaus Ziemer (Hrsg.), *Lexikon der Politik*, Vol. 4: *Die östlichen und südlichen Länder*, Beck Verlag, München 1997, pp.118–27 and 122; Philippe C. Schmitter, The International Context of Contemporary Democratization, in: *Stanford Journal of International Affairs* 2 (1993), pp.1–34; Dean McSweeney/Clive Tempest, The Political Science of Democratic Transition in Eastern Europe, in: *Political Studies* XLI (1993), pp.413 and 417; G. V. Hyde, Adrian Price, *Democratization in Eastern Europe*: the External Dimension, in: Geoffrey Pridham/Tatu Vanhanen (eds.), Democratization in Eastern Europe, London/New York 1994; Wolfgang Zellner/Pal Dunay, Ungarns *Außenpolitik 1990–1997*, Nomos-Verlag, Baden-Baden 1998; and

Mario Telò (ed.), *Démocratie et construction Européenne*, Editions de l'Université Libre de Bruxelles, Bruxelles 1995.

3   See, for example, Eric Remacle/Reimund Seidelmann (eds.), *Pan-European Security Redefined*, Nomos-Verlag, Baden-Baden 1998; Emil Kirchner/Kevin Wright (eds.), Security and democracy in transition societies. Conference Proceedings, University of Essex 1998, and *Journal of European Integration*, Special Issue *Problems of Eastern Europe*, No 2–3/1997.

4   See, for example, Mario Telò (ed.), Un défi pour la Communauté Européenne: Les bouleversements à l'Est et au centre du continent, Editions de l'Université de Bruxelles, Bruxelles 1991, Mario Telò (ed.), *L'Union Européenne et les défis de l'élargissement*, Editions de l'Université de Bruxelles, Bruxelles 1994; and Mario Telò/Paul Magnette (eds.), *Repenser l'Europe*, Editions de l'Université de Bruxelles, Bruxelles 1996.

5   There is no need to go into the discussion, whether the military capability of the WTO was equal to that of the West. Using the term relevance means that despite all asymmetries in military capability and because of mutual assured nuclear destruction the USSR constituted an 'equal' power in military dimension.

6   Such calculations are based on the assumption of rational cost-risk-benefit calculations. Although Western-Russian relations have a broad range of measures to secure and re-establish such rationality, it cannot be taken for absolutely granted.

7   See, for example, the process of 're-civilizing' or 'de-militarizing' Soviet/Russian foreign policy underlined by Russia's policies towards the second Yugoslavian war.

8   Military policing should not be confused with military aggression because of its special legitimacy, its goal-mean limitation, and its explicit reference to agreed political formulas. This concept of military policing as a legitimate mean to keep, to enforce, and to re-establish peace and security has been applied in peace-keeping in Bosnia-Herzegovina and in ending violations of the basic European consensus on democracy, minority rights, and so on, in Kosovo.

9   Such as in the former case of the participation of the FPÖ in Austria's government.

10 A recent case is Russia's military intervention in Chechnya.

11 For an overview see Reimund Seidelmann (ed.), *Crisis Policies in Eastern Europe*, Nomos-Verlag, Baden-Baden 1996.

12 Think, for example, of the remaining nuclear weapons and nuclear material.

13 For a detailed analysis of the European security architecture and its problems see, for example, Reimund Seidelmann, NATO's Enlargement as a Policy of Lost Opportunities. In *Journal of European Integration* No 2–3/1997, Special Issue on *Problems of Eastern Europe*, pp.233–45, simultaneously published in Cicero Paper Paris/Maastricht, No 3/1997, S. 41–55.

14 See, for example, Panos Tsakaloyannis, *The European Union as a Security Community*, Nomos-Verlag, Baden-Baden 1996.

15 See, for example, EU's activities towards its Mediterranean south.

16 See Reimund Seidelmann, The Old and New Soviet Threat: the Case for a Grand New Western Strategy towards the Soviet Republic in the 1990s in: Peter Ludlow (ed.), *Europe and North America in the 1990s*, CEPS Paper No 52, Brussels 1992, pp.69–88.

17 See Reimund Seidelmann, Amsterdam e la sicurezza europea. Un' opportunità nuova o perduta in: Europa/Europe No 1/1998, pp.66–86.

18 For a recent example of such a political ambiguity see Tony Blair, Time for Europe to Repay America the Soldier, in: *International Herald Tribune*, November 14–15, 1998, p.8.

19 The establishment of an effective and integrated military power projection capability is a matter of 10–15 years.

20 Another example but under different specific conditions is Ukraine; see, for example, Oleg Strekal, Nationale Sicherheit der unabhängigen Ukraine (1991–95). Zur Analyse der Sicherheitslage und der Grundlagen der Sicherheitspolitik eines neu entstandenen Staates, Nomos-Verlag, Baden-Baden 1999.

21 For details see Jens Fischer, *Eurasismus*, Nomos-Verlag, Baden-Baden 1999.

22 Compare Irina Zviagelskaia, Russia's Security Policy and Its Prospects, in: Eric Remacle/ Reimund Seidelmann (eds.), *Pan-European Security Redefined*, Nomos-Verlag, Baden-Baden 1998, pp. 305–18.

23 See, for example, the discussion in Janusz Golebiowski (ed.), *Poland, Germany, Russia: Perspectives on Collaboration*, University of Warsaw, Warsaw 1995.

24 See, for example, Michael R. Lucas, The CIS and Russia, in: Eric Remacle/Reimund Seidelmann (eds.), *Pan-European Security Redefined*, Nomos-Verlag, Baden-Baden 1998, pp. 319–51.

25 For a new analysis see Günther Trautmann, Russia and the Euro-Atlantic Community, in: *Journal of European Integration* No 2–3/1997, pp.201–32.

26 For details see Ivo Samson, *Die Sicherheitspolitik der Slowakei in den ersten Jahren der Selbständigkeit. Zu den sicherheitspolitischen Voraussetzungen der Integration der Slowakischen Republik in die euroatlantischen Verteidigungsstrukturen*, Nomos-Verlag, Baden-Baden 1999.

27 In addition to these developments tactical aspects played a role. Germany, which promoted Eastern enlargement, offered to drop Slovakia to overcome reluctance in other EU countries and to demonstrate German willingness to compromise.

28 See, for example, the 'Trojan-horse' dispute about countries like Poland, which are accused to be more US than EU-oriented and to use EU membership as a mean to limit further 'Europeanization'.

29 The political perception of globalization ranges from ignorance over highlighting the negative effects or the 'threat' of globalization to uncritical praise of the new opportunities.

Chapter 13

The EU and the Mediterranean: Open Regionalism or Peripheral Dependence?

George Howard Joffé

When the European Union produced its first truly integrated policy for the Mediterranean basin in late 1995, the question arose as to whether the new policy initiative would be an example of 'open' or 'closed' regionalism[1]. At the time, this was a significant issue in international relations as discussions of globalization were beginning to focus on the issue of whether or not its effects would manifested in a truly global economic system or whether a regionalist pattern would emerge in which foci of integrated economic activity might not also acquire other integrated characteristics which would seriously undermine the sovereignty of component states. This, in turn, would affect diplomatic and international relations between such regional agglomerations and might thus construct a new kind of international order. Indeed, the general argument applied outside the confines of economic change, for the end of the bilateral balance-of-power was not seen as necessarily introducing hegemonic stability, focused around the sole remaining 'hyperpower'[2]. Instead regional orders of hegemonic political hierarchy were also conceived as likely outcomes[3]. Behind these issues, the overall discussion subsumed two separate but related issues: firstly, that globalization would inevitably be regionalist in nature and, second, that economic integration would inevitably lead to political integration and, eventually to societal homogenization.

1 Region and state in the contemporary world

Events over the past ten years have largely resolved these issues. Globalization has proceeded apace in economic terms and has powerfully affected the international division of labour, but the economic hierarchy of the old 'triad' – the economic network between the United States, Europe and Japan that predominated during the latter stages of the Cold War – seems largely in place, even if somewhat expanded eastwards[4]. Japan has been replaced by South-East Asia and China, with India, perhaps, knocking at the door, but the triad structures still seems firmly in place – as yet unaffected by the World Trade Organisation and protected by progressive failure in the various GATT negotiation rounds. In political and diplomatic terms, the hyperpower, the United States, after a brief burst of aggressive brilliance, seems now in retreat and regionalism looks as if it may become the dominant theme of global politics in future. Regionalism, in short, is still a matter of considerable relevance to the contemporary world.

In this respect, the initiative of the European Union in introducing the Euro-Mediterranean Partnership as its flagship policy in the Mediterranean continues to be important for this was, perhaps, the first genuine attempt at creating an open regionalist system. It was, however, created for a very different world, in which the globalization paradigm had a much more powerful resonance. At least, this reflected the views of the Clinton administration, with its belief that, with the Cold War ended, geopolitics could give way to geo-economics in which a globalized world economy would be dominated by the United States and where neo-realist assumptions about the world community would be subordinated to economic realities and democratic peace – the essence, after all, of Francis Fukuyama's vision of the 'end of history'[5]. At that time, the more pessimistic prognostications of Samuel Huntington[6] seemed largely irrelevant, although the passage of time has altered this so that they have now become part of the spontaneous vocabulary of policy-makers and acquired a new relevance in academic discourse as well.

Fukuyama seems to recognize this, for he has recently admitted that force and coercion, to be applied by states with the necessary status to do so[7], may well be necessary to achieve his ideal outcome, a situation which reflects the rather more accurate analysis of the post-Cold War world – made at the start of the 1990s and still relevant today – by Adam Roberts, when he argued that the developed world was now a 'Grotian one, observing norms of cooperation, and perhaps even has its Kantian element: a civil society of civil societies'. However, outside this normatively ideal focus, '…parts of the world beyond are still Hobbesian, with force still a very active final arbiter within and between countries, and sovereignty loudly proclaimed.'[8]. That is, after all, very much the European Union's self-image and the one that allows it to legitimately regard itself as a politically relevant region in the contemporary world. The question is, however, to what extent are these concerns relevant to the Union's current interactions with neighbouring states and how far can those be said to reflect a regionalist paradigm?

As Stephen Calleya[9] has pointed out, the subject of regionalism has received relatively little analytical attention in recent years, not least because of the dominance of neo-realism in theoretical studies of international relations, in which the state and the international arena have been the primary referents. Nonetheless, the growing effects of multinational organizations and transnational corporations on the international scene, together with the implications of the phenomenon of globalization have begun to alter these assumptions although the obsession with state security since the events of 9/11 seems to run counter to that. At the same time, the experience of the European Union and its relationships with peripheral and semi-peripheral states and regions has thrown the issue into sharp relief within the world of practical politics and diplomacy.

A major problem, however, is to establish precisely what the term means. Neither geographic nor systemic definitions, taken alone, provide a comprehensive mechanism for its conceptualization. Geographic contiguity is clearly an essential component but does not, of itself, provide any insights as to what regionalism actually is, although it does imply that a plurality of states is involved. Indeed, other than for the purposes of geographic or economic analysis, the term 'regionalism' is meaningless unless defined in social or political terms as well. In short, the concept essentially relates to a process of economic, political, cultural or social interaction between specified entities within the region's geographical bounds. It is that process of interaction that gives the term meaning, for it has greater explicatory power and significance than is the case for any other group of geographically contiguous entities linked to it.

Nor is such an interaction a purely passive process; it also involves purpose and action that prioritize the key elements that animate the concept. It is, in essence, a constructed and shared socio-political reality, often involving a shared economic dimension, within a geographically contiguous international region[10]. This is important, because – as we shall see – although the Euro-Mediterranean Partnership was articulated in largely economic terms, the Barcelona Declaration which introduced it in 1995 made it clear that its signatories recognized the underlying social, political and security realities that it was to condition. Now that, ten years later, the Partnership is to be redefined as from 2007 within the context of European Neighbourhood Policy in more bilateral terms, questions arise as to what extent the old assumptions about regionalism and the Mediterranean region still apply.

How, for example, should the linkages between an integrated region, such as the European Union and states to which it relates in a form of open regionalism be conceptualized? Is the relationship an issue of a centre-periphery/hub-spoke relationship or are there more substantive, egalitarian relationships involved, of the kinds implied by the Barcelona Declaration's objective of a 'shared zone of prosperity and stability'? And what of the relationships between the states of the Southern Mediterranean shore in this context? Are these to be static or evolutionary and, if the latter, what is the outcome likely to be? The intervening decade and the very strikingly altered international environment have played their parts, of course, in determining what these will be, but to what extent do the original concepts of open regionalism still have relevance? Indeed was the concept merely a transitional stage towards a more profound regional relationship and, if so, what will happen now, given the events of recent years[11]?

2 Europe's Mediterranean policies

The Euro-Mediterranean Partnership initiative was, nonetheless, quite unlike the policy initiatives that Europe had adopted towards its southern periphery previously, for those had in large measure stemmed from the colonial inheritance. It was also designed to respond to quite specific policy objectives for the Union's member states – peripheral security over both regional conflict particularly in the Middle East but also to end the danger of spill-over effects involving violence, smuggling and drugs. Perhaps the most important of these involved the development of a mechanism designed to end the danger of mass-migration into Europe itself. As such, it was a defensive strategy, but the means it adopted were novel since it saw mutual confidence-building and shared strategies as the way forward. This was a complete break with the past but reflect much of the ethos of the Union itself and its policies towards new Accession states in the wake of the end of the Cold War.

Britain and France had been the major colonial powers in the Middle East and North Africa, although Italy had first colonized Libya before being expelled during the Second World War, and Spain had had interests in Northern Morocco and in The Western Sahara. This had left a legacy of economic dependence on Europe, as well as ambiguous cultural relationships, which the Union and its predecessor, the European Economic Community, had tried to address in a series of bilateral economic agreements from 1969 onwards, starting with North Africa and then, in 1976 extending to the Middle East Mediterranean littoral. With Israel and Turkey there had been separate but parallel agreements dating from the mid-1960s. The major driver for this was a growing problem of migration into Europe, mainly from Turkey and North Africa but later, too, from Egypt which European states found difficult to digest in social and cultural terms, despite the growing demand for migrant labour and the growing need of host countries for the remittances it generated. Parallel to this were accelerating flows of asylum-seekers, reflecting deficiencies in governance in the South Mediterranean region.

Now the new Partnership, more colloquially known as the Barcelona Process, swept all of these into a single policy. Inevitably, the economic dimension of the policy was the most detailed and comprehensive, not least because this approach had underlain the construction of the Union itself. It was also an extension of the original bilateral agreements that had been negotiated between Europe and the South Mediterranean states. However, whereas these had provided for free access to the European market for industrial goods and restricted access for agricultural produce, the new economic policies converted these trade agreements into free trade agreements, in which European industrial products would also be granted free access to South Mediterranean markets after lengthy transition periods when tariff and non-tariff barriers would be gradually reduced. Given the Union's dominant position within the trade patterns of the South Mediterranean, it was both the essential and inescapable partner for economic change, a position reinforced by European dependence on the region for energy.

Energy dependence is quite striking – in 2005, Europe imported 11,112 million b/d net of oil and refined products. The Middle East and North Africa generated 45.5 per cent of this total – 5.06 million b/d, of which 3.12 million b/d came from the Middle East and the Gulf (28.1 per cent of the total) and 1.94 million b/d from North Africa (17.5 per cent). As far as natural gas was concerned, the dependence was even more acute. In 2005, the Union imported 294.5 billion cubic metres of pipeline gas and 47.6 billion cubic metres of liquefied natural gas; a total of 342.2 billion cubic metres. The Middle East and North Africa supplied 22.5 per cent of this total and North Africa alone supplied 19.3 per cent. In the case of Algeria, the largest sole supplier to the Union from the South Mediterranean, 97 per cent of its gas output went to Europe – 62.3 per cent by pipeline and the rest in the form of liquefied natural gas[12].

Such dependencies, particularly on pipeline gas, had clear security implications for alternative sources of supply would not be easily available. Indeed, given the dependence of oil refineries on an homogenous crude input mix, similar considerations applied to crude oil supply as well. Both concerns had an immediate implication for relations with North Africa, particularly Libya and Algeria – where, at the time, a full-blown civil war was being waged. Concerns about security in the Middle East also reflected global concerns about energy security from the Gulf but also concerns about spill-over effects from the Arab-Israeli conflict, as the future of the Oslo Process appeared to be ever-more gloomy. Europe clearly had an acute interest in trying to stabilise the region and, given the nature of the Common Foreign and Security Policy which was then just being given sinews as the second pillar of the Maastricht Treaty, prescriptions for this derived from the collective European experience seemed the most appropriate.

In terms of external trade, the dependence of the South Mediterranean on Europe is equally as striking. Tables I and II in the Appendix below demonstrate that, although the South Mediterranean is marginal to European interests, representing only 7.5 per cent of its imports – including oil and gas which caused a peak in imports in 2004 and 2005 – and 9.5 per cent of its exports in 2005, the European Union was the regions major trade partner by far, supplying 46 of its imports and taking 47 per cent of its exports in 2005. Table II demonstrates a similar marginalisation in terms of direct foreign investment, for the region only absorbed 3.26 per cent of EU foreign investment in 2004.

The disaggregated figures are even more revealing for they demonstrate that dependence on access to Europe amongst the Maghrib states has been far higher that the average figures would suggest. Furthermore, the overall figures also conceal the importance of Turkey in the South Mediterranean relationship for variations in South Mediterranean trade faithfully replicate similar variations in trade between Turkey and the European Union. In other words, despite the importance of energy trade to Europe, the real determinant of trade patterns is Turkey which is not an energy exporter, although this feature will emerge in the coming years as the country becomes the terminal for oil and gas from the Caucasus and Central Asia. The simple fact is, however, that Europe will shape the economic futures of the South Mediterranean powerfully in the years to come, even if its share of South Mediterranean trade is in slow secular decline. It is worth noting that the South Mediterranean suffers from a trade deficit with Europe, even Europe itself is in deficit in its trade with the rest of the world.

This pattern of dependence stemming both from the colonial period and from Europe's pattern of energy supply meant that South Mediterranean economic development would be intimately connected to the region's access to European markets, both in terms of trade and in terms of driving migration as employment generation failed to keep pace with its demographic growth. Conversely, Europe would react to its perceptions of the security dilemma that migration would cause by seeking to use economic means to improve economic performance and thus remove the driver for migration that had existed since the First World War but that had become a dominant concern after 1945.This was the key dilemma that the Barcelona Process sought to resolve but it was the integrated, holistic nature of the policy that marked in out as an experiment in open regionalism, as portrayed in the Barcelona Declaration.

3 The Barcelona Process

There were two essential components to the new policy. It first sought the organisation of a series of bilateral free trade arrangements between individual South Mediterranean states and the European Union in industrial goods, thus exposing their industrial sectors – seen as the primary potential generators of growth and employment – to unfettered competition with European industry. This, it was anticipated, would force an optimal use of resources in the countries concerned and ensure appropriate economic reforms to meet the European challenge by modernising their economies. It was an approach that recalled the principles behind the Europe Union's own construction, culminating in the Single European Market. Secondly, this was paralleled with a series of multilateral partnership measures based on the confidence-building approach established by the Conference on Cooperation and Security in Europe, held in Helsinki in 1975 to initiate the process of détente, and repeated in the Italian-Spanish non-paper of 1990 which proposed a similar Conference on Cooperation and Security in the Mediterranean. This, together with free trade, provided the innovative elements of the new policy and would construct the shared zone of peace and stability whilst the expected integration of Southern markets, to exploit efficiencies arising from economies-of-scale and complementarity within an enlarged market space capable of stimulating endogamous growth would speed access to a shared prosperity.

However, although the new policy was based on the principles of economic integration with the implied assumption of free movement of capital and goods, it remained faithful to its underlying purpose of preventing further migration into Europe and did not include the essential third freedom, that of labour. Borders and divisions, in short, were to be preserved for economic and political reasons. Indeed, to this extent, it faithfully replicated the underlying principles of *détente* which had sought to create confidence-building measures designed to reassure the Soviet Union against its fears of military threat but not to assimilate it, with its alien political system, into Western Europe or the wider Western sphere. That would have to await internal change and the spontaneous disintegration of the Socialist Bloc in 1989 as the Cold War came to an end. In the same way, the Barcelona Process was designed to promote economic, social and political change within established boundaries and indirectly reinforced their effectiveness, thus primarily serving the objective of European security through Europe's preferred diplomatic instruments.

Thus, as outlined above, the basket of economic measures designed to set up the bilateral free trade areas with the Union – which were eventually intended to be integrated into a single South Mediterranean market to match the Single European Market – was matched by two other baskets of measures. One basket dealt with common security concerns in the Mediterranean with the objective of constructing a cooperative security regime, an objective that, given the ongoing crisis in relations between Israel and the Palestinians, has remained stillborn. It also advanced the prospect of democratic governance and institutional respect for human rights as an essential part of the modernisation package. The other basket addressed measures directed at creating mutual public appreciation of cultures and societies, alongside others designed to stimulate the development of civil society in the South Mediterranean[13]. It has to be said that there has not been much progress on either objective both because of the timidity of European politicians and because of Southern resentment of European xenophobia at home and interference abroad, not to speak of the wider implications of Western policy after the events of 9/11, in the United States.

What the new Euro-Mediterranean Partnership, better known as the 'Barcelona Process', did not do was to resolve the inherent contradiction between closer economic cooperation and the persistence of political division. This focused around the issues of migration and visas. Migration had originally been treated by the Union on the basis of a zero-inward migration policy and seen as part of the Justice and Home Affairs pillar of the Maastricht treaty. By the end of the 1990s, however, Europe had come to recognize that it had become an immigration area and that a policy of managed migration would be necessary – a concern of the Common Foreign and Security Policy because it would involve state-to-state negotiation[14]. Even though this implied that migration and thus labour flows would be permitted, it was still based on the idea that this would take place between states and thus across borders normatively defined as impermeable.

European visa policy maintained this, whether inside the Schengen Area or outside it, so that the difficulties in obtaining a visa began to become a major theme of complaint from the South to the North of the Mediterranean. Similarly, the rapidly increasing flows of illegal migration and asylum-seekers from the South highlighted the reality of the European external border and the growing tensions that it caused – as President Jacques Chirac learned on his famous official visit to Algeria in August 2003, when he was greeted by the mass chanting of 'visas, visas!' by the crowds who welcomed him. Their cries were also a salutary warning to European politicians of the potential failure of the Barcelona Process to achieve its declared objectives, as illegal migration into Europe rose inexorably towards 400,000-to-500,000 a year.[15]

The failure to control migration, however, has not been the only failure that has confronted the Euro-Mediterranean Partnership since its inception in 1995. As mentioned above, the security agenda was stymied by the continuing violent confrontation between Israel and the Palestinians. This meant that no consensus could be reached over a Charter for Peace and Stability in the Mediterranean, the embodiment of the Barcelona Process and its aspiration for cooperative security in the region, at the Marseilles Summit in November 2000 and the matter has now been postponed indefinitely.

The European Commission has also been unwilling to invoke the sanctions provided in the bilateral Association Agreements it has signed with its South Mediterranean partners over progress towards democratic governance and particularly over the issue of human rights observance, despite blatant abuses committed in Algeria during its civil war between 1992 and 2000, in Tunisia or as a result of the conflict between Israel and Palestinians in the Occupied Territories. It has argued that it is more effective to act quietly through diplomatic channels in a process of constructive engagement and that this has been done. There have not, however, been any evident positive outcomes and it is difficult to avoid the conclusion that the political and security basket of the Barcelona Process has had little effect.

More obvious has been the failure of the basket of economic measures contained in the bilateral Association Agreements and the objective of integration of economies in the South Mediterranean. Bilateral free trade areas have been created through the Association Agreements and parallel reforms have taken place in the South Mediterranean states concerned. Primarily, this has involved the gradual phasing-out of tariff barriers to imports and the replacement of lost customs revenue to the state by the imposition of value-added tax. In parallel to this, economic restructuring has taken place. This has been designed to liberalize the economies concerned, in terms of their external trade, monetary policies and exchange control regimes, together with the withdrawal of the state from the economic process and the development of institutions – domestic financial markets and legal systems – designed to encourage foreign private direct and equity investment.

These changes, which mirror precisely the prescriptions of the IMF and the World Bank, were intended to improve the climate for foreign investment which was seen as the necessary driver for industrial expansion and job creation. Unfortunately, except for the one-time realisations of privatization receipts, inflows of investment have been disappointingly low. In fact they have been little more than one half of expectations and, once again, because investors sense that, outside the oil-and-gas sectors, returns and security is far better elsewhere – in South East Asia, China or Latin America. This has proved to be the pattern of the region overall which has not only had the second lowest level of foreign investment worldwide on average in recent years – only Africa received less – but has also see its share of investment actually decline in proportion to global investment flows.[16]

The main reason for this has been the region's lack of comparative advantage in a world where low-cost Asian producers are now a dominant force. The implications of this were underlined in January 2005 when the end of the multifibre agreement meant that South Mediterranean textile exports to Europe – one of the mainstays of the expected growth in industrial exports – collapsed precipitously. In the first three months of the year, Moroccan textile exports to Europe, for example, dropped by 30 per cent. The consequences of this in terms of job creation have been compounded by the continuing demographic boom for, even though birth-rates in the last decade have fallen significantly, the massive bulge in population created in the twentieth century is now approaching the age range when it will be potentially economic active but the potential for job creation is simply not there.

This implies that one of the main, if unexpressed, objectives of the Barcelona process – the creation of economic opportunity and employment to soak up the potential well of emigrants – has simply not been achieved. Of course, had agriculture formed part of the original economic package, this would have provided a further outlet for the economies of the Southern Mediterranean, as had been the case with the agreements drawn up before 1995. Yet, even here it is not clear that this would have been the case, for the highly mechanized, capital intensive agriculture of the European Union with its subsidised production costs could have done untold damage to the protected cereal markets of the southern peripheral states – a problem they now face with the United States.

4 Challenges

The reality of this potential failure has been highlighted by two other developments that further reinforce it, despite their innate contradiction with the normative values of the Euro-Mediterranean Partnership. The first of these has been the European reaction to both this implicit failure of the Barcelona Process and the challenge to it offered by similar American policy proposals such as the US-Middle East Partnership Initiative (USMEPI) or the Broader Middle East-North Africa Initiative (BMENA). The second has been the increasing securitization of Europe's Common Foreign and Security Policy in response to the perceived threat of global terrorism in the wake of the Madrid train bombings in March 2004 and the London bombings of July 2005. This tendency had begun long before, after the events of September 2001, but it has accelerated dramatically in recent years and is now conditioning all other external policies.

Its significance lies in the fact that it targets an internalized enemy, Europe's poorly integrated migrant communities, and because it is increasingly being seen at the demotic and instinctive level as a cultural confrontation. Ironically enough, it was to these very problems that the social and cultural basket of the Barcelona Process was addressed and the on-going social crisis within Europe is yet another testament to the wider policy failure described above. Indeed, it could be argued that these tensions go even further back, into the heart of the European project itself with its own normative values of political secularism and intellectual tolerance. In many respects, these are being inverted into statements of cultural intolerance in that, unless they are accepted in their entirety by alien non-European groups within the Union – whether or not they are in the process of being Europeanized through assimilation or integration – such groups are to be excluded from the European project despite their residence in Europe in a deliberate process of migrant cultural and social 'ghettoization'.

The American challenge is more ambiguous, for Europe both wishes to embrace it and yet fears its implications for its own policies in the region. In essence Europe and the United States have a common interest in shaping the Mediterranean environment to enhance their security interests although those interests differ. For Europe, as described above, the dominant concern relates to the Southern European periphery and seeks to ensure border security within an environment of controlled migration. That concern has now been complicated by the growing security threats within Europe itself which are linked, in part to the external political environment and to the European reaction to it. The result has been an increasing tendency to internalize these political concerns and to redefine them in terms of a cultural confrontation within and outside Europe that manifests itself as globalized terrorism.

For the United States, the security concern is quite different in that threats in the Mediterranean remain geographically external to the United States itself and relate to its wider strategic concerns. These reflect the security of strategic lines of communication[17] through the Mediterranean itself, given the fact that these are dominated by a series of choke-points, and the situation in the Eastern Mediterranean with respect to Israel and the Persian Gulf. Of course, in the wake of the events of 9/11, the United States has, in effect, adopted Samuel Huntington's concept of the clash of civilisations[18] – an essentially culturalist interpretation of security threat

This means that it is quite prepared to follow the European example of identifying the cultural confrontation that is epitomised by globalized terrorism.

This has not, however, been internalized as is the case with the European Union but it has emphasized a coincident geographic and cultural boundary, particularly with respect to Israel, to which the United States, in addition, to its hard security response in the 'war on terror', has now adopted soft security responses in a similar fashion to the European Union. This, in essence, argues – as does Europe – that the adoption of certain specific cultural and political values and practices could eliminate the security threat, provided that innate and indigenous parallel values are discarded. Despite superficial differences between the two projects – European and American – at root, they are surprisingly similar, even if articulated in different ways.

Thus, on 12 December, 2002, the then secretary-of-state, Colin Powell, in an address to the Heritage Foundation in Washington introduced a new soft security policy for the Mediterranean[19]. This, the US-Middle East Partnership Initiative, was designed to compensate for deficiencies in governance, economic development, educational approaches and the empowerment of women, to which Congress had committed $302.9 million over a four year period for the multilateral initiatives, in addition to the $1 billion-worth of bilateral aid that the United States supplies to the region every year[20], quite apart from the special aid programmes for Egypt and Israel. In 2004, the United States opened two regional offices, in Tunis and Bahrain, to manage this initiative and has negotiated bilateral free trade areas with Jordan, Tunisia and Morocco. The initiative is also the vehicle through which the individual programmes of the Broader Middle East and North Africa Initiative, proposed by the United States and adopted by the G-8 group of states at the Sea Island meeting in 2004, are put into operation.

The interesting feature of this new American policy is that, even though its security justification is quite different, it is in direct competition with the Barcelona Process, at least as far as governance and economic development are concerned. At best, such duplication causes confusion and at worst it provides a mechanism by which Southern governments can avoid commitments they do not wish to undertake by playing off the European Union against the United States. It is not clear why cooperation between both major regional powers was not encouraged when the United States decided to adopt a soft security approach and, although Commission officials today claim that there is no conflict, the Commission presidency in 2002 had no doubt at all that the American initiative was designed, in part at least, to challenge Europe[21]. After all, the United States had been sidelined when the Barcelona Process had been introduced in 1995!

It is also clear that the American initiative also emphasizes the existence of a cultural barrier between a realm of assumed secular democratic tolerance and an external arena of cultural otherness characterized by violence and threat. This is to be corrected by the introduction of cultural and political change in a rather more intrusive fashion, particularly with respect to education and the status of women, than that practiced by the European Union, although the underlying assumptions are the same in both cases. Both arise from shared perceptions of a new international order, created by the hegemony of a single hyper-power, in which Europe must find its place, despite the contradictions this may create with its underlying interests, given the presence of domestic migrant communities and a turbulent periphery in which the turbulence is, in part, a consequence of the attitudes and policies of its dominant partner, the United States.

The policies of both the United States and the European Union towards the Middle East must, however, be seen against the wider context of the contemporary international order. Most analyses of international relations today start with an assumption that a new world order was essentially established upon the ashes of the Cold War. With the destruction of the prolonged stability of the Cold War, a new kind of stability emerged, predicated on the predominance of the United States in security and economic terms – a kind of uni-polar hegemonic stability – and on the universalization of the liberal democratic model and the market economy – the modern version of globalisation[22]. The first airing of this new world occurred in the aftermath of the expulsion of Iraq from Kuwait by the Multinational Coalition under the leadership of the first Bush presidency and under the aegis of a revived United Nations, now set, apparently, to operate as its founders had intended. Concepts of open regionalism, which innately respected the sovereignty of participating states fitted well into this background

During the 1990s, however, a series of new ideas began to emerge, building in part on new, postmodernist concepts of sovereignty. These allowed for intervention in the internal affairs of a state, indeed encouraged it, if the state in question in some way abused universal principles of human rights or, because it repressed its own population, could be considered to have forfeited its right to rule, since sovereignty was an expression of general will or collective legitimacy, not solely of the power of the state[23]. By the end of the decade, this had blossomed into a full-blown ideology of intervention, particularly in the Anglo-Saxon world, as typified by Tony Blair's Chicago speech on 22 April 1999[24]. These ideas, drafted originally by Sir Laurence Freedman, were given intellectual substance by Robert Cooper, a British diplomat, who first argued that the postmodern state would be a construct of a state within an ordered international community where sovereignty was voluntarily derogated. He subsequently proposed a reification of interventionism under the rubric of 'reluctant imperialism', which turned out to be suspiciously similar to concepts of liberalism imperialism as developed at the height of the Victorian era[25].

Such ideas meshed well with those that were to emerge when the Bush administration came to power in 2001 and the neo-conservative agenda became to dominate the foreign policy process. The new concepts not only involved the long-standing American conservative vision of the projection of national interest at a global level – first proposed and justified by President Reagan in the 1980s, as a kind of inversion of the moral status of American democracy into the international area as a justification of the practice of diplomatic neo-realism – but also added its own unique assumptions. These involved the practice of unilateral force where necessary, on a pre-emptive basis, if need be, to establish an international democratic environment sympathetic of and supportive to the United States and its allies. The neo-conservatives rejected the restraining influence of international organisations or of an international, law-based community[26]. They also distanced themselves from the European Community's endorsement of such an approach and its innate preference for soft security and the preferred European diplomatic technique of constructive engagement.[27]

The neo-conservatives were a product of the frustrations felt by the United States during the 1990s and of the underlying American distaste for any kind of restraint on its diplomatic activities. As such they were well within an American tradition reaching back, ironically enough, to Woodrow Wilson as well as to his Congressional critics at the time who had refused to endorse the international institutions created by the Treaty of Versailles. They also reflected many of the assumptions behind the geo-economics of the Clinton era, much though they decried Clintonian foreign policy. In a sense, they combined the universalism of Francis Fukuyama's vision and the scepticism of Samuel Huntington. Even more surprisingly, they echoed many of the assumptions behind the New Right in Europe, even though they rejected the European project.

Indeed, in many respects, their arrival to power, as articulated through the Bush administration and, subsequently, in the new national security doctrine enunciated by the new administration,[28] marks the end of a long period of transition from the Cold War to a genuinely new world order. This has little to do with a rule-based international society and much more to do with the revival of a neo-realist approach to the international arena, albeit now against a globalized economic background. And, of course, it is this conundrum that Europe is now struggling either to digest or reject because of the contradiction between innate, if rarely-voiced, European sympathy for such a project and overt European preference for international law as the leaven for international relations. It is a crucial contradiction for it provides the intellectual counterpart to the internalized cultural boundary that has emerged in recent years as a result of terrorist violence. The irony is that, despite the reverses that the neo-conservative vision has suffered in recent years, both in Iraq and in the wider Middle East, the essential principles of the ideology itself have been increasingly integrated into the contemporary general European weltanshauung.

It is against this intellectual environment that the implications of the events of 9/11 should be seen. Ironically enough, they acted as a catalyst for the application of the neo-conservative agenda to the Middle East and for the development of the associated 'war on terror' which now applies to the whole region, together with South East Asia, Afghanistan and Pakistan. They have resulted in profound changes in regional politics and geopolitics, as well as in the underlying assumptions behind American and, to a lesser extent European regional diplomacy. They have also generated a competition over soft security, as opposed to hard security responses in the Mediterranean region and in the Gulf. Most strikingly of all, they have nourished the development of a major, dispersed and fragmented terrorist threat, exploiting modern means of communication and benefiting from access to a coherent intellectual background that has profoundly affected the internal politics and security assumptions of states throughout Europe, as well as in the United States. And, most importantly, both sides in this conflict are increasingly interlinked through a dialectic of antiphonal, mutually reinforcing violence – a reification, as it were, of the 'clash of civilisations'. It is this that forms the background to both the failure of the Barcelona Process and the emergence of a parallel American policy which is unlikely to be more successful.

5 The European response

In the past four years, Europe has had to respond to these new challenges, as well as to some old ones. It has had to face the fact that the Barcelona Process has failed to realize its early promise; it must confront the challenge of American soft security policies in the Mediterranean; and it has had to confront the issue of terrorism within its external frontiers. It has also had to face the implications of Enlargement, especially in the East where new states now share its common external frontier, many of them also seeking membership of the Union itself.

The issue began to be faced in 2002, at the Copenhagen summit of the Council of the European Union. A fully developed policy was produced by the European Commission in May 2004[29] – the month of Eastwards Enlargement – directed towards the new frontier states of the Ukraine, Belarus and Moldova – Russia was excluded at its own request – as well as the ten remaining, partner-states in the Barcelona Process – Turkey was excluded because of its imminent accession negotiations but Libya was included because of its expressed desire to join the Euro-Mediterranean Partnership. Finally, in June 2004, the states of the Caucasus also joined the new frontier policy[30] as a result of a decision taken by the European Union's Council on 17 June, 2004.

The policy is designed to create a 'ring of friends' around the European Union and to respond to the problem that Enlargement cannot be indefinitely extended, although European security depends on political and economic change in neighbouring states, something which, therefore – as in the Barcelona Process – the Union would wish to encourage. As such, although much of the policy is copied from the Enlargement experience,[31] its roots lie in the European Security Strategy, developed in 2003.[32] In other words, in security terms, the new policy is primarily concerned with trafficking of drugs and people, organized crime, terrorism and similar trans-border issues including the environment. This is, of course, inevitable, once the decision was taken in Brussels to limit future Enlargement, although the fact that boundaries between the neighbour states concerned and the European Union are to be maintained is to be mitigated by encouraging cross-border cooperation.

The logic behind the policy is, however, unchanged from that behind the Barcelona Process or, indeed, behind the parallel American initiatives; namely that neighbourhood states must accept European values in terms of governance and economic policy to enable them to become 'friends' and 'neighbours' but that doing so only provides proximity to the European Union, not access. Thus the policy proposes that a series of individual bilateral relations be established between the Union and each state in which the non-European partner is encouraged to adapt its political and economic policies towards the norms of the European Union and, as this occurs, greater and greater access is provided to the instruments of the Union itself, except that participation in the actual governance of the Union will not be part of the agreement. In other words, through a process of positive conditionality, neighbourhood states are to encouraged to apply the European acquis communautaire,[33] on the assumption that this will reduce potential security threats as, in effect, such states adopt the Copenhagen criteria which lie at the root of the Enlargement process.[34]

The policy itself is articulated through a series of Action Plans. These consist of bilateral agreements between the Union and individual states in which a programme of action, over three-to-five years, is laid out to achieve the overall objective. The state concerned, in negotiation with the Commission, determines the content of the Action Plan, thus establishing what it would consider a reasonable programme, whilst the Union monitors progress through a process of benchmarking and provides political, administrative and financial support. From 2007, the old Barcelona MEDA (Mésures d'Ajustement) financing programme which provided funding for the Euro-Mediterranean Partnership, together with the old programmes for funding political and economic change in the East, such as the TACIS programme, will have been absorbed into a new financial instrument designed specifically for the European Neighbourhood Policy.[35] It seems impossible to consider such a policy, based specifically on bilateral relations across the Mediterranean, as being in any sense 'open regionalism', even if it does apply to a series of geographically contiguous states.

What, then, happens to the Barcelona Process? It seems clear that the new European Neighbourhood Policy runs directly counter to the underlying principles of the Euro-Mediterranean Partnership for it promotes bilateral relations between neighbour-states and the European Union, rather than the horizontal integration which was the ultimate purpose of the Barcelona Process. The Commission is determined to reject such a conclusion and, in the regulations laying down the final policy,[36] published in October 2006, it states that (paragraph 13) 'For Mediterranean partners, assistance and cooperation should take place within the framework of the Euro-Mediterranean Partnership...' It argues that, in effect, the European Neighbourhood Policy will enable states to enter the European Economic Area (paragraph 18) and thus, supposedly, will enjoy all the benefits offered under the Barcelona Declaration's 'zone of shared peace, prosperity and stability' proposed in 1995.

The problem is twofold; firstly all the measures to be adopted under the new European Neighbour and Partnership Instrument in reality emphasize the bilateral relationship between neighbour-states and the Union and undermine the South-South relationships which were the key to the Barcelona Process, and secondly, neighbourhood states have no compulsion for reform. Instead they set the reform agenda by negotiation with the Commission and suffer no inconvenience if they do not achieve the objectives they have set for themselves. It is true, of course, that there are rewards for states that do achieve their targets but no price is paid if they do not. Thus, clearly, if a foreign government feels that its priorities require that the priority accorded to the Neighbourhood Policy should be downgraded, it suffers no disadvantage in consequence.

In essence, therefore, unlike the Barcelona Process, the old principle of horizontal integration has disappeared and the new policy is resolutely bilateral in its conception, rejecting the multilateralism inherent in the Barcelona Process as a complicating factor which led in part to the failure of the Euro-Mediterranean Partnership. It thus entrenches the 'hub-and-spoke' concept which the Barcelona Process considered to be a temporary stage, to be overcome by horizontal integration in the political, security and social spheres, once economic integration had been achieved in the South. In security terms, it seeks to build what Attina regards as an amalgamated security community, as defined by Karl Deutsch[37]. As William Wallace has said, 'Western Europe faces the uncomfortable choice of importing insecurity from its neighbours, or of exporting to them security – which necessarily involves prosperity and stability'.[38]

The policy is thus overtly Eurocentric, avoiding any of the linguistic moderation of the Euro-Mediterranean Partnership, even if its underlying purpose is little different. In effect, its spirit and outcomes seem likely to be far closer to the 'closed regionalism' concept, in that it wishes to bind neighbouring states into permanent relationships governed by an agreed body of law, as in the European Union itself, but without any executive counterpart. Indeed, it is also imperial, for the satellite 'neighbours' will be, in effect, satrapies of the European core in which, in the end governance, security mechanisms, economic relationships and cultural paradigms will be imposable if the full benefits of partnership are to be realised. Once states have accepted the European embrace – the *acquis communautaire* – there will be no going back!

6 Conclusion

In a sense, the policy wheel has come full circle, although the European Commission insists that the global and holistic features of the Euro-Mediterranean Partnership will not be over-ridden by European Neighbourhood Policy when the two are amalgamated after 2007. Whether this is true or not will depend on the degree to which the political-security and cultural-social baskets of the Barcelona Process are sustained under the new, combined policy. In economic terms, however, the hub-and-spoke arrangement of independent bilateral agreements with the European Union will dissipate hopes of integration of the economies in the South Mediterranean into a single market to partner the European Single Market, through initiatives such as the Agadir Agreement and the moribund Maghrib Arab Union (UMA). Yet that, of course, was one of the major justifications for the Barcelona Process; that it would generate economic integration in the South that would provide a sustainable economic region that could ensure endogamous economic growth.

Yet, if the pessimistic conclusions voiced above are not to be realized, the real question is whether or not the new initiatives can achieve the aspirations of the Barcelona Declaration, of creating a zone of shared peace, stability and prosperity, and thus of providing Europe with the security it needs from uncontrollable immigration from the South Mediterranean and from the spill-over effects of regional violence as a result of economic and political failure there. In part, of course, this depends on the ability of Western policy to defuse, not exacerbate, regional problems and tensions. In part it depends, too, on the development of stable, participatory government there as well. Both, in turn, depend on resolving the two great crises in the region – the aftermath of the invasion of Iraq and the continuing crisis in the Palestinian territories – and that, too, is a European and American responsibility. And, increasingly, both are becoming tributary to the securitised obsessions inherent in the 'war on terror'.

However, even if both issues – and even the 'war of terror' – were addressed by appropriate policies, in which the European Union, because of its lack of effective, integrated military force, could only play a subsidiary role, this will still not resolve the underlying economic crisis. Here, even given the indulgence inherent in the European Neighbourhood Policy which does not prescribe economic restructuring as the Barcelona Process, in parallel to the Washington Consensus, did, success seems unlikely. In large part this is because of the dimensions of the economic challenges that exist and because of the theoretical and ideological implications of the responses proposed. The European experience, even that of the Accession countries, does not necessarily apply in the South Mediterranean and attempts to force the region into the European mould will almost certainly fail. The danger will then be that frustration in the region will produce violence and extremism so that policies intended to dissipate security threats may well create them instead!

Appendix

The tables below provide economic data referred to in the chapter.

Table I   **EU trade with Mediterranean countries***
(€ million)

	EU-world trade		EU-Mediterranean country trade			
Date	Imports	Exports	Imports	% Eu Total	Exports	% EU Total
2001	983,443	892,720	68,201	6.93	73,407	8.22
2002	941,885	900,424	67,638	7.18	76.781	8.53
2003	940,347	878,483	67,926	7.22	78,107	8.89
2004	1,031,999	964,652	75,364	7.30	91,625	9.50
2005	1,176,055	1,061,836	88,171	7.50	101,671	9.58

Source: EUROSTAT (Comtext; Regime 4)
Note: * Algeria, Egypt, Palestine, Israel, Jordan, Lebanon, Morocco, Syria, Tunisia, Turkey

Table II   **Mediterranean country* trade with the EU**
(€ million)

	Med-world Trade		Mediterranean Country-eu Trade			
Date	Imports	Exports	Imports	% Med Total	Exports	% Med Total
2001	150,658	118,074	70,296	46.66	58,482	49.53
2002	163,631	122,211	76,495	46.75	60,369	49.40
2003	164,238	122,262	79,736	48.55	61,569	50.36
2004	207,812	155,287	92,288	44.41	76,157	49.04
2005	238,836	172,373	109,443	45.82	81.071	47.03

Source: IMF Direction of Trade Statistics
Note: * Algeria, Egypt, Palestine, Israel, Jordan, Lebanon, Morocco, Syria, Tunisia, Turkey

Table III   **EU Foreign Direct Investment**
(€ billion)

	EU outward FDI			
Country	2001	2002	2003	2004
Maghrib	0.78	0.83	1.77	1.38
Mashriq	0.60	2.00	1.15	0.11
Israel	-0.33	0.20	0.12	0.23
Turkey	2.98	0.80	1.11	1.54
MED countries	1.05	3.04	3.05	1.72
World	286.35	133.90	135.42	99.95

Source: Chronos; EC Relex: External Trade: EuroMed Fact Sheet 10.03.2006
http://trade-info.cec.eu.int/doclib/cfm/doclib_section.cfm?sec=152&lev=2&order=date
Note: Maghrib: Algeria, Morocco, Tunisia Mashriq: Egypt, Jordan, Lebanon, Palestine, Syria
MED: Maghrib and Mashriq including Israel but excluding Turkey

Table IV   **European Union meda support**
€ million

	MEDA-1 (1995-1999)	MEDA-2 (2000-2004)	MEDA 1 & 2 (1995-2004)
Bilateral funding			
Algeria	164.0	232.8	396.8
Palestine	111.0	350,3	461.3
Egypt	686.0	353.5	1,039.5
Jordan	254.0	204.4	458.4
Lebanon	182.0	73.7	255.7
Morocco	660.0	677.1	1,337.1
Syria	101.0	135.7	236.7
Tunisia	428.0	328.6	756.6
Total bilateral	2,586.0	2,356.1	4,942.1
Regional funding	471.0	739.8	1,210.9
Total funding	3,057.0	3,095.9	6,152.9

Source: Europe Aid
Note: According to the MEDA budget projections, funding under MEDA I (1995-1999) was set at
€3,435 million, with an additional €4,808 million in soft loans from the European Investment Bank.
Funding under MEDA II (2000-2006) will have totalled €5,350 million, with European Investment
Bank loan funding up to 2007 of €6,700 million.

Table V   **Financial support under the Usmepi programme**
$ million

	2002	2003	2004	2005
Economic development	6	38	32	23
Political development	10	25	20	22
Educational development	8	25	22	14.4
Women's empowerment	5	12	15.5	15
TOTALS	29	100	89.5	84.4

Source: http://mepi.state.gov/mepi

Table VI   **Funding under the European neighbourhood and partnership instrument**
€million

Year	2007	2008	2009	2010	2011	2012	2013	Total 2007-2013
Amount	1,433	1,569	1,877	2,083	2,322	2,642	3,003	14,929

Notes

1   Open regionalism implies linkages between states that do not impinge directly upon their sovereign activities and rights. They therefore tend to be primarily economic in nature, even if, the explicit objectives of such regional organizations may involve common security or diplomatic factors. Closed regionalism involves explicit common policies in all areas and thus diminishes the sovereign powers of constituent governments (see Thomas G. (1998), "Globalisation versus regionalisation", in Joffé G. (ed), *Perspectives on development: the Euro-Mediterranean Partnership*, Cass (London): 63.

2   The term was originally coined by Peregrine Worsthorne in the *Daily Telegraph* in 1991. It was, however, revived in 1998 and popularized by Hervé Védrine, then French foreign minister, in a speech to the Association France-Ameriques in Paris on Monday, February 1, 1999.

3   Viz: Buzan B. (1991), 'New patterns of global security in the twenty-first century', *International Affairs*, 67 (3): 431–51.

4   Globalization, of course, is no new phenomenon but, in its contemporary guise, based on deregulated global financial markets powered by information technology, together with free trade dominated by the Triad of the United States, Europe and Japan, it alohas some quite unique characteristics. See Barber B.R. (1995, 2001), *Jihad vs. McWorld: terrorism's challenge to democracy*, Ballantine Books (New York).

5   Fukuyama F. (1989), 'The end of history?' *The National Interest* (Summer 1989). Democratic peace in this context involves the explicit rejection of neo-realist views of state interest and the security paradigm.

6   Huntington S. (1993), 'The clash of civilisations', *Foreign Affairs*, 72, 3 (Summer 1993). Here conflict is innate in the very existence of different civilizations and in their political contacts with each other.

7   Fukuyama F. (2006), 'Afterword', *The end of history and the last man*, (second edition), The Free Press (New York).

8   Roberts A. (1991), 'A new age in International Relations?', *International Affairs*, 67, 3 (July 1991).

9   Calleya S. (1997), *Navigating regional dynamics in a post-Cold War world*, Dartmouth (Aldershot): 15.

10   Ibid: 35–36.

11   Thomas, op. cit. 1998: 59–74.

12   British Petroleum, *BP statistical review of world energy 2006*, London (available only in electronic form at www.bp.com)

13   There is now an extensive literature on the Euro-Mediterranean Partnership, the correct title for the Barcelona Process. Two short introductions to it and to its main activities over the past ten years are provided by the European Commission and the Euro-Mediterranean Human Rights Network. See: http://europa.eu.int/comm./external_ relations/euromed; www.euromedrights.net/english/barcelona-process/main/html.

14   Aubarell G. and Aragall X. (2005), Immigration and the Euro-Mediterranean Area: keys to policy and trends, *EuroMeSCo Paper No. 47* IEEI (Lisbon): 8–9.

15   Jandl M. (2004), 'The estimation of illegal migration in Europe', *Studi Emigrazione/ Migration Studies*, XLI, 153 (March 2004): 150.

16   UNCTAD (2005), *World Investment Report 2005*, Table 1 (FDI flows by region and selected countries) 1993–2004: pp. 10–11.

17   Strategic lines of communication, as defined by the Pentagon, carry 99 per cent of global maritime trade by volume. Four of the nine critical chokepoints for global trade exist in the Mediterranean system – the Bosporus and the Dardanelles for access to the Black

Sea, the Bab al-Mandab and the Suez Canal which control access to the Red Sea, and the Straits of Gibraltar which controls access to the Atlantic. To these could be added the Straits of Hormuz which control access to the Persian Gulf and 70 per cent of the world's oil reserves. The Mediterranean itself, of course, is a major pathway for the transfer of oil to both Europe and the United States. A chokepoint is defined as a waterway narrow enough to be closed by simple military action involving artillery, air or naval power. These issues are studied in detail in Nincic D. J. (2002), 'Sea lane security and US maritime trade: chokepoints as scarce resources', in Tancredi S. J. (2002) (ed.), *Globalization and maritime power*, Institute for National Strategic Studies, National Defense University (Washington DC).

18 See endnote (7).

19 http://www.state.gov/secretary/former/powell/remarks/2002/15920.htm.

20 The detailed commitments are given in the appendix and can be compared with funding levels under the MEDA programmes for the Euro-Mediterranean Partnership also given in the appendix.

21 Personal communication.

22 See endnote (5).

23 For example, Weber C. (1995), *Simulating sovereignty: intervention, the state and symbolic exchange*, Cambridge University Press (Cambridge).

24 A useful and sympathetic review of the speech and its subsequent implications is provided by Bentley T. (2003), "Countdown to war: Tony Blair, issue by issue", *Le Monde Diplomatique* (English version)(February 2003).

25 Cooper R. (1998), *The post-modern state*, Demos (London); Cooper R. (2003), *The breaking of nations: order and chaos in the 21st century*, Atlantic Books (London).

26 See Halper S. and Clarke J. (2003), *America alone: the neo-conservatives and the global order*, Cambridge University Press (Cambridge): 76–81, 254–57.

27 Kagan R. (2003), *Paradise and power: America and Europe in the New World Order*, Atlantic Books (London).

28 *National Security Strategy of the United States of America*, White House, September 17, 2002.

29 See Commission of the European Communities, *European Neighbourhood Policy: Strategy Paper*, COM (2004) 373 final, Brussels 12.05.2004.

30 Smith K. (2005), 'The outsiders: the European Neighbourhood Policy', *International Affairs*, 81, 4 (2005): 760.

31 See Kelley J. (2006), 'New wine in old wineskins: policy adaptation in the European Neighbourhood Policy', *Journal of Common Market Studies*, 44, 1 (2006).

32 Aliboni R. (2005), 'The geopolitical implications of the European Neighbourhood Policy', *European Foreign Affairs Review*, 10.

33 The body of European regulation that goes to make up the shared legal system of the European Union and makes access to the Single European Market possible, as well as, in the case of members, access to the Union's policy-making and administrative activities. The implications of this could be very costly! See Tocci N. (2005), 'Does the ENP respond to the EU's post-Enlargement challenges?', *The International Spectator*, XL, 1 (2005): 30.

34 These were laid down at the Copenhagen summit in June 1993 as the basis upon which Enlargement could proceed as they determined the conditions Accession state would have to fulfil to actually join the Union. They are:

- political: stable institutions guaranteeing democracy, the rule of law, human rights and respect for minorities;

- economic: a functioning market economy;
- incorporation of the Community acquis: adherence to the various political, economic and monetary aims of the European Union (http://europa.eu.int/scadplus/glossary/accession_criteria_copenhague_en.htm).

35 The figures for the new financial instrument, known as the European Neighbourhood and Partnership Instrument (ENPI), in constant 2004 prices, are taken from Smith op.cit. and appear in the Statistical Appendix above. They can be compared with the budget for the East and the Mediterranean in 2004 (€ 1,420 million with € 953 million for the Mediterranean) but the figures are not fully comparable.

36 Official Journal of the European Union (09.11.2006), Regulation (EC) No 1638/2006 of the European Parliament and of the Council of 24 October 2006 laying down general provisions establishing a European Neighbourhood and Partnership Instrument, Brussels.

37 Attina F. (2004), 'European Neighbourhood Policy and the building of security around Europe', in Attina F. and Rossi R. (eds)(2004), *European Neighbourhood Policy: political, economic and social aspects*, Jean Monnet Centre, University of Catania (Catania); 16-17. Deutsch's concept of an amalgamated security community is one in which the community considers war as an obsolete instrument of conflict resolution. Deutsch K *et al* (1957), *Political community in the North Atlantic area*, Princeton University Press (Princeton).

38 Quoted in Balfour R. and Rotta A. (2005), 'The European Neighbourhood Policy and its tools', *The International Spectator*, XL, 1 (2005); 9.

Chapter 14

Europe: Trading Power, American Hunting Dog, or the World's Scandinavia?

Göran Therborn

On the world maps of the Peters Projection, Europe appears as a small far northern periphery of *peninsulae* and islands, out on the Western fringe of the huge Asian land mass, separated by the narrow Mediterranean waterway from the big central continent of Africa, and by the wide Atlantic Ocean from the impressive semi-continent of North America. In other words, Europe here looks very much like the Nordic countries on a standard European map, with the qualification that Scandinavia normally looks larger on the maps of Europe. A Scandinavian scenario, I am going to argue, is in the long run one of the most attractive futures left to an irreversibly ex-imperial continent.

The future standing of Europe in the world will depend on four complex variables, the relative weight, the relative specificity, and the relative unity of Europe, and finally, least predictable of all, the handling of these variables by the political leaders. As this decade has shown already, European assets may be squandered by reckless politicians.

1 Still heavyweight, but ...

Western Europe has long since abdicated from claims to rule the world, although the Dutch, the French and the Portuguese had to be ousted from their colonies by force. The bungled Anglo-French-Israeli attack on Egypt in 1956 was the last attempt to play world power. The recent War of the Yugoslav Succession demonstrated Europe's weakness even as a regional power. A long way has been travelled from Berlin 1878 to Dayton, Ohio 1995. In so far as the Soviet Union was a European power, its collapse entails a further weakening of Europe on the global theatre of power.

Commemorations are correspondingly scaled down with lowered aspirations. The start of Western Europe's outward expansion was remembered in the last World Exhibitions of the twentieth century, in Sevilla in 1992 and in Lisbon in 1998, in ecologically conscious theme parks for tourists, without any of the imperial glory and nation state *braggadoccio* of the pre-Second World War exhibitions, nor with the futurism of the Brussels 1958 Exhibition. The arrival of European modernity in 1789 was two centuries later turned into a pure media spectacle, while the politically correct opinion held that the French Revolution was both vicious and unnecessary.

Production and prosperity

Economically, Europeans are, of course, still among the primary league players. Among the seven large economies of the world in 2005, having a GDP of more than one thousand bi.llion dollars, four are European, Germany, France, UK and Italy. (The others are the USA, Japan and China.) After its latest expansions, the economy of the EU27 as a whole is clearly larger, about 9 per cent, than that of the USA, 30 per cent each of the world economy at prevailing exchange rates (Eurostat and UN data.).

In the IMF (1997:121) count, there are twenty-eight 'advanced economies' of the world in the mid-1990s. Eighteen of these are European, and five are European settlements, Australia, Canada, Israel, New Zealand and the USA. The resting five are East Asian, Hong Kong, Japan, Korea, Singapore and Taiwan. The World Bank (1997:215) list of 'high income economies' is fairly similar. With Iceland and Luxemburg added – excluded from the main table for their small population – and correcting for purchasing power differences among currencies, this list comprises twenty-nine countries, of which eighteen are European. Taiwan is missing for diplomatic reasons, and the oil sheikdoms of Kuwait and UAE have been added. With the recent climbing of Portugal and Greece, no Western European country is in division II of prosperity.

How significant average GDP per capita and its growth are among rich countries, is far from obvious, unless median incomes, the overall distribution, and the quality of life are taken into account. But anyway, the distance of Europe to the United States and to Japan in those respects should not be forgotten. If we put the GDP per capita in purchasing power parities of the EU 27 in 2005 to 100, the US figure would be 156 and the Japanese one 115. When compared with the EU15 there has been a European advance, from a US index figure of 163 in 1970 to one of 139 in 2005. The Japanese are still benefiting from their advances in the 1970s and the 1980s, moving from 95 to the EU15 in 1970 to 102 in 2005. (Eurostat, 2005: national accounts).

. Western Europeans are increasing their distance to the world as a whole, that is, very strongly to the world outside North America and East Asia. In the mid-2000s the per capita GDP (in PPS) of EU15 is about six and a half times that of the Third World, of 'the developing countries'. For the gap to narrow, the latter need to grow at an annual rate more than six and half times higher than the growth of Europe. But, in fact, since 1990 the growth per capita of all developing countries taken together (including the Chinese success story) has only been about one and half time that of Western Europe (UNDP, 2006: Table 14).

In summary, Europe, and above all Western Europe, is a rich corner of the world, and it is growing relatively more prosperous.

Western Europe has also maintained itself well on the markets of world trade.

Table 14.1   Shares of world exports (of goods and services) 1950–1996, percentages

	1950	1970	1976	2003
Western Europe	33	46	42	42
North America	21	20	17	14
Japan	1	6	7	6

Sources: UNCTAD, 1995: table 1.9 and 1.10; UN, 1995a: Special Table A; IMF 1996: table 1; World Bank, 2005: tables 4.5 and 4.7.

For Western Europe, as well as for the US, the OPEC price hike was much more important to its trade shares than the recent wave of globalization. The trade expansion of Eastern and Southeast Asia has had no net effect on the OECD countries. The Third World has had to bear the full brunt. In other words, Europe is not being out competed. In fact, in the first half of the 1990s, the EU was (by a small margin) a net exporter of manufactures to the so-called emergent economies. This may of course change, but Europe is so far less exposed to low-wage industrial competition than North America and Japan (OECD,1997:104–5).

By way of conclusion, Europe is hardly the centre of the world economy, although London is still the world's major financial centre. But Europe is still fully reproducing itself as a small semi-arctic outpost of prosperity, out of reach and increasingly so, to the bulk of the earth's population. Statistically average prosperity is, to some extent, being undermined, though, by a historical rise and stabilization of unemployment. However, in most countries – Britain under Thatcher and Italy in the mid-1990s – the European welfare state has been strong and generous enough to prevent any rise of poverty over the two decades (Eurostat, 2005; Lisproject, 2006).

Population

In sheer numbers Europe is becoming steadily lighter in the world. The EU27 has less than half the population of India, 7.7 per cent of the world.

The population projection reflects the fact that Europe, together with Japan, is close to a static natural population equilibrium. Birth and death rates are almost canceling each other out. Eleven of the EU27 countries had a surplus of deaths over births in 2005, all the new Eastern European members except Slovenia, plus Germany and Italy. (France and Britain are the main counterweights to the natural decline.) (Eurostat, 2005) Since the end of the Soviet Union, a dramatic excess of

Table 14.2   Europe's proportion of the world's population 1950–2025, percentages

1950	1993	2003	2025 (estimate)
22	13	10	9

Note: Europe includes Russia and the non Caucasian and non-Central Asian republics of the former USSR.
Sources: United Nations, 1995b:12; World Bank, 1995:210–11, 228: UNDP, 2006: table 5).

deaths over births has risen in Russia, Ukraine, Belarus, and in the Baltic Republics (Unicef, 1995: tables A1–2). Part of Europe is dying out.

The outcome of this demography is already visible in the age structure. In 1990 14.5 per cent of the population of Western Europe was over 65 years old, 12.3 of the US, 11.9 of the Japanese, but 4.8 of the other Central, East and South Asian population, 3.6 of the West Asian–North African population, and 4.6 per cent of the Latin Americans. By 2015 Eurostat predicts that 20 per cent of the EU population will be 65 or older.

Whereas population biology is tending towards a static state, migratory flows keep up a certain momentum, although not (yet) enough to stop estimates of a slight population decline in the first decades of the next century. Europe turned from almost half a millennium of net outward migration to an immigration continent in the first half of the 1960s. But it is only since the mid-1980s that the pace of migration into (Western) Europe has quickened. Between 1985–87 and 1992, the number of immigrants into Western Europe almost trebled. (Therborn, 1995a. 41ff, 50). In the 1990s, migration has constituted the bulk of the population growth in the EU15. Net migration into Germany in the 1990s has been more than twice that into the US, 6.7 and 3.3 per thousand population per annum, respectively. (Eurostat, 1996a: fig. 1, table 2) In the 2000s, Spain has been the main European receiver of migrants, with a net immigration of a stunning 16.7 per thousand population in 2002–03. (Eurostat, 2005:74)

The combination of the lack of military strength of Europe, its remaining political division, its originally stable, but clearly no longer predominant economic capacity, the high and visibly unthreatened prosperity of its citizens – though partly diminished by unemployment – and its aging and tangentially shrinking native population, suggests that Europe has little, if anything, to gain from entering a race for world championship. Furthermore, the worldview of the global business consultants, with their vision of an inexorable struggle for world competitive rank, seems no more founded on what matters to most people than the ideology of the 1930s of the inescapable struggle for Lebensraum. On the other hand, there is no evidence of European marginalization, neither pending nor current.

In sum, Europe is still heavyweight, but its right punch is not as hard as it used to be, by a long way. Part of the weight is fat rather than muscles, and it is getting slower. But it also looks unscathed, exuding good training and experience.

2 Specificity under pressure – and imitation

The specificities of European societies derive from the historical trajectory of Europe, ancient and modern. This writer would tend to give more weight to the European route to modernity than to its ancient traditions in accounting for contemporary European sociology (Therborn, 1995b), but the point will not be argued here. What seems to be called for, however, is some assessment of the future life expectancy of the peculiarities of the Europeans.

Synoptically summarized, there are two kinds of significant European specificities: one refers to the aggregate of European societies and their common characteristics in comparison with the rest of the world; the other is made up of 'Europe', as a supranational, supra-state collective or social *mega-network*.

Both kinds are being subject to *three sorts of challenges*. One is the possibility of the characteristics being eroded, by internal processes and/or under external pressure. Alternatively, the specific traits of Europe may recede into the background, as marginal or irrelevant in relation to broader and stronger global processes. Thirdly, Europe's special features may become increasingly difficult to discern, because they are taken up elsewhere, by imitation or by parallel developments.

European modernity: Class and welfare state

Among the many particularities of European social relations as aggregates, this chapter only touches upon two: the special significance in Europe of industrial class relations and of a socially interventionist, 'welfare' state. The two are, of course, historically related, the latter pretty much an outcome of the former.

Modernity in Europe was a completely endogenous development, of the continent taken as a whole. This meant that the bitter and violent conflicts for and against modernity all took the character of civil war. This endogeny had at least three important implications.

Firstly, the European route to modernity pitted socioeconomic classes against each other more clearly than elsewhere. That was endogenous, as classes are internal social divisions, but it was strongly reinforced by the unique importance of industrialization to European societies. Only in Europe did industrial employment become at least relatively dominant (of a trisectoral employment structure) (Therborn, 1995a:68ff). The polarized industrial division of labour gave a further push to class consciousness, class mobilization and class organization in Europe. Until this day, the Western European political party system derives from clear cut class cleavages, with one major party descending from specific working class representation, and the other, from a core of bourgeois and middle class representation, representing non-working class politics, either by claiming transcendence of class into nation or religion (Christian Democracy) or by representing agrarian or middle class interests.

Secondly, the internal conflict path meant that established religion was always clearly on the side of anti-modernity. When modernity finally won, this meant a serious defeat of established Christianity. Today, Europe is by far the most secularized part of the world once governed by what Max Weber called the world religions. (Therborn, 1995a:275. The Confucian area is not quite comparable to the rest of the religious world.)

Thirdly, the protracted internal struggles for and against modernity gave rise to a large set of elaborate doctrines and principled ideological systems. Europe was the womb of almost all the major isms of the nineteenth and the twentieth centuries, from Legitimism and Monarchism and Republicanism to Liberalism, Conservatism, Traditionalism, Radicalism, Socialism, Marxism, Fascism and Anti-Fascism. Only Fundamentalism is of non-European origin, coined in the US of the 1920s to designate anti-modern Christian Protestantism.

A historically class-cleavage based party system, relatively high class voting, still characterizes Western Europe. Trade unions carry more weight in Europe than elsewhere, especially in Germanic Europe. Their weakening in the 1980s and 1990s have not made the situation of Western European unions significantly more similar to that of American or Japanese ones (Therborn, 1995.309–10).

In terms of ideological doctrines, Europe is still the world's major producer of ideology, although the successful export drive has passed from the Soviet Union and the Socialist International to neo-Tory Britain. Recently, British Blairism is contending for a position as ideological 'beacon' to the world. The major item of ideological export is no longer 'socialism' but 'privatization' and (marketeering) 'economic reform'.[1] The relatively meagre ideological output – outside Christian Fundamentalism – by the US right, of the Reagan Presidency and of the Gingrich Congress is noteworthy, and the Bush doctrine of spreading 'freedom' by military 'shock and awe' has been clearly counterproductive in terms of appeal.

On the other hand, de-industrialization and its concomitant socio-political re-alignments have hit Europe. The industrial class basis of European politics is being cut under, although it retains a relative advantage. The unique European preponderance of industrial over agricultural and services employment, or at least over all non-agrarian employment – characteristic of Britain since about 1820 and of Western Europe since the early twentieth century – has been lost. Since 1980 Europe has even become less industrial than Japan, although the distance to the US is by and large kept up.

Now, sociological experience teaches us, that institutions usually do not go away for being undermined. The institutions of industrial class society are still in place in Europe, and they are not likely to evaporate in the foreseeable future. But their significance has diminished, as rallying-points of collective identity and behaviour, from class voting to May Day marching or meeting attendance. The party effort at distancing itself from the unions and their more direct class allegiance is palpable all across Europe in the 1990s, from Scandinavia to the Iberian Peninsula, via the British Isles.

There are no signs of any accelerating descent of class relations and class politics in Europe. Even the basis for predicting continuous linear erosion is flimsy. Electoral politics in Western Europe is still moving, up and down, right or left, within the classical social parameters. Also with regard to non-electoral social conflicts the current pattern of tendencies is complicated. Against, for instance, the resigned adjustment to permanent mass unemployment one should also notice the occasional flare-up of still potent class-based social protest.

The welfare state has come under siege, from global financial markets – generally manned by highly-paid young males, to whom social issues are as distant as the other side of the moon – and from the bulk of the economics profession, while internal support is increasingly withheld by an upper middle class, growing both in assertiveness and in preoccupation with itself. More options for the prosperous and more concentration on the very minimum for the 'really needy' are slogans in ascendance, while social rights, solidarity, and social integration are correspondingly being demoted. But how far has this new ideological discourse eaten into existing institutions of public social rights?

Table 14.3   Social security transfers and total current public disbursements 1960–2005, percentage of GDP

	1960		1974		1985		2005	
	Transf.	**Total**	**Transf.**	**Total**	**Transf.**	**Total**	**Transf.**	**Total(a)**
Europe	9.5	31.4	13.3	40.0	17.7	49.5	14.5	46.6
USA	5.0	27.2	9.5	36.4	10.9	37.0	12.0	36.4
Japan	3.8	17.5	6.2	32.9	10.9	32.3	11.8	37.3

Notes: Europe = OECD Europe 1960-85; 2005: unweighted average old (Western European OECD members ,excl. Iceland and Luxemburg)
a. Total government outlays.
Source: OECD (1996: tables 6.3 and 6.5.); OECD, 2006a:59–60

On the whole, the specificity of the European state has maintained itself well so far. It is clearer if social services are included. In 2001, total social expenditure in the EU15 (by OECD definition) was 23.9 per cent of GDP, to compared with 14.7 in USA, and 16.9 in Japan (OECD, 2006b). According to EU counting, 'social protection' amounts to a good 27 per cent of EU25 GDP in 2004, only slightly lower than the EU15 figure of 28.7 in 1993 (Eurostat, 2005: ch.3)

The two major characteristics of modern European societies, their industrial class pattern of social relations and conflicts and their sizeable social state, are not currently proud foci of European collective identities. Both are being undercut by powerful forces, internal as well as international. However, like all traditions and institutions, they also show a strong resilience, and de facto they continue to shape the continent in characteristic ways.

Beyond the nation state: bloc or model?

An intricate inter-state, or to begin with inter-princes, system has characterized Western Europe since the Middle Ages. From the mid-nineteenth to the mid-twentieth century that state system gave rise to a series of devastating wars, the later more so than the previous one. Finally, these experiences generated a specific set of supra-state institutions.

This is not the place to analyze the process of European unification, or even to summarize it. What needs to be underlined, though, is the global specificity of it, and thereby its high relevance to the standing of Europe in the world, of today and of tomorrow.

The actually ongoing building of 'Europe', which started after the Second World War, is a process of system integration, of building a loosely coupled, open system. As such, 'Europe' is a set of supranational, supra-state institutions social mega-network.

The European Union is the most concrete and tangible of this set, with a highly visible political apparatus and a substantial budgetary underpinning. The EU does not operate only as a 'common market' – its impact on trade has been uneven and unsystematic – but, more caracteristically, as a pooling of economic resources and initiatives, and as a normative area, governed by an extensive body of rules, vigilantly and strongly protected by a European judiciary, to which even nation states are held liable.

The Council of Europe, with the European Convention on Human Rights, its Commission and its Court of Human Rights, and its European Social Charter have made Europe into an area of human rights, more specific and more binding than any other area of the world. The rulings of the Strasbourg Court of Human Rights are accepted as binding by the states which have ratified the jurisdiction.

A third major institution of normative Europe is the Organization for Security and Cooperation in Europe, officially constituted in 1992 and 1994 (when the name changed from 'Conference' to 'Organization'), but going back to the institutionalized thaw of the Cold War, the Helsinki Agreement of 1975. The seventh section of the latter listed a set of fundamental freedoms and rights to act and provided for a review process. The now permanent OSCE has a special monitoring and dialogue-initiating office on democratic institutions and human rights, located in Warsaw.

The global specificity of the current sociology of Europe resides most visibly in supra-state 'Europe'. Not that the continental drawing together of the Western part of Europe is unique, nor even pioneering. Pan American efforts in this direction clearly antedates the European ones, starting with more or less regular Pan American state congresses in 1889, leading to a loose pre-war Pan American Union and a set of hemispheric professional recurrent conferences and institutions, like the Inter-American Child Institute in Montevideo, and in 1948 to the Organization of American States. Ex-colonial Africa has created its Organization of African Unity, and, particularly in West Africa, a number of regional organizations, one of which was rather more successful in its intervention in the civil wars in Liberia than the EU was in ex-Yugoslavia.

However, in contrast to the OAS and the OAU (now re-modeled as the African Union) the EU, and, for those countries that have ratified its Human Rights jurisdiction, the Council of Europe are supra-state, not just inter-state organizations. Upon ratification, the treaties and their judicial interpretation, are legally binding to member states. This is also functioning in practice, as the rulings of the European Courts of Justice and of Human Rights, and their de facto acceptance by member states, show. The European Commission represents a union, not just a set of sovereign member states. A rare combination of a relatively balanced internal composition of power, intensive socio-economic internal exchange, and big economic strength also on a global scale has made that 'Europe' (that is, the EU) is widely perceived in the world as one 'bloc'.

As such a bloc, Europe was encountered by the South East Asian countries at the summit of Bangkok in March 1996. As such 'Europe' has inspired looser economic groupings in the Americas in the 1990s, NAFTA, Mercosur and the agreement on an Andean Community. The European Commission and Court of Human Rights have provided models for the recently established American equivalents.[2] 'Europe' as a bloc of prosperity is what attracts a growing queue of applicants, from long and probably hopelessly waiting Morocco and Turkey to the ex-Communist East-Central strip of Europe, from Estonia to Bulgaria.

Europe's future standing in the world will largely depend on the future of its supra-state organizations and institutions. Their problem is not one of erosion and descent, but rather of over-extension and emulation. What will happen to Europe as a normative area if the Council of Europe accommodates continuous violent suppression of minorities, in Turkey, Croatia and Macedonia or Russia? Will a European Union of twenty-five–thirty members become more like the proposal of an All-American Free Trade Area than a European Community? Will the OSCE achieve anything or fail in its virtually impossible missions to post-war Bosnia, Chechnya and the Caucasus? In the best of worlds the Council of Europe would decrease in significance and specificity, to a strong UN system of human rights flanked by many regional institutions. Implosion by internal disunity is another risk, which will be dealt with in a section below.

As a unit, Europe may appear in the world, and to the world, either as a power bloc, as a normative or institutional *model*, or, thirdly, as a nullity without significance. The last possibility is not in sight for the foreseeable future, although not logically to be ruled out for ever.

The limits of globalization

Tendencies of globalization have acquired a large amount of attention in the recent decade or two. The transnational corporations flattening the earth into one chessboard of competitive locations; the financial markets interconnected across all the time zones of the globe and with a gambling turnover exceeding the annual GDP of any state on the planet; a worldwide mass culture enclosing the earth in satellite radiation, audible in the remotest corners, visible in the same gym shoes and jeans, and digestible as global fast foods; they are all real and well known. On a more modest scale, there are also some steps taken towards a *normative* globalization, with the big UN Conferences on human rights, on population, on the environment, and on poverty, with ensuing declarations and conventions, and sometimes monitoring reporting systems and evaluating committees. Increasingly powerful and ambitious international economic organizations like the IMF and the World Bank are pushing liberal economic and social policies, largely derived from US education, onto all poor and/or indebted states of the world.[3]

All this delimits Europe both as an economic power and as an institutional model. But there is little reason to assume that globalization trends are, or in the foreseeable future will, reduce Europe to any interchangeable chunk of the earth.

A global economic system is not a novelty of yesterday morning. Many would say it goes back to the colonial expansion of Europe in the sixteenth century. In a narrower sense, it is at least 150 years old, that is, at least since the Royal Navy opened up China to the international drugs trade ('the Opium War'). Far from being extinguished, different 'corporate cultures' have been discovered recently, by students and consultants of big corporate management. (See, for example, Hampden-Turner and Trompenaars, 1993 and, as a testimony from within the corporate worlds, Albert, 1991.)

Global mass culture is more recent, and is mainly American or American/British. The US and the UK, in that order, dominate both the music and the audiovisual markets. Among the OECD countries, only the USA, 2031 million dollars in 1992, and the UK, 25 million, run a surplus on film and TV rights (OECD, 1995: table A 21.) But culture is effective largely within institutional structures, and the latter are still strongly shaped by states and by situated ethnicities. Therefore, the global cultural radiation is largely received in forms of hybridization or creolization.

The 1990s have also seen one important turn towards de-globalization. The collapse of the USSR and the end of the Cold War meant the end of four decades of global cleavage and alignments. The Gulf War and the protection of the Kuwaiti oilfields proved a brief episode and not the beginning of a global *Pax Americana*, now widely discredited by the second Gulf War. In international power politics, regional powers and regional cleavages are currently mounting in significance, at the expense of globalism.

The main forces of globalization no longer derive from Europe, and have not since Europeans launched the Second World War. However, it is true that the global Cold War had its script from the rival ideologies of European modernity and its centre-stage in the heart of Europe. But of the two main actors, one was a European expatriate and the other a cousin from the Eastern countryside. However, there are so far no signs of the globe driving continental (or smaller) regions out of business. And in the global economic games being played, European players are well represented, although perhaps in the risk of running off side. Globalization is cutting into European specificity culturally, also European political and corporate culture, and in the longer run this will not go without leaving new institutional imprints. But we are not witnessing a disappearance of historical geography.

In other words, Europe will continue to have a standing in the world, whatever that standing may be.

3 Clouds over unity

Not only does the earth have difficulties with unification. So does Europe. However, from a worldwide future perspective the problems of the latter look somewhat different to what dominated the European public discussions prior to the 1996/97 EU Inter-governmental Conference (Amsterdam Treaty). Since Europe is unlikely to become a first rank global political and military power in the twenty-first century, the concerns about a unified foreign and security policy have little more than parochial interest. Nor is a European monetary union likely to have any crucial impact upon Europe's relative economic power in the world. The idea of the EMU is mainly a peculiar conception of a political union. Economically, its overriding concern is stability, neither competitiveness nor growth.

Only to the extent that future world markets will be carved up between protectionist blocks will European unity be very important to the economic power position of European corporations, trading sites and states. That direction is not where the current regionalization in the world is currently heading. On the contrary, the major thrust is on the opening of markets, albeit regional and not borderless ones. European economic power will not depend directly on the unity of 'Europe' as one organization or collectivity, but on the dynamism and luck of the major

Table 14.4   Standardized open unemployment rates in the EC/EU 1964–2005

1964-73	1974-79	1980-89	1991-97	2001-5
2.7	4.7	9.3	10.2	7.8(a)

Note: a. EU15. For the EU27 the figure was 8.8 per cent.
Sources: OECD, 1996: table 2.20; OECD, 1998b: Table A; Eurostat, 2005.

European players. But it is true that social desintegration in Europe might very well affect the dynamism of Eurpean actors negatively.

Unemployment and ethnic multiculturalism

The major social unity problems that Europe is facing are two. One is the mounting socioeconomic segmentation and polarization within the nations of Western Europe, a product of rapid ethnic diversification in the big cities and sluggish labour markets, with unemployment steadily rising from one business cycle to the next for twenty years. The other is the discrepancy between, on one hand, an institutional / cultural adaptation of Eastern Europe to Western models and, on the other, a drastic widening of an already large divide in resources and life-chances for the bulk of the population, as the cost of breaking up the previous institutional structures.

Neither problem is very likely to lead to any acute social disintegration in the foreseeable future, with the possible exception of Russia, Ukraine and some Balkan country. Both look for the time being containable within existing institutions, of the Western cities and national states and of the extensive forms of East-West cooperation. But if they are not tackled seriously and in a concerted and sustained way, of which there are hardly indications at the time of writing, the internal Western divides and the East-West divide are more likely to aggravate than to recede. They will then bear heavily and negatively upon both the quality of life of the whole European population. Virtually everybody is likely to have to pay a price for social exclusion, marginalization, poverty, and despair, a price of fear, crime and occasional but recurrent violence.

The employment problem is not only the unemployment rate, but also the dropouts, of the labour force as well as of school, early retirement, and unemployability disguised as disability. The self-imposed fiscal constraints of Maastricht are increasing the attempts at shuffle the problem around, raising the statutorily 'normal' retirement age, tightening the disability criteria. How is the labour market going to bear that? Well, at least not by any particularly expansionary economic policies of past Keynesianism, now held obsolete by economically current opinion. The only recipe around is the creation of a more dualistic labour market. Along the normal European labour market, there is to be one with much lower wages, few if any social rights, and without any security. To what extent this deliberate division of labour into two lanes will be carried out remains to be seen.

The traditionally rather monoethnic cities of Western Europe have in recent decades acquired a considerable amount of multicoloured diversity. That is, something of the rich multiculturalism characteristic of Eastern European cities, from Constantinople/Istanbul to Helsingfors/Helsinki before the waves of national assimilation and ethnic cleansings.

The change has been enormous because of its concentration to certain cities, mainly capital or otherwise central cities. In Amsterdam about half of school children are of immigrant background, and in Paris in 1990 a third of all youths below 17 lived in a family of immigration. In the early 1990s 'non-whites' made up a fifth of the Greater London population. In Frankfurt and Brussels a good quarter of the resident population are 'foreigners'. (Therborn, 1995:49–50)

Even if one, as this writer, considers multiculturalism as an asset, sociology and history teach us, that it is not unproblematic. What 'Europe' will mean to the West Indians or Bangladeshis in Inner London, to the Mahgrebins in the suburbs around Paris, to the Turks and the Kurds in Berlin and Frankfurt is far from self-evident. And if there will be little or no proper space for them on the labour market and for their cultures among the cultures of Europe, the ensuing society will not be the normative area of the Council of Europe with its recognition of the rights of diversity.

The prospects for a rich, peaceful, and stimulating multiculturalism versus those of ghettoization, crime and ethnic strife and violence are difficult to assess. Evidence available so far belies any straightforward extrapolation in either direction. Unemployment hits proportionately more immigrants and immigrants' children than natives. The immigrant population tends to have a higher crime rate than the native. Xenophobic and ethnic violence has become part of social life all over Europe. Nativist parties and politicians have gained widespread support in several countries, notably in Austria, Belgium, France, and Switzerland. Protest riots against racism and discrimination have occurred in Britain, France and Germany.

On the other hand, there are also a large number of positive inter-ethnic contacts, including marriages. Public policy and public opinion are strongly in favour of multicultural integration. The immigrants, for their part, are not reducible to passive objects of discrimination. As migrants they tend to represent the more vigorous and active part of their original population. Therefore it is not surprising that many of them, or their children, do very well at school. The raw school records do not take class into account, which gives a distorted picture of school performance and migration. In all countries there is a considerable new ethnic entrepreneurship, and also, in the areas of concentration, a new ethnic politics.

To conclude, even if disaster scenarios are unlikely, Western European societies of the future are likely to be less cohesive than in the past, harbouring more mechanisms of exclusion than in the 1960s and 1970s. And certainly, there will be less of any unity or social integration rooted in ancient European culture and identity. Even the memory of the fatal national wars will disappear as a centripetal force – already in a few years, when the generation of Helmut Kohl leaves the political front stage. However, there are as yet no tendencies of socioeconomic and/ or cultural polarization or segmentation in sight likely to break up the institutional inertia, either of 'Europe' or of the Western European nation states.

The East-West divide

The adoption of capitalist democracy in Eastern Europe has not turned out to be a quick fix of Northwestern European prosperity. But, how high the costs of systemic change have been, and for how long they will have to be paid, is controversial and uncertain, respectively. To analyze them is completely outside the scope of this chapter. However, in order at least to hint at the magnitude of making one Europe, a couple of indicators are needed.

Unicef data on life expectancy show a clear difference between, on one hand, the countries of the former Soviet Union and the Balkans and, on the other, Poland, Czechia, Slovakia, Slovenia, and, with qualification, Hungary. The latter group maintained their late-Communist mortality rates during the first years of the 1990s and have already started to improve, although not yet at the rate of improvement during the 1980s. The successor states of the USSR (including the Baltics) and the Balkans on the other hand, have experienced a dramatic decline of life expectancy, which was already considerably lower than in Western Europe even before 1989–91.(Unicef, 1995:24ff, 143) As increased life expectancy is one of the very few development indices in which even sub-Saharan Africa has been able to participate, the 1990s decline in post-Communist Eastern Europe is a serious sign.

By the turn of 1997–98 only Poland was at least back at its GDP of 1989 (in the Polish case somewhat above both the pre-crisis peak of 1978 and 1989). Eastern Europe (except the ex-USSR) as a whole was about 8 per cent below its level of 1989. Before the crisis of 1998, the GDP of Russia was less than 60 per cent of its 1989 level. Consumption expenditure figures give a somewhat brighter picture. According to them, the 1989 was reached by 1995–96 in Croatia, the Czech Republic, Poland, Romania and Slovenia. In the other countries, real consumption expenditure had not reached its level under Communism (UN, 1998:146–47).

Thereafter, there has been a substantial recovery. By 2005, only Bulgaria out of the latest EU members was still below its overall economic level of 1989. Latvia and Lithuania were about level, and the others significantly above the economically not very glorious year of 1989. Russia (index 88), Ukraine (59), and Serbia (58) were still well below, but not Belarus (123, on a par with the Czech Republic and Estonia) (UNECE, 2006:15). Nevertheless, there is a persistent gap between East and West. In 2004 the OECD (2004:194) calculated that with the growth rates of 1995–2003 it would take Poland thirty-seven years to close *half* of that gap, Hungary twenty-nine years.

The East-West divide and the internal polarization in the East will interact with the economic and the ethnic segmentations and tensions in the West, and with the political efforts at wider continental integration. This will probably involve an upper middleclass continental rapprochement – already palpable – a tendency to aggravate the frustrations of the working and of the unemployed classes both from the East and West, without bringing them closer to each other, and, thirdly, to complex webs of continental networks of crime and of illicit business.

Table 14.5   Kinds of standing in the world

	Relative Performance	Model	Power
Political	+/-	+/-	+/-
Economic	+/-	+/-	+/-

4 Conclusion: A second West Germany or Scandinavia enlarged?

The future of Europe in the world is a function of its weight, its specificity and its unity. Western Europe is still a global heavyweight, but it has lost some force and speed. The institutional specificity of European societies as an aggregate remains, but is being subject to erosion both from the inside and from the environment. Globalization is not trumping European-type regionalization. But the most dynamic specificity of Europe, the effort at building a supra-state 'Europe', alongside the continental system of nation states, is facing difficult tasks of unification, within the increasingly segmented Western European societies as well as bridging the recently much widened gap in life chances for the bulk of the population in Eastern and Western Europe.

We may summarize the important possible future positions in the world by Table 14.5.

A plus sign on either political or economic relative performance, in comparison with the average of the world according to prevailing criteria – which may be political efficiency and stability or armed might, and economic growth or level of wealth – is a prerequisite for influence or power. Negative signs on both means underdevelopment or marginalization. In order to distinguish sharply between power and influence I have here called the holder of the latter a 'model'. A model is taken as influential only to the extent that other people choose to regard it as such. Lack of plus signs on both influence (model capacity) and power means insignificance, irrelevance, whatever the objective level of performance. You may also have plus signs in all cells, having both economic and political model influence, as well as power.

Europe is not going to under develop or to be marginalized in the foreseeable future, neither politically nor economically. Europe in the next century will not become the, say, East Africa or Luxemburg of the twentieth century. But will it remain a significant, major player in the world? And if so, will this be as an institutional or policy model or as a power bloc?

'Europe' as a global role model might take on two appearances, not necessarily incompatible with each other. It might appear as an economic model, of market unification and supra-state economic organization, possibly but much less likely of economic institutions in general. 'Europe' might also be taken as a normative model, of human rights, citizenship, gender and generation relations, of supra-national norms and institutions.

As a power bloc 'Europe' is most unlikely to manifest itself in any other form than an economic one, as a continental 'trading-state' of the sort that the West Germans and the Japanese created so successfully after their military defeat. Even a successful EU agreement on a common foreign and security policy is unlikely to yield any globally impressive military power. And without the backing of force and willingness to use it, 'Europe' is unlikely to become a normative power, telling other parts of the world what political, economic and social institutions they should have.

What may happen in the short run, and there are currently clear signs of it, is that old colonial reflexes and secularized vestiges of Christian mission can enlist Europe as an auxiliary force, a global *Hilfspolizei*, of the United States. After some Balkan testing in the 1990s, German troops are at the time of writing proudly patrolling northern Afghanistan for the Americans. Not only the British government and the Polish warriors, but also the rightwing government of the previously very peaceful Denmark are currently relishing in fighting Islamists in Afghanistan and Iraq. It is difficult to see this hunting dog role as sustainable for Europe. The widespread intense British hatred of or contempt for Tony Blair because of his part in the war on Iraq seems to indicate that.

However, in human societies anything can happen. A negative scenario of European recruitment to an endless anti-Islamist crusade, supported by mounting xenophobia at home has become at least conceivable. Large sectors of the Danish and the Dutch populations have already shown how rapidly a liberal bonhomie may be dropped for the frenzy of a frightened petite-bourgeoisie. Also in Sweden, the liberal press was cheering on the American bomber squadrons and missiles against Afghanistan and Iraq.

Were that tendency to gain the upper hand, the influence as well as the power of Europe in the world would soon be gone. At best meaningless and irrational to the new economic heavyweights of East and South Asia, frustratingly incomprehensible to Latin Americans, and hated and despised by the whole Muslim world, a Europe bogged down in Afghanistan, Iraq, or some other American hunting ground has no positive relevance to the ASEAN, the Mercosur, or the African Union. And in the eyes of a ruling America Europe would still remain sissy, because most of the killing would be made by the Americans.

After all, Europe is more likely to keep a significant position in the world of the next century. But not all places in the sun look available. A position as a major politico-military power of global reach is to be ruled out for Europe, as far into the future as any eye can see – except among some nostalgic politicians in the ex-big-power countries, who are looking into their rear-view mirror Acceptance as a significant economic institutional model appears very unlikely, for the time being. Lacking the American back-up of military muscle, mass culture and elite economics education, European economic role-modeling would have to rely – at least to begin with – almost exclusively on clearly superior economic performance, once the inspiration to other regional market arrangements has been spent. There have hardly been any signs of that in the past twenty years, and it is unlikely that aging Europe will provide the world with any new economic achievements impressive enough to compare with either side of the Pacific.

This leaves us with two possible (positive) options, which do not necessarily exclude each other, but could very well mix in various combinations. One would be the position of a major purely economic power, the other that of a socio-political

Table 14.6   Europe's positive futures

	Model	Power
Political	'Scandinavia'?	-
Economic	-	'Trading state'?
		'Germany'

institutional model of some significance of influence, even if generally accepted as such. In the former case Europe would become a sort of post-war West Germany or Japan of the next century, that is, an economically prominent 'trading state'. The other, a Scandinavia writ large.

Both variants are variants of Europe, and have therefore a common background and certain common preconditions of relative success. Both represented a break with a, in the end disastrous, military power past – although the major Scandinavian defeats occurred in the century of 1709–1809. Instead, both followed a concentration on internal socio-economic construction, in neither case economically inward-looking and protectionist, though, but open to and reaching out for the markets of the world. Both the Federal Republic and the Scandinavian countries became eminently prosperous in that way.

They differ in two basic respects: most obviously, of course, in their size and significance in the world., but also in their interest in social experimentation and in universalistic social norms. 'No experiments', was once a winning electoral slogan in post-war West Germany, whereas 'social reform' has been a persistent aim of successful Scandinavian politics. Scandinavians have also been outstandingly active in pushing universalistic and supra-state norms, in the Council of Europe, in the United Nations and the UN Conferences and Conventions, in the Palme and Brundtland Commissions and in the most recent Commission on Global Governance. German foreign policy has had a strong supra-state component in the commitment to European unification, but has not shown any strong universalistic interests.

Both variants are built on strong, if differently organized, forms of social integration, and both require a well-managed prosperous economy. But there is one major difference in the economic prerequisites. The German-type economic power play requires the constant reproduction of a sharp competitive edge of a long economic blade. A Scandinavian-type role model only needs some sharply competitive niche capacity and maintenance of a certain amount of relative prosperity.

For the future, both a Germany- and a Scandinavian-type Europe will require some positive solutions to the two major problems of European unity – the economic-cultural divisions within Western Europe and the gaps between Eastern and Western Europe. A European 'Scandinavia 'will demand a maintenance of characteristically European institutions as well as new endeavours with regard to human and citizenship rights in the world. A European 'Germany' will have to produce new generations of large-scale competitiveness.

In the beginning of the twenty-first century, Europe has three major options. It can solidify its position as the world's leading trader, and as such a big economic power, which will not be very easy to achieve, given the surging economic dynamism of East Asia and India. But its skills in financial and other business services, and the pooled economic clout of the Union provide Europe with a fair chance in the intermediate run.

A disaster scenario, not to be ruled out, is Europe as the hunting dog of the United States, providing supporting bellowing, helping to drive the prey into the guns of the Americans, and taking care of the prey killed. It is certainly the explicit option of very few, but it might come about by politicians dreaming of re-gaining lost world power, of ideological zealots and crusaders dreaming of a world safe for 'Western values', and the support of angry xenophobes and racists.

A third option is to develop Europe as a social model, of economic efficiency combined with trans-national law, relative equality, social security, and humane social relations, of ecological awareness and commitment, of multi-national/multi-cultural coping. A social continent prepared to help others in need, but abstaining from ambitions to the dictate the good to others, as well as from bombardments and invasions.

Which ideal-typically stereotype option to choose is a matter of preference. But my guess is that at least by the second half of the twenty-first century the best Europeans can hope for is to constitute a nice, decent periphery of the world, with little power, but with some good ideas.

Notes

1   An interesting symptomatic reading of this new ideological export is provided by Galal and Shirley (1994), a publication oozing the zeal of true believers Justly, the editors recognize Lady Thatcher's United Kingdom as the 'pacesetting privatizer' (p.6).

2   The issue of human rights is, of course, much more serious and difficult in the Americas than in Western Europe, but according to Chilean human rights activists interviewed in Santiago in January 1996, the new American institutions are doing a good job.

3   A good example is the World Bank's country report on Hungary: 'International comparison shows that Hungary spends a far larger share [about the same as that of Austria or Italy] of its resources on welfare than other market economies at similar stages of development. .... if Hungary is to join the ranks of high-income countries, reforming its welfare system is a sine qua non.' (World Bank, 1995:b:25. Italics in the original.) The report then goes on to spell out, that if you don't severely cut pensions rights and abolish general family allowances you will never join the rich.

PART IV
Reconsiderations

Chapter 15

European Union, Regionalism, New Multilateralism: Three Scenarios

Mario Telò

1 New regionalist studies and European integration studies: Two bridges

To what extent is the discussion, concerning the European Union and its international role, a crucial part of the broader debate on new regionalism? The first bridge between European integration studies and comparative regionalist studies is the controversial international salience of the regional cooperation process occurring in Europe since 1945. We focused Part II of this volume on this side of the question. This books takes explicit distance from two extreme theses: the EU as 'the model for regional integration' in the classical 'Balassian' understanding, which has been even more recently revived and is rejected by all the authors of this volume, in clear terms by R. Higgott. Secondly, this volume rejects the opposite idea: according to several scholars, that all that we learned from comparative research is the European exceptionalism, that is the impossibility of a unique experience to interact, in terms of mutual learning, by deepening similarities and differences, with other paths to regional cooperation. In our understanding the European continent (and not just the EU, but also the Council of Europe, the OCSE, and so on) still provides the most complex, rich and elaborated workshop of regional cooperation/integration in the world, namely of institutionalized integration. That's why we absolutely need further comparative studies including the European case, out of teleological and evolutionistic models.

The second bridge between the EU experience and regional cooperation abroad is the main topic of the present concluding chapter: we will focus attention on the consequences of the occurring transformation of the EC/EU from a mere regional regime into an international actor in the making, establishing relations with other continents and regions and addressing the theoretical question of the nature of its 'power'. Many questions still remain open regarding both its institutional capabilities and its ability to cope with the uncertainties of the globalized world after the Cold War .[1] However, this major change is a matter of facts: the open question is whether the European international regime is moving towards a mere entity, or a player, or an actor, or already a new kind of power. Not only the article by B. Hettne but also several insights provided by Söderbaum, Vasconcelos, Seidelmann, Joffé and Therborn show how relevant the international size of the EU influence is both in the near and the far abroad, allowing to define it as the second global actor after the USA, to which it can be assimilated in terms of GDP (about 12 000 billions

Euros in 2006) and share of global trade (about 20 per cent). To what extent does a
regional kind of power entail several distinctive features as far as both the internal
governance and the contribution to external governance are concerned? To what
extent are its cooperative nature, support of regionalism elsewhere and setting of
inter-regional regimes, able to change the surrounding and global system, beyond
the anarchy, unipolarism and classical sphere of influence Realpolitik?

2 EU as an international actor in the making?

The self-consciousness of the EC/EU as a proactive region of the world and its
inter-regional cooperation are essential elements in understanding it as a new
international actor. To deepen the theoretical implications of this crucial topic, we
firstly need to focus on the empirical side of the evolving interaction between the
economic and political dimensions of EC/EU external relations.

2.1 The EC/EU as a global economic actor

Even in the difficult times of the bipolar world, the European Community was
considered as a highly significant example of the inadequacy of a state-centric
paradigm, the declining role of force and the growing importance of transnational
interdependence.[2] The famous K.Deutsch definition of an 'amalgamated security
community'[3] or area of peace, is a concrete consequence of intense regional
integration at economic and social levels according to the J. Monnet model, or of a
successful 'internal foreign policy', in Habermas' words. The very first definition
of Europe as a 'civilian power' has such a theoretical background. Tocqueville
already categorized trade policy as foreign policy. The Common Trade Policy is the
core of external economic relations.[4] In a few decades, the European Community
became an economic and trade power with growing influence. It was the first trade
power since 1996, a net exporter of products to the so-called emerging economies
and was the first foreign investor and aid provider. European states are no longer the
predominant economic powers they used to be pre-Second World War, however,
four members of the G8 are European and, similar to the US, European Union
constitutes one-fifth of the world's economy.[5]

It would be wrong to speak of the strength of *individual* Western European
countries: such an enhanced global economic weight is largely the consequence of
a successful regional integration process. Since the Single European Act and the
Maastricht Treaty, the EC/EU is becoming even more proactive as a multilateral
international entity. In fifteen years, the Community and Union have created both
on bilateral and increasingly on region-to-region bases, an important network of
institutionalized international agreements. Europe acts either as a supranational unit
(as it does within the WTO and international and interregional trade arrangements)
or by cooperation and coordination among member states.[6]

Summing up, whatever our critical evaluation of their differentiated impact
might be, several crucial 'post-Westphalian' tendencies have to be stressed as far as
the external relations of EC/EU are concerned: the successful enlargement process

and the association pacts and bi-regional agreements often explicitly supporting regional cooperation among partners. For example, the ACP Convention and the regional arrangements in Africa, the bi-regional agreements with MERCOSUR and other Latin American groupings, the ASEM process, the association agreements with Eastern European countries and the Mediterranean process, illustrate (with various degrees of success) an EC/EU strategic preference for *region-to-region cooperation*, even if often mixed to bilateral conditionality. Secondly, many international and domestic factors result in the border between economic and political dimensions of regional cooperation, no longer constituting a 'Chinese wall'. For example, the external representation and implications of the single currency are highly sensitive political issues, despite depending on the first pillar. The political impact of trade disputes and negotiations, particularly, the various difficult challenges related to the Uruguay Round, the Millennium Round, the Doha Round of the WTO were also a feature of this 'politization' of civilian issues. The political dimension of economic and trade external relations are becoming clear, and the realistic classic criticism of the European economic and trade power, as a mere part of the bipolar balance of power, was eventually questioned after the Cold War. To what extent is the scepticism expressed, by R. Gilpin among others, regarding, on the one hand, the huge dependency of EC regional integration on the 'pax Americana' (that is, on US hegemony), and on the other hand, the primacy of states, still a satisfying explanation?[7]

2.2 The Common Foreign and Security Policy

We are witnessing a spectacular evolution, spanning from the low profile of the very first decades after the Second World War, to the years after the end of the bipolar world. The growing expectations by third parties and the very ambitious self-defining aspirations asserted by the Treaty of European Union (TEU, Maastricht, 1992) are particularly significant in the next evolution. Recalling briefly the history of political cooperation may be helpful in better understanding its significance and limits.

After the failure of the European Defence Community in 1954, and the rejection of the 1961 'Fouchet Plans', the political dimension became a taboo. A step in a new direction was the Summit of The Hague in 1969, the first summit of the 'post de Gaulle era' and of the new 'Brandt era'. The six Heads of State and government called at that time for 'a united Europe capable of assuming its responsibilities in the world of tomorrow'. The first declaration for political cooperation came in the next Luxembourg Summit and, already by 1973; the Nine established the EPC (European Political Cooperation) and a principle of consultation among member states before taking political foreign policy decisions. Even if ineffective, the 1978 'Venice Declaration' on the Israeli–Arab conflict was the most famous example of this new activism and of the emergence of a partial disengagement from the previous identification to the American policy.[8] The 1981 'London Report', which associated the European Commission with the EPC process, replacing cooperation with joint action as an EPC main goal, and also the Single European Act of 1986, which institutionalized the ECP in the framework of the Treaty and partially associated the European Parliament to the process, were the next significant steps taken by the EPC. The EC identified nine areas in which European political cooperation could be developed: CSCE, Council of Europe, East–West, Cyprus, Middle East, Africa (South Africa and the Great Lakes), Latin America and the USA.

In the new international context, characterized by the declining power of Russia and by the increase in the weight of the unified Germany, the 1989 Franco-German initiative was historically important, even if not as yet sufficient to achieve a political union in Europe. The preference by new Germany for deepening European cooperation, instead of asserting its new national identity, has been the crucial background for any further development and, in general, the tendencies towards a 'renationalization of foreign policy' have been contained.[9] However, Maastricht's dual decision to create a monetary and political union (including a common security policy) was unable to correct the internal asymmetry of the integration process, namely the gap between the huge international weight of the EC, as an economic and commercial world player, and its political role.

Indeed the objectives set by the Treaty of Maastricht, establishing the so-called 'second pillar' (Common Foreign and Security Policy), independent from the European Community procedures but belonging to the same house,[10] the new European Union, emerged difficult to implement. The Lisbon European Council (1992) was a move in the evolution towards a settlement of concrete common priorities.[11] The European Councils of Essen (1994), and particularly after the Saint Malo meeting (Chirac-Blair) the ones in Cologne and Helsinki (1999) influenced the development of the so called European common defence policy. However, the balance of the achievements of the first years of CFSP and ECDP is widely considered modest by international literature. The pan-European and enlargement policies are more successful, as far as the pre-membership association agreements are concerned, than regarding partnership with neighbouring countries so far. By contrast, the Mediterranean dialogue is very problematic. European policies during the 1990s regarding civilian wars and tragedies in the former Yugoslavia are considered a 'Debutante Performance'.

As regards the global action, the ASEM process stated in 1996, the framework cooperation agreement with MERCOSUR, the bi-regional process started in 1999 in Rio and the new ACP Conventions have a double meaning. They give an initial answer to external expectations for an expanding and global role for the EU and they push the EU beyond the traditional trade dimension or cooperation policy. Political dialogue with the near abroad, and with Asia, Latin America and Africa increase European responsibilities in stabilizing world politics after the end of the Cold War. Nevertheless, there is no evidence that the previous large gap between stated aims and economic power on the one hand and, on the other, political actions, operational abilities and diplomatic representation has truly been overcome.[12] As far as common foreign and security policy is concerned, even if the Amsterdam Treaty increased visibility and allowed a more flexible decision-making process, the procedure still included, even in the Nice treaty, a veto right.[13] As a consequence, very contradictory facts characterize the beginning of the new century. On one side there exists the confirmed political and technological dependency of Europe on American leadership regarding the revival of 'power politics' (Kosovo war,

Iraqi war) and the reluctance of European states and peoples to provide for their military security. On the other side, the practice of collaboration, the institutional spillover and the willingness of several member states and of EU institutions to react collectively to external challenges, is making both external expectations and the European international role, stronger then ever before, even in the controversial and dangerous context following 2001(informal international terrorism and New US Security Strategy, 2002).

When analyzing the described mix of discontinuity and continuity in a global assessment of the EU external relations and actions, one should mention two main points. The first is the increasingly *extended multidimensional presence* of both the Union and member states worldwide after the end of the Cold War,[14] and secondly, the more 'active identity' of the EU.[15] The EU is the second global player and is considered thus by third parties. No doubt that since the end of the Cold War and the collapse of the USSR, European regional association is less dependent than previously on American security strategy and threat perceptions. Most of the chapters printed here underline such a discontinuity and, in particular, the importance of the inter-regional dialogue in the new institutional framework and international environment. Prior to the Treaty of Maastricht, the EC was an economic entity with initial political impact, playing a minor international role. The European states were under the umbrella of American multilateral hegemony. In the new international environment, however, the will of member states to cope more efficiently with external opportunities and responsibilities and also with the internal spillovers of the EC/EU process allow one to speak of a *new European regionalism*. That does not only refer to deepening integration policies but also to giving an active contribution – as a single entity and not only as a sum of member states – to filtering and shaping international economic and political relations.

3   Beyond the idealist concept of 'civilian power Europe'

The concept of 'civilian power Europe' is reoccurring, though with multiple meanings. One is a euphemism, a synonym of semi-sovereign power. Indeed, every observer notices that, if confronted with a revival of power politics (for example, the. Kosovo and Iraqi war), the EU remains under the American shadow or shows internal rifts. Despite the end of the Cold War and the EC/EU success story (Single Market and Monetary Union), the so-called 'French way' to international power[16] prescribed by H. Bull in the early 1980s, still seems beyond European capabilities. Bull described it as a notion of European political power 'comparable with the dignity of nations with the wealth, skills and historical position of those of Western Europe'. What is behind the reluctance of many European states and citizens to devote a part of their wealth in order to provide for their security? Firstly, different national visions, as far as the future of Europe in the world and as far as the relationships with the US are concerned,[17] play a role. Secondly, controversies surrounding the institutional form of Europe as a political power can also explain this reluctance: for many, enhanced supranational unity would be a weakness and not a strength in defence policy. Moreover, the current system of a rotating Council

Presidency is structurally weak because it is temporary, part-time, and is not as yet based on any diplomatic apparatus. Finally, as far as the internal feedback is concerned, the further external relations are extended, the more it is causing a huge coordination difficulty among the various dimensions of external relations (trade, cooperation policy, foreign policy, external implications of internal security, and so on) due to the pillar structure and the lacking coherence.[18]

However, the concept of 'civilian power Europe' is richer in nuances than the narrow notion of semi-sovereign power. There are two good reasons for dwelling on the analysis provided by F. Duchêne and R. O. Keohane and J. S. Nye during the Cold War. The European Community had already been defined as more than a mere economic power but not as 'a superpower in the making', by J. Galtung, in 1973. François Duchêne focused his pioneering notion of 'civilian power Europe' both on its internal and external roles of civilizing and domesticating relations between member states and also on spreading civilian and democratic standards. He wrote, 'this means trying to bring to international problems the sense of common responsibility and structures of contractual politics, which have been in the past associated exclusively with 'home' and not foreign, that is alien, affairs'.[19] In spite of the limits set by the bipolar world, the EC started to become an international entity, without any military dimension by focusing on norm setting. However, it was also able to exercise its influence on states, international and regional organizations, multinational corporations and other transnational bodies through a wide variety of diplomatic, economic and legal instruments. Furthermore, the aforementioned international relations scholars have studied the EC, emphasizing the external implications of its internal successful integration process. It has particularly been stressed that the concepts of power and of foreign policy are no longer as clearly defined as in the past and also that the traditional distinction between political and economic dimensions and between high and low politics are becoming quite obsolete, even within international relations theories.[20]

The famous 1989 letter by Kohl and Mitterrand proposing to the twelve to strengthen the European political dimension, in order to be able to cope with the new post-Cold War challenges and the Maastricht decision to create both a Monetary and Political Union, are symbolic of the EC/EU opportunity to tremendously increase its presence and to strengthen its international identity.[21] The external acknowledgements and expectations are helpful in so far as the EU institutions are seeking international and inter-regional agreements, with the aim of enhancing both the EU's visibility and internal legitimacy.

What about the terminus *ad quem* of such an evolution? According to a large part of the literature, the EU is becoming a global actor.[22] 'Actorhood' raises the question of the criteria of the actor's capability, in comparison with the model of the nation state and, more particularly, with the US: a community of interests, a decision-making system, an independent system for crisis management, a system of policy implementation, external communication channels and representation, an appropriated amount of common resources. To what extent has the EC/EU achieved a satisfactory degree of actorhood in the main areas of external relations? The previous type of semi-sovereign civilian power was able to cope as a second range power with the bipolar world, however there is no evidence that an enlarged EU, can, cope with the globalized and uncertain world of the twenty-first century.

Thirdly, there is a crucial theoretical problem: how and to what extent can a regional 'civilian power' evolve towards a more open political dimension without following the classical French pattern of 'Europe puissance', which was over-illustrated by H. Bull? It is not sufficiently clear what a non-state-like political Union can be, in terms of power definition. What kind of political and military capacity is necessary to overcome the current, already mentioned, picture of a '*Candide*' Europe and to act effectively as a more independent actor facing the new global and regional threats?

This volume focuses on the institutional variables: namely the evolving revision of the Treaties. The delicate topic of security policy, the 'Petersberg tasks', included within the Amsterdam Treaty (1997), the programme to build a military capacity approved in 1999 and the provisions for an 'enhanced cooperation' in the treaty of Nice (2000) represent modest but concrete innovations. This applies even if their implementation in the case of regional crises is far from evident and even if, ultimately, such an evolving European international identity is not as yet at the level of a fully achieved, coherent, reliable, credible international political power.[23]

The institutional dimension of external relations deserves an increasing place within international scientific literature. The EU's legal status is still unclear because the member states have not yet provided the status of an independent subject of international law, while in contrast the legal status granted to the EC and the Constitutional Treaty is not yet ratified.[24] But the most important point is that the decision-making process and implementation of foreign policy and external relations are particularly affected by the lack of centralization, which causes incoherence and inconsistency among the three pillars of the existing Treaty. There are actually three external relations systems: the EC, highly centralized (trade policy) the second and third intergovernmental pillars and finally the member states foreign policies, where decentralization makes the decision making a two level game (national and supranational). Notwithstanding the wishes of the article 3, two centres of decisions (Council and Commission) are diminishing the EU/EC external efficiency. Europe lacks hierarchical, centripetal, legitimized decision making, including – even if of course unlike the so-called 'Imperial Presidency' of the USA – a stable, full-time, legitimized central Council and European Council presidency.[25] This would constitute a realistic centralization in difficult political matters, balancing the internal polyarchy and the fragmentation of multilevel actors taking part in the decision and implementation processes. As T. J. Lowy pointed out, in the USA crucial foreign political issues, fragmented governance and polyarchy are centralized, better and clearly substituted by decisions of the unified élites[26] while, on minor issues, decisions and implementation are taken according to the fragmented or polyarchic pattern. What about the EU way?

The Constitutional treaty (2004) provides original solutions combining decentralized European multilevel governance with centripetal tendencies. The reformed European institutions, particularly the new Foreign Minister supervising both the European Commission and the European Council external competences, would support coordinated decisions and actions. This reform will be on the next agenda, whatever the destiny of the Constitutional treaty will be. Furthermore, the national Ministries' so-called Europeanization process, namely the routine of working jointly with fourteen partners and of regularly taking their points of view and interests into account when formulating national preferences, substantially changed thousands of high-ranking civil servants' vision and practice, especially those who attended the various specialized Councils of Ministers. It is provoking to a certain extent a dynamics of institutionalization of the Brussels regimes, a feeling of common identity, of shared values and aims.[27] Beside any teleological illusion, how to explain almost sixty years of progress, high citizen expectation and also some very ambitious statements and some steps accomplished even by Euro-sceptic member states?[28] However, the growing international role of the EU and its relations with other regions of the world is not only explained through the positive sum play within the Council but also by the converging dynamics of interests, values and institutions.

The current institutional evolution needs to be correctly interpreted. On the one hand, the European Union is not a state in the making. The causes of the still highly decentralized polity are of structural nature. Firstly, they are to be found in the heterogeneous national interests and different visions of the Union's future, as shown by the routinized bargaining between the supporters of an increased internal consistency and the defenders of the symbols and practices of national sovereignties.[29] Secondly, they are to be found in the overlapping and conflicting competencies, the internal pluralism and lobbying, the lack of hierarchies, the continuous negotiation among different levels and various bodies, the two poles of external relations (Council and Commission) and the multidimensional structure as far as European Commission external relations are concerned (divided among many DGs), which inevitably hinder the EU's ability to decide and to act as a state.

On the other hand, inter-governmentalist approaches underestimate the centripetal spillover provoked by converging interests and common policies, as far as the first pillar and EMU are concerned. They also underestimate the impact of institutions on state's behaviour: the simple fact that thousands of national civil servants and representatives of ministries have been accustomed, through routine cooperation of many decades, to paying fundamental and continuous attention to the EU-partners by stating positions and agendas has changed their national preferences. However, contrary to the federalist hopes, the second global player is not a state, neither is it a republic of republics, nor a unique and coherent political actor. It is instead a *regional polity*, an original institutional construction. The Constitutional Treaty would not fundamentally change this feature: it would, however, put an end to the most evident deficits in terms of external consistency and coherence: that the EU has no E. Council President, no single and hierarchical diplomatic body and no single Minister of Foreign Affairs; finally it would change the current lack of loyalty among states and between them and the EU: despite the fact that participating in the European common policy strengthens the international weight of the member states, the simple coordination of national foreign policies within international organizations as the UN and conferences sometimes happens.[30]

Our theoretical conclusion is that *institutions fundamentally matter when dealing with regional civilian powers*. Changes in rules and legal settlements might induce changes in the policies and behaviour of member states. They also largely explain, the strength and the weakness of fifty years' achievements, the *sui generis* nature of the EU, as a special kind of international actor, a 'strange power'. All in all, the EU contrasts with a classical state and particularly with a superpower, which gathers both soft influence and hard power, namely the means to implement its aims in different fields: ideology, politics, economics, finance, military field, nuclear technology. But regional integration is already so deeply advanced that the rescued European nation state does not have very much in common with the sovereign state of the first half of the twentieth century and very little option than underpinning the established regional polity.

4 New regionalism and multilateralism: three scenarios

The following three scenarios are based on different interconnections between EU, new regionalism and globalization. To conclude the present introduction by drawing scenarios seems to be a realistic way of expressing the uncertainty of the current developments both of the European Union and of the international system. This avoids 'would be thinking', that is challenging in a trivial way Europe as it is, as opposed to Europe as it should be, or presenting black/white pictures of the present debate between alternative options. The evolving international role and identity of the EC/EU are not analysed as the world's centre, but as a still salient aspect of evolving global trends.

4.1 Back from political regionalism to regionalization within a globalized economy?

This book does not trust that the over-simplified image (paradoxically proposed both by 'apocalyptic' and 'integrated' visions) of Europe as 'a mere free trade area' is a realistic option. The first scenario rather shows an apparent continuity with the existing low profile 'civilian power', however, under the condition of a stop in the deepening process of regional integration. In parallel, the already-decided or planned Eastern and Mediterranean enlargements of the EC/EU are creating a new geopolitical reality. There are two versions of this scenario. In the most optimistic hypothesis, the EU is conceived as diffusing the historical benefits of the European construction (peace, stability, democracy and prosperity) on a continental scale and in the near abroad. In the worst hypothesis, this '*Candide* Europe scenario' would be firstly shacked by the international security troubles. Secondly, given the widened economic gap between the many parts of Europe, the huge financial, social, political and cultural challenge linked to enlargement and the uncertainties regarding the Eastern border, the traditional positive trade-off between widening and deepening of the EC/EU would be interrupted. In case of further institutional inertia a major economic and political decline of political actorness and an increasingly overlapping and fragmented European polity.

Let's examine this scenario in more detail, regarding the other features of the EC/EU and their external role: EMU could either fail because of a lack of political authority, or it could survive. However, it would be very doubtful that the

Economic Monetary Union would do more than stabilize the economies of member states and prevent internal disintegration. The Single European Market would be largely diluted as a part of a continental and Mediterranean free trade area and within worldwide liberalization. The *acquis communautaire* would not disappear but would certainly be faced with gradual erosion. The 'Brussels model' of deep regionalism would be downgraded, by withdrawing to a special kind of regional grouping within American economic and political globalism.

What do we mean by a new, overlapping and fragmented European polity? According to the 'new-Medievalist' school of thought the European Union would only become a diplomatic coordination of apparently 'sovereign' nation states, occupying territorial spaces but no longer controlling what goes on in those spaces.[31] The political authority lost by nation states would not be centralized at supranational level but would mainly shift elsewhere, towards public and private bodies. Within European Studies, an important school of thought emerges, analyzing the consequences of the possible blockade of the dynamics of political integration. For an European polity, as a non-hierarchical, centrifugal, variegating, overlapping set of policies, including increasing problems of democratic legitimacy, the concept of '*condominio*' – a complex mix of functional and territorial constituencies and forms of governance remains relevant.[32] According to other observers a maintained intergovernmental cooperation including common rules and procedures, mutual expectations among partners could continue with a two-level game.[33] While the national level would rather be a voluntarist framework than a shell, really protecting what happens inside, the intergovernmental cooperation would be more like a mere set of international regimes, than a political community.[34]

Regarding the socio-economic contents of such a weak European polity, two versions have been outlined. For this European-rich corner of the world, the present book offers on the one hand, a relatively optimistic view: should a certain degree of territorial stabilization of such a new multilevel polity be possible, it would partly be comparable with the semi-sovereign Bonn Federal Germany of 1949–90. Europe could keep its international image of being a relatively ecologically and socially conscious continent, but politically divided and militarily weak. Such a heavyweight entity within the international economy, rich in specificity, would be challenged because of international competitiveness and of demographic changes (immigration flows and free movement of people, not only as a consequence of eastern enlargement). However, it is true that these latter threats are frequently overestimated by protectionists. According to several *longue durée* observers, for instance, Göran Therborn, 'there is no evidence of European marginalization either pending or current', in spite of the broadly diffused visions of an 'inexorable struggle' for world competitiveness and market. Under this condition, in spite of eastern and southern enlargement and globalization, Europe will continue to play an influence-role in the world.

On the other hand, less optimistic comments emphasize that the 'Bonn-GFR type' Europe, in order to maintain social integration and a prosperous economy, would require a sharp competitive edge to survive within the global economy. Most observers agree that this scenario would necessarily diminish, on a global level, the profile of the EC/EU as an economic and trade giant and its ambitions not only as a European power but also as a European influence is concerned. Somehow such a timid Europe would go back to the kind of regionalism, typical of the first decades of European integration. To mention the Federal Republic of Germany, which existed in the decades before German unity, reminds one of the famous picture of an economic giant and half-sovereign political dwarf. According to R.N. Rosencrance, the 'trading state' is a political system where economic growth has no relevant implications, as far as political power is concerned, because the latter remains firmly monopolized in the hands of the leading power of the alliance.[35] All in all, the weight of US and emerging powers could make of Europe the victim of globalization.

The current main supporters of this evolution are economic networks, transnational coalitions of social interests, not only in the US, but in many European countries, and more precisely in the United Kingdom and in the new member states. A way towards this scenario could also be a hierarchical version of a strengthened transatlantic inter-regional entity, including the EC/EU and the sole remaining superpower. Of course, the trade disputes, political obstacles, the failure of the American transatlantic project for a Multilateral Agreement on Investment (1998) and the troubles of similar most recent initiatives, show the huge problems existing between and within European states on this asymmetrical perspective, particularly after the troubles of the Doha Round.

What about its implication for new regionalism worldwide? At the end of the twentieth century, a 'European continental trading state' looked to be a potential part of a general trend: within the globalist strategy of '*emerging markets*', creating free trade mega-arrangements between US and Latin America, FTAA; between US and Asia-Pacific, APEC with EU, a stronger NTA. Such an evolution of the EC/EU would probably have important implications for other regions of the world, putting a stop to European support of the developments for deeper regionalism in Asia, Africa and Latin America. According to Vasconcelos: 'If Europe were only a trading region, then MERCOSUR would be reduced to a "backyard" of the United States'. Would it be the same for every regional association? Hettne's chapter provides relevant inputs on that issue. Every country and region would only have the choice between adjustment of national economies to the imperatives of global markets and catastrophic isolation. Nationalistic or fundamentalist movements, as a reaction to globalization imperatives, are likely to arise somewhere in the world, since these movements would no longer have a regional alternative, as a framework for setting a more gradual and compromising cooperative process. Less would be done against the current marginalization of the poorest countries, which would lose bargaining edges, allied within international organizations. In 2006, the limits of US power and trade strategy both at global and inter-regional levels and the declining interest of US in global governance are clearer and this scenario looks more controversial.

In conclusion, this scenario is relevant as far as economic and political research is concerned. However, something would be amiss, if we go on by variously combining 'New Medievalist' theories with US-imperialist theories, in spite of changes and failures. The twenty-first century starts by showing how controversial is the idea that the globalized international system would be increasingly characterized by what J. Rosenau called 'a bifurcation':[36] on the one hand, a fragmented multilevel soft governance and, on the other, a concentration of high-level political decision that is, a practical shift towards a perpetual dependency on US-centred globalism, both in economic and political terms. No doubt that new regionalism would fail in that scenario, as a dynamic third way of multilateral and polycentric world governance, between unipolar power politics and fragmentation.

4.2   The second scenario: a 'Fortress Europe' as part of a global new-mercantilist competition?

In the uncertain framework of the post-Cold War and post 9/11 world, given the increasing uncertainties of global multilateralism, Europe could strengthen current tendencies to set inward-looking priorities, reducing dependency from partners and allies, as a reaction to both external pressures and internal demands. Economic failures and international threats could exacerbate this. The combination of hard trade disputes and the social demands of economic security could force not only single MS but also the EC/EU to set defensive economic and protectionist policies, and, according to a part of the international literature,[37] also ease a spillover towards enhanced political and military security. The politicization of domestic pressures could be particularly evident in the case of growing instability in the eastern and/ or southern borders of the Union, the arch of crisis.[38] These two demands are not necessarily linked, but the first one creates a background that is favourable to the second one and vice versa. Thirdly, the demands of internal security also play a role in strengthening such a double trend. The perceptions of threats linked to migration flows, terrorism and criminality have already inspired defensive border-control policies at national and European level (as shown by some of the Schengen Treaty provisions regarding immigration and asylum policies).

A kind of institutional reform, fostered by new conflicts and threats in the surrounding world or by a degradation of the multilateral economic and trade system is not excluded, even if it would not occur in line with a federal pattern. In front of the undesirable consequences of the federal and functional patterns,[39] a new confederate polity would be the more realistic institutional consequence of that scenario.[40] The new polity would be based on the revival of the territorial sovereign logic as a major institutional principle, firstly at national level.

Broadly diffused fears and a negative perception of external threats could act in support of the old idea of puissance, the plea to revive the classical concept of international power. Paradoxically, such an evolution happens to be more likely in the case of the failure of the model of Europe as a civilian power that quietly contributes to peaceful external relations and world governance, as a regional stabilizer, and as a resource of economic dynamics for partners and neighbors. Indeed, even if the starting point were economic demands, the trend would be towards political and military power as the only one able to settle disputes and conflicts when the economic, juridical, and ideological powers fail.[41] Against the simple notion of influence, the myth of an European classical power, 'telling other parts of the world what political, economic and social institutions they should have' would cover neo-colonial practices, inward looking protectionist statements and re-nationalized policies.

To what extent is that scenario realistic in the early 21st century? Firstly, several socio-political streams in many Member States and interest networks openly support the idea of Europe, or European States, as a classical economic, political and military power. Relevant industrial and socio-economic sectors (interested in arms cooperation etc) need protection, as well as agricultural interests. Most importantly, the difficulties that emerged during the last decades for the EU in coping both with the challenges of a globalized economy make such a scenario less abstract than during the 1970s and the 1980s.

The latter challenge is on the very first point of the agenda. EU countries are still lagging behind Japan and the US in the areas of information and communication technologies (ICT), employment and growth, and economic competitiveness in strategic sectors. New demands for protecting the domestic market and subsidizing exports (including NTBs) are about to surface because of urgent domestic and sectorial problems. A vicious circle is possible since only a dynamic European economy can finance the costs of social cohesion and of enlargement, the stability plans in the Balkan subregion, the Mediterranean policies, and so on, and compensate the problems created by liberalization in sensitive economic sectors and local districts. Even if global economy provided in the last five years more growth than ever since 1945, large part of European population feels poorer and more marginal and demands for protectionist policies.

What would be the implications for new regionalism and world governance? A shift to multiple conflicts among competing regional blocs (and nations) could result out of the uncertainties of global multilateralism. As far as Europe is concerned, much more than it already does, it could oppose US interests with a general counter strategy of 'Europe-centred' inter-regional agreements and a myriad of 'EC centred preferential free trade areas',[42] whatever biregional or bilateral, including Eastern Asia, Russia, Africa and Latin America. The US is pushing in that direction by setting bilateral PTAs with singles Asian and Latino-American countries. Most Favored Nation clause could become a weapon in provoking trade wars. Setting global multilateral agreements would be increasingly difficult because of growing tensions as far as the global commercial, financial and monetary systems were concerned.[43] Furthermore, the costs of more blocs competition might be sidelined particularly in the developing countries and in the periphery, becoming the victim of struggles between spheres of influence, obliged to opt for one or another contender in the framework of inter-centres competition. The UN system could suffer because of increasing transatlantic conflicts. In conclusion, the fundamental opposition theory of regionalism versus globalism would be revived in a new form.

However, there are some important *caveats* about such an evolution towards scenarios of a kind of new-mercantilist contested globalization:

- It cannot but cause serious divisions among and within European States, according to various interests in expanding the open economy, to variations in the consequences of trade wars in defence of selected geo-economic interests and, lastly, to the various historical pressures of liberalism and protectionism.
- As for the political side of the demand for a harder European power politics, there are huge discrepancies according to national traditions. These include differences between the two nuclear powers themselves and the others,

between the neutrals and the nuclear states, between the five countries with greater experience of power politics (according to the consequence of WW2), and between the staunch defenders of symbols of national sovereignty and hard-line federalists. Lastly, an important cleavage is the people's acceptance of the cost of defence policy in terms of standard of living and of possible input into the democratic scrutiny of European and national decision making. The simultaneous explosion of some of these internal cleavages could possibly disintegrate the EU.

However, imagine the scenario of several regional powers managing the internal economic and political conflicts within their regions. What would be the international implications for world governance? As previously mentioned, global economic and trade organizations would be jeopardized. There would be no automatic spillover; however, the strengthening of defensive regionalism or economic nationalism elsewhere in America and Asia would support various demands for tighter economic protectionism and military security. Most probably, the EU and many regional organizations mentioned in this book would be profoundly transformed in the case of increasing trade and political disputes between trade blocs: either they would disintegrate or they would become hierarchical spheres of influence by a regionally dominating State. Secondly, according to Hettne, Söderbaum and others, even if not highly militarized, the EU would be a factor in the tendency towards a multipolar world. Of course, theoretically, there are many possible forms of a multipolar world. The military concept of multipolarism, replicating the negative experience of the thirties, is no longer relevant. The transformation of multilateralism into hard bargaining between trade blocs, or the emphasis on the classical dimension of power politics in an ambiguous way (whatever the main actors would be – mega-states or regional blocs), is not far from the vision of international relations recently expressed by leaders both in Asia and Europe. It could provide the background for a controlled nuclear proliferation. Traditional international theories consider the balance between various spheres of influence as a realistic basis for a better world government. However, is a step back to the international system of 'balance of power' in the early 21st century conceivable? Such a vision of multipolarism lacks realism, and not only because there is no evidence that the legacy of fifty years of world history could be easily deleted. Consider the primacy of US, the role of international and multilateral organizations, the tremendous development of transnational relations, the development of peaceful and cooperative new regionalism. Certainly, given the uncertainties of the new global framework, the shift from benevolent to malevolent behavior of regional entities should not be excluded. However, even the tendencies towards a new multipolar balance of power should cope with the historical transformations of the last decades at global, regional, domestic and transnational levels.

4.3 The third scenario: new regionalism as a pillar of a new multilateral world order

Research on new regionalist associations transforming into new kind of international actors entails various approaches, both normative and analytical, idealistic and realistic. Contrary to idealized pictures of civilizing and normative power, this volume brings some arguments in favour of a realistic understanding of the evolving regional polities, able to adjust their socio-economic features in the context of globalization, better able to cope with the evolving changing international environment, but unable and/or unwilling to build classical powers.

The European workshop is the most advanced and several authors as Sbragia, Higgott, Eliassen/Arnesen, Söderbaum do underline the differences between the 'Brussels model' and the other paths to regional cooperation. However, many regional entities are already providing their contribution to global governance, by their relationship both with neighbors and far abroad, with big powers and international organizations as WTO, IMF and UN. Under this respect EU is not entirely isolated as a regional entity transforming its internal context and external environment by its very existence. It is relevant for comparative studies and as proactive entity: many writers in this volume suggest new concepts for defining the European Union's international identity beyond the two previously mentioned scenarios. The contributions by Gamble and Padoan describe Europe as a 'strategic' economic actor. Hettne underlines its political relevance as the transatlantic rift and the very different global presence of EU and US are concerned, while keeping open the question of the nature of EU. Comparing with US and with the colonial legacies of European states, Söderbaum, Vasconcelos, Joffé among others well show how controversial is the balance between similarities on the one hand and alternative geopolitical interest and original external relations on the other hand. In our understanding 'civilian power' is matter both of external policies and of the implications of what the EU internal governance already is. While Göran Therborn elaborates the concept of 'Europe as a Scandinavia of the World' in his chapter, emphasizing the socio-economic contents and the potential international influence of Europe as such, R. Seidelmann includes the two distinctive notions of '*political responsibility*' and '*historical learning*' in his concept of 'soft power Europe'. These visions are important pillars of a new research, combining the question of civilian power Europe, with the evolving new regionalism facing the challenges of global governance and world order.

By overcoming the idealistic understanding of civilian power we don't come back to classical realism. By contrary, to show to what extent, in several regions of the world, past conflicts, shared interest and needs of common belonging bring states to opt in favor of cooperation with neighbours and apply the value 'responsibility' to external relations is to emphasize the need of radical innovation of the realist and neo-realist tradition. In some cases, calling for democracy, peaceful settlement of conflict and accountability in foreign policies puts in question the 'Chinese wall' between domestic democratic politics and international power politics, a perennial stake for democratic theory, since Rousseau, Kant, and Tocqueville. Furthermore, to explain EU, MERCOSUR, ASEAN internal foreign policy of reconciliation through shared values goes even beyond F. Duchêne's Euro-centric definition quoted above. In the sole European case, however, 'international responsibility' means, the weight of domestic democratic public opinion, and particularly on *memory of the past tragedies*: on the one hand, keeping alive the best legacy of 2,500 years of Greek *polis*, Roman right, Renaissance and Enlightenment culture,

Christian influences and so on, and, on the other hand, emphasizing the democratic learning process, making of past tragedies and aggressive policies (fascism, colonialism, intolerance, infra-European civilian war, and so on) a resource for people's understanding and good governance. For example, it is useful to compare the salient differences between the German/Italian/Portuguese/Spanish post-fascist learning processes and the Japanese post-war experience and with the tensions between Japan and its neighbours regarding memory of the past and its political impact. That helps by explaining the deep 'realistic' roots of the variously spread diffusion of the idea of peace in different regions of the world. Moreover, the relatively stronger weight of norms in Europe, given the normative multilateral internal network. Is Europe more globally responsible for the public good of world governance than, for example, the US, Japan or China? Are European foreign policies more consistent with the UN's and cosmopolitan values, by defending the common interests of humans (disarmament, peace, environment, economic growth, social justice, the fight against crime and drugs and so on)? This volume fosters impact studies on oscillations and incoherence, which cannot be something else than comparative studies.

We need to combine various disciplinary and theoretical approaches to understand such an original combination of interests and ideas and the practical influence of normative values within the European construction. Furthermore, current constructivist approaches focus on the weight of historical learning and memory, by building people's consciousness and by influencing national and supranational preferences in many policy fields particularly linked to international identity and global role. That is matter of fact in many European countries, either as a heritage of the post-fascist democratic reconstruction or as a traditional national commitment to democratic values, republican aims, or neutral proactive traditions. To what extent such an evolution is occurring also within MERCOSUR and other regional entities? Cognitive regionalism is to some help under this respect.

The realistic background as far as interests and historical forces are concerned has been strengthened after the end of the Cold War: diminishing the weight of nuclear threats and hard security issues, enhanced role of 'idealistic democracies', particularly Germany, Italy, Iberian countries, Benelux, Scandinavia within the European construction. Is Europe a post-modern island? The confidence building measures and the regional cooperation between Brazil and Argentina is considered the best success story of the declining Non Proliferation Treaty. The evolving cooperation between previous enemies Vietnam and Thailand/Philippines within ASEAN is proving the potential of peace setting through economic integration.

The incipient transformation of Europe and of several regional entities into new civilian actors is raising several theoretical questions. To focus more on long-term benefits than on purely short-term utilitarian criteria, as far as foreign relations are concerned, raises the question of the time frame of foreign policy. The theoretical opposition between the 'structural foreign policy' and the 'conjunctural' foreign policy of traditional powers needs to be theoretically deepened. The crucial question is: in which meaning do political dwarfs conceive and implement a 'structural' foreign policy? For example, the Therborn socio-economic perspective provides insights for a first step regarding the present and future European regionalism. His concept of Europe as a 'Scandinavia of the world' means much more than a mere economic entity and deepens explicitly an alternative to both the above-mentioned scenarios. A 'Scandinavian Europe' is not essentially a prescriptive rather an analytical concept, consistent with realized economic and social features and with the awareness of the impossibility of simply importing the American model.

The question is twofold: Firstly, is the European socio-economic model condemned to fail within the globalized economy or can it not only adjust and survive , but further influence the global environment? Secondly, is it one of several resilient regional socio-economic-institutional-values diversities (Europe, East Asia, Latin America, Africa) within the same global market as fundamental features of the world of 21st century? To the second question, this books clearly answers that, not only because of the fragile globalization, we will have more regionalism in the current century than in the last one. And what about the first question? Europe has maintained its peculiarities so far in spite of domestic and international troubles. The diffusion of social justice as a value influencing the social actors and the various national party systems, and, the relatively well developed welfare states demonstrate resilience and continue to shape the wider EU in characteristic ways. Moreover, the European Union is a specific set of intergovernmental and supranational institutions, a process of systemic integration, a 'social mega-network', a normative area, and at least partly governed by European law and common rules. It includes relatively binding human rights protection, and inspiring concentric organizations like the EU, the Council of Europe and the OSCE. A consistent set of common values regarding science and society (including control of genetic manipulation, the defense of human beings against the death sentence, and so on) is surviving globalization. Lastly, as a result of the *acquis communautaire* and the dynamics of European integration the 'EU is perceived in the world as one bloc and attracting many neighbour countries to apply for membership and to accept long and hard training to achieve it'.[44]

Of course, such a socio-economic model is challenged: it is currently facing a double erosion, both from inside (unemployment and huge demographic change) and from outside (competitiveness, immigration flows and so on). The future European socio-economic diversity in the 21st century cannot be the same as in the second half of the 20th century, when Western European states were able to adjust to a less developed economic internationalization by high-performing national welfare states, Keynesianism, 'Rhenan capitalism'[45] and functional regional integration. Even in defending the past achievements, Europe has to be more proactive within the international arena. The huge pressure towards economic convergence and the technological, financial and trade trends are challenging European regionalism to combine competitiveness, technological innovation, economic reforms and social cohesion in new terms. By new terms, we mean more research, more investment in human resources, growth policy, and also new methodologies of vertical and horizontal coordination and coherence among member states, going beyond the old federalism–confederalism debate. A concrete example of new regionalism with a strategic vision and innovation policy, including concrete benchmarking and monitoring, has been offered by the 'Lisbon ten years program' started in 2000.[46] The results are controversial, positive in northern Europe, limited in southern. Larger states resist to deeper regional coordination. However, awareness of lagging behind in the area of international competitiveness might break up the institutional inertia of Europe and of the member states pushing them to start a new era, with a new strategic concept giving a soul to new European Regionalism. Every regional entity is challenged by the building up of knowledge societies, while variously combined with development programs. Europe already is providing references and inputs to other regional paths by its experience and sophisticated modes of governance of national diversities (for example the 'open method of coordination'). Further coordination and deeper integration does not mean building a European state, and setting up a protectionist trade policy either. New forms of European governance on the one hand, and, on the other hand, the process of soft institutionalization of other regional entities is making two-ways communication easier than in the past.

Indeed, the troubles and tensions of global multilateral regulation show that new regionalism, if conceived as a mere assertiveness of regional interests against other regions and powers, would not be a responsible provider of the rare 'public good' of world governance. By its very existence, the EU, up to now, moderates both wild liberal and protectionist member state's policies, but its ability to cope with growing protectionist demands is an open question.[47] Mutatis mutandis, the same uncertainty exists for MERCOSUR, ASEAN and other regional entities. Our insight is that the future of 'Europe as a Scandinavia of the World', strictly depends on the necessary pre-condition that EU and other regional entities could provide the background for a new multilateralism at a global level.

To what extent do similarities between EU and other regional entities have to do with the concept of power? According to Göran Therborn, it is more realistic to talk about influence. Neither the marginalization of Europe nor the building of a superpower Europe, are very realistic, while its influence as a policy model is much more likely to be diffused inwards and outwards: 'a model is taken as influential only to the extent that other people choose to regard it as such'. Rather than a civilian power, he speaks about a civilian 'influence', namely of a particular interest in social experimentation and in universalistic social norms as Scandinavian countries have already demonstrated through their past action in the framework of the UN ('Bruntland Commission', 'Palme Commission', 'Global Governance Commission').

Let us moderate our agreement with some step forwards. The influence of national social and political cultures is an essential part of the European international socio-economic identity, including shared values and varying practices. However, the common institutions are more and more salient in reviving and spreading out such a legacy than in the past. Without strengthening its decision-making process and institutional capabilities and further developing towards a new path as a civilian power, 'Scandinavian Europe' would risk falling into a Volterian '*Candide*' Europe scenario, a victim of hard economic competition and political threats. Even worse, is the case of other regional entities who risk becoming marginal.

What do we mean by a more proactive and regulatory regionalism and, as a vanguard, a new civilian power Europe? We have already stressed the importance of the political global changes occurred in 1989 and 2001. They are challenging regional entities, and namely the EU, to step forwards from external influence to international power, from mere regional governance to an active role in shaping a rule-based multilateral world order. If regional actors, and namely Europe, as international entity have not the means fit to strengthen regional governance and shape the surrounding economic and political environment, malevolent actors, middle or great powers, will marginalize or even break up their values and interests.

Reassessing the relationship to USA within a more balanced and multilevel, multilateral framework is a crucial issue at stake, not only for Europe, but also for every regional entity. Respectively Vasconcelos, Söderbaum, Hettne and Higgott show how relevant the critical relationship to US in the three continents is for the political future of regional cooperation. In Europe, at the end of the bipolar world and particularly after 9/11 (informal terrorism) and the US New Security Strategy, neither founding member states of the EC nor Scandinavian and neutral states, can be satisfied living any longer (explicitly or not) in the shadow of the security provision offered by the traditional transatlantic relationship within a NATO in identity crisis. To become a classical political and military power with centralized leadership is not an option for the EU, nor for regional groupings. However, no doubts that (whatever the destiny of the Constitutional Treaty might be) the European agenda already entails strengthening of common institutions, improving the coherence of external relations, pushing peace-keeping and peace-enforcing missions in the near abroad and beyond, preventing trade wars, settling North–South relations, and defending common strategic interests. Pursuing such ambitious objectives as an isolated regional entity without strategic allies and dynamic and genuine interregional partnerships would be futile.

What concept can we use to describe such a new civilian, militarily limited, soft, responsible, democratic, long-term oriented, economic and political power? Both the member states and the EC/EU have already made some important steps forwards with their foreign policies in terms of conceiving and implementing a European international presence and role. It was the next best option, given the impossibility of becoming a traditional actor of power politics. According to the international scientific literature, the concept of 'structural foreign policy'[48] is able to describe such a strategic and practical evolution. A 'structural foreign policy' affects particularly the economic and social structures of partners (states, regions, economic actors, international organizations, and so on) and it is implemented through pacific and original means (diplomatic relations, agreements, sanctions and so on),[49] and its scope is not conjunctural, but rather, middle of the road and long range. However, the concept of 'structural foreign policy' should be deepened beyond its empirical side.

When speaking of structural power and structural policy within international relations theory, the main references are of the 'structural' new realism developed by Kenneth Waltz[50] and the concept developed within the international political economy. Contrary to Marxist thought, according to Waltz the word structural is not synonymous with economics opposed to the superstructural dimension, namely politics and culture. By 'structure' he means the political perennial structure of the international system. This structure is anarchical, centrifugal, and non-hierarchical. The definition of structural foreign policy should focus on the ability of an international unit to support, even gradually and partially, the changes brought about in such a structural feature of the international system through cooperation among states. The very existence of the EU, making war between former enemies impossible, is already the best example of 'internal' structural foreign policy. The relationship between Brazil and Argentina, between South Africa and neighbouring countries, and between Vietnam and some ASEAN member states, as well, are salient in this respect. This is particularly noteworthy if compared with the India– Pakistan conflict, which has put a stop to regionalism in Southern Asia because of the resilience of great states and of nationalism elsewhere in Asia. We can propose indeed the concept of 'cooperative power', able to prevent conflict and diminish security dilemmas, beyond a competitive international game.

Our general forecast is that, in the 21st century, new regionalism will not only remain a multidimensional feature of the fragile global system, but increase in political relevance. Of course we don't underestimate failures, as the chapter on Mediterranean well shows. The comparative analysis of the regional variations brings us to the conclusion that 'a structural policy' by the EU and by regional entities cannot succeed if it only occurs top-down: it can be successful only when and if deep domestic endogenous bottom-up trends exist within the region limiting anarchy among states. Only when successful regional arrangements emerge limiting the anarchical structure of the regional/global system can the interregional relationship help to further reduce fragmentation and conflicts and strengthen cooperation.

Our critical approach to Waltz new realism benefits from an established theoretical background. Regional cooperation studies benefit from the extraordinary development of the transnational complex interdependence theories and new institutionalism for more than thirty years. The concepts of regional institution and of civilian power would be inconceivable without the theoretical background of the critical analysis of neo-realism developed within the American and international political science field in the 1970s and 1980s.[51] Secondly, as an example of 'international regimes', regional arrangements establish various sets of common rules and procedures, providing mutual information and expectations among member states. This makes transnational interest coalitions easier, limiting uncertainty and security dilemmas. Even candidates for membership are influenced by the club's internal rules as far as their preferences are concerned. Thirdly, the growing network of multiple, informal and formalized, decentralized systems of governance do correct substantially the neorealistic, state-centered vision of a structural anarchy. Even the current deficit of world government, typical of a post-hegemonic era, does not necessarily revive the tendency towards anarchy, fragmentation and mere power politics. Our conclusion is that both the multiple functional networks and also the new regional territorial entities are providing a third level of governance, between local and national fragmentation on the one hand and, on the other, the global level, dominated by declining concentration of political and economic authority by the US.

The key issue at stake is the bridge between regional and global governance. Without being a 'model', the European experience appears to be relevant not only as partial governance of globalization and regulation of national diversities, but also because of its impact on international rules, other regional cooperation arrangements and global multilateralism. That can work only if Europe is not perceived as a 'post-national constellation', a 'post-Westphalian' or 'post-modern' entity, an island of peace, democracy and prosperity opposed to the rest of the world. Regional associations and regime, including the EU are nothing more than parts of a gradual process of revision of the classical state-centered Westphalian system. Take the example of the EU. Its main instrument is 'structural foreign policy', which can be, at least to a certain extent, interpreted as an export of the internal multilateral experience, setting peaceful political relations through economic interdependence. That is shown by means of external relations (economic agreements and sanctions, partnership with developing countries, and so on) and particularly by the so-called bilateral and interregional '*pactomania*', spreading out cooperation agreements over the world. Post-war reconstruction, and in general the so called 'Petersberg tasks', are an essential element of this European international assertiveness. This book takes into account critical views of European 'conditional' bilateral relations, underlining their possible evolution towards a new hegemonic sphere of influence opposed to others and reviving the theories of growing dependency centre-periphery. Our comparative research on regional groupings in Africa, Asia and America proves that external support to regional arrangements by the EU can be successful only if domestic pressures, coming from economic and political orientations within the partner member states, are autonomously pushing towards regional cooperation. It fails because of asymmetrical balance between internal and external factors.[52] In conclusion, structural foreign policies are efficient only if they interact with deep endogenous trends and set two-ways partnerships. Quoting Machiavelli, '*virtus*' is efficient only if combined with '*fortuna*': proactive policies need a favourable objective context.

The international political economy provides a second concept of 'structural power' opposed to the traditional realistic notion of 'relational power'. According to S. Strange, the structural powers are increasingly able to shape the hierarchies of the globalized world. They are indirectly condition the actors' way of acting, by changing the conditions of their behaviour and without forcing them to do something. With the end of the bipolar world, the security structural power is declining while the economic, financial and knowledge-based structural powers are enhancing their role in changing the international economy and affecting world politics.[53] If accepted, this international political economy approach recommends paying much more attention to the decline of the EC/EU in terms of ICT and the knowledge society than to its capacity gap in terms of military power. A regional organization, leader of the international trade and no longer disadvantaged as far as the technologies of knowledge are concerned, would maybe be able of balancing its minor defence power. Our second conclusion is that, within the new framework of evolving structural power, the realistic argument (mentioned among others by H. Bull in the 1980s), opposing the 'contradictory in terms' concept of civilian power to a European classical kind of military power is no longer as conclusive as during the Cold War. However, Bull is perfectly right in emphasizing Europe's need to develop an international actorhood 'compatible with the dignity of nations with the wealth, skills and historical position of those of Western Europe'. However, the huge transformations in the nuclear proliferation (Northern Korea, Iran, India, Pakistan, Israel) and the unstable international system, along with the consequence of the changing perception of threats (see Seidelmann), drastically limit the optimism of the 1990s regarding an emerging peaceful, decentralized global governance. That's to explain our focus on the problematic and controversial link between regional entities and power.

What are the current internal driving forces pushing the EC/EU beyond the previous minor stage of civilian power and structural foreign policy? In other words, to what extent is our third scenario realistic? The EMU and its international implications; the mentioned Lisbon strategy for a 'European way to a knowledge society'; a more strategic management of economic and trade power; the role of the EU as first investor and aid provider to the southern world; the network of interregional arrangements, the first step towards a EU security strategy ('Solana paper' of December 2003). On the other hand, what is missing is: a EU strategic concept of global order, the slow institutional reform and an enhanced coherence among several dimensions of external relations, the single EU voice within international organizations with the exception of WTO (IMF, World Bank, and what is particularly serious is the internal controversy on the enlargement of the UN security council), the problems by reforming the multilateral organizations on the basis of regional representation.

In conclusion, one point is increasingly crucial: the institutional settlement or regional organizations, namely of the EU. As mentioned above, to become more efficient in the long and middle term, to be more consistent and more adaptable regarding the external urgencies, a regional actor providing a structural foreign policy needs to enhance clarity and coherence among the various dimensions of internal multilevel governance and external relations. In itself, developing external relations can bring both more internal fragmentation and enhanced coherence of policies and political unification. Institutional models cannot but be different in various regional contexts. We share a comprehensive vision of institutionalization as both formalized and informal. However, institutional strengthening should, beyond the old state building models '(federal or confederational), might allow the EU and other regional entities to orient the current decentralized multilevel governance towards selected common goals, which looks unlikely given the new methods of governance and of coordination.[54] Secondly, without democratic scrutiny and increased legitimacy of foreign policy and external relations, no relevant international action can be implemented; even if was of a structural nature and with long-term scope, every regulation needs enhanced legitimacy. Thirdly, the institutional architecture of every regional grouping should conciliate deepening and widening, enlargement of membership and efficiency of the decision-making process. In Europe that means that an eventual efficient and open 'hard core' needs to appropriate treaty provisions supporting flexible integration and enhanced cooperation, as a sole alternative to the realistic way of problematic 'contact groups' and informal and controversial directorates of the largest countries. Fourthly, whatever the final institutional path of a regional organization, the issue of political leadership is becoming, according to many authors, the big challenge of the next decade (East Asia, Latin America, Africa, Europe).

Ultimately, new regionalism increasingly faces new threats (failing states, ecological disasters, illegal migration flows, poverty, endemic diseases) and security challenges (fighting informal terrorism and international criminality, isolating Islamic fundamentalism, balancing unilateral policies). As we understand it, contrary to the US perception, major threats and security challenges are mainly regional.[55] A realistic and innovative answer is represented by increased cooperation among neighbouring states, consolidating a bottom-up multilateralism. It is a very uncertain challenge, which will characterize the next decades. The gap between the increasing politization of regional groupings on the one hand and the downgrading of the international agenda, dominated by violence and war, on the other, looked to be growing dramatically in the years of the Iraqi War. Europe is confronted with the controversial issue of the future of its relationship with US. Of course, the historical roots of this alliance and of American primacy have the solid background of the victories against Fascism, Nazism, Stalinism and European militarism. The difficulties facing the UK and several states of a disengagement from the new American security agenda (post-9/11) carries a price in terms of the relationship with other regional organizations and world powers, as clearly shown by the reactions of Brazil, MERCOSUR, Japan, China, India, ASEAN, and so on. to the Kosovo War and to the Iraqi War.

The chances of involving the USA within a new multilateral regulatory framework are linked firstly to the USA itself: namely to what is happening within American society after the failure in Iraq. It is this which is making the global role of the country as a world leader more problematic than in the 1990s. The concept of 'American hegemony' looks as obsolete as Robert Keohane argued some years ago, while the defence of national interests is less so, and the military and economic primacy still survives.[56] In spite of declining leadership, because of its political, economic and cultural interests, the US will not leave East Asia, Latin America and Europe, but the balance between the US agenda and the global agenda will inevitably evolve. Secondly, geopolitical differences between the EU and the US are increasing, as far as economic interests, perceptions of security threats, and the vision of the post-Cold War world are concerned. The international vision and action of Germany, the 'junior European partner' of the US, is currently showing a more realistic balance between continuity and discontinuity. This makes Germany a potential – and partially already present – leader of European new regionalism, both as far as the security policy and the trade policy are concerned. According to the authors of this book, the issue of regional leadership is becoming a relevant one, in East Asia, Latin America and Africa.

In conclusion, the concept of civilian power is not at all an inert legacy of the past, declining within the new global post-Cold War and post-9/11 world system. On the contrary, under certain conditions and out of its idealistic understandings, it belongs to the *longue durée* evolution of the regional entities. However, many of the contradictory – even hypocritical – features of the concept, now belong to the past, since the very evolution of relations among states and of structural power is strengthening the chances of a new international role, of new international actors within the economic and political international system. More so than in the past, the EC/EU can find allies and partners elsewhere to construct less asymmetric world pluri-regional governance. New regionalism is not a panacea, but it could eventually provide further means to brake the tendency towards an increased fragmentation without imposing controversial globalist rules. Finally Europe is not only a laboratory to understand potentialities and limitations of 'de jure' regionalism, but also an actor in the making within the new globalized world, supporting regionalism elsewhere. The EU is not a model for other regions; however, the European experiment, could suggest new concepts to cope with a new reality: an international system in transition where new actors and new forms of multilateral governance emerge.

On the other hand, whereas global multilateral organizations have no dynamic future chances without a fundamental reform, new democratic and civilian regionalism cannot express its potential without a new economic and political multilateralism.[57] New regionalism is not only an instrument for multilateralism; but rather a driving force for a reformed world governance, far beyond the mere *aggiornamento* of the old (1948), aforementioned, art. 24 of the WTO.

Our third scenario shares with the first one the inevitability of growing economic convergence and globalization; however, it also shares with the second scenario the analysis of conflicts, unbalances and obstacles which the globalized economy provokes, with possible salient political implications. Protectionism can only be fought by enhanced world regulation, provided by informal governance but also by reformed multilateral central rules. New regionalism can be the best support of new multilateralism, limiting both arrogant unilateralism and nationalistic, ethnic or privatizing fragmentation of authorities and decision making. We do witness and we will witness in the next decade an array of evolving regional arrangements. Regional cooperation entails more than a set of policies: it is a pillar of world multilateral politics, adjusting the legacy of the former multilateral values within a less asymmetric framework. If so, new regionalism would combine what a large part of economic literature considers as non-compatible, that is, economic openness and representation of territorial economic, cultural and political variations. A new principle of territoriality is emerging between obsolete sovereignty and functional globalism.

While in the 1930s imperial regionalism was against worldwide multilateral arrangements and in the 1960s regional association was part of international multilateralism dominated by the liberal American hegemony, today a better balance is one of the scenarios on the agenda: new regionalism and inter-regionalism could maybe interact fruitfully with global multilateral regulation. We are witnessing a mix of continuity and discontinuity with the past decades, when the vocation of democratic capitalism was multilateral, but until the 1980s it was accompanied by strategic hegemonic power.

The conditioners and salient variables largely depend on systemic and endogenous factors and on the prevailing trends of the international economy and politics. However, new regionalism offers the EU the possibility of partnerships and worldwide alliances and partnerships with a view to implementing new multilateralism. The EU is particularly committed to strengthening this kind of alliance and cooperation between regional organizations. It can help to overcome the current gap between economic globalization and the multilateral political and economical institutional framework.

Is our analytical understanding of regional civilian powers exclusive of a normative research? Not at all. The new regionalism could also offer an opportunity for normative studies, deepening a third way between global regulation and fragmentation, globalism and relativism, universalism and stato-centric paradigms. In the framework of the current normative discussion about improving world governance and respect of human rights, we should mention the need to deepen new regionalism as an original path between cosmopolitan rhetoric and power politics.[59] Many authors of this book have been working on the question of to what extent Europe can be, thanks to its memory and values, the cradle of a universal idea of peace and cooperation, through its contribution to a pluralistic, multicultural and multilateral democratic government at national, regional and world levels. The conclusion of this book is against every Eurocentric understanding of the global role of the EU. Europe can only assert its values provided that other regional entities and state actors share the same goals. A new multilateralism is more than mere international regime-building and more than a bigger role for international organizations, it is matter of a transnational communication towards a global more legitimate and pluralistic global polity. While military and economic unilateralism corrode universal values and do not stop fragmentation, in times of low trust in global multilateralism, some new forms of institutionalized regionalism or of 'regulatory regionalism' look at providing incipient pieces of a better world governance, economic justice and respect of human rights through more structural symmetry among actors, economic and political dialogue, respect for diversities, and a cross-border pluralistic trans-national public sphere.[60] Reciprocally, an innovative concept of civilian power cannot seriously rise out of a new multilateral global framework based on a revised Westphalian system, that is on various forms of sovereignty pooling. Maybe it is not a 'grand design', but the market of political ideas in the uncertain globalized world of the early 21st century does not offer much better options.

Notes

1   C. Rhodes, ed. (1998) and R. Ginsberg, Conceptualizing the EU as an International Actor: Narrowing the Theoretical Capability-Expectations Gap, in *Journal of Common Market Studies*, 37(3): 429–54.

2   R. Keohane and J. Nye (eds.) (1970).

3   K. Deutsch et al. (1957) and E. Haas (1958).

4   As far as the economic dimension of external relations is concerned, the ECSC Treaty and the 1957 Treaties of Rome are the legal foundations of the EC's external competence: customs and trade policy, external implications of the common market and of all the common policies (agricultural, competition), cooperation with developing countries, and so on. According to the Treaties, the European Commission can, in part, act on behalf of member states and the communitarian procedures can be applied (Majority Voting Procedure in the Council, competence of the European Court of Justice, role of the European Parliament), while in part intergovernmental cooperation is requested.

5   Furthermore, no Western European economy is in division II of prosperity according to the World Bank and IMF lists, and they are behind the US and Japan as far as GDP per capita is concerned. They are, however, increasing their distance from developing countries.

6 Article 133 (ex–113) of the Treaty of Rome (TEC) provides one of the most important legal foundations of common external action, allowing the Commission to make commercial agreements with 'one or more States or international organizations'.

Though submitted to the unanimous agreement of the Council of Ministers, the new Treaty of Amsterdam (1997) provides for the extension of the Commission mandate, to 'international negotiations and agreements on services and intellectual property', for example the sensitive issues of the problematic 'Millennium Round' of the WTO. The European Commission, on the basis of articles 300–301 (ex–228 and 228A) can negotiate international agreements with states and international organizations. Articles 302–304 (ex–229–231) provide a legal basis for the EU's participation in international organizations: WTO, GATT, European Bank for Reconstruction and Development (for Eastern European countries), the Council of Europe, the OSCE, the UN and some of the UN organizations and agencies.

Moreover, a particular Treaty provision is particularly meaningful from economic and political points of view: art. 310 (ex–238) of the TEC describes the 'association making power', including 'reciprocal rights and obligations, common actions and special procedures', applied to the concerned state (s) and organizations.

There are different types of association status: States belonging to the 'Lomé Convention' (78 African, Caribbean and Pacific countries), Eastern European and Mediterranean states. Finally, applicant states for membership have special agreements, conceived as a kind of an antechamber. It is important to underline that from the very beginning of the integration process the successive enlargements (art. 49 of the TEU) were an essential part of European foreign policy as shown by the British and the Iberian enlargements and more particularly since 1989, by the Scandinavian and EFTA, the Central-Eastern European enlargements.

7 R. Gilpin, The Politics of Transnational Economic Relations, in R. Keohane and J. Nye (1970), pp.48–68.

8 By its emergence as an international political actor, the EC contributed already in the 1970s to the decline of US international hegemony. The ECP is hard to explain only as the outcome of an internal dynamic. The first coordination process of national foreign policies was a response by the EC to its international environment.

9 S. Hoffmann, R. Keohane and J. S. Nye (eds.) (1993). See also C. Hill (1996) and particularly the Introduction by C. Hill and W. Wallace.

10 The Preamble to the TEU stresses the aim to 'reinforce the European identity and its independence in order to promote peace, security and progress in Europe and the world' (par. 9). Art. 11 (ex-title V, article J) of the TEU is the legal basis for the Common Foreign and Security Policy, which is part of the political Union and strengthens the former European political cooperation with the aim of 'asserting its identity on the international scene', art. 2 (ex-art. B, par. 2). J.-M. Dumond and P. Setton (1999), *La Politique étrangère et de sécurité commune* (PESC), La Documentation française, Paris.

11 European Council, Lisbon 26/27 June 1992, Conclusion by the Presidency, European Commission General Secretary, 1992. The European Council emphasized the importance of strengthening the economic and political external relations of the European Community. It stressed the common interests and areas open to joint actions as far as external relations are concerned (Eastern Europe and Russia, Mediterranean, Latin America, Middle East, developing countries). Inter-regional relations are also mentioned: 'the easing of international tensions with the end of the Cold War provides new possibilities and resources for development but also favors the emergence of new forms of cooperation namely at inter-regional level' (p. 24).

12 See C. Piening (1997) pp. 193–7, Martin Holland, ed. (1997); K. A. Eliassen, ed. (1998).

13 See M. Telò and P. Magnette, eds. (1998), and particularly the articles by M. Telò and E. Remacle. The procedure of the Amsterdam Treaty is intergovernmental the very complex provisions of enhanced cooperation excludes security and defence issues (second pillar of the TEU) and art. 25 of TEU allows single member states to stop common external actions – the 'Nice Treaty' makes 'enhanced cooperation' easier in defence policy.

14 D. Allen and M. Smith (1990) Western Europe's Presence in the Contemporary International Arena, in: Review of International Affairs, (16): 19–37.

15 I. J.Manners and R. G. Whitman, International identity of the EU, in *Journal of European Integration*, (3): .231–49: the EU implements its 'active identity', according to the authors, through a significant array of tools: informational (strategic, specific, informational instruments and reactive statements), procedural (regional, bilateral, and so on), transference (6 per cent of the EU Budget for external actions in 1997) and overt (either on a transitory or on a permanent basis).

16 By 'French pattern' he means: 'endogenous nuclear weapons, control of foreign bases, loyalty to NATO but insistence on a distinct personality within it' in H. Bull (1982) p.160. Obviously, the international environment of the 1970s and early 1980s historically conditions the call by H. Bull for a distinctive European nuclear deterrent force, based on French-British collaboration.

17 C. Hill (1996).

18 The Treaty of Amsterdam expresses openly the wish to better coordinate these multiple dimensions, by strengthening art. 3 of the TEU (former art. C) requesting not only a coherence between the various dimensions of the external action but also a better coordination between the Council and the Commission. However, the current multiple responsibility system, including 'Mister CFSP' (General Secretary of the Council and of WEU, M. X. Solana since 1999), the Commissioner charged with external relations (Mr Patten, in the Prodi Commission) and the rotating Presidency of the Council, does not yet show a clear division of competence in policy implementation.

19 F. Duchêne (1973) The European Community and the Uncertainties of Interdependence, in: M. Kohnstamm and W. Hager , *A Nation Writ Large? Foreign Policy Problems before the EC*, London: Macmillan.

20 R. O. Keohane and J. S. Nye (1970); and more recently, R. B. Walker (1993); W. Carlsnaes and S. Smith eds. (1994), *European Foreign Policy: the EC and Changing Perspectives*, London: Sage.

21 R. G. Whitman (1998) see note 18.

22 C. Piening (1997), pp.193–7.

23 See the Helsinki European Council decision to build up a new capability, namely a European 'rapid reaction force' by 2003 (60,000 soldiers capable of being mobilized within a short period of time in the framework of the 'Petersberg Tasks' (Amsterdam Treaty).

24 See articles 228 and 238 EC Treaty, granting a Treaty-making power, even if submitted to unanimous vote by the Council and '*avis conforme*' by the EP; revised in the Amsterdam Treaty articles 300 and 310.

25 A. Schlesinger (1979), *The Imperial Presidency*, New York.

26 T. Lowi (1967).

27 W. Wessels and D. Rometsch (1996).

28 See for instance the statement presented by the General Affairs Council to the Vienna European Council (Dec. 1998) in order to increase the weight and coherence of the Union, with the title 'Common strategies', the proposals by Tony Blair concerning

defence cooperation (April 1999) and the progress made in 1998 and 2000 as far as defense cooperation is concerned (St Malo, 1998, Feira , Colone and Helsinki European Council starting the ECDP).

29 Particularly useful is the analysis of the various national interests and aims provided by the book edited by C. Hill (1996). However, Hill underlined in his 1993 article, The Capability–Expectation Gap, or Conceptualizing Europe's International Role (in *Journal of Common Market Studies*, n. 3, Sept.) four common external interests of EU member states: providing a second Western voice in international diplomacy; stabilizing Eastern Europe; managing the globalized economy and the world trade; relations with the South.

30 As regards the Amsterdam Treaty: better visibility by 'Mr. CFSP' even if he will not be much more than a spokesperson, dependent on the Council; improved decision-making process (even if the 'enhanced cooperation' clause cannot yet be applied to the 'second pillar'), strengthened Treaty-making power of the Commission (even if limited by the revised art. 300 and 310 and 133, submitting it to unanimous vote procedure of the Council).

31 S. Strange, Who are EU? Ambiguities in the Concept of Competitiveness, in Journal of Common Market Studies, 36(1) March 1998: 101–13.

32 This elaborated version of 'multilevel governance' takes into account the end not only of teleological visions of the EU, but also of the functional spill-over dominating the first three decades of European regional integration. The author considers non-realistic both the 'Stato' and 'Confederatio' scenarios, linked to the territorial logic; see P. C. Schmitter (1995). Examining the Present Euro polity with the Help of Past Theories and Imagining the Future of the Euro Polity with the Help of New Concepts, in G. Marks, F. W. Scharpf, P. C. Schmitter, and W. Streeck (1996).

33 The two-level game, analyzed by among others A. Moravsik (1998), is only to some extent compatible with such a neoliberal scenario.

34 S. D. Krasner (1983). In the same book, see Keohane, Strange and other congtributors.

35 R. N. Rosencrance (1986).

36 J. Rosenau has proposed for that scenario the concept of 'fragmegration' (combining fragmentation and integration); however the authors of this book, in general, do not share his functional optimism, as far as decentralized governance is concerned and focus on the crucial question of the role of new regionalism by providing a synthesis between the two dialectical tendencies mentioned by J. Rosenau. See J. Rosenau and Czempiel, eds., (1992) and Rosenau (2000) A Transformed Observer in a Transforming World, in *Studia Diplomatica, Les théories des R. I. à l'épreuve de l'après-guerre-froide*, edited by C. Roosens, M. Telò and P. Vercauteren, 52(1), 2000: 4–14.

37 R. Gilpin (1987) distinguishes between the 'benevolent' and 'malevolent' types of neomercantilism. See also Björn Hettne, The Double Movement: Global Market versus Regionalism, in R. Cox ed. (1997), pp.223–44 and Hettne (1999).

38 G Grevi and N. Gnesotto (eds.), *The New Global Puzzle.What World for the EU in 2025?* ISS, Paris, 2006.

39 A. S. Milward (1999), L'impossibile fuga dalla storia, in *Europa/Europe.Quale idea d'Europa? per il XXI secolo*, n. 5, edited by M. Telò, pp. 57–68.

40 A. Moravcsik (1999).

41 N. Bobbio (1981), and (1998), *Etat et démocratie internationale*, Complexe, Bruxelles, ed. M. Telò.

42 Bhagwati (1993) and A. Sapir (1998), pp. 717–32.

43 Kébabdjian, G. (1999), pp. 227–53.

44   On European exceptionalism, see W. Wallace (1994). On the controversial issue of the place and role of the so called European model see: Eu External Relations.Exporting the EU model of Governance? , in '*European Foreign Affairs review*' ,10(4), winter, 2005, see the chapters by M. Farell (editor), Ben Rosamond, Stephen Leibfried and Dieter Wolf, Bjorn Hettne and F. Söderbaum, C. Jörges and R. Higgott.

45   M. Albert has updated his famous concept of 'Rhenan capitalism' in Albert (1999), Il capitalismo europeo nel quadro della mondializzazione: convergenze e differenze, in *Europa /Europe, Quale idea d'Europa per il XXI secolo?* ed. by M. Telò, n. 5.

46   Portuguese Presidency of the EU (January 2000), *Employment, economic reforms and social cohesion. For a Europe of innovation and knowledge*, Lisbon, and *Conclusion of the Presidency* (Lisbon, 23/24. 3. 2000). See also European Commission (February 2000), *The Lisbon European Council. An Agenda of Economic and Social Renewal for Europe*, Brussels, 28.

47   For two opposite viewpoints, see: D. Piazolo (1998) and S. Bilal (1998), Political Economy Considerations on the Supply of Trade Protection in Regional Integration Agreements, in *Journal of Common Market Studies*, 36(1): 1–31.

48   S. Keukeleire (1998) has explored the empirical side of this approach in, *Het buitenlands beleid van de Europese Unie*, Deeventer, Kluwer. However, what is needed is to further develop here the theoretical dimension of the concept.

49   T. de Wilde d'Estmael (1998).

50   K. Waltz (1979); and R. Keohane, ed. (1986).

51   R. O. Keohane and J. S. Nye (1989 and Keohane 1984, 2004, 2005), examine the importance of transnational cross-border relations and the emergence of new private and public actors within the international system, and the decline of the traditional hierarchies of power and issues. These trends stop giving priority to security and question the traditional separation between inside and outside of the state; international cooperation becomes as a possible positive sum game even in absence of hegemonic power. Neo institutionalism provides a possible bridge between EU studies, comparative regionalism and international relations. That is possible thanks to an encompassing and comprehensive notion of institutions including several paths and levels of formalization, not only the EU one, even if customs unions evolve easily to deeper institutional settlements: See the chapter provided by Higgott and S. Haggard, Regionalism in Asia and the Americas, in E. Mansfield and H. Milner (1997), pp. 47–8 and Haftendorn, Helga , Keohane Robert O.,Wallander Celeste A.. (eds), *Imperfect Unions*, Oxford Un. Press (1999)

52   M. Telò, *Europe: A Civilian Power? EU,Global Governance, World Order*, 2005, Palgrave Macmillan.

53   S. Strange (1988).

54   The internal cohesion and consistency can be enhanced only through institutional reforms: a) strengthening the political leadership of the European Council as the strategic options as far as the long-term decisions are concerned (see the example of the Lisbon European Council on technological modernization, economic reform, knowledge society and social model); b) reforming the General Affairs Council, to be divided in two, in order to correct its current fragmentation and depolitization. On the one hand, the Council responsible for foreign affairs and security issues, and on the other hand, a General Affairs Council composed of superministers (Deputy Prime Ministers) responsible for coordinating and leading the implementation of intergovermental cooperation, acting as an internal reference for the European policies; c) improving the executive role of the European Commission, its external role of representation and its political accountability d) organizing a European diplomatic body, even if coordinated with member states.

55 Even part of French literature takes into account the need to overcome the past debate between the French and British security policies, both focusing on the nuclear threat. Cfr. N. Gnesotto (1998). As the EU is concerned, see the emphasis on comprehensive security in the 'Solana paper', approved by the EU Council in December 2003.

56 See P. Kennedy (1987) and R. Keohane (1984 and 2004). D. A. Lake (1999), D. L. Boren and E. J. Perkins, eds. (1999).

57 See John Gerard Ruggie (1993) *Winning the Peace*, Columbia, New York and R. Cox, ed. (1997), pp. 245–61, M. Telo, Multilateralism. Constructing a common language, paper for Bruges GArnet NoE JERP, Sept; 2006, and E. Newmann, R. Thakur and J. Tirman(eds.) Multilateralism. Under challenge?, United Nations University press, 2006.

58 B. Badie (1999), particularly the third part, Entre responsabilité et puissance, pp.223–85.

59 M Telò (1999) Lo Stato e la democrazia internazionale. Il contributo di N.Bobbio oltre globalismo giuridico e relativismo, in Teoria politica, XV, Turin edited by L.Bonanate, n.2–3, pp.533–62.

60 J.Habermas (1996), and Die europäische Nationalstaat unter dem Druck der Globalisierung, in *Blaetter fuer deutsche und internationale Politik* n.4 (1999). Regarding the international discussion on world governance, realism and cosmopolitism, F. D. Archibugi, D. Held and M. Koehler, eds. (1998), F. Cerutti, ed. (2000); H. Bull (1986) H. Kelsen and International Law, in J. J. L. Tur, W. Twining, eds. *Essays on Kelsen*, Oxford: Oxford University Press, and D. Zolo (1997).

Appendix:
List of Regional and Interregional Arrangements

Sebastian Santander

1 Regional arrangements

The organizations listed below are grouped by geographical area (Africa, Americas, Arab World, Asia, Europe and Oceania) and listed within each area in alphabetical order.

1.1 Africa

AU: African Union, 2001:

Purposes

The historical foundations of the African Union originated in the Union of African States, an early confederation established in the 1960s, as well as subsequent attempts to unite Africa, including the Organization of African Unity (OAU), which was established in 1963, and the African Economic Community in 1981. Critics argued that the OAU in particular did little to protect the rights and liberties of African citizens from their own political leaders. The idea of creating the AU was revived in the mid-1990s as a result of the efforts of the African Unification Front. The heads of state and government of the OAU issued the Sirte Declaration on September 9, 1999, calling for the establishment of an African Union. The Declaration was followed by summits at Lomé in 2000, when the Constitutive Act of the African Union was adopted, and at Lusaka in 2001, when the plan for the implementation of the African Union was adopted. The African Union was launched in Durban on July 9, 2002, by its first president, South African Thabo Mbeki, at the first session of the Assembly of the African Union. Its Constitutive Act declares that it shall 'invite and encourage the full participation of the African diaspora as an important part of our Continent, in the building of the African Union'. The African Union Goverment has defined the African diaspora as consisting of people of African origin living outside the continent, irrespective of their citizenship and nationality and who are willing to contribute to the development of the continent and the building of the African Union. The African Union also aims to have a single currency and a single integrated defence force, as well as other institutions of state, including a cabinet for the AU Head of State. The purpose of the union is to help secure Africa's democracy, human rights, especially by bringing an end to intra-African conflict and creating an effective common market. It also aims to create a sustainable economy. In order to reach the latter purpose the AU launched the New Partnership for Africa's Development (NEPAD).

http://www.africa-union.org/root/ua/index/index.htm

Members

Algeria, Angola, Benin, Botswana, Burkina Faso, Burundi, Cameroon, Cape Verde, Central African Republic, Chad, Comoros, Democratic Republic of the Congo, Republic of the Congo, Ivory Coast, Djibouti, Egypt, Equatorial Guinea, Eritrea, Ethiopia, Gabon, Gambia, Ghana, Guinea, Guinea-Bissau, Kenya, Lesotho, Liberia, Libya, Madagascar, Malawi, Mali, Mauritius, Mozambique, Namibia, Niger, Nigeria, Rwanda, Western Sahara (SADR), São Tomé and Príncipe, Senegal, Seychelles, Sierra Leone, Somalia, South Africa, Sudan, Swaziland, Tanzania, Togo, Tunisia, Uganda, Zambia and Zimbabwe

CEUCA: Customs and Economic Union of Central Africa, 1966

Purposes

CEUCA, in French Union douanière et économique de l'Afrique Centrale (UDEAC) is a free trade area and a customs union with a common external tariff for imports from other countries. It aims to establish an ever-closer union among member states so as to reinforce sub-regional solidarity, to promote the gradual and progressive establishment of a Central African common market, and subsequently, through establishment of this sub-regional grouping, to participate in the creation of a true African common market and the consolidation of African unity. CEUCA signed a treaty for the establishment of a Economic and Monetary Community of Central Africa (CEMAC) to promote the entire process of sub-regional integration trough the forming of monetary union with the Central Africa CFA franc as a common currency.

http://www.cemac.cf/

Members

Cameroon, Republic of Congo, Chad, Central African Republic, Equatorial Guinea, Gabon.

COMESA: Common Market for Eastern and Southern Africa, 1994

Purposes

Successor to Preferential Trade Area of Southern African States which was established on 22 December 1981. The aims of COMESA are the following:

- attain sustainable growth and development of member states by promoting a more balanced and harmonious development of production and marketing structures; promote joint development in all fields of economic activity and the joint adoption of macro-economic policies and programmes in order to raise the standard of living of the peoples in, and to foster closer relations among, member states; cooperate in the creation of an enabling environment for foreign, cross-border and domestic investment, including joint promotion of research and adaptation of science and technology for development; cooperate in the promotion of peace, security and stability among member states in order to enhance the economic development of the region, cooperate in strengthening the relations between the Common Market and the rest of the world and adopt common positions in international forums, contribute towards the establishment, progress and the realization of the objectives of the African Economic Community.

Nine of the member states formed a free trade area in 2000, with Rwanda and Burundi joining the FTA in 2004 and the Comoros and Libya in 2006.COMESA is one of the pillars of the African Economic Community.
http://www.comesa.int/index_html/view

Members

Angola, Burundi, Comoros, Democratic Republic of Congo, Djibouti, Egypt, Ethiopia, Kenya, Madagascar, Malawi, Mauritius, Rwanda, Seychelles, Sudan, Swaziland, Uganda, Zambia, Zimbabwe. Botswana and South Africa are under conditions stipulated by the members.

Former Members

Lesotho (quit in 1997), Mozambique (quit in 1997), Tanzania (quit on September 2, 2000), Namibia (quit in May 2004).

EAC: East African Community, 2001

Purpose

The EAC is a customs union in East Africa, originally founded in 1967. It was disbanded in 1977. In January 2001 the EAC was revived. The new EAC treaty paved the way for an economic and, ultimately, political union of the three countries. A further treaty signed in March 2004 set up a customs union, which commenced on 1 January 2005. Under the terms of the treaty, Kenya, the richest of the three countries, will pay duty on its goods entering Uganda and Tanzania until 2010. A common system of tariffs will apply to other countries supplying the three countries with goods. EAC is one of the pillars of the African Economic Community.
htt://www.eac.int

Members

Kenya, Uganda and Tanzania.

ECCAS: Economic Community of Central African States, 1983

Purposes

ECCAS, in French Communauté Économique des États d'Afrique Centrale (CEEAC), is an organisation for promotion of regional economic co-operation in Central Africa. It 'aims to achieve collective autonomy, raise the standard of living of its populations and maintain economic stability through harmonious cooperation'. ECCAS was established on by the CEUCA and ECGLC members (see below). Angola became member on 1999. It started functioning in 1985, but was inactive for several years because of financial difficulties and the conflict in the Great Lakes area. The war in the DR Congo was particularly divisive, as Rwanda and Angola fought on opposing sides. ECCAS has been designated a pillar of the African Economic Community, but formal contact between the AEC and ECCAS was only established in October 1999 due to the inactivity of ECCAS since 1992. The AEC again confirmed the importance of ECCAS as the major economic community in Central Africa at the third preparatory meeting of its Economic and Social Council (ECOSOC) in June 1999. The headquarters of the ECCAS are situated in Livreville, Gabon. The working languages of the Community are French, Spanish, and Portuguese.

http://www.africa-union.org/root/au/recs/eccas.htm

Members

Angola, Burundi, Cameroon, Central African Republic, Chad, Congo, Democratic Republic of Congo, Gabon, Equatorial Guinea, Rwanda, São Tomé and Príncipe.

ECGLC: Economic Community of the Great Lakes Countries, 1976

Purposes

ECGLC, in French Communauté Économique des Pays de Grands Lacs (CEPGL), is a sub-regional organization. It aims to establish a customs union. It got a series of specialized agencies for common development: in the banking, energy, agronomy and animal technology sectors.

http://acronyms.thefreedictionary.com/Communaute+Economique+Des+Pays +Des+Grands+Lacs Members

Burundi, Democratic Republic of Congo, Rwanda.

ECOWAS: Economic Community of West African States (CEDEAO in French), 1975

Purposes

To become a common market. To promote cooperation and development in economic activity, particularly in the fields of industry, transport, telecommunications, energy, natural resources, trade, monetary and financial questions and in social and cultural matters, for the purpose of raising the standard of living, of increasing and maintaining economic stability, of fostering closer relations among its members and of contributing to the progress and development of the African continent. The ECOWAS Secretariat and the Fund for Cooperation, Compensation and Development are its two main institutions to implement policies. The ECOWAS Fund was transformed into the ECOWAS Bank for Investment and Development in 2001. ECOWAS is one of the pillars of the African Economic Community.
http://www.ecowas.int/

Members

Benin, Burkina Faso, Gambia, Ghana, Green Cape, Guinea, Guinea-Bissau, Ivory Coast, Liberia, Mali, Niger, Nigeria, Senegal, Sierra Leone and Togo.

Former Members

Mauritania (quit in 2002).

MRU: Mano River Union, 1973

Purposes

The MRU is an international association established 1973 between Liberia and Sierra Leone. In 1980, Guinea joined the Union. It aims to establish a customs union, to expand trade, encourage productive capacity, and progressively develop a common policy and cooperation as regards harmonization of tariffs and regulations related to customs, qualifications and postal services. It also aims to promote joint development projects (hydroelectric construction, telecommunications, maritime activities) and to secure a fair distribution of the benefits from economic cooperation.

Due to conflicts involving the countries (Sierra Leone civil war and Liberian civil war) the objectives of the Union could not be achieved. However, on May 20, 2004, the Union was reactivated during a presidential top.
http://manoriverwomen.afrikart.net/index.htm

Members

Guinea, Liberia, Sierra Leone.

SACU: Southern Africa Customs Union, 1969

Purposes

SACU is a customs union among the countries of South Africa. It is the oldest Customs Union in the world. It entered into force in 1970 replacing the Customs Union Agreement of 1910. Its aim is to maintain the free interchange of goods between member countries. It provides for a common external tariff and a common excise tariff to this common customs area. SACU is developing external relations: by late 2004 it was negotiating a Free Trade deal with the United States.
http://www.sacu.int/

Members

Botswana, Lesotho, Namibia, South Africa and Swaziland.

SADC: Southern African Development Community, 1992

Purposes

Replaced the SADCC (Southern African Development Coordination Conference) which was established in 1980. The main purposes of this customs union are: deeper economic cooperation and integration, on the basis of balance, equity and mutual benefits, providing for cross-border investment and trade, and freer movement of factors of production, goods and services across national borders; common economic, political and social values and systems, enhancing enterprise and competitiveness, democracy and good governance, respect for the rule of law and the guarantee of human rights, popular participation and alleviation of poverty; strengthened regional solidarity, peace and security, in order for the people of the region to live and work together in peace and harmony. Particular concerns: human resources, science and technology, food security, natural resources and environment, infrastructure and services, finance, investment and trade, popular participation, solidarity, peace and security.
http://www.sadc.int/

Members

Angola, Botswana, Lesotho, Malawi, Mozambique, Swaziland, Tanzanie, Zambie and Zimbabwe.

Former Members

Seychelles left on 1 July 2004. However, in 2006, it appeared that the Seychelles would apply to rejoin.

WAEMU: West African Economic and Monetary Union, 1994

Purposes

The WAEMU, in French the Union économique et monétaire oust-africaine (UEMOA), replaced WAMU (West African Monetary Union), which was established in 1959. The WAEMU is a customs union and monetary union between some of the members of Economic Community of West African States (ECOWAS). The WAEMU aims to make the economic and financial activities of member states more competitive in the context of an open market based upon free competition, to set up a multilateral surveillance procedure to harmonize national legislations (particularly fiscal) and coordinate economic policies. To set up a common market and a common external tariff.

    http://www.uemoa.int/

Members

Benin, Burkina Faso, Guinea-Bissau, Ivory Coast, Mali, Niger, Senegal and Togo.

1.2   Americas (The)

ALADI: Latin American Association for Development and Integration, 1980

Purposes

The ALADI (by the English acronym LAIA) replaced the ALALC (Latin American Association of Free Trade). The Montevideo Treaty signed on August 12, 1980, is the global legal framework that establishes and governs ALADI. It is preferential trade area based in Montevideo. Its main purpose is to become a common market. The ALADI has contributed to transforming economic structures and creating the conditions for integration in countries where they were less favourable. It has contributed to establishing bilateral and multilateral relations among member states. ALADI is open to all Latin American countries and regional integrations as well as to other developing countries or their respective integration areas outside Latin America.

    http://www.aladi.org/

Members

Argentina, Bolivia, Brazil, Chile, Colombia, Cuba, Ecuador, Mexico, Paraguay, Peru, Uruguay and Venezuela.

Observers: China, Dominican Republic, El Salvador, Guatemala, Honduras, Italy, Nicaragua, Panama, Portugal, Romania, Russia, Spain, Switzerland.

CAN: Andean Community of Nations, 1969 (previously Andean Pact)

Purposes

The CAN, in Spanish Comunidad Andina de Naciones, was established in 1969 with the Cartagena Agreement. The CAN established the conditions for a common market within ALALC–ALADI (see below). Since 1995, the member states have been working on a customs union. From January 1, 2005, the citizens of the member states can enter the other Andean Community member countries without the requirement of visa. The passengers should present the authorities their national ID cards. The CAN together with MERCOSUR comprises the two main trading blocs of South America. In 1999 these regional organizations began negotiating a merger with a view to creating a South American Free Trade Area (SAFTA). On December 8, 2004 it signed a cooperation agreement with MERCOSUR and they published a joint letter of intention for future negotiations towards integrating all of South America in the context of the South American Community of Nations.
http://www.comunidadandina.org/endex.htm

Members

Bolivia, Colombia, Ecuador and Peru. Chile who was a founder member, withdrew in 1976. Venezuela who joined the CAN in 1973, announced in 2006 its withdrawal, claiming the FTA agreements signed by Colombia and Peru with the USA caused irreparable damage to the community.

Observer Members

Chile, Mexico and Panama

CACM: Central American Common Market, 1960

Purposes

The CACM, in Spanish Mercado Común Centroamericano (MCCA), is a regional trade organization which collapsed in 1969 with the 'Football War' between Honduras and El Slavador. The CACM was reinstated in 1991. Its main purpose is to establish a customs union and a political integration as a federation of Central American states. However, it has not achieved the goals yet. With the proposal of the Free Trade Area of the Amercias, it is possible that this new organization will replace the CACM (or make it redundant). Further, the implementation of the DR-CAFTA which is planned for 2006, may render this common market redundant.
http://www.mcca.com/

Members

Costa Rica, El Salvador, Guatemala, Honduras, Nicaragua.

CARICOM: Caribbean Community, 1973

Purposes

The CARICOM was established by the Treaty of Chaguaramas and replaced the 1965-1972 CARIFTA (Caribbean Free Trade Association), which had been organized to provide a continued economic linkage between the English-speaking countries of the Caribbean following the dissolution of the West Indies Federation (1958–62). The CARICOM has established a common external tariff and common market. A Revised Treaty of Chaguaramas establishing the Caribbean Community including the CARICOM Single Market and Economy (CSME) was signed by the Heads of Government of the Caribbean Community on July 5 2001. Part of the revised treaty includes the establishment and implementation of the Caribbean Court of Justice.
http://www.caricom.org/

Members

Antigua and Barbuda, The Bahamas (member of the Community but not of the common market), Barbados, Belize, Dominica, Grenada, Guyana, Haiti, Jamaica, Montserrat, Saint Kitts and Nevis, Saint Lucia, Saint Vincent and the Grenadines, Surinam, Trinidad and Tobago.

Associate members

Anguilla, Bermuda, British Virgin Islands, Cayman Islands and Turks and Caicos Islands.
Observer countries:, Aruba, Colombia, Dominican Republic, Dutch Antilles, Mexico, Puerto Rico, Venezuela.

DR-CAFTA: Dominican Republic-Central American Free Trade Agreement, 2005

Purpose

Originally, the agreement encompassed the United States and the Central American countries of Costa Rica, El Salvador, Guatemala, Honduras, and Nicaragua, and was called CAFTA. In 2004, the Dominican Republic joined the negotiations, and the agreement was renamed DR-CAFTA. The goal of DR-CAFTA is the creation of a free trade zone, similar to the North American Free Trade Agreement (NAFTA) which currently encompasses the US, Canada, and Mexico. DR-CAFTA is a stepping stone towards the Free Trade Area of the Americas (FTAA).
http://ustr.gov/Trade_Agreements/Bilateral/CAFTA/Section_Index.html

Members

Costa Rica, El Salvador, Guatemala, Honduras, Nicaragua and Dominican Republic.
   Grupo de los Tres: The Group of the Three, 1995

Purposes

The G3 is a free trade agreement that came into force in 1995. The agreement aims to liberalize goods, investment and services, and to facilitate public purchase. Venezuela decided in May 2006 to quit the trade bloc due to differences with its two partners.
   http://www.edomex.gob.mx/tlcs/grupo3.htm

Members

Colombia and Mexico.

Former Members

Venezuela.

MERCOSUR: Southern Common Market, 1991

Purposes

The MERCOSUR, in Spanish Mercado Común del Sur and in Portuguese Mercado Comun do Sul, was established with the Treaty of Asunción signed on March 26, 1991. Before the establishment of MERCOSUR, the biggest member states, Argentina and Brazil, passed through two important stages. The PICE (Integration and Cooperation Program, 1986) established the first link between them in pursuit of further economic integration. In 1989 the two countries reached a new agreement: the PICAB (Integration, Cooperation and Development Treaty), which aimed to abolish tariffs barriers and coordinate policy in some specific areas (customs, science, technology) as well as macroeconomic policy. In 1990 new modifications were introduced with the Acta de Buenos Aires (Buenos Aires Act), which aimed to facilitate the setting up of the common market in 1994. One year later the Treaty of Asunción extended the Buenos Aires Act to Paraguay and Uruguay established MERCOSUR. The former was later amended and updated by the 1994 Treaty of Ouro Preto which created new institutions and gave it to it a legal status in international law. MERCOSUR came into force on 1 January 1995. Its aims are both political and economic: to stabilize democracy, to develop the economies in the region, to provide global insertion of national economies and to reinforce the power of the members in the international system. An important aim of MERCOSUR is to be a mechanism for 'open integration'. The development of MERCOSUR was arguably weakened by the devaluation of the brazilian currency on January 1999 following by the collapse of the Argentine economy in 2002. It has still seen internal conflicts over trade policy. It has not achieved two important goals yet. The free trade area and the customs union are still unachieved. In spite of internal problems, MERCOSUR has been enlarged: Venezuela signed its membership agreement on 17 June 2006, and became a full member on 4 July of the same year. The organization has a South and Andean American integration vocation. In December 2004 it signed a cooperation agreement with the Andean Community and they published a joint letter of intention for a future negotiations towards integrating all of South America. MERCOSUR has developed interregional trade links with the EU; contacts in the field of trade have been made with, China, India and APEC; member states are taking part to the negotiations of a Free Trade Area of the Americas and are also planning a South American Free Trade Area (ALCSA or SAFTA.

http://www.mercosur.int/msweb/

Members

Argentina, Brazil, Paraguay, Uruguay and Venezuela.
 Associated members: Bolivia, Chile, Colombia, Ecuador and Peru.

NAFTA: North American Free Trade Agreement, 1994

Purposes

NAFTA, in Spanish Tratado de Libre Comercio de America del Norte (TLCAN) and in French Accord de libre-échange nord-américain (ALENA), is more than a simple free trade agreement of goods. It aims to liberalize movement of goods, capital and services. It aims to abolish more than 20,000 barriers to trade by 2010; to promote conditions of fair competition and increase investment opportunities; to provide adequate provision for intellectual property rights and environmental protection; to establish effective procedures for implementing and applying the Agreement and for resolution of disputes; to encourage further trilateral, regional and multilateral cooperation. Unlike other free trade agreements in the world, NAFTA is more comprehensive in its scope. It also was complemented by the North American Agreement for Environmental Cooperation (NAAEC) and the North American Agreement on Labor Cooperation (NAALC). While different groups advocate for a further integration into a North American Community, sensitive issues have hindered that process. The three countries have pursued different trade policies with non-members making the possibility of creating a customs union hard to attain. Security issues and sovereignty are also a controversial topic. Nonetheless the three countries have complemented NAFTA with the Security and Prosperity Partnership of North America (SPP). The later was born on March 23, 2005, in order to take new steps to address the threat of terrorism and to enhance the security, competitiveness and quality of life of their countries' citizens.

http://www.nafta-sec-alena.org/DefaultSite/index.html

Members

Canada, Mexico, United States.

SELA: Latin American Economic System, 1975

Purposes

Established by the governments of Latin America with the main purpose of reinforcing the region's capacity in international economic negotiations and contributing to the full development of the member states.
    http://www.sela.org/sela/

Members

Argentina, Barbados, Belize, Bolivia, Brazil, Chile, Colombia, Costa Rica, Cuba, Dominican Republic, Ecuador, El Salvador, Grenada, Guatemala, Guyana, Haiti, Honduras, Jamaica, Mexico, Nicaragua, Panama, Paraguay, Peru, Surinam, Trinidad and Tobago, Uruguay, Venezuela.

SACN: South American Community Nations, 2004

Purposes

SACN, in Spanish Comunidad Sudamericana de Naciones (CSN) and in Portuguese Comunidade Sudamericana de Nações (CSN), aims to unite two existing regional organizations (MERCOSUR and the Andean Community) with the participation of other South American countries in order to create a free trade area. The latter will eliminate tariffs for non-sensitive products by 2014 and sensitive products by 2019. The South American leaders announced also their intention to model the new community after the European Union, including a common currency, parliament, and passport by 2019.
    http://www.comunidadandina.org/sudamerica.htm

Members

Andean Community (Bolivia, Colombia, Ecuador and Peru), MERCOSUR (Argentina, Brazil, Paraguay, Uruguay and Venezuela), Chile, Guyana and Suriname.

Observer States

Mexico and Panama.

1.3   Arab World and Maghreb

ACM: Arab Common Market, 1964

Purposes

The Arab Common Market (ACM) has been established by the Council for Arab Economic Unity (CAEU) an organization that the Economic Council of the Arab League had founded in 1957. The ACM is not an independent organization and its implementation was overseen by the CAEU. The long-term goal of the ACM was to establish a full customs union that would abolish trade restrictions, trade quotas, and restrictions on residence, employment, and transportation. Since its founding the ACM has fallen short of this goal. The Arab world has always been divided between the wealthy oil states and the least-developed marginal states such as Mauritania, Somalia, Sudan and Yemen. Major political events such as the Cold War and the Gulf War (I and II), as well as differing internal institutions and external relations and policies, continue to hamper Arab economic integration.

   http://www.caeu.org.eg/English/Intro/

Members

Egypt, Iraq, Jordan, Libya, Mauritania, Syria and Yemen.

ACC: Arab Cooperation Council, 1989

Purposes

To be a more efficient forum for economic cooperation and integration among Arab countries; to promote among member states the coordination and harmonization of major economic policies in areas such as finance, customs and trade, industry and agriculture; to form an Arab common market. It is open to all Arab countries. The aim is eventually to bring together countries represented by organizations with more limited geographical coverage.

Members

Egypt, Iraq, Jordan, Yemen.

AMU/UMA: Arab Maghreb Union, 1989

Purposes

The goals of the AMU are to safeguard Maghrebian economic interests; to foster and promote economic and cultural cooperation among member states; to intensify mutual commercial exchanges as a necessary precursor to integration; and the creation of a Maghreb Economic Space (a free market in energy products; free movement of citizens within the region; joint transport undertakings, including a joint airline, road and railway improvements; formation of a Maghreb union of textile and leather industries; creation of a customs union).

http://www.maghrebarabe.org/

Members

Algeria, Libya, Mauritania, Morocco, Tunisia.

CAEU: Council for Arab Economic Unity, 1957

Purposes

To provide a flexible framework for achieving economic integration in stages. To undertake research into the economic conditions and outlook of the member states, to collect and to distribute the information and to offer consulting services; to prepare the way for a customs union; to develop industry and agriculture.

http://www.caeu.org.eg/English/Intro/

Members

Egypt, Iraq, Jordan, Kuwait, Libya, Mauritania, Palestine Authority, Somalia, Sudan, Syria, United Arab Emirates, Yemen.

CCASG: Council of Cooperation between Arab States of the Gulf, 1947

Purposes

The organization's main purpose is to pursue coordination, integration and cooperation in the economic, social and cultural fields.

http://www.gcc-sg.org/home_e.htm

Members

Bahrain, Kuwait, Oman, Qatar, Saudi Arabia, United Arab Emirates.

LAS: League of Arab States, 1945

Purposes

The main purposes of this association are to reinforce the links between member states. The League's charter states that the League shall coordinate economic affairs, including commercial relations; communications; cultural affairs; nationality, passports, and visas; social affairs; and health affairs. In recent years, some have questioned the efficacy of the Arab League's ability to fulfill its mission and ensure better conditions for Arab countries as political repression and poverty are still rampant throughout the Arab world; some, even within the Arab world, have called for it to be disbanded.

http://www.al-bab.com/

Members

Algeria, Bahrain, Comoros (1993), Djibouti, Egypt, Iraq, Jordan, Kuwait, Lebanon, Libya, Morocco, Mauritania, Oman, Palestine Authority, Qatar, Saudi Arabia, Somalia, Sudan, Syria, Tunisia, United Arab Emirates, Yemen.

Observers

Eritrea (January 2003) and Venezuela (July 2006) joined the Arab League as an observer.

1.4 Asia

ASEAN: Association of South-East Asian Nations, 1967

Purposes

According to its founding Bangkok Declaration, the objectives of the Association are: to accelerate economic growth, social progress and cultural development in the region through joint endeavors in the spirit of equality and partnership in order to strengthen the foundation for a prosperous and peaceful community of Southeast Asian Nations: to promote regional peace and stability through abiding respect for justice and the rule of law in relationship among countries of the region and adherence to the principles of the United Nations Charter; to promote active collaboration and mutual assistance on matters of common interest in the economic, social, cultural, technical, scientific and administrative fields; to provide assistance to each other in the form of training and research facilities in the educational, professional, technical and administrative spheres; to collaborate more effectively for the greater use of their agriculture and industries, the expansion of their trade, including the study of the problems of international commodity trade, the improvement of their transportation and communications facilities and the raising of the living standards of their peoples; to promote Southeast Asian studies; to maintain close and beneficial cooperation with existing international and regional organizations with similar aims and purposes, and explore all avenues for even closer cooperation among themselves.

The aims of ASEAN economic cooperation in the post-Cold War period include the following: to develop the region into a global base for the manufacture of value-added and technologically sophisticated products geared towards servicing regional and world markets; to enhance the industrial efficiency of the region through exploiting complementary location advantages based on the principles of market sharing and resource pooling; to enhance the attractiveness of the region for investment and as a tourist destination; to cooperate in enhancing greater infrastructural development which will contribute towards a more efficient business environment; to ensure that the rich resources (mineral, energy, forestry and others) of the region are exploited effectively and efficiently. It also aims to create a free trade area.

http://www.aseansec.org/

Members

Brunei, Cambodia, Indonesia, Laos, Malaysia, Myanmar, Philippines, Singapore, Thailand, Vietnam. Observer governments: Papua New Guinea.

CACO: Central Asian Cooperation Organization, 1994

Purposes

The Central Asian Cooperation Organization (CACO) is an international organization, composed of five member-states: Kazakhstan, Kyrgyzstan, Tajikistan, Uzbekistan and Russia. Observer status has been given to Georgia, Turkey and Ukraine. The objective of the Central Asian Cooperation Organization is to enchance 'the development of the economic integration in the region, the perfection of the forms and mechanisms of expansion of the political, social, scientific-technical, cultural and educational relations' among its members. The Central Asian Cooperation Organization (CACO) was first initiated by all five Central Asian nations in 1991 as the Central Asian Commonwealth. Later Turkmenistan followed a policy of isolation, withdrawing from participation in all regional forums. It continued in 1994 under the name of Central Asian Economic Union or CAEU and included Kazakhstan, Kyrgyzstan and Uzbekistan as members. In 1998 it was then renamed Central Asian Economic Cooperation with the entry of Tajikistan. In 2002 it was renamed yet again to its current name, the Central Asian Cooperation Organization or CACO. In 2004, Russia joined the organization. In the end of 2005 it was decided between the member states that Uzbekistan will join the Eurasian Economic Community and that the organizations will merge.

http://en.wikipedia.org/wiki/Central_Asian_Cooperation_Organization

Members

Kazakhstan, Kyrghizstan, Tajikistan, Uzbekistan and Russia.

Observers

Georgia, Turkey and Ukraine

SAARC: South Asian Association for Regional Cooperation, 1985

Purposes

To promote the welfare of the peoples of South Asia and improve their quality of life; to accelerate economic growth, social progress and cultural development in the region and give all individuals the opportunity to live in dignity and realize their full potential; to promote and strengthen collective self-reliance among the countries of South Asia; to contribute to mutual trust, understanding and appreciation of one another's problems; to promote collaboration and mutual assistance in economic, social, cultural, technical and scientific fields; to strengthen cooperation with other developing countries; to strengthen cooperation among members in international forums or matters of common interest; to cooperate with international and regional organizations with similar aims and purposes. In 1993, SAARC countries signed an agreement to gradually lower tariffs within the region. Nine years later, at the 12th SAARC summit at Islamabad, SAARC countries devised the South Asia Free Trade Agreement which created a framework for the establishment of a fee trade zone covering 1.4 billion people. This agreement went into force on January 1, 2006.

http://www.saarc-sec.org/main.php

Members

Afghanistan (in statu nascendi) Bangladesh, Bhutan, India, Maldives, Nepal, Pakistan and Sri Lanka.

1.5   Europe

BENELUX, 1947

Purposes

Benelux is an economic union in Western Europe. The treaty establishing the Benelux Customs Union was signed in 1944 by the governments in exile of the three countries in London, and entered into force in 1947. It ceased to exist in 1960, when it was replaced by the Benelux Economic Union. It was preceded by the (still extant) Belgium-Luxembourg Economic Union, established in 1921. Its founding contributed to the founding of the European Economic Community in 1957.

http://www.benelux.be/

Members

Belgium, Luxembourg, The Netherlands.

BSECS: The Black Sea Economic Cooperation, 1992

Purposes

The Black Sea Economic Cooperation Scheme (BSEC) has been established by 11 countries of the region during the summit meeting held in Istanbul on 25 June 1992. It is based on two documents, the 'Summit Declaration on Black Sea Economic Cooperation' and the 'Bosporus Statement'. The principles governing the BSEC are based on those of the Helsinki Final Act, the CSCE follow-up documents, the Paris Charter for a New Europe (1990). Since then (on 1 May 1999) with the entry into force of its charter, it has gained legal identity.

Its main purposes are: to achieve closer cooperation among the member states (and any other interested country) through the signing of bilateral and mutilateral agreements, in order to 'foster their economic, technological and social progress, and to encourage free enterprise'; to ensure that the Black Sea becomes a sea of peace, stability and prosperity, striving to promote friendly and good-neighbourly relations; to ensure economic cooperation to help implementing 'a Europe-wide economic area, as well as reaching a higher degree of integration of the Participating States into the world economy'.

http://www.bsec-organization.org/

Members

Albania, Armenia, Azerbaijan, Bulgaria, Georgia, Greece, Moldova, Romania, Russia, Turkey and Ukraine.

Observer nations

Belarus, Croatia, Czech Republic, France, Germany, Israel, Italy, Poland, Slovakia, Tunisia and the United States.

CEFTA: Central European Free Trade Agreement, 1992

Purposes

Through CEFTA, participating countries hoped to mobilize efforts to integrate Western European institutions and through this, to join European political, economic, security and legal systems, thereby consolidating democracy and free-market economics.

http://www.cefta.org/

Members

CEFTA is a trade agreement between Romania, Bulgaria, Croatia and the Republic of Macedonia. Former members are Poland, the Czech Republic, Slovakia, Hungary and Slovenia.

CIS: Commonwealth of Independent States, 1991

Purposes

It is an economic union which has been initiated by the leaders of Russia, Belarus and Ukraine after the dissolution of the Soviet Union (8 December, 1991). They announced that the new alliance will be open to all republics of the former Soviet Union. However, between 2003 and 2005, the leaderships of three CIS member states were overthrown in a series of 'colour revolutions': in Georgia, in Ukraine, and, lastly, in Kyrgyzstan. The new government in Ukraine has taken an especially clear pro-Western stance, in contrast to their predecessors' close relationship with the Kremlin. The new government of Georgia has likewise taken a pro-Western and anti-Kremlin stance. Moldova also seems to be quietly drifting toward the West, away from the CIS.

http://www.cisstat.com/eng/cis.htm

Members

Armenia, Azerbaijan, Belarus, Georgia, Kazakhstan, Kyrghizstan, Moldavia, Russia, Tajikistan, Ukraine, Uzbekistan. Turkmenistan, withdrew in 2005 and became an associate member since then.

EC/EU: European Community/European Union, 1957

Purposes

The European integration process has passed through several stages. In 1985 the European Economic Community (EEC) set up in 1957 by the Treaty of Rome was modified by the Single European Act, which brought together the European Coal and Steel Community (ECSC), the EEC and the European Atomic Energy Community (Euratom). The EEC became the European Community and then, in 1992, with the signature of the Maastricht Treaty, the European Union. The EU today has a three-pillar structure: (1) the Community activities pillar, managed by mainly supranational procedures; (2) the Common Foreign and Security Policy pillar, managed by an intergovernmental Council; and (3) the justice and home affairs pillar also based on intergovernmental cooperation.

The Union currently has a custumos union, a common single market, a single currency managed by the European Central Bank (so far adopted by 13 of the 27 member states), a Common Agricultural Policy, a common trade policy, and a

Common Fisheries Policy. The Schengen Agreement abolished passport control, and customs checks were also abolished at many of the EU's internal borders, creating a single space of mobility for EU citizens to live, travel, work and invest.

According to Article 2 of the Treaty of EU (Maastricht Treaty), the Union sets itself the following objectives: to promote economic and social progress which is balanced and sustainable, in particular through the creation of an area without internal frontiers, through the strengthening of economic and social cohesion, and through the establishment of economic and monetary union, ultimately including a single currency in accordance with the provisions of the treaty; to assert its identity on the international scene, in particular through the implementation of a CFSP including the framing of a defence policy cooperation; to strengthen the protection of the rights and interests of the nationals of its member states through the introduction of a citizenship of the Union; to develop close cooperation in the field of justice and home affairs; to maintain in full the acquis communautaire ensuring the effectiveness of the mechanisms and the institutions of the Community. The objectives of the Union should be achieved as provided in the treaty and in accordance with the condition of the schedule set out therein while respecting the principle of subsidiarity. Article C indicates that the Union shall in particular ensure the consistency of its external activities as a whole in the context of its external relations, security, economic and development policies.

The Treaty of Amsterdam (1997), which superseded the Maastricht Treaty, incorporated a number of changes: to sweep away the last remaining obstacles to freedom of movement and to strengthen internal security; to give Europe a stronger voice in world affairs. The Treaty of Nice (2000) had the main task to adopt the Union's institutional structure and to enable the Union to enlarge to new member states. On October 29, 2004, EU member state heads of government and state signed the Treaty establishing a Constitution for Europe. This has been ratified by 13 member states and is currently awaiting ratification by the other states. However, this process faltered on May 29, 2005 when the majority of French voters rejected the constitution in a referendum by 54.7%. The French rejection was followed three days later by a Dutch one on June 1 when in the Netherlands 61.6% of voters refused the constitution as well.

http://europa.eu/index_fr.htm

Members

Austria, Belgium, Bulgaria, Cyprus, Czech Republic, Denmark, Estonia, France, Finland, Hungary, Germany, Greece, Ireland, Italy, Latvia, Lithuania, Luxembourg, Malta, Poland, Portugal, Romania, Slovakia, Slovenia, Spain, Sweden, The Netherlands, United Kingdom. Any European state may apply to the Council to become a member of the Union, which acts unanimously after consulting the Commission and after receiving the assent of the European Parliament; ratification by each member state is requested.

Candidate countries

Croatia, Turkey, FYR Macedonia

EEA: European Economic Area, 1994

Purposes

Free trade area.
　http://ec.europa.eu/comm/external_relations/eea/index.htm

Members

EU and EFTA, minus Switzerland which rejected the EEA in a referendum.

EFTA: European Free Trade Association, 1960

Purposes

To promote in the area of the Association and in each member state a sustained expansion of economic activity, full employment, increased productivity and the rational use of resources, financial stability and continuous improvement in living standards; to secure conditions of fair competition in trade between member states; to avoid significant disparity between member states in the conditions of supply of raw materials produced within the area of the Association; to contribute to harmonious development and expansion of world trade and to progressive removal of barriers to this; to create a single market in Western Europe.
　http://www.efta.int/

Members

EFTA brought together the countries which did not want to join the Treaty of Rome in 1957: Austria, Denmark, Norway, Portugal, Sweden, Switzerland and United Kingdom. Today it consists of just four countries: Iceland, Liechtenstein, Norway and Switzerland.
　Visegrád, 1991

Purposes

The Visegrád Group created a free trade area between for Eastern countries in order to further the process of European integration. All four members of the Visegrád group entered the European Union on May 1, 2004.
　http://www.visegradgroup.eu/

Members

Czech Republic, Hungary, Poland, Slovakia.

1.6 Oceania

ANZCERTA (CER: Closer Economic Relationship, 1983)

Purposes

Established in 1983 as a successor to the New Zealand–Australia Free Trade Agreement (NAFTA) which had been set up in 1966. The Antipodean NAFTA applied only to certain products (excluding agriculture) and was therefore not a full free trade agreement. CER involved a stronger commitment to the establishment of free trade between the two countries, with trade in merchandise becoming fully free by 1990. There is also a commitment to economic integration in relation to services and the labour market. Integration has not been achieved in investment and currency matters; Australia unilaterally abrogated an agreement on a common aviation market in October 1994.

http://www.fta.gov.au/default.aspx?FolderID=283&ArticleID=229

Members

Australia, New Zealand.

SPC: South Pacific Commission, 1947

Purposes

The Commission was established by the governments of Australia, France, the Netherlands, New Zealand, the United Kingdom and the United States. It became an NGO providing the member states with technical assistance, scientific knowledge and economic assistance for development. On 1 January 1996 the United Kingdom decided to leave the Commission.

http://www.spc.int/

Members

Australia, Cook Islands, Guam, Eastern Samoa, Fiji, France, French Polynesia, Futuna, Kiribati, Marianne Island (North), Marshall Island, Micronesia, Nauru, New Caledonia, New Guinea, New Zealand, New Island, Palau, Papuasia, Pitcairn Islands, Solomon Islands, Tokelau, Tonga, Tuvalu, United States, Vanuatu, Wallis, Western Samoa.

2 Interregional organizations

EU-ACP relations: EU + Countries of Africa, Caribbean and Pacific, 1975

Purposes

Established by the EU through the Lomé Convention (Togo), replacing the Yaoundé Convention and the Arusha agreements. Its purpose is to establish cooperation for development among its member countries, some of which are former European colonies. The Lomé Agreement was suceeded by the Cotonou Agreement signed in Benin in June 2000. One of the major differences with the Lomé convention is that the partnership aims to reinforce ACP regionalism in order to conclude interregional arrangements with each regional groups. An other difference with the Lomé Convention, is that the Cotonou Agreement is extended to new actors like civil society, private sector, trade unions, local authorities, and so on. These will be involved in consultations and planning of national development strategies, provided with access to financial resources and involved in the implementation of programmes.

http://www.acpsec.org/

Members

The 27 Member States of the European Union and Angola, Antigua-Barbuda, Bahamas, Barbados, Belize, Benin, Botswana, Burkina Faso, Burundi, Cameroon, Central African Republic, Chad, Cook Island, Comoros, Congo, Cuba, Democratic Republic of Congo, Djibouti, Dominica, Equatorial Guinea, East Timor, Eritrea, Ethiopia, Fiji, Gabon, Gambia, Ghana, Green Cape, Grenada, Guinea, Guinea-Bissau, Guyana, Eastern Samoa, Haiti, Ivory Coast, Jamaica, Kenya, Kiribati, Lesotho, Liberia, Madagascar, Malawi, Mali, Marshal Island, Mauritius, Mauritania, Micronesia, Mozambique, Namibia, Nauru, Niger, Nigeria, Niue, Palau, Papua New Guinea, Rwanda, St Kitts and Nevis, St Lucia, St Vincent and Grenadines, Samoa, Solomon Islands, Sao Tomé and Principe, Senegal, Seychelles, Sierra Leone, Somalia, Sudan, Surinam, Swaziland, Tanzania, Togo, Tonga, Trinidad and Tobago, Tuvalu, Uganda, Vanuatu, Zambia, Zimbabwe, South Africa.

APEC: Asia–Pacific Economic Cooperation, 1989

Purposes

To serve as a forum for regular discussion on regional trade questions and cooperation; to sustain the growth and development of the region for the common good of its peoples and contribute to the growth and development of the world economy; to enhance positive gains, both for the region and the world economy, resulting from increasing economic interdependence, to include encouraging the flow of goods, services, capital and technology, developing and strengthening the open multilateral trading system in the interest of Asia–Pacific and all other economies; to reduce barriers to trade in goods and services among participants in

a manner consistent with WTO principles where applicable and without detriment to other economies. The main purpose is to set up a free trade area by 2020.
    http://www.apec.org/

Members

Australia, Brunei, Canada, Chile, China, Hong Kong, Indonesia, Japan, Malaysia, Mexico, New Zealand, Papua New Guinea, Philippines, Peru, Russia, Singapore, South Korea, Taiwan, Thailand, United States, Vietnam.

ASEM: Asia–Europe Meeting, 1994

Purposes

In 1994 the European Commission proposed a 'New Strategy for Asia' and the ASEAN member states approved the 'Singapore Project'. From both these initiatives emerged the principle of the Asia–Europe Meeting, with the main purpose of bringing the two continents closer. Launched in Bangkok in 1996 between the 15 member countries of the European Union, the European Commission and 10 Asian countries, the ASEM process has developed a global agenda and a new dynamic between two strategic partners, Asia and Europe. ASEM Summits have taken place every two years, alternating between Asia and Europe. ASEM potentially covers all issues of common interest to Europe and Asia. ASEM has a comprehensive approach, addressing the political, the economic, and the cultural and people-to-people dimensions of Asia's relations and partnership with Europe.
    http://asem.inter.net.th/

Members

The 27 Member States of the European Union and the European Commission; the seven member states of ASEAN; China, South Korea and Japan.
    Barcelona Process, 1995

Purposes

After 20 years of increasingly intensive bilateral trade and development cooperation between the EU and 12 Mediterranean partners, the Conference of EU and Southern Mediterranean Foreign Ministers in Barcelona (27–28 November 1995) marked the start of a new 'partnership' phase including bilateral, multilateral and regional cooperation. The conference was a first step towards a 'Euro-Mediterranean Partnership' (hence called 'Barcelona Process'). The Barcelona Declaration adopted at the Conference expresses the partners' intention to:

- establish a common Euro-Mediterranean area for peace and stability based on fundamental principles including respect for human rights and democracy (political and security partnership);

- create an area of shared prosperity through the progressive establishment of a free-trade area between the EU and its partners and among the Mediterranean partners themselves, accompanied by substantial EU financial support for economic transition and for the social and economic consequences of this reform process (economic and financial partnership);
- develop human resources, promote understanding between cultures and bring peoples closer together in the Euro-Mediterranean region, as well as develop free and flourishing civil societies (social, cultural and human partnership).
  http://www.euromedheritage.net/fr/rmsu/ateliers_rmsu/barcelona.htm

Members

The 27 EU member states, Algeria, Cyprus, Egypt, Israel, Jordan, Lebanon, Malta, Morocco, Palestinian Authority, Syria, Tunisia, Turkey. Observer: Libya.

FTAA: Free Trade Area of the Americas, 1994

Purposes

The project of the Initiatives of the Americas (1990) is at the root of the Free Trade Area of the Americas (FTAA, in Spanish: Área de Libre Comercio de las Américas (ALCA), in French: Zone de libre-échange des Amériques (ZLEA) and in Portuguese: Área de Livre Comércio das Américas (ALCA)). The latter has as main aim to liberalize goods, services and investments. The negotiations were launched by US President Clinton on December 11, 1994 at the Miami summit conference of thirty-four American countries. However, the FTAA came to public attention during the Quebec City Summit of the Americas in 2001, a meeting targeted by massive anti-corporatization and alter-globalization protests. The Miami negotiations in 2003 met similar protests, though perhaps not as large. The last summit was held at Mar del Plata, Argentina in January 2005, but no agreement on FTAA was reached. 26 of the 34 countries present at the negotiations have pledged to meet again in 2006 to resume negotiations.
    http://www.ftaa-alca.org/

Members

All the countries of the Americas except Cuba: Antigua and Barbuda, Argentina, the Bahamas, Barbados, Belize, Bolivia, Brazil, Canada, Chile, Colombia, Costa Rica, Dominica, El Salvador, Ecuador, the United States, Grenada, Guatemala, Guyana, Haiti, Honduras, Jamaica, Mexico, Nicaragua, Panama, Paraguay, the Dominican Republic, St Lucia, St Kitts and Nevis, St Vincent and the Grenadines, Surinam, Trinidad and Tobago, Uruguay and Venezuela.

NTA: The New Transatlantic Agenda, 1995

Purposes

On 3 December 1995 at the EU–US Summit in Madrid, European Commission President Santer, Spanish Prime Minister Gonzalez, as President of the European Council, and US President Clinton signed the New Transatlantic Agenda (NTA). The agenda is essentially a political gesture. The US and EU have agreed a NTA for making swifter and more effective progress towards the political, economic and security goals they first set for themselves in the Transatlantic Declaration of 1990. The Agenda drawn from a more detailed Action Plan identifies a joint work program in four areas: promoting peace, development and democracy around the world; responding to global challenges such as international crime, the environment and disease; contributing to the expansion of world trade and closer economic relations; building bridges across the Atlantic.

http://www.eurunion.org/partner/euusrelations/AgendasDialoguesSummits. htm

Members

United States of America and the 27 Member States of the European Union. Rio de Janeiro Process, 1999.

Purpose

The 'Rio de Janeiro Process' started in June 1999 in Brazil with the Euro-Latin American summit. The main purpose of this initiative is to bring the two continents closer, creating a strategic partnership. The objective of the Rio Summit was to strengthen the political, economic and cultural understanding between the two regions in order to encourage the development of a strategic partnership, establishing a set of priorities for future joint action in the political and economic fields. A second EU-LAC Summit was held in Madrid on 17-18 May 2002. This summit assessed progress made in the framework of the strategic partnership established at Rio, emphasising progress in the three main pillars of the relationship: political dialogue, economic and financial relations including trade and capital, and cooperation in a number of areas. On this occasion, new proposals were made for the further strengthening of this bi-regional partnership. The third EU-LAC Summit took place in Guadalajara (Mexico) on 28 May 2004. It achieved a great deal finding a common policy line to the 58 participating countries: 33 LAC + 27 EU states. Strong and concrete commitments were taken in three main domains: Social cohesion, Multilateralism and Regional Integration. The fourth EU-LAC Summit took place in Vienna (Austria) on 12-13 May 2006. Heads of State decided in particular, to launch negotiations for an Association Agreement between the EU and Central America.

http://ec.europa.eu/comm/external_relations/la/index.htm

Members

The 27 member states + the European Commission and all the countries of the Americas including Cuba and except the Canada and the USA: Antigua and Barbuda, Argentina, the Bahamas, Barbados, Belize, Bolivia, Brazil, Chile, Colombia, Costa Rica, Dominica, El Salvador, Ecuador, Grenada, Guatemala, Guyana, Haiti, Honduras, Jamaica, Mexico, Nicaragua, Panama, Paraguay, the Dominican Republic, St Lucia, St Kitts and Nevis, St Vincent and the Grenadines, Surinam, Trinidad and Tobago, Uruguay and Venezuela.

OSCE: Organization for Security and Cooperation in Europe, 1975

Purpose

The Organization for Security and Cooperation in Europe succeeded to the Conference on Security and Cooperation in Europe started on 3 July 1975, and originated the so-called 'Helsinki Process'. The basic act of the Conference on Security and Co-operation in Europe was signed on 1 August 1975 in Helsinki, by Heads of States or governments of 35 states.

Institutionalized as a permanent body on 21 November 1990 (Charter of Paris for a New Europe), the OSCE has been enlarged and further delineated by the Helsinki Document (July 1992). the current title has finally been adopted at the pan-European summit of Budapest, 5–6 December 1994, to be effective from 1 January 1995.

The OSCE is a security forum and its 55 participating States span the geographical area from Vancouver to Vladivostok. In this region, it is an important instrument for early warning, conflict prevention, crisis management and post-conflict rehabilitation. The OSCE includes three baskets: a) a comprehensive and co-operative approach to pan-European security; b) human rights and elections monitoring; c) economic and environmental cooperation. Members Albania, Andorra, Armenia, Austria, Azerbaijan, Belarus, Belgium, Bosnia and Herzegovina, Bulgaria, Canada, Croatia, Cyprus, Czech Republic, Denmark, Estonia, Finand, France, Georgia, Germany, Greece, Holy See, Hungary, Iceland, Ireland, Italy, Kazakhstan, Kyrghizstan, Latvia, Liechtenstein, Lithuania, Luxembourg, Malta, Moldova, Monaco, Netherlands, Norway, Poland, Portugal, Romania, Russian Federation, San Marino, Slovak Republic, Slovenia, Spain, Sweden, Switzerland, Tajikistan, the former Yugoslav Republic of Macedonia, Turkey, Turkmenistan, Ukraine, United Kingdom, United States of America, Uzbekistan, Federal Republic of Yugoslavia.

http://www.osce.org/

TEP: The Transatlantic Economic Partnership, 1998

Purpose

Announced at the Birmingham summit of the TEP is economic pillar of the New Transatlantic Agenda, to be achieved by 'progressively reducing or eliminating barriers that hinder the flow of goods, services and capital'. A new private sector group, the Transatlantic Business Dialogue (TABD), was established to define and promote the specific trade and investment agenda needeed to bring the marketplace to fruition. Thanks in large part to the TABD, Washington and Brussels reached agreement in 1997 – after years of effort – on a package of mutual recognition agreements (MRAs) eliminating duplicative testing and certification in six sectors. The US government estimates that this package, which covers about $47 billion worth of trade, eliminates costs equivalent to two or three percentage points of tariffs. In the meantime, other problems arose that soured the prospects for broader transatlantic economic cooperation.

    http://www.eurunion.org/partner/euusrelations/AgendasDialoguesSummits. htm

Members

United States of America and the 27 Member States of the European Union.

3 Other institutions

ECFA: Economic Commission for Africa, 1958

Purposes

United Nations initiative. To facilitate economic development and relations between member states.

    http://www.uneca.org/

Members

Algeria, Angola, Benin, Botswana, Burkina Faso, Burundi, Cameroon, Central African Republic, Chad, Comoros, Congo, Democratic Republic of Congo, Djibouti, Egypt, Equatorial Guinea, Eritrea, Ethiopia, Gabon, Gambia, Ghana, Green Cape, Guinea, Guinea-Bissau, Ivory Coast, Kenya, Lesotho, Liberia, Libya, Madagascar, Malawi, Mali, Morocco, Mauritius, Mauritania, Mozambique, Namibia, Niger, Nigeria, Rwanda, Sao Tomé and Principe, Senegal, Seychelles, Sierra Leone, Somalia, South Africa, Sudan, Swaziland, Tanzania, Togo, Tunisia, Uganda, Zambia, Zimbabwe.

ECLA: Economic Commission for Latin America (CEPAL in Spanish), 1948

Purposes

United Nations initiative. It has been working in the field of industrial development.
   http://www.eclac.org/

Members

Antigua-Barbuda, Argentina, Bahamas, Barbados, Belize, Bolivia, Brazil, Canada, Chile, Colombia, Costa Rica, Cuba, Dominica, Dominican Republic, Ecuador, El Salvador, France, Grenada, Guatemala, Guyana, Haiti, Honduras, Italy, Jamaica, Mexico, Nicaragua, Panama, Paraguay, The Netherlands, Peru, Portugal, St Kitts and Nevis, St Lucia, St Vincent and Grenadines, Spain, Surinam, Trinidad and Tobago, United Kingdom, United States, Uruguay, Venezuela.

ESCAP: Economic and Social Commission for Asia and the Pacific, 1947

Purposes

United Nations initiative (today ECAFE). The main purpose of ESCAP is to encourage economic and social development in Asia and the Pacific. It acts as a regional centre of the United Nations and constitutes the only intergovernmental forum for all Asia and the Pacific. It implements a whole series of development programmes through technical assistance, services for governmental cooperation, research, training and information.
   http://www.unescap.org/

Members

Afghanistan, Australia, Azerbaijan, Bangladesh, Brunei, Cambodia, China, Eastern Samoa, Fiji, France, India, Indonesia, Iran, Japan, Kiribati, Kyrgizstan, Laos, Malaysia, Maldives, Marshall Island, Micronesia, Mongolia, Myanmar, Nauru, Nepal, New Zealand, North Korea, Pakistan, Papua New Guinea, The Netherlands, Philippines, Russia, Solomon Islands, Singapore, South Korea, Sri Lanka, Tajikistan, Tonga, Turkmenistan, Tuvalu, United Kingdom, United States, Vanuatu, Vietnam.

ESCWA: Economic and Social Commission for West Asia, 1974

Purposes

United Nations initiative. To undertake or to support studies on economic and social perspectives in the region, to collect and to diffuse the information, and to offer consulting services. The main work of the ESCWA is being led in collaboration with other members of the UN.

http://www.escwa.org.lb/

Members

Bahrain, Egypt, Iraq, Jordan, Kuwait, Lebanon, Oman, Palestine Authority, Qatar, Saudi Arabia, Syria, United Arab Emirates, Yemen.

Rio Group, 1986

Purposes

Forum dealing with political and development problems of external relations and issues of regional integration.

http://es.wikipedia.org/wiki/Grupo_de_R%C3%ADo

Members

Argentina, Bolivia, Brazil, Chile, Colombia, Ecuador, Mexico, Panama, Paraguay, Peru, Uruguay, Venezuela.

Planispheres

Pablo Medina Lockhart

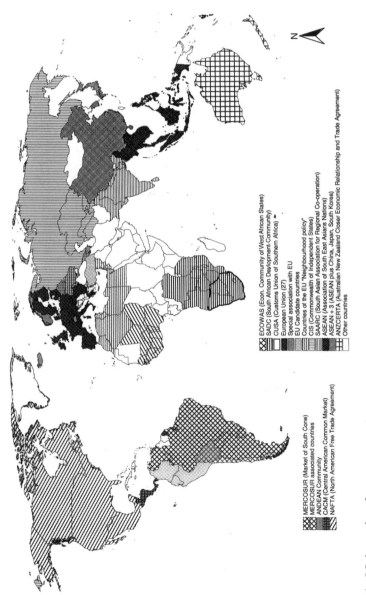

1 **Main regional arrangements**

MERCOSUR (Market of South Cone)
MERCOSUR associated countries
ANDEAN Community
CACM (Central American Common Market)
NAFTA (North American Free Trade Agreement)

ECOWAS (Econ. Community of West African States)
SADC (South African Development-Community)
CUSA (Customs Union of Southern Africa) ≈
European Union (27)
Special association with EU
EU Candidate countries
Countries of the EU "Neighbourhood policy"
CIS (Commonwealth of Independent States)
SAARC (South Asian Association for Regional Co-operation)
ASEAN (Association of South East Asians Nations)
ASEAN + 3 (ASEAN plus China, Japan, South Korea)
ANZCERTA (Australian New Zealand Closer Economic Relationship and Trade Agreement)
Other countries

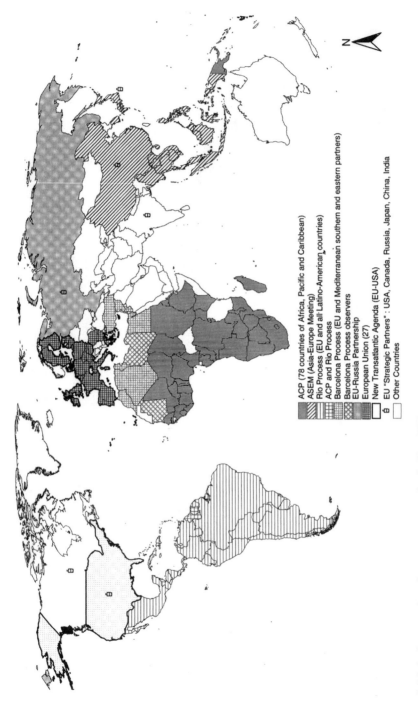

ACP (78 countries of Africa, Pacific and Caribbean)
ASEM (Asia-Europe Meeting)
Rio Process (EU and all Latino-American countries)
ACP and Rio Process
Barcelona Process (EU and Mediterranean southern and eastern partners)
Barcelona Process observers
EU-Russia Partnership
European Union (27)
New Transatlantic Agenda (EU-USA)
EU "Strategic Partners" : USA, Canada, Russia, Japan, China, India
Other Countries

2 Main interregional arrangements including EU

APEC (Asia-Pacific Economic Co-operation)
FTAA (Free Trade Area of the Americas)
USA (New Transatlantic Agenda + FTAA + APEC)
New Transatlantic Agenda

3 Main interregional arrangements including US

Bibliography

Abad Jr., M. C. (2003) The Association of Southeast Asian Nations: Challenges and Responses, in M. Wesley .(ed.) *Regional Organizations of the Asia Pacific: Exploring Institutional Change*, Gordonsville, VA: Palgrave Macmillan, pp. 40–59.

Acharya, Amitav (1997) Ideas, Identity and Institution-building: From the 'ASEAN way' to the 'Asia-Pacific way', in *Pacific Review*, 10(3), Department of Politics and International Studies, University of Warwick.

Acharya, A. (2001) *Constructing a Security Community in South East Asia: ASEAN and the Problem of Regional Order*: London: Routledge.

Acharya, A. (2004) How Ideas Spread: Whose Norms Matter? Norm Localization and Institutional Change in Asian Regionalism, *International Organisation*, 58(2): 239–75.

Acharya, A. (2005) Europe and Asia: Reflections on a Tale of Two Regions, in Douglas Webber and Bertrand Fort (eds.) *Regional Integration in Europe and East Asia: Convergence or Divergence*, London: Routledge.

Aggarwal, Vinod. (1994) Comparing Regional Cooperation Efforts in the Asia–Pacific and North America, in Andrew Mack and John Ravenhill (eds.), *Pacific Cooperation: Building Economic and Security Regimes in the Asia–Pacific Region*, St Leonards, New South Wales: Allen and Unwin.

Aggarwal, V. K. and E. A. Fogarty (2006) The Limits of Interregionalism: the EU and North America, in Söderbaum and Langenhove, pp 79–98.

Ahwireng-Obeng, Fred and Patrick J. McGowan (1998) Partner or Hegemon? South Africa in Africa: Part One, *Journal of Contemporary African Studies* 16(1): 5–38.

Albert, M. (1991) *Capitalisme contre capitalisme*, Paris: Seuil.

Alesina, A. and Grilli, V. (1993) On the Feasibility of a One-Speed or Multi-Speed European Monetary Union, in *Economics and Politics*, 5.

Aliboni, R. (1990) *Southern European Security*, London: Pinder.

Aliboni, R. (2005) The Geopolitical Implications of the European Neighbourhood Policy, *European Foreign Affairs Review*, 10.

Allen, D. and Smith, M. (1990) Western Europe's Presence in the Contemporary International Arena, in *Review of International Affairs*, 1990, no. 16: 19–37.

Almond, Gabriel A. and Verba, Sidney (1963) *The Civic Culture. Political Attitudes and Democracy in Five Nations*. Princeton, NJ: Princeton University Press.

Alter, Karen J. (1998) Who Are the 'Masters of the Treaty'? European Governments and the European Court of Justice, in *International Organization*, 52(1), Winter: 121–47.

Amato, Giuliano and Batt, Jud (1999) *Long-Term Implications of EU Enlargement: the Nature of the New Border*, Florence: Robert Schuman Centre.

Amin, Samir (1997) *Capitalism in the Age of Globalization*, Trieste: Asterios.

Andersen, Svein S. and Eliassen, Kjell A. (eds.) (1993) *Making Policy in Europe: The Europeification of National Policy-making*, London: Sage (2nd edn., 2001).

Anderson, Benedict (1987) *Imagined Communities*, London Verso.

Anderson, James and Goodman, J. (1995) Regions, States and the European Union: Modernist Reaction or Postmodernist Adaptation?, in *Review of International Political Economy*, 2(4): 600–31.

Anderson, M. (1989) *Policing the World: Interpol and the Politics of International Police Cooperation*, New York : Oxford University Press.

Anderson, Perry (1974) *Lineages of the Absolutist State*, London: Verso.

Archibugi, Daniele, Held, David and Koehler, M. (eds.) (1998) *Re-imagining Political Community. Studies in Cosmopolitan Democracy*, Cambridge: Polity.

Aron, Raymond (1998) L'Europe face à la crise des sociétés industrielles, in *L'Europe? L'Europe*, texts collected by Pascal Ory, Paris: Omnibus.

Asante, S. K. B. (1997) *Regionalism and Africa's Development. Expectations, Reality and Challenges*, Basingstoke: Macmillan.

Attina F. and Rossi, R. (eds.) (2004) *European Neighbourhood Policy: Political, Economic and Social Aspects*, University of Catania: Jean Monnet Centre.

Axelrod, R. and Keohane, R. O. (1986) Achieving Cooperation under Anarchy: Strategies and Limitations, in K. A. Oye, ed., *Cooperation under Anarchy*, Princeton University Press.

Aubarell, G. and Aragall, X. (2005) Immigration and the Euro-Mediterranean Area: Keys to Policy and Trends, *EuroMeSCo Paper No. 47* IEEI (Lisbon).

Ayoob, Mohammed and Samudavanija, Chai-Anan (1989) Leadership and Security in Southeast Asia: Exploring General Propositions, in M. Ayoob and Samudvanija, Chai-Anan, *Leadership Perceptions and National Security: The SE Asian Experience*, London: Routledge.

Bach, Daniel C. (1997) Institutional Crisis and the Search for New Models, in Lavergne, Reál (ed.) *Regional Integration and Cooperation in West Africa. A Multidimensional Perspective*, Trenton. NJ: Africa World Press.

Bach, Daniel C. (1999a) *Regionalisation in Africa. Integration & Disintegration*, London: James Currey.

Bach, Daniel C. (1999b) Regionalism Versus Regional Integration: the Emergence of a New Paradigm in Africa in Jean Grugel and Wil Hout (eds.), *Regionalism Across the North-South Divide. State Strategies and Globalization*, London: Routledge.

Bach, Daniel C. (2005) The Global Politics of Regionalism: Africa in Mary Farrell, Björn Hettne and Luk van Langenhove (eds.) *Global Politics of Regionalism. Theory and Practice*, London: Pluto Press.

Bache, Ian and Flinders, Matthew (eds.) (2004) *Multi-level Governance*, Oxford: Oxford University Press.

Badie, Bertrand (1999) *Un monde sans souveraineté. Les Etats entre ruse et responsabilité*, Fayard: Paris.

Balassa, Bela (1961) *The Theory of Economic Integration*, London: Greenwood.

Baldwin, Richard (1993) *A Domino Theory of Regionalism*, CEPR Discussion Paper 732, London: Centre for Economic Policy Research.

Baldwin, Richard (1994) *Toward an Integrated Europe*, London: CEPR.

Baldwin, Richard (1998) Le cause del regionalismo, in P. Padoan, ed., *Globalizzazione e regionalismo, Europa/Europe*, 6: 83–111, Rome.

Baldwin, Richard and Venables, Anthony (1994) Regional Economic Integration, in Gene Grossman and Kenneth Rogoff, eds., *Handbook of International Economics*, vol. 3, Amsterdam.

Balfour R. and Rotta, A. (2005) The European Neighbourhood Policy and its Tools, *The International Spectator*, XL, 1.

Barahona de Brito, Alexandra (1997) Condicionalidade politica e cooperação para a promoção da democracia e dos direitos humanos, in *Além do Comercio*, IEEI, Lisbon.

Barber, Benjamin, R. (1995) *Jihad vs. McWorld*, New York: Times Books.

Barro, R. and Sala-i-Martin, X. (1991) Convergence Across States and Regions, in *Brookings Papers on Economic Activity*, 1: 107–58.

Bauman, Zygmunt (1998) *Globalization. The Human Consequences*, Cambridge: Polity Press.

Baylis J. and Smith S. (2001) *The Globalisation of World Politics*, Oxford: Oxford University Press.

Bayoumi, Tamil (1994) *A Formal Model of Optimum Currency Areas*, CEPR Discussion Paper 968, Centre for Economic Policy Research, London.

Beeson, Mark (2005) Rethinking Regionalism: Europe and East Asia in Comparative historical Perspective, *European Journal of Public Policy*, 12(6): 969–85.

Beeson, Mark and Richard, Higgott (2005) Hegemony, Institutionalism and US Foreign Policy: Theory and Practice in Comparative Historical Perspective, *Third World Quarterly*, 26(7):1173–88.

Bellamy, Richard (2005) Still in Deficit: Rights, Regulation and Democracy in the EU, for the Democracy Task Force of the EU 6th Framework Integrated Project on *New Modes of Governance*, 1–31.

Benhabib, Seyla (1993) *Demokratie und Differenz. Betrachtungen über Rationalität, Demokratie und Postmoderne*. In: Brumlik/ Brunkhorst.

Ben-David, D. (1995) *Trade and Convergence Among Countries*, CEPR Discussion Paper Series 1126, London: Centre for Economic Policy Research.

Bensidoun, I. and A. Chevallier (1996) *Europe-Méditerranée: le pari de l'ouverture*, Paris: Economia-CEPII.

Berg, E. (1988) *Regionalism and Economic Development in Sub-Saharan Africa*, Washington DC: USAID.

Berger, Susan and Dore, R. (1996) *National Diversity and Global Capitalism*, Ithaca: Cornell University Press.

Bergsten, Fred (1996) Globalizing Free Trade, in *Foreign Affairs*, no. 3.

Bergsten, Fred (1997) *Open Regionalism*, Working Paper, Institute for International Economics, Washington DC.

Bergsten, Fred (2000) East Asian Regionalism: Towards a Tripartite World, *The Economist*, 15 July.

Bernard, Mitchell and Ravenhill, John (1995) Beyond Product Cycles and Flying Geese: Regionalization, Hierarchy and the Industrialization of East Asia, in *World Politics*, 47(2): 171–209.

Bertrand, G., A Michalski. and L. R Pench.) (1999), *Scenarios Europe 2010. Five Possible Futures for Europe*, Working Paper, European Commission, Forward Studies Unit.

Bhagwati, Jagdish (1991) *The World Trading System at Risk*, Princeton: Princeton University Press.

Bhagwati, Jagdish (1993) Regionalism and Multilateralism: An Overview, in Ross Garnaut and Peter Drysdale, eds., *Asia Pacific Regionalism: Readings in International Economic Relations*, Pymble: Harper Educational/ANU.

Bhagwati, Jagdish and Arvind, P. (1996) Preferential Trading Areas and Multilateralism: Stranger, Friends or Foes? in J. Bhagwati and A. Panagariya, eds., *Free Trade Areas or Free Trade?*, Washington DC: AEI Press.

Bhagwati, Jagdish, R. Haass,, R. Litan, E. M. Lincoln and M. Bouton (1998) Can Asia Recover?, articles published in *Foreign Affairs*, May/June 1998, 77(3).

Bhagwati, Jagdish (2002) *Free Trade Today*, Princeton: Princeton University Press.

Bhagwati, Jagdish and Hugh, Patrick (eds.) (1990) *Aggressive Unilateralism: America's 301 Trade Policy and the World Trading System*, Ann Arbor: University of Michigan Press.

Bhattacharaya, A., P. Montiel and S. Sharma (1996) *Private Capital Flows to Sub-Saharan Africa: An Overview of Trends and Determinants*, mimeo, *International Monetary Fund*, Washington DC.

Bøås, Morten (2003) Weak States, Strong Regimes: Towards a 'Real' Political Economy of African Regionalization, in J. Andrew and Fredrik Söderbaum eds. *The New Regionalism in Africa*, Aldershot: Ashgate.

Bøås, Morten, Marianne H. Marchand and Timothy M. Shaw (eds.) (1999) *New Regionalisms in the New Millennium*, special issue of *Third World Quarterly*, 20: 5 (October).

Bobbitt, Philip (2002) *The Shield of Achilles : War, Peace and the Course of History*, London: Allen Lane.

Bobbio, Norberto (1981) Stato potere, governo, in *Enciclopedia Einaudi*, vol. XIII, Einaudi, Turin.

Bobbio, Norberto (1998) *Etat et démocratie internationale*, Complexe, Brussels, ed. by M. Telò (translated by Vogel, Magnette and Giovannini).

Bomber, E. (1994) Policy Network on the Periphery, in *Regional Politics and Policy*, 4: 45–61.

Bouzas, Roberto (ed.) (2006) *Domestic Determinants of National Trade Strategies. A Comparative Analysis of Mercosur Countries, Mexico and Chile*, Paris, Sc.Po. Chaire Mercosur.

Bova, Russell (1994) Political Dynamics of the Post-Communist Transition: A Comparative Perspective, in *World Politics*, 44(Summer): 113–38.

Boyd, Gavin (1997) Regional Economic Cooperation: EU, NAFTA, and APC, in Gavin Boyd and Alan Rugman, eds., *Euro-Pacific Investment and Trade: Strategies and Structural Interdependencies*, Cheltenham: Edward Elgar.

Boyer, Robert, *et al.* (1997) *Mondialisation. Au delà des mythes*, Paris: La Découverte.

Braudel, Fernand (1949/1972) The Mediterranean and the Mediterranean World in the Reign of Philip II, 2 vols, London: Fontana.

Breslin Shaun and Higgott, Richard (eds.) (2000) Special Issue: Studying Regions, *New Political Economy* 5:3.

Breslin, Shaun (2005) Studying Regions: Comparativism and Eurocentrism, *Conference on China and Asian Regionalism*, Shanghai: Fudan University, January: 1–39.

Breslin, Shaun and Higgott, Richard (2000) Studying Regions: Learning from the Old, Constructing the New, *New Political Economy*, 5(3): 333–52.

Breslin, Shaun, Chris Hughes,, Nicola Phillips and Ben Rosamond, (eds.) (2002) *New Regionalism in the Global Political Economy: Theories and Cases*, London: Routledge.

Bressand, A. and K Nicolaidis (1990) Regional Integration in a Networked World Economy, in William Wallace, ed., *The Dynamics of European Integration*, London: Pinter.

Bretherton, Charlotte and John Vogler (1999) The European Union as a Global Actor, London: Routledge.

Brewer, A. (1990) *Marxist Theories of Imperialism*, London: Macmillan.

British Petroleum (various years: published annually), BP Statistical Review of World Energy, British Petroleum plc, London.

British Petroleum (2006) BP statistical review of world energy,, London.

Buchanan, James (1965) The Economic Theory of Clubs, in *Economica*, 37: 1–14.

Bull, Hedley (1977) *The Anarchical Society*, London: Macmillan.

Bull, Hedley (1982) Civilian Power Europe: A Contradiction in Terms? in *Journal of Common Market Studies*, 1/2: 149–64.

Bulmer, Simon (1994a) The Governance of the European Union: A New Institutionalist Approach, in *Journal of Public Policy*, 13(4): 351–80.

Bulmer, Simon (1994b) Institutions and Policy Change in the European Communities: The Case of Merger Control, in *Public Administration*, 72: 423–44.

Burbach, Roger and Jim Tarbell (2004) *Imperial Overstretch. George W. Bush and the Hubris of Empire*, London: Zed Books.

Buzan, Barry (1991) New Patterns of Global Security in the Twenty-First Century, in *Foreign Affairs*, 67(3): 431–51.

Buzan, Barry and Gerald Segal (1994) Rethinking East Asian Security, *Survival*, 36(2): 3–21.

Buzan, Barry (2003) *Regions and Power*, Cambridge: Cambridge University Press.

Cai, Penghong (1992) The Fourth ASEAN Summit Talk and its Influence over Regional Economic Cooperation, in *Asia–Pacific Economic Review*, 2: 16–18.

Calleya, S. (1997) *Navigating Regional Dynamics in a Post-Cold War World*, Aldershot: Dartmouth.

Caporaso, James and J. Keeler (1993) *The EC and Regional Integration Theory*, paper presented at the Conference of the ECSA, May 1993, Washington DC.

Cardoso, Fernando Henrique (1998) speech delivered at the closing session of the Fifth Euro-Latin American Forum, IEEI, Lisbon.

Charillon, Frédéric (2004) Sovereignty and Intervention: EU's Interventionism in its 'Near Abroad', in Carlsnaes *et al.*

Carr, Edward H. (1946) *The Twenty Years Crisis 1919–1939*, London: Macmillan.

Carlsnaes, Walter et al. (ed.) (2004) *Contemporary European Foreign Policy*, London: Sage.

Casella, Alessandra and James Feinstein (1990) *Public Goods in Trade: On the Formation of Markets and Political Jurisdictions*, NBER Working Paper 3554.

Castells, Manuel (1996) *The Rise of the Network Society*, Cambridge, MA: Blackwell Publishers.

Castells, Manuel (1997) *The Information Age. Economy, Society and Culture. Vol. II:The Power of Identity*. Oxford.

Cavalcanti, Geraldo H. (1990) As opções da América Latina face às transformações de hoje, speech delivered at the First Euro-Latin American Forum, Federação das Indústrias do Estado de São Paulo (FIESP) and IEEI, São Paulo.

CEC (1996) *Creating a New Dynamic in EU–ASEAN Relations*, report from the Commission of the European Communities, COM (96) 314 final.

Cerny, Philip G. (1990) *The Changing Architecture of Politics: Structure, Agency, and the Future of the State*, London: Sage.

Cerny, Philip G. (2000) Restructuring the Political Arena: Globalization and the Paradoxes of the Competition State, in *Globalization and its Critics: Perspectives from Political Economy*, Randall D. Germain, ed., Macmillan/St. Martin's Press, Basingstoke/New York.

Cerutti, Furio (1997) Identität und Politik, in *International Zeitschrift für Philosophie*, no. 2.

Chabal, Patrick and Jean-Pascal Daloz (1999) *Africa Works: Disorder as Political Instrument*, London: James Currey.

Chalermpalanupap, Termsak (1997) *Enlargement of ASEAN: Prospects for Closer Regional Cooperation*, paper presented to the international conference 'ASEAN at the Crossroads: Opportunities and Challenges', Malaysian Institute of Economic Research, November 1997, Kuala Lumpur.

Chirac, Jacques (1997) speech delivered to the Congress of the Federal Republic of Brazil, 12 March 1997, Brasilia.

Cho, Yong-sang and Chung, Chong-tae (1997) ASEM's Hopes and Apprehensions: An Interregional Organization in the 21st Century, paper presented to the International Political Science Association at the 17th World Congress, August 1997, Seoul.

Chourou, B. (1998) The Free-Trade Agreement between Tunisia and the European Union, in *Journal of North African Studies*, 3(1), Spring.

Clapham, Christopher (1996) *Africa and the International System. The Politics of State Survival*, Cambridge: Cambridge University Press.

Clapham, Christopher (1999) Boundaries and States in the New African Order, in Daniel C. Bach (ed.) *Regionalization in Africa: Integration and Disintegration*, Oxford: James Currey.

Clarck, Ian (1997) *Globalization and Fragmentation. International Relations in the Twentieth Century*, Oxford: Oxford University Press,.

Cohen, Benjamin J. (1993) Beyond EMU: The Problem of Sustainability, in *Economics and Politics*, 5.

Coleman, W. D. and G. R. D. Underhill (eds.) (1998) *Regionalism and Global Economic Cooperation*, London: Routledge.

Collier, Paul and J. Gunning (1996) Trade Liberalization and the Composition of Investment: Theory and an African Application, WPS/96–4, Centre for the Study of African Economies, Oxford: University of Oxford.

Collier, Paul and J Gunning. (1999) Explaining African Economic Performance, in *Journal of Economic Literature*, 37: 64–111.

Collignon, S. (1997) *European Monetary Union, Convergence and Sustainability* (The Sustainability Report), Paris: AUME.

Collinson, S. (1996) *From Shore to Shore*, London: Royal Institute of International Affairs,.

Commission Européenne (1997) *L'avenir des relations Nord-Sud*, Les cahiers de la cellule de Prospective, Bruxelles.

Commission on Global Governance (1995) *Our Global Neighbourhood*, New York: Oxford University Press.

Cooper, Richard (1994) World-wide Regional Integration: Is There an Optimal Size of the Integrated Area?, in Ross Garnaut and Peter Drysdale, eds., *Asia Pacific Regionalism: Readings in International Economic Relations*, Pymble: Harper Educational/ANU.

Cooper, Richard (1997) *The Postmodern State*, London: Demos.

Cooper R. (2003) *The Breaking of Nations: Order and Chaos in the 21st Century*, London: Atlantic Books.

Cornes, James and Todd, Sandler (1985) *The Theory of Externalities, Public Goods and Club Goods*, Cambridge: Cambridge University Press.

Cox, Robert W. (1996) *Approaches to World Order*, Cambridge: Cambridge University Press.

Cox, Robert W. ed. (1997) *The New Realism. Perspectives on Multilateralism and World Order*, United Nations University Press, Tokyo, New York, Paris.

Cox, Robert , with Timothy J. Sinclair (1996) *Approaches to World Order*, Cambridge University Press.

Cox, Robert W. (1999) Civil Society at the Turn of the Millennium:Prospects for an Alternative World Order, *Review of International Studies*, 25(1): 3–28.

Cox, Michael (2004) Imperialism and the Bush Doctrine, *Review of International Studies* 30(4): 585–608.

Cram, L. (1997) *Policy-Making in the EU: Conceptual Lenses and the Integration Process*,London: Routledge.

CREFSA (1997) The South-East Asian Crisis and Implications for South Africa, in *Quarterly Review*, October, Centre for Research into Economics and Finance in Southern Africa, London School of Economics, London.

Crouch, Colin and Wolfgang Streeck,, (eds.) (1997) *Political Economy of Modern Capitalism. Mapping Convergence and Diversity*, London: Sage.

Cryssochou, Dimitris N. (2001) *Theorizing European Integration*, London: Sage.

Cumings, Bruce (1984) The Origins and Development of the Northeast Asian Political Economy: Industrial Sectors, Product Cycles, and Political Consequences, in *International Organization*, 38: 1–40.

Dannreuther, Roland (ed.) (2004) *European Union Foreign and Security Policy. Towards a Neighbourhood Strategy*, London: Routledge.

Decaluwé, B., D. Njinkeu and L. Bela (1995) UDEAC Case Study, paper presented at the AERC workshop on Regional Integration and Trade Liberalization, Harare.

Defraigne, Jean Christophe, Heribert Dieter, Richard Higgott and Pascal Lamy (2005) *East Asian Integration: Opportunities and Obstacles for Enhanced Economic Cooperation, Report for JETRO*, Paris: Notre Europe.

de Grauwe, Paul (1992) *European Monetary Integration*, Oxford: Oxford University Press.

Deiter, Heribert and Richard Higgott (2003) Exploring Alternative Theories of Economic Regionalism: From Trade to Finance in Asian Co-operation, *Review of International Political Economy*, 10(3): 430–54.

Delanty, Gerard (1995) *Inventing Europe: Idea, Identity, Reality*, Basingstoke: Macmillan.

de Melo, Jaime, A. Panagariya and D. Rodrik (1993) The New Regionalism: A Country Perspective, in J. de Melo and A. Panagariya, eds., *New Dimensions in Regional Integration*, Cambridge: Cambridge University Press.

Dent, Christopher (2004) *The New Economic Bilateralism and Southeast Asia: Region Convergent or Region Divergent*, British International Studies Association, IPEG Papers in Global Political Economy, No. 7, April.

Dent, Christopher (2006) *New Free Trade Agreem ents in the Asia Pacific*, Basingstoke: Palgrave.

Desker, Barry (2004) In Defence of FTAs: From Purity to Pragmatism in East Asia, *The Pacific Review*, 17(1): 3–26.

de Senarclens, Pierre (1998) *Mondialisation, souveraineté et théorie des relations internationales*, Paris: Colin.

Deutsch, Karl, S. Burrell and R. A. Kan (1957) *Political Community in the North Atlantic Area*, Princeton: Princeton University Press.

de Wilde d'Estmael, T. (1998) *La dimension politique des relations économiques extérieures de la Communauté européenne, Sanctions et incitants économiques comme moyens de politique étrangère*, Bruxelles: Bruylant.

Diez, Thomas and Antje Wiener (eds.) (2003) *Theories of European Integration*, Oxford: Oxford University Press.

Dollar, D. (1992) Outward-oriented Developing Economies Really Do Grow More Rapidly: Evidence from 95 LDCs, 1976–1985, in *Economic Development and Cultural Change*, 40(2): 523–44.

Dowrick, S. and D. Nguyen (1989) OECD Comparative Economic Growth 1950–1985: Catch-up and Convergence, in *American Economic Review*, 79(5): 1010–30.

Dryzek, John S. (1996) *Democracy in Capitalist Times. Ideals, Limits and Struggles.* Oxford: Oxford University Press.

Duchêne, François (1972) *Europe's Role in World Peace*, in: R. Mayne, ed., *Europe Tomorrow. Sixteen Europeans Look Ahead*, London: Fontana.

Duchêne, F. (1973) The European Community and the Uncertainties of Interdependence, in M. Kohnstamm and W. Hager, *A Nation Writ Large? Foreign Policy Problems before the EC*, London: Macmillan.

Duff, A. (1994) The Main Reforms, in A. Duff, J. Pinder and R. Priye, eds, *Maastricht and Beyond*, London: Routledge.

Durand, Marie-Françoise and Vasconcelos, Alvaro (1998) *La Pesc. Ouvrir l'Europe au Monde*, Paris: Presses de Sciences Politiques.

Duynene de Wit, Thom/Ruud Koopmans (2001) *Die politisch-kulturelle Integration ethnischer Minderheiten in den Niederlanden und in Deutschland*. In: Forschungsjournal Neue Soziale Bewegungen.

ECSA World Conference (1998) *The European Union in a Changing World*, Brussels: European Communities.

Edwards, G. and D. Spence (1995) *The European Commission*, London: Longman.

Edwards, G. and E. Regelsberger (1990) *Europe Global Links: the EC and Inter-Regional Cooperation*, New York: St Martin's Press.

Edwards, S. (1993) Openness, Trade Liberalization and Growth in Developing Countries, in *Journal of Economic Literature*, 31(3): 1358–93.

Eichengreen, B. (1994) *International Monetary Arrangements for the 21st Century*, Washington DC: Brookings Institution.

EIU (1997) European Policy Analyst: Key Issues and Developments for Business, Regional Monitor, Economist Intelligence Unit, first quarter 1997.

Eizenstat, Stuart E. (1997) Our Future Trade Agenda, remarks before the House of Representatives, 24 September 1997.

Elbadawi, I. (1995) The Impact of Regional Trade/Monetary Integration Schemes on Intra-Sub-Saharan African Trade, paper presented at the AERC workshop on Regional Integration and Trade Liberalisation, Harare.

Eliassen, Kjell, A., ed. (1998) *Foreign and Security Policy in the EU*, London: Sage.

Ellwood, D. W. (1992) *Rebuilding Europe*, London: Longman.

Emerson, M. (1998) *Redrawing the Map of Europe*, London: Macmillan.

European Commission (1994) *The Economic Situation of the MENA Countries*, COM 94.

European Commission (1997) *Agenda 2000*, Brussels.

European Commission (1995) European Community support for regional economic integration efforts among developing countries, Communication from the Commission, June 16, Brussels: Commission of the European Communities.

European Commission (2000) Joint Statement by the Council and the Commission on the European Community's Development Policy, Brussels, November 2000, ‹europa.eu.int/comm/development/body/theme/consultation›, 24 February 2005.

European Commission (2004) *A World Player: The European Union's External Relations*, DG for Press and Communication, July 2004, pp. 1 and 3.

European Commission, *European Neighbourhood Policy: Strategy Paper*, COM (2004) 373 final, Brussels 12.05.2004.

Eurostat (1996) *Statistics in Focus: Population and Social Conditions*, no. 6, Luxembourg.

Eurostat (2005) *Europe in Figures. Eurostat Yearbook*. Luxembourg.

Evans, Paul M. (1994) The Dialogue Process on Asia Pacific Security Issues: Inventory and Analyses, in Paul M. Evans, ed., *Studying Asia Pacific Security*, University of Toronto–York University Joint Centre for Asia Pacific Studies and Centre for Strategic and International Studies, Toronto and Jakarta.

Evian Group (2005) East Asian Regionalism: Integrative versus Disintegrative Forces, *2005 Evian Hong Kong Initiative*, Hong Kong, 17–18 May: 1–12.

Falk, Richard (2004) *The Declining World Order: America's Imperial Geopolitics*, London: Routledge.

Fennema, Meindert/ Jan Tillie (2001) Civic Community, politische Partizipation und politisches Vertrauen- Ethnische Minderheiten in den Niederlanden. In: *Forschungsjournal Neue Soziale Bewegungen.*

Farrell, Mary (2006) A Triumph of Realism over Idealism? Cooperation Between the European Union and Africa, in Fredrik Söderbaum and Luk van Langenhove, eds., *The EU as a Global Player: The Politics of Interregionalism*, London: Routledge.

Fawcett, Louise (2005) Regionalism From a Historical Perspective, in Mary Farrell, Björn Hettne and Luk van Langenhove, eds., *Global Politics of Regionalism. Theory and Practice*, London: Pluto Press.

Fawcett, Louise and Hurrell, Andrew, eds. (1995) *Regionalism in World Politics: Regional Organization and International Order*, Oxford: Oxford University Press.

Feldstein, Martin (1988) Distinguished Lecture on Economics in Government: Thinking about International Economic Coordination, *Journal of Economic Perspectives*, 2(2): 3–13.

Ferguson, Niall (2004) *Colossus: The Rise and Fall of the American Empire*, London: Penguin.

Fidler, David P. (2004) *SARS. Governance and the Globalization of Disease*, London: Palgrave.

Fine, J. and S. Yeo (1994) *Regional Integration in Sub-Saharan Africa: Dead End or Fresh Start?*, mimeo, African Economic Research Consortium, Nairobi.

Finnemore, Martha (1996) Norms, Culture and World Politics: Insights from Sociology's Institutionalism, *International Organisation*, 50(2): 887–918.

Fischer, Jens (1999) *Eurasismus*, Nomos-Verlag, Baden-Baden.

Flaig, Bodo/Thomas Meyer/ Jörg Ueltzhöffer (1993) *Alltagsästhetik und politische Kultur. Zur ästhetischen Dimension politischer Bildung und politischer Kultur.* Bonn.

Fonseca, Gelson (1998) *A Legitimidade e outras questoes internacionais*, Paz e terra, Sao Paulo.

Foroutan, F. (1993) Regional Integration in Sub-Saharan Africa: Past Experiences and Future Prospects, in J. de Melo and A. Panagariya, eds., *New Dimensions in Regional Integration*, Cambridge: Cambridge University Press.

Fratianni, M. (1995) *Variable Interpretation in the EU*, mimeo, Indiana: Indiana University Press.

Fratianni, M. and J. Pattison (1982) *The Economics of International Organisations*, Kyklos.

Frey, Bruno (1984) *International Political Economics*, New York: Basil Blackwell.

Friedberg, Aaron (1993/4) Ripe for Rivalry: Prospects for Peace in Multi-Polar Asia, *International Security*, 18(3): 5–33.

From, J. and N. Sitter (eds.) (2006) *Europe's Nascent State? Public Policy in the European Union. Essays in the Honour of Kjell A. Eliassen*, Oslo: Gyldendal.

Froot, K. and D. Yoffie (1991) Strategic Policies in a Tripolar World, in *The International Spectator*, 3.

Fukuyama, Francis (1992) The End of History, *The National Interest*, Summer.

Fukuyama, Francis (1993) *The End of History and the Last Man*, London: Hamish Hamilton.

Fukuyama, Francis (2005) *State Building: Governance and World Order in the Twenty-first Century*, London: Profile Books.

Fukushima, A. (2003) The ASEAN Regional Forum in M. Wesley, ed. *Regional Organizations of the Asia Pacific: Exploring Institutional Change*. Gordonsville, VA: Palgrave Macmillan, pp. 76–96.

Furuki, Toshiaki (1998) *European Integration and the World-System*, ISS Chuo University papers, no. 3, Tokyo.

Gallant, Nicole and Stubbs, Richard (1996) Asia–Pacific Business Activity and Regional Institution-Building, in J. Greenwood and H. Jacek, eds., *Organized Business and the New Global Order*, London: Macmillan.

Galston, William A. (1991) *Liberal Purposes: Goods, Virtues, and Diversity in the liberal State*. Cambridge: Cambridge University Press.

Galtung, Johan (1973) *The European Community: A Superpower in the Making*, London: Allen and Unwin.

Gamble, Andrew (1993) Shaping a New World Order, in *Government and Opposition*, 28(3): 325–38.

Gamble, Andrew and Payne, A., eds. (1996) *Regionalism and World Order*, London: Macmillan.

Gamble, Andrew (2000) *Politics and Fate*, Cambridge: Polity.

Gamble, Andrew and Anthony Payne (2003) World Order Approach, in Fredrik Söderbaum and Timothy M. Shaw, eds. *Theories of New Regionalism. A Palgrave Reader*, Basingstoke: Palgrave.

GAO (1993) *North American Free Trade Agreement: Assessment of Major Issues*, vol. 2, Sept., US Government General Accounting Office, Washington DC.

GAO (1997) *North American Free Trade Agreement: Impacts and Implementation*, statement of Jay Etta Z. Hecker, Associate Director, International Relations and Trade Issues, National Security and International Affairs Division, testimony before the Subcommittee on Trade, Committee on Ways and Means, House of Representatives, 11 September, US Government General Accounting Office, Washington DC.

Garcia Marco Aurélio (2006) Conference IEEIbr/IEEI, As Novas Realidades e o Potencial de Cooperação entre a UE e a América Latina, São Paulo, 4–5 September.

Garnaut, Ross and Drysdale, Peter, eds. (1993) *Asia Pacific Regionalism: Readings in International Economic Relations*, Pymble: Harper Educational/ANU.

Garrett, Geoffrey, R. Daniel Kelemen and Heiner Schulz (1998) The European Court of Justice, National Governments, and Legal Integration in the European Union, in *International Organization*, 52(1): 149, Winter.

Ghanem, S. (1986) *The Pricing of Libyan Crude Oil*, Malta: Adams.

Gilbreath, Jan and Tonra, John Benjamin (1994) The Environment: Unwelcome Guest at the Free Trade Party, in M. Delal Baer and Sidney Weintraub, eds., *The NAFTA Debate: Grappling with Unconventional Trade Issues*, Lynne Rienner, Boulder, CO, pp. 53–96.

Gill, Ranjit (1998) *Asia under Siege: How the Asian Miracle Went Wrong*, Singapore: Epic Management Services.

Gills, B. K. (1997) East Asian Development in World Historical Perspective: Ascent, Descent, Ascent, paper presented to International Political Science Association at the XVIIth World Congress, August, Seoul.

Gilpin, R. (1970) in R. O. Keohane and J. Nye, *Transnational Relations and World Politics*, Cambridge, MA: Harvard University Press.

Gilpin, R. (1981) *War and Change in World Politics*, Cambridge: Cambridge University Press.

Gilpin, R. (1987) *The Political Economy of International Relations*, Princeton: Princeton University Press.

Gilson, Julie (2002) *Asia Meets Europe*, Cheltenham, UK: Edward Elgar.

Ginsberg, Roy (1999) Conceptualizing the European Union as an International Actor: Narrowing the Theoretical Capability–Expectations Gap, in *Journal of Common Market Studies*, 37(3): 429–54.

Gnesotto, Nicole (1998) *La puissance et l'Europe*, Paris: Presses de Sciences.

Goldstein, Judith (1996) International Law and Domestic Institutions: Reconciling North American 'Unfair' Trade Laws, in *International Organization*, 50(4): 541–64, Autumn.

Goldthorpe, J. H. (ed.) (1984) *Order and Conflict in Contemporary Capitalism*, Oxford: Oxford University Press.

Golebiowski, Janusz (ed.) (1995) *Poland, Germany, Russia: Perspectives on Collaboration*, Warsaw: University of Warsaw.

Gompert, D. C and S. Larrabee, (eds.) (1997) *America and Europe: A Partnership for a new Era*, Cambridge: Cambridge University Press/RAND Corporation.

Gowa, Johanne and E. Mansfield (1993) Power Politics and International Trade, in *American Political Science Review*, 87.

Gowan, Peter and P. Anderson (eds.) (1997) *The Question of Europe*, London: Verso.

Gramsci, Antonio (1975) *Quaderni del carcere*, Turin: Einaudi.

Grant, Andrew J. and Fredrik Söderbaum (eds.) (2003) *The New Regionalism in Africa*, Aldershot: Ashgate.

Gray, John (1998) *False Dawn. The Delusions of Global Capitalism*, Cambridge: Granta Publications.

Grayson, George W. (1995) *The North American Free Trade Agreement: Regional Community and the New World Order*, New York: University Press of America.

Greenwood, J. (1997) *Representing Interests in the EU*, London: Macmillan.

Greenwood, L. (2003) *Interest Representation in the European Union*, London: Palgrave.

Grieco, Joseph M. (1997) Systemic Sources of Variations in Regional Institutionalization in Western Europe, East Asia and the Americas, in E. D. Mansfield and H. Milner eds., *The Political Economy of Regionalism*, New York: Columbia University Press, pp.164–87.

Grossman, G. and E. Helpman (1991) *Innovation and Growth in the World Economy*, Cambridge, MA: MIT Press.

Grossman, G. and E. Helpman (1994, Protection for Sale, in *American Economic Review*, 84.

Grossman, G. and E. Helpman (1996) Sunk Costs and Liberalization Policies, in *European Economic Review*, May.

Grugel Jean and Wil Hoult (eds.) (1999) *Regionalism across the North-South Divide: State Strategies and Globalisation*, London: Routledge.

Guéhenno, Jean-Marie (1998) The Impact of Globalisation on Strategy, paper delivered at the 40th Annual Conference of the International Institute for Strategic Studies, Oxford, 3–6 September 1998.

Guerrieri, Paolo and P. C. Padoan (eds.) (1988) *The Political Economy of International Cooperation*, London: Croom Helm.

Guerrieri, Paolo and P. C. Padoan (eds.) (1989) *The Political Economy of European Integration: Markets, States and Institutions*, Brighton: Wheatsheaf.

Guerrieri, Paolo and Hans-Eckart Scharree, (eds.) (2000) *Global Governance, Regionalism and the International Economy*, Baden-Baden: Nonos-Verlag.

Haas, Ernst, B. (1958) *The Uniting of Europe. Political, Economic and Social Forces*, Stanford: Stanford University Press.

Haas, Ernst B. (1964) *Beyond the Nation state:Functionalism and International Organization*, Stanford: Stanford University Press.

Haas, Ernst, B. (1975) *The Obsolescence of Regional Integration Theory*, Berkeley, CA: Institute of International Studies.

Habermas, Juergen (1996) *Kant's Idee des ewigen Friedens aus dem historischen Abstand von 200 Jahren*, Frankfurt: Suhrkamp Verlag.

Habermas, Juergen (1999) Der Europäische Nationalstaat unter dem Druck der Globalisierung, in *Blaetter fuer Deutsche und internationale Politik*, no.4.

Habermas, Jürgen (1992) *Faktizität und Geltung.Beiträge zur Diskurstheorie des Rechts und des demokratischen Rechtsstaates*. Frankfurt/Main.

Habermas, Jürgen (1997) *Anerkennungskämpfe im demokratischen Rechtsstaat*. In: Charles Taylor, *Faktizitaet und Geltung*, Frankfurt am Main: Suhrkamp.

Haggard, Stephan (1997) Regionalism in Asia and the Americas in E. D. Mansfield and H. Miller, eds., *The Political Economy of Regionalism*, New York: Columbia University Press.

Haftendorn, Helga, Keohane Robert O.,Wallander Celeste A. (eds.) (1999) *Imperfect Unions*, Oxford: Oxford University Press.

Hall, J. (1996) *International Orders*, Cambridge: Polity Press.

Hall, Peter and David Soskice (eds.) (2001) *Varieties of Capitalism: the Institutional Foundations of Comparative Advantage*, Oxford: Oxford University Press.

Hall, Rodney Bruce and Thomas J. Biersteker (eds.) (2002) *The Emergence of Private Authority in Global Governance*, Cambridge: Cambridge University Press.

Halper S. and J. Clarke (2003) *America Alone: the Neo-conservatives and the Global Order*, Cambridge: Cambridge University Press.

Hamilton-Hart, Natasha (2005) The Chiang Mai Initiative and the Prospects for Closer Monetary Cooperation in East Asia, in Douglas Webber and Bertrand Fort, eds., *Regional Integration in Europe and East Asia: Convergence or Divergence*, London: Routledge.

Hampden-Turner, C. and A. Trompenaars (1993) *The Seven Cultures of Capitalism*, New York: Doubleday.

Hanks, P. (1986) *Collins English Dictionary*, Glasgow: Collins.

Harris, Stuart (2002) Asian multilateral institutions and their response to the Asian economic crisis: regional and global implications, in S. Breslin *et al. New Regionalisms in the Global Political Economy*, London: Routledge.

Hay, C. and B. Rosamond (2002) Globalisation, European Integration and the discursive construction of economic imperatives, *European Journal of Public Policy*, 9(2).

Henrikson, Alan K. (1995) The growth of regional organizations and the role of the United Nations, in: Fawcett and Hurrell, eds. *Regionalism in World Politics*, pp.122–68.

Hänggi, Heiner *et al.* (ed.) (2006) *Interregionalism and International Relations*, London and New York: Routledge.

Harvey, D. (1989) *The Condition of Post Modernity*, Oxford: Blackwell.

Harvey, David (2003) *The New Imperialism* Oxford: Oxford University Press.

Hay, Colin and David Marsh (eds.) (2001) *Demystifying Globalization*, London: Palgrave-Macmillan.

Heclo, Hugh (1978) Issue Networks and the Executive Establishment, in A. King, ed., *The New American Political System*, Washington DC: American Enterprise Institute.

Heitmeyer Wilhelm/J. Müller/J. Schröder (1997) *Verlockender Fundamentalismus: Türkische Jugendliche in Deutschland.* Frankfurt/Main.

Held, David (2004) *Global Covenant: the Social Democratic Alternative to the Washington*, consensus, Cambridge: Polity.

Held, David (1995) *Democracy and the Global Order. From the Modern State to Cosmopolitan Governance*, Cambridge: Polity Press.

Held, David and Anthony McGrew (eds.) (2000) *The Global Transformations Reader: An Introduction to the Globalization Debate*, London: Polity.

Henderson, Callum (1998) *Asia Falling? Making Sense of the Asian Currency Crisis and its Aftermath*, Singapore: McGraw-Hill.

Henning, R. (1996) Europe's Monetary Union and the United States, in *Foreign Policy*, Spring.

Hentz, James J (ed.) (2004) *The Obligation of Empire. United States' Grand Strategy for a New Century*, The University Press of Kentucky.

Héritier, A. (1999) *Policy-Making and Diversity in Europe: Escape from Deadlock*, Cambridge: Cambridge University Press.

Hernandez, Carolina G. (1996) Controlling Asia's Armed Forces, in L. Diamond and M. Plattner, eds,, *Civil–Military Relations and Democracy*.

Hess, A. C. (1978) *The Forgotten Frontiers: A History of the Sixteenth-Century Ibero-African Frontier*, Chicago: University of Chicago Press.

Hess, R. (2000) Constraints on Foreign Direct Investment, in C. Jenkins, J. Leape and L. Thomas, eds,, *Gaining from Trade in Southern Africa: Complementary Policies to Underpin the SADC Free Trade Area*, London: Macmillan.

Hettne, Björn, Andras Inotai and Osvaldo Sunkel (eds.) (1999–2001) *The New Regionalism Series. Vol. I-V*, Basingstoke: Macmillan.

Hettne, Bjorn, Andres Inotai and Osvaldo Sunkel, (eds.) (1999) *National Perspectives on the New Regionalism in the Third World*, London: Palgrave.

Hettne, Bjorn, Andres Inotai and Osvaldo Sunkel (eds.) (2000) *National Perspectives on the New Regionalism in the North*, London: Palgrave.

Hettne, Bjorn, Andres Inotai and Osvaldo Sunkel (eds.) (2001) *Comparing Regionalisms: Implications for Global Development*, London: Palgrave.

Hettne, Björn (1999) The New Regionalism: A Prologue, in Björn Hettne, András Inotai and Osvaldo Sunkel, eds., *Globalism and the New Regionalism*, Macmillan/St. Martin's Press, Basingstoke/New York.

Hettne, Bjorn and Fredrik Soderbaum (eds.) (1998) Special Issue: The New Regionalism, *Politeia*, 17(3).

Hettne, Björn (2005) Beyond the 'New' Regionalism, *New Political Economy*, 10(4), December.

Hettne, Björn and Bertil Odén (eds.) (2002) *Global Governance in the 21th Century: Alternative Perspectives on World Order* , Stockholm: EGDI.

Hettne, Björn *et al.* (eds.) (2000) *The New Regionalism and the Future of Security and Development*, Basingstoke: Macmillan.

Hettne, Björn and Fredrik Söderbaum (2000, Theorising the Rise of Regionness, *New Political Economy*, 5(3): 457–73.

Hettne, Björn and Fredrik Söderbaum (2005) Civilian Power or Soft Imperialism? The EU as a Global Actor and the Role of Interregionalism, *European Foreign Affairs Review*, 10(4): 535–52, Winter.

Hettne, Björn and Fredrik Söderbaum (2006) The UN and Regional Organizations in Global Security: Competing or Complementary Logics?, in *Global Governance*, 12: 227–32.

Hettne, Björn (2005) Beyond the 'New' Regionalism', *New Political Economy* 10(4): 543–72.

Hew, Denis and Soesastro, Hadi, (2003) Realising the ASEAN Economic Community by 2020: ISEAS and ASEAN ISIS Approaches, *ASEAN Economic Bulletin*, 20(3).

Higgott, Richard, Richard Leaver and John Ravenhill (eds.) (1993) *Pacific Economic Relation in the 1990s: Cooperation and Conflict*, Boulder, CO: Lynne Reinner.

Higgott, Richard and Richard Stubbs (1995) Competing Conceptions of Economic Regionalism: APEC versus EAEC, *Review of International Political Economy*, 2(3).

Higgott, Richard (1995) Economic Cooperation in the Asia Pacific: A Theoretical Comparison with the European Union, in *Journal of European Public Policy*, 2(3): 361–83.

Higgott, Richard (1997) Globalization, Regionalization and Localization: Political Economy, the State and Levels of Governance, paper presented to the 25th Joint Sessions of Workshops of the European Consortium for Political Research, February–March, Bern.

Higgott, Richard and S. Reich (1998) *Globalization and Sites of Conflict: Towards Definition and Taxonomy*, GSGR working paper 3.

Higgott, Richard (1997) *De facto* or *De Jure* Regionalism: The Double Discourse of Regionalisation in the Asia Pacific, *Global Society: Journal of Interdisciplinary International Relations*, 11(2): 165–83.

Higgott, Richard (1998) The Asian Financial Crisis: A Study in the Politics of Resentment, *New Political Economy*, 3(3): 33–56.

Higgott, Richard (1998a) The International Political Economy of Regionalism: Europe and Asia Compared, in William Coleman and Geoffrey Underhill, eds., *Regionalism and Global Economic Integration: Asia, Europe and the Americas*, London: Routledge.

Higgott, Richard (2004) The 'Securitisation' of U.S. Foreign Economic Policy in East Asia, *Critical Asian Studies*, 36(3): 425–44.

Higgott, Richard (2005) Economic Regionalism in East Asia: Consolidation with Centrifugal Tendencies, in Richard Stubbs and Geoffrey Underhill, eds., *Political Economy and the Changing Global Order*, Oxford: Oxford University Press.

Higgott, Richard (2005a) The Theory and Practice of Regionalism in a Changing Global Context, in Douglas Webber and Bertrand Fort, eds., *Regional Integration in Europe and East Asia: Convergence or Divergence*, London: Routledge, pp. 17–38.

Higgott, Richard (2005b) The Theory and Practice of Global Governance: Accommodating American Exceptionalism and European Pluralism, *European Foreign Affairs Record*, October 2005, forthcoming.

Higgott, Richard (2006) International (Political) Organisation(s) in Rod Rhodes and Bert Rockman, eds., *The Oxford Handbook of Political Institutions*, Oxford: Oxford University Press.

Higgott, Richard (2002) From Trade-Led to Monetary-Led Regionalism: Why Asia in the 21st Century will be Different to Europe in the 20th Century, *UNU/CRIS e-Working Papers 2002/1*, Bruges: UNU/CRIS.

Hill, Christopher (1993) The Capability–Expectations Gap, or Conceptualizing Europe's International Role, *Journal of Common Market Studies*, 3, Sept.

Hill, Christopher, (ed.) (1996) *The Actors in Europe's Foreign Policy*, London and New York: Routledge.

Hill, C. and M. Smith (eds.) (2005) *International Relations and the European Union*, Oxford: Oxford University Press.

Hirst, Monica (1995) A dimensão politica do Mercosul: especificadades nacionais, aspectos institucionais e actores sociais, in *Integração Aberta*, Euro-Latin American Forum/IEEI, Lisbon.

Hirst, Paul and Grahame Thompson (1996) *Globalization in Question: the International Economy and the Possibilities of Governance*, Cambridge, UK and Cambridge, MA: Polity Press.

Hirst, Paul (1994) *Associative Democracy. New Forms of Economic and Social Governance*, Amherst: University of Massachusetts Press.

Hix, Simon (1994) The Study of the European Community: The Challenge for Comparative Politics, *West European Politics*, 17(1).

Hix, Simon (1999) *The Political System of the European Union*, Basingstoke: Macmillan.

Hobsbawm, Eric (1994) *Age of Extremes: The Short Twentieth Century 1914–1991*, London: Abacus.

Hodge, Carl Cavanagh (2005) *Atlanticism for a New Century. The Rise, Triumph and Decline of NATO*, Pearson: Prentice Hall.

Hoekman, B. (1998) Free Trade Agreements in the Mediterranean: A Regional Path towards Liberalization?, in G. Joffé, ed., *Perspectives on Development: the Euro-Mediterranean Partnership Initiative, Journal of North African Studies* special issue, 3(2), Summer, London: Cass.

Hoffmann, Stanley, R. Keohane and J. S. Nye (eds.) (1993) *After the Cold War, International Institutions and State Strategies in Europe. 1989–1991*, Cambridge: Harvard University Press.

Hofstede, Geert (1980) *Culture's Consequences: International Differences in Work-Related Values*, Beverly Hills, CA: Sage.

Hofstede, G. (1994) *Cultures and Organizations: Intercultural Cooperation and its Importance for Survival*, New York: Harper Collins.

Hoge, James F. and Gideon Rose (eds.) (2005) *Understanding the War on Terror*, Council on Foreign Relations, New York: W.W. Norton.

Holland, Martin (ed.) (1997) *Common Foreign and Security Policiy. The Record and Reforms*, London: Pinter.

Holland, Martin (2002) *The European Union and the Third World*, London and New York: Palgrave.

Holland, K. M. (1994) NAFTA and the Single European Act, in T. D. Mason and A. M. Turay, eds., Japan, NAFTA and Europe: Trilateral Cooperation or Confrontation? New York: St Martin's Press.

Honneth, Axel (1992) Kampf um Anerkennung: zur moralischen Grammatik sozialer Konflikte, Frankfurt.

Honneth, Axel (Hrsg.) (1993) *Kommunitarismus. Eine Debatt.*

Hunt, D. (1998) Development Economics: The Washington Consensus and the Euro-Mediterranean Partnership, in G. Joffé, ed., *Perspectives on Development: the Euro-Mediterranean Partnership Initiative, Journal of North African Studies* special issue, 3(2), Summer, London: Cass.

Huntington, Samuel P. (1993) *The Third Wave: Democratization in the Late Twentieth Century*, Oklahoma: Norman.

Huntington, Samuel P. (1993) The Clash of Civilisation?, in *Foreign Affairs*, 72(3): 22–49.

Huntington, Samuel P. (1996) *The Clash of Civilizations and the Remaking of World Order*, New York: Simon and Schuster.

Hurrell, Andrew (1995) Regionalism in Theoretical Perspective, in Louise Fawcett and Andrew Hurrell, eds., *Regionalism in World Politics: Regional Organization and International Order*, Oxford: Oxford University Press.

Hurrell, Andrew (1995) Explaining the Resurgence of Regionalism in World Politics, *Review of International Studies*, 21(4).

Hurst, Paul and Grahame Thompson (2001) *Globalisation in Question*, Cambridge: Polity, 2nd edition.

Hurt, Stephen R. (2003) Co-operation and Coercion? The Cotonou Agreement between the European Union and ACP States and the End of the Lomé Convention, *Third World Quarterly*, 24(1): 161–76.

Hyde, G. V. and Price, Adrian G. V. (1994) Democratization in Eastern Europe: the External Dimension, in: Geoffrey Pridham and Tatu Vanhanen, eds., *Democratization in Eastern Europe*, London/New York.

IEEI (1998) Report of the Fifth Euro-Latin American Forum, *Setting Global Rules*, Lisbon.

ILO (1995) *World Labour Report 1995*, International Labour Organization, Geneva.

Ikenberry, John (2004) Liberalism and Empire, *Review of International Studies* 30(4): 609–30.

IMF (1988) *International Financial Statistics: Supplement on Trade Statistics*, International Monetary Fund, Washington, DC.

IMF (1995) *International Financial Statistics Yearbook 1995*, International Monetary Fund, Washington, DC.

IMF (1996) *Direction of Trade Statistics Quarterly*, September, International Monetary Fund, Washington, DC.

IMF (1997) *Direction of Trade Statistics Yearbook*, Washington, DC.

IMF (1997) *World Economic Outlook*, May, International Monetary Fund, Washington, DC.

Inglehart, Ronald and P. A. Abramson (1995) *Value Change in a Global Perspective*, Michigan: University of Michigan Press.

IRELA (1998) *European Direct Investment in Latin America*, Madrid.

*IRELA (*1998) *Latin America at the Brink? Effects on the Global Finance Crisis*, Madrid.

Isaksen, Jan and Elling N. Tjønneland (2001) Assessing the Restructuring of SADC-Positions, Policies and Progress,

Jaguaribe, Helio (1996) Uma nova concepção de segurança para o Brasil, in *Estrategia: Revista de Estudos Internacionais*, nos. 8–9, Lisbon.

Jaguaribe, Helio (1998) *Mercosul e as alternativas para a ordem mundial*, Instituto de Estudos Politicos e Sociais, Rio de Janeiro.

Jaguaribe, H. and A Vasconcelos (eds.) (2003) *The European union, MERCOSUL and the New World Order*, London: Cass.

Jameson, F. (1984) Postmodernism, or the Cultural Logic of Late Capitalism, in *New Left Review*, (146): 53–92.

Jameson, F. (1989, Marxism and Postmodernism, in *New Left Review*, 176: 31–45.

Jayasuriya, Kanishka (ed.) (2004) *Asian Regional Governance: Crisis and Change*, London: Routledge.

Jandl M. (2004) The estimation of illegal migration in Europe, *Studi Emigrazione/ Migration Studies*, XLI, 153, 150.

Jenkins, Carolyn (1997) Regional Integration is Not Enough, in Quarterly Review, April, Centre for Research into Economics and Finance in Southern Africa, London School of Economics.

Jenkins, Carolyn and Lynne Thomas (1998) Is Southern Africa Ready for Regional Monetary Integration? in L. Petersson, ed., *Post-Apartheid Southern Africa: Economic Policies and Challenges for the Future*, London: Routledge.

Jenkins, Carolyn and Lynne Thomas (2000) The Macroeconomic Policy Framework, in C. Jenkins, J. Leape and Lynne Thomas, eds., *Gaining from Trade in Southern Africa: Complementary Policies to Underpin the SADC Free Trade Area*, London: Macmillan.

Jenkins, Carolyn, J. Leape, and L. Thomas (2000) Gaining from Trade in Southern Africa, in Carolyn Jenkins, J. Leape and L. Thomas, eds. *Gaining from Trade in Southern Africa: Complementary Policies to Underpin the SADC Free Trade Area*, London: Macmillan.

Jenkins, Carolyn and Lynne Thomas (2001) African Regionalism and the SADC, in Mario Telò, ed., *European Union and New Regionalism. Regional Actors and Global Governance in a Post-Hegemonic Era*, Aldershot: Ashgate (first edition).

Joffé, Emil and George Howard (1997a) Southern Attitudes towards an Integrated Mediterranean Region, in R. Gillespie, ed., *The Euro-Mediterranean Partnership: Political and Economic Perspectives*, London: Cass.

Joffé, Emil and George Howard (1997b) Sovereignty in the Developing World, in M. Heiberg, eds., *Subduing Sovereignty*, London: Pinter.

Johnson, Chalmers (2005) No Longer the 'Lone' Supoerpower: Coming to Terms with China, *Japan Policy Research Institute, Working Paper 105*, San Francisco: March: 1–12. www.jpri.org/publications/wp105.html.

Johnson, Chalmers (2004, The Sorrows of Empire: Militarism, Secrecy and the End of the Republic, New York: Metropolitan Books.

Jourdan, Paul (1998) Spatial Development Initiatives (SDIs). The Official View, *Development Southern Africa*, 15(5): 717–25.

Julien, Ch-A. (1954) *L'Afrique du Nord en marche*, Paris: Presses Universitaires de France.

Kagan, R. (2003) *Paradise and Power: America and Europe in the New World Order*, London: Atlantic Books.

Kahler, Miles (1995) *Regional Futures and Transatlantic Economic Relations*, New York: Council on Foreign Relations Press.

Kahler, Miles (2000) Legalization as a Strategy: The Asia Pacific Case, *International Organization*, 54(3): 549–71.

Katzenstein, Peter, Robert O. Keohane and Stephen Krasner, (1998) International Organisation and the Study of World Politics, *International Organisation*, 52(4).

Katzenstein, Peter (1996) Regionalism in Comparative Perspective, working paper no. 1/96, ARENA, Oslo.

Katzenstein, Peter (2005) A World of Regions: Asia and Europe in the New American Imperium, Ithaca: Cornell University Press.

Kébabdjian, G. (1999) *Les théories de l'économie politique internationale*, Paris: Seuil.

Kehoe, Timothy J. (1994) Assessing the Economic Impact of North American Free Trade, in M. Delal Baer and Sidney Weintraub, eds., *The NAFTA Debate: Grappling with Unconventional Trade Issues*, Boulder, CO: Lynne Rienner, pp.3–33.

Kelley J. (2006) New wine in old wineskins: policy adaptation in the European Neighbourhood Policy, *Journal of Common Market Studies*, 44(1).

Kennedy, Paul (1987) *The Rise and Fall of the Great Powers*, London: Random House.

Kenwood, G. and A. L. Lougheed (1992) *The Growth of the International Economy 1820–1990*, 3rd edn., London: Routledge.

Keohane, Robert O. (1980) *The Theory of Hegemonic Stability and Changes in International Economic Regimes, 1967–1977*, Boulder, CO: Westview Press.

Keohane, Robert O. (1984, and 2004 with a new Preface) *After Hegemony. Cooperation and Discord in the World Political Economy*, Princeton: Princeton University Press.

Keohane, Robert O. (ed.) (1986) *Neorealism and its Critics*, New York: Columbia University Press.

Keohane, R. O. and J. S. Nye (1970) *Transnational Relations and World Politics*, Cambridge: Harvard University Press.

Keohane, R. O. and J. S. Nye (1989) *Power and Interdependence*, New York: Harper Collins.

Keohane, R. O (1989) *International Institutions and State Power: Essay in International Relations Theory*, Boulder CO: Westview Press.

Keohane, R. O., H. Haftendorn and C. A. Wallander (eds.) (1999) *Imperfect Unions*, Oxford: Oxford University Press.

Keohane, R. O. (2001) Governance in a Partially Globalised World, *American Political Science Review*, 95(1): 1–13.

Keohane, R. O. (2002) *Power and Governance in a Partially Globalized World*, London: Routledge.

Keohane, R. O. (2004) Global Governance and Democratic Accountability in David Held and Mathias Konig Archibugi, *Taming Globalization: Frontiers of Governance*, Cambridge: Polity Press.

Keukelaire, S. (1998) *Het buiterlands beleidvande EU*, Kluven, Deeventer.

Kindleberger, Charles P. (1973) Economic Integration, in *International Economics*, Illinois: Richard D. Irwin Inc.

Kindleberger, Charles P. (1973) *The World in Depression 1929–1939*, Berkeley, CA: University of California Press.

Kirchner, Emil and Kevin Wright, (eds.) (1997) Security and democracy in transition societies, Conference Proceedings, Essex 1998, and *Journal of European Integration, Problems of Eastern Europe*, nos. 2–3.

Kobrin, S. (1996) Back to the Future: Neomedievalism and the Postmodern World Economy, paper presented at the 1996 Annual Meeting of the International Studies Association, San Diego, California, 17 April.

B.Kohler-Koch (2003) *Linking EU and National Governance*, Oxford: Oxford University Press.

Kooiman, Jan (2003) *Governing as Governance*, London: Sage.

Koopmans, Ruud/Paul Statham (Hg.) (2000) *Challenging Immigration and Ethnic Relations Politics: Comparative European Perspectives*. Oxford: Oxford University Press.

Krasner, D. Stephen (ed.) (1983) *International Regimes*, Ithaca: Cornell University Press.

Kratochwil, Freidrich and John Ruggie, (1986) The State of the Art on an Art of the State, *International Organisation*, 40(4): 753–75.

Kratochwil, Freidrich and Edward Mansfield (eds.) (2005) *International Organisation: A Reader*, New York: Longman Publishers.

Krauthammmer, Charles (1991–92) The Unipolar Moment, *Foreign Affairs*, 70(1): 23–33.

Krauthammmer Charles (2001) Unilateralism is the key to our success, *Guardian Weekly*, 22 December 2001.

Krishna, K., A. Ozyildirim and N. Swanson (1998) *Trade, Investment and Growth: Nexus, Analysis and Prognosis*, Working Paper 6861, National Bureau of Economic Research, Washington DC.

Krugman, Paul (1993a) Regionalism versus Multilateralism: Analytic Notes, in R. Garnaut and P. Drysdale, eds., *Asia Pacific Regionalism: Readings in International Economic Relations*, Pymble: Harper Educational/ANU.

Krugman, Paul (1993b) Regionalism: Some Analytical Notes, in J. de Melo, A. Panagariya and D. Rodrik, eds., *New Dimensions in Regional Integration*, Cambridge: Cambridge University Press.

Krugman, Paul (1994) *Peddling Prosperity*, New York: Norton.

Krugman, Paul (1998) *La mondialisation n'est pas coupable*, Paris: La Découverte.

Krugman, Paul (ed.) (1986) *Strategic Trade Policy and the 'New' International Economics*, Cambridge, MA: MIT Press.

Kuznets, S. (1966) *Modern Economic Growth*, Cambridge, MA: Yale University Press.

Kupchan, Charles A. (2000) After Pax Americana: Benign Power, Regional Integration and the Sources of Stable Multipolarity, in Birthe Hansen and Bertel Heurlin, eds., *The New World Order: Contrasting Theories*, Basingstoke: Palgrave, pp. 134–66.

Kupchan, Charles A. (2004) The End of American Primacy and the Return of a Multipolar World, in Hentz, 2004.

Kymlicka, Will (2000) *Politics in The Vernacular: Nationalism, Multiculturalism, & Citizenship*. Oxford: Oxford University Press.

Kymlicka, Will/Wayne Norman (2000) *Citizenship in Diverse Societies*. Oxford: Oxford University Press.

Lafer, Celso (1999) *Comércio Desarmamento Diretos Humanos*, Sao Paulo: Paz e terra.

Lafer, Celso and Gelson Fonseca, (1995) A problemática da integração num mundo de polaridades indefinidas, in *Integração Aberta*, Lisbon: Euro-Latin American Forum/IEEI.

Lafer, Celso, Conference IEEIbr/IEEI (2006) As Novas Realidades e o Potencial de Cooperação entre a UE e a América Latina, São Paulo, 4–5 de September.

Lake, D. A. (1999) *Entangling Relations. American Foreign Policy in its Century*, Princeton: Princeton University Press.

Lake, D. A. and P. M. Morgan (1997) *Regional Orders. Building Security in a New World*, Pennsylvania Pennsylvania: State University Press.

Latham, Andrew (1997) *The Liberal Moment: Modernity, Security, and the Making of Postwar International Order*, New York: Columbia University Press.

Latouche, Serge (1998) *Il mondo ridotto a mercato*, Rome: Edizioni Lavoro.

Laursen, Finn (1991) The EC in the World Context: Civilian Power or Superpower, in *Futures*, pp.747–59.

Laursen, Finn (ed.) (2003) *Comparative Regional Integration. Theoretical Perspectives*, Aldershot: Ashgate Publishing Ltd.

Laursen, Finn (2006)The Politics of the Constitutional Treaty: Elements of Four Analysis, in J. From and N. Sitter, pp. 37–60.

Lavigne, Marie (1998) *L'intégration des pays d'Europe centrale dans l'économie mondiale: régionalisation ou mondialisation*, papier présenté au colloque OCDE, CEPII, Sept. 1998, Paris.

Lavigne, Marie (1999) *The Economics of Transition. From Socialist Economy to Market Economy*, London: Macmillan.

Lawrence, R. (1996) *Regionalism, Multilateralism and Deeper Integration*, Washington, DC: Brookings Institute.

LeClair, Mark S. (1997) *Regional Integration and Global Free Trade: Addressing the Fundamental Conflicts*, Aldershot: Avebury.

Lee, Eun-Jeung (1997) Konfuzianismus und Kapitalismu,. Münster.

Leonard, Mark (2005) *Why Europe will Run the 21st Century*, London: Fourth Estate Books.

Leslie, Peter M. (2000a) The European Regional System: A Case of Unstable Equilibrium?, in *Journal of European Integration. The Fuzzy Edges of Community*, edited by Peter Leslie and Charles Pentland, no.23.

Leslie, Peter M. (2000b) Abuses of Asymmetry: Privilege and Exclusion, in Karlheinz Neunreither and Antje Wiener, eds., *Amsterdam and Beyond: The European Union on its Way into a Twenty-first Century.* Oxford: Oxford University Press.

Lieven, Anatol (2004) *America Right or Wrong. An Anatomy of American Nationalism*, Oxford: Oxford University Press.

Lijphart, A. (1994) *Democracies*, London: Yale University Press.

Lim, Robyn (1998) The ASEAN Regional Forum: Building on Sand, in *Contemporary Southeast Asia*, 20(2): 115–36.

Lindberg, Leon (1966) *The Political Dynamics of European Economic Integration*, Stanford, CA: Stanford University Press.

Lisproject (2007) www.lisproject.org/keyfigurs (accessed 28.1.2007).

Little, R. (1989) Deconstructing The Balance of Power: Two Traditions of Thought, in *Review of International Studies*, 15(2): 92–7, April.

Lorenz, Ditlev (1992) Economic Geography and the Political Economy of Regionalization: The Example of Western Europe, in *American Economic Review*, 82(2): 84–97.

Lowi, Theodore (1967) Making Democracy Save for the World, in J. Rosenau ed., *Domestic Sources of Foreign Policy*, New York: The Free Press, pp. 295–331.

Lucas, Michael R. (1998) The CIS and Russia, in, Eric Remacle and Reimund Seidelmann, eds., *Pan-European Security Redefined*, Baden-Baden: Nomos-Verlag, , pp. 319–51.

Luttwack, George (1990) From Geopolitics to Geoeconomics. Logic of Conflict and Grammar of Commerce, in *National Interest*, Summer.

Maasdorp, G. (2000) Microeconomic policies, in C. Jenkins, J. Leape and L. Thomas, eds., *Gaining from Trade in Southern Africa: Complementary Policies to Underpin the SADC Free Trade Area*, London: Macmillan.

Mackinder, H. (1904) The Geographical Pivot of History, in *Geographical Journal*, 23.

MacLean, Sandra (1999) Peacebuilding and the New Regionalism in southern Africa, *Third World Quarterly*, 20(5): 943–56.

McCormick, J. (2007) *The European Superpower*, Basingstoke: Palgrave.

Mahjoub, A. (1998) Social Feasibility and the Costs of the Free Trade Zone, in G. Joffé, ed., *Perspectives on Development: the Euro-Mediterranean Partnership Initiative*, *Journal of North African Studies*, special issue, 3(2), Summer, London: Cass.

Maier, Charles (1987) *In Search of Stability: Explorations in Historical Political Economy*, Cambridge: Cambridge University Press.

Majone, Giandomenico (1996) *Regulating Europe*, London: Routledge.

Mann, Michael (2003) *Incoherent Empire*, London: Verso.

Manners, I. J. and R. G. Whitman, (1998) International Identity of the EU, in *Journal of European Integration*, 3: 231–49.

Mansfield, Edward and Rachel Branson (1994) Alliances, Preferential Trading Arrangements, and International Trade, paper presented at the annual meeting of the American Political Science Association, 1–4 September 1994, New York.

Mansfield, Edward D. and Helen V. Milner, (ed.) (1997) *The Political Economy of Regionalism*, New York: Columbia University Press.

Manupipatpong, W. (2002) The ASEAN Surveillance Process and the East Asian Monetary Fund, *ASEAN Economic Bulletin*, 1 (1): 114–15.

Marks, J. (1996) High Hopes and Low Motives: The New Euro-Mediterranean Partnership Initiative, in *Mediterranean Politics*, 1(1):1–24, Summer.

Marks, J. (1998) The European Challenge to North African Economies: The Downside to the Euro-Mediterranean Policy, in G. Joffé, ed., *Perspectives on Development: the Euro-Mediterranean Partnership Initiative*, *Journal of North African Studies*, special issue, 3(2), Summer, London: Cass.

Marty, Martin E. and R. S. Appleby (1991) *Fundamentalisms Observed*, Chicago: University of Chicago Press.

Marty, Martin E. and Scott R. Appleby (1996) Herausforderung Fundamentalismus. Radikale Christen, Moslems und Juden im Kampf gegen die Moderne, Frankfurt (u.a.): Campus.

Martin, Lisa (2003) Multilateral Organisations after the US-Iraq War of 2003, Harvard University, Weatherhead Centre for International Affairs, August: 1–17.

Mattingley, G. (1964) *Renaissance Diplomacy*, London: Penguin.

Mattli, W. (1999) *The Logic of Regional Integration. Europe and Beyond*, Cambridge: Cambridge University Press.

Mattli, Walter and Anne-Marie Slaughter (1998) Revisiting the European Court of Justice, in *International Organization*, 52(1), Winter.

Mayer, F. (1992) Managing Domestic Differences in International Negotiations: The Strategic Use of Internal Side-Payments, in *International Organization*, 46.

Mayhew, Alan (1998) *Recreating Europe. The EU's Policy towards Central and Eastern Europe*, Cambridge: Cambridge University Press.

Mazey, S. and J. Richardson, (eds.) (1993) *Lobbying in the EC*, Oxford: Oxford University Press.

McSweeney, Dean and Clive Tempest (1993) The Political Science of Democratic Transition in Eastern Europe, in *Political Studies*, XLI.

Meyer, Thomas (1997) *Identitäts-Wahn: Die Politisierung des kulturellen Unterschieds*, Berlin: Aufbau.

Meyer, Thomas (2001) *Identity Mania. Fundamentalism and the Politicization of Cultural Differences*, London: Zed.

Meyer, Thomas (2002) *Identitätspolitik. Vom Missbrauch kultureller Differenz.* Frankfurt/M.

Meyer, Thomas and Lew Hinchman (2007) *Theory of Social Democracy.* Cambridge: Polity.

Mezran, K. (1998) Maghrib Foreign Policies and the Internal Security Dimension, in *Journal of North African Studies*, 3(1), 1–24, Spring.

Milner, Helen V. (1995) Regional Economic Cooperation, Global Markets and Domestic Politics: A Comparison of NAFTA and the Maastricht Treaty, in *Journal of European Public Policy*, 2(3): 337–60.

Milner, Helen V. (1997) *Interests, Institutions, and Information*, Princeton: Princeton University Press.

Milward, Alan (1992, *The European Rescue of the Nation State*, London: Routledge.

Missiroli, Antonio (1999) European Security and Defense, the Case for Setting Convergence Criteria, in *European Foreign Affairs Review*, 4: 485–500.

Mistry, Percy S. (2003) New Regionalism and Economic Development, in Fredrik Söderbaum and Timothy M. Shaw (eds.), *Theories of New Regionalism. A Palgrave Reader*, Basingstoke: Palgrave.

Mittelman, J. and R. Falk (1999) Regionalism and Globalization in the Post-Cold War World, in Stephen Calleya, ed., *Regionalism in the Post-Cold War World*, Aldershot: Ashgate.

Montes, Manual F. (1998) *The Currency Crisis in Southeast Asia*, Singapore: Institute of Southeast Asian Studies.

Moravcsik, Andrew, (ed.) (1998) *Centralization or Fragmentation? Europe Facing the Challenges of Deepening, Diversity and Democracy*, New York: Council of Foreign Relations Press.

Moravcsik, Andrew (1999) *The Choice for Europe: Social Purpose and State Power from Messina to Maastricht*, Ithaca: Cornell University Press.

Moravcsik Andrew and K. Nicolaidis (1999) Explaining the Treaty of Amsterdam: Interests, Influences, Institutions, *Journal of Common Market Studies*, 37(1): 59–85.

Moravcsik, Andrew (1994) Preferences and Power in the European Community: A Liberal Intergovernmental Approach, in Simon Bulmer and Andrew Scott, eds., *Economic and Political Integration in Europe*, Oxford: Blackwells.

Moravcsik, Andrew (2004) Is there a 'Democratic Deficit' in World Politics? A Framework for Analysis, *Government and Opposition*, 39(3): 344–46.

Mullen, Paul (1998) Legitimate Options: National Courts and the Power of the European Court of Justice, in *ECSA Review*, European Community Studies Association, 11(1): 2–7, Winter.

Muchie, Mammo (ed.) (2003) The Making of the Africa-nation: Pan-Africanism and the African Renaissance, London: Adonis & Abbey.

Munakata, Nana (2003) The Impact of the Rise of China and Regional Economic Integration in Asia: A Japanese Perspective, *Statement to US-China Economic and Security Review Commission Hearings on China's Growth as a Regional Economic Power*, Washington, DC: December: 1–13.

Murithi, Timothy (2005) *The African Union. Pan-Africanism, Peace-Building and Development*. Aldershot: Ashgate.

Murphy, E. (1999) *Economic and Political Development in Tunisia: From Bourguiba to Ben Ali*, London: British Academic Press.

Nairn, Tom (1981) *The Breakup of Britain*, London: Verso.

Nathan, K. S. (2002) *The European Union, United States and ASEAN. Challenges and Prospects for Cooperative Engagement in the 21ˢᵗ Century*. London: ASEAN Academic Press.

Nelsen, B. F. and A. C-G. Stubb (eds.) (1994) The European Union: Readings on the Theory and Practice of European Integration, in *Cooperation and Conflict*, 28: 373–402.

Nesadurai, Helen (2003) *Globalisation, Domestic Politics and Regionalism: The ASEAN Free Trade Area*, London: Routledge.

Neumann, Iver B. (2003) The Region-building Approach, in Fredrik Söderbaum and Timothy M. Shaw, eds., *Theories of New Regionalism. A Palgrave Reader*, Basingstoke: Palgrave.

Nohlen, Dieter (1997) Demokratie, in: Dieter Nohlen, Peter Waldmann and Klaus Ziemer, eds., *Lexikon der Politik* Bd 4: *Die östlichen und südlichen Länder*, Beck Verlag, München, pp.118–27 and 122.

North, Douglass (1990) *Institutions, Institutional Change and Economic Performance*, Cambridge: Cambridge University Press.

Nugent, N. (2001) *The European Commission*, London: Palgrave.

Nugent, N. (ed.) (2004) *European Union Enlargement*, London: Palgrave.

Nye, J. (1968) Comparative Regional Integration: Concepts and Measurement, *International Organisation*, 22(4).

Nye, Joseph (1971) *Peace in Parts: Integration and Conflict in International Organisations*, Boston, MA: Little Brown.

Nye, Joseph (2002) *The Paradox of American Power: Why the World's Only Superpower Can't Go It Alone*, Oxford: Oxford University Press.

OECD (1995) *Services: Statistics on International Transactions*, Paris: Organization for Economic Cooperation and Development.

OECD (1996) *Historical Statistics 1960–1994*, Paris: Organization for Economic Cooperation and Development.

OECD (1997) Employment Outlook, June, Paris: Organization for Economic Cooperation and Development.

OECD (1998a) *National Accounts 1960–1996*, vol. 1, Paris: Organization for Economic Cooperation and Development.

OECD (1998b) *Employment Outlook*, June, Paris: Organization for Economic Cooperation and Development.

OECD (1998c) *Economic Outlook*, June, Paris: Organization for Economic Cooperation and Development.

OECD (1999) *Historical Statistics 1960–1997*, Paris.

OECD (2000) *Economic Outlook*, no. 67, Paris.

OECD (2004) *OECD Economic Outlook* no. 75. Paris.

OECD (2006a) *OECD in Figures 2006-2001*. Paris.

OECD (2006b) *OECD Factbook 2006*. Paris.

Ohmae, Kenichi (1993) The Rise of the Region State, in *Foreign Affairs*, 72.

Ohmae, Kenichi (1995) *The End of the Nation state. The Rise of Regional Economies*, London: HarperCollins.

Ohmae, Kenichi (1995) *The End of the Nation State: The Rise of Regional Economies*, New York: HarperCollins.

Oliveira Martins, Guilherme (1993) O enigma Europeu, Lisbon: Quetzal Editores.

Oliveira Martins, Guilherme and Vasconcelos, Alvaro (1995) A lógica de integração aberta, base de un novo multiregionalismo, *Integração Aberta*, Euro-Latin American Forum, Institute for Strategic and International Studies (IEEI), Lisbon.

Olson, Mancur (1965) *The Logic of Collective Action*, New Haven: Yale University Press.

Oman, Charles (1994) *Globalization and Regionalisation: The Challenge for Developing Countries*, Paris: OECD Development Centre.

Oman, Charles (1999) Globalisation, Regionalisation and Inequality in Louise Fawcett and Andrew Hurrell, eds., *Regionalism in World Politics: Regional Organisation and International Order*, Oxford: Oxford University Press.

Oye, Kenneth, A. (ed.) (1985) *Cooperation under Anarchy*, Princeton: Princeton University Press.

Oye, Kenneth A. (1992) *Economic Discrimination and Political Exchange*, Princeton: Princeton University Press.

Padoan, Pier Carlo (1997) Regional Agreements as Clubs: The European Case, in Mansfield and Milner (eds.)1995.

Padoan Pier Carlo (ed.) (1998) Globalizzazione e regionalismo, special issue of *Europa/Europe*, Rome no. 6.

Palmer, Norman D. (1991) *The New Regionalism in Asia and the Pacific*, Lexington, MA: Lexington Books.

Pape, Wolfgang (ed.) (1998) *East Asia by the Year 2000 and Beyond: Shaping Factors*, a study for the European Commission, Surrey: Curzon Press.

Patel, Saliem (1999) The Nature and Impact of South African Investment in Southern Africa, paper for the Sweden-South Africa Civil Society Encounter Student Conference.

Pekkanen, Saadia (2004) At Play in the Legal Realm: The WTO and the Changing Nature of US-Japan Anti-Dumping Disputes, in Ellis Krauss and T. J. Pempel, *Beyond Bilateralism: US-Japan Relations in the New Asia Pacific*, Stanford: Stanford University Press.

Pempel, T. J. (ed.) (2004) Emerging Webs of Regional Connectedness, *Remapping East Asia: The Construction of a Region*, Ithaca: Cornell University Press.

Pempel, T. J. (2005) Firebreak: East Asia Institutionalizes its Finances, *Institutionalizing North East Asia: Making the Impossible Possible?* Tokyo, UNU and Aoyama-Gakuin University, Sept. 20–22.

Peña, F. (2006) Dilemas do Mercosul a Cinco, *O Mundo em Português*, no. 63, October–November.

Pena, F. (2006) Interrogantes sobre el futuro: las negociaciones comerciales tras las elecciones en Brasil e en los EEUU', *O Mundo em Português*, November.

Peng, Dajin (1997) *An East Asian Model of Regional Economic Cooperation*, Oslo: Centre for European and Asian Studies, Norwegian School of Management.

Perraton, J., D. Goldblatt, D. Held and A. McGrew (1997) The Globalization of Economic Activity, in *New Political Economy*, 2(2): 257–78.

Perroni, C. and J. Whalley (1994) *The New Regionalism: Trade Liberalization or Insurance?*, NBER Working Paper 4626.

Petersen, Thomas (1998) *Realism and Regional Institutionalization. A Theory of Cooperative Hegemony*, paper presented at ISA meeting, Sept.ember.

Peterson, J. (1992) The European Technology Community: Policy Networks in a Supranational Setting, in D. Marsh and R. Rhodes, eds., *Policy Networks in British Government*, Oxford: Oxford University Press.

Peterson, J. (1995) Decision-making in the European Union: Towards a Framework for Analysis, in *Journal of European Public Policy*, 2(1): 69–93.

Peterson, John and Michael Shakleton (eds.) (2006) *The Institutions of the European Union*, Oxford: Oxford University Press.

Piazolo, D. (1998) European regionalism and Multilateral Trade Negotiations, in *Journal of European Integration*, 21(3): 251–71.

Piening, Christopher (1997) *Global Europe. The EU in World Affairs*, London: Rienner.

Pierre, Jon and Guy Peters (2000) *Governance, Politics and the State* London: Palgrave-Macmillan.

Poh, Steven (1997) Just Don't Expect a Feast, in *Asia Week*, 25(4).

Polanyi, Karl (1957) [1944] *The Great Transformation: The Political and Economic Origins of our Time*, Boston: Beacon Press.

Powell, R. (1994) Anarchy in International Relations Theory: The Neorealist-Neoliberal Debate, in *International Organizations*, (31): 313–44.

Prakash, Aseem and Jeffrey A Hart. (eds.) (1999) *Globalization and Governance*, London and New York: Routledge.

Preston, C. (1996) *Enlargement and Integration in the European Union*, London: Routledge.)

Putnam, R. (1988) Diplomacy and Domestic Politics: The Logic of Two-Level Games, in *International Organization*, 42.

Putnam, Robert (2000) *Bowling Alone. The Collapse and Revival of American Community*. New York.

Rapkin, David P. (2001) The United States, Japan, and the power to block. The APEC and AMF cases. *The Pacific Review*, 14(3): 373-410.

Rapkin, David (2005) Empire and its Discontents, *New Political Economy* 10(3): 389–412.

Ravenhill, John (2001) *APEC and the Construction of Pacific Rim Regionalism*. Cambridge: Cambridge University Press.

Ravenhill, John (2005) US economic relations with East Asia: From hegemony to complex interdependence, in Beeson, M., ed., *Bush and Asia: America's Evolving Relations with East Asia*, London: Routledge.

Rawls, John (1993) *Political Liberalism*. New York: Columbia University Press.

Regelsberger, Elfriede (1988) EPC in the 1980s: Reaching Another Plateau? in A. Pijpers, Elfriede Regelsberger, and Wolfgang Wessels, eds., *European Political Cooperation in the 1980s: A Common Foreign Policy for Western Europe?*, Dordrecht: Martinus Nijhoff.

Regelsberger, Elfriede (1990) The Dialogue of the EC/Twelve with Other Regional Groups: a New European Identity in the International System? in G. Edwards and E. Regelsberger, eds., *Europe's Global Links: The European Community and Inter-Regional Cooperation*, London: Pinter.

Reich, Robert (1991) *The Work of Nations*, New York: Knopf.

Remacle, Eric and Reimund Seidelmann, eds (1998) *Pan-European Security Redefined*, Baden-Baden: Nomos-Verlag.

Reno, William (1995) *Corruption and State Politics in Sierra Leone*, Cambridge: Cambridge University Press.

Reuber, Paul and Günther Wolkersdorf (2002) The Transformation of Europe and the German Contribution: Critical Geopolitics and Geopolitical Representations, *Geopolitics*, 7(3): 39–60.

Rhein, E. (1998) Euro-Med Free Trade Area for 2010: Whom Will It Benefit?, in G. Joffé, ed., Perspectives on Development: the Euro-Mediterranean Partnership Initiative, *Journal of North African Studies* special issue, 3(2), Summer, London: Cass.

Rhodes, Carolyn, (ed.) (1998) *The European Union in the World Community*, Boulder, CO: Lynne Rienner.

Rhodes, Carolyn and S. Mazey (1995) *The State of the European Union: Building a European Polity?* Boulder, CO: Lynne Rienner.

Richardson, Jeremy R. (1995) *Actor Based Models of National and EU Policy-making: Policy Communities, Issue Networks and Epistemic Communities*, in A. Menon and H. Kassim, eds., *The EU and National Industrial Policy*, London: Routledge.

Richardson, Jeremy R., (ed.) (1996) *European Union: Power and Policy-making*, London: Routledge.

Richardson, Jeremy R. and Grant Jordan (1979) *Governing Under Pressure: The Policy Process in a Post-parliamentary Democracy*, Oxford: Martin Robertson.

Risse-Kappen, Thomas, (ed.) (1995) *Bringing Transnational Relations Back In*, Cambridge: Cambridge University Press.

Robles, A. C. Jr., (2004) *The Political Economy of Interregional Relations. ASEAN and EU*, Aldershot: Ashgate.

Rodriguez, F. and D. Rodrik (1999) *Trade Policy and Economic Growth: A Skeptic's Guide to Cross-national Evidence*, Working Paper 7081, National Bureau of Economic Research, Washington DC.

Rodriguez, M. J. (ed.) (2002) *European Konwledge Economy*, London: Elgar.

Rodrik, Dani (1997) *Has Globalization Gone Too Far?*, Washington, DC: Institute for International Economics.

Roett, Riordan (1998) *The EU and Mercosur: US Perspectives*, text prepared for the Fifth Euro-Latin American Forum, Lisbon.

Roney, Alex (1995) *EC/EU Fact Book*, Chamber of Commerce and Industry, London.

Rosamond, B. J. (2000) *Theories of European Integration*, Basingstoke: Palgrave.

Rosamond, B. J. (2005) Conceptualizing the EU Model of Governance in World Politics, *European Foreign Affairs Review*, 10(4): 463–78, winter.

Rosenau, J. (1995) Governance in the Twenty-First Century, in *Global Governance*, 1: 13–43.

Rosenau, J. (2000) A Transformed Observer in a Transforming World, in *Studia Diplomatica, Les théories de R. I. à l'épreuve de l'après-guerre-froide*, edited by C. Rosens, M. Telò and P. Vercauteren, 52(1): 4–14.

Rosenau, J. and E. O. Czempiel (eds.) (1992) *Governance without Government: Order and Change in World Politics*, Cambridge: Cambridge University Press.

Rosenau, James (1990) *Turbulence in World Politics: A Theory of Change and Continuity*, London: Harvester Wheatsheaf.

Rosencrance, Richard N. (1986) *The Rise of the Trading State: Commerce and Conquest in the Modern World*, NewYork: Basic Books.

Ruggie, John G. (ed.) (1993) *Multilateralism Matters: The Theory and Praxis of an Institutional Form*, New York: Columbia.

Ruggie, John G. (1993) Territoriality and Beyond: Problematising Modernity in International Relations, in *International Organization*, 47(1):139–74.

Ruggie, John. G. (1996) *Winning the Peace*, NewYork: Columbia.

Ruggie, John G. (1998) *Constructing the World Polity*, New York: Routledge.

Ruggie, John G. (1993) Multilateralism: The Anatomy of an Institution, in John Ruggie, ed., *Multilateralism Matters: The Theory and Praxis of an Institutional Form*, New York: Columbia University Press.

Rüland, J. (2000) ASEAN and the Asian crisis. Theoretical Implications and Practical Consequences, in *Pacific Review*, 13(3): 421–52.

Sachs, J. and A. Warner (1995) Economic Reform and the Process of Global Integration, in W. Brainard and G. Perry, eds., *Brookings Papers on Economic Activity*, 1: 1–118.

Sachs, J. and A. Warner (1997) Sources of Slow Growth in African Economies, in *Journal of African Economies*, 6(3): 335–79.

SADC (1997) Review and Rationalisation of SADC Programme of Action. Volume 2: Main Report, Gaborone: SADC.

Sala-i-Martin, X. (1997) I Just Ran Two Million Regressions, in *American Economic Review Papers and Proceedings*, May 1997, 87(2): 178–83.

Sampson, Gary and Stephen Woolcock (eds.) (2003) *Regionalism, Multilateralism and Economic Integration: The Recent Experience*, Tokyo: UNU Press.

Sandholtz, Wayne and Alexander Stone Sweet (eds.) (1998) *European Integration and Supranational Governance*, Oxford: Oxford University Press.

Sandler, Todd and James Tschirhart (1980) The Economic Theory of Clubs: An Evaluative Survey, in *Journal of Economic Literature*, 18.

Santander, Sebastian (2006) The European Partnership with Mercosur: a Relationship based on Strategic and Neo-liberal Principles, in Söderbaum and Langenhove, pp 37–58.

Santos, Paulo (1993) The Spatial Implications of Economic and Monetary Union, in *European Economy*, no. 54.

Sapir, André (1998) The Political economy of EC Regionalism, in *European Economic Review*, (42): 717–32.

Sbragia, Alberta (1992) Thinking about the European Future: The Uses of Comparison, in Alberta Sbragia, ed., *Euro-politics: Institutions and Policy-making in the 'New' European Community*, Washington DC: Brookings Institution.

Sbragia, Alberta (1996) Environmental Policy, in Helen Wallace and William Wallace, eds, *Policy-making in the European Union*, Oxford: Oxford University Press,, pp. 235–56.

Sbragia, Alberta (1998) The Transatlantic Relationship: A Case of 'Deepening' and 'Broadening', in Carolyn Rhodes, ed., *The European Union in the World Community*, Boulder, CO: Lynne Rienner, pp.147–64.

Sbragia, Alberta and Jon Pierre (2000) The European Union as Coxswain: Governance by Steering, in Jon Pierre, ed., *Debating Governance: Authority, Democracy, and Steering*, Oxford and New York: Oxford University Press.

Scharpf, Fritz W. (1998) *Governing in Europe*, Oxford: Oxford University Press.

Schiavone, Giuseppe, (ed.) (1989) *Western Europe and South-East Asia. Cooperation or Competition*, London: Macmillan.

Schmidt, S.K. (1998) Commission Activism: Submitting Telecommunications and Electricity under European Competition Law, *Journal of European Public Policy*, 5(1): 196–84.

Schmitter, Philippe C. (1993) The International Context of Contemporary Democratization, in *Stanford Journal of International Affairs*, (2): 1–34.

Schmitter, Philippe C. and Lynn Terry Karl (1995) The Conceptual Travels of Transitologists and Consolidologists: How Far to the East Should They Attempt to Go?, in *Slavic Review*, pp. 111–27.

Schmitter, Phillipe (1971) A Revised Theory of European Integration, in Leon Lindberg and Stuart Scheingold, eds., *Regional Integration: Theory and Research*, Cambridge, MA: Harvard University Press.

Scholte, Jan Aart (2005) *Globalisation: A Critical Introduction*, London: Palgrave, 2nd edition.

Segal, Gerry, Hans Maull and Jusuf Wanandi (eds.) (1998) *Europe and the Asia Pacific*, London: Routledge.

Seidelmann, Reimund (1992) The Old and New Soviet Threat: the Case for a Grand New Western Strategy towards the Soviet Republic in the 1990s, in Peter Ludlow, ed., *Europe and North America in the 1990s*, CEPS Paper No 52, Brussels, pp. 69–88.

Seidelmann, Reimund, (ed.) (1996) *Crisis Policies in Eastern Europe*, Baden-Baden: Nomos-Verlag.

Seidelmann, Reimund (1997) NATO's Enlargement as a Policy of Lost Opportunities, in *Journal of European Integration. Special Issue Problems of Eastern Europe*, (2–3): 233–45.

Seidelmann, Reimund (1998) Amsterdam e la sicurezza europea. Un' opportunità nuova o perduta, in *Europa/Europe*, Rome, (1): 66–86.

Shambaugh, David (2005) China Engages Asia, *International Security*, 29(3): 64–99.

Simmons, Beth and Lisa Martin (2002) International Organisations and Institutions in Walter Carlsnaes, Thomas Risse and Beth Simmons, eds., *Handbook of International Relations*, London: Sage, pp. 192–211.

Sidaway, James and Richard Gibb (1998) SADC, COMESA, SACU: Contradictory Formats for Regional Integration in Southern Africa, in David Simon, ed., *Reconfiguring the Region. South Africa in Southern Africa*, London: James Currey.

Sigma- Institut, Mannheim, Germany (unpublished) Research Papers on socio-cultural milieu stratification in Japan, Thailand, Canada, USA, Germany, Great Britain, France and Italy.

Simon, David (2003) Development-Environment Discourses, Policies and Practices in Post-Apartheid Southern Africa, in Andrew J. Grant and Fredrik Söderbaum, eds., *The New Regionalism in Africa*, Aldershot: Ashgate.

Simon, José Luis (1998) Lessons from Paraguay, in *Open Integration Newsletter*, Lisbon: IEEI.

Sjôstaedt, G. (1977) *The External Role of the EC*, Farnborough: Saxon House.

Slaughter, Anne Marie (2004) *A New World Order*, Princeton: Princeton University Press.

Smith, Alisdair and Loukas Tsoukalis (1996) Report on Economic and Social Cohesion, mimeo, Bruges: College of Europe.

Smith, Karen (2005) The Outsiders: the European Neighbourhood Policy, *International Affairs*, 81(4).

Smith, Michael (1984) *Western Europe and the United States. The Uncertain Alliance*, London: George Allen and Unwin.

Snidal, Duncan (1991) Relative Gains and the Pattern of International Cooperation, in *American Political Science Review.*

Snitwongse, K. (1990) Meeting the Challenges of Changing Southeast Asia, in R. Scalapino, ed., *Regional Dynamics: Security, Political, Economic Issues in the Asia–Pacific Region*, Jakarta Jakarta: Centre for Strategic and International Studies.

Söderbaum, Fredrik (1995) *Handbook of Regional Organizations in Africa*, Uppsala: Nordiska Afrikainstitutet.

Söderbaum, Fredrik and Ian Taylor (eds.) (2003) *Regionalism and Uneven Development in Southern Africa: The Case of the Maputo Development Corridor*, Aldershot: Ashgate.

Söderbaum, Fredrik (2004a) *The Political Economy of Regionalism. The Case of Southern Africa*, Basingstoke: Palgrave Macmillan.

Söderbaum, Fredrik (2004b) Modes of Regional Governance in Africa: Neoliberalism, Sovereignty-boosting and Shadow Networks, *Global Governance: A Review of Multilateralism and International Organizations*, 10(4): 419–36.

Söderbaum, Fredrik, Patrik Stålgren and Luk van Langenhove (2006) EU as a Global Actor and the Dynamics of Interregionalism: A Comparative Analysis, in Fredrik Söderbaum and Luk van Langenhove, eds., *The EU as a Global Player: The Politics of Interregionalism*, London: Routledge, pp. 117–32.

Söderbaum, Fredrik and Luk van Langenhove (eds.) (2006) *The EU as a Global Player- The Politics of Interregionalism*, London: Routledge.

Soesastro, Hadi (2005) Realizing the East Asian Vision, *CSIS Economics Working Paper Series*, Jakarta, www.csis.or.id/papers/wpe090.

Soysal, Yasemin N. (1994) *Limits of Citizenship. Migrants and Postnational Membership in Europe*. Chicago: Chicago University Press.

Spencer, C. (1998a) The End of International Enquiries? The UN Eminent Persons Mission to Algeria: July–August 1998, in *Mediterranean Politics*, 3(3): Winter 127–34.

Spencer, C. (1998b) Security Implications of the EMPI for Europe, in G. Joffé, ed., *Perspectives on Development: the Euro-Mediterranean Partnership Initiative*, *Journal of North African Studies*, special issue, 3(2): Summer, Cass, London.

Stavridis, Stelios *et al.*, (eds.) (1999) *The Foreign Policies of the EU's Mediterranean States and Applicant Countries in the 1990s*, London: Macmillan.

Steinberg, Richard H. (1997) Trade–Environment Negotiations in the EU, NAFTA, and WTO: Regional Trajectories of Rule Development, in *American Journal of International Law*, (2): April 231–67.

Stevens, C. (1997) The EU and South Africa: Slow Progress Towards 'Free' Trade, in *Quarterly Review*, April.

Centre for Research into Economics and Finance in Southern Africa, London School of Economics.

Stiglitz, Joseph (2002) *Globalisation and its Discontents*, London: Penguin.

Stone Sweet, Alex (2004) *The Judicial Construction of Europe*, Oxford: Oxford University Press.

Strange, Susan (1988) *States and Markets. Introduction to International Political Economy*, London: Pinter.

Strange, Susan (1996) The Retreat of the State. The Diffusion of Power in the World Economy, Cambridge: Cambridge University Press.

Strekal, Oleg (1999) *Nationale Sicherheit der unabhängigen Ukraine (1991–1995). Zur Analyse der Sicherheitslage und der Grundlagen der Sicherheitspolitik eines neu entstandenen Staates*, Baden-Baden: Nomos-Verlag.

Stubbs, Richard (2002) ASEAN Plus Three: Emerging East Asian Regionalism, *Asian Survey*, 42(3): 440–55.

Stubbs, Richard (2005) *Rethinking Asia's Economic Miracle: War, Prosperity and Crisis*. Basingstoke: Palgrave.

Suite101.com (1997) Cambodia and ASEAN: A Separation of Economics and Politics, 25 July: see http:www.suite101.com.

Summers, Lawrence H. (1991) Regionalism and the World Trading System, in R. Garnaut and P. Drysdale, eds., *Asia Pacific Regionalism: Readings in International Economic Relations*, Pymble: Harper Educational/ANU.

Summers, Larry (ed.) (1991) *Policy Implications of Trade and Currency Zones*, and particularly, Regionalism and the World Trading System, Federal Reserve Bank of Kansas City, Kansas City.

Summers, Robert and Alan Heston (1991) The Penn World Table (Mark 5): An Expanded Set of International Comparisons, 1950–1988, in *Quarterly Journal of Economics*, 327–68.

Suzuki, Sanae (2004) East Asian Cooperation through Conference Diplomacy: Institutional Aspects of the ASEAN Plus Three (APT) Framework. Tokyo: Institute for Developing Economies, APEC Study Center, JETRO. Working Paper 03-04, No. 7.

Sweet, Alec Stone and Thomas L. Brunell (1998) Constructing a Supranational Constitution: Dispute Resolution and Governance in the European Community, in *American Political Science Review*, (1): March 63–81.

Sweezy, Paul (1942) *The Theory of Capitalist Development*, New York: Monthly Review Press.

Syrquin, M. and H. Chenery (1988) *Patterns of Development, 1950–1983*, World Bank Discussion Paper no. 41, Washington DC: World Bank.

Tanaka, A. (1996) *A New Medievalism: The World System in the Twenty-first Century*, Tokyo: Nihon Keizai Shimbun.

Taniguchi, Makoto (2003) Towards the Establishment of an East Asian Economic Zone: How can Japan, China and Korea Cooperate to Attain This Aim?' *Working Paper* 171, Tokyo, Research Instituteof Economy, Trade and Industry, June: 1–11.

Taylor, Charles (1997) *Multikulturalismus und die Politik der Anerkennung*. Including a contribution by Jürgen Habermas. Frankfurt/Main.

Taylor, Paul (1993) *International Organisation in the Modern World: the Regional and Global Process*, London: Pinter.

Taylor, Ian (2005) NEPAD. Toward Africa's Development or Another False Start? Lynne Rienner: Boulder.

Taylor, Ian and Paul Williams (2001) South African Foreign Policy and the Great Lakes Crisis: African Renaissance Meets Vagabonde Politique, *African Affairs*, 100: 265–86.

Telò, Mario (ed.) (1993) *Towards a New Europe?* Brussels: Editions de l'Université de Bruxelles.

Telò, Mario (ed.) (1994) *L'Union Europénne et les defis del'élargissement*, Preface by W. Wallace, Brussels: Editions de l'Université de Bruxelles,.

Telò, Mario (ed.) (1995) *Démocratie et construction européenne*, Brussels: Editions de l'Université de Bruxelles.

Telò, Mario and Paul Magnette (eds.) (1996) *Repenser l'Europe*, Brussels: Editions de l'Université de Bruxelles.

Telò, Mario and Paul Magnette, (eds.) (1998) *De Maastricht à Amsterdam. L'Europe et son nouveau traité*, Brussels: Brussels Complexe.

Telò, Mario and Sebastian Santander (1999) *Can EU Contribute to a Less Asymmetric World?* December 1999, Brussels: ECPR-IPSA.

Telò, M., P. Vercauteren and C. Roosens (eds.) (2000), *Studia Diplomatica les théories des Relations Internacionales á l'épeure de l'aprés-guerre-procòle*, 52(1), Brussels.

Telò, Mario (2005) *Europe: A Civilian Power?: European Union, Global Governance*, World Order London, Palgrave Macmillan.

Therborn, Göeran (1995) *European Modernity and Beyond. The Trajectory of European Societies 1945–2000*, London: Sage.

Thomas, G. (1998) Globalization versus Regionalization?, in G. Joffé, ed., *Perspectives on Development: the Euro-Mediterranean Partnership Initiative*, *Journal of North African Studies*, special issue, 3(2), Summer, London: Cass.

Thomas, Nick (2004) *An East Asian Economic Community: Multilateralism Beyond APEC*, Conference on Asia Pacific Economies: Multilateral versus Bilateral Relationships, Hong Kong, City University, 19–21 May.

Tranholm-Mikkelsen, Jens (1991) Neo-functionalism: Obstinate or Obsolete? *Millennium: A Journal of International Studies*, 20(1).

Thränhardt, Dietrich (2000) *Conflict, Consensus, and Policy Outcomes*. In Koopmans/Statham, 2000.

Thurow, Lester (1992) *Head to Head: the Coming Economic Battle between Japan Europe and America*, London: Nicholas Brealey.

Tibi, Bassam (1998) *The Challenge of Fundamentalism*, Berkeley, CA: University of California Press.

Tibi, B. (1995) *Krieg der Zivilisationen. Politik und Religion zwischen Vernunft und Fundamentalismus*. Hamburg: Hamburg University Press.

Tocci N. (2005) Does the ENP respond to the EU's post-Enlargement challenges? *The International Spectator*, XL.

Tovias, A. (1998) Regionalization and the Mediterranean, in G. Joffé, ed., *Perspectives on Development: the Euro-Mediterranean Partnership Initiative*, in *Journal of North African Studies*, special issue, 3(2), Summer, London: Cass.

Tovias A. (1999) Israel's Free Trade Agreement with the European Union, EuroMeSCo Occasional Paper no. 5, IEEI, Lisbon.

Trautmann, Günther (1997) Russia and the Euro-Atlantic Community, in *Journal of European Integration* (2–3): 201–32.

Tsakaloyannis, Panos (1996) *The European Union as a Security Community*, Baden-Baden: Nomos-Verlag.

UN (1995a) *International Trade Statistics Yearbook*, vol. 2, New York and Geneva: United Nations.

UN (1995b) *Statistical Yearbook*, 40th ser., New York and Geneva: United Nations.

UN (1998) *Economic Survey of Europe 1998*, no. 2, New York and Geneva: United Nations.

UN (1999) *Demographic Yearbook 1997*, New York.

UNCTAD (1995) *Handbook of International Trade and Development Statistics*, New York and Geneva: United Nations.

UNCTAD-UNICEF (1995) *Poverty, Children and Policy: Responses for a Brighter Future*, Economies in Transition Series, Regional Monitoring Report no. 3, UNICEF, Florence.

UNDP (2006) *Human Development Report 2006*, New York.

UNECE (2006) *Transition Report Update May 2006*, Geneva.

Van Langenhove and Nikki Slocum, Identity and Regional Integration in L.Van Langenhove, M. Farrell and B. Hettne, eds., *Global Politics of Regionalism*, London: Pluto Press.

Valladão, Alfredo (1993) *Le XXIe siècle sera américain*, Paris: La Découverte.

Varshney, Ashutosh (2002) *Ethnic Conflict and Civic Life. Hindus and Muslims in India*. London; New Haven: Yale.

Vasconcelos, Álvaro de (2003) Back to the future? Strengthening EU/Mercosul Relations and Reviving Multilateralism, Lecture, Chair Mercosul, Paris.

Verdun, Amy (2000) *European Responses to Globalisation and Financial Market Liberalisation: Perceptions of Economic and Monetary Union in Britain, France and Germany*, Basingstoke: Macmillan.

Vernon, Raymond (1991) The Community in the Global System: A Synthesis, in Armand Clesse and Raymond Vernon, eds., *The European Community after 1992: A New Role in World Politics*, Baden-Baden: Nomos-Verlag.

Walker, Rob B. J. (1993) *Inside/Outside: International Relations as Political Theory*, Cambridge, MA: Cambridge University Press.

Wallace, Helen (1996) The Institutions of the EU: Experience and Experiments, in Helen Wallace and William Wallace, eds., *Policy-Making in the European Union*, Oxford: Oxford University Press, 3rd edition.

Wallace, Helen (1989) The Best is the Enemy of the 'Could': Bargaining in the European Community, in Secondo Tarditi, Kenneth J. Thomson, Pierpaolo Pierani and Elisabetta Croci-Angelini, eds., *Agricultural Trade Liberalization and the European Community*, Oxford: Clarendon Press, pp. 193–206.

Wallace, William (1994) *Regional Integration: The Western European Experience*, Washington DC: The Brookings Institution.

Wallace, William (1995) Regionalism in Europe: Model or Exception?, in Louise Fawcett and Andrew Hurrell, eds., *Regionalism in World Politics: Regional Organization and International Order*, Oxford: Oxford University Press.

Wallerstein, Immanuel (1974) *The Modern World System*, New York: Academic Press.

Wallerstein, Immanuel (1991) *Geopolitics and Geoculture*, Cambridge: Cambridge University Press and Maison des Sciences de l'Homme.

Wallerstein, Immanuel (1984) *The Politics of the World Economy* Cambridge: Cambridge University Press.

Walt, Stephen M. (2005) *Taming American Power. The Global Responses to US Primacy*, London & New York: W.W. Norton.

Waltz, Kenneth (1979) *Theory of International Politics*, Reading, MA: Addison Wesley.

Walzer, Michael (ed.) (1995) *Toward a Global Civil Society*. Oxford: Providence.

Walzer, Michael (1991) The Idea of Civil Society. In: *Dissent.* Frühjahr.

Warleigh, Alex and Ben Rosamond (2006) Comparative Regional Integration: Towards a Research Agenda, Description of Workshop for the ECPR Joint Sessions, Nicosia, Cyprus, 25–30 April 2006.

Webb, Carole (1983) Theoretical Approaches and Problems, in Helen Wallace and William Wallace, eds., *Policy-Making in the European Union*, Chichester: John Wiley, 2nd edition.

Webber, Douglas (2001) Two funerals and a wedding? The Ups and Downs of Regionalism in East Asia and the Asia Pacific after the Asian Financial Crisis, *The Pacific Review*, 14(3): 339–72.

Weber, M. (1978) *Gesammelte Aufsätze zur Religionssoziologie*. Tübingen.

Weidenfeld, Werner and Joseph Janning (eds.) (1993) *Europe in Global Change. Strategies and Options for Europe*, Gütersloh: Bertelsmann Foundation Publishers.

Weiler, Joseph J. H. (1999) *Fundamental Rights and Fundamental Boundaries: Common Standards and Conflicting values in the Protection of Human Rights in the European Legal Space*, paper, Law School, Harvard.

Weintraub, Sidney (1997) The North American Free Trade Agreement, in Ali M. El-Agraa, ed., *Economic Integration Worldwide*, New York: St Martin's Press, pp. 203–26.

Weiss, Linda (ed.) (2002) *States in the Global Economy: Bringing Domestic Institutions Back In*, New York and Cambridge: Cambridge University Press.

Welsch,Wolfgang (1994)Transkulturalität: die veränderte Verfassung heutiger Kulturen, in *Sichtweisen. Die Vielheit in der Einheit*, Frankfurt am Main: Stiftung Weimarer Klassik.

Wendt,Alexander(1992)Anarchy is What States Make of it: The Social Construction of Power Politics, *International Organisation*, 46(3): 391–425.

Wendt, Alexander (2000) *Social Theory of International Politics*, Cambridge: Cambridge University Press.

Wessels, Wolfgang and D. Rometsch (1996) *European Union and Member States*, Manchester: Manchester University Press.

W. Wessels (2001) Nice Result: The Millennium IGC in the EU's Evolution, *Journal of Common Market Studies* , 39(2): 197–219.

Westerlund, Percy (1997) *Kan ASEM stärka den svaga länken i triangeln EU-Ostasien-Nordamerika?*, Directorate General I, European Commission, Brussels.

Whitehead, L. (1996), The International Dimension of Democratization: Europe and the Americas, Oxford University Press, Oxford.

Whitman, R. G. (1998), *From Civilian Power to Superpower? The International Identity of the European Union*, London: Macmillan.

White House (2002) *National Security Strategy of the United States of America*, September 17.

Widgren, Michel (1994) *The Relation between Voting Power and Policy Impact in the European Union*, CEPR Discussion Paper 1033, London.

Wijkman, Per Magnus and Eva Sundkvist Lindström (1989) Pacific Basin Integration as a Step Towards Freer Trade, in John Nieuwenhuysen, ed., *Towards Freer Trade Between Nations*, Oxford, New York: Oxford University Press, pp.144–62.

Winters, Alan (1993) Expanding EC Membership and Association Accords: Recent Experience and Future Prospects, in K. Anderson and R. Blackhurst, eds., *Regional Integration and the Global Trading System*, Brighton: Harvester Wheatsheaf.

Winters, A. (1999) Regionalism vs. Multilateralism, in *Market Integration. Regionalism and the Global Economy*, R. Baldwin, D. Cohen, A. Sapir and A. Venables, eds., CEPR, Cambridge: Cambridge University Press.

Wolf, Martin (2005) *Why Globalization Works* New Haven: Yale University Press.

World Bank (1994) *Averting the Old Age Crisis*, Oxford and New York: Oxford University Press.

World Bank (1995a) *World Development Report 1995*, Oxford and New York: Oxford University Press.

World Bank (1995b) *Hungary: Structural Reforms for Sustainable Growth*, Washington, DC: World Bank.

World Bank (1996) *From Plan to Market: World Development Report 1996*, Oxford and New York: Oxford University Press.

World Bank (1997) *The State in a Changing World: World Development Report 1997*, Oxford and New York: Oxford University Press.

World Bank (1998) *Global Development Finance*, Washington, DC: World Bank.

World Bank (2005) *World Development Indicator*,Washington DC.

Wrobel, Paulo S. (1998) A Free Trade Area of the Americas in 2005?, in *International Affairs*, 74(3):547–61.

Yearbook of International Organization (1998) V.I.A., München, New York, London and Paris.

Young, Soogil (1993) Globalism and Regionalism: Complements or Competitors?, in R. Garnaut and P. Drysdale, eds., *Asia Pacific Regionalism: Readings in International Economic Relations*, Pymble: Harper Educational/ANU.

Zellner, Wolfgang and Pal Dunay (1998) *Ungarns Außenpolitik 1990–1997*, Baden-Baden: Nomos-Verlag.

Zielonka, Jan and Alex Prava (eds.) (1997) Democratic Consolidation in Eastern Europe: International and Transnational Factors, in press, Dieter Nohlen, Demokratie in Dieter Nohlen, Peter Waldmann and Klaus Ziemer (Hrsg.), *Lexikon der Politik*, vol. 4. Die Östlichen und Südlichen Länder, Beck Verlag, München, pp.118–27.

Zielonka, Jan (1998) *Explaining Euro-Paralysis*, London: Macmillan.

Zolo, Danilo (1997) *Cosmopolis, Prospects for World Government*, Cambridge: Polity Press.

Zviagelskaia, Irina (1998) Russia's Security Policy and Its Prospects, in: Eric Remacle and Reimund Seidelmann, eds., *Pan-European Security Redefined*, Baden-Baden: Nomos-Verlag, pp. 305–18.

Zysman, J. (1996) The Myth of a Global Economy: Enduring National Foundations and Emerging Regional Realities, in *New Political Economy*, 1(2):157–84.

Index